History of the
Reformed Presbyterian Church
in America

Yours Sincerely,
W. M. Glasgow.

History of the
Reformed Presbyterian Church
in America

With Sketches of All Her Ministry, Congregations,
Missions, Institutions, Publications, Etc., and
Embellished with Over Fifty Portraits and Engravings

———◆◆———

by
William Melancthon Glasgow

Biographical Introduction by
Ray B. Lanning and Nathan P. Eshelman

REFORMATION HERITAGE BOOKS
GRAND RAPIDS, MICHIGAN

Biographical Introduction
Copyright © 2007
Ray B. Lanning and Nathan P. Eshelman

Published by
Reformation Heritage Books
2965 Leonard St., NE
Grand Rapids, MI 49525
616-977-0599 / Fax 616-285-3246
e-mail: orders@heritagebooks.org
website: www.heritagebooks.org

ISBN 978-1-60178-019-5

Originally published Baltimore: Hill & Harvey, 1888.

————————————

Undertaken with the approval of the Synod of the Reformed
Presbyterian Church in America, and by a resolution passed in its
session at Newburgh, New York, June 8, 1887.

*For additional Reformed literature, both new and used, request a free
book list from Reformation Heritage Books at the above address.*

PREFACE.

HUMAN history will not be complete until man has arrived at his destination to give in the final testimony. Among the many millions of human beings, however, who have come, lived, and gone from earth, there have always been some to fight the battles of right and to maintain the truth of God against error. Before passing hence, each generation of Christians built its stone of remembrance into the rising structure of the Church of God, and will continue to do so until the gilded dome of this divine institution shall penetrate the heavens. Recognizing this fact, no apology is made by the author for presenting to the members and friends of the Reformed Presbyterian Church this contribution to her history, and offering this stone of remembrance upon her two hundredth anniversary. No history of this Church has been written, although detached sketches have been printed in the magazines of the Church by the venerable historiographers, the Revs. Drs. James R. Willson and Thomas Sproull. This work is an attempt to place upon record an impartial, authentic, and continuous history of the Reformed Presbyterian Church in America. It includes, also, a biographical sketch and notice of every ordained minister and licentiate who has in any way been

connected with the Church in America. In this department, free use was made of memoirs of the older ministers, and the author did not study to avoid using the
exact language of the biographers where the event related was important, or where the sentiment expressed
suited his purpose. Most of the sketches, however, were
obtained directly from the families and descendants of
the subjects, the dates being carefully compared with the
ecclesiastical records, and are given as practically correct.
The living ministry have answered for themselves, and
delicacy forbade them speaking at length. Wherever a
life was out of tune, the chords have been touched as
softly as could be done in order to retain the truth and
yet cause the whole strain to be heard with profit. The
Church has chosen her own Moderators of Synods, and
these have been selected as the fairest representatives of
the Church and subjects for portraits, so far as the like-
nesses could be obtained. All the Moderators appear
but five, and these never had any pictures taken, viz.:
James Blackwood, John Cannon, William Gibson, John
Kell and Robert Lusk. Some of the original pictures
were in a very bad condition, and these portraits are
pronounced excellent considering the old faded cards,
oil paintings, and daguerreotypes, from which they were
made. They were photographed several times before they
were made into copper plates of a uniform size. The
"Ives Process," by Crosscup and West, Philadelphia, a
new invention, was the only one that could give a true
likeness at a reasonable price. These fifty illustrations
have greatly added to the expense, but correspondingly
enhanced the value of the book, which every reader

will appreciate. The best effect will be received by holding the portrait at a little distance from the eyes. Distance generally lends enchantment. This work contains, furthermore, a sketch of every living and extinct congregation; its location, date of organization, successive pastors, and the names of some of the prominent members. It also contains a history of every Mission conducted by the Church, as well as the Theological and Literary Institutions, Catalogue of Students not completing the course in the Seminary of the Church, a Chronological List of Synods, and the Magazines and Papers conducted in the interests of the Church and by her members.

The facts comprising much of the local history were obtained from magazine sketches, and often the memories of old members furnished interesting data. Much information of dates was obtained from the original and printed records of the Church. Many of the latter were found in ancient musty pamphlets which the tidy housewife had consigned to oblivion in the old trunk in the garret. These were perseveringly brought to light from all parts of the Church, and used in furnishing material for this volume. The principal authorities consulted in the historical introduction were: "Hetherington's History of the Church of Scotland;" "Wodrow's History of the Sufferings of the Church of Scotland;" "Reid's History of the Presbyterian Church of Ireland;" "Testimonies of the Reformed Presbyterian Church in Scotland, Ireland and America;" "Sprague's Annals of the American Pulpit;" "Lathan's History of the Associate Reformed Synod of the South;" "Scouller's Manual of the United Presby-

terian Church:" "Dr. Sproull's Historical Sketches," and
minor works and pamphlets found in the Congressional
Library at Washington.

To the many kind friends in Europe and America who
have aided in the preparation of this volume, the author
returns his sincere thanks, and asks their pardon for the
liberty he was compelled to take in condensing and cor-
recting some of the sketches.   He was under special
obligation to the late Mrs. Rebecca Junkin, of Steuben-
ville, Ohio, for the loan of a copy of the original diary
kept by the Rev. John Cuthbertson; to the late Rev.
Dr. John Forsythe for references; to the Rev. Dr. J. B.
Scouller for rare documents and references; and to Drs.
Thomas Sproull, T. W. J. Wylie, Josias A. Chancellor,
Revs. J. W. Sproull, D. B. Willson, C. D. Trumbull,
J. C. K. Milligan, R. M. Sommerville, D. S. Faris, Henry
Easson, A. M. Stavely, Robert Dunlop, and Messrs.
S. R. Burns, J. C. McMillan, W. N. Elder, Dr. S. B. W.
McLeod, and others, for numerous favors.   It is a gratification to know that among the many hundreds of
letters received, no less touching and kind were those
from ministers who have gone out from the Reformed
Presbyterian Church, thus showing that they have not
forgotten the home of their birth and training, and to
which they are much indebted.   The manuscript prepared
for the composition of this book was sufficient to make
two volumes each of the present size, and the copy had
to be cut down about one-half in order that the whole
scope of the contemplated work might be included in one
volume of reasonable size and price.

This work is far from being perfect, and the writer is

just as cognizant of that fact as any of his critics.
Indeed the result of his work gives little evidence of
the time and labor expended upon it, and he only regrets
that abler hands had not at an earlier period gathered
and published what is attempted in this volume. If
there is any eloquence in this book, it is that of *facts*
and not *sentiment*. While it has been a labor of years,
it has also been a labor of love. While it has been a
real task, it has also been a great pleasure to gather up
these leaves of history which had been blown in all directions ; to remove them from their otherwise unnoticeable
destiny; to place them in a bundle by arranging the
stems of events one upon the other; to unfold the incom-
plete parts by explanation ; to tie them together with
the cord of publication ; and now hang them upon the
wall of memory for preservation in the homes of the
friends of the Covenants. And, finally, the author feels
that he will be doubly compensated for the pains he has
taken, should his imperfect work prove acceptable and
interesting to those for whom it has been gathered, and
to whom it is now affectionately dedicated.

W. M. GLASGOW.

Baltimore, Md., June, 1888.

TABLE OF CONTENTS.

HISTORICAL INTRODUCTION.

POSITION OF CHURCH.

ORGANIC HISTORY.

CONGREGATIONS AND SOCIETIES.

MARITIME PROVINCES.

NEW ENGLAND.

CANADA WEST.

NEW YORK.

NEW JERSEY.

COVENANTERISM IN THE SOUTH.

THE CONGREGATIONS.

THE MINISTRY.

LIST OF PORTRAITS.

SKETCHES OF MINISTERS.

STUDENTS NOT COMPLETING THE COURSE.

THEOLOGICAL SEMINARY.

LITERARY INSTITUTIONS.

THE MISSIONS.

FOREIGN MISSIONS.

SKETCHES OF MISSIONARIES.

DOMESTIC MISSIONS.

SYNODS AND PRESBYTERIES.

PUBLICATIONS.

"THE kingdom is the Lord's; and He is the Governor among the nations. * * King of kings and Lord of lords. * * The wicked shall be turned into hell and the nations that forget God. * * Be wise now, therefore, O ye kings. * * Kiss the Son. * * For the nation and kingdom that will not serve Thee shall perish. * * The Lord reigneth. * * By Me kings reign. * * The powers that be are ordained of God." — *The Bible.*

"WE, the people of the United States, do ordain and establish this Constitution." — *United States Constitution.*

"THE Government of the United States of America, is not in any sense, founded on the Christian religion."—*U. S. Treaty with Tripoli.*

"IN vain does the nation attempt to purchase liberty with the best blood of her citizens, while delivering it into the keeping of men un-acquainted with, or regardless of, the supreme legislative authority of God." — *Rev. James McKinney.*

"No consideration will justify the framers of the Federal Constitution and the administration of the Government, in withholding a recognition of the Lord and His Anointed from the grand charter of the nation." — *Rev. Alexander McLeod, D. D.*

"IN the United States the refusal to acknowledge God in the Constitution has probably been more explicit than it ever was in any other nation." — *Rev. James R. Willson, D. D.*

"THE Federal Constitution of the United States does not recognize the existence of God, the King of nations; * * and shall a nation act as if independent of the God of the Universe and expect to be guiltless? * * The principles of reformation are not fashionable. They were once, however, considered as the glory of Presbyterians. For civil and ecclesiastical reformation, for a glorious covenanted cause, thousands bled and died. * * I have endeavored to advocate *that cause* because I thought it the doctrine of the Bible, and the cause of Christ." — *Rev. Samuel B. Wylie, D. D.*

BIOGRAPHICAL INTRODUCTION

William Melancthon Glasgow (c. 1857-1909)

The author of this *History of the Reformed Presbyterian Church in America* deserves to be remembered by Reformed Christians today for many reasons. In a comparatively short lifetime, William Melancthon Glasgow amassed an astonishing record of achievement in several fields as a journalist, as a church historian, and as a minister of the Word. He was also something of an ecclesiastical pilgrim, deeply rooted in his heritage as a Reformed Presbyterian or "Covenanter," but willing to embrace other branches of the Presbyterian family of churches in North America as his own views changed, and as he followed where his sense of calling led him.

Background: The Scottish Dissenting Churches

Glasgow was born July 1, 1857,[1] the son of Moses T. and Martha W. (Thompson) Glasgow, who were Reformed Presbyterians living in or near the hamlet of Northwood, in Logan County, Ohio. Never more than a crossroads village, Northwood was the center of a community of Scottish and Scotch-Irish immigrant families, and it was large enough to support two congregations: the Upper Miami Reformed Presbyterian Church, founded in 1833, and later, the Northwood United Presbyterian Church, organized in 1859. In 1880 the Miami congregation included 172 communicant members and boasted a Sabbath School enrollment of 159 "scholars." The United Presbyterian congregation came not far behind, with as many as 162 communicants in her fold.[2]

These congregations represented two bodies, the Reformed Presbyterian Church in United States of America, as it was then known, and the United Presbyterian Church of North America. Both belonged to the family of denominations known to Presbyterian church historians as the "Scottish Dissenting Churches," *viz.*, American churches with roots in Scotland, standing apart or "dissenting" from the "mainline" Presbyterian bodies in Scotland and the United States. Glasgow provides a fuller account of their history, so it will only be necessary to say a few words here.

---

1. Various sources give 1856, 1857, or 1858 as the year of birth; RP sources give the year as 1856; UP sources give 1857; and his memorial in Falls Presbyterian Church, 1858.

2. *History of Logan County and Ohio* (Chicago: O.L. Baskin & Co., 1880).

The Reformed Presbyterian Church in Scotland

The Reformed Presbyterians, or "Covenanters," are the oldest branch of the family. In 1689, at the close of a long period of strife between church and state, the newly crowned king of Great Britain, William III, moved quickly to put an end to the conflict by the shortest means. His proposal was known as the Revolutionary Settlement, and most of the Scottish Covenanters, worn down by the struggle of several generations, which cost them 18,000 people, accepted the king's proposal.

This settlement was at best a compromise of the aims of the famous Solemn League and Covenant of 1643, and intended to bring the churches of the three kingdoms of England, Scotland, and Ireland, into uniformity of confession, worship, and order, as summarized in the Westminster Standards. Instead, the king proposed to maintain Episcopal government and the use of the *Book of Common Prayer* in the Churches of England and Ireland, while the Church of Scotland would, by popular demand as it were, resume her historic Presbyterian polity and Reformed mode of worship.

It is no wonder then that some of the Covenanters rejected this settlement and stood aloof from the newly reconstituted national church. They took the name, "Reformed Presbyterians," *i.e.*, Reformed Christians who embraced Presbyterianism as an article of faith, over against those in the national church who, under the terms of the Revolutionary Settlement, were only Presbyterians by preference, custom, or mere indifference.

From her beginning, then, the Reformed Presbyterian Church in Scotland was a "testifying church," committed to the idea of a Reformed church whose liturgy and polity was nothing but the consistent outworking of her covenanted Confession of Faith, embraced and approved by all of her members and officers. This idea of a Reformed church set them apart from the more broadly-based national Church of Scotland, which was intended to be a church for all Protestant Christians in the realm, and of necessity having to allow at least some latitude of belief and practice.

The Associate Presbyterian Church in Scotland

In the first part of the eighteenth century, the Church of Scotland was beginning to reap the bitter fruits of the diversity of belief and practice embraced in the Revolutionary Settlement. A generation of conflict between the "Moderates," or broad churchmen, and the "Evangelicals," all of whom were committed exponents of evangelical Calvinism, resulted in the Secession of 1733. Four "Evangelical" ministers had been suspended from office, and rather than accept a proposed compromise that would have restored them to office, they chose to decline the authority of the courts of the Church of Scotland, and banded together as the Associate Presbytery in an historic meeting at Gairney Bridge on December 5, 1733.

From this small beginning grew the "Secession Church," a vigorous movement in Scottish church history, which resulted in two denominations of Associate Presbyterians, "Burgher" and "Anti-Burgher," preaching the gospel and planting churches all over Scotland. Fueled in no small measure by the fires of the eighteenth century Evangelical Awakening, the Seceders left their stamp on Scottish Christian history, and extended their influence to Northern Ireland. Associate ministers sent out from Scotland were prime movers in the planting of the Presbyterian Church in Canada as well.

COVENANTERS AND SECEDERS IN NORTH AMERICA

At the same time, large numbers of Scottish folk and their cousins in Northern Ireland, known as the Scotch Irish, were beginning to leave their homelands for a new life in the British colonies being planted along the Atlantic seaboard of North America. Among them were significant numbers of both Covenanters and Seceders, including whole congregations electing to emigrate with their ministers.

Soon there were enough societies, congregations, and ministers of both kinds, spread from Vermont to the Carolinas, to permit the erection of presbyteries and synods. The Associate Presbyterians were more or less concentrated in the middle colonies of New York and Pennsylvania; the Reformed Presbyterians were more widely scattered along a line forming the western frontier of colonial settlement.

The American Revolution was warmly supported by both groups, and in the wake of independence, there arose a conviction on the part of both that they were now in a new situation, in which the points of difference that had kept them apart in Scotland were no longer relevant. Nearly all the Reformed Presbyterians, and about half of the Associate Presbyterians, chose to unite as the Associate Reformed Church in North America in 1782.

So it came about that the infant republic was blessed with no less than three bodies of "dissenting" Presbyterians, the Reformed Presbyterians, the Associate Presbyterians, and the Associate Reformed Presbyterians. All three bodies grew vigorously, often side by side in the same rural communities and urban centers, and sometimes meeting in the same buildings.

All three agreed, whatever their differences, that the Presbyterian Church in the United States of America, newly constituted in 1789, was exactly the same kind of broad-based, latitudinarian denomination they had rejected in the form of the Church of Scotland as established by the Revolutionary Settlement. They therefore felt justified in standing apart from the larger body in America, as they had done in Scotland; and more than justified, when the PCUSA, early in the new century, abandoned the pure Psalmody of Scotland in favor of the *Psalms and Hymns* of the English Congregationalist, Isaac Watts.

Finally, in 1858, the Associate and Associate Reformed Churches saw fit to combine forces as the United Presbyterian Church of North America. The invitation to union was extended to the Reformed Presbyterians, who in 1833 had themselves divided into two bodies, as "Old Side" and "New Side" Covenanters; but neither body was inclined to join the newborn UPCNA. Sadly, remnants of the Associate and the Associate Reformed Churches also chose not to enter the union of 1858. As a result, in Glasgow's lifetime, there were no less than five distinct bodies of "Scottish Dissenting Churches" in the United States. Writing in 1882, Southern ARP historian Robert Lathan summed up the situation this way:

> It is painful to think that the psalm-singing churches are so divided. In the two branches of the Reformed Presbyterian Church in America there are about two hundred ordained ministers and nearly twenty thousand communicants. In America there are more than twelve hundred psalm-singing congregations, with a baptized membership of more than five hundred thousand, and fully one hundred and twenty thousand communicants. To these about one thousand ministers are preaching the gospel. Unfortunately they are not united. That they are interested in each other's welfare no one will deny; but still they are divided. That they disagree on minor points will be admitted. Absolute harmony exists only in heaven. In matters purely religious, Associates, Reformed Presbyterians, Associate Reformed Presbyterians and United Presbyterians never have differed. They are, today, one in doctrine, one in form of church government, one in worship and one in everything but—shall we say—politics; and this, and this alone divides them![3]

THE POLITICAL QUESTION

Since Glasgow himself was deeply interested in the "politics" that divided these "Scottish Dissenting Churches" in their American hey-day, it is important to appreciate the central question which gave rise to the divisions. Simply put, the question was, how ought Reformed Christians to relate to the constitution and government of the United States?

Beginning with the same confessional principles regarding civil government and the duty of Christians as subjects and citizens (Westminster Confession of

---

3. Robert Lathan, *History of the Associate Reformed Synod of the South, 1782-1882* (Harrisburg, Penn.: n.p. 1882) p. 255.

Faith, Chapter XXIII), these American bodies developed widely divergent ways of formulating and applying these principles. Retaining the Confession of Faith in its original form, the "Old Side" Reformed Presbyterians renounced American citizenship, and would not vote, hold office, or take oaths of obligation to the U.S. Constitution. They regarded it as fatally defective in its failure to acknowledge God as Creator, or the rights of Christ as King. They hoped to achieve reform of the national order by standing aloof from it and testifying against it.

The Associate Reformed and United Presbyterians took the opposite tack. At the beginning of their history, the ARPs had carefully revised the relevant passages of the Confession of Faith to accommodate America's constitutional separation of church and state. They accepted the U.S. Constitution, despite its acknowledged faults, and later, as United Presbyterians, they were warmly devoted to the cause of maintaining the powers of the federal government and the union of the states during the Civil War of 1861-1865. The United Presbyterians held that the best way to foster Christian civil government was to become fully engaged in the existing order and labor to reform it from within.

Glasgow began his ministerial career wholly devoted to the position of the "Old Side" Reformed Presbyterian Church. In time his views changed, and when efforts to reverse the long-standing practice of the denomination ended in frustration and division, Glasgow followed many like-minded RP ministers and entered the United Presbyterian fold.

Finally, perhaps in search of wider opportunities to bring the power of the gospel to bear on the life of America's growing urban centers, Glasgow found a place in the Presbyterian Church in the U.S.A. While there may have been few in the PCUSA who desired change in the federal constitution by way of an amendment "recognizing the dominion of Jesus Christ over the nations, and this nation's subjection to the Divine law," there were many who campaigned for the temperance and prohibition movements, and warmly endorsed the "progressive" measures urged by President Theodore Roosevelt, a devout member of the Reformed Church in America, and later by Woodrow Wilson, himself a Covenanter descendant and a Southern Presbyterian.

FAMILY BACKGROUND, EDUCATION AND EARLY CAREER AS A JOURNALIST

Glasgow seems never to have written an account of his family history, but a careful search of this volume and his later work, *The Geneva Book*, has turned up some interesting bits of information. The earliest mention of the Glasgow family appears in the account of the Pine Creek and Union congregations in Butler County, Pennsylvania (pp. 289, 290). Rev. Matthew Williams was installed as pastor in 1807; and during the years of his ministry until his death in 1828, John Glasgow was a member of the church session. Glasgow also records that "Mrs. Penninah Glasgow" was "very useful in social meetings and in giving the children instruction in the doctrines of salvation."

Next is a reference in the account of the Londonderry and North Salem congregations in Guernsey County, Ohio (pp. 215, 216), organized in 1822. The Glasgow family is listed among "old and prominent families" in Londonderry and North Salem. Glasgow says that these families had come from Harrison County, Ohio; and the families who had settled there, northeast of Guernsey County, "were mostly emigrants from Western Pennsylvania" arriving as early as 1806.

Finally, on the list of "old families and members at Northwood," Logan County, Ohio, in connection with the Miami congregation, Glasgow entered the name of his father, Moses T. Glasgow (p. 325). Covenanter families began settling in Logan County as early as 1828. There is some confusion at this point, since Glasgow also places "M.T. Glasgow" in Bellefontaine (p. 326), south of Northwood, and county seat of Logan County. It is possible that Moses made his start in life in Bellefontaine, but moved to Northwood when prospects for organizing an RP church in Bellefontaine faded.

Moses T. Glasgow appears to have been a restless and enterprising man, for in 1844 Glasgow places him in Cincinnati, and states that he was elected ruling elder for the newly reorganized RP congregation there. In a rare footnote, Glasgow credits his information about the origin of the Cincinnati congregation to "reminiscences by Hon. Washington McLean, Moses T. Glasgow, and others" (p. 331). In 1848, "Mr. Moses T. Glasgow, Cincinnati, Ohio" appears on the list of names of the first "Board of Inspection" for the newly-opened "Geneva Hall" (*The Geneva Book*, p. 19).

There was also a Hugh Glasgow connected with Covenanterism in Cincinnati, who at an earlier time was one of the few who "held the testimony intact," the wake of the division of 1833 (p. 332). To complete the record, the Glasgow name also appears among the old families connected with the Brush Creek congregation, organized in 1812, in southern Ohio's Adams County (p. 330); and Robert Glasgow is named as one of the men chosen as ruling elders of the congregation in Pittsburgh, Pennsylvania, when it was re-organized in 1865 (p. 302).

By 1855 Moses T. Glasgow was back in Northwood. His name appears regularly in the minutes of the Board of Trustees of Geneva Hall beginning in February 1855. Sadly, on June 15, 1857, when the board found fault with him for failing to carry out what was very likely an unpleasant assignment, Moses abruptly resigned his post as treasurer. Just a few days later, on June 24, he tendered his resignation as a member of the board. The resignation was laid on the table at the time, but by July 31, 1857, in a postscript to the minutes, the secretary recorded that Glasgow's resignation was accepted (*The Geneva Book*, pp. 19, 42-45).

During his time away from Northwood, Moses T. Glasgow appears to have begotten a son and older brother to William Melancthon Glasgow. He appears in *The Geneva Book* as "Robert Finley Glasgow [*Furniture and Carpet Manufacturer*], Born in the city of Cincinnati, Ohio, Oct. 2, 1844; reared at Belle Center, Ohio" (p. 241). Service in the U.S. Navy during the Civil War did not prevent Robert being graduated from Geneva in the class of 1864. After further training and service as a school teacher, Robert was engaged in "newspaper work" in Cincinnati, first in the years 1871 to 1874; then, after twelve years as a merchant in Boston, Massachusetts, Robert returned to Cincinnati in 1886 to spend two more years working as a "traveling advertising agent for the *Times-Star*." In 1887 Glasgow noted that his brother was a ruling elder in the Cincinnati congregation (*History*, p. 333). It is interesting to note that Robert, like William, ended his days in the fold of the Presbyterian Church in the U.S.A. (*The Geneva Book*, p. 242).

One more Glasgow family member appears in *The Geneva Book*, perhaps an older sister to Robert and William. Her name was Lois Ladd Glasgow. Like Robert, she was born in Cincinnati, on December 12, 1841, but "reared at Belle Center." She was graduated from Geneva College in the class of 1862, and returned to her home in Belle Center, where after several years of ill health, she died on June 18, 1870 (p. 237).

Glasgow passed his early years in Northwood and nearby Belle Center. Upon completion of his basic education in the local public schools, he followed Robert down to Cincinnati and first found employment as a printer with the *Daily Star*, and subsequently, in 1874, became agent and reporter for the same paper in Dayton, Ohio.

These youthful labors as a journalist left their stamp on Glasgow's subsequent writings. His major published works are full of the journalistic imperatives of "who, what, when, where, and how." They are reference books crammed with names, dates, and places, with significant events and achievements briefly noted and documented. It fell to Glasgow to compile several of these "data bases," on which subsequent historians have been grateful to rely for the nuts and bolts of their historical writings.

RETURN TO NORTHWOOD AND GENEVA COLLEGE

In 1877 Glasgow returned to Northwood, Ohio, to enroll in the small college located there and known in its early days as "Geneva Hall," founded as "a literary Institution upon Scriptural principles, making [*sic*] the Bible, with a selection of the best Christian authors in the Latin and Greek languages, as the text book."[4] Today this institution continues as Geneva College, located in Beaver Falls, Pennsylvania. Glasgow belonged to the last class of students to complete their studies at the Northwood campus before the relocation of the college to Beaver Falls in 1880.

Sponsored by Reformed Presbyterians residing in the immediate vicinity, the college had its beginnings in 1838 as a small class of young men meeting for instruction in the study of Rev. John Black Johnston, pastor of the Miami RP Church in Northwood. In 1848 a building was erected to house the fledgling institution, and the faculty was enlarged to three. Forty-two students were enrolled in the first class to meet in the new building.

Other buildings were added in following years, classroom buildings and residence halls, comprising the small campus that Glasgow would recall with great warmth and tenderness in *The Geneva Book* (1908), devoting a whole chapter to his "Last Visit to Northwood," including Charles S. Herron's poem of thirteen stanzas entitled, "The Old College Bell" (Ch. XI, pp. 116-119).

Glasgow excelled as a student athlete, and played for the college baseball team and held down the position of pitcher for the years 1877 to 1880. The team enjoyed winning seasons, and in Glasgow's senior year, went undefeated. Later he recalled that, "During the last season at Northwood, the team never lost a game, defeating the then-celebrated semi-professional club of Northwestern Ohio University twice in one day."[5]

Other extra-curricular activities included singing tenor in the Geneva College "Quintette Club." In *The Geneva Book*, Glasgow humorously reports that this singing ensemble "first startled, then charmed Western Ohio with music and oratory."[6] He joined one of the campus literary clubs, known as the Aletheorian Society. He also continued his work as a journalist, as editor of the monthly college publication known as *The College Cabinet*. In after years, Glasgow served as president of the Alumni Association, 1898-1901, compiled a *Catalogue of the Alumni of Geneva College* (1882), produced a *History of Geneva College* (1883), and, much later, published *The Geneva Book: Comprising a History of Geneva College* (1908).

SEMINARY, LICENSURE, ORDINATION AND FIRST PASTORATE
IN BALTIMORE, MARYLAND

When he finished his course at Geneva College, Glasgow made his way to Boston, Massachusetts, where his found employment for two years as a "collector," *viz.*, a clerk or agent whose assignment is to collect delinquent

---

4. *The Geneva Book*, p. 17.
5. *Ibid.*, p. 156.
6. *Ibid.*, p. 141.

accounts on behalf of a merchant or manufacturer. Most likely William worked for his brother Robert, who, as noted above, was a merchant in Boston at that time.

In the middle decades of the nineteenth century new congregations of Reformed Presbyterians were being organized among the Scottish immigrants arriving in Boston, among them large numbers of Scottish weavers recruited to provide skilled labor for New England's textile mills and carpet factories. It may have been contact with these new churches that moved Glasgow to consider training for the gospel ministry by enrolling in the denominational seminary.

The denominational theological "seminary" for a long while was in fact a free-floating program for ministerial training conducted in the parsonage or church building of the particular minister who had been chosen as the Synod's theological instructor. For a time it was located at Northwood, in connection with the college, until its removal to more or less permanent quarters in Allegheny, Pennsylvania, today's "Northside" Pittsburgh, in 1856. The seminary would remain there until 1923, when it was moved across the river to occupy "The Gables," former residence of department store magnate Durbin Horne, on Penn Avenue in the Point Breeze neighborhood of Pittsburgh, where it operates today as Reformed Presbyterian Theological Seminary.

Glasgow therefore headed for Allegheny to enroll in the seminary and train for the gospel ministry, finishing his course of study in time to be granted license to preach by Pittsburgh Presbytery on April 9, 1884. He then embarked on the business of "candidating" for a call, and made a tour of the Reformed Presbyterian congregations in Canada's Maritime Provinces. Called to the Reformed Presbyterian Church of Baltimore, Maryland, Glasgow was ordained to the ministry by Philadelphia Presbytery and installed as pastor of the Baltimore congregation on November 26, 1885.

Reformed Presbyterianism in Baltimore had a history reaching back to at least 1797. As a port city, Baltimore served as one of the American gateways for immigrants arriving from Scotland and Ireland, and the Covenanter society had slowly grown in size and resources, only to collapse quite suddenly with the division of the denomination in 1833. The small remnant of "Old Side" RPs had to sell their building, settle their debts, and begin all over again. The years of the Civil War also took a toll on the congregation, leaving it "greatly reduced," as Glasgow records, but it revived again in the years following the war. Glasgow's years in the Baltimore charge were not many, but he certainly took an interest in its one hundred year history of alternating periods of prosperity and adversity, devastation and renewal.

In addition to his labors as preacher and pastor, Glasgow began to write extensively for the denominational periodical, *The Reformed Presbyterian and*

Covenanter. Many of his contributions were sketches of the careers of RP ministers, and short histories of the congregations and presbyteries of the denomination. In time these articles were augmented and developed into the present volume, *The History of the Reformed Presbyterian Church in America: With Sketches of All Her Ministry, Congregations, Missions, Institutions, Publications, Etc., and Embellished with Over Fifty Portraits and Engravings.* This book, which may be regarded as Glasgow's *magnum opus*, was first published in 1888, while Glasgow was still serving the Baltimore congregation.

MARRIAGE AND SECOND PASTORATE IN KANSAS CITY, MISSOURI

Baltimore also provided Glasgow with his life partner. He married Miss Elizabeth Mullen on December 20, 1888. They had two children, daughters Miriam O. and Genevieve M. Glasgow. Six months later Glasgow was released from the Baltimore charge, on June 25, 1889. He headed west to a very different field of labor, helping to plant a new congregation in Kansas City, Missouri.

Glasgow was well aware of what was happening in that part of the country. Kansas City, Missouri, was already well established and rapidly growing as the "Gateway to the Southwest," situated at the confluence of the Missouri and Kansas Rivers, standing athwart the Santa Fe Trail just west of its eastern terminus in nearby Independence, Missouri. To the westward, Reformed Presbyterian congregations were being planted in many parts of Kansas. To assist in these church-planting efforts, Rev. James Milligan Wylie, General Secretary of RP Home Missions, had taken up residence in Kansas City, Missouri, where he took charge of gathering and organizing a new congregation soon after his arrival on the field in 1888.

Wearied, perhaps, with the effort to keep "ancient" Covenanterism alive and well in old Baltimore, Glasgow welcomed the opportunity to build up a new work in a young and thriving city. Brother Robert had once more led the way, leaving his newspaper work in Cincinnati and heading out to Topeka, Kansas, to make a new start as a furniture and carpet dealer, in 1888.

Glasgow took over the reins of the work from Secretary Wylie and "labored as Stated Supply for some time with the greatest success."[7] The designation, "Stated Supply," indicates that perhaps the congregation did not grow to sufficient size to be able to present Glasgow with a call during his time there. However, Glasgow's entry in his *Cyclopedic Manual of the United Presbyterian Church of North America* lists him as pastor of the Kansas City congregation, so it is likely that at some point he was called to that office by the congregation, and duly installed.

---

7. Owen F. Thompson, *Sketches of the Ministers, 1888-1930,* (Pittsburgh: Reformed Presbyterian Board of Publications, 1930) p. 132.

Third Pastorate: Beaver Falls, Pennsylvania

In 1893 the First Reformed Presbyterian Church of Beaver Falls, Pennsylvania, presented Glasgow with a call that he found impossible to decline, his "great success" in Kansas City notwithstanding. Returning eastward to Beaver Falls, Glasgow took up his labors as pastor in a prominent charge in the RP homeland, in close proximity with his beloved *alma mater*, Geneva College, now flourishing on its new campus there.

Though well situated in the Scotch Presbyterian Canaan of Western Pennsylvania, the Beaver Falls congregation was not very old when it welcomed Glasgow as its second pastor. From small beginnings in 1869, mission work in the vicinity bore fruit, and by 1874 a society of twenty-four members could be organized as a congregation. In 1875 this little band was so blessed as to secure the services of Robert James George as their pastor.

Settling into his work, George led a successful effort to relocate Geneva College to Beaver Falls, and won a place as secretary of both the college board of trustees and the seminary board of superintendents. He remained in Beaver Falls until 1892, when he was appointed professor of theology and church history in the RP Seminary at Allegheny, Pennsylvania, where he served until 1910. At least three volumes of George's *Lectures in Pastoral Theology* were published after his death, and they are a fitting monument to his many abilities, profound learning, and sterling character as a servant of God.

So it was that Glasgow was presented with the opportunity to build upon a foundation that had been well and truly laid. Sadly, the shadow of controversy had once more fallen across the Reformed Presbyterian Church. Earnest calls for changes in practice were being pressed on the church, only to be met with the stoutest resistance. Several generations of successful work to rebuild the fortunes of the "Old Side" Reformed Presbyterian Church were put at risk as the bands of denominational unity were strained to the breaking point.

Glasgow found it impossible to keep above the fray. Writing anonymously in George P. Hays' volume, *Presbyterians, A Popular Narrative of Their Origin, Progress, Doctrines and Achievements* (New York: J.A. Hill & Co., 1892), Glasgow reported that a meeting of persons aiming at change in church practice held in Pittsburgh's "East End" had resulted in the framing and circulation of the "East End Platform."

Among other things, this platform called for repealing the "term of communion" that bound Reformed Presbyterians to adopt the historic position of the church with regard to the "political question" discussed above. Reformed Presbyterians would no longer be required to express "political dissent" by not voting in elections. Brought speedily to trial, the ministerial framers of the "East End Platform" were suspended from office by their presbytery. This suspension was upheld by the synod in 1891, with the result that "most of the signers of the 'East End Platform' have since united with other denominations" (Hays, p. 424). It is said that ten percent or more of the church's members followed them out of the RP fold.

Though in 1892 Glasgow seems to have approved of the actions of the church courts in holding the line on the long-held, oft-controverted practice of "political dissent," he gave at least a hint that his own thinking may have been in flux at that time. He ended his chapter in Hays' book somewhat abruptly with this observation:

> Ministers and people insist that those who become dissatisfied with the position of the Church, instead of trying to revolutionize the denomination in a disorderly way, should quietly withdraw and join some other body of Christians.[8]

In 1899, that is precisely what Glasgow himself would do.

FOURTH PASTORATE:
THE UNITED PRESBYTERIAN CHURCH OF WELLSVILLE, OHIO

By 1899 Glasgow seems to have come to the point that he could no longer support or endure the entrenched resistance to change in the Reformed Presbyterian Church. He accepted a call to the United Presbyterian Church of Wellsville, a small community located southeast of the manufacturing center of East Liverpool, along the Ohio River in Columbiana County, Ohio.

United Presbyterianism in Wellsville dated back to the organization of the Associate Reformed Presbyterian Church there in 1848. The congregation had grown slowly but steadily through the years, and must have afforded Glasgow the stability and peace he needed to heal the wounds he had incurred in tearing himself loose from his lifelong moorings in the Reformed Presbyterian Church.

Glasgow fully engaged himself in the life and work of his new denomination, and set to work on another massive reference work that he gave to the world in 1903 as the *Cyclopedic Manual of the United Presbyterian Church of North America, Comprising a Brief History of Her Ancestral Branches, Ministry, Congregations, Institutions, Courts, Boards, Mission, Periodicals, Etc., and Embellished with the Portraits of the Moderators of the General Assembly since 1858* (Pittsburgh: United Presbyterian Board of Publication, 1903). Glasgow relied heavily on an earlier work by James Brown Scouller, *A Manual of the United Presbyterian Church of*

---

8. George P. Hays, *Presbyterians* (New York: J.A. Hill & Co., 1892), p. 424. Though the chapter on the Reformed Presbyterians is unattributed, Glasgow claimed it, and it has the marks of his style throughout.

North America, 1751-1881 (Harrisburg, Penn.: Patriot Publishing Company, 1881). Glasgow abridged much of Scouller's work, and augmented it with the necessary data to bring it forward to 1903. Sadly, Glasgow found it necessary to delete or abridge much anecdotal material included in Scouller's volume; users of Glasgow's manual should take note that the occasional citations attached to the ministerial profiles are taken from Scouller.

Glasgow's manual would itself be updated by Hugh Alexander Kelsey and issued as *The United Presbyterian Directory, A Half-Century Survey, 1903 to 1958* (Pittsburgh: The Pickwick Press, 1958), on behalf of the Committee on Centennial Celebration of the United Presbyterian Church of North America. These works of Scouller, Glasgow, and Kelsey are all the more important today as monuments and reference books inasmuch as the remarkable history and heritage of the UPCNA has been almost entirely eclipsed and forgotten since her union with the Presbyterian Church in the U.S.A. in 1958.

It is clear that Glasgow had come to embrace the United Presbyterian answer to the "political question" that had for so long divided the "Scottish Dissenting Churches." Engagement, not isolation, was the way to bring about the desired "national reform."

Addressing a presbytery-wide convention of the Young People's Christian Union, youth work agency of the UPCNA, held in Salineville, Ohio, in 1900, Glasgow declared:

> The State cannot justly claim to be Christian in its sphere without the acknowledgments in its national constitution of the sovereignty of God, the kingship of Christ, and the supreme authority of the Word of God to regulate its life.... Civic reform, constitutional and legislative, is a present need and duty.... No Church is more thoroughly committed to this work of national reformation than is the United Presbyterian. We believe in the headship of Christ over the nations of the earth, not simply as an essential denominational tenet, but as a Scriptural principle.[9]

These affirmations notwithstanding, Glasgow did not long continue in the communion of the United Presbyterian Church of North America.

FINAL PASTORATE:

FALLS PRESBYTERIAN CHURCH, PHILADELPHIA, PENNSYLVANIA

It should be remembered that all through his life, Glasgow had felt the drawing power of the nation's urban centers, old and new, whether it was

---

9. William Melancthon Glasgow, "The Christian's Duty as a Citizen," *The United Presbyterian*, November 8, 1900, p. 2.

Cincinnati, Boston, Baltimore, or Kansas City. In the first decades of the twentieth century, Americans in record numbers left their farms and rural villages for a new life in the nation's big cities.

This "migration to the metropolis" had serious consequences for denominations such as the Reformed Presbyterian Church and United Presbyterian Church, whose strength of numbers lay almost entirely in the bounds of rural America. The leaders of these denominations were slow to see that this huge shift in population was permanent; and likewise, they lacked the resources, skills, and flexibility needed to work effectively in the new urban environment.

Denominational loyalty was considerably weakened in the process of migration. RP and UP members who joined in the general movement of people to the big cities of the land were often lost to their ancestral churches. With few churches of their own kind in their new surroundings, sons and daughters of Covenanter and Seceder homes were inclined to cast in their lot with churches of other denominations.

Once again, Robert Glasgow had blazed a trail of sorts for his younger brother. Robert had finally settled in Topeka, Kansas for the long haul. It is likely that he supported efforts to gather a congregation of Reformed Presbyterians there, but such efforts, if they were made, came to naught. Robert joined the Presbyterian Church in Topeka and was honored with election to the office of ruling elder in his local congregation.

In 1904 William Glasgow accepted a call to the pastorate of Falls Presbyterian Church, located in a picturesque neighborhood known locally as "East Falls" or "Falls of the Schuylkill," lying along the Schuylkill River, just east of the Wissahickon Valley, not far up river from the center of Philadelphia, Pennsylvania. The names of charter members of the congregation suggest that it was composed of Scotch-Irish or Scottish immigrants, artisans and mechanics, like those mentioned earlier who were brought to New England to provide a skilled labor force for the growing manufacturing sector.

Even so, Glasgow was venturing into new ecclesiastical territory. It was one thing for a Reformed Presbyterian to join the Associate Reformed or United Presbyterian Church; many RPs had done so throughout the nineteenth century. As noted above, there was little or no difference in doctrine or worship among these "Scottish dissenting churches." However, the Presbyterian Church in the U.S.A. had a very different culture and practice.

Ethnically, the PCUSA was by no means an exclusive enclave of Scottish and Scotch-Irish Presbyterians, though large numbers of them adhered to it. Liturgically, although metrical Psalmody had a long history in the PCUSA, the denomination had readily accepted "uninspired" hymnody early in the nineteenth century, and later, the use of the pipe organ as more or less a necessary appurtenance to public worship. The latest book of praise authorized by the General Assembly, *The Hymnal* of 1895, edited by master hymnologist Louis F. Benson, contained almost nothing by way of metrical versions of the Psalms.

By 1904 the Presbyterian Church in the U.S.A. was beginning to divide along the battle line that ranged "conservative evangelicals" over against "theological liberals." The "evangelical" side of the denomination warmly embraced all the latest fads and fashions of American evangelicalism. Evangelist William A. ("Billy") Sunday was granted ordination as a Presbyterian minister in 1903. Conservative Presbyterians bought copies of *The Scofield Reference Bible* when it first appeared in 1907 and freely imbibed the hermeneutical scheme of "Dispensationalism" found in the copious footnotes. Paperback collections of the cheery, energetic "gospel songs" of Charles Gabriel and Homer Rodeheaver were introduced for use alongside the statelier hymns and tunes found in *The Hymnal*.

Leaders of the "liberal" side of the PCUSA were quietly at work to effect changes in the doctrinal tenets of the denomination, and to consolidate their hold on Presbyterian agencies and institutions, while pursuing liturgical "reform" designed to bring worship practice more into line with the "catholic" traditions of the Church of England. Under the guidance of preacher/poet Henry Van Dyke, afterwards an arch-foe of staunchly conservative J. Gresham Machen in the fight to save "Old Princeton," a complete liturgy was published in 1905 "for voluntary use" as *The Book of Common Worship*, very much in the mold of the Anglican *Book of Common Prayer*.

Philadelphia was the cradle of the Presbyterian Church in the U.S.A., and a citadel of "Old School" Presbyterianism, in the wake of the division of 1837. Although "New School" Presbyterians had a hand in its beginnings, the congregation of Falls Presbyterian Church cast in its lot with the "Old School" branch of the denomination when organized in 1856. The two branches had long since been reunited by 1904, but Philadelphia Presbytery ranked among the most conservative judicatories in the entire denomination. Glasgow could at least take comfort in the fact that he had landed in a place where the conservative influence of "Old Princeton" was very much in evidence.

Glasgow entered the PCUSA fold in the wake of intense controversy over revision of the Westminster Confession of Faith, intended to accommodate the reception of a large number of congregations from the anti-predestinarian Cumberland Presbyterian Church.

In 1903 two chapters were added to the Confession of Faith, together with some "declaratory" statements repudiating a strictly Calvinistic interpretation of the Standards. These alterations gave great offense to the waning numbers of doctrinal Calvinists in the denomination, but in 1906, two thirds of the Cumberlanders happily returned to the fold of the PCUSA.

The battle against confessional revision was lost, but the smoke still lingered over the field when Glasgow arrived in Philadelphia in 1904. He could not have been oblivious or indifferent to the fact that these alterations in the Confession of Faith represented a very substantial departure from the historic doctrinal position of the PCUSA. Calvinism was going into the discard, even among the "evangelical" ministers and leaders of the denomination.

We have no way of knowing from this distance, but it is possible that Glasgow had come to look upon "church reform" in the same way he had come to view "national reform." If the Presbyterian Church in the U.S.A. needed to be rescued from liberalism and restored to her historic confession of the Reformed faith, the best way to do it was by the way of engagement, *viz.*, to become involved and work from within the denomination. Or perhaps, like many other men in his situation, Glasgow simply decided to content himself with doing the best possible work as a preacher and pastor to his own congregation, and leave the denomination to look after itself. At least it can be said that there is no evidence to suggest that Glasgow himself ever questioned or discarded the Calvinism of the Westminster Standards, however much his view of public worship must have changed.

Glasgow was warmly welcomed to his new charge on December 6, 1904. A loyal "Old Princetonian," Dr. John Calhoun, then in the middle decades of his long and successful pastorate at Mount Airy Presbyterian Church in northwest Philadelphia, presided over the installation service. The sermon was delivered by another conservative voice in the PCUSA, Dr. Charles Erdman, pastor of one of the most prominent churches of greater Philadelphia, First Presbyterian Church of Germantown; later, as a professor of practical theology at Princeton Seminary, he would win fame as a popular preacher and conference speaker. Erdman is recalled today as the author of a series of brief "expositions" or commentaries on the New Testament, published by the Westminster Press and widely used down to the present time.

In 1905 Falls Presbyterian Church began to prepare to celebrate its fiftieth anniversary in the year to follow. The church building was enlarged and refurnished. A new platform for the choir and pulpit was built in the sanctuary, and a new pipe organ was installed. The manse was renovated. A series of meetings and services was held in March 1906 to celebrate and publicize these improvements, and later, in November 1906, another series of events marked the fiftieth anniversary, beginning with an "historical sermon" delivered by the pastor during Morning Worship on Sabbath, November 4th. As one would expect from a pastor's wife in those days, Mrs. Glasgow was president of the Ladies' Missionary Society and served on the refreshments and decorations committees.

FURTHER PUBLICATIONS AND DOCTORATE

While engaged in the many labors of his pastorate in Philadelphia, Glasgow found time to pursue his historical interests by compiling an illustrated *Register of Franklin College, Ohio*, published in 1908. Founded in 1825 and located in New Athens, Ohio, Franklin College is listed in Glasgow's *Cyclopedic Manual of the UPCNA* as the oldest of the many colleges "not directly under control of the Church, but manned and patronized largely therein" (p. 618). Franklin College closed its doors in 1921, but a museum to perpetuate its memory is maintained in the beautiful building that once housed the college. The museum's web site states that

> Franklin College boasted numerous influential graduates of national and international renown, including 8 U.S. Senators, 9 U.S. Representatives, 20 State Legislators, 47 physicians, over 113 educators, and over 440 ministers. A few of the more notable graduates include John Bingham, Congressman and author of the due process clause of the 14th Amendment to the Constitution and chief deputy prosecutor of President Lincoln's assassins; Titus Basfield, an ex-slave who was one of the first African-American graduates from an Ohio college; William Lawrence, first Controller of the U.S. treasury; John Kuhn, one of the founders of the Republican Party; and Joseph Ray, who authored "Ray's Arithmetic" books.

A register of the faculty and alumni of Franklin College would make fascinating reading, and William Glasgow was just the man to produce it. For this labor Franklin College rewarded Glasgow by conferring on him the degree of "Doctor Divinitatis" (D.D.) in the year of the book's publication, 1908.

Appearing the same year was a book even closer to Glasgow's heart, *The Geneva Book, Comprising a History of Geneva College, and a Biographical Catalogue of the Alumni and Many Students* (Philadelphia: Westbrook Publishing Company, 1908). The book is a densely-packed compilation of history, reminiscence, poems and college songs, lists of names and dates, and profiles of faculty and students, complete with hand-drawn maps and rare photographs of both the Northwood and Beaver Falls campuses, all suffused with the love and unwavering loyalty that small colleges evoke from the hearts of their sons and daughters. Glasgow abandoned all attempts to be journalistically objective or dispassionate about his subject, and his personal warmth and subjectivity set this book apart from his other historical productions.

FINAL ILLNESS AND DEATH

Glasgow was in the prime of life and work when he was stricken with a condition described as "intestinal rheumatitis." The sturdy frame that had supported him through years of constant preaching, lecturing, travel, research and writing, seemed to have suddenly given way. After several weeks of illness at home, Glasgow was taken into the hospital and died on March 2, 1909.[10] Newspaper accounts of his death reported that Glasgow was conscious until a few minutes before his death, and able to talk to his wife and two daughters, who were at his side.

A bronze plaque, "In memory of our beloved pastor, Rev. W. Melancthon Glasgow, D.D., 1858-1909," hangs today in the sanctuary of Falls Presbyterian Church. Inscribed on the plaque are words taken from the text of his last sermon:

> Blessed be God, even the Father of our Lord Jesus Christ, the Father of all mercies, and the God of all comfort; Who comforteth us in all our tribulation, that we may be able to comfort them which are in any trouble, by the comfort wherewith we ourselves are comforted of God. (2 Corinthians 1:3, 4)

Glasgow made his mark in Philadelphia as a forceful preacher, an active evangelist, and when hard times fell on his part of the city, a true friend of the poor. Consistent with his Covenanter background, he was a vocal supporter of reform efforts such as the prohibition movement and other campaigns against the vices and evils of society. He produced a goodly number of lengthy historical or reference works, and a veritable flood of shorter writings flowed from his never-resting pen.

Glasgow could not have known that his life would be cut short in its prime, but even so, brief as it was, his life was crowded with labors of many kinds, and no small amount of success and lasting achievement. Relatively few men that have lived far longer lives have accomplished nearly so much.

It is to be hoped that the republication of Glasgow's *History of the Reformed Presbyterian Church* will reawaken interest in both the author and the subjects that were dear to his heart. There is much that remains to be discovered about his life and work, and a fuller biography should be written. Glasgow himself tantalizes us with the statement that,

---

10. It is ironic that Glasgow should have left a confused record with regard to the year of his birth; and likewise that subsequent RP chroniclers should err with regard to the year of his death, giving it as 1911.

We are grateful to David McClenahan of Falls Presbyterian Church for confirming from the church records that Glasgow died in 1909—although those same records may be in error about the year of his birth.

The manuscript prepared for the composition of this book was sufficient to make two volumes each of the present size, and the copy had to be cut down about one-half in order that the whole scope of the contemplated work might be included in one volume of reasonable size and price.[11]

Where is that manuscript now? What further treasures of Reformed Presbyterian history does it contain? Perhaps in the future the manuscript will be recovered, and a new and greatly enlarged edition of this book will see the light of day.

Until then, Presbyterians of every kind, and all who love the *Magnalia Christi*, as Mather put it, "the great works of Christ," unfolded in the history of Christianity in our country, will be more than content to have this present volume in their hands once more. We all are deeply indebted to Dr. Joel Beeke, and to Reformation Heritage Books, for undertaking the republication of Glasgow's *History of the Reformed Presbyterian Church*.

Students of Presbyterian church history will discover a whole family of churches whose history sparkles with remarkable personalities and noteworthy achievements, however much they may have been forgotten in the years that followed. Reformed Presbyterians, Associate Reformed Presbyterians, and the dwindling numbers of those who once belonged to the United Presbyterian Church of North America, will all give thanks for the history that is brought to light in these pages. We "Scottish Dissenting Presbyterians" have a goodly heritage. We have much to discover about our forbears in the faith, and what they accomplished in their day; and much as well to consider with regard to how their distinctive principles and practices may have something vital to contribute to our churches and to our nation today.

— Ray B. Lanning and Nathan P. Eshelman

Grand Rapids, Michigan
May 2007

---

11. See "Preface," p. vii.

HISTORY OF THE

REFORMED PRESBYTERIAN CHURCH

IN AMERICA.

HISTORICAL INTRODUCTION.

THE Reformed Presbyterian Church in America is the
lineal descendant and true representative of the
Church of Scotland in her purest days, and embraces
in her Testimony the principles of the Second Reformation as exhibited between the years 1638 and 1649.
The Presbyterian Church of Scotland was a Covenanting Church, and the Reformed Presbyterian Church of
this age is not a branch of any Presbyterian body but
the remnant of the original stock. While the Synod
of this Church is among the small ecclesiastical assemblies, yet for that reason she should not be regarded
with reproach. Her principles are both scriptural and
unpopular, and neither the paucity of her members nor
the unpopularity of her principles prove that the position
of the church is unsound or impracticable. She claims
to be a Reformed Church, a Presbyterian Church, and

a Covenanting Church; and to fully substantiate this claim a cursory review of the history of the Christian church will be necessary.

From the earliest period in the world's history the church of God has been a Covenanting Church, and a dissenter from immoral constitutions of Church and State. The antediluvians bore faithful testimony to the character and moral government of God, and by the call of Abraham this covenanting society received a more perfect organization. The patriarchs were constant witnesses to the truth of God against idolatry and immorality either national or individual. Under the Mosaic dispensation also the nation of Israel was brought into a solemn league and covenant with God, and the Church erected in the wilderness was a witnessing society for the rights of God. When the "fullness of time" had come, and the predicted Messiah came into the world as the "Messenger of the Covenant," He was a witness for the truth, and not only bore constant testimony to His Sonship before Jewish priests, but also claimed His right to the Headship over the nations before the Roman government. These two articles have formed the chief points of Christ's witnesses in all ages, and are the cardinal principles of the Reformed Presbyterian Church in this age. When Christ commissioned His apostles to go forth and preach the gospel, He gave them to be witnesses for Him and to His rights upon earth, even to the end of the world. The commission then implies that every minister of Christ is to bear like testimony. At the organization of the Apostolic church and in accordance with the directions of the Divine Head, members were to be received into it by an expression of their belief in the Saviour, and a confession of the scheme of grace as revealed in God's Word, with a life and conversation as becomes the same profession. In this the requirements of the Christian church should be uniform. The government and order of the primitive church were evidently *Presbyterian.* It was distinguished for the purity of its doctrines and the simplicity of its worship. Nothing of human invention was tolerated and it was scriptural in all its appointments. In this system of government, moreover, the Headship of Christ and the subjection of all things to Him were clearly displayed. At an early period of the life of this scriptural church and covenanting society were the fires of persecution kindled, and they raged with increased fury because many had not grown weary of purity and witness-bearing. For three hundred years were they persecuted under Jewish bigotry, until Constantine the Great wrapped the imperial robe around him, and signally overthrew the policy of the Roman power, and established pure Christianity as the religion of the empire. Under his eventful reign Christianity spread rapidly, but co-incidently the spirit of Anti-Christ was at work. The condition of the church was such that men were not willing to return to the pure state of the primitive church, nor to become witnesses for the rights of King Jesus. Preachers of the gospel were lead to defection by vain philosophies and worldly ambition. Discipline was relaxed and the lives of members gradually became more corrupt. They had broken covenant with God and iniquity was being visited upon them. The union of Church and State doubtless promoted

defection and corruption, and the spirituality of the
church became very low. The favors of the State soon
developed a hierarchical system of Prelacy, which system
was directly antagonistic to the teaching of the Apostolic church. The same causes also gave rise to Papacy,
and the bishop of Rome assumed the title of the
Universal Bishop. Seemingly the whole world "wondered
after the beast," and the unmutilated Word of God
was not only prohibited to be read, but the worship
was conducted in an unknown tongue. During all these
periods of the prevalence of Papacy, there were faithful witnesses for Jesus to be found. Before the papal
power had reached the Western church, God had raised
up the faithful Athanasius to contend against the Arian
heresy ; Vigilantius to expose the strongholds of super-
stition, and the learned Augustine to overthrow the
Pelagian and Semi-Pelagian heresies.

Away to the north and west faithful witnesses for revealed
truth and scriptural church-life had been preserved, who
uncompromisingly refused to hold communion with the
church of Rome.   In England, Scotland and Ireland the
pure gospel was preached and the church conducted after
the Apostolic model.   Patrick and Columba, with their con-
temporaries and successors, multiplied witnesses for Jesus
and established a church in opposition to Rome. Many
of these witnesses were denominated *Ceilide*, or servants
of God, and have been known in history as *Culdees.*
They were *Covenanters* in theory, *Presbyterians* in
government, and *Reformed Presbyterians* in sentiment.
They held firmly to the Word of God and supremacy
of Christ, and maintained a separate existence until the

time of the Reformation. In parts of Europe, Roman persecutors found faithful witnesses for the rights of Christ, who opposed the Anti-christian system. The Waldenses in the valleys of Piedmont, and the Albigenses in the south of France, had continued their existence since Apostolic times. They were a covenanting society separated from, or rather never had been in connection with, the church of Rome, and propogated a truly evangelical creed and a Presbyterian form of government since the Apostolic age. This fact is admitted by nearly every historian. But these witnesses for Christ were soon discovered in vast congregations and caused to suffer most violent and terrible persecution. Many of them were banished, and, as so many sparks from the burning stake, they kindled anew their principles in other parts of Europe. They were afterward found in Germany, Bohemia, France and England. In the fourteenth century eighty thousand of these Covenanting Presbyterians were found in Austria and maintained their principles to the death. In the fifteenth century the Reformation from Popery began, although its work is generally attributed to the sixteenth century. Wyckliffe, John Huss, the Lollards, and Jerome of Prague espoused the principles of the covenanting Waldenses, and in their maintenance of truth prepared the way for the Reformation. All those in sympathy with the cause of pure religion formulated a covenant, which was entered into by the whole Waldensian Church. Some of the reformers of this period had been reared within the pale of the Romish Church and experimentally knew the errors against which they heroically contended. God brought out such eminent witnesses as

Luther, Zwinglius, Melancthon, Calvin and Farel, who in
Germany, Switzerland and France were the effective instruments in God's hand for propogating the cause of the
First Reformation, and shook Papal Europe to her very
foundations. As might be expected the Reformation met
with a great deal of opposition. The hands of the
reformers were held up by the Lutheran Church, which,
in 1534, solemnly swore the famous League of Smalkalde.
In 1537, a similar covenant was sworn by the followers
at Geneva. Unhappily the Lutherans and Reformed differed
in some points, and especially in regard to sacraments,
but with reference to the pure Word of God and the
errors of the Romish church they were agreed. The
Reformed churches of France and Hungary also swore
similar covenants and all were known as *Protestants*
against the corruptions of the church of Rome. The
cause of the Reformation did not find such rich soil
in England. The despotic Henry the Eighth was King.
He was a most irreligious man, and, in order to gratify
his own lusts, established the Church of England, and
arrogated to himself the power of a Pope at London.
Although this church was separated from that of Rome,
yet it retained much of the doctrine and order of the Papacy.
The Reformation made some progress under the brief
reign of Edward the Sixth, but its friends were caused
to pass through fiery persecution under the reign of
bloody Mary. Upon the accession of Queen Elizabeth
the protestant faith was again restored, but through the Erastian measures of the Queen the cause did not flourish. The
chief hindrance was from the fact that the anti-christian hier-
archy of the Romish church was retained almost unaltered

in the Established Church of England. For all intents and purposes it *was* Romish, and the bitter enemy of the Reformation. There were some again in England who contended for purity in doctrine and government, who were called *Puritans*, and because they would not take the communion of the corrupt English church, entered the role of *Dissenters*. The Reformation began to spread rapidly in Scotland in the early part of the sixteenth century, and owed little or nothing to the favor of the state. God raised up several eminent witnesses for the truth who suffered martyrdom, and, notwithstanding the fact that they sealed their testimony with their own blood, the truth continued to progress. Among these faithful witnesses were Patrick Hamilton, George Wishart and John Knox. The latter returned from the Continent in 1555, when the cause of the Reformation was languishing, and he was the means of awakening the multitude by his powerful preaching, and caused the Queen to fear his prayers more than an army of soldiers. Through his indomitable courage and consecrated devotion to the cause of the Reformation the people entered into several solemn covenants for the purpose of uniting the friends of the cause. Various covenants adapted to the times were sworn at Edinburgh in 1557; at Perth in 1559; at Stirling in 1560; and at Leith in 1562, in which they pledged their lives and their substance to maintain the cause of Christ.

In 1560, the Parliament abolished Popery, and the first General Assembly emitted the First Book of Discipline, fixing and defining the government and order of the church after a scriptural and Presbyterian plan. In 1578, a Second Book of Discipline was prepared and adopted and the Presbyterian Reformation was fully established. The most memorable step in the progress of the Reformation was the adoption of the NATIONAL COVENANT OF SCOTLAND. It was drawn up by Rev. John Craig of Edinburgh, and was the nation's solemn protest against Popery and the bond for the maintenance of the Reformed faith. It was sworn and subscribed by the King and most of the nobility with their households, in 1581. In all these covenants it is expressly agreed that the "Bible should be the supreme law, and that nations should frame their laws according to the Divine standard; that there is a conscience toward God paramount to human control, and the Word of God is the rule for the government of the conscience; that there is no lord of conscience but the Lord Jesus Christ who alone is the Head of the Church and the lawful Governor among the Nations; that it is the duty of every nation, as well as the individual, to incorporate these principles in its constitution and live a life in conformity to this profession."

In 1590, the National Covenant was again subscribed. In 1592, the Presbyterian form of church government was ratified by the King and parliament, and this has been denominated the GREAT CHARTER. In 1596, the General Assembly renewed the National Covenant again, at which time over four hundred ministers and elders with uplifted hands to God solemnly engaged in His name to purge the church of all corruption. This was a reviving time from the presence of the Lord, and the Reformation was in the meridian of its life.

Partly by craft and partly by arbitrary interference with ecclesiastical courts, James attempted to overthrow the Scottish Reformation and establish Episcopacy. This perfidious ruler favored Popery, interfered with the election of members to the highest judicatory of the church, and introduced prelacy in 1610. In 1618, the "Five Articles of Perth" were forcibly carried and ratified, and because some ministers refused to subscribe to these Popish requirements, they were ejected from their charges and visited with heavy penalties. At the accession of Charles the First to the throne, in March, 1625, the Presbyterian Church of Scotland witnessed a deadly foe, and his determination was to destroy every vestage of Presbyterianism and compel them to conform to the English Episcopal Liturgy. In 1536, a Liturgy and Book of Ecclesiastical Canons were introduced, and had the effect of abolishing the ecclesiastical polity of the Church of Scotland. Lamentably too many complied with these prelatic innovations and arbitrary measures. These tyrannical proceedings aroused the independent spirit of many of the Scotch, and, after earnest deliberation and fervent prayer, they resolved to flee to the strength received by their ancestors, and took steps to renew the National Covenants. The *Covenants* were the source of Scotland's strength and the crown of her glory! The National Covenant had served a good purpose in consummating the First Reformation, and it was brought into service in the Second.

To now adapt it to the circumstances of the church and nation, Archibald Johnston specified several acts of former Parliaments to prove that the course taken by the Covenanters was constitutional; and Alexander Henderson

applied the sacred bond to the condemnation and rejection
of all prelatical innovations. They say in this bond:

"We promise and swear by the great name of the Lord our God,
to continue in the profession and obedience of the true religion; that
we shall defend the same, and resist all those contrary errors and corruptions according to our vocation, and to the utmost of that power
which God hath put in our hands, all the days of our life."

And they also declare:

"We shall, to the utmost of our power, stand to the defence of our
Sovereign, the King, in the defence and preservation of the aforesaid
true religion, liberties, and laws of the kingdom."

And with regard to the original covenant that was now
renewed, they said:

"The present and succeeding generations in this land are bound to
keep the aforesaid national oath and subscription inviolate."

The Covenant was now sworn and subscribed at Grey-
friar's Church in Edinburgh, March 1, 1638, by sixty
thousand persons, amid scenes of joy and sorrow. They
laid the precious document upon the mossy tombs, and
many wrote their names with blood from their own veins,
while others were but permitted to subscribe initials, because
the document was full, and there was no more room.
The renewing of the Covenant was followed by the happiest
effects and manifest tokens of the Divine blessing. It was
the means of awakening the people to their vows and the
signal overthrow of Episcopacy. The Covenanters acted
with prudence and decision in demanding the General
Assembly to redress their grievances, and a meeting of
Parliament to rectify disorders. This assembly met in the
city of Glasgow, November 20, 1638, and was presided
over by the great Alexander Henderson. This assembly
condemned the "Five Articles of Perth," the Liturgy

and Canons, the Book of Ordination, the High Commission Court, and the civil places and powers of churchmen. Prelacy was rejected, bishops and prelatical leaders were deposed and excommunicated. The renovation of the Covenant was approved; the Presbyterian form of government was fully restored; the power of the church to convene in her annual assembly was granted, and the right of the church to preserve order, discipline, education and religious worship was acknowledged. These were among the purest days of the Covenanting Presbyterian Church of Scotland, and the faithful witnesses for Jesus were triumphant in their rights and liberties. Although armies were brought down to crush the success of the Covenanters and to restore prelacy, they were ineffectual in destroying the witnesses, and the work of the Scottish Reformation was fully confirmed by Parliament in 1640. The exiled ministers were recalled, the order of the church restored, and the ordinances of religion were again dispensed to the people to the utter dismay of the prelates, and Spottiswood, Archbishop of St. Andrew's, mournfully exclaimed, "Now, all that we have been doing these thirty years by past is at once thrown down."

While the cause was flourishing in Scotland, the Covenanters in Ireland were inhumanly massacred. Charles the First closed his ears against the cry for help, and he was justly suspicioned for his complicity with the Romish power.

By an application of the English Parliament, June 12, 1643, an assembly of learned and godly men was called, composed of one hundred and twenty ministers and thirty elders, the majority of which were strict Presbyterians.

This was called the WESTMINSTER ASSEMBLY, and met
in the Jerusalem Chamber, Westminster, London, July
1, 1643, and continued its sessions for a period of five
years, six months and twenty-two days. They drew
up from the Word of God the Confession of Faith,
the Larger and Shorter Catechisms, a Form of Church
Government and a Directory for Worship. These all
received the sanction of the English Parliament and
were adopted by the General Assembly of the Church
of Scotland. A joint application by the Parliament
and Westminster Assembly was made to the Convention of Estates in Scotland and the General Assembly,
August 17, 1643, to enter into a SOLEMN LEAGUE
AND COVENANT, embracing the civil and religious interests of the three kingdoms. A draft was made by
Alexander Henderson and cheerfully subscribed by the
Assembly of Divines at Westminster, by both Houses
of Parliament, and by persons of all ranks in England.
It was then carried over into Ireland and signed generally by the congregations in the province of Ulster.
This famous document bound the United Kingdoms to
the preservation of the Reformed religion, to its doctrines, discipline and government according to the Word
of God. It simply brought the Church back to its
Scriptural basis and its allegiance to King Jesus and
His Law in all transactions, civil and ecclesiastical. Had
it not been for the Solemn League and Covenant, the
three Kingdoms would have been cast into absolute
despotism, and the liberty and civilization of the world
would have received an irrecoverable shock. The great
principles of this sacred bond are those of God's Word,

and nothing more nor less. While England was not quite ready, but should have been, to fully adopt them as her principles of national government, yet they are none the less Scriptural, and there will a time come when all the Kingdoms of the earth will be united under a similar and one grand Solemn League and Covenant; when God's Anointed shall be practically acknowleded King of nations; and when these Scriptural principles of the heavenly-minded Covenanters of Scotland shall gloriously triumph. It cannot be otherwise, for the nations that neglect or refuse to enter into such a covenant with the King of Kings shall perish. No international document has ever been so much misrepresented and maligned as the Solemn League and Covenant. Statesmen should pause and read it carefully, compare it to the demands of God's Law, and fully digest what is in it, before they vent their eloquence in undue criticism. A sacred principle was then, and by this document infused, into the heart of that nation, which has never perished; and, having taken root in the new empire of America, may be regarded as the dawn of a better day for the cause of King Jesus. The Covenanters never attempted to force Presbyterianism upon England or any other nation, for they entered into the Covenant without any such stipulations, and it has always been contrary to their principles to *force* Christians to the acceptance of any position. But they do feel it their duty to teach men and nations their allegiance to Christ and to use every legitimate means to bring them to an acceptance and acknowledgment of the same.

James the First had signed the first National Covenant, and Charles the Second, on being crowned at

Scone, January 1, 1651, solemnly swore to keep both
the National and Solemn League and Covenant. And
when the oath to defend the Church of Scotland was
administered to him, kneeling and holding up his right
hand, he uttered the following solemn vow: " By the
Eternal and Almighty God, who liveth and reigneth
forever, I shall observe and keep all that is contained
in this oath."

A blessing followed the course of the Church at this
time, and many of the breaches in Church and State
were healed. The Solemn League and Covenant was
a necessity, and not until all nations are bound together and to God by a holy Covenant, and true liberty
flowing from Bible principles recognized, will universal
peace prevail. The attainments of the Second Reformation are worthy of record. The supreme Headship of
Christ over the Church was exhibited ; the Church was
priviledged to call her own assemblies ; the policy of
the government was brought into conformity to God's
Word ; the nation owned its allegiance to King Jesus ;
and rulers were to be set up who should be God's
ministers for good and a terror to evil doers. This
was the church's purest period and the nation's happiest
hour. The object of the existence of the Covenanter
Church in America as true witnesses for the royal
perogatives of King Jesus, is to bring this nation to
the enjoyment of the blessings and duty of this period
in the life of the British nation. It is the required
attitude of every church and nation to its Divine Head.

The period in which the nation continued to avow
and practically apply the principles of the Reformation,

was too brief to fully test the blessings of the nation whose God is the Lord. The beauty of the Covenanted Reformation was soon marred by the duplicity of an unprincipled king and his followers. England was the first to make defection, because the danger which threatened her civil liberty was past, and she imagined that she no longer needed the help of the King of Heaven. Scotland soon also broke her solemn covenant engagements and departed from her attainments. The invasion of England, in 1648, by the Duke of Hamilton's army, was a wilful breach of the Solemn League and Covenant, and was afterwards condemned by both the Parliament and General Assembly. Charles the Second was totally unworthy of the homage of a loyal people, and happy would they have been had they never placed the crown upon him. The people had committed their trusts into the hands of a treacherous man. There was undue attachment to the house of Stuart, which ultimately lead to untold calamities. The King was forced to exile, and Oliver Cromwell invaded Scotland with an English army, and gained a victory at Dunbar. Under Cromwell's usurped authority, and by intrigue, plans were formed to overthrow the Constitution. The faithful Presbyterians considered that they were bound to adhere to the Constitution ; and, because they opposed the malignants and their policy, were called *protestors*. Cromwell died in September, 1658, and his son Richard succeeded him. He was wanting in capacity and ambition, and Charles the Second was restored to the throne in May, 1660. From this date to that of the Revolution Settlement in 1688, the period is denominated the "killing

times." Now begin the sufferings of the Church of Scotland ;
and the history of this period may well be written in
characters of blood.   In 1661, the Parliament required
an oath of unlimited allegiance from all members instead
of a subscription to the Covenants.   The order and
government of the Church were reversed ; bishops were
restored ; all proceedings of the Church and State on
behalf of Reformation from 1638 to 1649 were pronounced treasonable ; the Covenants, National and Solemn League, were pronounced unlawful oaths ; and all
civil and ecclesiastical acts were regarded null and void.
The covenants were ordered to be burned in public at
Edinburgh, as they had been done at London ; and all
those who owned the covenants were subjected to the
penalties of treason.   Nearly four hundred ministers of
the Presbyterian Church were driven from their congregations by an act of the Privy Council.   The whole work
of the Reformation was overturned, and the Act of
Supremacy, making the King judge in all matters civil
and ecclesiastical, paved the way for the terrible persecution which immediately followed.   Amid these bloody
persecutions the Covenanter Church came into prominence as the faithful witnesses of the great principles
of the Reformation.   They bore constant testimony for
the divine authority of the Presbyterian Church as contrasted with Prelacy ; for the exclusive Headship of the
Lord Jesus Christ over the Church ; for the supreme
authority of the Mediator and His Law over the rulers
of the nation ; for the perpetual obligation of the
Covenants ; together with the rights and duties of subjects owning the authority of Christ to resist those

wicked rulers who had usurped their authority and trampled under their feet the rights and liberties of a religious and covenanting people. Such was the testimony which the Covenanters bore, and sealed it with their blood. Among the first victims of this irresponsible power were the Marquis of Argyle and Rev. James Guthrie, staunch Presbyterians and resolute defenders of the cause of the Redeemer. No less than twenty thousand Presbyterian and Covenanting witnesses suffered martyrdom in various ways, and many were banished to America and Jamaica ; and upwards of two thousand godly ministers were banished from their congregations in one day. Some renounced the Covenanted cause, but those who continued faithful were driven and chased like partridges on the mountains. The persecutions were horrible in their character, and one cannot read the history of this period without feeling his blood boil at the atrocious slaughter of the Covenanters by the thousands. They refused to wait upon the ministrations of curates who had been thrust upon them by the bayonet, and if they were found waiting upon any of the ejected Presbyterian ministers either in private houses or conventicles, they were heavily fined and cruelly punished. Among the principal non-conforming ministers were Richard Cameron, John Welsh, Thomas Douglas and John Kid, and a reward was offered for the heads of these faithful divines, dead or alive. Even to the death the martyrs of Jesus bore testimony against their persecutors, and when given an opportunity to speak in their courts, replied to the perjured prelates in the following manner : " Every immoral constitution is disapproved of God. No

2

man ought to swear allegiance to a power which God does not recognize. All kings are commanded to promote the welfare of the Church, and those who own allegiance to Christ cannot consistently pray for the prosperity of the Church's enemies, or for the establishment of thrones founded upon iniquity. It is certainly the duty of Christians to be meek and peaceable members of civil society. If they are permitted to enjoy their lives, their property, and especially their religion, without being required to make any sinful compliances, it is right that they should behave peaceably and not involve society in confusion, even though the power of the empire in which they reside be in evil hands. Every burden which God in His Providence brings upon them, they must cheerfully bear. But never are Christians called upon by their God to own as His ordinance anything which is contrary to His Law. The civil powers of which He approves are a terror to them who do evil. Tyrants and persecutors, usurpers and despisers of religion may be set up in His holy and just Providence to answer valuable purposes in His hand, but He himself declares in His Word that such Kings are set up not by Him. The Pagan Roman government is described in Revelation as the empire of the dragon, and all the kings that support anti-Christ are said in the same infallible Word to have received from Satan their authority. God has declared their overthrow and destruction, and no Protestant should recognize them as the ordinance of God to which they must yield conscientious support. The present King, Charles the Second, has violated the Constitution of Scotland ; he has broken the covenant

which he made with God and man; he has claimed as
an essential part of royal perogative, a blasphemous
supremacy in the Church; he has overturned our ecclesiastical order; banished the faithful ministry, and persecuted the most virtuous inhabitants of the land. Such a
perjured usurper and profligate tyrant cannot be considered as a lawful magistrate by the Reformed Presbyterian Covenanters."

These were the sentiments of the martyrs of Jesus, and
for these principles they freely gave their lives. Their
position was exceedingly unpopular, but in it were the
germs of future glory and greatness. Like John
the Baptist, they were the forerunners of greater
things, and like John the Baptist, many of them
were beheaded. For over twenty years this cruel
persecution lasted, and the Covenanting Church was reduced to a few ministers and members. As the faithful
remnant of the Church of Scotland in her purest days,
they continued to assemble for worship in such places
as they could, and their courts of judicature were prevented from meeting. They made several bold declarations of their principles, and aroused the indignation of
the King. At the first anniversary of the return of the
King, Charles the Second, May 27, 1679, bonfires had
been kindled in Rutherglen in commemoration of the
restoration. The Covenanters repaired to the scene, ex-
tinguished the fires, and burned the Acts of Parliament
and the Council as the Covenants had been burned.
They formulated the notable "Rutherglen Declaration
and Testimony," and after fixing it to the market cross,
peacefully retired. This was regarded as open rebellion

against the power, and produced the fiercest indignation among the prelatic party. It was among the first fearless declarations of the principles of the Covenanters, and lead to the battle of Drumclog, where Graham of Claverhouse was defeated. The Covenanters also issued the "Queensferry Paper" in June, 1680, in which they declared: "We do declare that we will set up over ourselves, and over what God shall give us power of, government and governors according to the Word of God; that we shall no more commit the government of ourselves and the making of laws for us to any one single person, this kind of government being most liable to inconveniences and aptest to degenerate into tyranny." This is strong language, and a bold sentiment of Republicanism. This was burning the bridge behind them, and they neither asked nor received any favors from the prelatic power or ministry. The Covenanters hereafter kept themselves aloof from prelatic assemblies and worshipped among themselves. Holding fast to the Covenants and the rights of the Church which had been established by the King and all subjects, they passed just sentence upon all backsliders and defectionists from the King to the humblest member of the once established Church. Rev. Donald Cargill excommunicated Charles the Second and six other noted profligates, September 17, 1680, in the presence of a vast congregation. They were guilty of the most atrocious crimes, and justly dealt with, but they were regarded as fit members of the Episcopacy. This again excited the blood-thirsty persecutors to frenzied madness. Richard Cameron, who was the leader of the Covenanters and a most fearless and pious man, fell at

Airsmoss, July 22, 1680, as a victim of the diabolical power. The blood-stained standard was not allowed to trail, and was borne aloft by Donald Cargill, until he also was apprehended and executed at Edinburgh, July 27, 1681. This left the Covenanters without a minister, but the followers were just as faithful to *their* King and the attainments of the Covenanting Church. They immediately organized a system of societies among themselves and met as often as they could. Correspondents from all the societies met in a general meeting, usually every three months, and determined the course of the whole body, but never assumed to dispense any official work. The minutes of these General Meetings were kept by Michael Shields and are published in the "Faithful Contendings." While they were deprived of public ministrations and sealing ordinances, the Covenanters could not conscientiously be administered unto by any minister who had taken "the indulgence." Mr. James Renwick, one of their worthy young men and a youth of good education, was sent to the University of Groningen, Holland, where he studied theology, and was licensed and ordained by the Classis of Groningen, May 10, 1683. The same fall he returned to Scotland, and, as the sole minister of the Covenanters, labored faithfully for the rights of Jesus and the liberties of his people. He suffered many annoyances and was frequently outlawed and persecuted. Every person was forbidden by the edict of the tyrannical King "to harbor him and his followers, or supply them with meat or drink; but to hunt and persue them out of all their dens, caves and most retired deserts, and to raise the hue and cry after them." Not-

withstanding these dangers and cruelties, the Covenanters
kept March 4, 1685, as "a day of thanksgiving unto the
Lord for the wonderful proofs of His love and good will,
manifested to a scattered and distressed remnant in this
land, by His delivering them in several places from the
power and rage of enemies when they were ready to
swallow them up." By the death of Charles the Second,
they enjoyed a brief breathing spell, and improved the
precious time by preparing the famous "Sanquhar Declaration," and nailing it to the market cross.* In 1682,
Rev. Alexander Peden was called from Ireland, and
assisted Mr. Renwick until his death, January 26, 1686.
In December, 1686, Alexander Shields, who had been
licensed by some Presbyterian ministers in London,
espoused the despised cause of the Cameronians. Mr.
William Boyd, educated in the Netherlands by the Covenanters, was licensed by the Classis of Groningen in
September, 1687, and all these held forth the rights of
"Christ's Crown and Covenant" with fearlessness and
power. Rev. James Renwick, the last martyr to the
sacred cause of Scotland, was executed February 17,
1688, for his devotion to the Crown rights of King
Jesus. His charge was: "You, James Renwick, have
shaken off all fear of God and respect and regard to
his majesty's authority and laws; and having entered
yourself into the society of some rebels of most damn-
able and pernicious principles and disloyal practices;
you took upon you to be a preacher to those traitors
and became so desperate a villain that you did openly

---

* For many of these notable documents, and the details of incidents,
the reader is referred to any reliable history of the Church of Scotland.

and frequently preach in the fields, declaiming against the authority and government of our sovereign lord, the King; denying that our most gracious sovereign, King James the Seventh, is lawful King of these realms; asserting that he was a usurper, and that it was not lawful to pay cess or taxes to his majesty; but that it was lawful and the duty of subjects to rise in arms and make war against his majesty and those commissioned by him." What is asserted was true; for the Covenanters held the principle that "the abuse of power abrogates the right to use it." With few exceptions, all Protestants accept this principle. Thomas Lining, also educated by the Covenanters, was ordained by the Classis of Embden, in August, 1688, after an examination of twenty-one days. Revs. Shields, Boyd and Lining maintained the faithful Covenanted testimony until the Revolution. Those Covenanters residing in Ireland were ministered unto by the revered David Houston. The Revolution Settlement of 1688, which dethroned James the Second and placed the crown upon William, Prince of Orange, is a memorable period, and one worthy of careful consideration in the history of the Reformed Presbyterian Church. The two hundredth anniversary of this event was celebrated by the Covenanter Church in America, as in other lands.

All true hearted Presbyterians looked with favor upon the Prince of Orange, and regarded the circumstances which placed the crown upon his head as a good omen and the dawn of a better day for Scotland. It was regarded as a Divine interposition in behalf of a loyal people, and the course pursued fully vindicated some of the principles held by the Covenanting witnesses. The Scottish convention passed the following : " That King James, by his abuse of power, had forfeited all title to the crown, and that it be conferred upon the Prince of Orange." The English Parliament also declared "that King James the Second, having endeavored to subvert the Constitution by breaking the original contract between the King and the people, did abdicate the throne." Now it is plain that both these acts establish these two principles, "that the abuse of power destroys the right to exercise it ; and that a people may depose their rulers." These same principles dissolved the union between the Colonies and Great Britain, and gave the United States their independence. The same principles now lead thousands of Covenanters to sacrifice their lives, and the principles will be admitted as sound by every intelligent reader. But the hopes of the faithful Covenanting witnesses were doomed to speedy disappointment. While the Presbyterian system was established in Scotland, the Church was left under Erastian control. The Revolution Settlement was unsatisfactory in many respects. It was characterized by several flagrant errors. The Covenants were blasphemously cast aside as worthless ; the civil institutions no longer pretended to possess scriptural qualifications ; and prelacy was retained in the National Church. If the Revolution of 1688, which overturned the house of Stuart, justified the course of those who rejected the authority upon the principle now accepted by all, then certainly the Covenanters were justified in rejecting the "settlement" of King William when he openly violated the very principles which brought him to the throne. He wilfully betrayed the very cause he solemnly swore to defend. Because the Covenanters regarded an oath of vast importance and binding until the ends for which it was made were accomplished; because they, and others, solemnly swore to adhere to the doctrine and order of the Church of Scotland as constituted between the years 1638 and 1649; because they were sworn to oppose Popery, Prelacy and Erastianism as all the Kings and subjects were bound; because the crown was offered to the new sovereign without the proper and required scriptural qualifications; because the evil institution, against which the whole Church of Scotland had borne constant testimony, was interwoven into the policy of King William; and because he became the acknowledged head of the Church, and exercised authority over it contrary to the Word of God and the previously avowed position of the Church of Scotland, the *Reformed Covenanting Church publicly protested against the "settlement,"* and remained separate from it, both in its civil and ecclesiastical relations. Their grounds of dissent are those of reason and justice. The Reformed Presbyterian Church, or because of its attachment to the Covenants, the Covenanter Church, of this day, occupies the same position as the Church of Scotland did between the years 1638 and 1649, and which was the purest and most blessed period in its history. The Covenanters hold that the Covenants were binding upon those who solemnly swore them, and who are represented in them, and they are not willing to speedily relinquish the testimony for which the life-blood of thousands of their brethern was sacrificed. While they stood aloof from the government because of principle and the reasons heretofore mentioned, as peaceful and law-abiding citizens they claimed the right of the protection of their lives and property, and paid all just dues in taxes, and bearing arms in defence of their country. Those in Scotland who held these principles of Bible civil government as they had always been maintained by a true scriptural policy, hoped for a reformation and a return to former attainments. As an expression of their hopes, at the first General Assembly after the Revolution "settlement" held in 1690, the Covenanter ministers, Revs. Shields, Boyd and Lining, presenting a paper asking the Assembly to carefully examine their position, to acknowledge and confess their sin of Covenant breaking, and the nation's sin of defection from the previous attainments. This they not only refused to do, but fully embraced the policy of the government, and subsequently deposed the Rev. John McMillan, a Presbyterian minister and a member of their own court, for no other cause than pleading for the obligations of the Covenants which they had solemnly sworn, and now violated with impunity.

In 1691, Revs. Thomas Lining and William Boyd made defection, and after being admonished for their faithfulness to the Covenanters, were received into the Established Church. After having preached the Gospel and held the principles of the Covenanting Church for several years at the risk of their lives, they could not withstand the unpopularity of their cause. They even persuaded Rev. Alexander Shields, the author of "The Hind let Loose," to leave the glorious principles he had so ably defended, and he also joined the Established Church. Rev. David Houston, in Ireland, was now the sole minister of the Reformed Presbyterian Church, and he held her principles intact until his death. Alexander Shields continued in his course of defection and became a chaplain in an army which fought under the Pope, and he died abandoned and distressed in Jamaica. The Covenanters were without a minister for sixteen years, and continued to hold that it was inconsistent with their position to wait upon the ministrations of a minister who had been unfaithful to Jesus and his solemn vows. They scrupulously contended for the whole truth once delivered to the saints, organized themselves into praying societies, and supplicated earnestly and importunately the Good Shepherd to send them a pastor for the scattered flock. They watched with interest the contendings of the Rev. John McMillan, who, until 1703, sought a recognition of the obligations of the Covenants, and had failed. Believing that he had received his commission to preach from Christ and not from men, and that he had been unjustly deposed by the Established Church, he resumed his ministrations among his former congregation, who cordially received him and embraced his views of the Covenants. After frequent conferences and serious deliberation, Mr. McMillan acceded to the Reformed Presbyterian Church in October, 1706, and began his labors among them in December, 1707. His labors were greatly blessed among scattered societies, and many were built up in their most holy faith. About this time, Mr. John McNeil, a licentiate of the Established Church, and who had been deprived of the priviledge of preaching in that body because of his fidelity to Reformation principles, also joined himself to the Covenanting Church, and assisted Mr. McMillan in displaying a banner because of truth. They drew up a Protestation and Declinature, in which they clearly set forth the principles of the Covenanting Church, and their reasons of dissent. The following is the title of this notable document: *Protestation and Testimony of the United Societies of the Witnessing Remnant of the Anti-popish, Anti-prelatic, Anti-erastian, Anti-sectarian, True Presbyterian Church of Christ in Scotland, against the sinful Incorporating Union with England and their British Parliament, Concluded and Established, May, 1707.* This famous document and many other copies of the original manuscripts of a similar nature, are in the possession of the author. In 1708, another paper entitled "Protestation, Declinature and Appeal," was prepared and signed by these ministers, in which they clearly exhibit their reasons for dissent from the Revolution Church and declare their unfaltering attachment to the standards of the once pure Church of Scotland. In 1707, the union of Scotland and England was effected, and in 1711, patronage was restored. These steps gave additional evidence of apostacy in the Church and Nation, and the Covenanters felt it their duty to take another stand against the incoming tide of Prelacy and Papacy. To this end, and to strengthen their hearts, they renewed the Covenants at

Auchinsaugh, Lanarkshire, July 23, 1712. All the societies assembled for this important transaction, and with their right hands lifted up to Heaven, solemnly pledged themselves to be for God, and not for another. This act of Covenanting was followed by a blessing. As Mr. McNeil was never ordained, Mr. McMillan was the only minister of the Covenanters for over thirty years. He was faithful in visiting the different localities where the societies assembled and preached to them with great power. While there was defection all around him and reproach cast upon him for his fidelity to a persecuted remnant of Christ's witnesses, he was unmoved in his course, and is an example of moral heroism unparalled in the history of the Christian Church. He was constantly treated with disrespect by Church and State, yet held fast the true position and the attainments to which every Church and Nation must reach, viz: allegiance to the Lord Jesus Christ as the Divine Head and King. In November, 1733, Rev. Ebenezer Erskine, who was subsequently joined by Revs. James Fisher, Alexander Moncrieff and William Wilson, seceded from the Established Church on account of thè evils flowing from patronage, and other tyrannical measures, and constituted the *Associate Presbytery*. In 1747, they divided on the "Burgess Oath" into two Synods, and grew rapidly. It was hoped some of them might join the Covenanters so that a Presbytery could be erected, but in this there was disappointment. In the testimony emitted by these men who constituted the first Associate Presbytery, it is admitted that grievous defects existed in the Revolution "settlement," and that rulers did not possess scriptural qualifications; yet these brethren continued to acknowledge that the government as constituted was an ordinance of God, and freely rendered it their support. They limited the Mediatorial Headship of Christ to the Church, and that as Mediator Christ does not govern the nations; that nations are not bound to acknowledge Christ or His religion; that magistrates are God's ordinance, no matter how immoral their characters may be; and that while scriptural qualifications may be desirable in rulers, yet they are not at all necessary. This view is simply placing the whole of the Reformation attainments into the grave and erecting a tombstone.

It is not at all strange that they and the Covenanters did not embrace each other. In the spring of 1743, however, one of the Associate ministers, the Rev. Thomas Nairn, did embrace the principles and joined himself to the Covenanters. He and the Rev. John McMillan now constituted the REFORMED PRESBYTERY, at Braehead, Parish of Carnwath, Scotland, August 1, 1743. Accession of ministers and increase of members soon followed, and the persecuted and despised Covenanter Church of Scotland began to exert an influence. In a popular sense, the Covenanter Church in Scotland was never very strong, because her principles were exceedingly unpopular, and not in harmony with the minds of the public. And, as Dr. Lathan, of South Carolina, truly says, "Her doctrinal standards were too high and her practical requirements too rigid to be at all palatable to the mass of the human family. Notwithstanding all this," he says, "the

Reformed Presbyterian Church has been, since its organization, a mighty power in the world. It stands among all other Christian denominations like a gnarled oak in a forest of dwarfed undergrowth." They again renewed the Covenants at Crawford-John, in 1745. THE ACT, DECLARATION AND TESTIMONY was adopted at Ploughlandhead in 1761, and soon afterwards published. The societies in Ireland, which, after the death of the Rev. David Houston, in 1696, were left without a minister, and only occasionally visited by the Rev. John McMillan. The societies in Ireland were placed under the care of the Reformed Presbytery of Scotland until the Reformed Presbytery of Ireland was erected in August, 1763. The Synod of the Reformed Presbyterian Church in Ireland was constituted at Cullybackey, May 1, 1811. The Church now regularly constituted in both Scotland and Ireland continues almost uninterruptedly to exist as a distinct denomination until the present time. The history of the Reformed Presbyterian Church is now transferred to America, and, after a brief statement of her beliefs and position, the organic history of the Church in this country will be recorded.

POSITION OF THE REFORMED PRESBYTERIAN CHURCH IN AMERICA.

———

IN her testimony the Reformed Presbyterian Church embraces the plain and cardinal truths of the Bible and brings them to bear practically upon the lives of her members.* From the following "Terms of Communion" and a brief statement of the distinctive principles of the Church, her true position may be learned:

TERMS OF COMMUNION.

1. An acknowledgment of the Scriptures of the Old and New Testaments to be the Word of God, and the only rule of faith and manners.

2. An acknowledgment that the whole doctrine of the Westminster Confession of Faith, and the Catechisms, Larger and Shorter, are agreeable unto, and founded upon, the Scriptures.

3. An acknowledgment of the divine right of one unalterable form of Church Government and manner of worship—and that these are, for substance, justly exhibited in that form of Church Government and the Directory for Worship agreed upon by the assembly of divines at Westminster, as they were received by the Church of Scotland.

4. An acknowledgment of public covenanting as an ordinance of God to be observed by churches and nations; and of the perpetual obligation of public covenants; and of the obligation upon this Church of the Covenant entered into in 1871, in which are embodied the engagements of the National Covenant of Scotland, and of the Solemn League and Covenant, so far as applicable in this land.

5. An approbation of the faithful contendings of the martyrs of

———

* See Testimony of the Reformed Presbyterian Church.

Jesus, and of the present Reformed Covenanted Churches in Britain and Ireland, against Paganism, Popery, and Prelacy, and against immoral constitutions of civil government, together with all Erastian tolerations and persecutions which flow therefrom, as containing a noble example for us and our posterity to follow in contending for all divine truth, and in testifying against all contrary evils, which may exist in the corrupt constitutions of either Church or State.

6. An approbation of the doctrines contained in the Declaration and Testimony of the Reformed Presbyterian Church in North America, in defence of truth, and in opposition to error.

These, together with due subordination in the Lord to the authority of the Synod of the Reformed Presbyterian Church in North America, and a regular life and conversation, form the bonds of our ecclesiastical union.

From this clear and concise declaration and testimony it is learned that the position of the Reformed Presbyterian Church in America is, and always has been, one of practical dissent from the Constitution of the United States. In this the practice of the Church has been uniform. The Constitution is radically and wilfully defective in that it does not recognize the existence of God, the supremacy of Christ the King of Nations, and the Word of God as the supreme law. On account of these radical defects, and the many immoralities which naturally flow from them, Reformed Presbyterians cannot recognize it as a scripturally constituted civil government, nor swear allegiance to it, however much they may admire its many excellencies.

The relation of Christ to the nation is that of a Sovereign to a moral subject—a moral person, upon whom the law of His Kingdom is binding.* While

* Lecture of Dr. J. R. W. Sloane.

3

civil society is founded in nature, it is one of the "all things" that are put under Christ as Mediator, and the nation flourishes or decays as it is obedient or disobedient to His law. Now as our highest allegiance is due not to the state, but to Christ, it is the duty of every Christian to stand aloof from such a government and refuse to incorporate with the political society which refuses or neglects to acknowledge the authority of Christ and His word in its fundamental law. The document reads: "We, the people of the United States * * * do ordain and establish this Constitution for the United States of America." This declaration is historically, philosophically and scripturally untrue. The Constitution in all its essential elements was in existence before the document thus called was penned; constitutions are not ordained of men, but grow; and the Scripture affirms that the powers that are legitimate powers at all, are ordained of God. These glaring defects, with the denial of any religious qualification, the absence of the name of God from the oath, and the license of immorality and crime upon which it sets its official seal, give the document, called the Constitution, such a character of infidelity and irreligion that no true Christian ought to give it his full sanction. For these reasons, Reformed Presbyterians have never voted at any of the elections, nor held office under the government. They have never refused, however, to recognize the authority of the government in things lawful, and its right to legislate for the well being of men. They pay their taxes cheerfully as a lawful obligation; bear arms heroically in its defence and for the protection of their rights; and give it their moral support in every way that does not involve them in its evil. They heartily aid the government in all that is right and true. They enter the role of defenders and not traitors; reformers and not revolutionists. Theirs is the highest kind of patriotism. Theirs is a love of country which would lead them to make any sacrifice to bring it into the enjoyment of the blessedness of that nation whose God is the Lord.

Reformed Presbyterians hold that the Church and State are two divine institutions, supreme in their own spheres, yet touching at so many points that they cannot be entirely separated. The one should not arrrogate to itself the powers of the other, for under Christ the one is His spiritual kingdom, and the other His moral dominion. They should, however, assist each other in dangerous emergencies, and in the universal spread of the gospel.

The National Reform Association, organized with the hearty support and indorsement of the Reformed Presbyterian Church, in 1863, has for its object "the maintenance of the existing Christian features in the American government; the promotion of needed reforms in the action of the government touching the Sabbath, the institution of the family, the religious element in education, the oath, and public morality as affected by the liquor traffic, and other kindred evils; and to secure such an amendment to the Constitution of the United States as will declare the nation's allegiance to Jesus Christ, and its acceptance of the moral laws

of the Christian religion; and so indicate that this is
a Christian nation and place all the Christian laws,
institutions, and usages of our government upon an
undeniable legal basis in the fundamental law of the
land." This Association has drawn to its support
many of the most learned theologians and able jurists
in the country, and all true Christian patriots are falling into line with this theory of civil government as
the only safe and true course for the preservation of
America. It is often asked, Is the Reformed Presbyterian Church a necessity? This question is answered
in the affirmative. It is the only distinct religious
body in America that is bringing its principles to bear
on the government for its reformation, and has the
grandest object for which to live and labor. A *practical* protest against evil is the only testimony that is
weighty. The intelligent reader can understand the
necessity and attitude of this Church, and that it is
not for a trifling reason that Reformed Presbyterians
forego priviledges dear to every freeman, and subject
themselves to the reproach of men.

As it is not the province of the historian to discuss
theological differences between Christians, an elaborate
argumentation of the distinctive principles of the Church
will neither be expected by the readers, nor required
by the author to carry out the design of this book.
The distinctive principles will be briefly stated. Reformed Presbyterians hold that social religious Covenanting is an ordinance of God to be entered into by the
individual, the church, and the nation. They acknowledge the perpetual obligation of the National and

Solemn League and Covenant entered into by their fathers in Scotland, so far as they are applicable in this land, and until all the objects therein specified are accomplished. While they acknowledge that many of the objects for which those precious documents were sworn have been accomplished, yet they are binding upon the present Covenanting Church in America until Papacy is removed from our land, and this Man of Sin recognizes the perogatives of Christ. In 1871, they entered anew into Covenant with God, the bond of which will be found on another page. There is no doctrine of the Bible more clearly revealed than the descending obligation of Covenants. We recognize the principle every day in our commercial and national life, and it is alike applicable in our spiritual life. Because Reformed Presbyterians hold tenaciously to former Covenants of the Church and conscientiously display the principle, they are rightly called *Covenanters*.

Reformed Presbyterians exclude from their communion all members of secret oath-bound societies. They regard all such associations as the creatures of the Prince of darkness. The example and the spirit of the religion of Christ condemn such societies, for He said nothing in secret, and His acts of charity were done towards those very characters which are excluded from secret societies. Did Christ not minister to *woman* in all her needs? Did He not minister to the *maimed*, the *halt* and the *blind*? And yet these special objects of Christ's love and charity are the very ones secrecy excludes from any benefit. Charity towards the rich, the famed, and the healthy, is not *charity*, but rather selfishness and malevolence. Secrecy is held up in a very unfavorable manner in the Eighth Chapter of Ezekiel. Neither the Church nor the State has ever delegated to any association of men the power to administer the horrible oaths that are administered to the unfortunate candidates of secrecy, and who are in the dark as to what they are swearing to perform. On account of their blasphemous oaths, irreverent use of God's titles and attributes. banding together for selfish and wicked purposes, Christless Scriptures which are used to accommodate all classes of persons and beliefs, and the tyrannical measures and dreadful penalties for revealing their benevolent (?) work, Reformed Presbyterians forbid their members to join or to belong to associations of this character.

Reformed Presbyterians do not use hymns of human composition in the service of divine worship. They believe that God has given to His Church the matter of praise in the Book of Psalms, and has never delegated to any uninspired man the authority to substitute human for divine matter of praise. The Psalms of the Bible were used in the temple and synagogue worship and it would have been considered a corruption of the worship to substitute any thing else. Christ and the Apostles used the Psalms in divine worship under the present dispensation, and on the night of the institution of the eucharistic feast they sang a part of the Great Hallel, i. e., a portion of the six Psalms from the one hundred and thirteenth to the one hundred and eighteenth, inclusive. Hymns, or human compositions, were unknown in the Christian Church until several centuries after Christ. It is a remarkable fact that the periods in which Hymns were introduced were generally those characterized by defection and spiritual ignorance. The Presbyterian Church never introduced human compositions into worship until she made defection from the attainments of the Second Reformation, and in some parts of the world this Church still clings to the Songs of Zion. For the reasons that God has not delegated to an uninspired person the right to introduced into His worship that which is already provided ; that Christ and the New Testament Church sanction the use of the songs of the Bible ; that many of the hymns are untrue, frivolous and sectarian, the Reformed Presbyterian Church use exclusively the one hundred and fifty Psalms of the Bible in divine worship, and they have always found them beautifully adapted and truly comforting in all the circumstances of the Church, and pre-eminently so because they are the words of God to all His people.

Another peculiarity of the Reformed Presbyterian Church is that no instruments of music are used in divine worship. They believe that instruments were used in the tabernacle and temple worship by the Levites, and at the time of the offering up of sacrifices by the priests. As these services were wholly typical and were done away with at the coming of Christ, so also all the accompaniments and material supports of that service. At the advent of Christ the building was completed and the scaffolding was taken down. Christ and the Apostles never used an instrument of music in the synagogue worship, although they used the Psalms. If instruments had been necessary to acceptable worship, the example or direction of Christ in this matter would have been given. Christ requires a spiritual service—the melody of the heart with the fruit of the lips. The leading writers and fathers of the Church give instruments no place in the worship. They were introduced by Pope Vitalian, in A. D., 660, to "augment the *eclat* of religious ceremonies." Being of Romish origin, all true Protestants should look upon the innovation with suspicion. The true principle of Christian worship is "What has the Lord required," and not what He has not forbidden. All Presbyterians recognize the Westminister standards, and the Confession of Faith says we are to "sing *Psalms* with grace in the heart," and "the acceptable way of worshipping the true God is instituted by Himself, and is so limited by His own revealed will that He may not be worshipped according to the imaginations and devices of men." It is an admitted fact that instruments and operatic choirs destroy congregational singing, and substitute a meaningless service for that which every heart should render unto God. Instruments are used for the express purpose of making the service attractive, and the praise offering is often rendered for the worshippers by those whose lips and hearts have never been touched by the love of God. When the worship is thus rendered by machinery, God is robbed of that heart service and spiritual communion which each worshipper should have with Him in the ordinances of grace.

Among the forms still retained in the Church are the distribution of tokens at the communion season,

the "fencing of the tables," with table addresses, and
an explanation of a portion of a Psalm each Sabbath morning. They are opposed to any change
with reference to the doctrines and practice of the
house of God. Their services are plain and simple,
and aim at the purity rather than the attractiveness of
divine worship. While many of their doctrines and
practices are unpopular, Reformed Presbyterians choose
to bear the criticism, and even the reproach, of men,
if they can only please God and bring glory upon
His name. They desire to be approved of God in the
maintenance of a purely scriptural Church, and to bring
prominently before the world the sacrificial and mediatorial work of the Lord Jesus Christ. While often
despised of men for their exclusiveness, they do not
expect their reward for their accommodations to the
likes of sinful men, but for their fidelity to Christ and
and His truth, and whose angel speaks to them as to
the Church of Smyrna, "Be thou faithful unto death
and I will give thee a crown of life." They plead
the promise to the Apostles, "Fear not, little flock,
for it is your Father's good pleasure to give you
the kingdom." They maintain these doctrines and principles in the spirit of love and charity for all men
and Christians, and with the sanguine belief that their
principles will ultimately prevail and fill the whole
earth with liberty and happiness.

ORGANIC HISTORY OF THE REFORMED PRES-
BYTERIAN CHURCH IN AMERICA.

DURING the persecution in Scotland, members of the Reformed Presbyterian Church were banished, or voluntarily found an asylum, in America. They mostly settled in Eastern Pennsylvania, New York and South Carolina; and where two or three families were located in the same community, they organized themselves into a society upon the basis of the Reformation, and kept themselves distinct from other denominations. The majority of the Covenanters previous to 1750, were settled in Eastern Pennsylvania. Those residing in the vicinity of Octorara were joined by the Rev. Alexander Craighead of the Presbyterian Church, who espoused their principles in 1743, lead them in Covenanting, and dispensed the ordinances to them for several years. A session was constituted, and among the first elders were Robert Laughhead and Josiah Kerr. The congregation was often called the "Craighead Society." In maintaining the principles of the Covenanters, Mr. Craighead aroused the displeasure of his former brethren and the civil society. He published a pamphlet of a political nature, in which he set forth his peculiar views on civil government which were offensive to the Presbyterian Church because it was loyal to the Crown. After co-operating with the Covenanters for

several years, and failing to obtain help for them from
the mother country, he abandoned the society, returned
to the Presbyterian Church, and removed to North
Carolina.

The societies were again left destitute of a minister,
and made urgent applications to the Reformed Presbytery of Scotland for help. The first Covenanter minister who came to America was the Rev. John Cuthbertson, from Scotland, who arrived in August, 1751.
He continued to visit the scattered societies of Covenanters throughout Pennsylvania, New York, and other
States, for a period of twenty-two years. He made
his home at Little Octorara, Lancaster County, Pennsylvania, where the chief society was located. A few
rude log houses of worship were erected, but the preaching services were held either in the open air in some
pleasant grove, or in private houses and barns, and his
travelling was wholly done on horseback. The amount
of travel, and the hardships endured by this pioneer
missionary are perfectly marvelous, and almost incred-
ible to those enjoying the accommodations and luxuries
of this age.

In 1759, the Rev. Alexander McDowell left the
Presbyterian Church, and espoused the cause of the
Covenanters. He ministered principally to the societies
in Connecticut and Massachusetts, but assisted Mr.
Cuthbertson in Eastern Pennsylvania. He was called to
the congregation of Rock Creek (Gettysburgh), but declined, and in a few years returned to New England,
and was lost to the Church. In 1766, the Reformed
Presbytery of Ireland sent out the Rev. Daniel

McClelland, who ministered to the societies in Connecticut and Eastern Pennsylvania for a few years, but neither of these ministers was of any material assistance to the cause. Mr. Cuthbertson had a great deal to contend with in several ways. He suffered many annoyances from the British government, which was doing all in its power to subject the struggling colonist to carry the doubly grievous yoke of tyranny and Episcopacy. He encouraged the societies to assert their rights as freemen and to fight for the defence of their country. He inspired them to perseverance and the hope that God would vindicate the cause of the oppressed and give them civil and religious liberty. In 1772, the Rev. William Martin came out from Ireland with a colony of his people and settled along Rocky Creek, in South Carolina.

In the Spring of 1773, a Commissioner was sent to Ireland from Paxtang society, Pennsylvania, to secure one or two ministers to come to the assistance of Mr. Cuthbertson. He was successful in his mission, and the Reformed Presbytery of Ireland sent out the Revs. Matthew Linn and Alexander Dobbin, who landed in Philadelphia, December 13, 1773, where they were met by Mr. Cuthbertson and conducted to his home. Revs. John Cuthbertson, Matthew Linn and Alexander Dobbin constituted the first REFORMED PRESBYTERY IN AMERICA, at Paxtang, Dauphin County, Pennsylvania, March 10, 1774. At this time each of these ministers was assigned to his respective field of labor in Eastern Pennsylvania, and with Mr. Martin in South Carolina, these four ministers held forth the cause of the Reformation in the new world.

The country was now thrown into the excitement and turmoil of the Revolutionary war, and every colonist who loved civil and religious liberty was called upon to defend his country and his rights. To a man the Covenanters were Whigs. An unsound Whig made a poor Covenanter, and a good Covenanter made a loyal Whig. The colonists declared themselves independent of Great Britain, July 4, 1776, at Philadelphia, and a five years' war ensued. North and South the Covenanters went hand and heart into the struggle for independence. When the Rev. Alexander Craighead removed to North Carolina he was thoroughly imbued with the principles of the Covenanter Church, and disseminated them among the Scotch-Irish Presbyterians of that community. The consequence was the First Declaration of Independence was emitted by his followers in May, 1775, a year or more previous to the National Declaration. From reliable histories a few interesting facts are gleaned. Mr. Bancroft says: "The first public voice in America for dissolving all connection with Great Britain came not from the Puritans of New England, the Dutch of New York, nor the Planters of Virginia, but from the Scotch-Irish Presbyterians of the Carolinas." He evidently refers to the influence of Rev. Alexander Craighead and the Mecklenberg Declaration; and this influence was due to the meeting of the Covenanters of Octorara, where in 1743, they denounced in a public manner the policy of George the Second, renewed the Covenants, and swore with uplifted swords that they would defend their lives and their property against all attack and confiscation, and their consciences should be kept free from the tyrannical burden of Episcopacy. Here was the fountain of Southern patriotism, and the Octorara meeting was the original germ of American independence which was transplanted in Charlotte and then in Philadelphia. More than this. Thomas Jefferson says in his autobiography, that when he was engaged in preparing the National Declaration that he and his colleagues searched everywhere for formulas, and that the printed proceedings of Octorara were before him, and he used freely the ideas in the Mecklenberg Declaration.* No doubt this accounts for the similarity of expressions in the two documents. Sometimes it does happen that the discover or the inventor does not enjoy the right which should be bestowed upon him.

A writer in the *New York Review*, reviewing the "Life of Thomas Jefferson," by Tucker, clearly shows that the Preamble to the Bill of Rights, the Mecklenberg Declaration, and the Virginia Bill of Rights contain nearly everything of importance in the Declaration of Independence of July 4, 1776, upon which rests so much of Mr. Jefferson's fame.† Of this latter instrument, and the Mecklenberg Declaration, Judge Tucker, says: (Vol. II., p. 627.) "Every one must be persuaded, at least all who have been minute observers of style, that *one* of these papers had borrowed from the other." (See also the observations in the writings of Thomas Jefferson, by H. Lee, Philadelphia, 1839).

---

* Wheeler's Reminiscences, p. 278, in Congressional Library,

† Wheeler's Reminiscences, p. 278.

The spirit which moved Rev. Alexander Craighead to the use of expressions frequent in documents prepared and used on similar occasions in Scotish history, evidently influenced the mind of Thomas Jefferson, when he indited the National Declaration of Independence. The printed proceedings of Octorara and Mecklenberg were both in circulation in Philadelphia at that time, and account for kindred expressions.

It is now difficult to tell whether Donald Cargill, Hezekiah Balch or Thomas Jefferson wrote the National Declaration of American Independence, for in sentiment it is the same as the "Queensferry Paper" and the Mecklenberg Declaration.

The "rash" declaration of Rev. Donald Cargill, the Covenanter, was, "We do declare that we shall set up over ourselves and over what God shall give us power of, government and governors according to the Word of God ; that we shall no more commit the government of ourselves and the making of laws for us to any one single person, this kind of government being most liable to inconveniences and aptest to degenerate into tyranny." This sentiment of thorough Republican independence was in circulation long before Balch or Jefferson was born, and the proceedings of Octorara preceeded those of Charlotte or Philadelphia fully a third of a century. "Honor to whom honor is due." To stigmatize Covenanters as "anti-government people" is unjust aud untrue, and they are only objects of derision because their accusers are totally ignorant of their principles. They are heartily in favor of *government*, and the *republican form of government*, and only object to the Constitution for its *omission to acknowledge the source* from which all government comes, and a practical application of that doctrine.

These humble and sincere followers of Jesus, who would conscientiously desire to erect a church and government after God's pattern, have been the truest and best friends the American government has ever possessed, and to a man they have been faithful to their country and to their God in every national struggle. To them, more than to any other people, the American government is indebted for liberty, and they demonstrated to the world that "there can be a church without a bishop and a government without a king."

At the house of Captain Paxton, in Eastern Pennsylvania, July 2, 1777, after a patriotic and powerful sermon, the Rev. John Cuthbertson, and many of the Covenanters, swore fidelity to the cause of the Colonists. They took no immoral oath to an immoral constitution, for there was none in existance; they simply said they were heartily in favor of the Revolution, and would be faithful to its cause. It was a similar act to that of Rev. Alexander Craighead and the Covenanters in 1743. In South Carolina, the old Covenanter minister, William Martin, than whom no man in the South was better known, was doing all in his power for the cause of the Whigs. He preached rebellion against an unlawful and tyrannical King, and incited the people to rise up in arms against British oppression. For the expression of his sentiments he was apprehended by the Tories, and lay in the prison-house at Rocky Mount

and Camden for over six months. When he was
brought before Lord Cornwallis at Winnsboro, he made
no retraction of his sentiments, and said he might
do with him as he pleased. The Covenanters went
heartily into the bloody conflict, and the battles of
Fridus Fort and Eutaw Springs were so fierce and
hotly contested, that their guns came to a blue heat
in the conflict.* Such bravery in battle as was displayed by William Anderson, John Smith, John Faris,
Thomas McClurkin, Thomas Neil, and other Covenanters, deserves record. Wherever Covenanters and staunch
Presbyterians were settled, there were the strongholds
of the cause of American independence.

While the colonists had a right and just reason to
declare their independence of Great Britain in 1776,
they had not a right nor a just reason for declaring
their independence of the God of battles in 1789.
The Declaration of Independence was right, but the
Constitution of the United States was wrong. The
spirit of liberty that animated the Revolutionary patriot
was the same spirit that beat in the true heart and
unyielding courage of the Scotch Covenanters, although
many of the heroes and patriots of the struggle were
irreligious men. The trouble was, French infidelity
mingled with American patriotism at the helm of
State, and was the cause of the perversion of loyalty
to the Divine Being in the instrument of the newly
erected government.

During this excitement of war, and the disturbed
state of the country, there was a slight change going

* Rev. D. S. Faris, in R. P. & C., 1876, p. 56.

4

on in the minds of some of the Covenanters in Eastern
Pennsylvania. The religious element in this country at
that time was in a chaotic state. It was a new
country being settled up by emigrants from the old.
There, they were trammelled with tyrannical measures
in church and state; here, they were free to assert
their independence of thought and action, and they
were not as cautious as they should have been.
Covenanters enthusiastically threw themselves into the
struggle without immorality, thinking for aught they
knew the Constitution when framed would be of the
nature and make the acknowledgments which they
desired. In this state of things Covenanters freely
mingled with other Christians without respect to national
or denominational peculiarities. The Covenanters hailed
with joy the destruction in America of the government that had oppressed and persecuted them to the
death in Scotland. Besides this, another branch of the
Scottish Church was taking root in the same community, which had originally been of the same stock
and race in Britain, and now cotemporaneously planted
in America. These circumstances all pointed to the
practicability of seeking a union of the Covenanters
and the Associate Church. Churches ought to unite
and cause the body of Christ to become one when
there is no immorality or departure from principles
demanded. So far as the practical application of this
movement at that special period was concerned it was
a good move, but theoretically it was a bad movement. When the union was effected there was no
Constitution, moral or immoral, but the Seceders held

the *principle* that we are bound to recognize as the ordinance of God *any government* that may be set up without respect to qualifications, and here the Seceders showed their inconsistency. They bitterly opposed the Covenanters in Scotland and America for disowning the British government as an ordinance of God, and now they turn around and do all they can to overthrow that very government which they declared was an ordinance of God. Under the same government they were loyal in Scotland and disloyal in America, and seek union with a body that was always opposed to an unscriptural, tyrannical and oppressive government. The Seceders declared at the Revolutionary war that the doctrine of passive obedience, which they had cherished with seeming sincerity, was simply absurd; and that the principles of the Covenanters, and those upon which the colonists acted, were true, and that "we are not bound to own as God's ordinance every one, without exception, who may providentially have power in his hands."

In the coalescence, the Covenanter ministers never thought of giving up their principles, but they should have known the dangers of a compromise of principle. No sooner had the fair building of Covenanterism been erected in America upon Reformation principles, than the builders began to hew down the carved palace by affiliating with men who were opposed to the design of the structure. And this thing was not done hastily. They had been deliberately agitating the question for at least five years, and consummated it in the erection of the Associate Reformed Church, November 1, 1782.

They called the new organization by both names, although it was practically an Associate Church still. As soon as the Constitution was framed a few years later, they all came under it as the Associate Church had done in Britain; they swore allegiance to it as the ordinance of God, although God, or Christ, or the Bible, is not recognized in it. If not in 1782, certainly in 1789, it became an Associate Church, and we are not surprised to learn that some of the Covenanter ministers hung their heads in shame and regretted the step they had taken.

The Reformed Presbytery lost its name and organization in America. No doubt Matthew Linn was the best Covenanter among them. In all the conferences, the minutes of which are published in "Miller's Sketches," hot debates were prevalent, and all the differences between the two bodies were discussed with marked ability. Upon one occasion the blood of the old Covenanter Matthew Linn became stirred, and he concluded an able and eloquent address upon a proposition in these words: " You may agree to what propositions you please, but we Covenanters will agree to none but with this interpretation, that all power and ability civil rulers have are from Christ the Prophet of the Covenant; and all the food and raiment mankind enjoy are from Christ the Priest of the Covenant." And if he and his colleagues had added that no government is lawfully constituted without the acknowledgment that Christ is the King of nations, and clung to these sentiments, there would have been no disastrous union. The following is the basis of union finally agreed upon and adopted:

1. That Jesus Christ died for the elect only.

2. That there is an appropriation in the nature of faith.

3. That the Gospel is indiscriminately addressed to sinners of mankind.

4. That the righteousness of Christ is the alone proper condition of the Covenant of grace.

5. That civil power originates from God the Creator, and not from Christ the Mediator.

6. That the administration of the kingdom of Providence is committed to Jesus Christ the Mediator; and magistracy, the ordinance appointed by the moral Governor of the world to be the pillar or prop of civil order among men, as well as other things, is rendered subservient by the Mediator to the welfare of His spiritual kingdom, the Church, and beside the Church has the sanctified use of that and every common benefit, through the grace of our Lord Jesus Christ.

7. That the law of nature and the moral law revealed in Scripture are substantially the same, although the latter expresses the will of God more evidently and clearly than the former; and therefore magistrates among Christians ought to be regulated by the general directory of the Word as to the execution of their offices in faithfulness and righteousness.

8. That the qualifications of justice, veracity, &c., required in the law of nature for the being of a magistrate, are also more clearly and explicitly revealed as necessary in Scripture. But a religious test any farther than an oath of fidelity can never be essentially necessary to the being of a magistrate, except when the people make it a condition of government; then it may be among that people necessary by their own voluntary deed.

9. That both parties, when united, shall adhere to the Westminster Confession of Faith, Catechisms Larger and Shorter, Directory for Worship, and Propositions concerning Church Government.

10. That they shall claim the full exercise of church discipline without dependence on foreign judicatories.

The union was consummated at the house of William Richards, in the city of Philadelphia, November 1,

1782, at which time and place the Synod of the Associate Reformed Church was constituted, with the Rev. John Mason, Moderator. The following members composed the new body as then organized:

Associates: Revs. James Proudfit, Matthew Henderson, John Mason, Robert Annan, John Smith, John Rodgers, Thomas Clark, William Logan, John Murray and David Annan. Elders—Joseph Miller, Thomas Douglas and William McKinley.

Covenanters: Revs. John Cuthbertson, Matthew Linn, Alexander Dobbin and David Telfair. Elders—James Bell, John Cochran and Dr. Robert Patterson.

The great majority of the Covenanters in the North followed their misguided pastors into the union. Rev. William Martin, in South Carolina, was the only Covenanter minister left in America, and no doubt he would have gone in too if he had been in good standing and had had the opportunity. The Covenanters in the South were little effected by the union. While in the ten articles of agreement there are many concessions to the principles of the Reformed Presbyterian Church, yet there are some radical departures. To the concessions all the Seceders did not agree, and to the departures all the Covenanters did not agree. The consequence was, three bodies were formed instead of one. While it is said "in union there is strength," it depends largely upon the basis of that union. The moral strength of the Church depends upon purity of doctrine and not upon the mass of individuals. The sparkling rill from the mountain side is smaller and purer than the large turbid river that flows through the valley. Two ministers of the Associate Church did not go into the union, and this Church was re-organized and grew rapidly.

In an edition of their Testimony, emitted about fifty years after the union, we read: "Nearly fifty years have now elapsed since the organization of the Associate Reformed Church; and the correctness of the [former] remarks on her Constitution, has been clearly exhibited. For some time she continued to observe the usages of the Associate Church from which she separated. But becoming numerous and popular some of her ministers began to manifest symptoms of dissatisfaction with many of these usages, acted contrary to them, wrote against them, and attempted their abolition." Among their devisive courses enumerated were the doing away with days of fasting and preperation before communion, holding open communion, singing hymns, freely exchanging pulpits with all denominations, and agitating a union with the Presbyterian Church. The history of the Associate Reformed Church was marked with so much declension, that the body divided into three distinct Synods in the North, South and West.

The Covenanters were worse off than the remnant of the Associate Church, for they had no minister. But God graciously preserved the germs of Covenanterism, and the few faithful ones rallied around the old flag. With the heroism of their martyred ancestry, they clung to their blood-bought principles and gathered themselves again into the praying societies. The Covenanter Church has a mission to fill and a grand object for which to live, or God would not have so tenderly and marvelously preserved her from total extinction both in Scotland and America. Nearly every, if not every, other denomination has either departed from some of her principles or become thoroughly Americanized ; but the old Covenanter Church retains her ancient principles intact, with her rugged Scottish forms of worship, and has successfully weathered every storm of innovation.

The scattered societies of Covenanters now called loudly for help from Scotland and Ireland. They waited patiently seven years before their request could be granted. In the summer of 1789, the Reformed Presbytery of Scotland sent out the Rev. James Reid to examine into the condition and needs of the societies. He made an investigating tour among all the societies from New York to South Carolina ; preached and held communions, organized new societies and congregations, and returned to Scotland in a little less than a year. Doubtless in his elaborate report to the Scottish Presbytery, Mr. Reid showed the need of . immediate action and the pressing claims of the American Covenanters. His visit lead the Churches in Europe to take immediate steps for sending ministerial help to this country. The Rev. James McGarragh was first sent out by the Reformed Presbytery of Ireland, and he arrived in South Carolina in the Spring of 1791. Rev. William King was also commissioned by the Reformed Presbytery of Scotland, and arrived in South Carolina in the Fall of 1792. Revs. McGarragh and King were now directed to act as a Committee of the Scottish Presbytery and to judicially manage the affairs of the Church; they restored the Rev. William Martin, and he was added to the Committee. In the Spring of 1793, the Rev. James McKinney came out from Ireland as an exile for liberty, and preached throughout the Northeastern States and cities with great power and success. He also was connected with the work of the Committee, which now acted as a regularly constituted Presbytery in subordination to the Reformed Presbytery beyond the ocean. In August, 1795, Mr. McGarragh was suspended on account of intemperate habits, and Mr. Martin was silenced for the same reason, thus leaving Mr. King alone in the South to manage the affairs of the Church. Mr. McKinney held that it was not satisfactory to judicially manage the affairs of the Church in America by a Committee from Scotland; but to understand and judiciously apply the provisions for the needs of the societies, the Church here should have a separate and distinct Presbytery. This was necessary on account of the vast number of emigrants which were arriving, and efforts were made to carry this idea into execution.

The Reformed Presbytery of Ireland was placed in a critical position with reference to the Irish insurrection, and their troubles proved advantageous to the Church in America in the way of receiving ministers and members. For many years the Covenanters in Ireland were the sole advocates of liberty from the Crown. While they deeply sympathized with the cause of the oppressed, they could not join the society of

United Irishmen, but disapproved of their proceedings.
This society was organized at Belfast by Theobald
Wolfe Tone. In a document published in 1796, entitled
"A Seasonable and Necessary Information," the Reformed Presbytery of Ireland vindicated its character
in reference to this society known as the United Irishmen, by declaring its "highest abhorence of all such
tumultuous meetings and disorderly societies," and
signified its disapproval of "anything said or done
prejudicial to the peace, safety and property of any
individual or society." This document was published
in the *Northern Star*, October 3, 1796, and was done
in the name of the Covenanter Church in the counties
of Antrim and Down.* Being thoroughly in sympathy
with the cause that might overthrow monarchy and
prelacy, Covenanters were suspected by the government
of being in connection with this society, and were often
so regarded. They did sympathize with, but not adopt
the methods of, this society, and many of them fled
to America for safety and peace. Among those coming
in the Fall of 1797, were the Rev. William Gibson,
with John Black and Samuel B. Wylie, students of
theology. Revs. King, McKinney and Gibson now
made arrangements to constitute a Presbytery in
America, but Mr. King died before it was effected.
Revs. Gibson and McKinney, with ruling elders, constituted the REFORMED PRESBYTERY OF AMERICA, at
Philadelphia, in May, 1798, which had been dissolved since
the coalescence of 1782. This court was fully recognized by the Presbyteries in Ireland and Scotland, and

---

* Reid's History of the Presbyterian Church in Ireland.

a friendly correspondence was established with them. They were not placed under the same circumstances as the brethren in 1774, and the objectional features of the Constitution of the United States were clearly pointed out and testified against. Its wilful omission of all reference to God the Author, Christ the King, and the Word of God as the Supreme Law of nations and civil government; its sanction and protection of human slavery, and other permissions of evil, excluded all conscientious Covenanters from swearing allegiance to it. The position of the Church was then, as it is now, one of practical dissent from the Constitution for these just and good reasons, and so it remains without change either in the testimony or the practical application of these principles.

Among the first judicial acts of the Reformed Presbytery worthy of special notice, was the deliverance of this body, in 1800, on the subject of human slavery. They had always held this system to be a sin, and previous to 1798, the ministers in South Carolina had warned members against it. The matter was brought before them by Rev. Alexander McLeod refusing to accept a call to Coldenham, New York, because there were some members who owned slaves. The Presbytery enacted, without a dissenting voice, that "no slaveholder should be allowed the communion of the Church." They also appointed a Committee, consisting of Revs. James McKinney and Samuel B. Wylie, to repair to South Carolina with the message of this court that the Covenanters there must either emancipate their slaves or be refused the communion of the Church. "The Committee were no less surprised than delighted to find with what alacrity those concerned came forward and complied with the decree of Presbytery. In one day, in the small community of Covenanters at Rocky Creek, not less than three thousand guineas were sacrificed upon the altar of principle," and the Church then and forever cleansed her hands from the guilt of human slavery. Covenanters were far in advance of other denominations in this matter. The Associate Reformed Synods of the North and West gave a very mild deliverance in 1826, but the Synod of the South never made a deliverance upon the subject. Previous to the Revolutionary war there were few negroes in the South, but the traffic in human souls began immediately afterwards and the nefarious business became a great trade and industry. With the annual growth of slavery the annual emigration of Covenanters increased. They were thorough-going abolishionists, and established "underground railways" from the South into Canada.

In 1802, the Rev. Samuel B. Wylie was sent as a commissioner to the sister judicatories of Europe, with the instructions of the Reformed Presbytery that he shall "give them a just representation of our present situation as a church in North America; to intimate our unfeigned wish for a friendly connection and express our sorrow that the court had so long neglected making intimation to this effect; and to endeavor to procure as many ministerial laborers as may be conveniently obtained." Although the Presbytery had been constituted four years, the fact had not been officially announced to the Presbytery under whose care they had been. This state of affairs would seem to indicate the necessity of a common judicatory or supreme court under which Covenanters in all lands could be united. Mr. Wylie was received with cordiality everywhere, and all the objects of his mission were obtained so far as practicable.

The next important item in the organic history was the provision made for the emission of the Testimony. While they went upon the principle that truth is not local, and they desired a testimony that would be applicable in all lands, yet they felt the need of a testimony to apply to the Church in America in contending for all truth and testifying against local evils. A committee was appointed in 1802, to draught such a system and ask the co-operation and assistance of all the ministers in America and the Presbyteries in Scotland and Ireland. Rev. Alexander McLeod was the chairman of the committee, and different departments were assigned to different ministers.

In 1804, the Reformed Dissenting Presbytery proposed a union with the Covenanters, but they could not be admitted upon their basis, and the matter was dropped. In May, 1806, the "Declaration and Testimony of the Reformed Presbyterian Church in America" was unanimously adopted and ordered to be published with all convenient speed. At this meeting it was also enacted that "sitting on juries in the civil courts of the United States, or in any State, is inconsistent with the Testimony;" and "an oath may be made before the constituted authorities provided such magistrates understand that the person doing so does not recognize thereby his official right to administer it, but the individual makes the oath voluntarily to the Supreme Being." In 1807, a committee was appointed to make a draught of a covenant, "embracing the spirit and design of the vows entered into by our fathers in the Reformation." This work was never attended to, and not until sixty-five years thereafter was the original purpose carried out. The "Terms of Communion" now in use were prepared, and the fourth term was changed in 1878 to apply to the renovation of the Covenants in 1871. At the same time the "Directory for Worship" was prepared by Rev. John Black, and the "Book of Discipline" by Rev. Alexander McLeod. They were both adopted in 1819; but it seems the "Book of Discipline" was rewritten, several years spent in making amendments, and it was not authoritatively published as the law of the Church until 1863. The Presbytery also decided to establish a Theological Seminary, and it was opened in Philadelphia, May, 1810, with the Rev. Samuel B. Wylie as the professor.

The Synod of the Reformed Presbyterian Church in America was constituted at Philadelphia, May 24, 1809, which court ratified all the deeds of the Reformed Presbytery and changed the three Committees into Presbyteries.

The next national struggle was what is known as the "War of 1812." On account of "the impressment of American seamen, depredations on commerce and attacks upon armed vessels, the United States Congress declared war against Great Britain." The majority of the Covenanters thought it their duty to again come to the defense of the country and their interests. As there were many members who were aliens and would not take the naturalization oath, and, for fear they would be suspected as enemies of the States, the Synod of 1812, made a statement to Congress of her position as a Church. As no immoral oath was required of them, the Covenanters were hearty supporters of the nation's rights and cheerfully bore arms in defense of the country. The failure of many of the Christian ministers of other denominations throughout the country to support the nation in its rights, many of whom were loyal to Great Britain and opposed to the measures adopted by the United States, lead the Rev. Alexander McLeod to preach a series of "War Sermons," which for truth and eloquence are unexcelled in modern sermonizing. They were published and received a large circulation.

At the meeting of Synod in 1817, the following resolution was passed : "WHEREAS, A judicial testimony for truth and against errors and immoral practices, unaccompanied with an argumentative defence of the one and refutation of the other, must be defective— and as a promise has been given by the highest judicatory of this Church, that such a defence and refutation, as a third part of our testimony, may be expected ; therefore,

Resolved, "That a Committee be appointed to inquire into the subject, and report on the propriety of redeeming their pledge at this time, and to suggest the fittest mode for accomplishing that purpose.

Resolved, " That this Committee consist of three members, viz : Revs. McLeod, Milligan and Lusk." The Synod also made arrangements for a more hearty and systematic support of the Seminary.

At the meeting of Synod in 1818, the following distribution of articles for the Testimony was made : " The Directories " to Rev. John Black ; the " Book of Discipline " and " Form of Covenanting " to Rev. Alex. McLeod ; " Form of Church Government " to Rev. J. R. Willson ; " Forms of Process " to Rev. Gilbert McMaster ; and an " Address " to accompany the Covenant to Rev. Thomas Donnelly. These were to be ready by the next meeting. The most of the sessions of 1819 were consumed in considering the " Book of Discipline " and the " Directory for Worship." The tasks assigned at the previous meeting were not completed and the writers were continued. A Committee consisting of Revs. S. B. Wylie, Alex. McLeod and J. R. Willson was appointed to " address the sister Synods in Britain and Ireland and propose to them the propriety of entering into a Solemn League and Covenant, mutually binding us to God and to each other in the support of the cause of the Reformation in which we are all engaged ; and recognizing the obligation by which we are bound by the Covenants of our ancestors."

At the meeting of Synod in 1821, a paper was received from Mr. James Willson, of Kaskaskia, Illinois, asking for information with respect to the law of the Church in civil affairs, and especially on the subject of sitting on juries. The Synod stated " that no connection with the laws, the offices, or the order of the

State is prohibited by the Church, except what truly involves immorality." This action of Synod has frequently been used as an excuse and apology by those who subsequently became citizens. Now it is clear that there is no surrender of the position of the Church in this act, for the Testimony of the Church has declared over and over again that there was "immorality interwoven with the general and state's Constitutions," and members uniformly dissented from them. Until the Church published her Testimony it passed an act prohibiting members from sitting on juries, for jurors are executive officers created by the Constitution and represent the Nation in giving a verdict according to the law and testimony. The Synod gave no new deliverance on the question in 1821, and if Mr. James Willson had read the authorized Testimony he would have found that the law of the Church, as made in the meeting of Presbytery in 1806, was that " sitting on juries in the civil courts of the United States, or in any State, is inconsistent with the Testimony." This law never was repealed and it was not disannulled by the act of 1821. Although this act unsettled the minds of some who were anxious to lay down the Testimony, and lead to complaints from others who thought the Church was laying down her principles, the Synod in 1825, gave this clear and difinite deliverance which forever after should have closed the mouths of latitudinarians : " Some misunderstanding having occurred relating to the meaning of the act passed at our last session respecting serving on juries, the Synod passed the following resolution :

"*Resolved*, That this Synod never understood any act of theirs relative to their members sitting on juries as contrary to the old common law of the Church on these subjects." The "old common law" was prohibitory and did hold sway, but there was a disposition on the part of some leading members of Synod to change the position of the Church as dissenting from the government, which lead to the formation of the party which abandoned this distinctive position in 1833.

In 1823, the constitution of the supreme judicatory was changed into a General Synod by the following action:

Resolved, That a General Synod of the Reformed Presbyterian Church, to meet bi-ennially, be formed by delegates from the several Presbyteries; that each Presbytery shall have the right of sending two ministers and as many ruling elders, and that the ratio of increase of the number of delegates be, until further order be taken on the subject, two ministers and as many ruling elders, for every three ministers of which the Presbytery consists.

By many this change was regarded as uncalled for and the means by which power was acquired to effect a change in the relation of the Church to the government. History confirms the fact that these suspicions were well-grounded. At this meeting also they reiterated the law of the Church that "no slaveholder can be held in the communion of the Church," and the Committee appointed to act on cases of discipline recommended Synod "to insert under the Chapter of Oaths, a new article to testify against the oaths taken by free-masons."

In 1825, the General Assembly Presbyterian Church proposed a plan of correspondence, and delegates were appointed from the Reformed Presbyterian Church. They framed a treaty which was ratified by the General Assembly, but rejected by the Synod of our Church. This was not satisfactory to those who were imbued with the spirit of the treaty and who manifested a disposition to not heed the decisions of Synod. Thus began a discord, and the peace and harmony of the Church were again disturbed. Those who began to maintain these principles of latitudinarianism, and consider the testimony and decisions of the Church as of no force, are responsible for the disruption that soon followed. In 1827, the Synod was called upon to vindicate its course in criticizing the position of the Associate Church, and, as this body had begun a correspondence with Synod upon the subject of union, after a free and full discussion of the principles of each body, the Synod, in 1828, declared that it would be useless to endeavor to effect a union with them, and the matter was dropped.

In 1830, the Committee previously appointed to "report concerning the propriety of making application to the several civil authorities of our common country respecting the existing relations of this community to the Commonwealth," reported in an able and earnest paper that "there could be no change in the existing relations of the Church to the Nation in consistency with her testimony as witnessing for the authority of Christ as King of nations." This faithful report was galling to some who desired to modify the position of the Church, and, after a good deal of discussion, it was finally agreed to commit it to the examination of a Committee of four, and if they saw fit, to publish it as an overture before the next meeting of Synod. The Committee framing the paper, and that to examine it, were made one, and it was hoped that the valuable part of it would be preserved and the position of the Church maintained. The following is the action of the Synod of 1831, with reference to it:

The object of appointing a committee on the civil relations, is to inquire into the propriety of making application to the civil authorities respecting the relations in which the members of this Church stand to them. The said committee accordingly submit to Synod a resolution in these words:

That an application be made to the Congress of the United States, when it shall have been ascertained from influential statesmen that such application shall probably prove successful, for a grant of the rights of citizenship to the members of this Church, not otherwise recognized as citizens, on other terms than swearing an oath of allegiance to the existing civil institutions of the land.

Your committee are of opinion that influential statesmen have not, as yet, opened the door for a successful application to Congress, and therefore deem it most prudent to recommend to Synod a postponement of the subject.

While this report fails to accomplish the design for which the Committee was appointed, it certainly exalts the position and authority of the Synod in forbidding her members to swear allegiance to the government. A "rising party" was not yet satisfied because the iron laws of the Church held them down to a submission to her Testimony. They wanted to breathe more freely, and so, at the same meeting of 1831, it was "resolved that this Synod recommend that the points of difference on the application of our principles to the civil institutions of the United States be discussed through the medium of the *American Christian Expositor*, under the head of "Free Discussions," and that every member of Synod have full liberty to avail himself of this vehicle."

Now the law of the Church and the acquiescence of members to the report both plainly declared that members of the Reformed Presbyterian Church could not, consistent with their position of dissent, swear allegiance to the government. As upon this vital question there was no difference of opinion, how could it be a matter of discussion? It was simply an occasion to repeal the action of Synod prohibiting incorporation with the government. The consequence was the pulpit and the press now became vehicles for the dissemination of doctrines subversive to the position of the Church. Some of the learned doctors, who had grown weary of testimony-bearing, wrote articles to show how easily Covenanters, in consistency with their principles, could incorporate with the government and not be charged with complicity in the sins of the nation. This was "new light" to those who had thought and held that the Constitution was defective and licensed immorality, and those who swore allegiance to it were justly implicated in the evil. Some of the leading men, who had spent their best days in upholding the principles of the Church and emitting publications in her defense, now "changed their minds" and repudiated the sentiments held when they were "beardless boys."

We have now come to a period in the history of the Reformed Presbyterian Church when those errors, which were given too much countenance at first, developed into open rebellion against the true and historic position of the Church. It is now fifty-five years since the unpleasant controversy and division of the Church; and, while we have no desire to revive the trouble, we have an earnest desire to vindicate the position of the Reformed Presbyterian Church. It is granted that mistakes and bad temper were displayed upon both sides; that the war of words and pamphlets aggravated the controversy and widened the separation; but back of all this debris there was a righteous position to be held and a Bible principle to be maintained. Neither the righteousness of the cause nor the validity of the course consisted in which side had the learned doctors, the most worldly ambition, held the most property, exerted the most influence in society, or held or withdrew from material buildings. All this is simply *dust*. The question is, Which side held the true Bible theory of civil government, and which departed from the recognized position of the Reformed Presbyterian Church in America?

Now the trend of Scottish history, and the Testimony of the Reformed Presbyterian Church officially adopted in 1806, testify to the fact that Covenanters are dissenters from immoral Constitutions of Church and State. No candid and intelligent reader can deny this fact. No one thoroughly acquainted with the godly instruction of Covenanters and the true character of the American government could be mistaken as to the attitude of Reformed Presbyterians. Hear the Testimony of 1806:

Since the adoption of the Constitution in 1789, the members of the Reformed Presbyterian Church have maintained a constant testimony against these evils. They have refused to serve in any office which implies an approbation of the Constitution, or which is placed under the direction of an immoral law. They have abstained from giving their votes at elections for legislators or officers, who must be qualified to act by an oath of allegiance to this immoral system. They could not themselves consistently swear allegiance to that Government, in the Constitution ot which there is contained so much immorality. In all these instances their practice has been uniform.

And who wrote these sentiments? A man who was now repudiating them! And not only in the "Historical Part" of the Testimony, but in the "Doctrinal Part," which was adopted at the same time, the holding up of the United States government as an ordinance of God was an error to be condemned and testified against. The sessional records all over the country reveal the fact, that, previous to the "new light" which dawned upon the Church in 1833, members who sat on juries or voted at any elections were *centured*, and they either confessed their sin or left the Church.

Without fear of contradiction it is affirmed, and synodical reports corroborate the statement, that it was the settled policy and position of the Reformed Presbyterian Church in America to refuse allegiance to the United States government on account of its defects and immoralities. The constitutional law of the Church has always been that members are absolutely prohibited from affiliating with the government in any way that would involve them in its evil or give sanction to it as the ordinance of God.* The act of Synod in 1831, by which

---

* This position of the Church is admitted in the *Reformed Presbyterian Advocate*, the organ of the New School Church, January, 1888.

members were given the priviledge of free discussion, in
no way gave them the liberty to *change the constitutional
law* of the Church. The law on this subject was fixed,
and it never was repealed, and stands to-day to the condemnation of those who departed from it.

At the meeting of the Eastern Subordinate Synod,
held in New York, April 25, 1832, a paper, which was
designed to be a pastoral letter to the Churches, was
drawn up by the Chairman of a Committee appointed
for that purpose. This paper embodied high enconiums
and commendations of the United States government,
which government was the same as it had been when
the same gentleman had previously condemned it for its
immoralities, and denounced those who were faithfully
maintaining the Church's Testimony. This paper was
adopted, after many malicious paragraphs were expunged
because they were directly subversive to the principles
of the Church and highly abusive of some of the
members of Synod. Contrary to the decision of Synod,
and in insubordination to the highest judicatory of the
Church, the Chairman of this Committee, and a
minority of the members of the court, gathered together and made arrangements for publishing the whole
document with explanatory notes, and they spread the
dangerous publication all over the Church. As a point
of law, it is not whether the standards of the Church
are correct or whether the pastoral letter taught doctrines
contrary to them ; but, those who held these views,
must either *clear themselves according to the constitutional law of the Church, or abandon her position.* The
existing law of the Church, however, condemned the

expunged paragraphs and the sentiments of those who sympathized with them, and they were compelled to do the other thing—*leave the Church.* If men do not believe the principles of the Church they are at liberty to step down and out. But many of these misguided brethren, by their writings and speeches, would condemn the standards and justify their opinions.

In this state of things it was necessary to stay the progress of defection. The only and the proper thing to do, was to call a meeting of the court to which those who were departing from the principles were amenable. This was done. The Moderator of the Eastern Subordinate Synod, on the requisition of two Presbyteries, called a *pro re nata* meeting which was held in New York, November 25, 1832. The Synod was regularly constituted by prayer and the object of the meeting sustained. As might be expected, protests came in from six ministers upon whose conduct the meeting was to act. The Clerk refused to produce the minutes of the court, and, after three regular citations to do so, was suspended for insubordination. The meeting then proceeded to examine the "original draft of a pastoral letter" and the paragraphs which had been expunged, and a libel was founded thereon against those who signed it. The counts in the libel were five in number, viz: 1. Following divisive courses. 2. Contempt of the authority of Synod. 3. Error in Doctrine. 4. Abandonment of the Testimony of the Church. 5. Slandering Synod and its members. Copies of the libel were sent to all those to whom it applied, and they were cited to appear before the regular meeting of Synod, April 9, 1833, and answer to the charges in the libel.

The pastor of the First congregation of New York paid no attention to the act of Synod, and introduced the suspended Clerk of Synod into the pulpit to the discomfiture of the majority of the members. These members who would be law-abiding and recognize the validity of the court of God's house, were excluded from church priviledges without charge, citation or trial, because they would not hear a suspended minister. In order to evade centure by the Presbytery for this conduct, the pastor of the First congregation applied to the Philadelphia Presbytery to be taken under its care, with the congregation, for there were sympathizers with this divisive course in that city. Now everybody knows that such conduct as that would not be tolerated by any orderly body; and besides this matter of order, the Synod had fixed the boundaries of the Presbyteries, and neither congregations nor Presbyteries had the power to alter them. The Philadelphia Presbytery, or some members of it, now installed the suspended minister over the congregation in New York. The congregation was placed under the Philadelphia Presbytery, a call moderated, the pastor settled, and one hundred and forty members expelled in less than three days. Certainly the "King's business required haste." Any one at all acquainted with the rules and usage of the Presbyterian Church law at once will say that such transactions were unlawful and unpresbyterial.

At the meeting of the Eastern Subordinate Synod,

April 9, 1833, the court was regularly opened with a sermon and constituted by prayer by the Moderator. The suspended Clerk attempted to force himself upon the court, but was checked by a motion to appoint a Clerk *pro tem*. When this point of order was settled, the leader of the parties against whom the libel was framed, called upon his colleagues and they withdrew to another house without any officers. Here they set up an independent Synod, which they styled the "Eastern Subordinate Synod." They felt sure the regular court would sustain the libels, and they sought this mode of contending for the rights of the suspended Clerk in order to escape the application of discipline. Though these offenders had withdrawn, the Synod agreed that they were not free from their jurisdiction, and they proceeded with the citations to appear and answer the libels. After citing them three times to appear, and notifying them if they did not, they would be proceeded against as if they were present, the Synod, after patient waiting, proceeded to examine the conduct of those libeled. The Synod resolved that the parties were guilty of the five counts in the libel, and were thereupon suspended from the exercise of the ministry and priviledges in the Reformed Presbyterian Church. The five suspended ministers were duly notified of the action of the Eastern Subordinate Synod.

The General Synod of the Reformed Presbyterian Church met in Philadelphia, August 7, 1833. The former Moderator of this Synod was among those suspended, and for this reason was disqualified for taking his position until his case was adjudicated and he

restored. The Synod, and the people whom they represented, were not willing to trust their interests to those
who had no regard for the high position of the Church
as a witness for Jesus, and · who trampled all Presbyterial law and order under their feet. They must make
amends or be self-excluded from participation in the
transactions of the court. Supposing the proceedings
of the Eastern Subordinate Synod were held by some
to be invalid or unjust, the General Synod could neither
disannul nor act upon them, until it was constituted
and the matter came regularly before it. The Moderator's alternate was then called upon to open the Synod
by a sermon. At this juncture a disturbance was
created; and, as the church in which the Synod met
was in possession of the party against whom the
charges were made, and because they had invoked the
aid of the police in case of a disturbance, for the
sake of peace, the majority, who held the testimony
intact, withdrew from the house, and met in another
place where the sermon was preached and the Synod
regularly constituted. It is not customary for majori-
ties to secede, especially when they are in the right,
but because of the peculiar circumstances of this case,
and for the sake of peace, the majority manifested
the Christian spirit and withdrew from the brethren
who were walking disorderly. While those who
abandoned the principles of the Church were minis-
terially in the minority, the membership throughout the
Church was about equally divided. The misguided
brethren set up an independent Synod and styled it
that of the "Reformed Presbyterian Church." Since

that day the two denominations have been known as the " Old Light " and " New Light," because the one adheres strenuously to the distinctive principles of the Church as they had always been held, and the other abandoned them in 1833.

Now in order to show which party adheres to the true position of the Church, and is thereby entitled to the name, a comparison of the " Terms of Communion " may be helpful.

TERMS OF 1806.

1. An acknowledgment of the Scriptures of the Old and New Testaments to be the Word of God.

2. An acknowledgment that the whole doctrine of the Westminster Confession of Faith, and the Catechisms, Larger and Shorter, are agreeable unto, and founded upon, the Scriptures.

3. An acknowledgment of the divine right of one unalterable form of Church Government and manner of worship—and that these are, for substance, justly exhibited in that form of Church Government and Directory for Worship agreed upon by the assembly of divines at Westminster, as they were received by the Church of Scotland.

4. An acknowledgment that Public Covenanting is an ordinance 'of God, to be observed by Churches and Nations under the New Testament Dispensation—and that those Vows, namely, that which was entered into by the Church and Kingdom of Scotland, called the NATIONAL COVENANT, and that which was afterwards entered into by the three Kingdoms, Scotland, England, and Ireland, and by the Reformed Churches in those Kingdoms, usually called the Solemn League and Covenant, were entered into in the true spirit of that institution—and that the obligation of these Covenants extends to those who were represented in the taking of them, although removed to this or any other part of the world, in so far as they bind to duties not peculiar to the Church in the British Isles, but applicable in all lands.

5. An approbation of the faithful contendings of the martyrs of Jesus, and of the present Reformed Covenanted Churches in Britain and Ireland, against Paganism, Popery and Prelacy, and against immoral

Constitutions of civil government, together with all Erastian tolerations and persecutions which flow therefrom, as containing a noble example for us and our posterity to follow in contending for all divine truth, and in testifying against all contrary evils which may exist in the corrupt Constitutions of either Church or State.

6. An approbation of the doctrines contained in the Declaration and Testimony of the Reformed Presbyterian Church in North America, in defence of truth and in opposition to error.

These, together with due subordination in the Lord to the authority of the Reformed Presbytery in North America, and a regular life and conversation, form the bonds of our ecclesiastical union.

———

Those were the Terms in use by the whole body previous to 1833. Now we will place side by side the Terms of each body at the present time for comparison with those of 1806:

Present Terms of Old School Body.	*Present Terms of New School Body.*
1. An acknowledgment of the Scriptures of the Old and New Testaments to be the Word of God, and the only rule of faith and manners.	1. An acknowledgement of the Scriptures of the Old and New Testaments to be the Word of God.
2. An acknowledgment that the whole doctrine of the Westminster Confession of Faith, and the Catechisms, Larger and Shorter, are agreeable unto, and founded upon, the Scriptures.	2. An acknowledgment of the doctrines of the Westminster Confession of Faith. Catechisms, Larger and Shorter, and Reformation Principles Exhibited, the Testimony of the Church—as embodying, according to the Word of God, the great principles of the Covenanted Presbyterian Reformation, to the maintenance of which this Church is obliged by solemn Covenant engagements.
3. An acknowledgment of the divine right of one unalterable	3. An acknowledgement that the Lord Jesus Christ, the only

form of Church Government and manner of worship—and that these are, for substance, justly exhibited in the form of Church Government and Directory for Worship agreed upon by the assembly of divines at Westminster, as they were received by the Church of Scotland.

4. An acknowledgment of public Covenanting as an ordinance of God to be observed by Churches and Nations; and of the perpetual obligation of public Covenants; and of the obligation upon this Church of the Covenant entered into in 1871, in which are embodied the engagements of the National Covenant of Scotland and of the Solemn League and Covenant, so far as applicable in this land.

5. An approbation of the faithful contendings of the martyrs of Jesus, and of the present Reformed Covenanted Churches in Britain and Ireland, against Paganism, Popery, and Prelacy, and against immoral Constitutions of civil government, together with all Erastian tolerations and persecutions which flow therefrom, as containing a noble example for us and our posterity to follow in contending for all divine truth, and in testifying against all contrary evils which may exist in the corrupt Constitutions of either Church or State.

Redeemer and Head of His Church, has appointed one permanent form of ecclesiastical government; and that this form is, by divine right, Presbyterian.

4. An acknowledgment that public, social covenanting, upon proper occasions, is an ordinance of God, and that such moral deeds as respect the future, whether ecclesiastical or civil, are of continued obligation, as well as upon those represented in the taking of them as upon those who actually covenant, until the ends of them be effected.

5. An acknowledgment of the faithful contendings of the martyrs of Jesus, and a recognition of all as brethren, in every land, who maintain a Scriptural Testimony in behalf of the attainments and cause of the Reformation, against all that is contrary to sound doctrine and the power of godliness.

6. An approbation of the doctrines contained in the Declaration and Testimony of the Reformed Presbyterian Church in
North America, in defence of
truth, and in opposition to error.

These, together with due subordination in the Lord to the
authority of the Synod of the
Reformed Presbyterian Church in
North America, and a regular life
and conversation, form the bonds
of our ecclesiastical union.

6. A practical adorning of the
doctrine of God our Saviour, by a
life and conversation becoming the
gospel, together with due subordination in the Lord, to the authority of the Synod of the Reformed
Presbyterian Church in North
America.

According to the spirit of the doctrines and history
of the Covenanter Church, the Old School body renewed the Covenants in 1871, after the example of
their ancestors, and their fourth term of communion
was changed in 1878, to embrace this step, and
embodies in it all that is implied in the term of 1806.
Previous to 1878, the term was precisely the same as
that of 1806. At a glance, and with a clear perception of truth, the candid reader can see that the New
School brethren have cast out of their terms the
peculiar and distinctive profession of the Reformed
Presbyterian Church. In the second term they slyly
drop out the word "whole" from the Westminster
standards in order to make them more palatable to
the tastes of those bodies with which they hoped to
unite. In the third term they make no reference whatever to the document which is the standard of the
Church, and they have cut out all that refers to a
form of worship, in order to leave matters open for
the reception of innovations in the future. In the

fourth term, which is the distinguishing and important one, they make no allusion whatever to Churches and Nations Covenanting ; they have broken the link that bound them to the past ; they do not acknowledge any peculiar connection with the Covenants of our fathers in Scotland ; they have never Covenanted in America, and hence have repudiated the entire principles of the Reformation, and yet claim and demand the name *Covenanter!* In the fifth term, which is a strange conglomeration compared to the genuine one, they fail to give the true import of that term ; they leave out all that relates to "contending against immoral Constitutions of civil government," and yet claim and demand the name *Reformed Presbyterian!* They make no reference to the witnessing Church in Britain and Ireland, and, on the whole, this term is so indefinite that any Protestant could take it no matter what his views were about the martyrs of Scotland, or whether he knew that for which they so heroicly contended. In the " Historical Part " of the Testimony it is a remarkable fact that they have left out that part which assigns a distinguished place to the Covenants. This omission is remarkable because the omitted paragraph is the only one which gives the organization of the first Reformed Presbytery, and refers to two occasions upon which the Church renewed the Covenants. That all may see the force of this important omission by the New School brethren, this paragraph will here be inserted :

" For more than a third of a century, Mr. McMillan sustained alone the banner of a Covenanted Reforma-

6

tion, until, by the accession of Mr. Nairn, the way was opened for the constitution of the REFORMED PRESBYTERY. This important event took place, August 1, 1743. In the meantime, however, the scattered remnant had met at Auchinsaugh, July 24, 1712, and there renewed the Covenants, National and Solemn League, with confession of sins, and an engagement to duties ; as they also did, after the constitution of Presbytery, at Crawford-John, in the year 1745."*

We regard that paragraph as of great importance, both for the date of the constitution of our Church and for the fact that they then Covenanted. In the "Doctrinal Part" they have failed to bring up their Testimony to contend against evils of the present day, such as intemperance, secrecy, and others. No paragraph appears against slavery. Now we believe that while divine truth is unchangeable, the testimony of the Church is progressive, and should be brought up to apply to new aspects of evil as they arise. This is what the Testimony requires of the Church when it says :

"Every generation is to take care that the truth, as stated and defended by their predecessors, shall be maintained and faithfully transmitted together with the result of their own contendings to the succeeding generation."

We have no quarrel with our New School brethren because they do not believe as we do, but we do insist that they have no claim upon our name. It has been clearly shown that they neither dissent from immoral

* Omitted from New School Testimony, page 111.

Constitutions nor hold or renew the ancient Covenants, and since these two positions constitute it a Reformed Presbyterian Covenanting Church, they have no just claim to such a name. After the setting up of an independent body in 1833, they flourished for awhile, but affiliating too freely with other bodies they lost their foreign mission ; and not only did ministers leave them, but whole congregations and Presbyteries went into other denominations, and they have ceased to publish any statistics by which to determine their strength.* The obvious reason for their marvelous declension is that they have no distinct ground upon which to stand.

The Synod of 1833, at Philadelphia, took the following action in regard to those who had separated from it :

That the members of our subordinate and inferior judicatories, and all our people, be and hereby are warned not to recognize the authority, or admit the interference of such ministers as have been suspended for the maintaining of principles opposed to the standards of our church on the subject of civil government ; as likewise of all such ministers and others who may be confederated with them in corrupting the doctrine, contemning the authority, and violating the order of the church; inasmuch as these last, as well as the first, are, and hereby are declared to be, from the nature of the opinions they maintain, and the divisive course they pursue, prohibited from holding a seat in our courts, or exercising authority, or any way interfering in the judicatories or congregations of the Reformed Presbyterian Church, while maintaining such principles and pursuing such practices.

At this same meeting, the Synod re-affirmed its attachment to the historic and true position of the Church in this country, by the following resolution :

---

* The minutes of the General Synod of 1887, reveal the fact that they have twenty-four ministers, fourteen of whom are settled pastors ; and, by the accession of a native, they have one missionary in India.

That as it has always been in the proceedings and history of the
Reformed Presbyterian Church, both in the land of our forefathers and
in this land, a great and leading object to bear an explicit and practical testimony to the truth respecting civil government as the ordinance
of God, and the subjection of the nations to Messiah; so it is utterly
inconsistent with our doctrinal standards and judicial acts for any member of this church to sit on juries, to hold offices, or swear allegiance
to the Constitution of the United States.

From that day to this the Reformed Presbyterian
Church has had little or no trouble in applying the
principles of the Church, and the members feel that it
is their duty to separate themselves from that civil
institution which refuses to own Christ as its King, and
His Word as its supreme law. If any pastors or sessions allow any members to violate the law of the
Church in this respect, they deserve the same condemnation as those brethren who separated from us
in 1833. If any such there be, the fact is unknown
to the Church, and when discovered will be dealt with
as an offence.

In the session of 1834, at Pittsburgh, the names of
some ministers, who had identified themselves with the
New School body, were stricken from the roll. Papers
on important subjects were read and ordered published
in overture. Measures were adopted for devising a
plan by which young men could be prepared for the
service of the ministry until the Theological Seminary
was resuscitated. Arrangements were also made for
the publication of another edition of the Testimony.

At the meeting of Synod in 1836, at Pittsburgh, it
was apparent that the Church was in a flourishing
condition, and many ministers had been settled in

pastoral charges. At this meeting strong ground was taken against the sin of slavery. The Synod disapproved of the plan of the Colonization Society considered as opposed to the manumission of slaves. It was on the supposition that this Society would be favorable to the abolition of human slavery that the Synod had previously given it countenance. The Synod continued to maintain the duty of the immediate and universal emancipation of the enslaved, and disapproved of their transportation to Africa. Parts were assigned to different ministers to write pieces for the argumentative part of the Testimony. Drafts of a "Book of Discipline" and also of "Church Government" were read and referred. The Theological Seminary was revived, located at New Alexandria, Pennsylvania, and Rev. Dr. J. R. Willson was chosen professor. It was also resolved, "That we recommend to our people, totally to abstain from traffic in ardent spirits." Ministers were instructed to preach on the sin and danger of Sabbath profanation. The "Book of Discipline and Church Government," as also the "Argument on the Arminian Controversy" were published in overture.

The Synod of 1838, met in New York. Rev. William Sommerville, missionary to Nova Scotia, was present and made an address on the cause of the Reformation in that country. For disorderly conduct and abusive language, a licentiate, and some persons associated with him, were suspended from ecclesiastical priviledges. As there were some difficulties in the way of establishing one Theological Seminary, according to the resolution of the previous meeting, the Synod now agreed to abandon the idea of locating it at New Alexandria, and rescinded their former action. It was then resolved to establish two Seminaries—one at Coldenham, New York, in which Rev. Dr. J. R. Willson was continued professor; and the other at Allegheny, Pennsylvania, in which Rev. Thomas Sproull was chosen professor. Boards of Superintendents were chosen, whose duty should be to arrange the course of study. The Church's relation to the Anti-Slavery society again came up for settlement, and the Synod declared its approbation and patronage of the *cause* of abolition, but warned its members against "voluntary associations" with men of erroneous principles and corrupt practices. If it was to become a political society, then Covenanters must withdraw. The Synod then passed the following resolution:

"That the Testimony of this Church is directed against, not only the practical evil of slavery, but also against the immoral principles in the Constitution of the United States, by which this wicked system is supported; we, therefore, declare to the Church and to the world, that from all associations which propose, by an act homologating the Constitution of the United States, to remove the evil of slavery, it is our duty and determination to stand aloof."

The Synod of 1840, met in the city of Allegheny. A letter from the Rev. Dr. John T. Pressly of the Associate Reformed Church in behalf of a "Convention of Reformed Churches" was received. The Committee appointed to examine the letter reported, in substance,

that " while this Synod laments schism in the Church,
yet knowing that societies and individuals are more
solicitous about the *removal* of evils than to ascertain
their *causes* and *natures;* and because most of these
schisms exist from the departure of some from Reformation attainments ; and as there is no disposition on
the part of those who have departed to retrace their
steps, but desire to strike out of certain articles of
agreement the doctrine of the power of the civil magistrate
from the Confession ; and, as this Synod will not do
any act that would be construed as implying an abandonment of any part of her terms of communion, resolved
that they could not comply with the invitation to attend
such a Convention." On motion Synod decreed the
union of the Eastern and Western Theological Seminaries under the joint care of both the professors, and
the Seminary was located in the city of Allegheny.
The members , of the Church were urged to a hearty
support of this important institution. A resolution was
again presented to prohibit the traffic in ardent spirits
or intoxicating liquors by members of the Church.

The Synod of 1841, met at Utica, Ohio. A
memorial from the Missionary Society of the Philadelphia congregation was received, urging the Synod
to take steps for the immediate establishment of a
Foreign Mission. Since the last meeting of Synod, two
ministers of the Ohio Presbytery had followed divisive
courses and left the communion of the Church for the
alleged reason that the Synod had postponed its
deliverance on " voluntary associations," and they regarded the Synod as unfaithful to its duty. These

misguided men erected the " Reformed Presbytery," and
a few disciples gathered around them. The conduct of
these schismatics brought the Synod to the fuller consideration of the question, and now adopted the following resolutions :

1. That our solemn covenant obligations demand our social as
well as individual adherence to the whole law of God, in dependence
on whose grace all our endeavors and engagements are to be made
for the performance of every duty and the attainment of every lawful
object.

2. That those confederated associations for declared moral purposes,
which pay no express regard to a belief in the Lord Jesus Christ
for salvation, nor to a dependence on His Spirit for guidance in all
duty, and in the special duties of such associations in particular, but
are based on principles of legalism, and admit promiscuously all
classes of their members to perform religious as well as other duties,
are not entered into in the true spirit of the solemn deeds of our covenant forefathers.

3. That our ministers and people be admonished to refuse uniting
unnecessarily in associations with the erroneous and wicked, when a
bond of confederation is required to be signed implying identity with
such persons.

4. That in associations also of a merely civil nature, when in the
prosecution of their respective charters they are known to have been
guilty of immorality, such as turnpike companies, steamboats, &c., in
the desecration of the holy Sabbath, Reformed Presbyterians should
have no participation.

If those men who went out were grieved only because of Synod's negligence to do as it now did, they
would have returned to the Church of their fathers.
This they never did. The one died in obscurity in
1845, and the other strenuously maintained his peculiar
views alone until his death in 1887.

The subject of the traffic in intoxicating liquors
had often been a matter of consideration by Synod,

and, against this sinful and nefarious business the Synod had taken only too mild measures. As the subject had been fully investigated, and the destructive employment fully exhibited by Committees previously appointed, the Synod was now prepared to adopt the following preamble and resolutions:

WHEREAS, The traffic in ardent spirits for *luxurious purposes and as a beverage* has been a fruitful source of scandal and crime; therefore resolved,

1. That members of this church be and hereby are prohibited from engaging in or continuing in this traffic; and

2. That wherever there are individuals employed in this traffic, sessions are hereby directed to deal with them immediately in such a way that this evil may be removed from the church in the best and speediest manner.

As the Church had always held as a term of communion that "the Scriptures of the Old and New Testaments are the *only rule of faith and manners*," this latter clause was directed to be inserted in its proper place in the first term of communion. A Committee was also appointed to continue the "Historical Part" of the Testimony with emendations of the same. A Committee was appointed to prepare a "draft of the National Covenant and of the Solemn League and Covenant, adapted to the present circumstances of the Church and of the world." Mild complaints occasionally came before Synod in the matter of reading out the lines in pubic worship, but the court did not consider these difficulties of sufficient magnitude to justify the formation of a fixed law on the subject. Efforts were made for the permanent support of the Seminary.

The Synod of 1843, met in the city of Rochester, New York. The friendly correspondence with the Synod of Ireland, which had been disturbed by the gross misrepresentations of the Church by those who had abandoned her testimony in 1833, was now resumed, and a most affectionate letter from the brethren beyond the sea was received. Friendly relations and fraternal greetings have since been annually exchanged with the Covenanted brethren in both Scotland and Ireland. The reports from all the Presbyteries were of an encouraging character, and revealed the fact that the number of congregations and missionary stations, as well as ministers and licentiates, had greatly increased since the last meeting. The Committee previously appointed for the purpose, reported the draft of a Covenant, which was published in overture, and sent down to the inferior courts for them to report upon at the next meeting. Copies were also sent to the sister judicatories in Scotland and Ireland for the same purpose. Several cases of discipline of a local interest were adjudicated, but nothing of vital importance was transacted at this meeting.

The Synod of 1845, met in the city of Allegheny, Pennsylvania. Many new ministers appeared in this session. Reports revealed the fact that several new congregations had been organized in the West, and that missionary work was being done among the colored people who had fled to the North. The Church generally was in a healthy condition. There was manifest a general awakening on the subject of missions at home and abroad. The Committee previously appointed to designate a field for missionary operations, and had selected the Island of St. Thomas, now were prepared to report that on account of the peculiar hindrances in the way in that field they were undecided as to the practicability of beginning operations in that Island. A special Committee on Covenanting was appointed, and the matter referred for the present. The subject of the "deacon" again came regularly before the Synod, and, after some amendments and discussion, the following preamble and resolutions were unanimously adopted :

WHEREAS, The office of deacon is a divine institution, the functions of which are declared in the Form of Church Government to be "To take special care in distributing to the necessities of the poor," and of which it is said in Reformation Principles that he "has no power except about the temporalities of the Church," and—

WHEREAS, Said office has fallen very extensively into neglect for many years ; and—

WHEREAS, It is the desire of this court that uniformity in practice be maintained in all our congregations ; and—

WHEREAS, Some misunderstanding seems to exist in relation to the ground of our Covenanted uniformity in practice in respect to the subject of deacons as settled at the Second Reformation ; and—

WHEREAS, Faithfulness to the Church's Head requires the re-assertion of this ground of practical uniformity as it then obtained : therefore—

Resolved, 1st, That our Covenanted uniformity does not recognize as of divine right the congregational trustee, but the Scriptural deacon as stated in the preamble.

Resolved, 2d, That said Covenanted uniformity does not recognize as of divine right a Consistory of ministers, elders and deacons, having authority to enact, govern and control the Church, either in her spiritual or temporal concerns, or as having any authority or power whatever, except for consultation and advice for the well ordering of the temporal affairs of the congregation.

A Board of Domestic Missions was appointed, consisting of six members, their duties being to receive and disburse monies to needy stations, and to open up new fields of labor at home. A plan for completing the "Argumentative Part" of the Testimony was considered, and subjects and writers were assigned for the completion of this work. Some changes took place with reference to the Theological Seminary. Rev. Thomas Sproull resigned his professorate; the location was changed from the city of Allegheny to the city of Cincinnati, Ohio; the Board of Inspection resigned and a new one was appointed; and Rev. Dr. J. R. Willson continued to be the professor in the Seminary.

The Synod of 1847, met in the city of Allegheny, Pennsylvania. By an appointment of the Board of Foreign Missions, the Rev. J. B. Johnston had made an exploring tour through the Island of Hayti, and the Board reported the selection of this Island as the field of operations, and the city of Port au Prince as the starting point and center of work. Several young men were chosen as missionaries, but declined, and finally the Rev. Joseph W. Morton and Mr. Robert J. Dodds accepted appointments. Mr. Morton entered upon the work in Hayti the same year, a history of which Mission will be found in another part of this volume. Several generous bequests were made to the Theological Seminary, and efforts were made for the establishing of a literary institution under the care of the Synod.

The Synod of 1849, met in the city of Philadelphia, The Lakes Presbytery reported that they had founded "Geneva Hall," at Northwood, Ohio, April, 1848, and that the institution was under the superintendence of the Rev. J. B. Johnston. The Pittsburg Presbytery also reported the establishment of Westminster College and Female Seminary, at Wilkinsburg, Pennsylvania, and that buildings were about to be erected. This enterprise was largely carried on by the generous donations of Mr. James Kelly. The missionary to Hayti having changed his beliefs in reference to the Christian Sabbath, appeared in court, and, having been libeled, was cited to appear and answer the charges. The following is the report of Synod on this case:

Order of the day, viz: the case of Mr. Morton called for, the libel was then read by the Clerk; when Mr. Morton having, in reply to the Moderator, answered that he was prepared for trial, the substance of the libel was again stated in his hearing. Mr. Morton was then called upon, according to the rule provided for such cases, either to confess the charge or put himself upon his trial. Mr. Morton in return acknowledged that he had denied that the day commonly called the Christian Sabbath is so by Divine appointment, and then proceeded to plead the irrelevancy of the charge by endeavoring to prove the perpetuity of the law for the observance of the seventh day. While so doing he was arrested by the Moderator, who informed him that the charge contained in the libel was such that Mr. Morton could only prove its irrelevancy to censure by proving that the appropriation of the first day of the week, known as the Christian Sabbath, to secular employments, or teaching so to do, is not relevant to censure, which attempt the Moderator would consider disorderly, and would not allow.

From this decision a member appealed, when the Moderator's decision was unanimously sustained. Upon this, Mr. Morton declined the authority of the court.

Resolved, That Mr. Morton's appointment as missionary to Hayti be revoked.

Resolved, That inasmuch as Mr. Morton has now publicly declined the authority of this court, he be suspended from the exercise of the Christian ministry, and from the privileges of the Reformed Presbyterian Church. The Moderator then publicly pronounced the sentence of suspension on Mr. Morton, agreeably to the above resolution.

By this defection the Hayti Mission was abandoned, and Mr. Dodds was not sent out as was expected. Two ministers were admonished and warned that in the future they were not to teach doctrines contrary to the standards of the Church which are founded upon the Word of God. The Committee to which were referred certain memorials on the subject of slavery reported the following :

The petitioners, lamenting the prevalent ignorance of our testimony against this great evil, and the countenance given to it by most Christian denominations in the United States, respectfully ask Synod, 1st, To re-assert their position in regard to the exclusion of slave-holders from her fellowship, and her dissent from the United States Constitution, on this, with other grounds. 2d. They ask that, if practicable, some more efficient means may be employed for the diffusion of our doctrines and testimony on this subject, particularly that a remonstrance may be addressed to the principal slave-holding Churches.

In regard to the first of these petitions, we remark that the declarations contained in the Historical part of our testimony, published, of course, by the Presbytery itself, furnish ample testimony of the position occupied on slavery by this Church. We refer to the following statements, "The Presbytery resolved to purge the Church of this dreadful evil : they enacted that no slave-holders should be retained in their Communion." "The Presbytery required of their connexions a general emancipation." "No slave-holder is since admitted to their Communion." See Hist. Test. pp. 154, 155, Ed. 1835. Now, while it is true, as stated in one of the memorials, that we have not in our hands the original acts, excluding all slave-holders, we have the Presbytery itself as evidence that this was the purport and design of their actions. This, with the uniform practice of the Church—for in the language of the testimony, "No slave-holder is since (1800) admitted to their Communion"—in the judgment of your committee as completely defines the position of this Church in regard to ecclesiastical fellowship with slave-holders as it is possible to do. A sight of the original acts might gratify curiosity, but could not shed any additional light upon that which is already as clear as the noon-day. *No* slaveholder *can* have privileges in the Reformed Presbyterian Church. We say the same of our position **as** a Church in relation to the civil institutions of the country. The Historical Testimony, pp 152, 153, 154, and the frequent incidental actings since are sufficiently explicit on this point. Covenanters have not sworn, and do not swear oaths to the institutions of the country, among other reasons, because the Constitution of the United States contains compromises with slave-holding interests, and guarantees for the institution itself protection so long as it exists in the slave-holding States. We have no further action to recommend on either of these points.

2d. In regard to a remonstrance to be addressed to slave-holding Churches, we agree with the petitioners that it is important that this Church take some measures to bring her testimony more directly before the Churches, and would recommend that a Committee of three be appointed to prepare a remonstrance of the kind contemplated, embodying the views and position of this Church on the whole question, said Committee to publish the remonstrance on their own responsibility, as to the arguments and expressions which they may see fit to employ.

The Theological Seminary was removed from Cincinnati to Northwood, Ohio, and it and the Literary Institution were taken under the care of Synod. Students now frequently persued their literary and theological courses at the same time. Rev. Dr. J. R. Willson was continued professor, and received the assistance of the professors of Geneva Hall in some departments of study.

The Synod of 1851, met in the city of Allegheny, Pennsylvania. Quite a number of ministers had been ordained and installed over pastoral charges, and took their seats in the court. Several important cases of discipline came up for adjudication, and were judiciously disposed of. Some of these related to the organization of congregations without deacons. Events arising out of conflicting interests and personal feelings, the Synod

deemed it proper to suspend the Theological Seminary
for the present, and the students were directed to prose-
cute their studies under the care of their respective
Presbyteries.   Dr. Willson was honorably retired as
emeritus professor.   The library and all monies were
given into the hands of Committees to hold in trust for
Synod.   The Board of Domestic Missions reported that
much money had been contributed and that many promising stations had been opened up.   A systematic
plan for the operations of home missions was inaugurated,
and much interest manifested in this part of the work
of the Church.   The Committee appointed to express
the views of the Church in reference to the Fugitive
Slave Law, reported the following preamble and
resolutions :

As human enactments are to be tested by the Divine law ; and as
it is the duty of the church to testify against all that is in opposition
to the law of God : and as her Head came "to proclaim liberty to
the captive," so she should open her mouth for the dumb. Therefore,

1. *Resolved*, That this Synod reiterate its uncompromising opposition to the institution of slavery as a system of complicated and
unmitigated wrong, and utterly repudiate all• the arguments and excuses
of slaveholders and their abettors for its continuance ; and recommend
to all our people more vigorous and persevering efforts for its removal.

2. That the fugitive slave law is essentially tyrannical ; not only
securing the enslavement of those who are in fact free, but in forbidding freemen to exercise the sympathies of Christian compassion,
and commanding them to assist in returning men to cruel bondage.
It brings deserved infamy upon our land, dishonors God, and is
expressly contrary to the plainest precepts of this law—"Thou shalt
not deliver unto his master the servant which is escaped from his
master unto thee." "Bewray not him that wandereth." "Relieve the
oppressed." And it is the duty of all not only to refuse compliance
with its provisions, but to show others its hideous enormity.

3. That the main element of the fugitive slave law naturally

flows from the provisions of the Constitution of the United States upholding slavery. Art. 4, Sec. 2. "No person held to service or labor in one State, under the laws thereof, escaping into another, shall, in consequence of any law or regulation therein, be discharged from such service or labor; but shall be delivered up on claim of the party to whom such service or labor may be due." Art. 4, Sec. 1. "Full faith and credit shall be given in each State to the public acts, records and judicial proceedings of every other State." And we see in this another exemplification of the immorality of the United States Government, and it shows clearly the evil of swearing oaths of allegiance, and thus sustaining slavery.

4. That those ministers of the gospel who teach the binding obligation of this law to be obeyed for conscience's sake, and the conduct of those Christians who sustain the law, hypocritically professing to love God while they hate the negro, bring reproach upon religion, encourage infidelity, and rivet still more tightly the chains of the oppressed.

5. That it is the duty of the ministers of Christ to teach clearly that magistrates in Christian lands should yield to the authority of God's law, and that any law that is in opposition to the precepts of the Bible does not bind the conscience, and ought to be resisted by every means consistent with religion ; for we must obey God rather than men.

6. That we recognize with gratitude the hand of God in making this infamous law the means of showing many the enormous evil of slavery, and convincing them of their practical and constitutional connection with slavery ; and that we rejoice in the efforts that are making to free some of the Churches from the incubus of slavery. And we trust that the " Free Churches " will, ere long, see the sin of upholding a government that rejects the law of God ; and that they and we, upon the broad ground of Christian principles, may labor to bring this nation into submission to God's higher law.

The Rev. William Wilson of the New School body, who desired to return to the communion of the Reformed Presbyterian Church upon certain conditions contained in papers laid before the court, learning that

7

he could not enter the body without a full reception
of all her principles, withdrew his papers.

The Synod of 1853, met in the city of New York.
Synod re-affirmed its deliverance of 1847, that the consistory, an assembly composed of the pastor, elders
and deacons to manage the temporalities of the Church,
is not an ecclesiastical court. The special Committee
to which was referred the subject of civil legislation
against the traffic in ardent spirits, reported the following which was adopted by Synod :

The Church of Christ is a divinely instituted association, organized,
not only for the conversion of sinners and sanctification of saints, but
for the reformation of society ; and as a reformatory association, she
should be in advance of the world in all reformatory movements. In
the temperance reform we would not only be active, but until the object
of that reform is accomplished, would use all the means in our power
to give a proper direction to the efforts put forth by others. We would
not close our eyes to the fact that the tide of intemperance, now flood-
ing this land, is truly alarming, calling not only for mourning and com-
miseration, but for greater activity on the part of the Church to stem
that torrent that the appalling amount of crime and misery, consequent
upon the use of intoxicating drinks, may be speedily diminished, and
the evil wholly removed.

The principles involved in the law of the Church, and particularly
set forth in the action of this Synod in 1841, should be carried out
in civil legislation so as to forbid, and wholly prevent, the traffic in
intoxicating drinks as beverages. Civil government is intended, among
other objects, to protect the people against the wrongs inflicted by
venders of ardent spirits. This can be done effectually only by utterly
prohibiting the traffic. Therefore,

Resolved, 1. That we hail with joy the efforts that have been made
recently in several of the States to suppress entirely the traffic in
intoxicating drinks, and we earnestly hope that the work may go on
until there be no place where license will be given, or the protection
of law afforded to that traffic, so wicked and so ruinous in its
consequences.

Resolved, 2. That this Synod gives its hearty approbation to the principles involved in the law commonly called the Maine Liquor Law, viz : the right and the duty of civil government to wholly prohibit the sale of intoxicating drinks, except for medicinal, chemical, mechanical, and sacramental purposes.

Resolved, 3. That in the temperance reform we depend wholly upon the Spirit of God for success, and regard the gospel of Jesus Christ as the only efficient means of permanently removing the evil.

The Synod embodied the following reformatory sentiment in its proceedings at this session :

There are two great evils which must be removed from the world before the state of society can be healthy : Popery, which directly enslaves the soul and indirectly the body ; Slavery, which directly enslaves the body and indirectly the soul. We cannot, consistently, claim the character of Reformers if we do not untiringly employ the armour of light on the right and left against these great, and alas ! yet growing evils in our land. We may incur some temporary odium, and, perhaps, not only be reproached, but persecuted on this account ; but, assuredly. the advocates of impartial liberty for the souls and bodies of men will prevail, and their memories be savory if they die in the field of contest ; and their persons will be honoured if they survive the strife.

The Synod of 1855, met in the city of Allegheny, Pennsylvania. The reports of Presbyteries revealed the fact that there had been great emigration to the Western States and Territories, and that mission stations were springing up in various places, demanding the care of the Mission Board. A delegation from the New School body invited the Synod to attend a farewell missionary meeting in Pittsburg, and also expressed the Christian affection and respect of the body they represented. The Committee preparing a " Form of Covenant," reported, and it was published in the appendix to the minutes of Synod. Arrangements were

made to renew the Covenants, at the next meeting
of Synod, if the way should be open. The organization of a Foreign Mission was recommended, as well
as the resuscitation of the Theological Seminary.

The Synod of 1856, met in the city of Philadelphia,
Pennsylvania. The Board of Foreign Missions selected
Syria as the field of operations, and, after several
elections, the Rev. Robert J. Dodds and Mr. Joseph
Beattie, licentiate, accepted appointments to that field.
They left the same Fall for the scene of their labors.

The Theological Seminary was reorganized, and
located in the city of Allegheny, Pennsylvania, where
it has since remained. Revs. Drs. James Christie and
Thomas Sproull were chosen professors. A friendly correspondence was carried on with the Associate Presbyterian Church and New School body, but nothing
agreed upon as a basis of union.

The Synod of 1857, met in Northwood, Ohio. There
was a large delegation and much interest manifested
in all the proceedings. The vexed question of "the
deacon" disturbed some parts of the Church for many
years, and the following paper, after being amended,
was adopted, and is as follows:

WHEREAS, Much of our troubles in the Church, and at our meetings
of Synod for some years past, has originated in the attempts, too often
successful, to form congregations on the principle known as that of
"elective affinity;" as also in the formation of congregations by commissions of Synod, and not by Presbyteries to whom the business of
organizing congregations belongs; therefore,

Resolved, 1. That hereafter no congregation shall be organized by
any Presbytery on the principle of elective affinity, to evade discipline,
or reconcile parties at variance, or to settle difficulties which properly

belong to the discipline of the Church, or upon a difference in principle, or the meaning of the Standards of the Church.

Resolved, 2. Synod shall hereafter leave the organization of congregations to the Presbyteries to whom it belongs ; and

WHEREAS, The Form of Church Government recognizes deacons as ordained officers in the Church, and "requisite" among the officers of a particular congregation, and this by the will and appointment of the Lord Jesus Christ ; and

WHEREAS, The Form of Church Government defines the duty of the deacon to be "to take special care in distributing to the necessities of the poor," and the Testimony declares that the "deacons have no power except about the temporalities of the Church ;" and

WHEREAS, This office has not yet been exemplified in all our congregations ; therefore

Resolved, 1. That Presbyteries be directed to exercise due care and diligence to have deacons chosen and ordained in congregations where they are still wanting, with no other powers than those defined in the Standards.

Resolved, 2. That Presbyteries be enjoined in organizing new congregations, to see to it that deacons be chosen and ordained in them.

Resolved, 3. That no action of last Synod was intended to rescind or repeal the resolutions of 1845 and 1847, on the subject of the deacon's office, the trustee or consistory, nor were they so affected.

An elaborate and convincing report on "Systematic Beneficence and a Sustentation Fund" was submitted and its claims enforced. The reports from all the Presbyteries were full, satisfactory, and represented the Church to be in a generally good condition. Another lengthy report was submitted on the subject of slavery, and the Church resolved to plead with more earnestness for the cause of the oppressed, and work more diligently for the emancipation of the slave. Large contributions and bequests were made to the support of the Theological Seminary, and a plan of endowment was submitted. The Foreign and Domestic Mission Boards reported affairs to be in an encour-

aging condition, and the Church was generally support-
ing these departments of her work. The Synod was not
yet ready to enter into the work of Covenanting.

During the year 1858, a conference of two Com-
mittees from the Synod and the General Synod of the
Reformed Presbyterian Churches, met in the city of
Allegheny, Pennsylvania, to confer on the subject of
union. There were present of the Synod, Revs.
Thomas Sproull, J. B. Johnston and J. M. Willson.
Of the General Synod, Revs. Hugh McMillan, A. W.
Black, William Wilson and J. N. McLeod. Dr. Sproull
was chosen Chairman, and Dr. McLeod, Secretary.
After much discussion and the reading of letters which
had passed between the Committees and the Synods,
and after holding several sessions, the delegates finally
submitted the grounds upon which a union could be
effected. Rev. J. B. Johnston submitted the following,
in behalf of the Synod, as the only ground upon
which a reunion could be effected:

The Committee present the brethren, the Committee of the other
Synod, the following theses, as embracing for substance the ground on
which we understand the Reformed Presbyterian Church stood in
regard to *civil relations* anterior to 1833, and as the only ground on
which we can give any encouragement to our brethren to expect that
a re-union of the two Synods can be effected.

1. That we dissent from the Constitution of the United States,
because of its immoralities.

2. That this dissent from the Constitution requires to abstain from
the oath of allegiance, and from oaths of office binding to support
the Constitution.

3. That it prohibits voting for officers who must be qualified by
an oath to support the Constitution.

4. That it prohibits sitting on juries, as explained by our Testimony, understanding that such juries do not include various other

juries, where there is neither an incorporation with the government, an oath to an immoral law, nor any implied engagement to support the Constitution.

Rev. Andrew W. Black then read the following statement on behalf of the General Synod, in reply to the theses already presented:

1. The ground occupied by the Reformed Presbyterian Church in reference to the civil institutions of the United States, State and Federal, prior to the disruption, is as expressed in her own language in 1821, "That no connection with the laws, officers, or the order of the State, is forbidden by the Church, except what truly involves immorality."

2. That in the application of the above principles, we regard ourselves as dissenters from immorally constituted civil establishments; that is to say, whenever the recognition of an immoral law is made essential to the action of the juror; or to the exercise of the elective franchise; or to holding civil office; or to the discharge of any other civil duty. Reformed Presbyterians must abstain from all such acts, as involving immorality.

3. That the moral character of the Federal Constitution of the United States, being a matter of opinion, and undecided by any competent authority, the recognition or non-recognition of it should not be made a term of ecclesiastical communion.

4. We therefore recommend, that as the two churches are united in their views of the great principles of civil government, and in the belief and declaration of the fact that no communion should be held with immorality, the ground of the re-union should be the exercise of forbearance in regard to those special governmental questions by which they are now divided. It is the belief of this Committee that the Reformed Presbyterian Church was divided, not by difference of religious principles, but by other causes, as is shown in the letter, to which a reply is expected.

5. Should the brethren of the other Committee and the Synod not agree to these grounds of re-union, we recommend to the ministers and members of these Churches to treat each other with Christian courtesy and respect, and to co-operate as far as possible on the large common ground they occupy as Reformed Presbyterians.

A re-union of these bodies has never been effected
for the reason that the one party is not willing
to come back to the high position from which it
departed in 1833, and the other is not prepared to
abandon the historic and true position of the Church.

The Synod of 1859, met in the city of Allegheny,
Pennsylvania. A communication from the General
Assembly of the United Presbyterian Church was
received, with a basis of union. The following is the
reply:

DEAR BRETHREN—Your letter containing a resolution of your Reverend
Body, and inclosing a copy of the Basis of Union of the United Presbyterian Church, was received during the session of our Synod.

Your kind and fraternal greeting we most heartily reciprocate, and
unite with you in the prayer that "the great King and Head of the
Church will direct the way by which the friends of Zion and of the
truth shall be led to see eye to eye." We have His sure promise
that He will accomplish this in his own time.

The steps by which you have arrived at your present position we
have watched with attention and interest. It gives us joy to find in
your Basis of Union the statement and assertion of some of the
principles for which we have long contended. The supreme dominion
of Messiah as Lord of all—Prince of the Kings of the earth—occupies
a place in your Testimony, and our hearts rejoice on this account.
It is the application of this and kindred principles to the civil institutions of the country that has placed us in the position of dissenters from a government that ignores the claims of our Prince. In our
view it is only by maintaining this position that we can consistently
carry out our principles, and succeed in bringing our land into subjection to its Lord and King. Our present standing has been deliberately taken, and in the strength of Divine grace we purpose to
hold on till the great end—the enthronement of Messiah—shall be
effected.

In order to bring up the Testimony of the Church
to prevaling evils, the following preambles and resolution were adopted:

WHEREAS, Secret Associations and Slavery are present evils of enormous magnitude, and are rapidly extending their power and pernicious influence in this land ; and

WHEREAS, In our present Testimony, there is no direct and explicit utterance against these sins proportionate to their prevalence and heinous character ; and

WHEREAS, There is a demand for a new edition ;   therefore,

Resolved, That Synod proceed to take, at once, the requisite steps for adding a section on Secret Societies, and a chapter on the subject of Slavery.

The Reformed Presbyterian Church has always been consistent with her position and held that human slavery is a sin against God and men. In the fearless advocacy of the cause of the oppressed, the ministers of this Church have been mobbed, stoned, egged and burned in effigy. All manner of reproachful epithets have been pronounced upon them. Notwithstanding the unpopularity of the cause, they proclaimed fearlessly the sin of the nation and the outrage committed upon humanity until God heard the cry of the oppressed and sent them deliverance.

A vacancy being created in the corps of professors in the Theological Seminary, the Rev. James M. Willson was chosen a professor. Geneva Hall was taken under the care of Synod and left under its present management. The reports from the Foreign and Domestic Missions pronounced both these departments in a flourishing condition. The following memorial was prepared, generally signed throughout the Church, and transmitted :

To the Senate and House of Representatives of the United States:

The memorial of the Synod of the Reformed Presbyterian Church, now in session in Allegheny, Pennsylvania, showeth—That, desirous to promote the best interests of the country, and knowing that "the Most High ruleth in the kingdom of men ;" that the Lord Jesus Christ is "Prince of the kings of the earth " and "Governor among the nations ;" and that the law of God is the "law ;" knowing, also, that nations and rulers should acknowledge God and submit to our Lord Jesus Christ, obeying God's commands, your memorialists are also convinced that this nation does not thus submit itself to God in its Constitution, and exposes itself to the denunciations of God's wrath—"the nations that forget God shall be turned into hell"—We, therefore, pray you to take measures for the amendment of the Constitution, so that it may contain,

1. An express acknowledgment of the being and authority of God.

2. An acknowledgment of submission to the authority of Christ.

3. That it should recognize the paramount obligation of God's law, contained in the Scriptures of the Old and New Testaments.

4. That it may be rendered, in all its principles and provisions, clearly and unmistakably adverse to the existence of any form of slavery within the national limits.

The Synod of 1861, met in the city of New York. The dark political horizon indicated a speedy clash of arms, and the war. of the rebellion broke out. The position and duty of the Church in the present crisis were presented in the following report:

That in view of the calamities brought upon this land by the iniquitous war now raging, *in the interest of slavery*, against the United States, Synod feels called upon to present, for the information of all whom it may concern, a brief outline of our position as a Church ; and

1. We heartily acknowledge the numerous excellencies of the civil institutions of this land ; we appreciate its code of laws, as, in general, wholesome and just ; we prize the privileges and protection we here enjoy in our personal pursuits and rights, and take a deep interest in this land of our birth or adoption, endeared to us as the early refuge of the friends of civil and religious liberty, as the scene of a noble conflict for national freedom and independence, as our home and that of our children.

2. Notwithstanding all this, we are constrained, in conscience, to maintain, as we and our fathers have heretofore done, a state of dissent from the Constitution of the United States, inasmuch as there

is in this instrument no acknowledgment of the name of God, Most High and Eternal; no recognition of the supremacy of His law contained in the Scriptures of the Old and New Testaments; no profession of subjection to the Mediatorial authority of the Son of God, who is "King of kings and Lord of lords:" while on the other hand, this Constitution contains certain "compromises" in the interest of slavery and slaveholders.   On these grounds we are compelled to withhold from said Constitution our oath in its support, and thus to deny ourselves certain privileges which we would gladly enjoy could we do so with good conscience toward God.   But

3. That our position may be fully and definitely understood, we declare,

(1.) That we disclaim allegiance to the government of any foreign nation.

(2.) That we "consider ourselves under obligations to live peaceably with all men, to advance the good of society, and to conform to its order in everything consistent with righteousness."

(3.) That we disown all sympathy, even the least, with the traitors styling themselves "the Confederate States," now in arms against these United States.

(4.) That we will, as true patriots, defend this, our common country, against these and all like enemies.

The Synod re-affirmed its position on the jury question, and exhorted the members to firmness and confidence in this respect.

The Synod of 1862, met in the city of Allegheny, Pennsylvania. The Domestic Mission Board established Mission Schools among the freedmen in several localities in the South, and several missionaries were sent out to Port Royal, South Carolina, and other vicinities where the way was open for mission work. The Theological Seminary received the attention of Synod, and the professors reported a good attendance of students and an addition to the library.

The Synod of 1863, met in Sharon, Iowa. The

Domestic Mission Board reported the establishment of mission schools in South Carolina, Florida, Mississippi and Arkansas, and missionaries and teachers had been sent to these respective fields. The Foreign Mission and Theological Seminary were in a flourishing condition and received the generous contributions of the Church. The Synod appointed a Committee to go to Washington and confer with the President of the United States, and heads of departments, in reference to the duty of the nation to submit to King Jesus. Presbyteries were directed to minister to the sick and wounded soldiers in the military hospitals within their bounds. Some objection being brought against the army oath, a Committee framed the following oath and sought the proper authorities for the sanction of the same, when members of the Church entered the army: "I do swear by the living God, that I will be faithful to the United States, and will aid and defend them against the armies of the Confederate States, yielding all due obedience to military orders." This oath neither encouraged members unduly to enter the conflict, nor pledged them to support an immoral Constitution. Covenanters regarded the government justifiable in the war so far as it was waged to maintain the integrity of the country and to overthrow the iniquitous system of human slavery. Taking this position the members of the Church generously supported the cause of the Union with their substance and their lives. There was not a rebel within the pale of this Church. They believed that the Southren Confederacy was a conspiracy against God and humanity, and that her members were doing God's service when they enlisted to break it up. While recognizing this fact they still claimed that the secession from a human government was not to be compared to rebellion against the divine government, and they would embrace every opportunity to teach the nation this truth and insist upon the recognition of the same. There was no sin or inconsistency in aiding the government in a lawful and righteous work, and while Covenanters heroicly defended their homes and their country by suppressing their enemies, they in no sense became responsible for the immoralities of the government although some wicked men were the brave leaders in the conflict.

In February, 1863, a number of ministers and members of several Christian denominations met in Xenia, Ohio, for the purpose of discussing the subject of amending the National Constitution. At a subsequent meeting in the city of Allegheny, Pennsylvania, circulars were addressed to the supreme judicatories of several Christian denominations to appoint delegates to a convention in July, 1863, but to these invitations no bodies responded but the two Synods of the Reformed Presbyterian Church. This was the origin of the present National Reform Association, and the Reformed Presbyterian Church has ever since been the chief supporter of the movement. Mr. John Alexander of Philadelphia, is, in many respects, the father of the Association, and has been the chief supporter of it in the way of personal contributions. Not a single religious paper in the country had a word of cheer to offer, and when the

Christian Statesman was founded for the propogation of the principles of the Association, some sneered at the project and others passed it by in silence. What a wonderful change in sentiment in twenty-five years! The most able ministers and jurists of the country are now wheeled into line with its glorious principles, and soon the cause which it advocates will finally triumph. The good which this Association has done in the last quarter of a century is incalculable, and at the present time lecturers are in the field from different denominations.

The Synod of 1864, met in the city of Philadelphia. Among the first resolutions was this :

Resolved, That this Synod recommend to the members of the Church entire abstinence from the use of tobacco.

The Committee previously appointed to wait upon the President of the United States, made the following report :

The Committee appointed to confer with the President and heads of Departments touching the duty of the nation to recognize God and the claims of His Word, have attended to the duty imposed upon them. About the beginning of February we visited Washington, and had a pleasant and satisfactory interview with the President. We proffered and read in his hearing an address expressing the well-known views of our Church in regard to the duty of nations, and of the duty of this nation in particular, in the present exigency. A copy of the address is herewith submitted. The Committee also prepared, and caused to be laid before the National Congress, a memorial craving such changes in and amendments to the Constitution of the United States as are set forth in the address.

The Committee took no steps toward securing an acceptance by the proper Department of the form of oath prepared by Synod. In view of the circumstances of the case, it was deemed unnecessary to do so. The Committee understand that the prescribed form of oath was specially intended to meet the case of those who might be drafted under the new conscription law of the United States. It was ascertained that under this law no oath of any kind was required of the soldier, and also that in the case of those who had felt it to be their duty to offer their services to the nation in special emergencies, they had been accepted without any oath. Under these circumstances no end was to be gained by pursuing the matter any further.

The Synod of 1865, met in Utica, Ohio. Resolutions on slavery, and Committees to present the same to the President, were passed. Geneva Hall was revived for the education of colored persons as well as all others. The Mission Boards reported great encouragement and large results from the efforts put forth at home and abroad. The Theological Seminary was not as fully attended as usual owing to the disturbed state of the country. As the rebellion was now put down the Synod adopted the following resolutions:

Resolved, 1st. That this Synod congratulate the country upon the utter overthrow of the slaveholders' rebellion, which has for the past four years filled the land with mourning and aimed at the destruction of the nation.

Resolved, 2d. That we recognize in the death of President Lincoln by the hand of an assassin, a severe chastisement from Almighty God, and the legitimate fruits of that system of wrong and bloodshed which inspired and animated the Southern conspiracy.

Resolved, 3d. That inasmuch as it is a principle of the divine government that "he that justifieth the wicked, and he that condemneth the just, even they both are an abomination to the Lord;" it is our calm and deliberate judgment, that it is the duty of the government, to inflict the penalty of death upon the leaders of the late rebellion.

Resolved, 4th. That we recognize in the late war a signal manifestation of the divine wrath against the sins of the nation, especially the rejection of the authority of Messiah and oppression of man.

Resolved, 5th. That we heartily rejoice in every step which has been taken for the destruction of slavery, and urge the carrying forward of the work, until every man in the nation, without regard to color, stands upon a perfect equality before the laws.

Resolved, 6th. That we again call upon the nation to abandon its rebellion against God, acknowledge His name, submit to His authority, and recognize the mediatorial claims of His Son.

The Synod of 1866, met in the city of Rochester, New York. Rev. R. J. Dodds, missionary from Syria, was present and addressed the court and presided over the deliberations. The question of voting for proper amendments to State Constitutions came up, and received the following answer:

That while there may be instances in which it would not be wrong to do so, yet as there are other ways by which countenance and approbation may be given to what is proper, as by petition, and by public and private expression, Synod does not recommend such a course.

Strong resolutions were passed against the use or sale of intoxicants, and Synod gave its promise to aid the cause of temperance in every way. Cheering reports were received from the Southern and Foreign Missions, and the work of evangelization and reformation was hopefully progressing in all the Church's departments.

The Synod of 1867, met in the city of Allegheny, Pennsylvania. A plan for the endowment of the Theological Seminary was set before the Church. A weekly paper was established for the dissemination of the principles of the National Reform Association. Rev. Samuel O. Wylie was chosen professor of Theology to fill the vacancy occasioned by the death of Rev. Dr. James M. Willson. To an inquiry whether a member of the Church living in Canada may hold office in a case where no oath is required, the following answer was given:

The principle involved in this question is not local but general in its application. The position of the Reformed Presbyterian Church in regard to accepting office, the committee understand to be, not that it is sinful in itself and wrong in all cases, but that it may become sinful either by the imposition of an immoral oath or by involving an obligation to perform a sinful service. When either of these conditions exists, the law and practice of the church forbid the holding of office.

Rev. Joseph McCracken was chosen President of Geneva Hall and Seminary, at Northwood, Ohio. The education of colored persons at this institution promised to be a success, and the Church was deeply interested in this work of elevating the condition of the sable race.

The Synod of 1868, met at Northwood, Ohio. The Theological Seminary and Geneva Hall received special attention. Rev. Samuel O. Wylie having declined the professorate in the former institution, the Rev. J. R. W. Sloane was chosen to the position. Arrangements were made for Covenanting in the near future. Synod re-affirmed its position on the jury question and intemperance, viz: that members are prohibited from sitting on juries, and that they are to cease touching intoxicants in any way. The law of the Church was declared to be positively prohibitory in these respects. Rev. Joseph McCracken having resigned the Presidency of Geneva Hall, Mr. S. J. Crowe, student of theology, had been appointed by the Board as Principal, and conducted the school several years in a most efficient manner.

The following deliverance of Synod upon the voting for amendments was given:

The Reformed Presbyterian Church has deliberately taken the position of dissent from the civil institutions of the United States, not

8

on the ground that participation in all the functions and operations of government is sinful in itself, but on account of the immoral character of the Constitutions and laws under which the citizen must act. Hence the Church has applied this principle by prohibiting her members from holding office and voting at civil elections.

The inquiry now demanding an answer is, Does voting for an amendment of State Constitutions involve, as in the other cases already determined by the Church, anything sinful or inconsistent with the principle and practice of the Church? Synod answers unequivocally, that it does. Inasmuch as voting for this object or any other, involves incorporation with the national society and imperils our dissent from it. Is. 8:12, "Say ye not, A confederacy, to all them to whom this people shall say, A confederacy." It exposes the members of the Church to temptation. 1 Cor. 8:12, "But when ye sin so against the brethren and wound their weak conscience, ye sin against Christ." It encourages other Christians to continue their sinful connection with an ungodly nation, and renders nugatory the discipline of the Church. On these, and other grounds, Synod is resolved to abide by the distinctive principles of the Church, and to apply the law of her exalted Head. "Abstain from all appearance of evil." 1 Thess. 5:22. "Lo the people shall dwell alone, and shall not be reckoned among the nations." Numb. 23:9. And ere long "the kingdom and dominion and the greatness of the kingdom under the whole heaven, shall be given to the people of the saints of the Most High." Dan. 7:27.

To the two inquiries: 1st. In a State where there is no objection to the school law, except that it requires of all officers an oath of allegiance to the Constitution of the United States, as well as an oath to discharge the duties of their office, can members of the Church hold the office of school director, if they are only required to take an oath to discharge the duties of the office, provided they let it be known that they will not take the oath of allegiance prescribed by law? 2d. Can members of the Church vote for an individual for school director who will take the oath of office with the above limitations and explanations? In accordance with the principles stated in the foregoing case, Synod answers, No.

The Synod of 1869, met in the city of Newburgh, New York. A most stirring and hopeful report was given of the cause of National Reform. The educational and Missionary Departments of the work of the Church were in a most healthy condition, and several new organizations of congregations and settlements of ministers were reported. The following resolutions on Secrecy were unanimously adopted :

Resolved, That this Synod views with deep concern the reviving growth and influence of the Secret Orders in the United States.

Resolved, That we condemn these associations, because their effect is to establish spurious and artificial social relations among men and a new code of duties founded upon these relations ; because the secrecy they practice and enjoin is inconsistent with the candor be-coming the Christian character ; and because they virtually assume to establish a religion distinct from the religion of Jesus, and therefore false. On these grounds we renew our traditional testimony that those who enter these associations are unworthy of ecclesiastical fellowship.

Resolved, That we welcome with great satisfaction the rise of an earnest and wide-spread opposition to the Secret Orders, and we trust it shall increase and prevail till society be delivered from the dangers and purified from the corruptions which they occasion.

The Synod of 1870, met in the city of New York. The Church was encouraged to organize Sabbath Schools in all the congregations, but not in such a manner as to supplant parental training or home in-struction. The Reformed Presbyterian Church has always excluded members of oath-bound secret societies from her Communion, the reasons for which action are embodied in the following timely report on the subject :

WHEREAS, Secret Orders are institutions avowedly setting before themselves ends of no mere temporary character, but permanent as those of the Church and State ; and

WHEREAS, Their boasted efforts of friendship and beneficence are designed not for the benefit of all men, nor for the aid of society and the Church in their work, but for the advancement of the orders themselves as rivals of the Church and State ; and

WHEREAS, The social relations formed by membership in these orders must therefore be artificial and false, and the performance of the duties imposed by their obligations an injustice to all outside, including the families of members; and

WHEREAS, Secrecy, which is an essential feature of these orders, however justifiable in exceptional circumstances, is in all ordinary cases needless, opposed to candor, unworthy of a benevolent enterprise, and unscriptural; and

WHEREAS, These orders become to many of the members a church and their ritual and services virtually a religion, and thus not only tend, as proved by fact, to keep men from uniting with the Church, but also induce professing Christians to abandon her; and

WHEREAS, In many of these orders the members are bound together by oaths, horrible in themselves, and administered by no civil or ecclesiastical authority, and may thus become ready instruments in the hands of designing leaders for the overthrow of our civil and religious liberties; therefore,

Resolved, 1. That we emphatically condemn all these orders as wrong in principle and necessarily injurious in their operation.

2. That it is as much the duty of the Church to prohibit the connection of her members with these orders as to forbid their participation in a system of rebellion or oppression.

3. That in view of the advocacy of Secret Orders by influential papers, and even by respected Christian men and ministers, we pledge ourselves to labor for the thorough agitation of the subject, believing that a clearer understanding of their character and influences will lead to the withdrawal of their most effective support.

There was a general and earnest desire upon the part of the Church to now go forward with the act of Covenanting, and definite arrangements were made to enter upon this important work at the next meeting.

The Synod of 1871, met in the city of Pittsburgh, Pennsylvania. It is the most notable meeting because during its sessions the Synod entered into the solemn act of Covenanting. The "bond" of the Covenant and the "Confession of Sins" had been overtured by the Church. This important event in the history of the Reformed Presbyterian Church in America took place in the Pittsburgh Church, May 27, 1871, after a sermon on "Covenanting" by Rev. Andrew Stevenson, D. D. Rev. James M. Beattie then read the Covenant, Rev. J. R. W. Sloane, D. D., addressed the Synod on "The Spirit in which we should Covenant," and Rev. Thomas Sproull, D. D., offered prayer. After a few moments of silent prayer, the Covenant–oath was taken by the members of Synod and others who joined them. The Covenant was then again read by Rev. Thomas Sproull, D. D., and at the close of each section all responded "Amen." At the close of the last section all repeated in concert Exodus 24: 7, "All that the Lord hath said will we do, and be obedient." The Covenant was then subscribed by seventy-four ministers, seventy elders, and by five licentiates, four students of theology, and nineteen elders not members of the Synod at that session. After the bond was signed, the Rev. William Milroy delivered an address on "Covenant-keeping," and the service closed by singing Psalm 72: 17–19.

As the proceedings of this memorable occasion have been preserved to the Church in the "Memorial Volume," it is thought proper to insert nothing in this volume but the Covenant itself, in order that this sacred bond may meet the eye of the casual reader.

COVENANT.

"We, Ministers, Elders, Deacons, and Members of the REFORMED PRESBYTERIAN CHURCH IN NORTH AMERICA, with our hands lifted up, do jointly and severally swear by the Great and Dreadful Name of the LORD OUR GOD:

1. "That coming into the presence of the Lord God with a deep conviction of His awful majesty and glory, of His omniscience, His purity, His justice and His grace; of our guilt and total depravity by nature, and our utter inability to save ourselves from deserved condemnation to everlasting punishment; with renunciation of all dependence on our own righteousness as the ground of pardon and acceptance with God, we receive for ourselves and for our children the Lord Jesus Christ as He is offered in the Gospel, to be our Saviour—the Holy Spirit to be our Enlightener, Sanctifier and Guide—and God, the Father, to be our everlasting portion; we approve and accept of the Covenant of Grace as all our salvation and desire, and take the moral law as dispensed by the Mediator, Christ, to be the rule of our life, and to be obeyed by us in all its precepts and prohibitions. Aiming to live for the glory of God as our chief end, we will, in reliance upon God's grace, and feeling our inability to perform any spiritual duty in our own strength, diligently attend to searching the Scriptures, religious conversation, the duties of the closet, the household, the fellowship meeting and the sanctuary, and will seek in them to worship God in spirit and in truth. We do solemnly promise to depart from all iniquity, and to live soberly, righteously, and godly in this present world, commending and encouraging, by our example, temperance, charity and godliness.

2. "That after careful examination, having embraced the system of faith, order and worship revealed in the Holy Scriptures, and summarized as to doctrine in the Westminster Confession and Catechisms, and Reformed Presbyterian Testimony, and, as to order and worship, justly set forth in substance and outline in the Westminster Form of Church Government and Directory for Worship, we do publicly profess and own this as the true Christian faith and religion, and the system of order and worship appointed by Christ for His own house, and, by the grace of God, we will sincerely and constantly endeavor to understand it more fully, to hold and observe it in its integrity, and to transmit the knowledge of the same to posterity. We solemnly reject whatever is known by us to be contrary to the Word of God, our recognized and approved manuals of faith and order, and the great principles of the Protestant Reformation. Particularly, we abjure and condemn Infidelity, under all its various aspects; Atheism, or the denial of the divine existence; Pantheism, with its denial of the divine personality; Naturalism, with its denial of the divine Providential Government; Spiritualism, with its denial of the Bible redemption; Indifferentism, with its denial of man's responsibility; Formalism, with its denial of the power of godliness. We abjure and condemn Popery, with its arrogant assumption of supremacy and infallibility; its corrupt and heretical teachings; its dogma of the Immaculate Conception; its hostility to civil and religious liberty, to the progress of society in civilization and intelligence, and especially its denial, in

common with Infidelity, of the right and duty of the State to educate in morality and religion by the use of the Bible in schools enjoying its patronage and support. Believing Presbyterianism to be the only divinely instituted form of government in the Christian Church, we disown and reject all other forms of ecclesiastical polity, as without authority of Scripture, and as damaging to purity, peace and unity in the household of faith. We reject all systems of false religion and will-worship, and with these all forms of secret oath-bound societies and orders, as ensnaring in their nature, pernicious in their tendency, and perilous to the liberties of both Church and State; and pledge ourselves to pray and labor according to our power, that whatever is contrary to godliness may be removed, and the Church beautified with universal conformity to the law and will of her Divine Head and Lord.

3. "Persuaded that God is the source of all legitimate power; that he has instituted civil government for His own glory and the good of man; that he has appointed His Son, the Mediator, to headship over the nations; and that the Bible is the supreme law and rule in national as in all other things, we will maintain the responsibility of nations to God, the rightful dominion of Jesus Christ over the commonwealth, and the obligation of nations to legislate in conformity with the written Word. We take ourselves sacredly bound to regulate all our civil relations, attachments, professions and deportment, by our allegiance and loyalty to the Lord, our King, Lawgiver and Judge; and by this, our oath, we are pledged to promote the interests

of public order and justice, to support cheerfully whatever is for the good of the commonwealth in which we
dwell, and to pursue this object in all things not forbidden by the law of God, or inconsistent with public
dissent from an unscriptural and immoral civil power.
We will pray and labor for the peace and welfare of
our country, and for its reformation by a constitutional
recognition of God as the source of all power, of Jesus
Christ as the Ruler of Nations, of the Holy Scriptures
as the supreme rule, and of the true Christian religion ;
and we will continue to refuse to incorporate by any
act, with the political body, until this blessed reformation has been secured.

4. "That, believing the Church to be *one*, and that
all the saints have communion with God and with one
another in the same Covenant ; believing, moreover,
that schism and sectarianism are sinful in themselves,
and inimical to true religion, and trusting that divisions
shall cease, and the people of God become one Catholic
Church over all the earth, we will pray and labor for
the visible oneness of the Church of God in our own
land and throughout the world, on the basis of truth
and Scriptural order. Considering it a principal duty of
our profession to cultivate a holy brotherhood, we will
strive to maintain Christian friendship with pious men
of every name, and to feel and act as one with all
in every land who pursue this grand end. And, as a
means of securing this great result, we will, by dissemination and application of the principles of truth
herein professed and by cultivating and exercising
Christian charity, labor to remove stumbling blocks,

and to gather into one the scattered and divided friends of truth and righteousness.

5. "Rejoicing that the enthroned Mediator is not only King in Zion, but King over all the earth, and recognizing the obligation of His command to go into all the world and preach the gospel to every creature, and to teach all nations, baptizing them in the name of the Father, of the Son, and of the Holy Ghost, and resting with faith in the promise of His perpetual presence as the pledge of success, we hereby dedicate ourselves to the great work of making known God's light and salvation among the nations, and to this end will labor that the Church may be provided with an earnest, self-denying and able ministry. Profoundly conscious of past remissness and neglect, we will henceforth, by our prayers, pecuniary contributions and personal exertions, seek the revival of pure and undefiled religion, the conversion of Jews and Gentiles to Christ, that all men may be blessed in Him, and that all nations may call Him blessed.

6. "Committing ourselves with all our interests to the keeping of Him in whom we have believed: in faithfulness to our own vows, and to the Covenants of our fathers, and to our children whom we desire to lead in the right ways of the Lord; and in love to all mankind, especially the household of faith in obedience to the commandment of the everlasting God to contend earnestly for the faith once delivered to the saints, we will bear true testimony in word and in deed for every known part of divine truth, and for all the ordinances appointed by Christ in his king-

dom; and we will tenderly and charitably, but plainly and decidedly, oppose and discountenance all and every known error, immorality, neglect or perversion of divine institutions. Taking as our example the faithful in all ages, and, most of all, the blessed Master himself, and with our eye fixed upon the great cloud of witnesses who have sealed with their blood the testimony which they held, we will strive to hold fast the profession of our faith without wavering, in hope of the crown of life which fadeth not away. Finally, we enter upon this solemn act of covenanting before the Omniscient God, with unfeigned purpose of paying our vow. All sinister and selfish ends and motives we solemnly disavow, and protest that we have no aim but the glory of God, and the present and everlasting welfare of immortal souls. And our prayer to God is and shall be, to strengthen us by His Holy Spirit to keep this our promise, vow and oath, and to bless our humble attempt to glorify His name and honor, His truth and cause with such success as will bring salvation to our own souls, the wider spread and triumph of truth and holiness, and the enlargement and establishment of the kingdom of our Lord and Saviour Jesus Christ, to whom, with the Father and the Spirit, one God be glory in the Church throughout all ages, world without end. AMEN."

With a very few exceptions, all the members of the Reformed Presbyterian Church in America entered into and subscribed this same Covenant in the respective congregations. The Rev. Samuel R. Galbraith was chosen missionary to Syria, to fill the vacancy caused by the death of the Rev. Robert J. Dodds. Rev. David McAllister was appointed by Synod to give his whole time to the interests of National Reform.

The Synod of 1872, met in York, New York. An offer was made by Mr. James Kelly of Wilkinsburgh, Pennsylvania, and also by friends in Newburgh, New York, for the location of the Theological Seminary. The Pittsburgh Presbytery donated the buildings of Westminster College to the Seminary Board. Wilkinsburgh was chosen as the seat of the new Theological Seminary. Elaborate reports on Missions, Education, National Reform, and other vital departments of the Church's work were submitted. The Committee on the "Homestead Oath" reported:

That they have examined the Homestead laws of the United States, and find that every applicant must swear that he is a citizen, or that he has filed his declaration of intention to become such, as required by the naturalization laws of the United States. (See Brightley's Digest of the Laws of the U. S., p. 288, sec. 41.) At the time the patent is made out, he must swear that he has borne *true* allegiance to the government of the United States. (*Idem.*, page 288, sec. 42.)

There never has been a question in the Church as to the first oath. It has always been deemed wrong. As to the second, which both natives and foreigners must take, a majority of the Committee think it inconsistent with our refusal to incorporate, by any act, with the government of the United States.

The Committee recommended that Synod take steps to obtain such a modification of these oaths as may be consistent with our dissent.

The Rev. H. H. George was chosen President of Geneva College, and has since continued to hold that position.

The Synod of 1873, met in Northwood, Ohio. For several reasons the location of the Seminary at Wilkinsburgh was not satisfactory to some parts of the Church, and the Synod adopted the following resolution:

Resolved, That a Committee of seven persons be appointed to locate and erect the Theological Seminary Building in the city of Allegheny, and that the place and style of building and appurtenances be left to the judgment of the Committee; and that the limit of expense be thirty thousand dollars ($30,000).

The Synod of 1874, met in the city of Philadelphia. The Committee appointed to report on the "Patrons of Husbandry" or "Grangers," after ascertaining facts, report the following:

1. That this order was organized by Freemasons and Oddfellows; is modelled after their forms in its rites, ceremonies and officers; is largely under their control, and as a matter of fact furnishes recruits for these detestable orders.

2. That it is in itself a secret and substantially oath-bound society, the candidate for admission being required to pledge his sacred word and honor, in the presence of God, to keep secrets, obey laws and assume responsibilities wholly unknown to him, and utterly incompatible with Christian integrity and simplicity.

3. That the order in its constitution assumes the false and impossible position of neutrality both with respect to religion and politics, and as a consequence of this its religious services are conducted indiscriminately in a Christian or Anti-Christian and pagan manner; and instead of being neutral in politics, it is practically a political party.

We therefore emphatically and unequivocally condemn this and all other secret orders as ensnaring, deceptive and sinful in themselves, as prejudicial to the best interests of society, and as a lawless and inefficient way of obtaining redress of grievances. We also recommend that Synod enjoin it upon all sessions not to fellowship members of this or any secret order, and to warn all under their care to beware of the ensnaring influences of such organizations. "Have no fellowship with the unfruitful works of darkness, but rather reprove them."

The Synod, as the representative of the Church, again pledged itself to the hearty support of the

principles incorporated by the National Reform Association, and has unceasingly carried forward the pledge
embodied in the following resolutions:

Resolved, That this Synod, and the whole Church, in whose interests
it is met, regard with the liveliest interest all efforts to reform our
nation, and to bring it, in its constitution, and administration, and
into conformity with the revealed will and written Word of God.

Resolved, That a distinct constitutional recognition of Jesus Christ,
the Mediator between God and man, as the legislative head and ruler
of nations is the indispensable duty of this nation, and that any proposed form of amendment to the national constitution, or States constitution, in which such recognition is omitted, is and will be held
by this Church to be fundamentally defective.

Resolved, That we will pray and labor for the reformation of our
nation, nor cease our efforts until we see it a Christian state, administering its authority in subserviency to the kingdom of Christ, in suppressing blasphemy, idolatry, licentiousness, and every other form of
public hindrance to its progress, and in giving positive countenance,
encouragement, and support to the Christian Church throughout the
commonwealth as the great restorer and conservator of the true religion, which, as a leaf of the tree of life, restores and heals the nations.

The Synod of 1875, met in Coultersville, Illinois.
Rev. David B. Willson was elected to a professorate
in the Theological Seminary. All the reports from
the different agencies of the Church were full and
satisfactory, and, with the exception of direction in the
settlement of a few local cases of discipline, the
proceedings of this Synod were routine.

The Synod of 1876, met in the city of Allegheny,
Pennsylvania. Rev. Joseph Beattie, of Syria, was present, and presided over the sessions of Synod.

Strong and definite resolutions bearing upon the
different reforms of the day were passed at the meeting,
and they were of such a character as to conclusively

show that this Church is composed of thorough reformers.

The Synod of 1877, met in the city of Allegheny, Pennsylvania. The following report explains itself :

The Committee appointed to confer with a similar Committee appointed by the General Synod of the Reformed Presbyterian Church, reports that, after several meetings of the joint Committee, it was agreed to report to the respective Synods, that while we recognize with thankfulness the identity in faith, and practice and testimony in many important respects of these closely related branches of the Church of Christ, we are constrained to admit that the obstacles in the way of organic reunion appear, for the present, to be insuperable.

The special Committee, to which were referred petitions relating to inviting clergymen of other denominations into our pulpits, report :

1. That, while desiring to cultivate and cherish the most friendly and fraternal relations with our brethren of other evangelical denominations, it has never been the custom of the Church to invite them to minister to our people in the preaching of the Word.

2. That we see no good reason, in the present condition of the visible Church of Christ, for departing from existing usage.

The Synod of 1878, met at Linton, Iowa. With reference to the conference on union with the New School body, the Committee made the following report :

After a frank, earnest and friendly conference, it was agreed that there was not, at present, any special encouragement to take steps in the direction of attempting to heal the breach between these two branches of the Reformed Presbyterian Church, and while it was agreed that we should foster in all proper ways friendly, fraternal feelings, that it was not advisable to continue the conference further.

Synod thought it proper for women to speak and lead in prayer in social praying societies. The Fourth Term of Communion was revised, and is as printed.

Synod advised the Missionary among the Chinese to baptize such persons as give evidence of "intelligent and unfeigned faith and repentance." Synod also regarded "the language of the Testimony on the duties of the Christian magistrate as the exhibition of the doctrines we hold upon this subject, and as properly interpreting the Confession of Faith."

The Synod of 1879, met in the city of New York. Rev. David Metheny, M. D., Missionary to Syria, was present, and was chosen to preside over the sessions. Rev. A. M. Stavely, of New Brunswick, was also present, and addressed the meeting.

The following resolutions on tobacco were unanimously adopted by Synod:

Inasmuch as tobacco is extensively used throughout society, and in its use is a positive evil, which manifests itself—1. As an injury to physical health; 2. As an offence to good manners; 3. As an unnecessary expenditure of money; 4. As it is associated with much vice; 5. As it exerts a demoralizing influence upon the youth; 6. As it is inconsistent with moral and spiritual purity. Therefore,

Resolved, 1. That this Synod condemn all indulgence in the use of tobacco.

Resolved, 2. That we urge our people to abstain from it in every form except as prescribed by competent medical authority, and use all lawful and wise means to eradicate this evil from society.

Resolved, 3. That Presbyteries be hereby advised to license no one to preach the gospel who indulges in the use of tobacco; and sessions be advised not to ordain any officers in the Church who practice this habit for mere carnal gratification.

Resolved, 4. That this Synod condemn the cultivation, manufacture, and sale of tobacco.

With its earnest desire, and with the hearty concurrence of the Irish Synod, the Presbytery of New Brunswick and Nova Scotia was received uuder the care of this Synod. The change of the location of Geneva College having been agitated for some time, the Synod now chose to remove the institution from Northwood, Ohio, to Beaver Falls, Pennsylvania, on the condition that ten acres of ground and twenty thousand dollars were given for the erection of buildings. This offer was made by the Economite Society and accepted by Synod. The College first opened in Beaver Falls in September, 1880, and the building erected for the purpose was occupied the following year. The Synod re-affirmed the law of the Church with reference to marriage with a deceased wife's sister, that it is prohibitory. In a concrete case of a member of the Church being summoned to sit upon a jury in Pittsburgh, and the Judge refusing to excuse him, a Committee of Synod was appointed to wait upon the Judge, who decided that he would not excuse the member, but was willing to accept, instead of the usual juror's oath, such an oath as would be approved by the Reformed Presbyterian Church.

The Synod of 1880, met in the city of Philadelphia. General Rules for the organization and government of Geneva College were submitted. The following report explains the manner in which affairs were settled by the removal of the College to Beaver Falls:

That the notes given to the endowment by persons in the vicinity of Northwood, on the condition that the College remain in that place, be returned to those who make this request.

That the Board of Education, as connected with the College in Northwood, Ohio, be continued in existence until all business matters relating to the transfer of the College to Beaver Falls shall be fully accomplished, and that the Executive Committee of the Board be authorized to make a quit claim deed to a Committee to be appointed by members of the Church at Northwood, of all the buildings there belonging to Synod, on condition that the Northwood Committee meet all the expenses afterwards accruing.

That the movable property of the College, such as the library, apparatus, &c., be removed to the College building at Beaver Falls.

The Synod of 1881, met in the city of Pittsburgh, Pennsylvania.   The following preamble and resolutions were adopted :

WHEREAS, It is important for the interests of the Church to place before our people and others a statement and vindication of the principles professed by us, and to justify the practice grounded upon these principles, and particularly in connection with questions made of immediate and pressing urgency from the circumstances of the times ; therefore,

Resolved, 1. That Synod take measures for the issuing of a series of tracts, of not more than 4 pages, 12 mo., for distribution among our people, and for general circulation, so far as it can be accomplished.

2. That D. S. Faris be appointed to write on the duty of our members in regard to the exercise of the Elective Franchises, Dr. Sloane on Psalmody, James Kennedy on Instrumental Music, Professor Willson on Dancing, J. Lynd on Temperance, D. M'Allister on the Jury Question, and Dr. Sproull on the Testimony of the Church, in regard to Christian people who are in political fellowship with nations, which disown the Kingship of the Lord Jesus ; and that these papers be published at once in the magazines of the Church.

On the question of voting for temperance amendments, the Committee say :

On this paper we report that as the Synod by its action of 1866 and 1867 refused to authorize such voting on the part of the members of the Church, and as it not only appears to many inconsistent with our position on the jury question, and in some measure an incorporating with government, but also inconsistent with the position, solemnly taken in our act of Covenanting of 1871, that therefore Synod should distinctly declare that it disapproves of and discourages such voting on the part of our members as if not positively a breach of their testimony, at least in many respects dangerous and ensnaring.

Synod thought that members acceding to our Communion in Syria from the Greek Roman Catholic Church should be baptized. Not only in this but in all similar cases baptism is to be administered. Rev. W. J. Coleman was chosen to labor in the interests of the. National Reform Association as the representative of this Church.

The Synod of 1882, met in New Concord, Ohio. From the following resolutions it will be seen that this is a temperance Church :

1. *Resolved*, That we unite in sincere thanksgiving to God for the firm hold the cause of Temperance has taken in the public conscience, for the able instrumentalities that are raised up in its advocacy, and for its marked progress in the Church and throughout the Nation.

2. *Resolved*, That we hereby lift up an uncompromising testimony against the use, manufacture or sale of intoxicating liquors, including beer, ale, wine and hard cider, as a beverage ; against the renting of property for the manufacture or sale of intoxicating liquors ; against the selling the fruits of the earth for the purpose of being manufactured into intoxicating drinks ; and against giving countenance in any way to the .nefarious traffic or use.

3. *Resolved*, That the ministers, officers and members of the Church be enjoined to take a public stand in the present Temperance movement, and openly wage, in all legitimate ways, an unceasing warfare against the atrocious liquor business and the pernicious evils of intemperance.

4. *Resolved*, That sessions see to it that members of the Church act consistently with her public position on the Temperance question, and that the discipline of the Church be rigidly applied in all cases where the law of the Church in this regard is violated.

5. *Resolved*, That the Sabbath Schools make Temperance a part of their instruction ; and that teachers and scholars be urged to pledge themselves to total abstinence from intoxicating liquors, and to earnest work in the Temperance cause.

6. *Resolved*, That Synod reiterate its former recommendation against the use of intoxicating wine in the Lord's supper.

7. *Resolved*, That we rejoice at the progress of legal Prohibition in

our country; and that we put forth every effort, consistent with our position as a Church, to secure an amendment to the United States Constitution, and also to the Constitutions of the different States, forbidding the importation, manufacture and sale of intoxicating liquors as a beverage.   •

8. *Resolved*, That the time has come when our Church should take an advanced step in the temperance cause by incorporating in her written Testimony an article forever prohibiting the manufacture, sale and use of intoxicating liquors as a beverage.

9. *Resolved*, That this Synod express its hearty approval of the action of the legislature of this State in closing the liquor saloons on the Lord's day.

10. *Resolved*, That Synod renew, in more emphatic terms, its condemnation of the production, manufacture, sale and use of tobacco, as it is injurious to the best interests of man socially, morally and spiritually; and that Presbyteries be enjoined to refuse licensure to any candidate who is in the habit of indulging in the use thereof.

Synod declared itself opposed to the action of the government in closing the western gate, while through the east gate a far more dangerous class of emigrants is received with no restrictions:

Resolved, That this Synod express its condemnation of the recent Anti-Chinese bill which has passed both houses of Congress, and been signed by the President, as a breach of treaty obligations, opposed to · the spirit of the age, a gross violation of the law of God, and as calculated to arrest the earnest missionary efforts now being put forth for the Christianization of that numerous people.

Rev. Henry Easson, missionary from Syria, was present and addressed the court. A suitable notice was taken of the providential death of President Garfield. A Committee was appointed to prepare an edition of the Book of Psalms with verbal corrections and suitable music.

A long and able discussion of the true and historic position of the Church was entered into in reference to the question of voting for temperance amendments in some of the States. The question was "Could Covenanters, consistent with their position, vote for amendments to State Constitutions? The following was the deliverance of Synod on this subject:

Resolved, 1. That this Synod declares anew our position of dissent, on moral grounds, from the Constitution of the United States, and rejoices in the evidence which this discussion has afforded of unabated and unanimous convictions in support of this position.

2. That it has always been regarded as the privilege and the duty of our members to unite in all civil action which is not inconsistent with this dissent.

3. That in view of the varying conditions under which constitutional amendments are submitted in different States, we leave it with Presbyteries and sessions to administer the discipline of the Church in harmony with these principles.

The Synod of 1883, met in the city of Allegheny, Pennsylvania. It was largely attended and much important business was transacted. The Commission visiting the Churches in the Maritime Provinces made an interesting report. A charter for Geneva College was submitted.

A memorial from Nova Scotia with reference to the validity of sacraments, received the following answer:

Whilst we are in full harmony with the Memorialists as to the nature and Scriptural mode of administering the ordinance of baptism, yet we cannot acquiesce in their prayer, asking this court to pronounce baptism by immersion to be in all cases invalid, and that applicants from the Baptist connection, seeking fellowship with us, should be required to receive baptism before admission, according to the mode of administration followed by us, for the following reasons:

1. Because it has never been, either in principle or practice, recognized as necessary in the Reformed Presbyterian Church, in this or any other country, that such a condition of admission to our membership should be required on the part of such applicants.

2. Because, while we strenuously contend for the Scriptural admin- istration of religious ordinances, we cannot admit the principle that mere imperfections in the mode of administration do invalidate them or destroy their efficacy. The Westminster divines declare that "The sac- raments become effectual means of salvation, not from any virtue in them, or in him that doth administer them;" therefore when the appointed sign is employed in baptism, and when it is applied as directed, in the name of the Father and of the Son and of the Holy Ghost, and that in an avowed symbolical and sacramental sense, and for a symbolical and sacramental purpose, then there are present substantially all the elements constituting a real administration of that ordinance.

3. Because, as the validity and efficacy of a sacrament do not depend on the amount of the material sign employed on the occasion, but upon the right apprehension, in its use, of its spiritual import and significance as an appointment of Christ, it is not impossible to realize the spiritual benefits of baptism even when administered by immersion. The leading idea in employing water in baptism is that of purifying from defilement, and as in ordinary life, from which the term is taken, this is sometimes effected by applying water to the object to be made clean, and sometimes by putting it into the water, we do not think that the ends contemplated in baptism cannot be reached, or that the ordinance is invalidated when the mode of administering is by immersion, any more than that the Lord's Supper is invalidated when in some Evan- gelical Churches it is administered in a manner which we cannot regard as altogether Scriptural.

4. Because we cannot refuse to accept the validity of this ordi- nance, as administered by Baptists without unchurching the connection, or in other words refusing to acknowledge them as a part of the true church of Christ. This we do in relation to Rome by refusing to accept her baptism and ordination, but we think it would be utterly unjustifiable to place Baptist Churches in the same category.

The following sentiment with reference to an old form and custom of the Church is interesting :

1. That the distribution of tokens on a week day evening previous to the administration of the ordinance of the Lord's supper has never been considered an integral element of the ordinance.

2. That it is in no sense an act of worship, nor is the token a religious symbol.

3. That it is simply a custom relating to the well ordering of the Church that has come down to us from persecuting times, and as such has a strong hold upon the minds of many in the Church.

4. That it cannot in any way be productive of mischief unless elevated into a prominence and significance that does not in any sense attach to it.

5. In view of these considerations we advise all our people to observe the custom as heretofore until such time as the Church in its wisdom may deem it proper to dispense with it.

An article on Temperance was inserted in the Testimony.

The Synod of 1884, met in Northwood, Ohio. While there was a large attendance of delegates, the business was interesting but of a routine character. The principal question that demanded the especial attention of this Synod was that of voting for amendments. The following is the report of this item :

1. Does voting for amendments to State Constitutions involve anything sinful or inconsistent with the principles and practice of the Church ?

2. Has the deliverance of this Synod in 1868 on the question of voting for amendments been repealed ?

To the first of these inquiries the following answer is submitted :

That it is a fundamental principle of the Church, in regard to which we are persuaded there is no diversity either of sentiment or practice amongst us, that all acts performed under the government, that either require or imply an oath to the National Constitution or to the Constitution of any of the States, are manifestly acts of incorporation with the government; and although the service should be right in itself, yet it becomes wrong and sinful by reason of the sinful condition involved.

It should, however, be borne in mind that in guarding with watchful jealousy against the sin of identification with an unscriptural government, the Church, both in the practice of her members, and in the deliverances of Synod, has wisely avoided the evil of being led aside into any unwarranted extremes, as regards our relation to the Nation, and its government.

In order that we may take no step of departure from our peculiar position, either to the right hand or to the left, it requires to be studied and observed with special care. There are forms of civil action in which our members have always held it their privilege to engage, without fear of complicity in the sin of an unholy confederacy. Among the latest utterances of Synod on this subject are these words : "The general rule for guidance is that participation in acts of civil administration is not in itself wrong and sinful, but becomes so when any sinful condition in the way of an immoral oath is involved." And, "that it has always been regarded as the privilege and the duty of our members to unite in all civil action which is not inconsistent with our dissent " from the Constitution of the United States.

Upon an examination of the entire ground occupied by these questions the following conclusions appear safe and just :

All civil action that involves an immoral oath is sinful and wrong. There are certain acts that do not involve an immoral oath, that are not acts of incorporation with the government, and that our members have always claimed the right to perform.

The simple act of voting for such an amendment to the State Constitution as will secure some important principle of moral right and reform such as the prohibitory amendments recently submitted to the people of Kansas, Iowa and Ohio, belongs to the class of acts consistent with the principles and position of the Reformed Presbyterian Church.

Act of 1868.—To the second inquiry the following answer is respectfully returned :

That we should recall the peculiar circumstances under which the deliverance of 1868 was given.

It is a matter of history that the report was taken up at the last hour, immediately before the final adjournment of the court. There was almost no opportunity for the examination and discussion of its merits. It was adopted amid much confusion and at a time when the attention of only a fraction of the court could be secured. Such ill considered action thus hastily taken must be wanting in force of authority, and cannot be expected to command the hearty respect and united submission of the Church.

Again, in so far as this deliverance prohibits all civil action, not only when the service is right in itself, but even when no immoral oath is involved, it contravenes the historical position of the Church, and the repeated deliberate utterances of this court.

Finally, although this measure has never, in so many words, been formally rescinded, yet by the well-known rule of law, that subsequent action necessarily sets aside prior action of a contrary nature, the deliverance of 1868, in the respect and to the extent already defined, has, by the action of 1875, re-affirmed in 1882, been virtually and really repealed.

Other members of the same Committee submitted the following report :

Voting for amendments to State Constitutions involves an act of voluntary incorporation with the governing political body, of which we say in our Covenant, "We will not incorporate with it until Reformation is secured."

We therefore recommend that our people be enjoined to abstain from voting for amendments to State Constitutions.

An interesting letter was received from the Associate Reformed Synod of the South recommending a Convention of all the Churches holding the same doctrinal symbols and who use exclusively the Psalms of the Bible in worship.

The Synod of 1885, met in Morning Sun, Iowa. The delegates to the Conference of Psalm–singing Churches reported that on account of our relations on civil affairs no union could be effected. The Synod took the following action with reference to weekly offerings of worship :

1. That Synod reaffirm the principle that the tithe is the law of God under the New Testament dispensation and that it is the least measure of liberality.

2. That the envelope system of weekly offerings be approved as in harmony with Scripture and wisely adapted for the end, and that our congregations be advised to consider it for adoption.

3. That in discussing this subject the preferences and convictions

of all parties be duly and kindly considered, and that forbearance be shown in reconciling differences; and whatever plan is adopted by a congregation we most earnestly urge and exhort the minority, since it is not a matter of conscience but of expediency, that they cease opposition and cordially acquiesce in it until by Christian persuasion a change is effected.

The following resolutions on Temperance were adopted:

1. We urge all our people to recognize the importance of the temperance cause, and its claim on their active and earnest support. That our Presbyteries be enjoined to hold temperance institutes or conventions, for the discussion and advocacy of this cause. That sessions be urged to give practical force to the recently adopted article on temperance, in admitting members, and faithfully to enforce the discipline of the church, in all cases where the law is violated.

2. We denounce the whole license system, as wrong in principle and most pernicious in practice—involving the nation in the guilt and shame of the liquor traffic to which it gives its consent, as ineffectual for the restraint or suppression of the evil, and an utter violation of the high trust God has committed to civil government as His ordinance.

3. Support of political parties that favor or ignore this nefarious business, or even incorporation with the government, is inconsistent with fidelity to Christ, and involves those who continue in such alliance in the guilt and ignominy of the liquor traffic.

4. That it is our duty as a Church to give to all scriptural measures, moral, political or legislative, for the suppression of this traffic, all that support and advocacy which is consistent with our position of political dissent; and especially that our women be encouraged to co-operate with the W. C. T. U. in its noble work of faith and labor of love.

5. We re-affirm the former actions of this court, enjoining sessions as far as possible, to use only unintoxicating wine in the administration of the Lord's Supper.

Having a concrete case before it, the Synod directs members of the Church to "take no part in the use of uninspired hymns in any service that may be regarded as the worship of God." Synod also says: "It is most expedient that the Moderator of a Church court be a minister of the Gospel."

The Synod of 1886, met in the city of Rochester, New York. On Secret Societies the Committee reported:

Speculative Freemasonry, the type of all modern secret societies, originated at Appletree Tavern, London, in 1717. The idea is borrowed from the heathen. Secret societies have been known in all lands in connection with the worship of false deities. Some of these claim the highest degree of piety ; others still claiming to worship their God, are expressly designed for criminal purposes.

The immediate parentage of Freemasonry were the guilds of operative masons, in the middle ages, their object being to control architecture, like the present trades unions. They are, therefore, necessarily of a selfish character, and charity is the veil to hide the real end.

The principal feature of secret societies is the oath or promise of perpetual concealment, and this often with horrible penalties annexed. The effect of such engagement is to take away the right of private judgment and to put another's conscience in place of one's own.

The penalties have been understood by the lodges themselves to be literal, and to forfeit life, property and character. Foul murders and implacable persecutions have followed the attempt of good men to free conscience from lodge tyranny.

Yet they claim to be religious—more religious and charitable than the Church. The Masons boast of the universal religion in which all men agree. This places Jew, heathen and Christian on a common platform, on which God, under the name of Grand Architect, is worshipped without Christ. Other societies model after the same pattern.

These orders also are in spirit and forms despotic, as their own authorities affirm. They are readily used by bad men to screen them from the just punishment of their crimes. The so-called *benevolent* societies provide and hold in readiness the machinery which bad men use for the destruction of life and property.

Socialists employ them for revolutionary purposes, and conspiring and plotting in secret have filled the world with horror and alarm. They hinder the freedom of manufacture and business, and force trade into ways injurious to the public.

How should the Church stand toward such organizations? If Baal worship was the abomination that God hated of old, surely he hates the abomination done in secret lodges ; all good men should hold their

Among other things the report on the tobacco question says :

The cultivation, manufacture, sale and use of tobacco are in measure under ban in the Reformed Presbyterian Church. Tobacco is prohibited to theological students. Presbyteries are enjoined to refuse license to any who are addicted to its use. Presbyteries are justified in refusing appointments to any laborer who may be assigned to them, and is a user of tobacco. Ministers, elders, deacons and Sabbath School teachers are admonished to abstain from the use of this filthy weed. Members of the Church are warned against its use as a blemish on Christian character.

The following strong resolutions on the same subject were passed :

1. We hold that the habitual use of tobacco in the usual forms, as well as the cultivation and sale of tobacco for such use, are inconsistent with the Christian profession, and our members are solemnly enjoined not to engage in or continue in this business.

2. We earnestly and affectionately urge every member of the Church who is addicted to its use in any form, to break off the habit at once.

3. That we renew the injunction to Presbyteries, not to license any one to preach, nor to ordain any one to the ministry, who persists in the use of this filthy weed.

4. That Sessions be enjoined not to ordain any one to the office of elder or deacon, who is addicted to this habit.

5. That Sessions be instructed to strongly urge youthful applicants for membership in the Church, to refrain from using tobacco.

Rev. James Kennedy was chosen professor of Theology to fill the vacancy occasioned by the death of the Rev. J. R. W. Sloane, D. D. Mr. Kennedy, however, declined the position, and the Rev. R. J. George temporarily filled the chair for the following winter. Synod condemned the organization and methods of the Knights of Labor, for the following reasons :

1. Because they are confessedly organized on the principles of secrecy, contrary to our standing Testimony.

2. The form of their society is that of absolute despotism, the members being under obligation to render unqestioning obedience in carrying out the dictates of their leaders, right or wrong, often in violation of the rights of their fellow-citizens.

3. Because they assume to dictate to the employer, not only the wages to be paid for service, but the persons to be employed, and all the conditions of the service, leaving him a helpless slave in the hands of a society with which he holds no relation.

4. They forbid non-union men to labor, and contractors to employ them, thus by the grossest tyranny monopolizing all rights and privileges to themselves.

5. They compel manufacturers and dealers to discharge freemen, or refuse them the right to buy or sell or carry on their business.

6. They interfere with the rights of the government by dictating to legislators and executors of law, and by making void all authority save their own.

7. All this they do, following the example of Freemasons, by secretly pursuing the objects of their vengeance, and hunting down their reputation and their business in a way that prevents obtaining redress by the law.

We, therefore, declare that Reformed Presbyterians cannot belong to these Associations without renouncing all the traditions of their history in favor of civil and ecclesiastical liberty and the rights of God and man. Further, we declare that our members ought to suffer rather than sin, by partnership in such practices. And further, we enjoin the members of our Church, rich and poor, to stand shoulder to shoulder in opposition to this tyranny, and we pledge ourselves and our members that we will not permit the poor to suffer unaided, but will consider what is done to persecute the least as done to all, and we will not stand by and see our dear brethren driven under the cruel lash of this new task-master, but will come to their aid with our goods, and if need be, with our lives.

Synod gave the following deliverances : That in cases where our ministers conduct services in other Churches, they must not give out hymns of human composition, but use any good version of the Psalms ; and, if instrumental music is used, they must have it understood that they do not sanction that part of the service. Members were urged not to sit on juries where an immoral oath was required. The Synod adopted the following resolutions :

WHEREAS, This Church has occupied a position of dissent from the government of the country on account of the infidel character of the National Constitution ; and,

WHEREAS, This reason of dissent is not removed ; therefore,

Resolved, 1. That voting on amendments to State Constitutions, or to the Constitution of the United States, or to revised forms of Constitutions, when conditioned on an expressed or implied approval of the National Constitution as a compact of government, is inconsistent with our position of political dissent.

Resolved, 2. That Presbyteries be directed to take no notice of inconsistencies which may have occurred during the discussion of this question by Synod.

Resolved, 3. That Synod will hold Presbyteries hereafter strictly responsible for the maintenance of discipline on this point.

The Synod of 1887, met in the city of Newburgh, New York. The meeting was a large and harmonious one, and the papers and discussions were of a most interesting character. The Synod re-affirmed her distinctive position, leaving no misunderstanding about what she believed and practiced. Rev. R. J. George was twice elected to fill the vacancy in the Theological Seminary, but declined. The Rev. J. K. McClurkin was then chosen, and accepted. Revs. J. P. Dardier of Switzerland, and Dr. A. P. Happer of China, addressed the court on the cause of evangelization in those countries. Rev. W. J. Sproull, returned missionary from Syria, addressed the Synod. A Committee was appointed to make a suitable revision of the Psalms. With reference to the character of mission work that may be properly done by students of theology, the Synod says:

That while students of theology are not authorized to preach the gospel until they are licensed by Presbytery; yet there is a large amount of work in which they may be profitably employed. They may act as colporteurs; organize and teach in Sabbath Schools, and under the direction and supervision of the Presbytery to which they belong, they may be employed in such evangelical work as Presbytery may designate.

With a concrete case before it, Synod decided that mutes, who are members of the Church, are entitled to all privileges as such, and have a right to vote in elections of the congregations, and to pay all their quotas to the schemes of the Church. A pastoral letter was directed to be written touching upon the matters that were before Synod, and press them on the attention of the people. Plans for the establishment of an Indian Mission, for the better support of the Theological Seminary, and for a fund for Ministers' Widows' and Orphans' were laid before the court. In the report on the jury question it is plainly and satisfactorily shown that Reformed Presbyterians cannot take the immoral oath required, and serve the designs of that office in consistency with their avowed position of dissent from the Constitution of the United States. A revision of the Book of Psalms for the use of the Church was completed in the fall of 1887. The Committee performing this work consisted of Revs. David McAllister, T. P. Stevenson, R. M. Sommerville, J. C. K. Milligan, and elders Henry O'Neil, William Neely and W. T. Miller. The work will be presented at the meeting of Synod in May, 1888. A Committee of

Synod met a similar Committee of the United Presbyterian Church to formulate a basis of union. While there seemed to be a general agreement as to the doctrine of the headship of Christ, the latter body was not prepared to make a practical application of that principle, and it is not likely that a union can be effected.

The principal deliverances of Synod, touching upon the distinctive principles of the Reformed Presbyterian Church, have been noticed, leaving the members of this Church inexcusable, and others instructed, with reference to her peculiar principles. It is believed that her principles are Scriptural and her conduct consistent with her high profession, and that the cause for which Covenanters contend will ultimately prevail.

From the reports of 1887, the following condition of the Church is gathered:

Ministers, 114; Licentiates, 11; Students of Theology, 20; Congregations, 121; Communicants, 10,832; Total Contributions, $24.04 per member for the year.

The Synod of 1888, meets in the city of Allegheny, Pennsylvania, during the sessions of which the Bi-Centenary of the Revolution Settlement will be suitably observed.

CONGREGATIONS AND SOCIETIES.

NEW BRUNSWICK.

SAINT JOHN. This city was settled by loyalists who fled from New England during the American Revolution, and it now contains, with its suburbs, a population of nearly fifty thousand inhabitants. It possesses an excellent harbor and is a city of considerable commercial importance. Very early in the present century, a few Covenanters from Scotland and Ireland found abode in this city, and for many years worshipped together without the form of an organization. In the year 1820, these people made application to the Northern Presbytery of the American Church for preaching ordinances. The matter was brought before that court at the following meeting, and, in the spring of 1821, the Presbytery sent the Revs. James R. and Samuel M. Willson on an exploring expedition to these Provinces. As a result of their visit they found in the city of Saint John, seven families regularly certified from the Covenanter congregations beyond the sea, and organized them into a praying society. The missionaries then opened up a correspondence with the sister Churches of Scotland and Ireland, related to them of their success and the needs of their countrymen, and urgently requested them to send missionaries to these

10

destitute yet steadfast people. The Irish Church regarded it as a Macedonian cry. The Synod of Ireland organized the Home and Foreign Missionary Society in 1826, and sought for a suitable person to send as a missionary to the British North American Provinces. During the following winter, while the great Sheridan Knowles was giving readings in Belfast, which were held in the largest theatre in the city, one of the Presbyteries sent a Committee to the theatre to wait upon Mr. Alexander Clarke, then a theological student, to have him go as a missionary to Nova Scotia. He felt that it was the call of his Master and accepted the appointment. The following spring he was duly licensed and ordained for this field, and, in August, 1827, arrived safely in the city of Saint John. In 1828, he organized the congregation of Saint John with forty-five members. In 1833, a comfortable house of worship was erected in that portion of the city known as the Lower Cove. Mr. Clarke continued to preach to them, and societies adjacent, for several years, and then removed to the more inviting field of Eastern Nova Scotia. Saint John being now destitute of regular preaching, the needs of the congregation were repeatedly presented to the notice of the Church in Ireland and to the Society which was sustaining the Mission. These applications, however, were not answered until the spring of 1841, when Mr. Alexander McLeod Stavely offered his services as a missionary to this city. His offer was joyfully accepted, and, for this purpose, he was ordained by the Northern Presbytery at Kilraughts, Ireland, May 12, 1841. He sailed from Greenock in June, and arrived safely in Saint John in August, 1841. He found a congregation of about seventy-five members, to whose spiritual wants he at once devoted his labors with energy and success. The old house of worship in Lower Cove was sold in 1850, because it was neither in a desirable nor central location. The congregation erected a well-appointed church and manse on the corner of Sydney and Princess streets. Here the people worshipped for twenty-seven years, and gradually grew in numbers and Christian influence. The church and manse, with all their contents, were swept away by the great conflagration of June, 1877, when two hundred acres of the best of the city were laid in ashes. This great loss to the Covenanter congregation at a time when a serious financial depression immediately followed, disheartened many of the people, who left the city to seek their fortunes in a western clime. With that courage which knows no defeat, and which is characteristic of the Scotch-Irish, these people, encouraged by their pastor, began the erection of the present commodious and convenient church building in 1878, situated on the corner of Carleton and Peele streets. Notwithstanding the encouragements that presented themselves, Mr. Stavely resigned the congregation in July, 1879, and returned to his native Ireland. Licentiates were now sent from the States and Saint John was one of the vacancies. The Rev. A. J. McFarland spent a part of the winter of 1881 in the congregation. Having received a unanimous call to become their pastor, he accepted, and was duly installed

August 4, 1882. The church and manse, which are models of neatness and convenience, were completed in the fall of 1883, and the congregation began a new lease of life. In the spring of 1887, the congregation suffered a severe financial stroke by the failure of one of the chief supporters and most efficient members. The Church in the States nobly contributed to the cause, and soon these worthy people will be lifted out of their straits. Among the fathers and heads of families who have been prominent in the life of the Saint John congregation are: Thomas Maclellan, John Boyd, George Suffren, Robert Ewing, John Millen, William Dougall, George Bell, John McMaster, Samuel Reid, John Toland, James Miller, Mrs. Russell, Mrs. Cunningham, James Dunbar, Neil Morrison, R. A. H. Morrow, John Baxter, J. O. Miller, W. G. Brown, Dr. Morrison and Thomas A. Dunlap.

BARNESVILLE. This is a beautiful little villa cosily nestled among the evergreen hills between the Hammond River and the lakes of Loch Lomond, twenty miles south-east of the city of Saint John. The congregation now derives its name from the village but was formerly known as South Stream. The Rev. James Reid Lawson, who came as a missionary from Ireland in 1845, after visiting several localities, settled in this place the following year when there were only two Covenanters in this section of the country. In 1856, he resigned the charge and accepted a call to the congregation of Boston, Massachusetts, but after a year's labor in that city, he returned to his first charge at Barnesville. Here he continued his labor of love, not only preaching to his own congregation, but making missionary tours through all parts of the Province. Suffering from a stroke of paralysis, which rendered almost useless his left side, he was compelled to resign the charge in the spring of 1882, since which time he has lived in comparative retirement at his country home in the suburbs of Barnesville. For five years the congregation was supplied by the Central Board of Missions, and the services were kept up pretty regularly. The Rev. Thomas Patton became the pastor in May, 1887, and the Covenanters of Barnesville have the prospect of becoming a flourishing congregation. Among those who have long been connected with the Barnesville congregation are the families of Rev. Mr. Lawson, Dr. Brady, Parks, Curry, Millican, Toland, Kelso, Henderson, McCracken, Armstrong, Barnes, Bell, and others.

MILL STREAM. This was a Mission Station about fifty miles east of the city of Saint John, and was established by the Rev. A. M. Stavely about 1858. A small house of worship was erected near Queenstown, and the society, which at one time was composed of thirty members, frequently received preaching by the ministers in the Provinces. It was an out-of-the-way place, and by emigration and death it is nearly extinct. The Elders, Gaileys and Grindons, were among the principal families.

MONCTON. This is a live young city of some eight thousand inhabitants, situated ninety miles east of Saint John and within fifteen miles of the Strait of Northumberland. Having received many urgent invitations from members of the congregations of Barnesville and

Saint John, who were living in this city, the Rev. A. J. McFarland visited them in the spring of 1884. His services were followed by those of several licentiates from the States, who preached in Ruddick's Hall and the old Union Church in Steadman street. Quite a congregation gathered from those who were dissatisfied with the human inventions of other Churches, and a few disaffected members of the Presbyterian Church joined them. In the fall of 1885, Mr. McFarland organized them into a mission station and they continued to receive occasional supplies. Among the principal members and supporters are the families of A. J. Millican, Charles Elliot, Dr. Ross and the Misses Grindon. There were other places in the Province of New Brunswick where the ministers frequently preached, but no organizations were effected. Among these are Quaco, Black River, Chepody, Hopewell, Neripis, Londonderry, Jerusalem, Salt Springs and Passakeag. Rev. Alexander Clarke established mission stations in Sackville, Nappan and Murray's Corner, but these passed under the control of the New School brethren in 1847, and are since about extinct.

NOVA SCOTIA.

AMHERST. The Rev. Alexander Clarke, missionary from Ireland, first visited this region in 1828, and this was the scene of most of his labors for forty years.

When he came to this part of the Province he found a few adhering to Reformation principles scattered over a vast area of country, but the outside world was a vast moral wilderness. If he had followed the method of many missionaries in a new country, and admitted indiscriminately persons to the privileges of the Church, he could have had large accessions. But this he would not do. He preferred the purity of the Church to the number of her members, and gave applicants a careful examination before he admitted them to the privileges of the Church. He dispensed the first Covenanter Communion in the fall of 1830, and a large audience waited upon the services. Fifty communicants from New Brunswick, Nova Scotia and Prince Edward Island sat down at the table of the Lord for the first time in their adopted country.* In 1831, the Rev. William Sommerville and Mr. Andrew Stevenson, Catechist, were sent to Nova Scotia as missionaries by the Church in Ireland. Revs. Alexander Clarke and William Sommerville, with Elders, constituted the Reformed Presbytery of New Brunswick and Nova Scotia, under the care of the Synod of Ireland, April 25, 1832. The congregation of Amherst was placed under the charge of Rev. Alexander Clarke, and was composed of numerous branches. Among the preaching stations, which subsequently became congregations, were Shemogue, River Hebert, Goose River, Port Elgin, Rockland, Truro and Pictou. In the year 1847, Mr. Clarke identified himself with the government which the Covenanters under the British Crown had been endeavoring to reform for many years, and the same government which had inflicted the persecution upon his forefathers in Scotland. He connected himself, and all the societies he represented,

---

* Report to Irish Synod, 1831.

with the New School body of the United States, and
by defection, death and emigration, New School Covenanterism is almost extinct in this region.

HORTON. The congregation which was gathered in
the historic village of Grand Pre, was commonly called
Lower Horton, from its location in the township of
Horton.   It is near the Basin of Minas, sixty-two
miles north-west of the city of Halifax. This was the
land of the Acadians, and where, in 1755, over two
thousand souls were exiled from peaceful homes and
fruitful fields which they had built by their own
industry and reclaimed from the sea by hard labor.
There may be viewed to-day the ruins of their church
and those of hundreds of dwellings, as well as the
place of the graveyard and home of Evangeline, and
the beach at the mouth of the Gaspereaux from
which they embarked in the ships which had been
prepared for them.*   Horton was first supplied with
regular preaching in 1765, by the Rev. John Murdock,
a Presbyterian minister from Ireland. His connection
with this congregation ceased in 1790, on account of
his intemperate habits.   In 1829, the Rev. Alexander
Clarke visited them and preached in this community
several Sabbaths.   In 1832, the Rev. William Sommerville was invited by these people to settle in Horton.
They promised him the use of a free house and garden
owned by the congregation, and as much money as
they could possibly raise for preaching every alternate

---

* The situation and incidents of the expulsion of the peaceful Acadians
have been minutely described by the lamented Longfellow in his "Exile
of the Acadians," and the pathetic story of "Evangeline."

Sabbath. They agreed also to sing the Psalms of David and comply to other practices of the church, and gradually the congregation became in theory and practice a Covenanter congregation. He accepted their invitation and terms, and became the regular pastor in 1835. This same year he was also presented with a call from the people of West Cornwallis for a part of his time, which was by him accepted, and from this date to that of his death, in 1878, he was pastor of the united congregations of Horton and Cornwallis. His increased labor, and that under physical decline, demanded the assistance of another minister. To meet this requirement, his son, the Rev. Robert M. Sommerville, was ordained and installed co-pastor, October 16, 1861. He soon afterwards built a church in Wolfville for the better accommodation of some of the people of that community, where he preached until 1873. The building was afterwards sold and the services all conducted at Horton congregation in the village of Grand Pre. The church building here is in the southern part of the historic village, with the accustomed large grounds and spacious graveyard. It was built about 1810, and is decidedly antique in architecture, having the regulation high pulpit, sounding board, box pews and commodious gallery. In the summer of 1881, the Rev. Thomas McFall became the pastor at Cornwallis, and preached here a part of his time, until it became disorganized by the death of an elder in 1886. Among the families in this branch are those of Harvey, McDonald, Chase, Trenholm and Newcomb.

CORNWALLIS. This congregation derives its name from the township in Kings County, in the central part of the Province, and is situated some eighty-five miles north-west of Halifax. The valley is a very fertile one and the orchards are luxuriant. It is a fruitful garden and has long been occupied by a thrifty and industrious people. About the beginning of the present century, the Rev. William Forsythe, a Scotchman, whose remains lie in the silent graveyard of Grand Pre, labored here as a Presbyterian missionary for nearly thirty years. In 1831, the Rev. William Sommerville entered the field and occasionally preached to Presbyterians generally, and over a vast extent of territory, until the spring of 1835, when he became the pastor, and remained until his death in 1878. The Presbytery had made arrangements previous to his death for the supply of the pulpit, and, during the summer of 1878, Mr. W. J. Sproull, licentiate, and late missionary to Syria, filled the pulpit with so much acceptance that they tendered him a unanimous call, which, however, he saw fit to decline. In the summer of 1881, the Rev. Thomas McFall was ordained and installed pastor, and after the adjustment of certain difficulties about baptism, the congregation has been in a harmonious and flourishing condition. The church building is not far from the village of Somerset, and the parsonage, which was burned in November, 1887, was located in the village. There are preaching stations at North Mountain, Ross' Corners and the public hall in Somerset. Among the faithful followers of Covenanterism in this section are the families of Mortons, Newcombs, Cochrans, Colemans, Woodworths, Magees, Sommervilles, and others.

WILMOT. This small mission station is fifteen miles west of the Cornwallis congregation. It was begun in 1834, when Mr. John Allan, a Covenanter who had emigrated from the north of Ireland to this place, travelled forty miles to Grand Pre to visit Mr. Sommerville and have him come and preach to his countrymen on Handly Mountain. This visit lead to the organization of a society, which was occasionally visited until 1849, when the Rev. Robert Stewart took charge of it, and where he remained until 1881. He also preached in Margaretville, Lawrencetown, and other places, and gathered quite a congregation. The church building is a neat and comfortable frame structure near Melverne Square. Since 1881, the congregation has enjoyed supplies sent out by the Central Board of Missions, and a good deal of interest was manifested in reviving the work. The families of Mr. Stewart, Mr. Kerr and Mr. Outhit have done much to keep the cause alive.

MAINE.

HOULTON. The few families of Covenanters which settled five miles north of Houlton, were from Donegal, Ireland, and were organized into the Littleton Society in 1859. These thrifty people reside on both sides of the line between Maine and New Brunswick, and are tenaciously attached to Reformation principles. For many long years they kept up the society meetings and read one of Dr. Houston's sermons as a substitute for a discourse delivered with the living voice. They built a meeting house which was replaced by a comfortable frame church in 1883. Mr. J. A. F. Bovard labored here during the summer of 1880, under appointment of the Central Board of Missions. He was ordained to the office of the holy ministry in the summer of 1881, and settled as a missionary among them, and remained until the spring of 1884. He was instrumental in gathering the people together and rebuilding their house of worship. The Central Board of Missions has almost constantly supplied them during the summer months. The several families of Hendersons, and their connections, form the great majority of the membership. They are worthy to be mentioned as the only Presbyterian Church in the State of Maine for many years.

NEW HAMPSHIRE.

No congregations of Covenanters were ever organized in the State of New Hampshire. Doubtless individuals and families found abode within its limits, but not in an organized capacity. In his diary, the Rev. John Cuthbertson says he visited New Hampshire in the fall of 1766, but he gives neither the names of the places nor the families he visited. In a missionary tour through this State in 1845, the Rev. James R. Willson, D. D., found but two members—one living in the village of Lyman Plains, and the other near the city of Concord.

VERMONT.

RYEGATE. The Ryegate society of Covenanters may be regarded as the parent of all the congregations in Vermont. It is situated on the Connecticut river and in the south-eastern corner of Caledonia County. Dr. Witherspoon was the original owner of the land in this section, and encouraged the Scotch emigrants to settle upon it about a century ago. In 1789, these people petitioned the Associate Presbytery for preaching, and, as the outcome of their earnest desires for services, the Rev. David Goodwillie was installed the pastor of Ryegate and Barnet, February 8, 1791, and continued in this relation until his death in 1830. Some of these Scotch settlers, however, did not connect with the Associate Church. Among these were the Whitehills, Holmeses, and others. They continued to hold society meetings among themselves and would not wait upon the ministrations of others, in this respect following the example of their forefathers in Scotland. At the formation of the Reformed Presbytery in the spring of 1798, they petitioned for the services of a Covenanter minister; and, according to their wishes, the Rev. William Gibson was sent to them the same fall. In the winter of 1798, the Rev. James McKinney also visited them, and encouraged them to call Mr. Gibson to be their pastor. This they did, and, accepting, he was duly installed pastor of the Ryegate congregation, and societies adjacent, July 10, 1799. In March, 1800, he also became town minister. Here he labored assiduously in defence of the principles of the

Church for fifteen years, and until his release in 1815.
The congregation languished for a little, and in many
respects became very disorderly. A call having been
importunately presented, the Rev. James Milligan was
installed pastor in 1817. The elders at this time in
the different societies were Messrs. Whitehill and Caldwell of Ryegate; Hindman of Barnet; McKeith and
McNeice of Topsham. Mr. Milligan's administration
was not free from serious trouble, yet he labored faithfully for over twenty years, and, when he left the
congregation in 1839, the parent Church was twice as
large as he found it, and two others were organized
from it. In 1844, the Rev. James M. Beattie was
settled over the congregation, and the elders at the
time were Messrs. Johnston, Coburn and McClure of
Ryegate; and Whitehill 'and McLaren of Barnet. Mr.
Beattie labored faithfully among them for thirty-eight
years, and resigned on account of the state of his
health in 1882. In 1883, the Rev. Hugh W. Reed
became the pastor, and, after three years of labor, he
resigned the charge, and efforts have been made to
obtain a pastor. Of the old members in Ryegate are
James Whitehill, Josiah Quint, Robert Dickson, John
Nelson, William Nelson, Jonathan Coburn, John Maclain,
James McLam, William Bone, Charles B. Harriman,
David Lang, Duncan Ritchie, James Beattie, Walter
Buchanan, William Johnston, John Dunn, Thomas
Hastie, Allan Stewart, John Brock, John Davidson,
Henry E. Whitehill, Archibald Ritchie.

BARNET. The present Barnet congregation was a
part of the Ryegate charge until its separate organiza-

tion in 1872. Rev. Daniel C. Faris was installed pastor in 1873, and is still in charge. Of the old members at Barnet are mentioned, William McLaren, William Keenan, William Whitehill, A. W. McLam, Robert McLam, Alexander Shields.

CRAFTSBURY. The Craftsbury congregation of Covenanters is pleasantly situated in Orleans County, some twenty-five miles directly south of the Canada line. It occupies an extensive and beautiful table land between two ranges of the Green mountains.* The first Covenanter in this vicinity was Mr. Robert Trumbull, originally from Cambuslang, Scotland, and who removed from Wilbraham, Massachusetts, to this place in 1788, as one of the first settlers of Craftsbury. Mr. Trumbull was a member of the Established Church of Scotland, and, in coming to America, connected with the Congregational Church, so prevalent in New England. He never was satisfied with this body of Christians on account of their heterodox views respecting the atonement of Christ, and their loose practices in many ways. He earnestly desired and ceaselessly labored to secure a return to puritanic orthodoxy. After unsuccessful attempts in this direction, he waited upon the Congregational services at Peacham and Barnet, but things were no better in these churches. It was suggested to him that no denomination would fit his ideas and principles unless it was the "McMillanites" down at Ryegate, who had the Rev. William Gibson for their pastor. He determined to hear Mr. Gibson. It was a communion Sabbath,.

---

* Sketch in *Covenanter*, Vol. 2, p. 343.

and the preacher was unusually comforting and eloquent
on this occasion.   Mr. Trumbull remained until the
close of the services on Monday, and then returned
to Craftsbury contented and cheered because he had
found a denomination of Christians with which he
could fellowship in all his views. In June, 1807, the
Rev. Mr. Gibson preached in Craftsbury in compliance
with a cordial invitation extended by Colonel Crafts,
Mr. Trumbull, and others. This was the first Covenanter preaching known to have been given in Craftsbury.   In the spring of 1808, Mr. Trumbull and
his family connected with the Covenanter congregation
of Ryegate. Mr. Gibson preached his last discourses
in Craftsbury, September 4, 1814. The subject of his
morning lecture was a part of the fifty-third chapter
of Isaiah, and in the afternoon he preached upon the
sixth verse of the same chapter.   On the following
Sabbath, the Rev. Mr. Farren, the Congregational
minister, argued against the doctrine of the substi-
tutionary sacrifice of Christ, which Mr. Gibson had
taught, and maintained the doctrine of universal atonement, which was the system known as the "Hopkinsian
heresy." This discourse of Mr. Farren gave offence to
many of his hearers, and a considerable number left
the communion of the Congregational Church and kept
society meetings with Mr. Trumbull. In the winter of
1815, the Rev. John Cannon, then a licentiate, preached
with great acceptance, and convinced many of the
impropriety of the New England custom of beginning
the Sabbath on Saturday evening and ending it at
sundown on the Lord's day. In September, 1816, the

first session meeting was held at the house of Mr. Robert Trumbull, and the Craftsbury society became a regularly organized congregation. Among the first members enrolled were: Robert Trumbull, Lucy Babcock Trumbull his wife, his children James, Mary, Nancy, Clarissa, and his nephew James Trumbull; John Babcock, Elizabeth Babcock, Leonard Morse, Elizabeth Morse, Mrs. Johnston, Phebe Johnston, Benjamin Morse, Ephraim Morse, Mrs. Rodgers and Mrs. Wylie. The society continued to enjoy the ministrations of the Rev. James Milligan of Ryegate until 1833, when they felt they were able to support a pastor themselves. In the spring of 1833, the Rev. Samuel M. Willson became the pastor when their membership numbered sixty communicants. Mr. Willson labored diligently for twelve years and gathered many into the church. He resigned in 1845, and returned to the State of New York. In 1846, the Rev. Renwick Z. Willson, nephew of the former pastor, took charge of the congregation. At this time the elders were James Trumbull, Alexander Shields, John A. Morse, Stephen Babcock, Leonard Harriman and John Anderson. After nine years of service, Mr. Willson resigned in 1855. Henceforth the pastorates were of short duration owing to the severity of the climate and the paucity of members. In 1857, the Rev. John M. Armour was installed pastor and remained until 1865. Three years it was a vacancy. The Rev. Archibald W. Johnston took the charge in 1868, and resigned in 1871, on account of the impaired health of his wife. Since 1873, the Rev. John C. Taylor has been the pastor,

11

and has done a good work. The congregation is small, but they are a worthy people, and have a noble history for faithfulness to Reformation principles. Other worthy members are Aurelius Morse, John Wylie, James Mitchell, John Gillies and James Anderson.

TOPSHAM. The Topsham society was a part of the Ryegate and Barnet congregation until its separate existence in the fall of 1818. The elders in this branch were Robert McNeice, William McNutt and Thomas McKeith. In the fall of 1820, they succeeded in getting a pastor in the person of the eminent Rev. William Sloane. Including the societies of Tunbridge and New-bury, they numbered forty members. In a short time the congregation nearly doubled its numbers and many worthy Christians were added to the Church. Mr. Sloane resigned in 1829, and removed to Ohio. For twenty-three long years it was a vacancy, but held its organization, and enjoyed occasional supplies by Presbytery. In 1852, the Rev. Nathan R. Johnston was installed pastor, and labored under many difficulties and sacrifices for thirteen years. He resigned in 1865. For four years they were without pastoral oversight. In 1869, the Rev. James M. Faris undertook the office of pastor among them, but resigned in 1872. Since 1874, the Rev. J. C. K. Faris has been the efficient pastor, and the Covenanter cause is still maintained with many tokens of the Divine blessing. Of old members are Daniel Keenan, John Peabody, Josiah Divoll, John McNeice, Parker McNeice, Ebenezer Currier.

SAINT JOHNSBURY. This is a new field. The Rev. W. R. Laird, then a licentiate, began labor in this growing city in the spring of 1879, and was the first Covenanter minister to preach in this community. By his public ministrations in the pulpit and his indefatigable labors among the people, he saw the fruits of his work in the organization of a congregation of thirty eight members in the summer of 1879, only a few months after he entered the field. Having received a call from these people, Mr. Laird was duly ordained and installed pastor of the Saint Johnsbury congregation in May, 1880, and is yet in charge. They soon erected a beautiful and comfortable church building, and the congregation has steadily grown in numbers and influence.

MASSACHUSETTS.

According to the diary of the Rev. John Cuthbertson there must have been a society of Covenanters at Pelham, Hampshire County, a little east of the Connecticut river. Mr. Cuthbertson visited this region in the fall of 1759, and preached on his way at different places in Connecticut. His places of preaching in Massachusetts were Sheffield, Berkshire County ; Westfield, Hampden County ; Northampton and Pelham, .Hampshire County. He preached in the latter place several Sabbaths, and on October 28, 1759, he preached in *the* meeting house, which seems to imply that the Covenanters had such a place of worship in that town. The Rev. Alexander McDowell was a disaffected minister once placed over the Presbyterian congregation at Colerain, in the same neighborhood, and who, in

1759, seems to have left that body and associated himself with the Covenanter societies of Massachusetts and Connecticut. Mr. Cuthbertson remained in this region for two months and returned to Pennsylvania in the middle of December, 1759, and probably did not visit this part of the country again. In the fall of 1845, the Rev. James R. Willson, D. D., made a missionary tour through this State and found a few families of Covenanters. In the city of LOWELL he found five families, all from the congregations of Vermont, who procured a church and he preached to them and others who composed a respectable audience.* These families were organized into a society, applied for preaching, which they occasionally received for some time.

BOSTON. Mr. Willson also visited the city of Boston, and called upon William Lloyd Garrison and Wendell Phillips, † who were heartily in sympathy with the principles of the Covenanter Church, especially in its relation and attitude towards the sin of slavery. Mr. Willson only found one family of Covenanters in Boston, but the Rev. A. M. Stavely found several families and preached to them shortly afterwards. In 1850, another worthy family arrived from Ireland, and still later another branch of the same family, and, in 1853, these people made application to the New York Presbytery for preaching, which was granted. They rented a comfortable hall, centrally located, and Covenanterism began to grow in the cultured metropolis of New England and the Hub of the Universe. The

---

* *Covenanter*, Vol. I, p. 150. † *Covenanter*, Vol. I, p. 241.

congregation of Boston was regularly organized by a
Commission of the New York Presbytery, consisting of
the Rev. Samuel M. Willson and elders James Wiggins
and Andrew Knox, July 12, 1854. The congregation
numbered twenty members, two elders and one deacon.
The Rev. James R. Lawson was the first pastor,
installed November 20, 1856. The congregation then
worshipped in a hall on the second floor of the building
at the corner of Province and Bromfield streets.* Mr.
Lawson remained less than a year, and returned to
his former charge in New Brunswick. The rent of halls
became so burdensome that the congregation frequently
moved. For nearly three years the congregation was
a vacancy. In March, 1860, the Rev. William Graham,
then a licentiate, supplied them, and until his settlement as the pastor, July 12, 1860. At the time of
his ordination there were thirty-nine members and some
adherents. Mr. Graham is still in charge. On account
of some discord, the seeds of which had been sown
many years before, a grant was given for another
organization. This was effected by a Commission of
the New York Presbytery, November 21, 1871. Thirty-
one members were certified from the First congregation, and two elders and two deacons were chosen.
For many years they met in halls on Hanover and
Tremont streets for worship. In 1873, the First congregation erected a magnificent church edifice at the
corner of Ferdinand and Isabella streets, at a total
cost of sixty-three thousand dollars. In 1878, the
Second congregation bought a large and commodious

* Sketch by Rev. W. Graham, R. P. & C., 1885, page 332.

church at a very reasonable price on Chambers street. The Rev. David McFall was installed pastor of the Second congregation, July 11, 1873, and is now in charge. Both the congregations are well housed and increasing in numbers and usefulness. The importance of Boston as a commercial and cultured city gives our people a prominence that is seldom equalled. The Warnock family have been connected with the cause from the beginning. The names of Mitchell, Riley, Gillespie, Grier, Stevenson, Warnock, Larkins, Graham, Ross, Adams, McClosky, Spragg, Calderwood, Oliver, Semple, Glasgow, Caldwell, McClelland, Burnett, and many other faithful standard bearers, should find mention in this connection.

CONNECTICUT.

There never were any regularly organized congregations in the State of Connecticut, but, no doubt, there were a few families who found abode within the borders. When the first Covenanters were banished to America, historians say that some of them "went to Connecticut and found employment after their several trades." It is not recorded who they were, or where they settled. In the fall of 1759, the Rev. John Cuthbertson visited this region and remained several weeks. He preached at Ridgefield, Danbury and Newtown in Fairfield County; Woodbury in Litchfield County; and at Waterbury in New Haven County. Doubtless the Rev. Alexander McDowell visited these same people and they were in sympathy with the principles of the Reformed Covenanting Church.

CANADA WEST.

RAMSEY. The region of Ontario south and west of the city of Ottawa, and bordering on the St. Lawrence and the lakes, was early settled by a religious and thrifty people from Scotland and Ireland.* In the year 1815, large numbers of Scotch people settled in the County of Lanark, and in 1820, at Dalhousie and Ramsey. Many of them were consistent members of the different branches of the Presbyterian family, and a few trained in the faith of the Covenanter Church. In 1816, they petitioned the Associate Church of Scotland to send them a minister. Their request was granted, and in the spring of 1817, the Rev. William Bell settled among them. In 1821, the Rev. Dr. John Gemmill was sent to this Scotch settlement by the London Missionary Society, and in 1822, the Rev. George Buchanan of the Relief Church arrived in this country. In a few years all these ministers, and many of the people, joined the Presbyterian Church of Canada in connection with the Established Church of Scotland. There were a few Covenanters, however, who did not follow their brethren, and they were joined by others, and a praying society was formed of those living in the township of Ramsey. About this time the families of Walter Gardner, John McEuan and James Smith emigrated from Scotland and joined the Covenanter society. In 1828, the Rev. James Milligan of Vermont visited this region and preached to these people. On his second visit in 1830, he

* From sketch by Rev. R. Shields, in *Banner*, 1877, pp. 33, 68, 107.

organized them into a congregation, dispensed the
sacraments and constituted a session. James Rea, William
Moir and William McQueen were chosen and ordained
ruling elders. Among the members enrolled at the organization of the first Covenanter congregation in Canada,
were: James Rea and his wife, William Moir and wife,
William McQueen and wife, James Smith, Thomas Craig
and wife, Alexander Duncan and wife, Robert Duncan,
Duncan Ferguson, John Fulford, Walter Gardner and
wife, John Graham, John Hutcheson and wife, David
Kemp, Thomas Kennedy, Mrs. John Kilpatrick, William
Lindsay and wife, John McEuan and wife, Thomas
McKean and wife. In the fall of 1830, they were
visited by the Rev. Robert McKee, and in 1831, by
Rev. John H. Symmes, and others. In 1831, the congregation received strength by the accession of the
family of James Waddell from Scotland. Mr. Waddell
was directed by the congregation to write to the Committee of the Covenanter Synod of Scotland urging
them to send a minister to them. In answer to this
petition, the late Rev. James McLachlane arrived in
the summer of 1833. At this time a serious division
was taking place in the Covenanter Church in America,
and it effected this congregation to the extent of
losing most of its members and its organization. Mr.
McLachlane reorganized the congregation with nine
members under the care of the Synod of Scotland.
James Rea, William Moir and James Waddell were
chosen ruling elders. Preaching services were also
dispensed at Packenham, Lanark and Carleton Place.
David Moffet of Carleton Place was ordained a ruling

elder February 16, 1834. During the summer of 1834, a comfortable log church was erected on the "Eighth line of Ramsey," about one mile from Bennies Corners. Carleton Place had grown to a considerable society and now received one-half the time of Mr. McLachlane. During the summer of 1835, another log church was erected by the people on the "Second line of Ramsey," and near the spot where the village of Clayton now stands. In the fall of 1835, a petition was received from PERTH for a part of Mr. McLachlane's time, and he preached every fifth Sabbath in this settlement. The Perth congregation was organized in April, 1836, and John Brown and John Holliday were ordained ruling elders, and Francis Holliday and John Walker, deacons. Among the original families at Perth were those of John, James, Francis, George and David Holliday, Lachlan Arthur, James Brice, John Brown, Thomas Dobbie, Adam Elliot, John Graham, John Grierson, Thomas Oliver and John Walker—in all about thirty members. In the summer of 1837, for the better convenience and comfort of all concerned, Carleton Place, Perth and Ramsey were organized into three distinct and separate congregations and each had a session. The session of Carleton Place was composed of David Moffet and James Waddell; that of Perth of John Holliday and John Brown; and that of Ramsey of James Rea, William Moir and Andrew Given. John McWhinnie was added to the latter session, February 1, 1838. Mr. McLachlane preached frequently at Clarendon, Bristol, Toronto, Hamilton, Guelph and Galt. At a general meeting of the three sessions, held February 7, 1839, the matter of the pastor missionating came up for adjudication. The strife was so great and the feeling so bitter that elders James Rea and William Moir of Ramsey were deposed, and many members were suspended on various charges. The present church occupied by the people of Carleton Place was erected in 1841. In the summer of 1847, Ramsey being without a session of its own, James Waddell and Andrew McKenzie were chosen elders. In the fall of 1850, the question of accession to the Covenanter Synod of the United States came up before the session, and the Canadian congregations were taken under the care of the Rochester Presbytery, October 7, 1851. A Commission repaired to Perth to settle certain difficulties existing between Mr. McLachlane and his people. After hearing the whole case, the Commission decided that, for the peace and comfort of all concerned, the pastoral relation should be dissolved. This caused a division in the congregation, a part of which strenuously adhered to Mr. McLachlane. A second congregation was organized at Perth, June 12, 1852, and those who followed Mr. McLachlane were known as the First congregation. John and Francis Holliday were ordained ruling elders in the new organization. The Rev. John Middleton was installed pastor of the Second congregation of Perth in October, 1854. A large and convenient house of worship was erected in the town of Perth, but the debt was so heavy upon it that the building was sold a few years afterwards. In the fall of 1855, Mr. McLachlane resigned the charge of First Perth, and removed to the congregation of Lisbon, New York. In the fall of 1856, Mr. Middleton resigned the pastorate of Second Perth, and these congregations never again enjoyed a settled pastor. For nearly ten years there was not a settled Covenanter minister in Canada, and by defection and emigration the cause began to look like speedy extinction. In the summer of 1861, the Rev. David Scott reorganized the Ramsey congregation by the election of James Waddell and John Lindsay ruling elders, and James Smith and John Waddell, deacons. At this time there were only twenty members. Supplies were sent as often as practicable and the cause began to revive. The Rev. Robert Shields was ordained and installed pastor, July 13, 1865. During his pastorate, Messrs. John Rorison, James Thom, John Waddell, David Holliday, David Thom, and others, have been connected with the session. Mr. Shields died in 1883, greatly lamented by the Church, and especially by the community and congregation where he had done yeoman service for his Master. The congregation has enjoyed almost constant preaching sent out by the Central Board of Missions, and has made efforts to obtain a pastor.

LOCHIEL. The village of Lochiel is situated between the St. Lawrence and Ottawa rivers, and about sixty miles east of the city of Ottawa, or half way towards Montreal. This society is of a more recent settlement than Ramsey and Perth. It was fully organized in the summer of 1861, as Glengary, and the name was changed to Lochiel in 1867. Elders Andrew Brodie and William Jamison have been instrumental in securing supplies and keeping the cause alive in this section. There are about twenty-five members and they have a house of worship and a manse. The Rev. R. C. Allen was settled as the pastor in the fall of 1887, and the principles of the Church are being faithfully presented in that part of Canada. ONEIDA and HAMILTON were mission stations, and made out a call for the Rev. James McLachlane in 1852, which he did not accept. The cause in the city of Hamilton was presented by the Rev. Joseph Henderson, who, in 1854, made defection, and took some members with him into the Free Church. North-west of the city of Hamilton were the stations of GALT and GUELPH, which were cultivated awhile with some degree of encouragement, but dropped from the list.

TORONTO. The city of Toronto was long the abode of a few families of Covenanters. In 1850, these people raised quite a sum of money for preaching, and the Revs. Robert Johnson, David Scott, and others, were sent as supplies. In the spring of 1851, a congregation of twenty members was organized, soon a church was secured, and the cause began to flourish. The Rev. Robert Johnson was installed pastor in the fall of 1852, and built up a flourishing congregation, which he resigned in 1859. He was an able preacher and a fearless advocate of the cause of Protestantism against the evils of Roman Catholicism. After his departure, the congregation made several unsuccessful efforts to obtain a pastor, and Rev. David Scott preached a great deal for them. The congregation became disorganized in 1868. The church property

was in jeopardy; and after being in litigation before
the courts for a considerable time, was fully secured
to the Church. The congregation was reorganized in
the winter of 1872, and consisted of nineteen members.
The Rev. J. L. McCartney was called, but declined.
Not succeeding in getting a pastor, and often not
supplies, the people became discouraged and rented
the church. They lost their organization in 1875, and
a number of the members connected with other
Churches. The church property is again in dispute and
is in the hands of the Rev. John Graham of Rochester,
who represents the Church in the settlement of affairs.
MORPETH. There was another station at Morpeth,
about sixty miles east of Detroit and near Lake Erie.
It was visited several times, and, in the spring of
1852, the Rev. James Neill was appointed stated supply,
and remained over a year. Mr. William McClure, a
late elder in the congregation of Belle Centre, Ohio,
was the leading member, and the cause was liberally
supported for some time. By emigration and death
Covenanterism has become extinct in that part of
Canada.

NEW YORK.

NEW YORK CITY. So far as is known the first
Covenanters settling in the city of New York were
Mr. John Agnew and his wife, who emigrated from
Ireland and settled in the city of Philadelphia in 1784,
where they resided three years.* In 1787, they

---

* *Covenanter*, Vol. 3, p. 371. *Presbyterian Historical Almanac*, Vol. 4, p.
251. R. P. & C., 1877, p. 294. *Stone of Help*, a pamphlet by Dr. J. N.
McLeod. Church Records.

removed to the city of New York, where Mr. Agnew became a prosperous merchant and the founder of Covenanterism in the metropolis of America. In the summer of 1790, when the Rev. James Reid, of Scotland, was making a missionary tour in America, and when about to embark for his native land, he was providentially introduced to Mr. Agnew, who was then doing business in Peck's Slip, near the East river. Mutual friends of the Covenant were highly gratified at the discovery, and Mr. Reid preached in the house of Mr. Agnew the following Sabbath, and baptized two of his children. Among those who heard Mr. Reid preach at this time was Mr. James Donaldson, a native of Scotland, and a worthy Covenanter. He joined Mr. Agnew in forming a praying society, and these meetings were regularly held until the arrival of the Rev. James McKinney in 1793. Among those who heard Mr. McKinney preach, was Mr. Andrew Gifford, a Scotchman brought up in the Covenanter Church, but now a member of the Scotch Presbyterian Church under the pastoral care of the Rev. John M. Mason. He, however, now joined the Church of his birth, and the society held regular preaching services in school houses and halls. In 1795, the society was strengthened by the arrival of John Currie, James Smith, James Nelson and David Clark. In October, 1797, the Rev. Willliam Gibson, and some private members, had emigrated from Ireland, some of whom settled in the city of Philadelphia. The Rev. William Gibson gave one-half of his time to the congregation of New York, and the cause began to flourish. The

first Covenanter congregation in the city of New York
was organized by the Rev. William Gibson, December
26, 1797. The first session was then constituted and
consisted of James Nelson, John Currie, John Agnew,
Andrew Gifford and David Clark. The number of
communicants was fifteen. They were very liberal, and
paid seventy-five dollars rent annually for the occasional
use of a school house for public services. They paid
the ministers twelve dollars per Sabbath for their
services and entertained them hospitably in their
homes. The sacrament of the Lord's Supper was first
dispensed in August, 1798, in a school room on Cedar
street. Revs. James McKinney and William Gibson
conducted the services. The number of communicants
was eighteen, six of whom were from a distance.
Mr. McKinney alluded very touchingly to the paucity
of their members, but said the number was greater
than that present in the upper room when the
Supper was first administered by our Lord. Among
the communicants were John Black, S. B. Wylie
and Alexander McLeod, students of theology.
On the following Tuesday, the Reformed Presbytery met
in "the Orchard," the country residence of Mr. John
Agnew. Here these theological students gave specimens
of improvement and had others assigned to them. In
the fall of 1800, this congregation made out a call, in
connection with Coldenham, for the services of Alexander McLeod. Several matters at Coldenham having
been rectified, Mr. McLeod was ordained and installed
the first pastor of the congregation of New York, July
6, 1801. In 1803, he resigned the Coldenham branch

and devoted his whole time to the rapidly growing congregation in New York, where he remained thirty-two years, and until his death in February, 1833. In 1804, a frame church building was erected on Chambers street east of Broadway. The same year the eldership was increased by the election of Dr. Samuel Guthrie, Hugh Orr and William Acheson. In 1812, there were one hundred and thirty-eight members, and this year Mr. William Pattison was added to the session. In 1817, Thomas Cummings was made an elder. In 1818, the first church building was found to be too small to accommodate the worshippers, and it was taken down, and a more commodious brick structure was erected upon the same site. Directly opposite the church on Chambers street stood the city Alms House. A poor widow, and a member of the Church, by the name of Mrs. Grant Bussing, formed a class among these poor and destitute children, and this was the first Sabbath School established in New York city. In 1819, Joseph McKee and William Cowan were ordained ruling elders, and in 1827, Robert Pattison, Hugh Galbraith, John Brown and John Wilson were added to the session. At the close of the year 1827, a few members living in the upper part of the city purchased a house of worship formerly occupied by the Dutch Reformed congregation of Greenwich, and, on January 11, 1828, offered it, with all the papers, to the consistory. It stood at the corner of Waverly Place and Grove street. The object of this movement was to furnish preaching to the members and others who lived far from Chambers street. The offer, however, was opposed by the down

town people, who were in the majority. Notwithstanding the opposition to the enterprize the place
was opened for public service, and Dr. McLeod and
others preached there. Over this step in the right
direction great bitterness and strife arose, and Dr.
McLeod left the scene of contention and went to
Europe for his health. The up town people applied
and secured a second and separate organization, June
11, 1830. The Presbytery made a geographical division of the congregation, and all the members residing
above this given line were to be recognized as
members of the Second New York congregation. This
division included elders Andrew Gifford, John Brown
and Thomas Cummings in the new organization. In
December, 1830, and soon after his arrival, Dr. McLeod
was presented with calls from both the congregations.
He decided to remain with the mother congregation,
which was the First congregation of New York. The
Second congregation then presented a call to the Rev.
Robert Gibson, who, having accepted it, was duly
installed pastor, May 31, 1831. The health of Dr.
McLeod began to fail very rapidly and he desired
the help of an associate pastor. His son, the Rev.
John N. McLeod, was installed pastor as his father's
successor against the wishes of many of the congregation, January 14, 1833. Dr. Alexander McLeod died
February 17, 1833. At this time the New School
controversy was agitating the Church, and Rev. J. N.
McLeod, and the majority of the congregation, went
into the New School body. Mr. Gibson, who took a
prominent part in the discussions, remained true to

12

the distinctive principles of the Covenanter Church. Of the eldership, Andrew Gifford, John Brown and Thomas Cummings, with their families and connections, of the Second congregation, also went into the New School body. This left the congregation in a distressing condition, as those departing were the main support of the cause. The faithful remnant, however, retained the church property and continued their services. As the members were generally poor and laboring people, Mr. Gibson was compelled to add to his ministerial work the additional labor of teaching a classical school in order to sustain himself and family. Notwithstanding the poverty of his devoted flock, they maintained the cause, and also furnished means to send Mr. Gibson to Europe, in the spring of 1837, for his health. He returned to New York the same fall not much improved, appeared but once in the pulpit, and died of consumption, December 22, 1837. As the majority of the First congregation had gone into the New School organization, it involved a long law suit for the property, which terminated after reaching the Court of Errors by a compromise. Soon after this the faithful remnant of the First congregation purchased a church in Sullivan street, and Rev. James Christie, D. D., was installed pastor, November 16, 1836, and remained in charge twenty years. The elders of the First congregation then were William Acheson, John Greacen, John Culbert, James McFarland, Andrew Bowden, John Brown, John Carothers and James C. Ramsey. The Rev. Andrew Stevenson was ordained and installed the pastor of the Second congregation, November 14, 1839,

who remained in charge until May, 1875, and emeritus
pastor until his death, June, 1881. When he became
the pastor in 1839, there were nearly two hundred
members and an efficient session, but the congregation was heavily in debt, possessed an uncomfortable
church building, and the members were very poor.
In August, 1841, James Wylie, John Kennedy and
James Wiggins were added to the eldership. In 1845,
there were three hundred and nineteen members. In
1846, the deacon controversy arose and seriously
effected this congregation. A division of sentiment
was prevalent as to the lawfulness of the management
of the temporalities, and the Presbytery, failing to
amicably settle the question or reconcile the parties,
granted a new organization. The church property was
sold at auction in January, 1848, and equally divided
between the two parties. The Third congregation of
New York was then organized, March 14, 1848, with
nearly two hundred members. An arrangement was
made by which the new congregation worshipped in
the old church on Waverly Place, while the Second
congregation rented the lecture room of the Presbyterian Church at the corner of Waverly Place and
Hammond street, and soon afterwards erected a large
church on Eleventh street near Sixth Avenue. The
Rev. John Little was installed pastor of the Third congregation in June, 1849. He was suspended in April,
1852, for preaching doctrines subversive to the principles of the Covenanter Church. The Rev. J. R. W.
Sloane was installed the pastor in 1856. The same
year the Rev. Dr. Christie resigned the First congrega-

tion to accept the chair of Theology in the Allegheny Seminary. The Rev. J. C. K. Milligan was installed as his successor in the spring of 1858, and is still in charge. The Third church, on Twenty-Third street, was erected in 1860. In 1868, Dr. Sloane resigned the charge of the Third church and accepted the chair of Theology in the Allegheny Seminary. In 1869, a division occurred in the Third congregation, and the Fourth congregation of New York was organized, February 21, 1870. The Rev. David Gregg was installed pastor of the Third congregation, February 23, 1870. The Rev. James Kennedy was installed pastor of the Fourth congregation, November 13, 1870, and is now in charge. The First congregation had, some years previously, bought a church from the United Presbyterian brethren, many of whom connected with the Covenanter Church, on Twenty-Eighth street near Ninth Avenue. The Fourth congregation secured a large and commodious church in Forty-Eighth street near Eighth Avenue in 1873, which is their present place of worship. In 1875, the Rev. Andrew Stevenson was retired as emeritus pastor of the Second congregation, and the Rev. Robert M. Sommerville was installed the pastor, and is now in charge. They sold their church in Eleventh street and purchased a Jewish Synagogue of magnificent architecture in Thirty-Ninth street near Sixth Avenue, which is the present imposing church building of the congregation. The Third church was burned, February 17, 1878, and immediately rebuilt. In January, 1887, the Rev. David Gregg left the communion of the Church, and as his successor the

Rev. Finley M. Foster was installed pastor of the
Third congregation, September 7, 1887. The First
congregation sold their church in Twenty-Eighth street
in 1883, and for nearly four years worshipped in
Trenor Hall, corner of Broadway and Thirty-Second
street. In 1887, they erected a large and well appointed church in Harlem, in One Hundred and
Nineteenth street near Fifth Avenue, where they are
now worshipping in one of the handsomest churches in
the body. The Covenanters of New York are an
energetic and liberal people, and are nearly one
thousand in number. The *First* congregation was
organized December 26, 1797 ; the present church
building is on One Hundred and Nineteenth street,
near Fifth Avenue, Harlem, and the pastor is the
Rev. J. C. K. Milligan. Members recorded are Andrew
Acheson, William Acheson, William Sterritt, John
Culbert, William Cowan, John Greacen, James C.
Ramsey, Joseph Thomson, Andrew Bowden, Matthew
Bowden, John W. Bowden, Charles Gillespie, John
Nightingale, Hamilton Biggam, John Whitehead, C. B.
French, James Thomson, Robert Bowden, John Lynch,
John Angus, John Carothers, William Fleming,
William Hazlett, E. N. Shields, William Law, James
Bell, Thomas Rusk, W. J. Cromie, David Henderson,
James Cowan, Frederick E. Milligan, W. J. Clyde,
Alexander Livingstone, David Bell, John McFarland,
Robert Smith, Edward McLean, J. C. Milligan. The
Second congregation was organized June 11, 1830 ;
the present church building is on Thirty-Ninth street
near Sixth Avenue, and the pastor is the Rev. Robert

M. Sommerville. Of old members are James Wylie, John S. Walker, Joseph Wiggins, James Wiggins, John Kennedy, Jacob A. Long, Joseph Torrens, David Torrens, Melancthon W. Bartley, Andrew Alexander, Samuel Miller, Henry O'Neil, Samuel K. McGuire, Matthew Miller, James Warnock, Thomas E. Greacen, William McCullough, William McLean, John Taylor, John J. McKay, Robert McCracken, Francis L. Walker, John Sharpe, W. H. Cochran, John Aikin, William Park, Hugh McCreery, J. J. Montgomery, James Dunlap, Thompson O'Neil, John Adams. The *Third* congregation was organized March 14, 1848; the present church building is on Twenty-Third street near Eighth Avenue, and the pastor is the Rev. Finley M. Foster. Of the membership are named William Neely, Walter T. Miller, A. J. Echols, Andrew Knox, John Mc-William, Alexander McNeil, Thomas Bell, Hugh Glassford, James Carlisle, Andrew C. Bowden, Robert Cairns, Hugh Young, William Brown. The *Fourth* congregation was organized February 21, 1870; the present church building is on Forty-Eighth street near Eighth Avenue, and the pastor is the Rev. James Kennedy. Of the principal membership are named Hugh O'Neil, Edward H. Pollock, John Kennedy, Hugh Thomas, Hugh Carlisle, Dr. Samuel Murtland, William McAfee, Robert McAfee, Hugh Getty, Robert Leishman, Dr. J. M. Harvey, David Houston, James Fischer, James Dunlap, David Donneghy, George Kennedy, Robert Kennedy, William Kilpatrick, Dr. W. C. Kennedy, James Bryans, William Pollock, Samuel Stevenson. Evangelistic work has been done among all the congregations by Mr. James M. McElhinney, and his efforts. have been crowned with fruitful results.

BROOKLYN. An organization was granted to the Covenanters residing in the city of Brooklyn, June 15, 1857. A comfortable church building was purchased in an eligible location, but the property was so heavily mortgaged that the small congregation found themselves unable to retain it.* The second property which they bought was located at the corner of Fayette Avenue and Ryerson street. It was primarily built for a chapel or Sabbath School room, and the church proper was never built. The Rev. James M. Dickson was the first pastor installed in November, 1857. He preached with great acceptance for five years and joined the Presbyterian Church. In the winter of 1864, the Rev. John H. Boggs was installed pastor. After a pastorate of sixteen years, he followed the example of his predecessor and went into the Presbyterian Church in 1880. Quite a number of influential members followed him, and are now found in the various Churches of Brooklyn. Mr. T. A. H. Wylie supplied the pulpit for nearly a year. In the winter of 1881, the Rev. S. J. Crowe was installed the pastor, and remained three years. During his pastorate the congregation not only increased in numbers, but in unity and liberality. In 1883, the present commodious church and chapel, situated at the corner of Willoughby and Tompkins Avenues, were purchased. They were erected for Miss Anna Oliver, a Methodist preacher, whose efforts to build up a congregation under her own

---

* *Banner*, 1883, p. 309.

ministry signally failed. Mr. Crowe resigned in the
fall of 1884, on account of the state of his health.
Rev. John F. Carson, the present pastor, was ordained
and installed, May 20, 1885. The congregation and
Sabbath School have greatly increased in numbers,
and the Church has a very prosperous following.
Among the members are named James A. Patterson,
William F. Bell, Francis Culbert, James Hughes, R. J.
Culbert, Thomas Kinkead, M. M. Henry, Henry Fergu-
son, John Shannon, James Warnock, John Boyd, James
Frazer, John W. Pritchard, Thomas Moore, Robert
Taylor, Leatham Teaz, James Williams, Alexander
Frazer, James Hunter, Dr. Palmer.

NEWBURGH. The city of Newburgh is pleasantly
situated in one of the picturesque regions of the famous
Hudson river, sixty miles above the city of New York.
It was the headquarters of General Washington for
some time during the Revolutionary War, and where
the American army was disbanded after national independence had been achieved from Great Britain.* The
first family of Covenanters settling in this city was
that of Mr. Josiah Gailey, in 1787. In 1793, Mr.
Thomas Johnston joined him, and they held society
meetings until Mr. Johnston removed into the neighboring vicinity of St. Andrews. In 1802, James Clarke
emigrated from Scotland, with some of his connections,
and in the fall of that year, the first Covenanter
society in Newburgh was organized. The leading
members were Josiah Gailey; Robert Johnston, James
Clarke and John Curry. The society was soon

* *Covenanter*, Vol. I, p. 373. *Banner*, 1876, p. 121. *R. P. & C.*, 1885, p. 148.

strengthened by the accessions of James King and James Robb. For many years, and until the organization in 1817, the society met at the house of Mr. James Clarke, and afterwards at the house of Mrs. Gillespie, an aged disciple. The society was a part of the Coldenham congregation, and, in 1817, received one-fifth of the time of the Rev. James R. Willson, D. D. In 1810, Samuel Jameson joined them, and, in 1811, they were much encouraged by the arrival of the families of William McCullough, James Orr, John Lawson, William Barclay, Sr., James Barclay, John Barclay and William Barclay, Jr. The Rev. James Milligan, pastor at Coldenham, occasionally supplied them and preached in the Academy. Infidelity had a strong hold in the village, but began to disappear before the tide of Reformation principles and practices. In 1819, this growing society erected a church building, and Dr. Willson was secured for one-half of his time. His eloquence and public spirit attracted many to wait upon his ministrations, and Presbyterianism took a deep hold upon the people. In 1824, having increased to eighty-six members, Newburgh obtained a separate organization from Coldenham. The elders at this time were James Clarke, John Lawson and Samuel Wright, all of whom had been elders in the Coldenham congregation. In 1825, William Thompson and William M. Wylie were chosen deacons, and the former soon afterwards was added to the session. On September 16, 1825, the Rev. James R. Johnston was ordained and installed the first pastor of the congregation of Newburgh. Mr. Johnston was a popular preacher. He

remained four years and then connected with the
Presbyterian Church. Rev. Moses Roney was installed
pastor, June 8, 1830, and remained eighteen years,
until his health demanded his release in 1848. During
his pastorate the elders were Matthew Duke, William
Thompson, David T. Cavin, William Brown and David
Stewart. The deacons were Edward Weir, John Little
and John Lawson. Other names worthy of perpetuation
are those of Kirkpatrick, Fleming, Ramsey, Wiseman
and Stewart. In the fall of 1849, the Rev. Samuel
Carlisle was installed pastor, and continued in this
relationship for thirty-eight years, and until his sad
death, by paralysis, in the summer of 1887. In the
winter of 1854, a Second Congregation was organized.
They worshipped one year in the Court House, and
then erected a neat church building. In the winter of
1855, the Rev. James R. Thompson, son of elder
William Thompson, was ordained and installed pastor,
and is the present incumbent. The first church of the
First congregation was rebuilt in 1877, and stands in
a favorable location on Grand street. The Second
church is in a beautiful spot on the same street and
a few squares away. Among the early members of the
Second church are the names of Little, Lawson, Hilton,
Cameron, Boyne, Fleming, Wilson and Young. Among
the members of the First congregation have been
William McCullough, J. W. McCullough, William Hilton,
John Hilton, John F. Beattie, Robert Campbell,
Alexander Wright, William Willson, William Lynn,
William Brown. Of the members of the Second con-
gregation have been William Thompson, James Frazer,

John Frazer, John Magee, Andrew Little, John T. Brown, James Jamison, John Burnett, John K. Lawson, Francis Willson, Isaac Cochran, William Johnston, R. M. McAllister, W. B. Hall, Robert Hilton.

COLDENHAM. The settlement of Covenanters upon the Wallkill, in Orange County, was the first of this Church in the State of New York, and began about 1748. The location is one distinguished for grazing and the products of the dairy, and is some nine miles west of the city of Newburgh on the Hudson river.* In the year 1748, the family of Mr. James Rainey removed from the city of Philadelphia and settled a little beyond the Wallkill river. Here he continued to stand aloof from communion with other denominations, and consequently was deprived of public ordinances for several years. In 1753, two other families joined him, and a praying society was formed. In September, 1759, the Rev. John Cuthbertson made his first missionary tour to the Wallkill people, and preached in this vicinity three or four weeks. On September 20, 1759, he constituted a session,† and baptized Susannah and David, children of James Rainey; Mary and Archy, children of Archy McBride; Daniel and Jean, children of William Wilkins; John, Helen and Agnes, children of John Gilchrist. In August, 1764, Mr. Cuthbertson, accompanied by elder Phineas Whiteside, of Pequea, Pennsylvania, visited the society again, and preached and baptized some children. During the year 1766, he again visited the Wallkillians when they had grown to a considerable society. In the fall 1769,

---

* *Covenanter*, Vol. 1, p. 283.   † Cuthbertson's Diary.

he made his fourth visit to these worthy and staunch Covenanters, and the most noted heads of the families were James Rainey, John Gilchrist, Archy McBride, James Thomson, William Wilkins, James McCord, John Archibald and Henry Trapp. Mr. Cuthbertson ordained James Rainey and William Wilkins ruling elders, October 29, 1769. This pioneer missionary visited the Wallkill society also in September, 1774, in October, 1775, and in November, 1779. On this latter visit he called upon the Rev. Mr. Annan of the Associate Church, and had much friendly intercourse with him, and he and Mr. Cuthbertson soon afterwards effected a union forming the Associate Reformed Church in 1782. At this coalescence the whole Wallkill Covenanter society went into the new body, except Mr. David Rainey, son of the late elder James Rainey. Covenanterism was now about extinct in this fertile valley, and they continued in this distressing condition for a number of years. All honor is due James Rainey for *establishing*, and David Rainey, his son, for *maintaining*, Covenanterism in Orange County. In the year 1790, the Rev. James Reid, missionary from Scotland, preached a few Sabbaths to the people. Soon after Mr. Robert Johnston joined Mr. Rainey, and they kept up a society meeting between the two families. In 1793, the Rev. James McKinney visited them, and found these two men loyal to Reformation principles. Mr. Robert Beattie acceded to the Covenanter Society in 1795, from the Associate Reformed Church. He was a remarkably generous and public spirited man, and entertained all the ministers and the families coming from a distance to worship. The cause again began to flourish, and they became a considerable society occasionally visited by Revs. James McKinney and William Gibson. The congregation was regularly organized by direction of the Reformed Presbytery, August, 1798, by the election and ordination of David Rainey and Robert Beattie, ruling elders. In June, 1799, the Reformed Presbytery met in the barn of Robert Beattie, and John Black, Thomas Donnelly, Alexander McLeod and Samuel B. Wylie were licensed to preach the gospel. This same year the first church building was erected on the plot of ground now occupied by the church of the Coldenham congregation, and was removed in 1838, to make room for the present edifice. At the meeting of the Reformed Presbytery held at Little Britain, November 7, 1800, a call was entertained from the united congregations of New York City and Wallkill.* It was found that an equal number of votes was cast for Samuel B. Wylie and Alexander McLeod. Mr. Wylie renounced all further connection with the call, and informed the court to take measures accordingly. The court then agreed to address those persons who had voted for Mr. Wylie, whether they would be willing to append their names to the call for Mr. McLeod. To this they willingly assented, and the call was modified by appending the names of all the electors to the call on Mr. McLeod, and it was presented by the Moderator for his acceptance. Mr. McLeod hesitated, and requested another day to consider the matter. After some reasoning with him, Mr. McLeod

---

* Minutes of Reformed Presbytery.

consented to accept the call only conditionally. One condition was that those holding slaves and who had signed the call, should be required to free them and have no more to do with the sinful institution of slavery. Agreeing to this, Mr. McLeod then accepted the call, with the other condition that three years thereafter he was at liberty to accept of either one of the congregations or none, as he thought proper. This the court agreed to, and he gave his pieces as trials for ordination, and was duly installed pastor of the united congregations of Wallkill and New York City, July 6, 1801. The salary and division of time were as follows: *New York*, thirty-one days in the year at eleven dollars per day; *Wallkill*, twenty-one days in the year at seven dollars per day; making the whole salary $488 per annum. In 1803, Mr. McLeod resigned the Wallkill branch to give his whole time to the rapidly growing congregation of New York. In 1807, a call was presented to Mr. James R. Willson, licentiate, but he declined it. In 1808, Mr. Gilbert McMaster was called, and declined. For several years they enjoyed almost constant supplies, but failed to obtain a pastor. In 1812, the Rev. James Milligan was installed pastor, and labored among them for five years, and left them in a good condition in 1817, when he removed to Vermont. Rev. James R. Willson was again called, and having accepted, was installed pastor in August, 1817. At this time there were about seventy members, with societies in Newburgh and beyond the Wallkill river. The congregation was now called Coldenham. At first Mr. Willson gave the Newburgh people one-fifth of his time, subsequently one-half, and in 1824, they became a separate organization and he remained at Coldenham until his resignation in 1830, when he removed to Albany. Dr. Willson returned to the pastorate of the Coldenham congregation in the fall of 1833, and remained in this relation seven years. In 1836, he was appointed professor of Theology in the Eastern Seminary located at Coldenham, and also conducted an Academy, where many of the ministers received their early education. Dr. Willson resigned the charge in 1840, and accepted a professorate in the Allegheny Theological Seminary. For four years Coldenham was a vacancy. In May, 1844, the Rev. James W. Shaw became the pastor. At this time there were nearly one hundred members and six praying societies. The elders were John Beattie, James Beattie, Samuel Arnott, William Elder and Daniel Wilkins. Mr. Shaw spent his whole pastoral life of thirty-eight years among these people, and resigned in 1882, on account of failing health. Several calls were made upon young men, but by them declined. In the spring of 1884, the Rev. Robert H. McCready became the pastor and is now in charge. He resuscitated the cause, inspired the members with new zeal, repaired and refurnished the church, and by no means does it look as if Covenanterism will soon become extinct in Coldenham or Orange County. Among the old members are David Rainey, Adam Rainey, James Clark, William Beattie, John Beattie, Israel O. Beattie, Dr. Charles Fowler, Edward T. Bradner, Matthew Park, William Park, James Thomson, David Elliot, Jephtha Williams, Samuel Arnott, Samuel Wright, William Shaw, William J. Shaw, Francis Wallace, J. Morrison, Nathaniel Fleming, M. Roney Fleming, William Fleming, Reuben Frazer, John Cochran, Robert Fleming.

ARGYLE. This settlement of Covenanters is now known as the congregation of West Hebron, Washington County, New York. It is east of the city of Albany and near the Vermont line. It is probable the first Covenanters settled in this vicinity, and that of Cambridge, as early as 1755, but as to their names and numbers nothing is definitely known. The Rev. John Cuthbertson first visited them in August, 1764, and preached at the house of Mr. Ephraim Cowan. He baptized Edward, son of William Selfridge; and Martha, daughter of Oliver Selfridge. From the amount of visiting he did in this neighborhood, it is probable there was quite a respectable society. In 1766, Mr. Cuthbertson visited them again and passed over into Vermont and New Hampshire. On his third tour in 1769, Mr. Cuthbertson constituted a session, and William Selfridge and John McClung were ordained ruling elders, October 22, 1769. He also spent some time in visiting among the people in September, 1774, in October, 1775, and in November, 1779. The principal members at this time were Ephraim Cowan, Samuel Clark, William Selfridge, Oliver Selfridge, John McClung and Phineas Whiteside. The latter had some time previously removed from Pequea, Pennsylvania. The organization continued for over fifty years without a settled pastor. In August, 1825, a call was made upon the Rev. James W. Stewart, which, being accepted, he was duly ordained and installed the first pastor of the Argyle congregation, October 13, 1825. The small congregation was poor in this world's goods, and it had great difficulty in raising the meagre salary.* Pews were auctioned off to the highest bidder, and often the pastor had to forgive a portion of the stipends in order to secure the remainder. Soon the little congregation was rent into factions as the New School controversy agitated the Church, and for sundry reasons Mr. Stewart was released from the charge in April, 1832. At a meeting of the session held November 15, 1832, and the last in which Mr. Stewart moderated, a petition was prepared and ordered to be forwarded to Synod, requesting that court to take the congregation from under the care of the Northren Presbytery and place it under the Western. Against this action elders William Shaw and Samuel Jackson protested, and these were the only members of session who adhered to the principles of the Church at the division of 1833. The whole congregation went with Mr. Stewart into the New School body. They held the church building, and after running it in debt for supplies, sold it back to the few faithful Covenanters who held the Testimony intact. Less than a half dozen Covenanters resorted to the praying societies, and occasionally enjoyed a day's preaching. In May, 1862, one of these elders died, and Argyle lost its organization. They embraced an opportunity to sell the old church at Argyle and bought the present church property near the village of West Hebron. The New York Presbytery re-organized them as the West Hebron congregation in August, 1866. Fourteen members were found in regular standing and

* From notes by Rev. J. A. Speer.

13

thirteen others united by profession of faith. They liberally supported the gospel, repeated their call for a pastor nearly every year, and trusted that in due time the Lord would send them an under-shepherd. In this they were not disappointed. The Lord heard their prayers and gave them a pastor. The Rev. James A. Speer was duly ordained and installed, July 28, 1875, and was the only pastor since 1832. He is now in charge. The congregation now owns a substantial and comfortable church property free from debt. For over fifty years previous to 1825, and for forty-three years since 1832, these people maintained the unpopular principles of the Covenanter Church without a pastor with a heroism and faithfulness without a parallel in history. Some of the old members of Argyle are Dr. David Lister, Eli Gifford, James Shaw, William Shaw, Henry Mehaffay, Alexander Mehaffay, James Stewart, John McQueen, John Selfridge, William Dennison, George Keys, John McNeil, James F. Mehaffay, John Dennison, Samuel Jackson.

TROY. This city contained a society of Covenanters as early as 1818, and was visited with supplies with LANSINGBURGH in Rensselaer County. Dr. Christie of Albany frequently preached here, and Troy and Lansingburgh were given an organization in 1828. Rev. Robert McKee was the first and only pastor, installed in 1830. In 1835, he connected with the Presbyterian Church. These places were supplied with preaching by Presbytery until 1848, when the field was abandoned. Peter McKinnon and Robert Campbell were elders.

ALBANY. Covenanters resided in the city of Albany as early as 1760. In August, 1764, the Rev. John

Cuthbertson came to this city from Wallkill, Orange County, and preached. He also visited the city in 1766 and 1769. He usually preached at the house of Mr. John Boyd,* with whom he lodged while remaining in the city. In the latter part of the past century supplies were given by the Revs. James McKinney and William Gibson, and, after the formation of the Reformed Presbytery, by other ministers. The society was organized into a congregation in 1815. The first pastor was the Rev. James Christie, D. D., who was settled in this city in the spring of 1822. He also conducted a Grammar School in connection with his ministerial duties, and was regarded as a preacher and educator of considerable influence in Albany. The church stood in Waterloo street. Dr. Christie demitted the charge in 1830. The people were not long in securing a pastor, for the Rev. James R. Willson, D. D., was installed the same fall. Here was a field for the display of his great powers as a preacher and writer, and he at once inaugurated a battle against the wickedness of the city and the ungodliness of the State legislature. In the fall of 1833, Dr. Willson resigned the charge and returned to Coldenham. For three years the small, but active, congregation was in a distressed condition. In the spring of 1836, the Rev. David Scott was installed pastor and remained in this capacity six years. He demitted the charge in the spring of 1842, for the people were not able to sustain a pastor of his ability and keep up the other expenses of the congregation. The field was supplied

---

* Cuthbertson's Diary.

with preaching for many years, but gradually by emigration and death, Covenanterism has become extinct in Albany. The family of the great Rev. James McKinney lived and died in this city, and other members were Robert Trumbull, M. J. Johnston, Samuel Graham, Robert Campbell and James Frazer.

MOHAWK VALLEY. This is one of the richest and most beautiful valleys in the State of New York. Lying a few miles west of the city of Albany and along the picturesque Mohawk river, are the towns of SCHENECTADY, DUANESBURGH and PRINCETOWN. About 1780, a few families from the Highlands of Scotland settled in this vicinity, and also in the neighborhood of GALWAY, MILTON and BROAD ALBIN. Not far distant were the flourishing societies of GALLOWAY, CURRIESBUSH and JOHNSTOWN. These Scotch people organized themselves into praying societies, and awaited God's time to send them a preacher. No religious society ever embraced a creed with more intelligence, and maintained it with more faithfulness, than these unsophisticated Scotchmen accepted the principles of the Covenanter Church.* In 1793, the Rev. James McKinney came among them and preached alternately in all the societies for about five years. In 1798, his labors were mostly confined to the Duanesburgh and Galway congregations, although he exercised a superintending control over all the societies on either side of the Mohawk. The elders at Duanesburgh were Walter Maxwell, Robert Liddle, John Cullings and George Duguid. Among other leading and influential

---

* Memoir of Dr. A. McLeod.

members were the families of Andrew McMillan, Alexander Glen, John Burns, Robert Spier, Hugh Ross and James Dunse. It is said, moreover, that the families of Andrew McMillan and James Dunse were the only ones in Duanesburgh who held the principles of the Covenanter Church previous to the arrival of the Rev. James McKinney in 1793, but the others soon afterwards embraced them under his eloquent and persuasive presentation of truth.* Mr. McKinney first preached in the old stone church near Princetown, erected by the community but under the control of the Presbyterian Church. He resigned this charge in the spring of 1802, and removed to South Carolina. The first church building erected in Duanesburgh was in 1804. The lot was given by Hon. Judge Duane, and a lot for the parsonage was donated by his daughter. The parsonage was not built until 1829. In the fall of 1807, the united congregations of Duanesburgh and Galway called the Rev. S. B. Wylie, who declined it. In the spring of 1808, the Rev. Gilbert McMaster was called. He accepted, and was duly ordained and installed August 8, 1808. The salary promised Mr. McMaster amounted to twelve hundred and fifty dollars a year and a parsonage. The number of communicants at Duanesburgh was fifty-four. They were an opulent and liberal people. Besides those mentioned previously were the families of William Turnbull, Daniel Stewart, John McCollum, Alexander Liddle, Alexander McFarlan, James McBean, John McClumpha, Charles Tulloch, James Ingersoll, George Turnbull, James Young

---

* Sermon by Rev. S. M. Ramsey, Duanesburgh, 1876.

and Thomas Hays. In 1818, Dr. McMaster resigned the Galway branch and devoted his whole time to the flourishing congregation of Duanesburgh. The first deacons were elected in 1818, and were John Tulloch, John Liddle, James Maxwell, Thomas Kelly and William Cummings. At the division of the Church in 1833, the large majority of the congregation went with their pastor into the New School body. The minority soon emigrated to other parts of the Church and reunited with their brethren.

SCHENECTADY was practically a part of the Duanesburgh congregation until its separate organization in 1831. Rev. John McMaster was installed pastor, January 25, 1832, and the following year, he, and the great majority of the congregation, went into the New School body, and in a few years afterwards the cause declined and finally died out in this learned city. Among the leading members at Schenectady were John Anderson, William Cunningham, Robert J. Brown and James Logan.

GALWAY was a good congregation connected with Duanesburgh until 1818. It was located in Saratoga County, and attached to it were the congregations of MILTON and BROAD ALBIN, in the neighboring County of Fulton. Among the families here were those of McKinley, Adams, Rodgers, Guthrie, Williams, Wilson, Dannon, McQueen, and others. In the fall of 1821, the Rev. Samuel M. Willson was installed the first pastor, and remained among these worthy people six years. In 1829, the Rev. John N. McLeod became the pastor, and held this charge three years, and removed to New York City. In April, 1833, the Rev. Algernon S. McMaster was installed, and in a few months afterwards he and many of the congregation identified themselves with the New School body. The faithful remnant were reorganized, and, in 1835, called Mr. Francis Gailey, licentiate, but he declined. It was regarded as a mission station until recent years. A small congregation of Covenanters was organized in the city of UTICA, Oneida County, in the fall of 1837, and also at NEW HARTFORD, same County, at the same time. These congregations were supplied by Dr. W. L. Roberts, David Scott, and others, for several years, but were finally abandoned. There was also a small society organized at MILFORD, Otsego County, but it never flourished and received little or no attention.

KORTRIGHT. This congregation is situated in the north-eastern part of Delaware County. It was settled in the early part of the present century by emigrants from Scotland. It was long a preaching station and probably received its regular organization as a con- gregation in 1814. In 1820, the Rev. Melancthon B. Williams became the pastor, and remained about ten years. He built up a good congregation of honest tillers of the soil, who afterwards engaged extensively in the dairy business. Mr. James Douglas preached frequently to them, and Mr. Francis Gailey was called to be their pastor. They were a great many years without a pastor, and owe much to the fidelity of elder Robert Spence for the maintenance of the cause during the New School controversy. The Rev. Samuel

M. Willson was installed pastor in the fall of 1845,
and remained until his death in 1864. In 1866, the
Rev. John O. Bayles, the present pastor, was installed.
Among some of the old and leading members at
Kortright have been George Spence, David Orr,
William McCracken, Robert S. Orr, James Spence,
Joseph Spence, Samuel Mehaffay, Andrew S. Gilchrist,
Andrew McNeely, J. W. Kelso, Seth Kelso, Henry
L. Orr, James H. McLowry, Robert Henderson.

BOVINA. This was settled about the same time as
Kortright, by Scotchmen, and is situated some fifteen
miles west of Kortright and at the headwaters of the
Delaware river. It was a preaching station supplied
for many years, and organized into a congregation in
1814. In 1820, it was under the pastoral care of the
Rev. Melancthon B. Williams, who was released from
them in 1823. In 1825, they invited Mr. James Douglas
of New York, who had been licensed in Scotland, to
preach to them. This he did for six years, and, in
1831, received ordination from the True Dutch
Reformed Church and continued to minister to the
people of Bovina until 1847, when he was restored,
his ordination deemed valid, and he was regularly
installed pastor of the congregation. Mr. Douglas died
in 1857, and for four years they were vacant. The
old stone church built in 1825, was now abandoned,
and a new one built in the village of Brushland.
Rev. James T. Pollock became the pastor in 1861,
and, after three years of service, connected with another
denomination. In January, 1865, the Rev. Joshua
Kennedy was installed, and remained with these worthy

people twenty years, when his health failed, and he resigned in the spring of 1885. The Rev. O. Brown Milligan was installed pastor in June, 1887; the church building was refurnished, and under most favorable circumstances the congregation continues its work of saving souls. Some of the old members are Andrew Thomson, William Telford, Daniel Arbuckle, Patrick Sanderson, James Miller, James Russell, James H. Thomson, William Thomson, James Thomson, James R. Douglas, James Dean, John Campbell, David B. Russell, Andrew T. Russell, Andrew Thomson, Jr., A. S. Gilchrist.

WALTON. This is a live young city, and the largest town in Delaware County. In this vicinity Francis Gailey made some disciples in early times. A few families lived in this community and held their membership in the Bovina congregation until the spring of 1861, when they received a separate organization. In 1863, the Rev. David McAllister was ordained and installed the first pastor. He resigned in 1871, and accepted an appointment of Synod to labor in the interests of the National Reform Association, and the congregation was vacant four years. Mr. McAllister was re-installed pastor in 1875, and again released in the fall of 1883, to teach in Geneva College. Rev. Samuel G. Shaw, the present pastor, was ordained and installed in the summer of 1884. In 1874, the old church in .the country was abandoned, and a large and commodious building of more modern architecture was erected in the town of Walton. The congregation is in a healthy condition. Among the representative men of Walton have been D. G. McDonald, R. F. McGibbin,

Henry Easson, James Alexander, Robert Jameson, Calvin McAllister, T. H. Thompson, J. E. Arbuckle, Smith St. John, A. J. Easson.

Not far from the town of Walton was the society of COLCHESTER, in a mining district. This was cultivated by Dr. Joshua Kennedy in connection with Bovina, and at one time contained about twenty-five members.

WHITE LAKE. South of Delaware County and between the Delaware and Hudson rivers is the congregation of White Lake, in the centre of Sullivan County. These people are living amid silver streams and placid lakes, the resort of many a weary New Yorker in the heated season. It is not definitely known at what time the first Covenanters settled in this region, but it was early in the present century. In 1820, the Rev. Melancthon B. Williams preached here as a part of his charge. For about twenty-five years they were a vacancy, and some made defection in 1833. They enjoyed supplies until 1850, when the Rev. John B. Williams, the present pastor, was ordained and installed in charge. Mr. Williams has been an untiring worker and has been a power for good in this community. Among the old families of White Lake have been those of William Pattison, William Stewart, John Tacey, John McClure, Joseph Forsythe, Robert Alexander, David McAllister, Clark Brown, James Frazer, Jacob Dubois.

SYRACUSE. About the year 1840, a few families of Covenanters found a home in this city, to whose spiritual wants the Revs. W. L. Roberts, John Fisher, David Scott, and others, ministered quite frequently.

The little society grew in numbers and faith until they received an organization in the fall of 1849. In the spring of 1851, they succeeded in obtaining the Rev. John Newell for a pastor. He remained but two years, and in 1854, they lost their organization. They were re-organized in 1858, and in the spring of 1859, they again beheld their teacher in the person of the Rev. Josiah M. Johnston. He remained in charge seven years, a part of which time he was engaged in mission work in the South. In 1867, the Rev. John M. Armour became the pastor, and remained six years. In the winter of 1874, the Rev. Samuel R. Wallace, the present pastor, was installed. The church building was erected in 1852, and is a comfortable house of worship. The Covenanters in the city of Syracuse have never been numerous or wealthy, but they have maintained the principles of the Church in a manner which deserves commendation. Of the old families at Syracuse have been those of John McClure, James McClure, Solomon Spier, John Service, William J. Park, William Cannon, James Cannon, Hugh Scott.

ROCHESTER. This city was frequently visited, previous to 1830, by Dr. W. L. Roberts who preached to a few families who had removed hither. The congregation was organized in the summer of 1831, and the Rev. John Fisher, of York, was in charge for four years. In the spring of 1837, the Rev. Charles B. McKee became the pastor, and also conducted a flourishing classical school. He was released from this charge in the summer of 1842. In the summer of 1844, the Rev. David Scott, who had often supplied the congregation, became the pastor and remained until the summer of 1862. In the spring of 1863, the Rev. Robert D. Sproull was installed pastor, and was released in October, 1880, when he left the communion of the Church. In the spring of 1881, the Rev. John Graham was ordained and installed in charge, and is the present efficient pastor. Recently the old church on North Union street was sold, and a beautiful and convenient church on Alexander street was purchased and refitted for worship. Rochester has had some worthy members, of whom have been Angus McLeod, John Campbell, Hugh Mulholland, James Edmonds, Robert Knowls, David Dorn, Samuel Gormley, Robert Kyle, David Logan, James Montgomery, Robert Willson, William Marshall, James Campbell, Hugh Robinson, Hugh McGowan, Robert Aiton, James Aiton, Abraham Ernissee, Thomas S. Linn, Joseph B. Robinson, James Keers, Thomas Logan, Simon Cameron, John Boyd, Thomas Percy, James S. Peoples.

BUFFALO. A few families of Covenanters residing in this city were supplied with preaching for some time, and organized into a congregation in 1838. They made out several calls but none were accepted. They continued steadfast in their endeavors to build up a Church, and while they did not enjoy the labors of a settled pastor, supplies were almost constant. A small church building was erected in 1849. Mr. George G. Barnum was the leading spirit in founding a Covenanter Church in Buffalo, and to whom the Church is much indebted for his public spirit and unceasing interest. Failing in their righteous attempt the church property was disposed of with much reluctance and difficulty.

'YORK. The congregation of York, in Livingston County, together with GALEN and CALEDONIA, originated from the preaching of the indefatigable pioneer and missionary, the Rev. James Milligan. As early as 1815, he began preaching in the Genesee Valley, and the congregation was organized in the fall of 1823.* The first elders were ordained at that time, and were James Guthrie, Sr., James Guthrie, Jr., James Milroy and James Cullings. The communion was dispensed at the same time by the Rev. William Sloane. Dr. W. L. Roberts was the pastor for part of his time from 1826 until 1830. Rev. John Fisher was installed as the first pastor of the York congregation, July 21, 1831. He preached in two school houses, three miles apart, and equally distant from the village of York. In 1834, a commodious church was erected, and this was occupied until 1872, when the present large and better building was completed. Mr. Fisher died in the summer of 1845, after a successful pastorate of fourteen years. In the winter of 1846, the Rev. Samuel Bowden was installed the pastor. The congregation grew rapidly under his ministrations until his release in 1876. Some internal troubles arose soon afterwards when he was recalled, and he left the communion of the Church, with some others. The breach, however, was healed, and in the fall of 1882, the present pastor, the Rev. W. C. Allen, was ordained and installed. The names of Milroy, Guthrie, McMillan, Gay, Logan, Cowan,

* R. P. & C., 1872, p. 85.

McCracken, Donnan, Hart, Morrow, Jamison, Cullings, and others, have long been connected with the cause in that region.

STERLING. Sterling, Cayuga County, and CLYDE, Wayne County, were long supplied with preaching and organized into a congregation in 1823. Dr. W. L. Roberts became the first paster in 1826, and remained until 1830, and preached in different localities which became societies and congregations. He was re-installed pastor of Clyde and Sterling in the fall of 1837, and released in 1855. The following year the Rev. Matthew Wilkin became the pastor, and was in charge until 1867. For three years they were vacant. In the summer of 1870, the Rev. S. R. Galbraith was installed pastor, and resigned in the following year to accept an appointment as a missionary to Syria. Four years they were without a pastor. In the fall of 1875, the Rev. T. J. Allen was installed, and remained twelve years. He built up a good congregation and many improvements were made in the church property. In 1883, the Sterling manse was burned with the furniture and library of Mr. Allen. Another parsonage has been erected. Mr. Allen resigned in June, 1887, and the Rev. J. C. B. French was ordained and installed pastor, January 12, 1888. Among the leading members have been James Hunter, John Hunter, Hugh Crocket, Samuel Cox, Alexander McCrea, John B. Crocket, M. W. Calvert, John McCrea, Robert McInroy.

LISBON. This congregation is situated north of the centre of St. Lawrence County, New York, and near the St. Lawrence river. The first Covenanter family

settling in this region was that of Mr. William Coleman, who came from the Kellswater congregation,
Ireland, in 1820.* In 1823, a society was formed,
which met at the house of Mr. John Smith, and was
composed of the families of William Coleman, John
Smith and William Glass. They had no public preaching until 1830. In 1828, Mr. William Coleman learned
from Ireland the address of the Rev. J. W. Stewart
of Argyle, New York, and Mr. William Craig, a
member of the Associate Reformed Church, wrote to
Mr. Stewart, but got no reply. Soon afterwards, Mr.
John Smith wrote and got an answer from Mr. Stewart
in February, 1829, who promised to send them a
preacher. This messenger came in the person of the
Rev. James Milligan, in the spring of 1830, who organized a society and dispensed the sacraments. In
the fall of 1832, Rev. J. W. Stewart, who had been suspended by the Northren Presbytery for defection from the
attainments of the Reformation, came and organized a
society in March, 1833, without authority. He, with
elder John Smith, withdrew and identified themselves
with the New School body in August, 1833. When the
deception of Mr. Stewart was exposed, and the proceedings of the division of the Church were published,
the misguided brethren tried in vain to destroy the
publications in order to keep the people ignorant of
their defection. Many of the people now returned to
the Church and were visited by Rev. James Milligan
in 1837. They began to be regularly supplied with
preaching by John Holmes, Dr. W. L. Roberts, and

* Extract from Sketch by Rev. W. McFarland.

others. In October, 1840, Rev. John Fisher of York, and elder John Campbell of Rochester, regularly organized the congregation and admitted thirty-four members. They were now supplied by William Neill, W. L. Roberts, John Middleton, and others. A church building was erected, but the property, in passing through the civil courts, was illegally conceded to the New School body in 1843. In 1845, a new church building was erected, and in the winter of the previous year, the Rev. John Middleton was ordained and installed pastor, and resigned in 1854, on account of the deacon controversy. In the summer of 1856, the Rev. James McLachlane, formerly a Scotch missionary to Canada, was installed pastor, and for eight years he taught and maintained the principles of the Church with fidelity. He died in 1864. For seven long years the congregation was a vacancy. Several calls were made and declined. The present pastor, the Rev. William McFarland, was ordained and installed in charge, May 18, 1871. Among those who have borne office in the Lisbon congregation are John Smith, William Glass, James Ballantine, John McCullough, John Coleman, John Hargrave, Charles Gillespie, elders ; and John Campbell, John Aiton, William W. Glass, James Smith and John C. Glass, deacons. The congregation is in a good condition, and Reformation principles are faithfully presented in the region of the St. Lawrence.

NEW JERSEY.

Perth Amboy. In 1685, George Scot, Laird of Pitlochie, was given his liberty in Scotland provided he transported to East Jersey many of the Covenanters who had refused to take the oath of allegiance to a tyrannical and profligate ruler. Thus authorized, he proceeded to gather his company from those confined in the tolbooth of Leith. He had to give security to land them there prior to September, 1686, and the penalty was to be five hundred merks in case of failure in any instance. In May, 1685, Scot chartered the "Henry and Francis" of New Castle, a ship of three hundred and fifty tons and twenty great guns, with Richard Hutton as master. On the eve of their banishment, twenty-eight of them signed the following conjunct testimony, bearing "That now to leave their own native and Covenanted land by an unjust sentence of banishment for owning truth and standing by duty, studying to keep their Covenant engagements and baptismal vows, whereby they stand obliged to resist and testify against all that is contrary to the Word of God and their Covenants; and that their sentence of banishment ran chiefly because they refused the oath of allegiance which in conscience they could not take, because, in so doing they thought they utterly declined the Lord Jesus Christ from having any power in His own house, and practically would, by taking it, say, He was not King and Head of His Church and over their consciences. And, on the contrary, this was to take and put in His room a man whose breath is in his nostrils; yea, a man who is a sworn enemy to religion, an avowed papist, whom, by our Covenants, we are bound to withstand and disown, and that agreeably to Scripture:

14

'When thou art come unto the land which the Lord thy God giveth thee, and shalt possess it, and shalt dwell therein, and shalt say, I will set a King over me, like as all the nations that are about me, thou shalt in anywise set him King over thee, whom the Lord thy God shalt choose: one from among thy brethren shalt thou set King over thee: thou mayest not set a stranger over thee, which is not thy brother.'"—*Deut. 17: 14, 15.* They then bore their testimony against the defections of the day, and for preaching in the fields and houses, and then signed their names. As Wodrow has given these names of the banished, we have thought it proper to insert them here. Their names are: ††Robert Adam, *Lady Athernie,*† John Arbuckle,* *Rev. William Aisdale,*† John Black, George Brown, Robert Campbell, David Campbell, John Campbell, William Campbell, Christian Cavie, John Crichton, John Corbet, Andrew Corbet, John Casson, *Agnes Corhead,* Barbara Cowan, Marjory Cowan, *William Cunningham,* Patrick Cuningham, Charles Douglas, William Douglas, Isabel Durie, John Frazer, *Thomas Finlater,* Elspeth Ferguson, Janet Ferguson, Mary Ferret,* John Ford,* James Forsythe,* John Foreman, John Gray, *Thomas Gray, Thomas Graham,* Grisel Gamble, *William Ged,*† Fergus Grier, James Grier, Robert Gilchrist, John Gilfillan,* Bessie Gordon, Annabel Gordon,* Katharine Govan, John Harris,* John Harvie,* John Henderson,* Adam Hood,* Charles Honyall,* *John Hutchinson, John Hodge,*

---

†† REMARK: † Voluntarily left Scotland.   * Left a written protest. Those in *italics* died on the voyage.

Thomas Jackson,* William Jackson, George Johnston,* John Johnstone,† James Junk, John King, *John Kippan*, John Kincaid,* James Kirkwood, *John Kirkland*, John Kellie, *Katherine Kellie*, John Kennie, Margaret Leslie,* Janet Linthron, Gawen Lockhart, Michael Marshall, John Marshall, John Martin, Margaret Miller' George Muir,* *Gilbert Monorg*, Jean Moffat,* John Muirhead, James Muirhead,* William McCalmont, John McEwen, Walter McEwen,* Robert McEwen,* John McQueen,* Robert McLellan, *Margaret McLellan*, *Andrew McLellan*, *John McKenman*, *William McMillan*, John McGhie,* William Nevin,† William Oliphant, Andrew Patterson,* John Pollock, *John Ramn*, Rev. *Archibald Riddell*,† Mrs. *Archibald Riddell*,† *William Rigg*,† Marian Rennie, *John Renwick*, James Reston, *Thomas Russell*, Peter Russell,* Christian Strang,* William Sprat, Agnes Stevens,* William Sproull,* Thomas Shelston, *John Swinton*, *John Smith*, John Seton,* *George Scot*,† *Margaret Scot*,† *Eupham Scot*,† Janet Symington,* James Sittingtown,* John Targat, John Turpine, William Turnbull, Patrick Urie, John Vernor,† Mrs. Vernor,† John Watt, Patrick Walker, *James Wardrope*, Elizabeth Whitelaw, Girzel Witherspoon, William Wilson, Robert Young.* The charge for transportation was five pounds sterling for each adult, and to each of those who were unable to pay for their passage was promised twenty-five acres of land and a suit of new clothes on the completion of four years of service; for children under twelve years of age, fifty shillings; sucking children, free; one ton of goods, forty shillings. These have been known in

American History as "Redemptioners." Many of these
passengers had endured much suffering. After some
delay, the ship sailed from the road of Leith, September 5, 1685. We hear of no untoward event until
after they had turned the "Land's End," when a fever
began to prevail with virulence, particularly among the
prisoners who had been confined in the great vault of
Dunnotter. Many were sick when they came aboard,
and the health of the others was endangered by the
condition of the provisions laid in by the Captain.
The meat began to putrefy and was not eatable. In
a month the fever assumed a malignant type. Few
escaped its ravages, and three or four bodies were cast
overboard every day. Most of the ship's crew, except
the Captain and boatswain, died. Pitlochie, who had
freighted the ship, with his lady, died likewise, and
so enjoyed nothing of the gain of nearly one hundred
prisoners gifted him by the Council, and upwards of
seventy persons died at sea. Death and unwholesome
food were not the only evils the unfortunate Covenanters had to encounter ; the master of the ship
was most cruel to the prisoners. Those who were
placed under deck were not allowed to go about
worship, and when they attempted it the Captain
would thrown down great planks of timber to disturb
them and endanger their lives. The ship sprang a
leak twice, and frequent storms added to their anxiety.
After the death of Pitlochie, the prisoners fell into
the hands of John Johnstone, his son-in-law. Captain
Hutton began to tamper with Mr. Johnstone, and
urged him to carry the prisoners to Virginia or

Jamaica, either place presenting better opportunity for disposing of them than New Jersey, and offered as an inducement to charge himself with the disposal of the prisoners and to account to him for them in the productions of the country. But the wind changed and they were forced to sail straight for New Jersey. They landed at Perth Amboy, New Jersey, in the middle of December, 1685, having been about fifteen weeks at sea. Before going ashore, Johnstone endeavored to stop them by urging them to sign an agreement to serve four years at that place in consideration of the expense incurred by the departed Scot. This they would not agree to, but joined in another protest against their banishment and recounted their harsh treatment during the voyage. When they came ashore, the people who lived on the coast and had not the gospel preached to them, were inhospitable and showed them no kindness. A little way up in the country, however, there was a town (supposed to be Woodbridge), and a minister settled, and the inhabitants were very kind to them. When they learned who the prisoners were and their circumstances, they invited all who were able to travel to come and live with them, and sent horses for the rest, and entertained them freely and liberally that winter. In the following spring, John Johnstone pursued them and had them all cited before a legal tribunal of the Province. After hearing both sides, the Governor called a jury to sit and cognosce upon the affair, who found that the pannels had not of their own accord come to that ship, nor bargained with Pitlochie for money or service, and therefore, according to the laws of the country, they were assoiled. Those who had so agreed had their suits come before the Court of Common Rights, and Captain Hutton was remunerated. The prisoners then scattered throughout Eastern Pennsylvania, New York and Connecticut, where they were kindly entertained and found employment according to their different trades.* At different times the persecuted Covenanters were banished to New Jersey, Delaware and South Carolina, but in the latter part of the seventeenth century this cruelty ceased. At this time no organized society of Covenanters has an existence in New Jersey.

PATERSON. For some years previous to its organization into a congregation, a few families of Covenanters resided in the city of Paterson. They were usually supplied by the students of the Philadelphia Seminary and received the organization in the fall of 1818. The Rev. William L. Roberts was the first pastor ordained and installed in charge in May, 1824. The congregation was small and rent with factions, and he resigned the charge in December, 1825. The Rev. William Gibson took charge of the congregation in 1826, and was stated supply for several years. In 1833, the great majority of the members went into the New School body and the cause gradually declined. The few faithful followers of the Church were supplied but they lost their organization in October, 1836. Of the eldership were James W. King, John McIntire and Thomas Lindon.

---

* Wodrow, Vol. 4, p. 331.

NEWARK. A number of Covenanters residing in this city and holding membership in the congregations of New York City, petitioned for an organization, which was granted, and the Newark congregation was organized, June 17, 1874, with eighteen members. David Houston and William J. Douglass were chosen ruling elders. They were supplied regularly by Presbytery and worshipped in Irving Hall. The Rev. David H. Coulter was installed pastor in December, 1874. He resigned in October, 1875, and for three years they were supplied; but failing to maintain the cause, were disorganized in October, 1878.

DELAWARE.

WILMINGTON. Previous to its organization, the congregation of this city was supplied by students of the Philadelphia Seminary. An organization was effected in December, 1832, at which time Samuel M. Gayley was ordained and installed in charge. In the following year, he, and the congregation, went into the New School body, and, in 1837, over to the Presbyterian Church.

PENNSYLVANIA.

PHILADELPHIA. Early in the eighteenth century Covenanters from Scotland and Ireland settled in the inviting Cumberland Valley in Eastern Pennsylvania, and doubtless some of them resided temporarily in the city of Philadelphia. The first account of any Cove-

nanters in Philadelphia was in 1740,* when a family
by the name of Boyd emigrated from Ireland. Mr.
Boyd died soon after his arrival in this country, and
his family took rooms in the household of James
Rainey, an emigrant from the same country. Mr.
Rainey was furnished Covenanter literature, and, no
doubt, moral suasion by Mrs. Boyd, and he soon embraced the principles of the Church. In 1748, Mr.
Rainey removed to the Wallkill, in Orange County,
New York, and the Boyd family are henceforth unknown to history. After the arrival of the Rev. John
Cuthbertson, the first Covenanter minister that came
to America, we find him preaching in Philadelphia. †
He preached at the house of Mr. George Graham, in
this city, November 26, 1754, at which time he
baptized Jane, daughter of George Graham. In October,
1761, Mr. Cuthbertson accompanied the Rev. Alexander
McDowell to Philadelphia, and the latter preached in
the city. About this time a family by the name of
Galbraith settled in the city, and Mr. Galbraith died
soon afterwards. In 1774, Mr. Thomas Thomson and
his family, from the congregation of the Rev. William
Stavely, in County Down, Ireland, arrived, and social
religious worship was conducted in his house for many
years. In November, 1774, the Rev. John Cuthbertson preached in the city and called upon the Rev.
Mr. Marshall, of the Associate Church. The Reformed
Presbytery met in Philadelphia, November 26, 1774,
and a Committee consisting of Revs. John Cuthbertson, Matthew Linn, Alexander Dobbin, and elder

---

* *Covenanter*, Vol. 1, p. 314. † Cuthbertson's Diary.

William Brown, rectified some irregularities existing among the people. Mr. Cuthbertson again preached to the Philadelphians in November, 1779. In 1784, Mr. John Agnew emigrated from Ireland, and, after a residence of three years in this city, removed to that of New York. In 1788, Mr. John Wallace emigrated from Ireland, but, failing to find any Covenanters, was starting to New York to return to his native land, when, at his lodging place, he providentially met with an acquaintance of Thomas Thomson, and directed him to his house in Camden, opposite the city. Mr. Wallace remained, and he and Mr. Thomson formed a society, which was held in the latter's house for many years. In 1790, the Rev. James Reid, missionary from Scotland, preached in Mr. Thomson's house, and this was the beginning of the Philadelphia congregation. In 1792, the society was augmented by the accessions of Andrew McLure, William and James McGowan, Samuel Campbell and Joseph Sterrett. In 1793, the Rev. James McKinney, from Ireland, came among them and preached. In 1795, the following families were added to the society: John Stewart and Stephen Young from Scotland; and Charles Huston, John Wallace, William Acheson, Andrew Acheson and Samuel Radcliff from Ireland. Mr. McKinney preached to them occasionally in a school house in Gaskill street below Fifth. He now procured a lot in St. Mary's street, above Sixth, and began the erection of a church building. The work progressed very slowly and was not finished until 1803. In October, 1797, the society received a large contribution of members from Ireland,

among which company were the Rev. William Gibson
and family, John Reilly, Thomas McAdam, and Messrs.
John Black and S. B. Wylie, students of Theology.
Mr. John McKinley, a teacher in New Jersey, visited
the society occasionally. Then there came the families
of Joseph McClurg, Hugh Miller and Robert Orr from
Ireland. Rev. William Gibson now preached to them
one half of his time, and the other half in New York.
Rev. William Gibson formally organized the first congregation in Philadelphia in the Gaskill street school
house, January 28, 1798. He brought on elders Andrew
Gifford and David Clark from New York, to constitute
the session. At this time, Thomas Thomson, John
Stewart and Stephen Young were ordained elders of
the new congregation. In May, 1798, the Reformed
Presbytery, which had been dissolved since the coalition of 1782, was constituted in the same school house
by Revs. William Gibson and James McKinney.
William Henry, Thomas McAdam and John Reilly
were ordained ruling elders, August 5, 1801. Mr.
Stephen Young had previously returned to Scotland
and was a bookseller of renown. The first sacrament
of the Lord's supper was dispensed in Philadelphia by
Revs. Alexander McLeod and S. B. Wylie on the first
Sabbath of June, 1802, to about thirty-five persons,
among whom were Mr. and Mrs. Thomas Thomson,
Mr. and Mrs. John Reilly, Mr. and Mrs. William
Henry, Mr. and Mrs. Thomas McAdam, John Wallace,
Catharine and Mary Gilleland, Mr. and Mrs. Service,
Catharine and Jane Service, Miss Hall, Mrs. Kidd, Miss
Creighton, Hugh Miller, James Vertue, Mrs. Gray, Charles

Huston, Mr. and Mrs. James Black, Mr. and Mrs. George Graham, Miss Purvis, John McLean and James Campbell. In the fall of 1802, the Rev. S. B. Wylie was presented with a call from the united congregations of Philadelphia and Baltimore.* He accepted the call on the conditions that he should be allowed to spend a year in Europe, that his pastoral relation should begin on his return, and that at the end of two years he might be at liberty to select one or the other, or neither of the congregations, without further action of the Presbytery. He was duly installed pastor of the united congregations of Philadelphia and Baltimore, November 20, 1803. He found the congregations in both the cities in a feeble condition, although public ordinances had been dispensed as frequently as possible. The edifice in Philadelphia was poor and in an undesirable location. It was thought proper to abandon the old unfinished church. This was not done, however, and the building was repaired and rendered more comfortable. The term of his connection with the united congregations having expired, Mr. Wylie demitted the charges, although he was earnestly invited to remain in Philadelphia. In the fall of 1807, he also received a unanimous call from Duanesburgh, New York, but finally decided to accept the call from Philadelphia, and he was duly installed the pastor. At the next communion twenty-five persons were admitted to Church privileges and the whole aspect of the field became more encouraging. In 1808, John McKinley, James Robinson and Robert Orr were ordained ruling

---

* Pamphlet by Dr. S. B. Wylie, 1847.

elders. In 1809, Mr. John Reilly was licensed to preach and his connection with the congregation ceased. In 1816, the old church in St. Mary's street was sold and a more commodious building was erected on Eleventh street, below Market, and was opened for service, June 21, 1818. In the mean time they worshipped in the Second Associate Reformed Church in Thirteenth street, above . Market. In 1819, Isaac Campbell, John Murphy and Samuel Bell were ordained elders, and, in 1820, Caleb Gray was recognized as a member of session. In 1824, Hugh Hardy, of Ohio, and in 1829, Henry Sterling, of Pittsburg, were added to the eldership. In 1829, the church building was enlarged by utilizing the rooms in the rear of the building. At the division of the Church in 1833, this congregation suffered a great loss because the pastor was the leading spirit among those who withdrew from the communion of the Church. Out of a membership of about four hundred and fifty, three hundred went with the pastor into the New School body, including all the elders, and they retained the church property. Without a session, the faithful Covenanters, who adhered to the principles of the Church, were immediately organized into a congregation by the ordination of Walter Bradford, Joseph Frazer and William Caldwell, ruling elders. They had, previous to the division, become dissatisfied, and purchased a church in Cherry street, below Eleventh, in which the General Synod met in August, 1833. The sacrament was administered on the first Sabbath of December, 1833, to one hundred and forty-five communicants. The Rev. James M. Willson

was ordained and installed pastor, November 27, 1834.
In 1838, deacons were ordained to manage the temporal
affairs of the congregation, and this soon lead to an
unpleasant feeling among a part of the people. The
Second congregation of Philadelphia was organized,
August 10, 1842, and the Rev. Samuel O. Wylie was
installed pastor, December 5, 1844, and, after a long
and successful pastorate, was released by death, August
22, 1883. In October, 1862, the Rev. J. M. Willson
resigned the First congregation to fill the chair of
Theology in the Allegheny Seminary, and the Rev.
T. P. Stevenson, the present pastor, was ordained and
installed as his successor, May 5, 1863. In 1867, the
church in Cherry street was sold, and for two years
they worshipped in halls. In 1869, they worshipped
at Seventeenth and Filbert streets, and for ten years,
and in 1879, the present large and well appointed
church at Seventeenth and Bainbridge streets was
erected. In the winter of 1851, the Third congregation was organized in Kensington, and held their
services in Commissioner's Hall. The following year
the present house of worship was erected on Deal
street near Frankford Avenue. The officers were Robert
Forsythe, Samuel Cameron, W. O. Lindsay, William
White, William Young, William Brown and William
Dunlap. The Rev. A. M. Milligan was the first pastor
installed in December, 1853, and released in October,
1855. Rev. John Middleton was installed in November,
1856, and resigned in May, 1862. Rev. Robert J.
Sharpe was ordained and installed pastor in April, 1866,
and was released in April, 1879. Rev. John M. Crozier

was installed in May, 1880, and released by sudden
death in September, 1881. The Rev. R. C. Montgomery, the present pastor, was ordained and installed,
March 27, 1883. A Fourth congregation was organized in the summer of 1853. In July, 1854, the
Rev. David McKee was ordained and installed pastor,
and after laboring for five years, the congregation was
disorganized and the members returned to the other
congregations. After the death of Dr. S. O. Wylie,
the Second congregation called the Rev. Prof. J. K.
McClurkin, of Westminster College, who was ordained
and installed pastor, October 9, 1884. The old church
building was taken down, and the handsome edifice
in which they now worship was erected. Mr. McClurkin
resigned the charge, August 25, 1887, to accept the
chair of Theology in the Allegheny Seminary. Among
other prominent members identified with the cause of
the Reformation in Philadelphia have been of the *First
Congregation*: Walter Bradford, Joseph Frazer, John
Ford, John Service, Matthew Mackie, William Craw-
ford, John Evans, Samuel McMahon, Henry Floyd,
Samuel McMullin, William White, John Alexander
William Young, David Smith, William Dunlap,
William Echols, James Dunlap, James Stevenson, Robert
Keys, William W. Keys, Hugh Lamont, John Wright,
William Carson, William McKnight, Robert Patton,
William Anderson, Matthew McConnell, Andrew Mc-
Murray, John M. Graham, James Crawford, Hugh
Graham, Samuel Irwin, Hugh Lilly, John Marshall, John
Lyons, John Cunningham, William G. Carson, Charles
Pullinger, Daniel Morrison, T. S. McDonald, James

Patterson. Of the *Second Congregation*: William Brown, Ebenezer Craig, Charles Craig, John Caldwell, George Orr, James Anderson, David Eccles, John Brown, Ezekiel Sterritt, Robert Sterritt, Samuel Fulton, James McKnight, William Walker, Thomas Walker, James Carlisle, J. B. Stewart, Thomas Brown, William Stewart, James Keys, Samuel Patterson, D. J. McIlhatton, William J. Ferguson, James McKee, William Lackey, William Walker, Jr., Robert Clelland, Dr. A. Caldwell, Robert J. Jamison. Of the *Third Congregation*: William Cochran, Alexander Mackie, Samuel Cameron, Adam Lindsay, William O. Lindsay, Robert Forsythe, William Young, Hugh Lamont, Thomas Laughlin, James Blair, William Steele, William McHatton, Hutcheson McCandless, Joseph Service, A. J. H. Mackie, George Alexander, John Grier, Joseph Steele, John McQuigg, Thomas J. Crozier.

CUMBERLAND VALLEY. The Commonwealth of Pennsylvania has no more productive region within its borders than the Cumberland Valley, extending from Harrisburgh south into Maryland and Virginia; and no section of this valley is richer in agricultural, mineral and manufacturing resources, than the fertile fields, rugged hills and busy towns of Franklin County. Early in the eighteenth century the persecuted Covenanters found an asylum in this inviting region and settled down to the honorable vocation of husbandmen. The principal settlements were along the *Conococheague* Creek, which word, in the Indian language, means "indeed a long way." Settlements were also made along the Octorara, Pequea, Conestoga, Swatara,

and other small streams that flow into the Susquehanna from the east.   These clusters of families scattered all over the eastern part of Pennsylvania had
been trained in the faithful practices of the Covenanter
Church beyond the sea, and did not fellowship with
other denominations in religious worship, but after the
example of their ancestors met at each other's houses
for social worship.   In 1720, a society formed at
Paxtang, Dauphin County, and among the families
were those of McClure, Wilson, Wills, Foster, Gilmore, Gray, Rutherford and Espy.   Still farther north
on the Susquehanna near Milton, Northumberland
County, dwelt the families of Hugh Wilson, John
Boyd and Samuel Brown, as early as 1728.   In 1731,
there were a few families on "The Barrens" in York
County.   In Adams County they settled upon an
immense tract of land in 1736, called the "Manor of
Maske," which was given by the Province.   The
principal settlements were at Octorara, Lancaster
County; Paxtang, Dauphin County; and Conococheague,
Franklin County.   The forefathers of the Willson
family, and the ancestors of the ministers of the
Church by that name, settled in Franklin County
about 1730, and about 1750, removed to the Cove
valley, a little west of the Blue Ridge, and some
twenty-five miles from Chambersburgh.   The McCon-
nells, also, who subsequently became related to the
Willson family, resided in the Cove at the time of
the Indian massacre in 1756.   They all migrated to
the region of the Yough, in Western Pennsylvania,
in 1769.   In the vicinity of Octorara, Lancaster County,

a considerable society of Covenanters had been collected previous to 1740. Rev. Alexander Craighead, a minister in connection with the Presbyterian Church at that place, withdrew from that body because that Church did not ratify the Westminster Standards. Mr. Craighead identified himself with the languishing cause of the Covenanters. He accepted their principles and became their preacher. Had he not done so, those faithful and conscientious Covenanters would not have followed him, neither would they have heard him preach nor received the sacraments from his hands. Mr. Craighead was deeply imbued with the spirit of the Scottish Covenants, and contended earnestly for the descending obligation of Covenants upon all whose ancestors were parties to the same, and insisted upon making the adoption of the Solemn League and Covenant and the National Covenant of Scotland a term of Communion for members of the Church in the Colonies as well as in the mother country. He claimed that the sea did not absolve the relation nor remove their obligation. He testified continually to the Headship of Christ over the Nation, and the responsibility of all rulers to Him; a failure of whose allegiance to Him would forfeit the allegiance of the people to the ruler. He preached these good old Covenanter doctrines with a zeal and courage that commanded admiration, and brought down upon him the censure of the Synod and the odium of the Governor.* On November 11, 1743, Mr. Craighead gathered all the Covenanters together at a meeting

---

* Rev. Dr. A. W. Miller, in Sermon, May 14, 1876, Charlotte, N. C.

15

at Octorara, Lancaster County, and, after various
religious services, he and the congregation renewed
the Covenants—National and Solemn League. After
denouncing George II. as an unfit King, they then
swore with uplifted swords to "keep their bodies,
property and consciences against all attacks; to defend
Christ's gospel and the purity of the Church; to
submit to no ruler who would not submit to Christ,
and to defend their liberty from fears without and
within." This declaration immediately disturbed the
political as well as the religious waters, for Governor
Morris, in his message to the Assembly, denounced
these people for their "aspirations and machinations
to obtain independency."* The following spring another
General Meeting was held, the minutes of which have
been handed down to posterity by Mr. Thomas
Wilson, of Marsh Creek, who was doubtless the
Secretary, and are inserted as a fair specimen of their
proceedings.

"THE GENERAL MEETING.

"*Middle Octorara*, March 4th, 1744.

"The G. M. constituted by prayer. Mr. Creaghead
chosen præs. The following commissioners being present commissionated from their respective correspondents, viz:

"From over Susquehanna, Christopher Houston; from
Paxton, James Mitchel and Andrew Smith; from ye
Barrens, Saml. Jackson and Saml. Hathorn; from Mr.
Creaghead's, Robert Laughead and Josiah Kerr; from

---

* Wheeler's Reminiscences, p. 276.

Muddy Run, John Brownlee and Joseph Bell; from Pequea, Jos. Walker, Neal McNaught and Wm. Ramsey; from Marsh Creek, Thomas Wilson and David Dunwoodie.

1*st*. "It is agreed upon by ye G. M. that no persons are to be admitted into our G. M. except those that are commissionated by their respective C's, except those of our community that have any particular business with the G. M.

2*dly*. "The alteration of our Society Rules that were altered by a committee is approven by the G. M.; the G. M. allows that each correspondent get a copy of ye Rules as they are now altered.

3*dly*. "It is agreed upon by ye G. M. that none of our community hire or employ a papist in our families, or be employed by any papist in their houses.

4*thly*, "It is agreed upon concerning ye Levy that it be paid, until that there be some other end that contradicts our testimony.

5*thly*. "It is agreed upon concerning Phineas Whiteside that Saml. Jackson and Saml. Hathorn go to Mr. Allison's concerning his learning, and to agree for his boarding where most convenient.

6*thly*. · "It is agreed upon by ye G. M. that Joseph Irwin withdraw from ye Society until his case be cleared in respect of ye scandal laid against him.

7*thly*. "It is agreed upon that Mr. Creaghead, John Brownlce and James Wilson are ordered to revise the minutes of our G. M.'s before ye next G. M.

8*thly*. "The G. M. agrees that John Walker was found guilty in ye affair laid against him, in not giving timous warning to Matthew Patterson to attend at ye running out of a line betwixt them.

9thly. "It is agreed upon that each private Society of our community give in their subscriptions for Mr. Creaghead's stipends against our next G. M., and that they make conscience to pay ye same yearly; if any society fails herein, they may expect that ye G. M. will take a particular account of them."

The meeting severely condemned mixed marriages and infairs held at the same, and finished the protracted meeting with lengthy causes of fasting.

Mr. Craighead, however, did not possess stability, and, terminating his connection with the Covenanters in 1749, returned to the Presbyterian Church and removed to Virginia, thence to Mecklenberg, North Carolina, where he died in 1766. The societies were again left in a destitute condition. They returned to the society meetings and prayed for an under-shepherd. In answer to their urgent entreaties, the Rev. John Cuthbertson was sent to the lonely societies in America by the Reformed Presbytery of Scotland. The information of names and places of settlements is taken directly from his diary. He landed at New Castle, Delaware, August 5, 1751, having been forty-six days at sea from Derry Loch. He praised God for His superintending care during the voyage. He first lodged with Thomas Griffith, and the next day rode twenty miles on horse back to the home of Moses Andrews, and on the third day he rode fifteen miles further south to the house of Joseph Ross, near the line between Pennsylvania and Maryland, where he met a

Presbytery (supposed to be the New Castle Presbytery of the Presbyterian Church), and conversed about some difficulties. On Friday, August 9, 1751, he preached his first sermon in America at the house of Joseph Ross. His text was Jonah 2 : 8, "They that observe lying vanities forsake their own mercy." The travels of Revs. Cuthbertson, Linn and Dobbin are so extensive that the societies will be taken in the order of their locations and the names of the early members given under each.

NORTHUMBERLAND COUNTY. On October 21, 1751, the Rev. John Cuthbertson stopped at the Indian wigwam not far from the present town of MILTON and conversed with several persons concerning Church doctrines, and preached at the house of Mitchell Clyde. He remained in the neighborhood and preached the next Sabbath and baptized George, son of James Gray, and Jean, daughter of Mitchell Clyde. Not far distant were the families of George Gray, James Gilmore and James McPherson. At the coalition of 1782, a good many went into the Associate Reformed Church. In 1798, they were again organized, and, in the early part of the present century they were sometimes visited by ministers while passing between Philadelphia and Pittsburgh. An incident is related to show the great value placed upon preaching and the belief in prayer. There had been a long interval during which they had enjoyed no preaching, and, their letters failing to bring a reply, they agreed to observe a fast day and pray for the desired blessing. This they did, and, at the close of the service, one of the devout worshippers was noticed to retire to an obscure place and there he poured out his soul in secret prayer. Another watched for his return to the company, and, as he drew near, his countenance indicated that his prayer was not in vain. To the inquiry, "What speed?" the reply was, "It is neither new moon nor Sabbath, but it shall be well." The same evening the Rev. John Black, of Pittsburgh, arrived on horseback and preached on the following Sabbath.* The society was not regularly organized into a congregation at Milton until the fall of 1830. Previous and subsequent to the organization it was supplied by students from the Philadelphia Seminary. The Rev. William Wilson was installed pastor in the summer of 1832, and the following year he and the congregation became identified with the New School body, and the cause is now extinct.

MIDDLE OCTORARA, LANCASTER COUNTY. There was a society of Covenanters in this vicinity as early as 1740, and here the Rev. Alexander Craighead joined them and lead them in the renewing of the Covenants in 1743. The Rev. John Cuthbertson permanently located here and lived about two miles from the stone church, which edifice was used until 1849, or a period of nearly one hundred years. The grant of one hundred acres of land was made to Rev. Alexander Craighead and his elders, when he ministered to the Covenanter society, by the proprietaries of William Penn, for church and school purposes, and six acres for a grave-yard. The Presbyterians have since held the church property by right of possession, although it was

---

* Dr. Sproull's Sketches.

originally granted to the Covenanters. On August 11, 1751, Mr. Cuthbertson first preached here at the tent three miles from the house of Joseph Walker. He returned from a monthly trip in September, 1751, crossing into Lancaster County near Columbia, and married Robert Love and Rachael Sloane at the river. On Sabbath, September 8, 1751, he preached in the Octorara tent and baptized Joseph, son of Joseph Kincaid; Mary, daughter of Alexander Lackey; Jean, daughter of William Patterson; Hannah, daughter of Robert Galbraith; John, son of Andrew Little; Jean, daughter of Jeremiah Murray; Samuel and Andrew, sons of Joseph Walker; and Mary, daughter of Moses Laughhead. At the house of Robert Laughhead, November 29, 1753, Mr. Cuthbertson presided in an election of ten persons for ruling elders. These were chosen at the General Meeting and were for all the societies. Those for Octorara were Robert Galbraith and Thomas Ramsey, ordained October 20, 1754. At the same time and place, Phineas Whiteside and William Galbraith were ordained for Pequea; John McMillan and John Duncan for Muddy Run, both of whom afterwards removed to York County; and Walter Buchanan for Junkin Tent in Cumberland County. At the communion at Octorara, October 27, 1754, there were five tables and two hundred and sixty sat down and communed. At the next communion on October 19, 1755, two hundred and twenty communed. After the marriage of Mr. Cuthbertson, February 25, 1756, he took up his permanent residence at Octorara and lived the remainder of his life on a farm bought from

Josiah Kerr, which was about two miles from the church. Revs. Alexander McDowell and Daniel McClelland frequently preached here and accompanied Mr. Cuthbertson on his tours. Mr. McClelland assisted at a communion here April 20, 1766, and also on May 31, 1767, but his services were not highly appreciated. After the arrival of Revs. Matthew Linn and Alexander Dobbin, in December, 1773, they frequently preached at Octorara for Mr. Cuthbertson. After the organization of the Reformed Presbytery in 1774, it frequently met at Octorara. After the union of 1782, Mr. Cuthbertson removed to Lower Chanceford, and the Octorara congregation was under the care of the Rev. John Smith. Mr. Cuthbertson was buried in the Lower Octorara graveyard. Nearly all the Covenanters of Octorara went into the Associate Reformed Church in 1782, and continued in that relation until 1823, when, on its own application, the congregation was received by the Associate Presbytery of Philadelphia. In 1858, Octorara went into the union and is now a United Presbyterian congregation.* Covenanterism is totally extinct in this region. The following were heads of families and members of the Covenanter Church at Octorara previous to 1774: Joseph and John Walker, William Robinson, James, Robert and Moses Laughhead, William Dunlap, Arthur Scott, Joseph Kincaid, Daniel and David McClelland, Alexander and Samuel Lackey, William and Thomas Patterson, Thomas Paxton, Robert Galbraith, Josiah and Joseph Kerr, Andrew Little, Thomas and Robert

---

* Aikin's Sketch of Cuthbertson.

Ramsey, James Wilson of Nottingham, Henry Coulter, John Neilie and Joseph Wishart.

MUDDY RUN. This society was situated about four miles from the present town of McCall's Ferry, on the Susquehanna river. The first log church was built previous to 1750. The first visit they enjoyed from a Covenanter preacher was on October 2, 1751, when the Rev. John Cuthbertson preached in the log meeting house. At this time he baptized Agnes, daughter of John Reed; Joseph and Margaret, children of Joseph McMillan; and Agnes, daughter of Peter Patterson. John McMillan and John Duncan were ordained ruling elders, October 20, 1754. Among the principal families were those of John Reed, Peter and John Patterson, John Brownlee, Joseph and John McMillan, John Duncan and William Mitchell. In 1782, the society went into the Associate Reformed Church and subsequently into the Associate Church. At the present time a few United Presbyterians hold an organization.

PEQUEA. This society was located about sixteen miles north of Octorara in the Pequea valley. It is not probable that the Covenanters had a house of worship here, but held the services in the neighboring house of Humphrey Fullerton. The Rev. John Cuthbertson visited the society August 14, 1751, and the services were four hours long. He held a communion here August 24, 1755, at which one hundred and ninety persons communed, and the services were ten hours in length, conducted without any assistance. At a meeting held October 20, 1754, Phineas Whiteside and William Galbraith were ordained ruling elders; and on October 4, 1767, Humphrey Fullerton, Thomas Girvan, James Ramsey, Cornelius Colins and John Robb were added to the session. The union between the Seceders and Covenanters was culminated here in 1782, and the majority of the Covenanters went into the Associate Roformed Church and under the pastoral care of the Rev. James Proudfit. Among the early Covenanters of this society were the families of Humphrey Fullerton, Matthew McClurg, Neil McKnight, Robert McCurdy, Thomas Montgomery, John Boyd, Phineas Whiteside, Cornelius Colins, William Galbraith, Alexander Lackey, James Ramsey and John Robb. There was a Covenanter living there as late as 1830, a Mr. McGill, and for several years the Rev. James Douglas of Bovina, New York, would come once a year and preach for the godly old man, who would harness up his one ox in his cart, place a chair in it, and drive the minister around among the hills of Brandywine, and give the people an opportunity to hear a good Covenanter sermon.*

DONEGAL. Mr. Cuthbertson frequently stopped and preached here at the house of the widow Carson when on his way between Pequea and Derry.

COLERAIN. This was the home of Mr. Daniel McClelland, and was situated about eighteen miles from Lancaster. Mr. Cuthbertson preached here occasionally, and, on September 24, 1751, he had a protracted public debate with a Mr. Craighead. It is not known what the dispute was about, but Mr. Craighead was won over to Mr. Cuthbertson's views. There

---

* Aikin's Sketch.

were probably but five places of preaching in Lancaster County; the principal ones being Octorara, Muddy Run and Pequea.

PAXTANG, DAUPHIN COUNTY. This society was situated about four miles east of the present city of Harrisburgh. Covenanters settled here as early as 1740, and were holding society meetings. The Rev. John Cuthbertson first visited them August 15, 1751, and lodged at the house of William Brown. He baptized Eliza, daughter of Andrew Stuart; Helen, daughter of Matthew Taylor; and Mary Ann, daughter of Joseph McKnight. A communion was held August 25, 1754, and about two hundred and fifty communed. Mr. Cuthbertson says that an awful thunder storm, accompanied by fearful lightning, occured during the blessing of the elements, and that four horses and a dog were killed, and a tree shattered by lightning not more than forty yards from the tent. On the following Sabbath, Mr. Cuthbertson had some unusual appearances of death. William Brown, Henry McCormick, Thomas Mitchell and Benjamin Brown were ordained ruling elders, February 24, 1771. While visiting the society in November, 1772, Mr. Cuthbertson was prevented from preaching on account of a great storm. In the spring of 1773, elder William Brown was sent to Ireland as a commissioner to procure two additional ministers and was especially instructed to get, if possible, the Rev. Matthew Linn, of Aghadowey. He was successful, and Mr. Alexander Dobbin, specially licensed and ordained for this purpose, accompanied him to America. The first Reformed Presbytery in

America was constituted in this place, March 10, 1774,
and the Rev. Matthew Linn was then placed in charge
of Paxtang and adjacent societies. After the union of
1782, the cause gradually declined and finally became
extinct. Among the early families connected with the
Paxtang society were those of William, James, Alexander and Benjamin Brown, John Graham, Andrew
and Alexander Stuart, George Williams, Matthew and
John Taylor, Bartholomew Hains, Joseph McKnight,
Joseph and John Mien, John Chambers, John and
Henry McCormick, Thomas and James Finney, Alexander Swan, John Thorn and Thomas Mitchell. When
the war of independence was over, the German population
literally crowded out the Scotch-Irish, and, in a few
years, Covenanterism was completely exterminated.
The old log church was thus disposed of: "On September 11, 1795, James Byers and James Wilson executors
of William Brown, Esq., deceased, of Paxtang, offered
for sale a log house near the residence of Mr. Brown,
and formerly occupied as a house of worship by the
Rev. Matthew Linn." It was subsequently used as a
sheep pen and but recently disappeared.

DERRY. This society was located about nine miles
east of Paxtang and was first visited by the Rev.
John Cuthbertson in September, 1751, when he preached
and lodged at the house of David McNair. In October,
1751, he returned and preached, and called at the
house of Alexander Swan, on the Blue Mountain near
by, when he baptized James, son of John Thomson,
and Agnes, daughter of Alexander Swan. The principal
families here were those of John Thomson, Alexander

Swan, Thomas Montgomery and David McNair. They mostly worshipped with the people at Paxtang.

LOWER CHANCEFORD, YORK COUNTY. This place is situated about twenty-two miles southeast of the city of York, and in the section of country known as "The Barrens." The Rev. John Cuthbertson preached at Chamber's tavern, York, December 9, 1751, and three days afterward preached at Chanceford, at the house of William Wilson. The first baptism here was that of George, son of John Buchanan, April 15, 1752. He frequently visited this society, for it was a large one, and ordained William Gabby and Daniel Sinclair ruling elders, March 27, 1771. After the organization of the Reformed Presbytery in 1774, this society fell under the charge of Mr. Cuthbertson with Octorara. During the last few years of his life, Mr. Cuthbertson preached principally in this society and generally at the house of William Maughlin. His last sermon was preached here September 20, 1790, and he died in the following March. . The names of the principal members previous to 1774, were William Wilson, George, John and William Buchanan, Hugh Ross, William Smith, James Anderson, Robert Greer, Samuel Dickson, Elizabeth Ayers, Joseph and John Brownlee, William Fullerton, William Young, Samuel Nelson, John McMillan, William Maughlin, William Nichol, Samuel Hawthorn, Daniel Sinclair, John and Robert Duncan, William Gabby, John Marlin, Daniel Sloan, John Reed, John Patterson, William Mitchell, Alexander Ewing and George Henry. At the union in 1782, the whole congregation went into the Associate Reformed Church, and, in 1858, into the United Presbyterian Church.*

ROCK CREEK, ADAMS COUNTY. The old church stood about one mile northeast of the present site of Gettysburgh. It was early erected and was used until 1805. There were a few Covenanters here previous to 1750, and they had a tent about two miles from David Dinwiddie's, who lived near Marsh Creek. In some of the early records the society was termed Marsh Creek, but the organization was known as Rock Creek, and subsequently as Gettysburgh. When the Rev. John Cuthbertson came to this country from Scotland in the summer of 1751, he was accompanied by a colony of Covenanters, among which was his brother-in-law, Archibald Bourns, who married Wattie Cuthbertson. They settled at the base of the Blue Mountains on "The Tract," near Gettysburgh. The descendants of the family are now in connection with the Conococheague congregation. The names of Archibald, John, Jeremy and Anthony Burns were long connected with the history of Covenanterism in that region. The Rev. John Cuthbertson visited this vicinity immediately after his arrival in this country. He first preached in the tent about two miles from the house of David Dinwiddie, September 1, 1751. At this time he baptized Jean, daughter of Thomas Anderson; Isabel, daughter of Robert McCullough; Rose Ann, daughter of Joseph Hutchison; James, son of Joseph Broomfield; and Mary, daughter of David Dinwiddie. On November 3, 1752, Mr. Cuthbertson bought one hundred acres of

* Aikin's Sketch.

land situated between Marsh Creek and Antietam. David Dinwiddie and Jeremiah Morrow, father of the late Governor Morrow, of Ohio, were ordained ruling elders, April 8, 1753. It is probable that the Rock Creek congregation was regularly organized at this time. The Rev. Alexander McDowell assisted Mr. Cuthbertson at communion seasons, and this congregation made out a call for him, October 12, 1761, which he declined. John Murphy and Andrew Branwood were added to the session, May 16, 1764. At the organization of the Reformed Presbytery in 1774, the Rev. Alexander Dobbin assumed the charge of this flourishing congregation. Previous to 1774, the principal members of this congregation were Archibald Bourns, David and Hugh Dinwiddie, Jeremiah Morrow, John Watt, Thomas Wilson, Joseph Little, Thomas Anderson, Neil McKnight, Robert McCullough, Thomas Neillie, Joseph Hutchison, Mary Silbuck, Joseph Broomfield, John Murphy, Mary Mair, Robert Stevenson, John Crook, Alexander Patterson, Andrew Branwood, John Finney, James Blackburn, John and William Morton. At the union of 1782, with a few exceptions, the whole congregation went with Alexander Dobbin into the Associate Reformed Church, and, at the union in 1858, it became a United Presbyterian Church, now located in Gettysburgh. The ground then occupied by the Covenanter congregation of Rock Creek has now become historic as the Gettysburgh battle field and the National Cemetery.

CUMBERLAND AND FRANKLIN COUNTIES. The societies in these Counties are so intimately connected both in location and history that they will be considered together as the branches of a single congregation known to-day as "Conococheague." The following were the places of preaching in Cumberland County as early as 1750: Junkin Tent, West Pennsboro, Big Spring, Carlisle, Stony Ridge, Newville and Shippensburgh. In Franklin County the societies were Lurgen, Roxbury, Strasburgh, Southampton and Greene, Scotland, Rocky Spring, Fayetteville, Guilford, Greenwood, Green Castle, Shady Grove, Waynesboro, Mercersburgh and Hamilton. At these different places there was usually a tent, consisting of a simple stand with a shelter over it, under which the minister stood, and a board set in between two trees for a rest for the Bible. The people most probably had some rude seats or logs on which to sit in front and around the preacher. In later times the services were held in orchards and barns, until meeting houses were erected for the purpose. Since the union of 1782, most of the Covenanters resided in Franklin County and built churches respectively in Greenwood in 1817; in Scotland in 1825; and in Fayetteville in 1840. JUNKIN TENT, in Cumberland County, was a preaching place in 1751. It was first situated on the farm of Joseph Junkin, near the present town of Kingston, about nine miles from Carlisle, and eleven miles from Harrisburgh. The tent was afterwards removed one mile west to the farm of James Bell, who was a ruling elder. The Rev. John Cuthbertson first visited this place, August 20, 1751, and stopped at the house of Walter Buchanan. He preached the following day and baptized Joseph, son of Joseph Glendenning; John, son of Joseph McClelland; and Jean, daughter of Henry Swansie. Mr. Cuthbertson held his first communion in America at this tent, August 23, 1752. A preparatory fast day was observed, tokens of admission to the table were distributed, and the services on the Sabbath lasted nine hours. He paraphrased the Fifteenth Psalm and preached from John 3: 35. After the sermon he prayed fervently and the people sang a Psalm. He then expounded the words of institution, fenced the tables, and the communicants came forward singing the Twenty-fourth Psalm. After four tables were served he gave a parting exhortation to the communicants. After an interval of half an hour, he preached from John 16: 31. On Monday he preached from Ephesians 5: 15. About two hundred and fifty communed and they were gathered from all parts of the country. To many it was the first time they had gathered around a communion table in America. No doubt it awakened memories of other days and scenes across the sea, and their tears were mingled with joy and gladness. Such tangible evidences of the tender care of the Good Shepherd strengthened every heart and quickened every grace as they sang that triumphant song which so often sustained and cheered their ancestors on the moors of Scotland : —

> God is our refuge and our strength,
> In straits a present aid ;
> Therefore, although the earth remove,
> We will not be afraid.

The communions were dispensed yearly in the

16

principal societies and the majority of the members attended each one. Walter Buchanan was ordained a ruling elder, October 20, 1754. Previous to 1774, the following were the principal members at Junkin Tent: Walter Buchanan, Joseph Junkin, John Leiper, Samuel Gay, James McKnight, William and Isaac Walker, Joseph McClelland, Henry Swansie, Samuel and Adam Calyhoun, Joseph Gardner, Robert Bonner, Alexander Lafferty, David Mitchell and William Rose. After 1774, the Rev. Matthew Linn had charge of this station, and, in 1782, the great majority went into the Associate Reformed Church. The faithful remnant joined with the societies in Franklin County.

CARLISLE. This was a preaching station visited by the Rev. John Cuthbertson, November 10, 1751, when he preached at the house of Joseph Patterson, and baptized Robert, son of Horace Bratton. Other members were Andrew Griffin, Frank McNeickle, James McClelland, William Patterson and Alexander Young. There was preaching at BIG SPRING, situated about four miles from Newville, at the house of Andrew Ralston, August 22, 1751. On November 12, 1751, Mr. Cuthbertson preached in the Pennsboro meeting house near by, and baptized several children. After 1774, Rev. Matthew Linn had charge of this society. Among the leading members at that time were Andrew Ralston, Robert Gibson, Samuel Calhoun, James McClurg, Andrew Giffin and Charles Kilgore. In 1782, they all went into the Associate Reformed Church, and, in 1858, into the United Presbyterian Church, and at the present time there is a large and flourishing congregation of the latter body in Newville.* Previous to 1774, the principal preaching places in Franklin County were Rocky Spring and Green Castle. ROCKY SPRING was situated about four miles northeast of Chambersburgh, and the tent was near the home of George Mitchell. Mr. Cuthbertson preached here, August 24, 1751, and the people got up a subscription paper for preaching. He baptized Andrew and Moses, sons of James Mitchell; James and Eliza, children of James Lowry; Martha, daughter of James Thomson; Sarah, daughter of Joseph Mitchell; and Rebecca, daughter of Joseph McClurg. George Mitchell was ordained a ruling elder April 8, 1753. The leading members of the Rocky Spring society were Andrew, James, George and Joseph Mitchell, John McCleary, James and John Lowry, James Thomson, John Wylie, Joseph McClurg, David Carson, James and Joseph Reed, John Sharp, Joseph Espy and Thomas Cross. The majority of the members went into the union of 1782, and it is due to the memory of Alexander Thomson and John Renfrew to say that they kept the Covenanter cause alive and maintained the principles of the Church. Among other faithful ones at this time were William Galbraith, the only ruling elder, Thomas Paxton, James Finney, Thomas Cross and Sarah Morrow. They organized a society which is the original of the present Conococheague congregation. In 1751, Mr. Cuthbertson visited a few families living in the vicinity of GREEN CASTLE, among whom were those of George Reynolds, George Clark and Samuel McColloch. They went into

* Dr. J. B. Scouller.

the union of 1782, and Matthew Linn was the pastor
of the Associate Reformed Church in that place.   After
the disastrous union of 1782, the faithful Covenanters
of Franklin and Cumberland Counties gathered themselves into a General Meeting, which was usually held
at the house of Alexander Thomson, near the present
village of Scotland.   Alexander Thomson, to whom more
is due than any other man for keeping the old blue
banner from trailing in the dust, deserves a passing
notice.   He was a Scotchman, and sailed from Greenoch
in July, 1771, and arrived in Boston, September 10,
1771.   A Scotch colony was being organized for
Caledonia County, Vermont, while numerous others
were going to settle in South Carolina.   He considered
the valley of the Kittatinny the most inviting, and
removed thither in 1773, purchasing five hundred acres
of land, embracing the site of the present village of
Scotland.   These Covenanters here settled on the
Conococheague Creek and built saw, grist and sickle
mills.   The house of Alexander Thomson was the
meeting place for worship and business, and where all
the distant members found hospitable entertainment.
The following were the

RULES OF ORDER FOR CONGREGATIONAL MEETINGS.*

I.   Let the meeting be constituted by prayer.

II.   Let the former Presis (or the Clerk in his
absence) call for the Commissions.

III.   Let a Presis be chosen by a vote of the

---

* For many of these hitherto unpublished documents the author was
under obligation to the late Samuel Rea Burns, of Scotland, Pa., whose
ancestors came with Rev. John Cuthbertson to this country in 1751.

meeting: the former Presis taking the votes beginning on his left hand, and in case of his absence let the Clerk of the meeting proceed in the same manner, and ye person having a majority of votes shall be Presis.

IV. Let the Presis then take the chair; call the meeting to order, and call upon the Clerk to read the Rules.

V. Let the Presis then pose the members with the following queries: 1. Do you carefully and conscientiously attend upon social meetings with your brethren both on Sabbaths and week days when deprived of more public ordinances? 2. Are you punctual and conscientious in maintaining the worship of God in your family morning and evening in all the parts thereof; and also secret prayer at the same seasons regularly? 3. Have you observed the last day of Fasting or Thanksgiving (as the case may be)? 4. Do you endeavor to adorn the doctrines of Christianity by a life and conversation becoming the gospel, and are you in habits of peace and friendship with your brethren of mankind? And are you satisfied upon inquiry that the members of your society duly attend the above duties?

VI. Let the Clerk read the minutes of the preceeding meeting and let unfinished business be taken up in order.

VII. Let the Presis enquire if there is any more business to come before the meeting, and when it appears there is no furthur business, let him put the question, "shall the meeting be concluded?" And if carried, let the meeting be concluded by prayer. 1. During the time the meeting is constituted, let no person withdraw from the house without the consent of the Presis. 2. Let no conversation be among the members. 3. Let each member speak to the question under consideration in rotation, beginning on the left of the chair, and let each speaker stand and address the Presis. 4. Let no motion be taken under consideration until made and seconded. 5. The above Rules shall be altered or amended from time to time as the Meeting may judge proper.

FURTHER RULES.

1. The most punctual attendance to the time of meeting; all the members being careful to assemble precisely at the hour appointed, and if any shall be absent after the constitution, he shall be censured, unless his reasons be sustained by vote of the court.

2. After the constitution the first thing to be done is the reading of the minutes of the last sederunt.

3. Unfinished business is always to be taken up as first in order.

4. All papers presented to the court shall be filed in the order in which they are read, being properly numbered and endorsed accordingly.

5. Every proposition or question which appears to be warmly litigated shall be stated in writing by the mover thereof and given to the Presis.

6. No motion can be admitted unless it be previously seconded.

7. No personal reflections are in any case to be

suffered, whether they respect members of the court or others.

8. A becoming gravity is to be observed by all the members; no whispering is to be admitted, but a close attention is to be paid to the matter in hand.

9. All prolix and declamatory harangues are to be avoided; the speaker confining himself exclusively to the question.

10. No person shall be allowed a silent vote; but all the neutrals shall be viewed as voting with the majority.

11. In taking votes, the Presis shall begin with the youngest members and proceed according to juniority. [Sometimes they blind-folded them.]

12. No speaker is to be interrupted, except he be out of order, or to correct mistakes or misrepresentations.

13. The votes by which a decision is made, shall not be recorded unless at the request of one-third of the members.

14. No member may leave the house without the permission of the Presis.

15. No member is to return home so as not to attend the termination of that session, without the consent of two-thirds of the court.

16. The Clerk shall keep a faithful record of every decision made by the court; the minutes of it shall be read while the matter of it is fresh in the memory of the members.

17. The Presis shall determine all questions of order that shall arise during the session, and his decision shall be submitted unto, unless it appears by

an appeal to the court a majority is against him.

The following is inserted as a form of commission to the General Meetings :

"We, the society of *Guilford*, being met and constituted by prayer, do appoint and commissionate *Anthony Burns*, being one of our number and free from public scandal so far as known to us, to go to the Congregational Meeting, to be held at the house of Alexander Thomson, on *Wednesday, April 17, 1790,* and there in our name to consent and agree to every thing in agreeableness to the Word of God and Reformation Principles as attained to by the Church of Scotland particularly between the years 1638 and 1649, inclusive. Signed in our name and by our appointment.

"JOHN RENFREW, Presis.

"THOMAS DUNCAN, Clerk."

For eight years after the defection of 1782, the faithful Covenanters and witnesses for Christ in this region were left as sheep without a shepherd. In 1790, they were cheered by the visit of the Rev. James Reid of Scotland. On August 17, 1791, a number of persons wishing to adhere to Reformation attainments, met at the house of Alexander Thomson and constituted themselves into a social capacity and entered into the following resolutions :

1. "It was resolved that two societies for prayer and Christian conference be erected to meet at such convenient times and places as each society shall from time to time agree upon, and that a General Meeting be held at this place on the third Wednesday of October next.

2. "It is resolved that any person of a character unknown to this society desiring to become a member, shall bring a certificate from the society he has been in communion with heretofore; or in case he hath not been in communion with any, then he shall bring a *character* from his reputable neighbors."

On October 19, 1791, a large delegation was present at the General Meeting, and, among others, the following resolution was passed:

"It was resolved that the Rev. James Reid's former letter be further pressed by John Renfrew and Robert Kidd who were in correspondence with the Scottish Presbytery."

These societies were endeavoring to secure the services of the Rev. James Reid for pastor, but in this they were unsuccessful. In the spring of 1793, the Rev. William King, who had the year previously emigrated to South Carolina, visited them and preached; and, at a General Meeting held August 17, 1793, they resolved to "lay out money which belonged to the meeting, and which amounted to £10. 14s. 10d., for defraying the Rev. William King's expenses in coming to visit them and laboring among them; considering it as agreeable to the intention for which the money was collected." In the spring of 1794, the Rev. James McKinney, recently from Ireland, visited them, and they were so well pleased with his labors that in October, 1794, they sent the following petition to the Reformed Presbytery of Ireland to have him transferred and settled in Conococheague:

"*To the Remnant members of the Reformed Presbytery, to meet when and wherever this may reach you*:

"The humble petition of the Old Covenanters in the Counties of Cumberland, Franklin, and parts adjacent, humbly sheweth that your petitioners are, and have been, for a long time in a very destitute condition as to the Gospel being administered among us according to what we judge to be the pattern showed us in the Mount; and having had the opportunity of having heard a member of your court, viz: the Rev. James McKinney, for some time past; and we hope his labors have not been entirely without their use among us, and that if he was to be settled in these parts, he might still be farther useful in calling the attention of this sleepy generation to their duty. We do, therefore, through your medium, invite him to remain and abide with us as our pastor, if you shall see meet to lose him from his pastoral relation in Ireland; and hope in such love that you will instruct the Committee here what measures they are to adopt in order to bring said settlement to a regular Presbyterial issue. We having at present no session, and being in a very scattered situation, cannot be supposed to write so formally as might otherwise be expected. But we are convinced that you, as a court of Christ, will stand when there is no formality in a matter of this kind. Our situation is, at the present, extremely pressing and loudly calls for aid from our brethren in Britain and Ireland. Mr. McKinney himself, who has been among us, can, and we hope will, more fully represent these matters to you than we

can at present pretend. In case you should see cause
to dissolve his pastoral relation in Ireland and consent
to his settlement among us, we hope we shall yield
all dutiful obedience to him in the Lord, and afford
such worldly support to him as our circumstances
will admit of, not doubting but he will sympathize
with us and be willing to bear his share in the
difficulties which at present effect us, until the Lord
shall be pleased to render us somewhat stronger,
which we hope might be the case in a short time
if the Lord was pleased to give us a fixed pastor;
and, in the meantime, earnestly desiring the advancement of the Redeemer's Kingdom with you, sym-
pathizing with you under the yoke of civil oppression,
we pray that in this our particular request, and in
all your other deliberations, you may be guided by
the blessed Head till you and us meet in that blessed
General Assembly where the Lord God and the Lamb
Himself will be our common lamp.

"Signed in the name of our General Meeting, and
by their order, by

"WILLIAM GUTHRIE, Presis.

"JOHN THOMSON, Clerk.

"*Conococheague, October, 1794.*

The sum subscribed amounted to about £25, and the
list was signed by the following persons: Alexander
Thomson, John Renfrew, John Thomson, William
Erwin, James Stevenson, Thomas Paxton, Thomas
Duncan, John Steel, Jr., John Steel, Sr., John Guthrie,
John Walker, William Guthrie, William Crow, George
McClure, John Ewen, Samuel Patterson, David Cowan,

David Dickey, John White, Finla McClure, William Speer, William Paton, Alexander McHaffy and Samuel Sterling. The following were the eight societies composing the General Meeting: Green and Southampton, Guilford, Green Castle, Mercersburgh, Strasburgh, Big Spring, Hamilton and Newton. At a meeting held at Alexander Thomson's, September 15, 1795, the following persons from the different societies were present and endeavored to effect the permanent organization of a congregation with the expectation of having the Rev. James McKinney as the pastor: William Galbraith, John White, John Renfrew, William Guthrie, John Walker, John Steel, John Stevenson, Alexander Thomson, William Love, Robert Davidson, Anthony Burns, Thomas Duncan, John Guthrie, Thomas Paxton, William McCrea, William Speer, John Busel, David Busel and John Thomson. The following were chosen elders: John Renfrew, William Guthrie, John Thomson and William Speer. At a meeting held April 20, 1796, a petition was received from the societies west of the Allegheny mountains desiring a part of Mr. McKinney's time. For one-half his time the Conococheague people agreed to pay Mr. McKinney at the rate of £125. annually. They did not give up the hope of securing Mr. McKinney, and continued their petitions each year, until he settled permanently in Duanesburgh and Galway, New York, in 1797. When Thomas Donnelly, of South Carolina, began to preach in 1799, he delivered about his first sermon at the Red tent near Carlisle, and was greatly lacking in confidence. He kept his eye constantly upon his little

Bible, scarcely looking his audience in the face at all. An old lady who heard him that day, on being asked after the sermon what she thought of the young preacher, she replied, "He did pretty weel; but he read ower muckle." The congregation was formally organized by a Commission of the Reformed Presbytery in 1802, by the election of John Thomson, William Guthrie, John Renfrew and James Bell, ruling elders. The first sacrament of the Lord's Supper was dispensed April 17, 1803, by Revs. William Gibson, Thomas Donnelly, John Black and Alexander McLeod. It was not until August 12, 1816, that they enjoyed the stated labors of a pastor, and, at that time, the Rev. Robert Lusk was ordained and installed in charge. His time was thus divided: "One-fourth time at Newville and Walnut Bottom; one-fourth at Shippensburgh; one-fourth in Green township; one-fourth at Lurgen and Waynesboro, days for other places to be taken out of the whole as occasion may serve." At this time the elders were John Thomson, John Renfrew, John Steel and John Scouller. About this time a log church was erected at Greenwood, and in 1818, the Roxbury society was added to Shippensburgh. The Synod of the Reformed Presbyterian Church met here in 1819. In 1821, several aggravated cases of *occasional hearing* came up before the session for adjudication, and two ladies were severely admonished for attending a Methodist camp-meeting at Shippensburgh on a week day. The ministry of Mr. Lusk was neither a happy nor a prosperous one, and, on account of certain monetary difficulties he was released from the charge,

October 15, 1823. The people then invited the Rev.
Samuel W. Crawford to supply them. On January
26, 1824, the Rev. John Gibson, of Baltimore, moderated
in a call which was unanimous for Mr. Crawford.
The following were the signers of the call: John
Renfrew, John Thomson, John Steel, Jeremiah Burns,
John Brown, Samuel Renfrew, John Renfrew, Jr.,
Alexander Thomson, Hannah Thomson, Mary Gill,
Ann Morrison, Ann McCloy, Nancy Renfrew, Sarah
Steel, Martha McCloy, Rebecca Steel, Elizabeth Ritchie,
Ann Thomson, Nelly Ann Steel, Samuel Hays, William
Stevenson and Samuel Thomson. The salary promised
was $300 in regular half-yearly payments. Mr. Craw-
ford accepted the call and was duly installed pastor
August 26, 1824. His time was thus divided: one-
third time in Waynesboro; one-third at John Renfrew's;
one-third at John Thomson's, and one day at James
Kennedy's near Green Castle. In 1825, the present
stone church at Scotland was erected. Mr. Crawford
resigned the charge in May, 1831. During the controversy and division of the Church in 1833, but a
few members left the Church. For eleven years they
remained without a pastor, notwithstanding repeated
efforts were made to obtain one. In 1840, the present
brick church in the town of Fayetteville was erected,
and the preaching services were principally held here
and at Scotland. In the winter of 1842, the Rev.
Thomas Hanna, recently from Scotland, was installed
pastor. His labors were well received but interfered
with by ill health, and he resigned the charge in the
fall of 1844. In the fall of 1845, the Rev. Joshua

Kennedy was ordained and installed pastor. He revived
the cause in Cumberland County and the congregation
flourished under his ministrations. The elders at that
time were James Kennedy, John Renfrew and Samuel
Thomson. In addition to his pastoral work, Mr.
Kennedy opened a school for both sexes in Fayetteville in the spring of 1852, called the "Fayetteville
Academy and Seminary." At the close of the first
year, the female department was suspended for a time
until a large and commodious building was erected on
the same ground by a company of stockholders. The
school possessed a corps of efficient teachers and was
conducted successfully until 1860, when Mr. Kennedy
resigned the school and congregation and went as a
missionary to Florida. The school was discontinued
during the war, the building was sold and is now
used for a private dwelling.* Since 1860, the Conococheague congregation has never enjoyed the labors of
a settled pastor. For twenty-eight years they have
been a vacancy, but have enjoyed almost constant
supplies. At different times the congregation has
suffered in the reduction of its members by emigration.
The old people have passed away by death, and,
without a pastor, the young and baptized members
have not remained in the Church. Centering at the
Fayetteville church, with occasional preaching at Shady
Grove and Scotland, there are about thirty members
in full communion. The elders are John Kennedy and
Robert McCoy. Some of the members live a great
distance from the church, but at the communion

* History of Franklin County, Pennsylvania.

season each summer they all gather around the Lord's table and renew their vows of loyalty to Jesus after the customs of their fathers.

FULTON COUNTY. There was a society at Licking Creek and Cove, in this County, near the Franklin County line and about ten miles west of Mercersburgh, as early as 1748. It was sometimes called Timber Ridge. The Wilson family were the principal members, who afterwards migrated to Western Pennsylvania. The Rev. John Cuthbertson first visited this society, November 19, 1751, preached at the house of James Wilson, and baptized Hannah, daughter of James McMihan; Martha and James, children of Joseph Martin; George, son of Joseph Cochran; Eliza, daughter of John Wilson; and Elizabeth, daughter of James Wilson. James and George Wilson were ordained ruling elders April 8, 1753, and John Cochrane was added November 11, 1770. Among the members in this vicinity previous to 1774, were James, John, Joseph and George Wilson, Robert McCullough, Joseph Martin, James Irwin, James McMihan, Robert and Adam McConnell, John and Joseph Cochrane, Joseph McMeehan and James McClelland. On account of emigration this society was discontinued and the few remaining members worshipped with the societies of Franklin County. The Rev. Joshua Kennedy, D. D., of Green Castle, has, through his father-in-law, Mr. James Bell, some of the original tokens used by Rev. John Cuthbertson and the societies in 1752. They were made of lead, about a half an inch square, with raised letters on both sides. On the one side are the letters "R. P.," and on the other, "L. S., 1752." Mr. Kennedy also possesses the book-case used by the Rev. James McKinney. The fertile Valley of Cumberland once occupied by numerous and thrifty Covenanter societies, at the present time contains but the two branches of one small congregation worshipping at Fayetteville and Shady Grove. While the Thomson and Renfrew families were for over one hundred years connected with the Church in this region, it is sad to relate that not one by the name of Thomson is now in connection with the Church there. The West has presented strong inducements to many and while the cause is diminishing in the Cumberland Valley, the Head of the Church is stretching forth the curtains of her habitations in the boundless country beyond the Mississippi even to the foot of the Rocky Mountains.

BRADFORD COUNTY.

BALLIBAY. In the early part of the present century a few Covenanters settled along the Susquehanna and Wyalusing rivers, in Bradford County, and not far from the New York line. They were occasionally visited by a passing minister, but were not organized into a congregation until the winter of 1832, when, according to the appointment of the Southern Presbytery of the Eastern Subordinate Synod, the Rev. David Scott organized them into the Wyalusing congregation by the ordination of William Gamble and William Morrow, ruling elders. In 1833, Mr. Gamble and some of the members went

17

into the New School body and the congregation was
disorganized. Mr. Morrow and the remnant continued
faithful to the principles of the Church. For some
time they enjoyed the labors of Mr. Francis Gailey,
licentiate. They appreciated his labors, and, in 1838,
when he withdrew from the Church and proclaimed
himself the only faithful representative of the Covenanter Church, he readily won their confidence and
they all followed him. Under his ministry they adhered
to Reformation principles, read their Bibles and the
old authors, but were lead to believe that all Churches
had ceased to be Churches of Christ by apostacy.
In 1859, having previously failed to obtain
ordination from any branch of the Christian Church,
Mr. Gailey wickedly assumed ministerial functions and
rebaptized all his followers. This opened their eyes,
and, finding that the Covenanter Church had been
basely misrepresented, they abandoned him and sought
a return to the Church of their fathers. Being far
distant from any congregation they were not cared
for until some had died and others had connected
with other denominations. A Commission of the New
York Presbytery, met at Ballibay, September 30,
1868, and received eight persons into Church privileges, among whom was Robert Morrow, the only
surviving member of the original organization. The
society was organized into the Ballibay congregation,
August 28, 1875, by the ordination of Dr. F. G.
Morrow and Richard Graham, elders, and John Branyen
and Newton J. Morrow, deacons. There were seven
members in good and regular standing, and twelve

persons were received by profession of their faith. A liberal subscription was raised for preaching and a request granted for the moderation of a call. In 1877, they called Mr. Robert McKinney, licentiate, who died before any action was taken. By emigration, death and defection the congregation was reduced, and disorganized, June, 1886.

INDIANA COUNTY.

CLARKSBURGH. About the year 1820, Richard Wasson and Andrew Stormont, emigrants from Ireland, settled near Kelly's station in this County.* They waited on the ministrations of the Rev. John Cannon, of Greensburgh, and requested him to come over and preach in this vicinity, which he did on week days. Before any church was built, Mr. Cannon usually preached in the barn of John Coleman or in the orchard of James Gray. About 1825, an organization was effected in connection with New Alexandria and Greensburgh, called Black Legs, but afterwards changed to Clarksburgh. The first elders were Moses Thomson and Robert Henry. The first church was erected in 1831. Among the early members of the Church at Clarksburgh are: Robert, John and Mrs. Margaret Henry, Moses Thomson, David, Robert and Alexander Henderson, John, Robert and William Coleman, James Gray, Thomas, James and Ann Gailey, Andrew, Samuel and Jane McCreery, Daniel Euwer, Samuel Gilmore, Nancy White, John McCurdy, John Morrison, Thomas Gemmil, James McKelvy, Mrs. Martha Smith, Nathan Douthett, Samuel

* History of Indiana County, Pennsylvania.

and Mrs. Frances Barr, John and Mrs. Kirkpatrick and Mrs. Kimball. The Rev. John Cannon continued to preach here until his death in 1836. For seven years the congregation was a vacancy occasionally supplied, when, in 1843, in connection with Greensburgh, they enjoyed the pastoral labors of the Rev. Samuel O. Wylie, until the fall of 1844. In 1847, the Rev. Robert B. Cannon was installed, and he was released in the spring of 1854. The following year New Alexandria was added to the charge, and, in the spring of 1856, the Rev. A. M. Milligan became the pastor for one-fourth of his time. He was released in the spring of 1866. Clarksburgh received a separate organization, October 8, 1867, and the following autumn they obtained the Rev. James A. Black as the pastor. He revived the work by the organization of a Sabbath School and a Missionary Society. In 1871, the old church was removed, and a handsome frame structure was erected near the old site. Mr. Black demitted the charge in the spring of 1882, since which time the Rev. John J. McClurkin has been stated supply.

BEAR RUN AND MAHONING. These societies are in the northren part of the County and were formerly connected with the Salem and Rehoboth congregations, and were organized into a separate congregation in the fall of 1870. It continued to be supplied by Presbytery until the fall of 1874, when the Rev. John F. Crozier became the pastor, and is in charge. Among the old members here were David White,

Alexander White, John McElwain, James Graham, James Stewart, James Sharpe, Samuel Gilmore.

JEFFERSON COUNTY.

REHOBOTH AND SALEM. For many years previous to an organization, Covenanters scattered into small groups all over this and the adjoining Counties of Armstrong and Clarion. In the fall of 1847, six of these societies were organized into a congregation and it was called "Rehoboth," because they had plenty of room and they trusted that the Lord would make them fruitful in the land. In the spring of 1852, they succeeded in getting the Rev. Robert J. Dodds for the pastor. His labors were very extensive, as his people were distributed over an area of about forty-five miles in length by thirty in breadth, and many of them lived in distant parts of four Counties. Mr. Dodds continued to labor here until the spring of 1856, when he was chosen by Synod as a missionary to Syria. In the spring of 1859, the Rev. Thomas M. Elder became the pastor. The field was too great and his health would not permit of so much travelling. The Presbytery then agreed to divide the congregation, which they did in the fall of 1860. Three of the societies in the southern part of the County retained the name of Rehoboth, and three in the western part assumed the name of Salem. Mr. Elder continued in charge of the Rehoboth branch, and, in the winter of 1862, the Rev. Armour J. McFarland became the pastor of the Salem congregation. Houses of worship were erected in nearly all the branches and the pastors distributed their time

among them. Mr. Elder resigned his congregation in
the spring of 1866, and the cause languished. In 1874,
it was associated with the congregation of Bear Run
and Mahoning, in Indiana County, and has since enjoyed
the faithful labors of the Rev. John F. Crozier. The
Salem congregation grew rapidly under the care of Mr.
McFarland, there being two principal places of preaching—the Bethel branch near Baxter station, and
Belleview in the village of Stanton. Mr. McFarland
was released from the Salem congregation in the spring
of 1882. For five years they were vacant, but enjoyed
almost constant preaching. In the summer of 1887,
the Rev. Harry W. Temple was ordained and installed
the pastor. The names of McFarland, Hill, Campbell,
Millen, Reed, Becket, Hanna, Sterritt, Dill, McKee,
Sharpe, McGiffin, Stewart, Martin, Temple, Wallace,
White, Graham, McIsaac, Fry, and others, have been
connected with the eldership and the best interests of
the cause in Jefferson County.

WESTMORELAND COUNTY.

NEW ALEXANDRIA. The first Covenanter to settle in
this vicinity was Samuel Patterson, who emigrated to
this region in the closing years of the past century.*
In 1800, the Rev. John Black was settled in the vicinity
of Pittsburgh and occasionally preached at Greensburgh.
To wait upon his ministrations Samuel Patterson rode
ten miles, and soon afterward Mr. Black preached twice
a year in Mr. Patterson's house near New Alexandria.
In the course of time small societies of Covenanters
sprang up in all parts of the County and became the

* R. P. & C., 1871, p. 363; 1872. p. 60.

nucleus of the present New Alexandria congregation. A congregation was organized at Greensburgh, by the Rev. John Black, about 1813, and Robert Brown, who did more for the cause in that vicinity than any other man, was ordained a ruling elder. He was a liberal supporter of the cause and his home furnished hospitable entertainment for all the ministers and the members from a distance. Rev. John Cannon became the first pastor in the fall of 1816, and he continued in this relation until his death in 1836. New Alexandria became a regular preaching station in 1819, when the Associate Reformed congregation was a vacancy. A subscription paper was gotten up for ten days' preaching and Mr. Cannon gave them that much time from his labors in Greensburgh. In 1822, a few families from the Associate Reformed and Presbyterian Churches joined the Covenanters, and the congregation of New Alexandria was organized. The Greensburgh church was built in 1823, and Rev. Alexander McLeod, of New York, preached the first sermon in it. After the death of Mr. Cannon in 1836, the Rev. James R Willson was called to the pastorate, but declined. In the fall of 1839, the Rev. James Milligan, of Vermont, was installed pastor. In 1841, Greensburgh joined with Clarksburgh and secured the labors of the Revs. S. O. Wylie and R. B. Cannon until 1854. Mr. Milligan continued his labors in the flourishing congregation of New Alexandria until the year 1848, and, the same fall, his son, the Rev. A. M. Milligan, succeeded him. The latter was translated to Philadelphia in 1853, and for three years New Alexandria, and for two years Greensburgh, were vacancies. In 1855, they were re-united under one charge and recalled the Rev. A. M. Milligan. He accepted, and was installed pastor May 6, 1856. In the spring of 1866, Mr. Milligan was released from the charge. The following year Clarksburgh received a separate organization, and New Alexandria and Greensburgh were regarded as one charge. Rev. Thomas A. Sproull was installed pastor in June, 1868, and was removed by death, April 8, 1878. The Rev. James L. Pinkerton was installed pastor in May, 1881, and, after two years of labor, was compelled to resign the charge on account of bodily affliction. The Rev. John W. F. Carlisle was ordained and installed, June 20, 1884, and released January 26, 1888. An occasional day is given to Greensburgh, but the great majority of the members are in the vicinity of New Alexandria. This congregation has always possessed good houses of worship. The first building occupied was a log church built about 1810, and was used by all denominations as a union church. In 1835, the congregation erected a substantial brick church, which, in 1870, gave place to the present well-appointed building. The old graveyard contains the dust of many a worthy Covenanter who devoted his life to the cause of Christ in this community. Long will be remembered the names of Johnston, Brown, Elder, Stewart, Du Shane, Henry, McClure, Dornon, Beattie, Nevin, Gemmil, Lowry, Steele, Hice, Temple, Purvis, Shaw, Allen, Simpson, Patterson, Thompson, Miller, Cannon and Gray.

BROOKLAND. Under this heading will be included all the societies which have been known by different names, and located in the north-western portion of Westmoreland

County and along the Allegheny River. This is an old settlement of Covenanters.* The pioneer of this region was Robert Sproull, the father of the Rev. Dr. Sproull of Allegheny. About 1796, he emigrated from Franklin County and settled in this vicinity within one mile of the Allegheny River. Here for twenty years he maintained the principles of the Church alone. In 1817, he was joined by David Houston, who married Mrs. Scott, and these families organized a praying society. In 1820, Thomas Sproull, nephew of Robert Sproull and father of Revs. T. C. and W. J. Sproull, acceded to the society. About the same time, John Dodds, father of the Rev. Josiah Dodds, from the Secession Church of Ireland, and, in 1821, John Bole, also from Ireland, strengthened the society by their membership. Revs. John Black and John Cannon supplied them occasionally and they were organized into a congregation in 1822. Rev. Jonathan Gill was the first pastor, installed October 23, 1823. The society grew rapidly, and, in 1830, they were joined by the families of Robert Armstrong, Joseph McKee, James Bole, Archibald Dodds and Joseph McElroy from Ireland. During the unpleasant controversy and subsequent division of the Church in 1833, the congregation was sorely tried and some of the members went with Mr. Gill into the New School body. The congregation as a whole stood by the old flag and maintained the principles of the Church. At this time the elders were Ebenezer Gill, Joseph Cowan, Samuel Milligan, Thomas Dunn and Joseph McElroy. Joseph McElroy was the delegate to the Synod of 1833, and walked the whole

*R. P. & C., 1886, p. 50.

way to Philadelphia to attend that notable session. Rev.
Hugh Walkinshaw was installed in April, 1835. The
congregation then was made up of many branches, and,
at the division of the extensive charge in 1841, both
branches were anxious to obtain the pastor, but he
remained with those on the east side of the Allegheny
until his death, April 19, 1843. During his ministry the
ruling elders were James Dougherty, John Rowan,
Thompson Graham and Robert Euwer. Rev. Oliver
Wylie was installed June 24, 1846. He did not possess
a robust constitution, and was released in the fall of 1851.
During his pastorate the ruling elders chosen were
Joseph Dodds and Samuel Henning. In June, 1854, the
Rev. Robert Reed was installed pastor. The extensive-
ness of the field had been somewhat curtailed by the
organization of new congregations, and, beside the
Brookland charge he ministered to the branches of
Manchester and North Washington. In the Manchester
branch were the Rowans, Hunters, Andersons and
Nelsons. Another society was composed of the Cope-
lands, Boyds, Reeds and Millers. The old log church
was soon abandoned and a handsome brick edifice was
erected. The elders during Mr. Reed's pastorate were
David Armstrong, William Copeland, R. C. McKee,
John Reed, Alexander Miller, John McKee, David
McElroy, Samuel McCrum and A. Dodds. In 1870, the
congregation was reduced nearly one hundred members
by the organization of the Manchester and Parnassus
congregation. The Manchester branch is five miles east
of Parnassus. Mr. Reed continued in charge of the
Brookland congregation, and Middletown in Butler County

was attached to his charge. The Rev. Josiah M. Johnston was installed pastor of the newly organized congregation at Parnassus in June, 1871. He was a popular preacher, but in less than two years he resigned the charge and left the communion of the Church. In June, 1874, the present pastor, the Rev. James C. McFeeters, was installed in charge. Rev. Robert Reed resigned the Brookland congregation in the spring of 1882, and, after receiving supplies for four years, the charge was united to Parnassus under Mr. McFeeters, November, 1886, and the Middletown branch was given a separate existence. The elders are A. B. and S. B. Copeland, R. A. Armstrong, Robert Dodds, John Reed, John Hunter and Alexander Miller. Brookland has furnished the Church no less than eleven ministers, twenty ruling elders and several missionaries.

BUTLER COUNTY.

MIDDLETOWN. This small society is situated about twelve miles northeast of the town of Butler. It was organized about 1825, and was under the pastoral care of the Rev. Thomas C. Guthrie. After 1833, it was under the care of the Slippery Rock congregation and ministered unto by Revs. 'James Blackwood, Thomas Hanna and J. C. Smith. It was known as the Sunbury branch and subsequently as North Washington. In 1869, it was annexed to the Brookland congregation and under the care of the Rev. Robert Reed. He demitted the charge in the spring of 1882, and for four years they only received an occasional day of preaching and the dispensation of the sacrament once a year. In November, 1886, they were given a separate organization. The church is a comfortable frame one situated in the village of Middletown.* Among the old families of this society were the Dunns, Doughertys, Euwers, Barbers, Gills and Osbornes. In later years the leading spirit was John Osborne, whose house was always open for the entertainment of the friends of the cause. The elders are Robert McCracken and Peter C. Young. Henry Blair, Thomas Banks and Mrs. Osborne are also among the loyal members of this congregation.

PINE CREEK AND UNION. This congregation lies principally in Butler County and about thirty miles northeast of Pittsburgh. All the societies lying along the Allegheny and its tributaries were a part of the charge of the Rev. John Black as early as 1800.† In 1807, the Rev. Matthew Williams was installed pastor of these branches northeast of Pittsburgh. They were eight in number and scattered over several Counties. He was almost constantly in the saddle, reaching places of preaching in the then thinly settled courtry, part of which was an almost unbroken forest. In 1815, the congregation was divided, and Mr. Williams now confined his labors more particularly to Pine Creek, Union and Deer Creek. He removed his family to Pine Creek and continued in this field until shortly before his death. The ministry of Mr. Williams was remarkably successful in the gathering of a large congregation, and they were bound together by the closest ties. Often as many as three hundred gathered around the communion table and those were the seasons of festive

* R. P. & C., 1883, p. 20.   † Covenanter, Vol. 3, p. 278.

joy. Mr. Williams had an able session composed of James Magee, John Glasgow, William Wright, Samuel Sterrett, Joseph Douthett, James Miller, Robert Anderson and David Dickey. The original house of worship was very primitive in its style of architecture and simple in construction. It was a log house with a clap-board roof fastened down by cross-beams and had very small windows. They usually had no fire, and one day when it was very cold and a heavy snow upon the ground, no one grumbled, but Andrew Barr remarked at the close of a long service, "We were not troubled with mosquitoes to-day."* In 1826, the Rev. Thomas C. Guthrie became the pastor. In 1833, he and about one-half of the congregation became identified with the New School body. The faithful remnant were now left without a pastor, but for two years were supplied by Presbytery. In 1835, the Rev. Hugh Walkinshaw was installed pastor, and, at the division of the congregation in 1841, he chose the Brookland branch, and Pine Creek was again a vacancy. In June, 1843, the Rev. John Galbraith, who now remains at North Union, was installed the pastor. There were two places of preaching and both became large societies. The elders were John and Robert Dodds, Thompson Graham and James Campbell. In 1870, the societies each received a separate organization and Mr. Galbraith remained pastor of the North Union branch. The Pine Creek and Union branch remained a vacancy for six years. In May, 1876, the Rev. Alexander Kilpatrick, the present pastor, was installed in charge.

---

* Rev. J. B. Williams in *Banner*, 1877, p. 224.

Among the old families in this region were those of the Magees, Douthetts, Glasgows, Millers, Andersons, Creswells, Arbuthnots, Campbells, Wrights, Crowes, Forsythes, McKinneys, Sproulls, Dodds, Deans, Cunning-hams, Gillelands, Sterretts, and others. It is said that Mrs. Penninah Glasgow and Margaret Cunningham were very useful in social meetings and in giving the children instruction in the doctrines of salvation. The people lived in Arcadian simplicity and were noted for their piety and integrity.

VENANGO COUNTY.

OIL CITY. Not a few Covenanters were attracted to this city and region during the oil excitement, and sufficient members being gathered together they were organized into a congregation in the summer of 1865. They then erected a house of worship and asked for the moderation of a call. Rev. David McFall was installed pastor in May, 1871, and remained two years. For ten years it was a vacancy, during which time it was greatly reduced in numbers. They manifested an enterprizing spirit, however, and made out several calls. Uniting with Oil Creek they succeeded in getting a pastor in June, 1884, when the Rev. J. A. F. Bovard settled among them for part of his time. The venerable elder William Magee has been the leading spirit, and among other representative men might be mentioned John Quinn, Joseph G. Garrett, William Thompson, Robert J. Brown and John Love.

CRAWFORD COUNTY.

OIL CREEK. This small congregation is situated seven miles north of Titusville and twenty-five miles from Oil City. The four societies of Perry, Oil Creek, Conneautville and Sugar Lake applied and received an organization, February 14, 1860, and it was called Oil Creek, as this society was the largest and most central. In later years Conneautville received a separate existence as a mission station, and is now defunct. Perry and Sugar Lake were ultimately abandoned, and the preaching was held at Oil Creek, where a small frame church was erected. The Rev. Daniel Reid was installed pastor in December, 1861, and was removed by death in March, 1875. For nine years the con- gregation was occasionally supplied, and, in the sum- mer of 1884, uniting with Oil City, secured a part of the time of the Rev. J. A. F. Bovard. Among the elders and members were R. J. Brown, Hugh McDill, Jacob Boggs, Henry Wright, Marcus Stewart, William Steele, James Moody, Robert P. Randall, Thomas Pollock and George Dunlap.

ADAMSVILLE. This was for many years a mission station, under the care of the Slippery Rock congrega- tion, and subsequently under that of Springfield. It was organized into a distinct congregation in Novem- ber, 1873. By the death of elder Thomas McFeeters the congregation was disorganized in October, 1874, and the members were re-certified to the Springfield congregation. They have a house of worship and are regarded as a mission station. William Blair, William Steel and Thomas Hays were old members.

MERCER COUNTY.

SPRINGFIELD. This was long one of the numerous branches of the Slippery Rock congregation.* As

_____

* Rev. J. C. Smith in *R. P. & C.*, 1885, pp. 147, 172.

early as 1825, those living in this vicinity were
organized into a society, and, in 1828, became the
Mercer branch of the Shenango and Neshannock congregation.   In 1832, the Rev. A. W. Black became
the pastor, who, in 1833, with many of the people,
went into the New School body.   In 1834, the remnant
were attached to the Slippery Rock congregation under
the pastorate of the Rev. James Blackwood.   The elders at
this time were Samuel and William Rodgers, Robert
Allen, Sr., and Robert Allen, Jr.   In 1838, they were
included in the Little Beaver congregation and enjoyed
the labors of the successive pastors of that field.
Springfield, Sandy and Greenville were organized into
a separate congregation in the summer of 1852.   The
first pastor was the Rev. John J. McClurkin, installed
September, 1854, and remained until October, 1873.
In June, 1877, the Rev. James R. Wylie became the
pastor, and resigned April 10, 1888.   Among the elders
may be named William and Samuel Rodgers, Thomas
Barr, William Cochran, William Hunter, Robert and
Cochran Allen, James, S. R. and A. C. McClelland,
J. R. McElroy and J. C. Montgomery.

CENTERVILLE.   This congregation is situated in the
north-west corner of Mercer County and in early times
was the Ryefield branch of the Slippery Rock congregation.   Previous to 1833, it was a branch of the
Shenango and Mercer congregation under the pastoral
care of the Rev. A. W. Black.   In 1834, the Rev.
James Blackwood became the pastor.   The old church
stood in a rye field about two miles from the present
two of Centerville, and was often call the "Granary."

The elders at this time were Joseph Kennedy, Thomas Blair and J. Campbell. In 1852, the Rev. Thomas Hanna became the pastor and continued in this relation for nine years. In 1863, the Rev. J. C. Smith became the pastor, with other branches. In 1867, Centerville and Sunbury (now Middletown) were made mission stations. In 1869, Middletown was attached to Brookland, and Centerville continued a mission station until 1871, when it was attached to the New Castle congregation. The Rev. S. J. Crowe became the pastor in May, 1872. Centerville was organized into a distinct congregation, September, 1879, and Mr. Crowe continued pastor until his resignation in April, 1881, at which time the congregation was attached to that of Springfield. Rev. James R. Wylie was installed pastor in July, 1882, and resigned in November, 1887. The elders are Robert McKnight, William McKee, William Jack and Hiram Snyder. The Kennedys, Blairs, Fishers, and other old families, abounded in hospitality.

LAWRENCE COUNTY.

SHENANGO. The first pioneer in Shenango was Samuel Rodgers who settled here in 1798.* He was soon followed by Hugh Cathcart, Thomas and Samuel Hays, Thomas Smith and William Campbell. They formed a praying society and the Rev. John Black occasionally visited them. Samuel Hays was the ruling elder. The societies subsequently organized at Mercer and Neshannock were associated with this, and enjoyed the labors of Revs. Robert Gibson and George Scott. These were

---

*Wm. Cochran in *R. P. & C.*, 1885, p. 176.

18

organized into a separate congregation, and the Rev.
Andrew W. Black was installed the pastor, January
18, 1832. In 1833, the pastor and the majority of
the congregation became identified with the New
School body and held the church property. Those who
remained true to the distinctive principles of the
Church were the families of Samuel Rodgers, Samuel
Cochran, Reed and William Porter, Charles Love and
George Logan—in all about twenty members. In 1834,
they were associated with the Greenville branch of the
Slippery Rock congregation and enjoyed the labors of
the Rev. James Blackwood. In 1838, they were attached
to the Little Beaver congregation and subsequently
under the pastoral care of Revs. Joseph W. Morton
and Samuel Sterrett. In 1852, they were attached to
the Springfield congregation and under the pastoral
care of Revs. J. J. McClurkin and J. R. Wylie. At
Greenville there are about forty members. In 1865,
the old church building was sold and they worshipped
at Adamsville. Among the old members were William
and Robert Rodgers, William Porter, William Cochran,
Thomas McFeeters, Elizabeth Mathers, Nancy Love,
Jane Porter and Jane McElhaney.

SLIPPERY ROCK. This congregation is situated
principally in Crawford County, and has been known
at different times by different names.* The branches
peculiar to this, and not to other congregations, were
Camp Run, Harlansburgh and Portersville. The first
preaching at Harlansburgh was held in the bar room
of the hotel, and afterwards in the Baptist church,

* Rev. J. C. Smith in *R. P. & C.*, 1885, pp. 147, 172.

until James Martin was *sprinkled*, and then the brethren told them to hunt other quarters. All these branches were under the pastoral care of the Rev. John Black until 1814, when they were included under the Little Beaver congregation. Rev. Robert Gibson became the pastor in 1819, and was released in 1830. In 1831, Rev. George Scott became the pastor, and, in 1833, he and some of the members went into the New School body. In the spring of 1834, the Rev. James Blackwood became the pastor. The elders within the bounds of the present congregation were James Wright and Samuel Sterrett of Camp Run; Thomas Willson and Thomas Speer of Harlansburgh. About 1836, Harlansburgh dropped its name and was known as Slippery Rock and Hautenbaugh. In 1838, churches were built in these places, but the one in Hautenbaugh was never finished and was abandoned. Mr. Blackwood died in 1851. During his pastorate William Wright, Matthew Stewart, John Love and James Anderson were ordained elders. In 1852, the Rev. Thomas Hanna became the pastor and remained in charge nine years. The Camp Run branch was abandoned, and here dwelt the Methenys, Sterretts, Wrights and McElwains. In the spring of 1863, the present pastor, the Rev. J. Calvin Smith was installed. At this time the branches were Slippery Rock, Portersville, Hautenbaugh and Lackawannock. The elders were Thomas and Robert Speer, David Pattison, A. F. Kennedy, Thomas Young, Robert Wylie, Robert McCaslin, J. B. McElwain, George Magee, George Kennedy and Dr. J. M. Balph. In 1871, Hautenbaugh and Lackawannock were included in the New Castle congregation, and Slippery Rock and Portersville now compose the organization. In 1833, Thomas Willson was the delegate to Synod in Philadelphia, and he walked all the way to attend that notable session. Such men as Thomas Willson, George Magee, Dr. Cowden, Thomas Speer, William Boyd, and others, were conductors on the Underground Railway and fearless advocates of the cause of the oppressed slave.

NEW CASTLE. A society of Covenanters was organized in the vicinity of this city as early as 1825, and was under the pastoral care of Revs. Robert Gibson and George Scott. In 1833, some of the members went into the New School body. In 1834, the Rev. James Blackwood became the pastor of the congregation of which this was a branch, and David Pattison was the elder. In 1852, the Rev. Thomas Hanna became the pastor, and during his ministry George Boggs and Robert Speer were added to the eldership. In 1863, the Rev. J. C. Smith began to preach a part of his time in this field and continued in this relation for seven years. The congregation was regularly organized, January 9, 1871. The elders installed at this time were Robert Speer, David and D. C. Pattison. Rev. S. J. Crowe was the first pastor installed in May, 1872, and built up a flourishing congregation. He demitted the charge in April, 1881. The Rev. J. Milligan Wylie was installed in June, 1883, and released in December, 1887. Rev. W. R. Laird was installed pastor in May, 1888. The first church building was erected during Mr. Hanna's pastorate and was then situated in the suburban town of Reynoldsville. It is a comfortable frame building and now within the limits of the stirring city of New Castle. Other elders are William Boyd, Robert McKnight, P. A. Mayne and Dr. T. J. Blackwood.

BEAVER COUNTY.

LITTLE BEAVER. This once widely scattered congregation is now concentrated, and worships in a comfortable church building in the town of New Galilee. As early as 1804, a ·few families were residing within the limits of this County, and in 1805, they were joined by James Cook from Canonsburgh. The society continued to grow and was occasionally visited by Rev. John Black. It was organized into a regular congregation in 1814, and for five years enjoyed supplies. The first pastor was the eloquent Robert Gibson, installed in September, 1819, and for eleven years he continued to draw large audiences wherever he preached, and built up a flourishing congregation. He resigned the extensive field in October, 1830, on account of impaired health. The next pastor was the Rev. George Scott, installed in April, 1831. At the division of the Church in 1833, he, and many of the congregation, went into the New School body, but the remnant retained the church property. This, however, so reduced their members that they were attached to the Slippery Rock congregation.* The elders who stood fast to the principles of the Church were James Cook, John and James Young, and James McAnlis. The Rev. James Blackwood was installed the pastor,

---

* Rev. J. C. Smith in *R. P. & C.*, 1885, p. 147.

with other branches, in May, 1834, and during his pastorate Robert Gray and Robert Gilmore were added to the session. In October, 1838, Little Beaver and the adjacent societies in Ohio, were organized into a separate congregation. The Rev. Joseph W. Morton was installed the first pastor in November, 1845, and was released in June, 1847, when he was chosen as a missionary to Hayti. Rev. Samuel Sterrett was installed pastor in June, 1848, and remained in charge until May, 1860, when Little Beaver became a distinct congregation and he retained the branches in Ohio. For four years they received supplies. Rev. Nathan M. Johnston was installed in April, 1864. He remained in charge twenty-two years, during which time the congregation grew extensively and a new church building was erected in the town of New Galilee. Mr. Johnston resigned the charge in June, 1886, and Rev. James R. Wylie was installed pastor in May, 1888. Among the families long connected with the Church in this vicinity are those of Cook, McAnlis, Porter, Calderwood, Young, Gray, Gibson, Gilmore, Duff, Carson, Qua, Campbell, McGeorge, Dodds, Boggs, Patterson, Acheson and Sharp.

BEAVER FALLS. The first Covenanter preaching in the city of Beaver Falls was given by the Rev. N. M. Johnston in the winter of 1869, when only one member of the Church lived there. This, and the station of Rochester, received an occasional day, and, for some time previous to the organization, Beaver Falls enjoyed services regularly once a month. The congregation was organized November 10, 1874, with twenty-four members, at which time Robert Paisley, John Cook and J. D. McAnlis were chosen ruling elders. Rev. Robert J. George, the present pastor, was installed in June, 1875. The same year they purchased a frame building,. which has since been replaced by the present comfortable and beautiful edifice. Mission and pastoral work have rendered this a most flourishing congregation and a center of influence in the Church. Since the organization, W. R. Sterrett, R. A. and R. J. Bole, and William Pearce have been added to the eldership.

ALLEGHENY COUNTY.

PITTSBURGH AND ALLEGHENY. The vicinity of these two cities was very early settled by an element strongly imbued with Presbyterianism, and a few Covenanters removed into this region from beyond the sea and the Allegheny mountains. The Rev. John Cuthbertson speaks of being in Pittsburgh in the fall of 1779, but mentions no names. Previous to 1797, the most of the Covenanters resided at the "forks of the Yough." In the fall of 1799, and shortly after his licensure, the Rev. John Black was assigned to labor among the societies west of the Allegheny mountains and in the vicinity of these cities. When Mr. Black first came to this part of the country as a preacher, he settled on a farm about twelve miles east of Pittsburgh, in what was known as the Thompson Run society. On the corner of this farm a log church was built and a graveyard surrounded it. He afterwards removed to the city of Pittsburgh, and the property was held by Synod. A congregation centering around Pittsburgh was organized

under the general name of "Ohio," and Rev. John Black
was installed the pastor, December 18, 1800.* The
services at the ordination were held in the old Court
House on Market street west of the Diamond, Pittsburgh, and were conducted by Revs. James McKinney
and Samuel B. Wylie. For two or three years the
congregation worshipped in the old Court House and
also in the Evangelical Lutheran Church at the corner
of Sixth and Smithfield streets. In 1803, the famous
Oak Alley church was built, which stands near Liberty
street and not far from the present Union Depot.
Here the congregation harmoniously worshipped for
thirty years. Among the first corps of elders were
John Hodge, William Gormley, John Armstrong, John
Aikin, John Cowan, James McVickars and Thomas
Smith. In after years there were added to the session
Alexander Harvey and Samuel Henry. At the division
of the Church in August, 1833, Dr. Black, and the
great majority of the members, departed from the
distinctive principles of the Church and went into the
New School body. They also retained the church
property. In fact there were only about thirteen
members who adhered to the principles, and they were
of the poor and less influential of the former congregation. From these few and poor, but true, witnesses
of the Reformation, four large and wealthy congregations have sprung, while the New School brethren are
about extinct in Pittsburgh. The congregation was

---

* Rev. J. W. Sproull in *R. P. & C.*, 1884, p. 173. Memoir of Dr. A.
McLeod, p. 51. *Presbyterian Historical Almanac*, Vol. 2, p. 182 ; Vol. 5, p.
404. Dr. Sproull's Sketches.

re-organized September 9, 1833, with thirteen members. On the first Sabbath of December, 1833, the first communion was conducted by Revs. John Cannon, James Blackwood and Thomas Sproull, and the services were held in the Associate Reformed Church in Allegheny. One hundred and twenty communicants sat down at the table of the Lord, and they were collected from the societies in the vicinity. Samuel Henry and Alexander Harvey were the only elders who adhered to the principles, and they were continued in office in the new organization. Rev. Thomas Sproull was installed the pastor, May 12, 1834. Being without a church building, for two years they worshipped in other churches and halls, and, after a good deal of discussion about a location, they finally agreed to erect a church at the corner of Lacock and Sandusky streets in Allegheny, which they did in 1836. Andrew Gormley insisted that they should erect the church in Pittsburgh, because if they did not they would lose the Oak Alley property which rightfully belonged to them. When the case came into the civil courts and was tried in 1855, Andrew Gormley was found to be correct, and the rightful owners lost the property by a change of name and location. There is something in a name. William Haslett, John Campbell, Hugh Harvey and William Adams were added to the session, October 1, 1836. For thirty years the congregation continued to worship in the old church in Allegheny, during which time James Carson, Robert Adams, Robert McKnight, H. A. Johnston, David Gregg, George Boggs, Thomas Newell, Daniel Euwer, Henry Stewart,

Isaac McKenry, W. C. Bovard, John Boggs and William Wills were added to the eldership. In October, 1865, fifty-eight members were certified to form the Pittsburgh congregation, and Robert Glasgow, Alexander and Robert Adams were chosen ruling elders. Rev. A. M. Milligan became the first pastor of the newly organized Pittsburgh congregation in May, 1866. They worshipped for a short time in the City Hall, and for four years in the Fourth Ward School House on Penn street. In 1870, the present commodious church building on Eighth street, below Penn, was erected. In 1866, Dr. S. A. Sterrett and John A. McKee, and in 1871, Daniel Euwer and Robert McKnight were added to the session. Subsequently Samuel McNaugher and Samuel M. Orr were chosen elders. For nineteen years Dr. Milligan preached with great power and success in Pittsburgh. His health failed in 1884, and he died of an incurable disease in May, 1885. In October, 1887, Rev. David McAllister was installed pastor. The congregation sustains a mission in Allegheny, a school for Chinese and mutes, and has a flourishing Sabbath School. This is one of the largest, wealthiest and most influential congregations in the Church. Among other influential members aside from the eldership are James R. McKee, John R. Gregg, James S. Arthurs, John Tibby, Matthew Tibby, John D. Carson, Dr. William Hamilton, Daniel Chestnut, James McAteer, John Hice, Samuel Sloane, William M. Dauerty, James Martin, John Hanna, John Ross, Robert Carson, Robert Gray. After the organization of the Pittsburgh congregation in 1865, the Allegheny congregation continued to worship in the old church at the corner of Lacock and Sandusky streets, and had about three hundred and fifty members. In December, 1868, they removed to the present large church building at the corner of Sandusky and Diamond streets. Dr. Sproull resigned the charge in October, 1868. For two years the congregation was vacant, and in the meantime a division occurred, resulting in the organization of the Central Allegheny congregation, October 24, 1870. The Rev. David B. Willson was installed pastor of the Allegheny congregation in November, 1870, and they continued to worship in the new church. Rev. John W. Sproull was installed pastor of the Central Allegheny congregation in April, 1871, and they worshipped in the chapel of the United Presbyterian Seminary until the occupation of the present church on Sandusky street below Ohio. Among the elders in this congregation are David Gregg, Robert Gibson, John and Robert Aikin, William Anderson, Hugh McKee, Matthew Steele, John Logan, Henry Stewart, William Haslett and Theophilus Sproull. Rev. D. B. Willson resigned the Allegheny congregation in October, 1875. Rev. J. R. W. Sloane was installed pastor in June, 1877, and continued in this relation, in addition to his Seminary work, until his health failed, and he was released in May, 1884. The Rev. J. R. J. Milligan, the present pastor, was ordained and installed in October, 1885. Among the elders and members in this congregation were John and James Boggs, James B. McKee, Daniel Euwer, John T. Morton, James Best, William Martin, John C. McKee,

Martin Prenter, Robert Morton, Clark Morton, Isaac Taylor, David A. Grier, James McFall, Donald M. Sloane, John Allen, James Patterson, Prof. McAnlis, James Knox, William Boggs. The Central congregation is conducting a mission school at Spring Garden, in the north-eastern part of Allegheny. In November, 1887, a congregation was organized in the East End, Pittsburgh, and a flourishing Sabbath School is being conducted. Among the officers in this new congregation are John C. Calderwood, Alexander M. Denholm, William Blair, J. Calvin Ewing, Samuel Denholm and Thomas C. Johnston. In the congregations of Allegheny and Pittsburgh there are about eight hundred members, closely attached to the principles of the Church, abundant in labors and liberal supporters of the gospel. There is a strong and healthy element of Covenanterism around Pittsburgh, which gives tone to the cause and influence to the Church in that vicinity.

WILKINSBURGH. Mainly through the instrumentality of Hugh Boyd and James Kelly, a house of worship was erected in this village in 1845, and a congregation organized in the summer of 1848. They had formerly belonged to the Pittsburgh and Allegheny congregation, and now included the preaching station of Deer Creek. The Rev. Thomas Hanna was stated supply for some time, and they also enjoyed the labors of the young men of the Church. The Rev. Joseph Hunter was installed pastor in April, 1852, and continued in this relation thirty years. The Rev. W. W. Carithers was installed pastor in June, 1883, and is in charge. The congregation has erected a neat parsonage and soon will build a new church edifice. Among the elders and prominent members in Wilkinsburgh have been James Kelly, Hugh and John Boyd, Robert Bovard, Samuel Henning, Samuel Henry, W. J. Dougherty, Dr. Wadsworth, David Osborn, Hugh Dean, William Wills, William Blair, Thomas Newell, Robert Barr, Thomas Black, A. C. Coulter, William Wylie, W. M. Pierce, James Barron, J. D. McCune, Isaac Kitchen, and others.

MCKEESPORT. For many years this was a branch of the Monongahela congregation, and enjoyed the labors respectively of Revs. John Crozier, J. W. Sproull, T. C. Sproull and W. J. Coleman. It was organized into a separate congregation in April, 1882, and for three years was supplied by Presbytery. Rev. Joseph H. Wylie was the first pastor, installed in June, 1885, and released in June, 1887. The congregation for many years worshipped in a school-house, and a few years ago secured a good church building in an eligible location. Among the members are S. O. Lowry, John McConnell, James Gemmil, Thomas Adams, J. G. McElroy, Knox C. Hill, Joseph Steele, William McCarthy, Joseph L. Stewart, David H. Sarver, James Bell, John Jenkins, William Littlejohn, William McCaw, G. W. Warren.

MONONGAHELA. This congregation occupies a prominent place in the history of the Church, and in early times was distributed over a large area of country lying along the Monongahela and Youghiogheny rivers, some twenty miles south-east of the city 'of Pittsburgh. The central point was the "forks of the Yough," as the space between these two rivers, and for a considerable distance above their confluence, was denominated. Other branches

were Jefferson, ten miles north-east; Redstone, thirty
miles south-east; and Miller's Run in Washington County.
Under "Monongahela" will be considered the history of
Covenanterism principally in Elizabeth Township, Allegheny County.* Perhaps the earliest settlement was in
1769, when James Willson, and his son Zaccheus, left the
Cove Mountain east of the Alleghenies, and settled in
this vicinity. The following year, accompanied by Robert
McConnell, Mr. Willson removed to the "forks of the
Yough." Soon after this they were joined by the
families of Robert and Matthew Jamison, Andrew
McMeans and Matthew Mitchell, and a praying society
was formed. The Rev. John Cuthbertson made his first
and only tour to this region in the autumn of 1779.
On the evening of September 17, 1779, he arrived at
the house of Mr. Simpson, at the "forks of the Yough,"
and on the next day rode to the homes of Colonel Cook
and Zaccheus Willson. On the Sabbath he preached in
a tent on the farm of Zaccheus Willson, and baptized
Mary, daughter of Robert Jamison. On Monday he rode
five miles down the Yough to Joseph Caldwell's and
Joseph Morton's, and on September 21, he preached and
baptized Thomas and Elizabeth, children of Charles
Boal. He also visited James Finney and David Robinson.
On the next Sabbath, September 26, 1779, he preached
at the house of John Drennen, and baptized Susan,
daughter of Josiah Willson; James, son of Aaron Willson;
Hannah, daughter of Joseph Laughead; David and Martha,
children of John Drennen; and Susannah, daughter of
James Patterson. On Monday he visited the homes of

Covenanter, Vol. 2, p. 152.   Cuthbertson's Diary.

Matthew Mitchell and John Reed, on the Monongahela, and then passed over into Washington County. He returned to the house of John Reed on October 3, and preached near by and baptized John, son of John Reed. He then went back to Washington County with John Reed. Mr. Cuthbertson appears to have returned the second time to the "forks of the Yough," preaching to and catechizing fifty persons. He also baptized William, son of Matthew Mitchell; Janet, daughter of Ebenezer Mitchell; Isabel, daughter of John Mitchell. He then went again to Miller's Run. On Sabbath, October 17, he passed this way on his road home and preached, and baptized Martha, daughter of James Finney; Hannah, Sarah and William, children of John Robinson. He then returned to Eastern Pennsylvania and never visited this region again. It would appear from Mr. Cuthbertson's diary that the principal Covenanter families in this vicinity in 1779, were those of James Simpson, Zaccheus, James, Josiah and Aaron Willson, Joseph Laughead, Joseph Caldwell, John Drennen, Thomas Morton, James Patterson, Robert and Matthew Jamison, Andrew Mc-Means, Matthew, John and Ebenezer Mitchell, James Finney, John Reed, Charles Boal, David and John Robinson. At the union of 1782, the whole society, with the exception of the single family of James Finney, went into the Associate Reformed Church. Soon Mr. Finney was joined by the families of John Laughead and Mrs. Parkhill from over the mountains. For ten years they lived without public preaching and maintained the principles of the Church. In 1792, they were cheered by a visit from the Rev. William King, who had recently emigrated to South Carolina. In 1794, the Rev. James McKinney visited them, and aroused such an interest by his eloquence, that as many as three thousand persons gathered to hear him from all parts of the country. In the autumn of 1799, the Rev. John Black, then a licentiate, was sent to the region beyond the Alleghenies. He was ordained in December, 1800, as pastor of all the societies in the vicinity of Pittsburgh, and gave part of his time to Monongahela. John Drennen and Zaccheus Willson returned to the Covenanter Church, and the society was now joined by Samuel Wylie, Benjamin Brown, William Madill, and others. The services were usually held at the house of James Finney, on the bank of the Monongahela. In 1801, the society was regularly organized, and James Finney and Zaccheus Willson were chosen ruling elders. The first communion was held in 1802, and was conducted by John Black and Samuel B. Wylie. The services were held in a grove near the "forks of the Yough," and a large number of communicants from all the western Counties assembled at the feast. Another communion was held by the same ministers on the farm of Samuel Scott, about eight miles south of Pittsburgh, and here the Rev. Samuel B. Wylie preached his celebrated sermons, "The Two Sons of Oil" and "Covenanting."* Soon the congregation so rapidly increased, that, in 1806, Dr. Black divided his extensive charge and continued to supply these people. The session was then increased by the election of Samuel Wylie, John Anderson and William Gormley, ruling elders. In the Redstone settlement were the Parkhills; and at

---

*Dr. Sproull's Sketches.

the "Sanhedrim," or Mifflin society, were the families
of William McElree, James Tennent and David Love.
The first pastor of Monongahela and Canonsburgh was
the Rev. William Gibson, who was installed in the fall
of 1817. He remained in this relation for nine years.
In the fall of 1827, the Rev. Gordon T. Ewing was
installed pastor. His health was very poor and he
resigned in May, 1830, and returned to Ireland. During
the controversy and division of the Church in 1833,
they were left without a pastor, but they were so well
grounded in the principles of the Church, that very few,
if any, left the communion. The Rev. John Crozier
was installed pastor in May, 1834, and remained in
this relation for thirty-one years, and until his release
in April, 1865. Rev. John W. Sproull was installed in
April, 1866, and released in April, 1871. Rev. T. C.
Sproull was the pastor from October, 1871, until May,
1876. Rev. W. J. Coleman was installed in June, 1879,
and released in July, 1881. Rev. John M. Wylie was
installed in April, 1883, and released in April, 1884.
Rev. Robert Reed was stated supply for some time.
By emigration and death, the cause which one hundred
years ago was so flourishing, is now languishing at the
"forks of the Yough." Among the old families and
elders of this historic congregation might be named
Zaccheus and John Z. Willson, Samuel Wylie, James,
William and Robert Finney, Thomas Reynolds, Walter
McCrea, Samuel Rodgers, William, James and David
Parkhill, James Patterson, John Huston, John Elliot, Sr.,
John Elliott, Jr., John and William McConnell, R. C.
McKee and John S. Patterson.

19

WASHINGTON COUNTY.

MILLER'S RUN. Previous to the year 1842, this congregation was a part of Monongahela, and was settled about the same time. The Rev. John Cuthbertson visited "Shirtee" (Chartiers) in September, 1779, and found the families of Alexander McConnell, James Scott, George Marcus and Samuel Willson in this vicinity. He preached at the house of John McGlaughlin and baptized James, son of James McGlaughlin; Francis and John, sons of Matthew McConnell; Sarah and Mary, daughters of Robert Walker. On September 4, 1779, accompanied by John Reed, Mr. Cuthbertson rode to his "Plantation" which he had previously bought. This farm was situated near West Middleton, and was occupied by his son John, who was a physician, and his only daughter lived with him. It was known as the Cuthbertson farm, and the daughter lived there until her death in 1835. After a visit again to the "forks of the Yough," Mr. Cuthbertson preached at the house of Samuel Willson and baptized Elizabeth, daughter of Samuel Willson; John and Margaret, children of Samuel Scott. From this diary it is probable to reckon that the principal families in Washington County, in 1779, were those of Alexander and Matthew McConnell, James and Samuel Scott, George Marcus, Samuel Willson, John and James McGlaughlin, William Patterson and Robert Walker. In 1782, all these went into the Associate Reformed Church and were the nucleus of the present United Presbyterian congregations in that vicinity. In 1794, the Rev. James McKinney visited this region and found a few families of Covenanters who had recently moved in, and organized them into a society. In 1799, and for many years thereafter, the Rev. John Black preached in this settlement. The congregation took the name of Canonsburgh in 1806, and was a part of Dr. Black's charge, but he soon confined his labors to Pittsburgh. In 1808, a log church was erected in the village of Canonsburgh, which had now become famous as the seat of Jefferson College, and a lot for a burial ground surrounded the old church.* In 1809, the Rev. David Graham began to supply them. He was a most eloquent preacher, and, in 1810, they gave him a unanimous call to become their pastor, which he accepted. Before his installation, however, some charges were brought against him, and, in 1811, he was deposed. He joined the Associate Reformed Church for a while, and many of the Covenanters followed him into that body, plainly declaring that they were more attached to the man than they were to their principles. They mostly returned to the faith of their fathers. Among the early families were those of John Slater and Robert George, who have numerous descendants in the Church of that County. Uniting with Monongahela, Canonsburgh succeeded in obtaining the Rev. William Gibson as pastor in October, 1817, who was released in May, 1826. In October, 1827, the Rev. Gordon T. Ewing became the pastor. He was a popular preacher and had a prosperous following. At his suggestion the old log church in Canonsburgh was torn down with the design of building a new church. His health

---

* History of Washington County, Pennsylvania.

failing, he resigned the charge in May, 1830, and upon the foundation laid for the church a dwelling was afterwards erected. It stood on the west side of Main street and a few graves may yet be seen at the west end of the lot.* In May, 1834, the Rev. John Crozier became the pastor. In 1835, the church site was changed from Canonsburgh to the present location five miles north, and a neat brick church was erected. The congregation now became known as Miller's Run, because the first preaching in this locality was conducted at the house of Mr. George near this stream. In October, 1842, Mr. Crozier was released from this branch of his extensive charge. In May, 1843, the Rev. William Slater was ordained and installed the pastor, and continued uninterrupted in this relation for forty-four years, and until his resignation in April, 1887. In 1870, the old brick church was removed, and the present commodious frame structure was built on the site. Miller's Run is a strong congregation. They have been thoroughly indoctrinated in the truths of the Bible and the principles of the Covenanter Church. Among the old families, and who have descendants now in connection with the Church, are those by the names of George, Slater, Scott, Roney, Orr, Wallace, Hunter, Ramsey, Maxwell, Toner, Houston, Thompson, Robb, McBurney, Walker, Conner, Burnside, McFarland, and others.

WEST VIRGINIA.

MIDDLE WHEELING. This small congregation is located in the "Pan-handle," east of the city of

* History of Washington County, Pennsylvania.

Wheeling, and not far from the Pennsylvania line. The settlement was made about 1825, and, as a part of the Canonsburgh and Miller's Run congregation, this neighborhood was occasionally visited by the Revs. Gordon T. Ewing from 1827 until 1830; by John Crozier from 1834 until 1842; and by William Slater from 1843 until April, 1860, when it was organized as a distinct congregation. The Rev. Armour McFarland was installed for a part of his time in April, 1866, and demitted this branch in April, 1873. The Rev. Samuel R. McClurkin, the present pastor, was installed in September, 1876. They possess a neat and comfortable house of worship recently erected. Among the eldership and members of this congregation have been John Roney, Alexander, James, Creighton C. and T. J. Orr, Samuel McCoy, John Cochran and James Roney.

OHIO.

YOUNGSTOWN. This congregation has been known at different times by different names; first as Austintown, then Poland and North Jackson, and finally as Youngstown. The congregation is situated principally in Columbiana and Mahoning Counties, Ohio, and along the Pennsylvania line. Austintown was a branch of the Little Beaver congregation as early as 1814, and enjoyed the labors of the Rev. Robert Gibson from 1819 to 1830, and those of the Rev. George Scott from 1831 until 1833, when he, and a part of the congregation, went into the New School body. In 1834, the congregation was attached to Slippery

Rock under the pastoral care of the Rev. James Blackwood. The elders at this time were William Guthrie and John Ewing. In 1838, Austintown and Little Beaver formed a separate congregation, and the first pastor was the Rev. Joseph W. Morton from 1845 until 1847. In 1848, the Rev. Samuel Sterrett became the pastor of the united charge. Austintown became a separate congregation in May, 1860, and Mr. Sterrett continued in charge until his release in October, 1867. Rev. Robert J. George was the next pastor installed in May, 1870, and released in April, 1875. Rev. T. C. Sproull was installed in July, 1876, and released in July, 1879. For six years they enjoyed occasional supplies in Poland and North Jackson, but were so reduced in numbers by emigration that they could not support a pastor. In October, 1885, they were re-organized as the Youngstown congregation and the principal place of preaching is in this city. They have secured a hall, and Rev. H. W. Reed was installed pastor in May, 1888. Among the elders and leading members in this congregation have been William and John Guthrie, John and Gibson Ewing, George Hamilton, J. B. Jordan, J. E. Gault, W. S. Kernohan, W. R. Sterrett, William McConnell, and others.

GREENFIELD. This congregation was situated in Harrison County, and included the adjacent societies of Londonderry, McMahon's Creek, Salt Fork and Steubenville. Covenanters settled in this region as early as 1806, mostly emigrants from Western Pennsylvania. The congregation was not regularly organized until about 1822. The first pastor was the Rev. William Sloane, installed in November, 1829, and released in October, 1838. Rev. James Love was installed in June, 1839, and released in May, 1847. The congregation soon diminished, and, in 1849, was dropped from the roll and soon became extinct. Nathan Johnston, James McKinney, Thomas McFetridge, Joseph Boyd, James Kirk, William Pollock, James W. Thomson, Matthew Wilkin, George Orr, James Herron, James Darrah, John Adams and Thomas Patton were among the leading members.

LONDONDERRY AND NORTH SALEM. Early in the present century a few families of Covenanters settled in Guernsey County and were occasionally visited by a passing minister. The congregation was organized about 1822, and included many branches with those farther east in Harrison County. Rev. William Sloane became the first pastor in November, 1829, and remained in this relation nine years. In June, 1839, the Rev. James Love succeeded him in the pastorate, and remained in this branch until Oetober, 1864. Rev. James A. Thompson was installed in October, 1866, and released in September, 1875. In April, 1879, the North Salem branch received a separate organization, and, in 1880, the Rev. James R. Latimer became the pastor of the united charges. He resigned in May, 1882, since which time they have not had a settled pastor. Among the old and prominent families here are those by the names of Hutcheson, Galbraith, Kernohan, Walkinshaw, Law, Martin, Cairns, Thompson,

Forsythe, Glasgow, Love, Reed, McKee, Logan, Walker, Blackwood, Moffett, and others.

BROWNSVILLE. This small congregation was located in Monroe County, and was supplied many years previous to its organization in 1854. Previous to that date, and until his death in October, 1856, the Rev. Oliver Wylie was stated supply. In August, 1859, the Rev. James A. Thompson became the pastor and was released in June, 1865. For ten years they were occasionally supplied by Rev. Armour McFarland, and others. In September, 1876, the Rev. Samuel R. McClurkin was installed for part of his time, but was released in the following year, and occasionally supplied it. The cause is now about extinct. John Barber, Henry Boyd, John McKaige, Robert Allen, John Adams, James Waltenbaugh, Joseph Eakman and William J. Anderson were among the leading members.

NEW CONCORD. This flourishing congregation is situated in the eastern part of Muskingum County, and, until 1871, was known as Salt Creek. The first Covenanter known to settle in this vicinity was Matthew Mitchell, who came with his family from the "forks of the Yough," in Pennsylvania, in 1804.* In 1810, John Jamison came from the same region, and in 1812, William Robinson and Neal McNaughton emigrated from Conococheague and settled on Salt Creek, twelve miles south of New Concord. In 1814, Samuel McCutcheon emigrated from Ireland and settled about six miles below New Concord. These families constituted a praying society and unfurled the banner

---

* Dr. H. P. McClurkin in *Banner*, 1876, p. 169.

of the Covenant. They were occasionally visited by
Revs. John Black and Matthew Williams. In the summer of 1814, Rev. Robert Wallace, who is the father
of Covenanterism in Ohio, began missionary work
principally at Utica and Chillicothe. In 1815, he
providentially met Neal McNaughton, at a hotel in
Zanesville, who took him to his home where Mr.
Wallace preached the following Sabbath. The society
continued to grow under his occasional ministrations
until the organization of the congregation in June,
1821, by the election of John Auld and John Jamison ruling elders. The communion was soon afterwards dispensed and Mr. Wallace was assisted by the
Rev. Charles B. McKee. The services were held in
the woods near the farm of Mr. McCutcheon, and the
following forty members communed at the first sacra-
ment: John and Mary Auld; John and Margaret Jamison;
Mrs. Black; Robert and Elizabeth Brown; Matthew,
Mary, Rachel and Rebecca Calhoun; Betsy Cunningham;
Eleanor Forsythe; Alexander and Mrs. George;
Matthew, Sr., Matthew, Jr., and Mrs. Mitchell; Samuel,
Isabel, Sr., Isabel, Jr., James and Anna McCutcheon;
Neal and Mary NcNaughton; William Robinson;
Joseph, Ann, James and Jane Sterrett; Thomas, Mary,
Sr., Mary, Jr., William, James and Archibald Steven-
son; David and Mary Sim; Jacob and Anna Wortman.
All these are now dead. In October, 1823, Mr.
Wallace was installed pastor, and also preached at
Jonathan's Creek, Muskingum, Tomica and Will's Creek.
Mr. Wallace died in July, 1849. In October, 1850, the
Rev. Hugh P. McClurkin was installed, and remained

almost uninterruptedly for thirty-two years, and until his release in October, 1882. The Rev. James M. Faris, the present pastor, was installed in July, 1884. Among the many officers who have served in this congregation are John Auld, John Jamison, David and Benjamin Wallace, David Hawthorne, Richard and Thomas McGee, Archibald and William Stevenson, Walter McCrea, David Stormont, William and Thomas Wylie, John Gibson, William Forsythe, William Speer, William Elliot, Thomas Stewart, John Taylor, James McCartney, Samuel Mitchell, James R. Willson, Hugh Patterson and John C. Robb.

MUSKINGUM AND TOMICA. This was long a part of the Salt Creek congregation and under the pastoral care of the Rev. Robert Wallace. It received a separate organization in October, 1831. The first pastor was the Rev. John Wallace, installed in April, 1833, and continued in this relation for twenty-two years. On account of some Church troubles he resigned in 1855. For ten years they were a vacancy, and the Rev. Armour McFarland frequently supplied them. In December, 1865, the Rev. J. C. K. Faris was installed pastor, and was released in April, 1871. For six years they were again vacant but enjoyed the labors of Rev. Armour McFarland and others. Rev. William S. Fulton was installed in December, 1877, aud released in April, 1883. Rev. John M. Wylie, the present pastor, was installed in January, 1885. There are two branches with good houses of worship, and the cause is in a healthy condition. Among the officers have been James Sloat, Robert and John Irwin, William Dunlap,

James McQuigg, William and James McGlade, William and John Robeson, John and William Wylie, James Beattie, James and John Stitt, and R. H. Kilpatrick.

JONATHAN'S CREEK. This congregation is situated along the Haysville pike and about eight miles southwest of the city of Zanesville. The first family settled in this vicinity in 1815. A society was formed in 1823, and was attached to the Salt Creek congregation under the care of the Rev. Robert Wallace. For thirty years they continued to be visited by the pastors in the vicinity. The branches of Rocky Fork, West Bedford and Irville were organized into a congregation in August, 1853, with twenty-three members, and James Stitt, James Beall and Walter B. Finney were chosen ruling elders. The name then was the Eden and Irville congregation, and, in 1855, the name was changed, by the transfer of preaching, to Jonathan's Creek. Rev. Armour McFarland became the pastor in the summer of 1853, and continued in this relation until his health caused his release in April, 1876. In 1880, the Rev. T. C. Sproull became stated supply for one year. The Rev. Robert B. Cannon, D. D., became the pastor in September, 1886, and is now in charge. They possess a very neat house of worship, near the town of Newtonville, and the cause has revived under the present pastorate. Families by the names of McFarland, George, Thomson, Kirkpatrick, Ardrey, Wylie, Johnston, Gladstone, Harvey, and others, have long held up the "Banner of the Covenant" in that locality.

UTICA. This is a pleasantly situated town in the

northren part of Licking County. As early as 1805,. the family of James Dunlap settled along the Licking Creek near this place.* In 1809, Robert Kirkpatrick settled in the same community ; and in 1810, the families of Nathaniel and Peter Kirkpatrick, Joseph Fulton, John McNaughton, Samuel Kirkland, Joseph and John Campbell, Samuel Duffield and Joseph Jameson settled in the same neighborhood, and a praying society was formed. They were regularly organized into a congregation in October, 1813, by the ordina- tion of James Dunlap and Nathaniel Kirkpatrick ruling elders, with thirty-five members. Rev. Robert Wallace was the first pastor installed in charge in November,. 1814, and preached in many other localities. He demit- ted the charge in the summer of 1822. William Mitchell was added to the session in 1822. The congregation was vacant for fifteen years, during which time they were almost constantly supplied, and many were added to the membership. They had no house of worship,. and held the services in a tent on the hill east of town, near the residence of J. M. Kirkpatrick, who was long a ruling elder. In 1830, a comfortable house of worship was erected. During this period, John McDaniel and Peter Kirkpatrick were added to the session. The Rev. Armour McFarland was installed pastor in October, 1837, and released in May, 1853. During his pastorate one hundred persons were added to the Church, and John Day, Hugh and James Hervey,. and William Adams were chosen ruling elders. In November, 1856, the Rev. John C. Boyd became pastor

---

* Extracted from sessional records by Mr. James Watson.

for a part of his time; and, from 1867, until his release in October, 1882, he devoted all his time to Utica. In 1857, James M. Kirkpatrick was chosen an elder, and William Stevenson, Robert McFarland and Wait Wright elected deacons. In 1860, William Dunlap, Walter B. Finney and James Beall; and in 1865, James Watson, were added to the session. In 1864, the congregation erected a new church building. William Hervey and Robinson Johnston were subsequently elected elders. After the resignation of Mr. Boyd they were vacant nearly four years. The Rev. W. J. Coleman was installed in charge, April, 1886, and resigned in November, 1887. Among the prominent families here have been those of Dunlap, Kirkpatrick, Kirkland, Campbell, Jameson, Mitchell, McDaniel, Day, Wright, Hervey, Adams, Watson, Beall, Stevenson, McFarland, Finney, Deary, Darrah, Bovard, Reynolds, McDermott, Boyd, Wallace, Hass, Dillon, Johnston, and others.

MANSFIELD. This is a growing city and a railroad center, situated in the northren and central part of the State. In the spring of 1877, the Rev. Samuel A. George, then a licentiate, was appointed by the Central Board of Missions to labor in this city, and began work when there were only three Covenanters in the city. The congregation was organized, October 11, 1878, with forty members. The elders have been W. P. Clarke, James Railt, William Gregg, Johnston McKee, Michael George, S. H. Garrett and J. B. Jordan. Rev. Samuel A. George was ordained and installed pastor, November 20, 1878, and has built up a good congregation of faithful and energetic people. In 1884, they erected a handsome brick church edifice in the heart of the city and upon a public thorough-fare.

SANDUSKY. This congregation was situated upon the Little Sandusky river in Crawford County, and not far from the present city of Crestline. The first Covenanter who settled here was William Jameson, in 1832, having emigrated from Western Pennsylvania. The Rev. J. B. Johnston, and others, occasionally visited the few families located here before the organization. It was organized in October, 1843, and was supplied for four years. The Rev. John C. Boyd became the pastor in May, 1847, and was released in November, 1867, after twenty years of faithful labor. Not securing another pastor, the congregation gradually weakened until its disorganization in April, 1876. Among the leading families were those of Jameson, Marshall, Robeson, Moore and Reynolds.

MIAMI. Under this heading will be included all the Covenanters in Logan County, and around the historic village of Northwood. In early times Cherokee was the post town. As early as 1828, a few families of Cove-nanters settled upon the head waters of the Miami river, among whom were Robert Scott, Samuel, Matthew, Jr., and Matthew Mitchell, Sr., Abram and Isaac Patterson, John Young, Joseph and Thomas Fulton, Mrs. Hays and Mrs. Margaret King.* They formed a praying society, and were occasionally visited by Revs. Hugh and Gavin McMillan, until the latter minister organized them into

---

* Items from Mrs. James Wylie, Northwood, Ohio.

a congregation in October, 1831, by the election of Abram Patterson, John Young and Matthew Mitchell, Jr., ruling elders. In June, 1834, the Rev. John B. Johnston was ordained and installed pastor. The congregation was rapidly built up, and they erected a log church on the Creek near the present West Geneva Cemetery. In time this was replaced by a large brick church in which they worshipped for many years. The deacon question caused a division in the once harmonious flock, and the Second Miami congregation was organized by a Commission of Synod, in August, 1851, and they erected a frame church building in the village of Northwood. In July, 1853, the Rev. J. C. K. Milligan was installed co-pastor with Mr. Johnston over the First congregation, and they continued to teach in the College. Those members residing in the vicinity of Rushsylvania were organized into a separate congregation in November, 1853, and soon afterwards erected a frame building for church purposes. The Rev. William Milroy was installed the first and only pastor of the Second Miami congregation in October, 1854. The Rev. J. R. W. Sloane, then President of Geneva Hall, was installed pastor of the Rushsylvania congregation, in January, 1855, and thus the three congregations enjoyed the labors of four eminent ministers. Dr. Sloane resigned the Rushsylvania congregation in May, 1856, and removed to New York. In 1858, the First Miami congregation lost both of its pastors. Mr. Johnston connected with the United Presbyterian body, and Mr. Milligan resigned and removed to New York. In November, 1860, Rushsylvania succeeded in getting the Rev. Preston H. Wylie as their pastor,.

and in November, 1861, the Rev. John L. McCartney was settled over the First Miami congregation. In 1866, the First Miami congregation removed from the old brick church on the Creek, and erected the present large frame church in the village of Northwood. In September, 1875, the Rev. J. L. McCartney was released from this pastoral charge, and in May, 1876, Rev. P. H. Wylie was released from Rushsylvania. In October, 1876, those members residing in and around Bellefontaine received a separate organization, and were supplied for four years. The Rev. William Milroy, pastor of the Second Miami congregation and Professor of Latin in Geneva College, died in November, 1876, and thus the four congregations were left without pastors. In April, 1877, the First and Second were consolidated, forming the United Miami congregation, and have since worshipped in the commodious First Church building, and those members residing in Belle Centre were granted a separate organization. The congregations have since been four in number, with Northwood (United Miami) as the center; Rushsylvania, four miles east; Bellefontaine, eight miles south; and Belle Centre, three miles north. A new brick church was erected in Belle Centre, and the Bellefontaine people purchased a church building. In May, 1878, the Rev. H. H. George became the pastor of the Rushsylvania congregation, and the Rev. George Kennedy that of United Miami. In January, 1879, the Rev. John Lynd was installed at Belle Centre, and in May, 1880, Rev. Finley M. Foster was installed at Bellefontaine. In May, 1880, Dr. George was released from Rushsylvania, and in August, 1880, the Rev. John Lynd was installed as his successor, with Belle Centre. In June, 1882, the Rev. George Kennedy was released from the United Miami congregation, and for four years the people made several unsuccessful efforts to obtain a pastor. In April, 1885, the Rev. John Lynd was released from Belle Centre and Rushsylvania; and in April, 1886, the Rev. Josiah J. Huston was installed pastor of Belle Centre, and, in July, 1886, over Rushsylvania, which are his present charges. In May, 1886, the Rev. Ruther Hargrave, the present pastor, was installed over the United Miami congregation at Northwood. In August, 1887, the Rev. F. M. Foster was released from Bellefontaine. By emigration and death, Rushsylvania and Bellefontaine are greatly reduced in numbers, and, alone, are not able to support pastors. Among the old families and members at *Northwood* were Robert and Joseph Scott, Abram and Isaac Patterson, Samuel Hyndman, Samuel and Matthew Mitchell, James Gray, James Wright, George Hartin, John and James Trumbull, Cornelius, Samuel and Russell Jameson, Moses T. Glasgow, Stephen Bayles, John Crawford, John Young, Robert Patton, Jonathan Ritchie, William, Samuel P. and James S. Johnston, Robert and David Boyd, David Milroy, Robert McClure, Matthew Wilkin, William Rambo, Thomas Hosack, William and Matthew Pollock, James Keers, Robert Wylie, Allan Reid, Hugh Parks, Drs. Carter and Jenkin, Joseph Murphy, David Clark, George Johnston, James Steele, Joseph Clyde, Hugh Harvey, Archibald Lamont, John Day, John and James Reid, William Reed, James and William Dunlap, T. C. Speer, David Alexander, William C. Johnston, Thomas Logan, John K. Mitchell,

20

Joseph Forsythe, Ebenezer Milroy, John Campbell, James Fulton, John Keys, and others. *Rushsylvania:* John and Matthew Mitchell, James Qua, Thomas M. Hutcheson, Henry and Michael George, James Wylie, Francis Halliday, George and Renwick Day, John McCullough, Martin Johnston, and others. *Bellefontaine:* David Boyd, James Forsythe, James Guthrie, William Funk, Samuel and Archibald Foster, M. T. Glasgow, David Fulton, John McClure, W. B. Keys, Renwick Elliot, and others. *Belle Centre:* Cornelius Jameson, Dr. M. D. Willson, William McClure, J. B. Temple, A. G. Patterson, J. B., J. W., and S. M. Torrence, William Johnston, John and William Fulton, Joseph and Alexander McConnell, William and George Crawford, David S. McKinley, Alexander and Oliver Liggett, Abram P. Wylie, Cornelius J. Ferguson, and others. Miami congregation is closely connected with the educational history of the Church, for in her midst Geneva College was founded and fostered for thirty-two years; Geneva Female Seminary was in existence thirty years; and the Theological Seminary remained here for several years. Many ministers and private members can look back upon "Miami" as the place where they received much of their mental and spiritual instruction, and the name of "Northwood" will be a household word for many generations.

MACEDON. This small congregation is situated on the low rich plains at the head waters of the Wabash river, in Mercer County, in the central western part of Ohio. It was a preaching station as early as 1846, when Alexander George settled in this region, and continued as a preaching station until its organization in July, 1852.* The Rev. William F. George was the first pastor installed in September, 1853. About 1855, the typhoid fever raged with such fatality that many fell under its power and others moved away. Mr. George was released from the charge in April, 1858. In January, 1861, they secured part of the time of the Rev. P. H. Wylie, who, in May, 1876, continued to give them all of his time. Here he labored faithfully under many discouragements until his release in March, 1887. The congregation is much reduced and has lost its organization. Among the old families were those of George, McGee, Woodburn, Fishbaugh, McDonald, Gray, McMillan, Porterfield, and others.

CEDARVILLE. This congregation is situated in the northren part of Green County, and was formerly known by the two branches of Xenia and Massie's Creek. This country was first settled by Covenanters in 1804.† That year the family of David Mitchell from Kentucky, and that of James Miller from Scotland, settled along Clarke's Run and held society meetings for some time. In 1808, Mr. James Reid, from Kentucky, and Mr. William Moreland were added to the society, and the following year they were visited by Revs. Thomas Donnelly and John Kell. They were afterwards visited by Rev. John Black, who constituted the society and dispensed the sacrament to about ten members. The next few years brought several more families, and the supplies preached in the barns and log houses. In 1812, they erected the first church

---

* *Banner*, 1878, p. 60.

† Sketch by Rev. J. F. Morton, D. D., and from other sources.

building, which was a rude log structure with a clap-
board roof, and stood on the farm of James Miller
some seven miles from Xenia. The Rev. John Kell
preached for them about one-fourth of the time until
1816. In May, 1816, the Rev. Jonathan Gill became
the pastor, and remained in this relation for seven
years. In 1823, the Rev. Gavin McMillan, of Beech
Woods, gave one-fourth of his time for six years. In
the fall of 1828, the Rev. Hugh McMillan, of South
Carolina, visited them, and, receiving a call, and
bringing a part of his congregation with him from
the South, settled as the pastor in September,· 1829.
In 1824, a new house of worship was erected upon
the banks of Massie's Creek, two miles from Cedarville.
At the division of the Church in 1833, there were one
hundred and sixty-four members, one hundred and
twenty-seven of whom went with the pastor into the
New School body. The trouble about the church
property was settled by allowing the faithful remnant
to occupy it every fourth Sabbath and during the
communion seasons. They continued to receive occasional supplies until the disorganization in August,
1841. They resorted to the prayer meetings and held
fast to their principles. They were re-organized as the
Cedarville congregation in June, 1850, and were supplied
for eight years by· the students of the Northwood
Seminary, and others. Uniting with Cincinnati, the
Rev. Henry George was ordained and installed pastor
in June, 1858, and was released from this charge in
August, 1866. Rev. Samuel Sterrett became the pastor
in May, 1868, and was removed by death in October,

1871. The Rev. Patterson P. Boyd was installed in charge in May, 1872, and released in July, 1874. For seven years they were a vacancy almost constantly supplied. The Rev. Thomas C. Sproull, the present pastor, was installed in June, 1881. Among the old families have been those of Reid, Miller, Mitchell, Moreland, McMillan, Hemphill, Willson, Grier, George, McConnell, Reynolds, Watt, McIntire, Williamson, Foster, Erwin, Sterrett, and others.

BRUSH CREEK. This small congregation is situated in Adams County and in the southern part of Ohio. The society was first called Chillicothe, and was first visited by Rev. John Kell. In 1814, the Rev. Robert Wallace began to give it a part of his time which he continued to do for six years. The Rev. Charles B. McKee was the first pastor, installed in August, 1821, and released in the fall of 1822. For five years they struggled for an existence. In April, 1827, the Rev. James Blackwood became the pastor and remained but two years. In June, 1831, the Rev. David Steele was installed the pastor. He had two principal places of preaching; one being at Mill Creek, in Kentucky, and often in other localities on both sides of the Ohio. In September, 1840, Mr. Steele and some followers went into the "Reformed Presbytery," and Francis Gailey, who also claimed to be the only true Covenanter, made some disciples, and thus the congregation was weakened. The Rev. Robert Hutcheson was installed pastor in September, 1842, but by defection, emigration and death the congregation was so reduced that he demitted the charge in May,

1856. The congregation now became disorganized, and, for twenty-five years, continued in this condition, although a few Covenanters resided there. It was re-organized in November, 1881, with thirty-three members, and enjoyed the stated labors of Revs. R. J. Sharpe, William McKinney, R. C. Allen, T. C. Sproull, and others. Among the old families here were those by the names of George, McIntire, Glasgow, Wright, Stevenson, Bayles, Milligan, Burns, Copeland, Hemp-hill, McKinley, Torrence, Foster, Ralston, Montgomery, and others.

BEECH WOODS. The original of this congregation was situated in the western part of Preble County and along the Indiana line, and was a part of the Garrison charge. It was settled early in the present century by emigrants from South Carolina. It was supplied by ministers passing to and from the South and increased rapidly in numbers. The Rev. John Kell took charge of the con-gregation in April, 1816, and remained among them for three years. Samuel Robinson, whose relatives lived here, supplied them, with others. In May, 1823, the Rev. Gavin McMillan became the pastor, and the congre-gation grew rapidly under his faithful ministrations. During the division of August, 1833, he hesitated, but finally cast in his lot with the New School brethren and remained pastor of a portion of his former flock. The remnant were then attached to the Garrison congregation in Indiana and enjoyed the labors of its pastor. The Robinson and Ramsey families, with their connections, were among the leading members at Beech Woods.

CINCINNATI. The commercial importance of this rapidly growing city attracted Covenanters from the mother country and from the South, very early in the present century. The congregation was organized in October, 1816, by the ordination of elders John McCormick and James McLean, father of Hon. Washington and John R. McLean, of the *Cincinnati Enquirer.** In March, 1818, Archibald Johnston became stated supply, and by his rare powers as a preacher gathered quite a congregation. He died the same fall. Rev. Samuel Robinson then took charge of the congregation, and was deposed for intemperance in the summer of 1821. The Rev. Charles B. McKee was installed pastor in November, 1822. He was an acceptable preacher and taught the classics in Cincinnati College. The young congregation, which had worshipped in private houses and public halls for many years, now erected a brick church on George street, near Race, in 1827, on a plat of ground donated by James McLean. In 1831, Mr. McKee was released from the charge and they were supplied. At the division of the Church in 1833, while the Rev. James W. Stewart was preaching for them, the whole congregation, with a few exceptions, went into the New School body and retained the church property. Among the most influential members who went into the new body at that time were: John McCormick, James McLean, John Hunt, John Fullerton, Joseph Beggs, William Monford, John Hazlett, James Sample, James Morton, John Edsworth, John

---

* Reminiscences by Hon. Washington McLean, Moses T. Glasgow, an d others. Also *Banner*, 1878, p. 59.

Walker, James Gray, James Mann and Dr. Killough. Those who held the testimony intact were: Hugh Glasgow, John and Mrs. Gray, William Carson and Mrs. Mary A. Murphy. They continued to hold society meetings, and occasionally enjoyed a day's preaching, for ten years. The congregation was re-organized with thirteen members, August 22, 1844, by the election of Moses T. Glasgow and John Gray, ruling elders. In 1845, the Theological Seminary was removed to this city from Allegheny, and for four years they enjoyed the stated labors of Dr. James R. Willson and the students. The first year the Seminary was conducted in a frame church on Elm street belonging to the Methodists, and the following winter, in a hall at the corner of Vine and Eleventh streets, where the congregation worshipped. In 1847, the spirited congregation leased a lot on Vine street above Twelfth, and erected a frame church upon it, with stores below. Here the Seminary also remained until 1849. They made out many calls, but they did not succeed in getting a pastor for several years. In 1853, James Brown and Alexander Bovard were added to the session. Uniting with Cedarville they succeeded in getting the Rev. H. H. George as the pastor in June, 1858. In 1860, the congregation bought a church on Clinton street, near Central Avenue, and, after remodeling it, they continued to worship in this place. In August, 1866, Mr. George began to give all his time to Cincinnati. Being called to the Presidency of Geneva College, Mr. George demitted the charge in August, 1872. The Rev. R. M. Sommerville was the stated supply for a year. In December, 1877, the Rev.

James M. Foster was ordained and installed pastor, and continued in this relation until April, 1886. The elders are Andrew McIntire, R. F. Glasgow and William Dearness. Among the names of old families may be mentioned those of Murphy, Gray, Glasgow, Finley, Brown, Bovard, Lusk, McIntire, Johnston, Thompson, Martin, Mitchell, McCullough, Crawford, Dearness, Adams, Edgar, and others.

MICHIGAN.

CEDAR LAKE. This congregation is located principally in Branch County, Michigan, and partly in Steuben country, Indiana. A few Covenanters emigrated to this country from Ohio, and succeeded in getting the organization of a congregation in April, 1841. For nine years they were supplied by Presbytery and students of Theology. The Rev. John French was installed the pastor in September, 1850, and continued in this relation for thirty years, and until his very sudden death in October, 1880. For four years they were vacant, and, after some troubles were settled, by which the California Mission Station was again joined to the congregation. The Rev. R. C. Wylie, the present pastor, was installed in charge in October, 1884. The Covenanters of Cedar Lake are intelligent and strongly attached to the old customs of the Church. Among the families long connected with the Church are those by the names of Jameson, Chestnut, Speer, French, Duguid, Mitchell, McNaughton, Morrow, Judson, Stewart, Logan, Elsey.

DETROIT AND NOVI. The city of Detroit contained a few Covenanters, who, in connection with the society of Novi, in Oakland County, were organized into a congregation in April, 1854. The Rev. Boyd Mc-Cullough was installed pastor in September, 1855, and remained in this relation for sixteen years, and until his release in May, 1871. At this time the congregation had become so reduced by emigration that it was disorganized, but continued as a mission station under the care of Presbytery. In 1876, and for several years, W. M. Shanks was stated supply. The field is now practically abandoned. Hugh Woodburn, Walter Calhoun, Andrew L. McCurdy, Robert Torrens, William Wray, Robert Laird and George McCarroll were among the chief supporters and elders.

SOUTHFIELD. This is the oldest and strongest congregation in Michigan. It is situated near the town of Birmingham, in Oakland County, and some seventeen miles north-west of the city of Detroit. David Stewart was the first Covenanter settling here in 1832, who was honored of God as the chief instrument in the organization of the congregation in May, 1834, and was a liberal supporter and efficient elder until his death.* For nine years the congregation was supplied and gradually increased in members. The Rev. James Neill was the first pastor, installed in May, 1843, and released in October, 1851. The Rev. James S. T. Milligan was installed pastor in November, 1853, and remained among these worthy people for eighteen years. The Rev. James R. Hill was installed in May, 1872, and released in May, 1876. In June, 1878, the Rev. Joseph McCracken, the present pastor, was

---

* *Reformed Presbyterian*, Vol. 16, p. 61.

installed in charge, and he has built up a large and flourishing congregation of intelligent and well-to-do Covenanters. Among the families long connected with the Southfield congregation are those of Stewart, Blackwood, McClung, Sloat, Parks, Bell, Cannon, Grier, Hemphill, Woodburn, McMullen, Marshall, McKinney, McLaughlin, McCarroll, Kirkpatrick, McCurdy, McDonald, Morrill, and others.

FAIRGROVE. This is a comparatively new field and was cultivated by the Central Board of Missions for several years. It is situated in Tuscola County, nearly one hundred miles north of Detroit and about twenty miles from Saginaw Bay. It was organized in December, 1878, with twenty-six members. The Rev. J. Ralston Wylie was installed pastor in November, 1879. The congregation rapidly increased and a substantial church building was erected in the village of Fairgrove. Mr. Wylie was released from the charge in October, 1887. Among the elders are Thomas Wylie, John Kirk, W. L. Robey and John Morrow.

INDIANA.

GARRISON. This small congregation of people was situated in Fayette County, and was a part of the Beech Woods congregation in Ohio. Emigrants from the South settled here as early as 1805, and occasionally enjoyed the services of a passing minister. It was organized in 1812, and the Rev. John Kell became the pastor in April, 1816, and remained in charge over three years. Samuel Robinson, and others,

were supplies. In May, 1823, the Rev. Gavin Mc-
Millan became the pastor, and, during the division of
1833, he and many of the people became identified
with the New School body. The largest part of the
congregation was now in Indiana, and the remnant
at Beech Woods was added to Garrison. For many
years they were supplied by John Holmes, Nathaniel
Allen, and others. The Rev. Josiah Dodds was
installed the pastor in October, 1847, and continued
in charge for eighteen years. The congregation was
greatly reduced by emigration, and the Beech Woods
branch was given up. In May, 1871, the Rev. Thomas
P. Robb was ordained and installed pastor, and remained
in charge three years. Six years again they struggled
for an existence, and in August, 1880, the Rev. John
J. McClurkin was installed in charge. He remained
four years, and the congregation lost its organization
in September, 1884, by the death of elders and the
removal of members. Among the old Covenanter families
at Garrison were those of Milligan, Stevenson, Gamble,
Dill, Huston, Russell, McMillan, Culbertson, Alexander,
Craig, Cook.

INDIANAPOLIS. Immediately after the war of the
rebellion a few Covenanters gathered into this city,
and the Central Board of Missions began to cultivate
it as a mission field. In the spring of 1866, the Rev.
John Crozier took charge of the mission, built a comfortable house of worship in a desirable part of the
city, and preached to appreciative audiences, among
which were members of the Legislature. The congregation was organized May 10, 1867, with twenty-

four members, and Mr. Crozier continued in charge. The good cause so auspiciously begun gradually declined, the congregation was disorganized in May, 1870, and the church property was sold by the Illinois Presbytery at a small sacrifice.* Dr. J. T. Boyd, B. F. Breedon and David Fulton were among the leading members.

WALNUT RIDGE. This small congregation was situated seven miles from Salem, the capital of Washington County, and in the southern part of the State. It was settled by emigrants from Tennessee and South Carolina about 1820. It was organized in May, 1822, and was supplied occasionally by Revs. John Kell, Samuel Wylie, and others. The Rev. Robert Lusk became the pastor in October, 1824, and the following year he was suspended on charges regarding monetary matters with his neighbors. Here he lived in comparative obscurity for ten years, when he desired to have his case investigated, and the local *fama clamosa* against his character averted.† This was done by a Commission of Synod, and he acknowledged he was sorry for being the occasion of so much trouble in the Church, and, after receiving an admonition, was restored by Synod in May, 1835, and continued to preach in his old charge for five years. In September, 1840, Mr. Lusk went with David Steele, and formed the "Reformed Presbytery," taking some members with him. In June, 1843, the Rev. John J. McClurkin was installed for part of his time, and

---

* *R. P. & C.*, 1872, p. 82.   † Reminiscences by Dr. David Steele, Sr., and Minutes of Synod, 1834, 1836.

remained in this relation until April, 1851. For ten years it was occasionally supplied and lost its organization in May, 1862, and was regarded as a mission station for several years. The cause was soon extinct, as the members had either emigrated or died. Among the old families here were those of Carithers, Reid, Marks and McElravey.

PRINCETON. This is the county seat of Gibson County and situated in the south-western corner of Indiana, not far from the confluence of the White and Wabash rivers. The first Covenanters settling here were Samuel Hogue from Blount County, Tennessee, and Robert Archer, from Chester District, South Carolina, in 1805.* In 1809, Mr. Hogue, having returned to Tennessee on business, met the Rev. John Kell, who, according to promise, visited the families of Princeton in 1810, and constituted a praying society. He continued to visit the scattered families from house to house in the then wilderness, and held the first communion at the house of Robert Archer, in October, 1813, at which time the congregation was organized by the ordination of Samuel Hogue and Thomas Archer, ruling elders. There were about twenty-five communicants. The congregation continued to grow by local accessions and emigration, and, in 1814, Robert Stormont and James W. Hogue were added to the session. The services were usually held in a log church owned by the Baptists and situated about one mile north-west of the town of Princeton. In 1817, James Lessly and Robert Milburn were added

---

* *Presbyterian Historical Almanac*, Vol. 5, p. 382.

to the eldership. The Rev. John Kell was installed the first pastor in June, 1820. William Crowe, having removed from Kentucky, was now recognized as a member of session. They erected the first church building in Princeton in the fall of 1820. It was a small frame structure and was occupied for sixteen years. At the division of the Church in 1833, Mr. Kell and the great majority of the congregation went into the New School body, and they retained the church property. Robert Stormont was the only elder that stood fast to the principles of the Church. The small but faithful remnant clung together, re-organized in July, 1836, and received supplies. In 1840, they called the Rev. Samuel McKinney to become the pastor; he accepted the call, but, before his installation, he removed to the South. Uniting with Walnut Ridge they received a part of the time of Rev. John J. McClurkin in June, 1843, who continued in this relation for seven years. The Rev. John Stott was installed pastor of Princeton in October, 1851, and was suspended from the ministry in June, 1868, when some of the members left, and the congregation became disorganized. It was re-organized in April, 1869, with twenty members, and James Little was ordained a ruling elder. The members adhering to Mr. Stott were suspended from the privileges of the Church.* The Rev. Daniel C. Martin was installed in November, 1872, and released in April, 1888. Among the old families here are those by the names of Stormont, Little, Lockhart, Archer, Watt, Hogue,

* *R. P. & C.*, 1869, p. 186.

Peoples, Crowe, Davis, Orr, Foster, Dickson, Faris, Mooney, Carithers, and others.

BLOOMINGTON. This city is the capital of Monroe County and the seat of the University of Indiana. The Covenanters left the sunny South in the early part of the present century on account of the prevalence of slavery, and found abode principally in Indiana and Illinois. This settlement was made in March, 1820, by John and Thomas Moore, from South Carolina. The society increased by emigration from the South, and was organized in October, 1821. At this time there were only eight members, and John Moore and Isaac Faris were chosen elders.* In 1823, they lost the organization by the death of John Moore and the removal of Isaac Faris. They were re-organized in 1825, by the ordination of Thomas Moore and James Blair, ruling elders. The Rev. James Faris became the first pastor in November, 1827. At this time there were twenty members. In 1830, David Smith and D. B. Woodburn, of South Carolina, were added to the session. The congregation now grew rapidly by accessions from the South, and others who were attracted to Bloomington by her educational advantages. At the division of the Church in 1833, there were about one hundred and twenty members, and they were divided into two nearly equal parts, the one becoming identified with the New School body, and the other standing fast to Covenanter principles. The pastor, and elders David Smith and Thomas Moore, remained true to the old flag. The congregation continued its work with about sixty

* Rev. D. J. Shaw in *Banner*, 1879, p. 238.

members, and, in 1835, Thomas Smith, Robert Ewing and John Gamble were added to the session. The congregation had never possessed a house of worship, and, in 1836, erected a brick building two miles east of Bloomington. In 1838, James Faris was added to the session. In 1847, they suffered the loss of their church building by fire, and a better structure was speedily erected. The pastor, the Rev. James Faris, departed this life in May, 1855. The Rev. David J. Shaw, the present pastor, was installed in May, 1856, and has labored faithfully and successfully in this field for thirty-two years. The elders added to the session have been Charles McCaughan, John Smith and David Faris in 1862; John R. Hemphill in 1867; James B. Faris, David M. Smith and Robert Ervin in 1873; James S. and John M. Faris in 1879. In 1877, they removed from the country and built a handsome brick church in the city. The different families by the names of Faris and Smith, with their connections, have formed a large part of the membership.

LAKE ELIZA. This was a small congregation situated in Lake County, and not far from the city of Chicago. It was settled by Covenanter emigrants from the Eastern States in 1850. The society was organized into a congregation in September, 1852. The Rev. Preston H. Wylie became the pastor in May, 1855, and remained in this relation nearly six years. In September, 1865, the Rev. R. M. C. Thompson became the pastor, and labored under many difficulties and discouragements for sixteen years. They enjoyed the visits of itinerants for several years, and the stated

21

labors of Robert Clyde in 1884. Gradually diminishing by emigration, the congregation was disorganized in 1886. Here lived the families of Young, McKnight, Kirkpatrick, Bovard, Russell, McFarland, Davidson, McLaren, and others.

ILLINOIS.

Early in the present century, Southren Illinois became a popular settlement for Covenanters who left the South on account of the prevalence of human slavery. They settled principally in Randolph and Washington Counties, and became the nucleii of the present con-gregations of Old Bethel, Bethel, Church Hill and Elkhorn.*

OLD BETHEL. The first Covenanter minister to visit this region was the Rev. Samuel Wylie in the summer of 1816. In the summer of 1818, he was ordained by Synod as a missionary and sent to this locality. He made his principal preaching station at the " Irish Settlement " a few miles south-west of the present town of Sparta, and among a few members of the Associate Reformed Church. The first Covenanter con-gregation organized was in June, 1821, with thirty-five members and the promise of a salary of about two hundred dollars per year. The elders were Samuel Little and William Edgar, who had the year previously emigrated from Tennessee. The Rev. Samuel Wylie was at that time installed in charge and the congre-gation was called " Eden," sometimes " Bethel," and

---

* *Presbyterian Historical Almanac*, Vol. 1, p. 197.   *Banner*, 1875, p. 156.
R. P. & C., 1884, p. 379.

the post town was Kaskaskia on the Mississippi river. Soon afterwards, James McClurkin, from the Associate Reformed Church, and James Monford, recently from South Carolina, were added to the session. Emigration soon augmented their numbers and Covenanters flocked from the South and settled around the orginal society. In 1823, a comfortable frame church building was erected, surrounded by a spacious graveyard. Soon the house of worship became too small, for there were nearly three hundred and fifty communicants, and arrangements were made for a new church. Strife arose in settling the location, and during the erection of the building, in 1832, the original congregation was divided, and those at Hill Prairie received a separate organization. At the division of the whole Church in 1833, these congregations were again divided, and Mr. Wylie took many with him into the New School body. The remnant of the old Bethel congregation continued to hold their organization. The Rev. James Wallace became the pastor in August, 1840, and continued steadfast to his post for twenty-seven years, when he was released in May, 1867, to labor in the interests of the National Reform Association. In October, 1869, the Rev. William J. Gillespie was ordained and installed pastor, and the following year left the communion of the Church. For four years they were vacant and made efforts to obtain a pastor. In July, 1874, the Rev. Patterson P. Boyd was installed in charge, and was released in December, 1887.

BETHEL. In 1832, the Hill Prairie branch of the

old and original charge assumed this name, and lost members at the division in 1833. For many years they received supplies, and, in August, 1840, the Rev. Hugh Stevenson was installed pastor. He was a faithful minister, and, after six years of labor, departed this life in May, 1846. In October, 1848, Rev. James Milligan was installed in charge and remained seven years. In October, 1857, the Rev. David S. Faris, the present pastor, was ordained and installed in charge. In the spring of 1875, the congregation left the old church at Eden where their fathers worshipped for over a half a century, and occupied the new and present church building in the town of Sparta.

CHURCH HILL. This congregation surrounds the village of Coultersville, and was organized from the Bethel congregations in October, 1854. The first pastor was the Rev. William F. George installed in March, 1860, and released in May, 1871. In 1873, they erected a new house of worship, which is a comfortable one and well adapted for the purpose. The Rev. James M. Faris was installed pastor in June, 1873, and remained in charge eleven years. The Rev. John Teaz, the present pastor, was ordained and installed in charge in July, 1885. The congregation has done good work among the colored people of the neighborhood.

ELKHORN. This congregation is situated a little north-east of the others, near Oakdale, in Washington County. It was first settled in 1831, by the families of John and Archibald Hood and James McClurkin from South Carolina. They located near the present site of the church, and the Rev. Samuel Wylie supplied them for a short time. Soon they were joined by others, and the congregation was organized in July, 1834, at the house of Archibald Hood, with nineteen members. John and Thomas McClurkin and John Donnelly were chosen ruling elders. The Rev. Samuel McKinney was installed pastor in April, 1835, and released in May, 1840. The Rev. William Sloane was installed his successor in September, 1840, and remained in charge nearly eighteen years. In July, 1859, the Rev. Andrew C. Todd was installed and he remained twelve years, when he, and a colony of his people, emigrated to Colorado. The Rev. David G. Thompson, the present pastor, was installed in charge in October, 1872. The congregation is large and has been active in all Church work. All the congregations enjoy tokens of the Divine blessing, because of their faithfulness to Covenant obligations and Reformation principles. The Old Bethel, Bethel, Church Hill and Elkhorn congregations are so closely related in their history and members, that the names are grouped together as representative families of the Covenanter Church in Southern Illinois. Among these are Samuel Little, William Edgar, John, Thomas and James McClurkin, James Monford, Archibald Hood, John and Thomas Donnelly, Thomas G. Armour, John Hunter, William Kennedy, Alexander Moore, John G. and Charles R. Miller, William and John Weir, John M. Sloane, James Coulter, Joseph Patton, James and Hugh Matthews, Andrew Todd, John Robinson, A. J. and R. S. Edgar, John Steele, W. A. Stevenson, M. K. Mawhinney, David H. Coulter, James Beall, James and Thomas Finley, W. B. Whittaker, John Houston, John and J. M. Wylie, W. J. S. Cathcart, Robert H. Sinclair, Daniel Dickey, Samuel McCloy, William and Samuel Woodside, Robert McAfee, Robert Ramsey, Francis Torrens, D. F. McClurkin, A. W. Hunter, J. D. Elder, John E. Willson, L. M. Patterson, R. G. McLean, R. K. Wisely, J. R. Keady, and others.

STAUNTON. This congregation is situated around the thriving mining town of Staunton, in the south-eastern corner of Macoupin County, and some forty miles northeast of the city of St. Louis. A few Covenanters settled here a few years previous to the organization of the congregation in July, 1863. The Rev. John Middleton was installed the pastor in May, 1865, and was released in August, 1870. The Rev. William F. George was installed in charge in May, 1872, and after many trials, died in April, 1880. For seven years they were without a pastor, although they made efforts to obtain one, and received almost constant supplies. Uniting with St. Louis they secured a part of the time of the Rev. Ellsworth M. Smith, in May, 1887, who is now in charge. The congregation is small, but they possess a comfortable house of worship, and are earnest in their endeavors to maintain the Reformation cause. Among the principal elders have been Daniel and W. H. Williamson, Silas Smith, W. J. Dripps, William and Hugh Patterson. A few members have lived in the city of Chicago, and other localities, but no societies were ever organized.

WISCONSIN.

VERNON. The first Covenanters settling in this region, some twenty-five miles south-west of the city of

Milwaukee, were William and Mrs. Ann McLeod, from Rochester, New York, in the spring of 1844.* About the same time John McNeil emigrated from York, and they enjoyed the preaching of Mr. Nathaniel Allen, licentiate, who conducted services in a log school-house. In the spring of 1845, the family of James Wright, from York, and, in the summer of 1846, that of James S. Cumming, from Toronto, Canada, arrived. In June, 1847, a society was constituted by elder Daniel Mc-Millan of York, which met regularly at the house of Mr. Wright. In the early part of 1848, William Turner arrived with his family from Coldenham, New York. They now received a few days preaching from Revs. James Love, James Wallace and W. A. Acheson, and the services were usually conducted in "Weir's barn." The congregation was organized as "Waukesha," October 18, 1848, with fourteen members, among whom were the families of Wright, Turner, McNeil, McLeod, McConnell, McKinney and Cumming. James Wright, James McConnell and William Turner were chosen elders. In 1849, the congregation was taken under the care of the Rochester Presbytery, for in those days there were no railroads, and New York was nearest by way of the lakes. In June, 1850, the Rev. Samuel Bowden preached and dispensed the communion, at which time fourteen members were added to the Church, and the Rev. Robert Johnson preached two or three months. By the death of elder James Wright, and the removal of elder James McConnell, the congregation was disorganized November 18, 1850. The present church

---

* Sketch by Rev. Isaiah Faris, in *R. P. & C.*, 1883, p. 332.

building was erected in the town of Vernon in 1853, and the congregation was re-organized by a Commission of the Illinois Presbytery as "Vernon," September 16, 1856. William L. Wright with William Turner were the elders. The Rev. John Middleton was called to the pastorate, but declined. The Rev. Robert Johnson was installed the first pastor in November, 1859, and remained in charge until December, 1867. In October, 1871, Ebenezer Milroy and John Gault were added to the session. After several unsuccessful attempts to obtain a pastor, the Rev. Robert B. Cannon, who was called the second time, was installed September 13, 1872, and remained nearly six years. In September, 1873, James Mann was added to the session. The Rev. Isaiah Faris, the present pastor, was installed in November, 1878. The principal families have already been mentioned.

WAUPACA. This city and vicinity were cultivated as a mission station by the Rev. James L. Pinkerton, in 1876, but no congregation was organized, as there were but a few families of Covenanters in that locality.

MINNESOTA.

ELLIOTA. This congregation is situated in Fillmore County, on the Iowa state line, and about forty miles west of the Mississippi river. It was settled by a few Covenanters as early as 1865, and was under the North West Mission. In May, 1867, the Rev. James S. Buck was sent as a missionary to this place, and labored amid much physical weakness for several years. The congregation was organized in November, 1868, with sixteen members, and they erected a comfortable house of worship. Mr. Buck continued in charge until shortly before his death in October, 1870. For eight years they were supplied by the Central Board of Missions, and Revs. N. R. Johnston, Robert Hutcheson, and others, were stated supplies. The Rev. John W. Dill was installed pastor in April, 1878, and remained among them three years. In February, 1886, the Rev. Robert Clyde, the present pastor, was ordained and installed in charge. The families of Rice, McKinney, Lemmon, and others, have long resided there.

SAINT PAUL. In 1855, Mr. James Aiton, of Rochester, New York, removed to this city, and for six years endeavored to establish a congregation, but in this he was not successful. At different times it was visited by a Covenanter minister, and some families resided there. At the present time efforts are being made to organize a society.

LAKE RENO. Along the shores of this beautiful lake, five miles from Glenwood, Pope County, and about one hundred and fifty miles north-west of Saint Paul, is located the growing congregation of Lake Reno. Several years previous to its organization, Covenanters from Illinois and Indiana had settled here, and were organized into a congregation in October, 1869, with thirty-three members. Revs. Daniel C. Faris and Robert Hutcheson were stated supplies for some time, and the field continued under the care of the Central Board of Missions for many years. The Rev. Edward G. Elsey was installed pastor in July, 1882, and is now in charge. Among the families here are those of

William Hogan, William Matthews, David Campbell, J. L. Ewing, James and Thomas Semple, Joseph M. Wylie, Dr. W. C. Allen, Prof. Z. G. Willson, and others.

ALEXANDRIA. This is a thriving town some ten miles north of Lake Reno, where some families reside belonging to the Lake Reno congregation, and is now regarded as a mission station.

ROUND PRAIRIE. This society settled upon this prairie, in Todd County, about thirty miles north-east of Lake Reno, in 1865. It was settled by emigrants from Indiana and Illinois, and was organized into a congregation in May, 1873, with eighteen members. They have since been under the care of the Central Board of Missions and never enjoyed the labors of a settled pastor. The families of Russell and Ewing have long been connected with the cause in that place.

IOWA.

SHARON. The first Covenanters settling within the limits of Iowa were the family of Robert McElhinney and his son-in-law, John Baird, from Philadelphia, in May, 1840.* They journeyed the whole distance in wagons, crossed the Mississippi at the village of Burlington, and pitched their tents on the banks of Honey Creek in the northren part of Des Moines County. In November, 1840, they were re-inforced by the arrival of the families of Samuel McElhinney and Thomas Cummings, and soon afterwards the Rev. Samuel Mc-

* Sketch by Rev. T. P. Robb, in *R. P. & C.*, 1884, p. 111.

Kinney, of Illinois, preached to them at the house of John Hamilton. In 1844, Robert Brown, Robert and Aaron Willson joined the society, which was then constituted. They were now supplied with preaching by the Revs. William Sloane, James Milligan, James Wallace, John Holmes and Nathaniel Allen, from time to time. The society soon became so large that it was divided, and the first Covenanter congregation in Iowa was organized by Revs. William Sloane and James Wallace, at the house of Samuel McElhinney, September 26, 1846, with seventeen members, and it was then called Linn Grove and Cedar. The elders chosen were Thomas Cox and Samuel McElhinney. The first pastor was the Rev. James M. McDonald, ordained and installed in charge, May 17, 1851. In 1852, a church building was erected on the present site, not far from the village of Linton, and the name of the congregation was changed to Sharon. The increase was large, but from time to time members were certified to constitute other congregations or removed farther West. By declining health, Dr. McDonald was compelled to resign the pastorate in June, 1872, and died a few months thereafter. The Rev. Thomas P. Robb, the present pastor, was installed in July, 1874. They occupy a commodious church building, and, in many ways, Sharon is one of the best country congregations in the body. Among the eldership and principal families here have been those of McElhinney, Baird, Willson, Glasgow, Faris, Sloss, Reid, Montgomery, Hays, McConaghy, McIntire, Huston, Henderson, Walkinshaw,

Elliott, Hensleigh, Robb, Carithers, Cubit, Cunningham, Stevenson, Marshall and Robinson.

KOSSUTH. This congregation was also situated in Des Moines County, and was formed by members from Sharon, September, 1865. Rev. Robert Johnson was installed pastor in January, 1868, and was released in July, 1875. By the death of elder William O. Lindsay, the congregation was disorganized in the winter of 1876. It was re-organized in October, 1877, and they sold their church, and erected another in the village of Mediapolis, two miles distant. Not receiving another pastor, and being greatly reduced by emigration, the congregation was disorganized in April, 1879, and the remaining members were certified to Linn Grove.

LINN GROVE. This was formed from the original Cedar society of the Sharon congregation, and organized in September, 1846, and now situated around the village of Mediapolis in Des Moines County.* Those opposed to the office of deacon petitioned and were granted the organization of a separate congregation, but the Commission of Presbytery appointed for this work refused to do so because a deacon could not be obtained to accept the office. The matter was then carried up to Synod, and its Commission consisting of Revs. William Slater and William Milroy, with elder David Boyd, organized the Linn Grove congregation, without deacons, in September, 1856. There were twenty-five members, and Samuel Hawthorne and Daniel Cook were chosen ruling elders. The first pastor

* Sketch by Rev. J. W. Dill, in R. P. & C., 1884, p. 437.

was the Rev. Charles D. Trumbull, ordained and installed in charge in January, 1864. At this time they erected the present church building. Mr. Trumbull remained in charge ten years, and until his release in April, 1874. The Rev. Matthew A. Gault was ordained and installed pastor in May, 1875, and released in October, 1877. The Rev. John W. Dill was installed pastor in July, 1881, and was released in September, 1887. The elders have been Samuel Hawthorne, Daniel Cook, John Logan, Thomas McConnell, Stephen Bayles, William J. McClemment and A. A. McKee.

MORNING SUN. Around this thriving town a congregation was gathered, and formed from that of Sharon in July, 1873, with forty-six members. A comfortable frame church was erected in Morning Sun, and they have enjoyed a good degree of prosperity. The Rev. Charles D. Trumbull, the first and present pastor, was installed in April, 1874. Among the elders here have been Stephen Bayles, A. W. Cavin, George Cunningham, John McIntire and S. E. McElhinney.

REHOBOTH. In the spring of 1854, a colony of Covenanters emigrated from Pennsylvania and settled near the present town of Wyman, in Louisa County, and were organized as the Rehoboth congregation in October, 1854. In December, 1854, the Rev. Robert B. Cannon, from whose congregation in Pennsylvania most of the members had emigrated, was installed the pastor. He remained in charge thirteen years, and gathered quite a flourishing congregation. In August, 1874, the Rev. Edward G. Elsey was ordained and installed in charge, and remained nearly seven years, and until his release in April, 1881. In February, 1886, the Rev. James A. Black, the present pastor, was installed. They possess a good house of worship. Of the eldership have been A. Charleton, Jacob W. Willson, Joseph Purvis, William McCrea, John Dougherty, H. F. and L. M. Samson, William Martin, Thompson Graham, J. B. Dodds and Thomas G. Dunn.

WASHINGTON. The congregation now collected in Washington was organized as Washington and Amboy, in November, 1863. The Rev. Samuel M. Stevenson, who had missionated in this field for several years, was installed pastor in February, 1865, and remained until October, 1871. In October, 1873, the Rev. W. Pollock Johnston was installed in charge. He built up a good congregation and conducted a flourishing Academy. He was released in August, 1881. In December, 1882, the Rev. Thomas A. H. Wylie, the present pastor, was ordained and installed in charge. The Amboy branch was dropped, and the members of the old Ainsworth congregation were received in October, 1873. Of the elders here are mentioned Hugh Thompson, David Porter, John Rowan, J. R. Kirkpatrick, W. J. Clyde, J. H. Willson, R. M. Stevenson, David Love, W. S. Wylie, W. B. Hay and H. F. Samson.

BURLINGTON. At different times the city of Burlington offered possibilities for becoming a center of Covenanterism, and, in 1879, was regarded as a mission station. In 1881, the Rev. T. A. H. Wylie labored here with a good degree of success under the Central Board of

Missions. The members there are in connection with the Sharon congregation.

DAVENPORT. In some respects the city of Davenport was the most promising point in the State of Iowa. For many years it was the only place above St. Louis where the Mississippi was spanned by a bridge, and, being situated most beautifully at the foot of the Rock Island rapids, in a healthy location and commanding commercial importance, was a field well worth cultivating. A congregation was organized in this city in September, 1864, principally through the efforts of John B. McElroy. It received supplies from Presbytery, but, by the removal of members, it became disorganized in May, 1869, and continued to occasionally receive supplies as a mission station until May, 1883.

HOPKINTON. Covenanters settled in Delaware County, and in the vicinity of this village, as early as 1850. In the fall of 1855, the Rev. William L. Roberts, D. D., removed from Sterling, New York, and took charge of this promising field.* The congregation was organized in April, 1856, and was called "Maquokcta," after the river that flows past the village of Hopkinton, and was changed to the present name in 1879. Robert Gilmore and J. B. Whittaker were chosen elders, and James Kilpatrick, deacon. Mr. Roberts continued as stated supply until May, 1860, when he was regularly installed pastor. In December, 1864, the pastor was removed by death. In April, 1867, the Rev. David H. Coulter was ordained and installed pastor, and remained in charge until October, 1874. In June, 1875, the Rev. Robert

* Items from Mr. James Grier, Sand Spring, Iowa.

C. Wylie was installed, and demitted the charge in October, 1882, to labor in the interests of National Reform. In September, 1886, the Rev. Thomas H. Acheson was ordained and installed in charge, and is the present efficient pastor. Of the principal members have been James Grier, Robert Gilmore, Peter Guthrie, James Kilpatrick, Andrew Orr, J. B. Whittaker, William McGlade, James Douglas, William Morrison, H. M. Johnston, Patterson O. Joseph, R. L. Wallace, William McCullough.

GROVE HILL. Emigrants, chiefly from southern Ohio, settled in the vicinity of Grove Hill, in Bremer County, in 1856, and continued to gather until the congregation was organized in October, 1861. The Rev. Robert Hutcheson continued to supply them until his installation as pastor in April, 1863. He resigned the charge in May, 1867, and supplied them until the congregation was disorganized by emigration in May, 1869.

HICKORY GROVE. A few families of Covenanters from Ohio settled in Monroe County, and not far from Albia, in 1863. They were followed by the Rev. James Love in 1864, and he ministered to them until the organization as Albia in October, 1865. The name was changed to Hickory Grove in May, 1872. In April, 1866, Mr. Love was installed pastor, and continued in this relation until old age caused his release in September, 1881. In September, 1882, the Rev. James A. Thompson, the present pastor, was installed in charge. Of the elders have been Joseph Purvis and James Boyd.

WALNUT CITY. A society of Covenanters settled in

Appanoose County, and near this city, in 1865, and were organized into a congregation in March, 1868. In September, 1870, the Rev. Isaiah Faris became the first and only pastor, and was released in May, 1877. Not obtaining another pastor, many emigrated, and the congregation was disorganized in April, 1884, and was regarded as a mission station. James W. Dougherty, Matthew Chestnut, Samuel Milligan and Joseph Stevenson were among the elders.

. CLARINDA. Emigrants chiefly from Sharon congregation settled in the far west Page County, as the nucleus of the present Clarinda congregation, in 1852. In those days there were no railroads in this country, and, by journeying in wagons through an almost unsettled country they found a resting place on the rolling prairie along the Nodaway river.* In December, 1855, they received an organization when there were thirteen families and thirty-three members. In the fall of 1856, the Rev. Joseph McCracken found his way among them as the pastor-elect, but, by the badness of the roads and the isolated location, the Commission did not install him until July, 1857. He remained in charge less than two years. In September, 1862, the Rev. David McKee, the present pastor, was installed in charge. Since his settlement the country has been wholly transformed by the building of numerous railroads and the fine cultivation of the rich prairies. Of the families are those of Willson, Hutcheson, Glasgow, Brown, Gilmore, Linn, Caskey, McDowell, Tippin,

---

* *Reformed Presbyterian*, Vol. 20, p. 128.

Connerry, Neill, Aikin, Whitehill, McKee, Pinkerton, McCalla, McFarland.

LONG BRANCH. A little south of Clarinda, and along the Missouri State line, is situated the flourishing congregation of Long Branch. They were organized in April, 1877, and for two years enjoyed the stated labors of the Rev. Matthew A. Gault. Mr. Gault was installed the pastor in October, 1880, and remained in charge two years, when he was released to enter upon the work of National Reform in the West. In October, 1887, the Rev. B. Melancthon Sharp was ordained and installed pastor, and is now in charge. Among the elders here are J. H. Walkinshaw, William McCrory and John McElroy. The congregation suffered the loss of their church building by a cyclone a few years ago, but a more commodious one was soon erected in the town of Blanchard.

MISSOURI.

SAINT LOUIS. The natural location of the city of Saint Louis on "the father of waters," with the boundless resources of the agricultural West, with its mineral, manufacturing and commercial advantages, with transportation by water and rail, at once commanded the name of the chief city in the Mississippi Valley. A few Covenanters had gathered in this emporium of the West as early as 1840, but with no opportunity to wait upon their own services. The congregation was organized in the old Associate Reformed Church, April 2, 1846, by Rev. James Wallace, with elders

James Finley and John Donnelly, of Illinois.* Henry Dean and John Moffit were chosen ruling elders. They worshipped principally in the Associate Reformed Church. In July, 1852, the Rev. Andrew C. Todd was ordained and installed pastor, and at that time there were forty members. In the following year, through the liberality of A. G. Gamble, Esq., then Postmaster of Saint Louis, they were put in possession of a lot of ground, now at the corner of Gamble Avenue and Mercer street, where they erected a church building. Mr. Todd resigned the charge in April, 1857. The Rev. Joseph McCracken was installed pastor in October, 1859, and was pastor for fifteen years, when he was translated to Geneva College in September, 1874. In September, 1877, the Rev. James R. Hill was installed pastor, and released in April, 1885. Uniting with Staunton, Illinois, they obtained a part of the time of the Rev. Ellsworth M. Smith, who was ordained and installed in charge in May, 1887. Among the principal families here may be named those of Henry Dean, Dr. John McKinley, John Moffit, George Thomas, Thomas Cox, Silas and Robert J. Smith, Daniel Williamson, James Kirk, Samuel W. McClurkin, Thomas Matthews, John Gass, William Patterson, James Orr, Henry and James Martin, Rev. James Wallace, John Ingram, William C. Bovard, Zaccheus G. Willson, J. P. Montgomery.

SYLVANIA. A few Covenanters settled in Dade County, south-western Missouri, and were gathered into a society chiefly through the efforts of the Rev. James

---

* *Covenanter*, Vol. 2, p. 21.

Wallace. They were organized into a congregation, August 10, 1871, with forty-nine members. Fourteen of these were received from the Free Presbyterian, United Presbyterian, Cumberland Presbyterian, Methodist and Roman Catholic Churches.* For nearly five years they were supplied by Presbytery, and, in 1876, the Rev. Josiah Dodds labored among them for two years. He was installed pastor in May, 1878, and is now in charge. W. M. Edgar, William Taylor, R. C. McGee, Thomas Crozier, James Coulter, Philip Eckard, Hugh McCluey and Dr. Robert Dunlap have been active and representative members.

CAMERON. This was a mission station, and for several years supplied by the Rev. Robert B. Cannon. No congregation was organized.

KANSAS CITY. A few Covenanters are now living in this rapidly growing city, and, chiefly through the efforts of Mr. David Boyd, arrangements are being made for the organization of a mission of which Rev. J. Milligan Wylie is in charge.

KANSAS.

The congregations in the great West have been so recently organized, and the membership so changeable, that the history of Covenanterism in this vast region is not ready to be written. With few exceptions, they have at one time been cultivated by the Central Board of Missions, and some of them are now receiving help from that source. Numerous also have been the

---

* *R. P. & C.*, 1871, p. 317.

laborers who have spent a few months in different localities. Societies are springing up all over the West and loudly calling for help. Home Mission work is employing laborers whose duty it is to gather scattered families into societies and congregations.

OLATHE. This is a growing town and destined soon to became a suburb of Kansas City. It is the capital of Johnston County, and in the eastern part of the State. The congregation was organized in April, 1865, through the labors of the Rev. William W. Mc-Millan. Mr. McMillan was installed pastor in March, 1866, and labored for nearly twenty years and until his release in October, 1885. The Rev. Joseph H. Wylie was installed pastor in October, 1887. Among the families here are those of Dr. Bell, Samuel Dickey, J. M. Hutcheson, Joseph Thompson, W. S. Mitchell, Thompson and Alexander Moore, John Robinson, Walter McCrea, Samuel and Robert Galbraith, James M. Renfrew, John Acheson, James Ritchie and James Hunter.

PLEASANT RIDGE. A few miles from Olathe, in Johnston County, Pleasant Ridge is located, and was originally a part of the former congregation. It received a separate organization in August, 1871. The Rev. Matthew Wilkin was the first pastor, installed for a part of his time, in May, 1874, and was removed by death in July, 1880. In October, 1881, the Rev. R. M. C. Thompson, the present pastor, was installed. Among the elders have been J. M. Marvin, John Sterritt, T. M. and James Hutcheson.

WINCHESTER. This is the largest congregation of

Covenanters in Kansas, and surrounds the growing town of Winchester, the capital of Jefferson County. It was built up chiefly through the labors of the Rev. Josiah Dodds, and was organized in September, 1868. In November, 1868, Mr. Dodds became the pastor, and remained in this relation eight years. In August, 1877, the present pastor, the Rev. David H. Coulter, was installed in charge. Among the members here are James Thompson, John Moore, David Faris, George Thomas, W. R. Curry, Hugh Selders, John R. Reynolds, Samuel and David Dill, William McCrea, David Logan, James R. McIntire, James White and John Carson.

NORTH CEDAR. North-west of Winchester, and in the adjoining County of Jackson, is the flourishing congregation of North Cedar. It was cultivated by the Rev. J. S. T. Milligan and organized in October, 1871. Since October, 1872, Mr. Milligan has been the pastor. Of the elders have been James Keers, J. M. Law, J. L. Wright and William Wylie.

ESKRIDGE. This promising congregation is located in Wabaunsee County, south-west of the city of Topeka, and was organized in April, 1884. In August, 1886, the Rev. Nathan M. Johnston became the pastor, and is in charge.

HEBRON. There are two congregations in Clay County, and near Clay Centre. They were organized in November, 1871, as Republican City and Eagle Bend, and changed to Hebron in May, 1876. The Rev. J. S. T. Milligan supplied it for several years. The Rev. Samuel M. Stevenson was installed pastor in October, 1874, and released in April, 1876. In

November, 1876, the Rev. Matthew Wilkin was installed for part of his time, and was removed by death in July, 1880. In August, 1882, the Rev. James R. Latimer, the present pastor, was installed in charge. J. B. Porter, John T. Sanderson and A. Copeland have been elders.

TABOR. The other congregation in Clay County, and near Clay Centre, is Tabor. It was originally a part of the Republican City and Eagle Bend congregation, and received a separate existence in October, 1873. Since October, 1874, the Rev. Samuel M. Stevenson has been the pastor. Of the elders are W. B. Whittaker, William Rodgers and W. B. McElroy.

JEWELL. On the northern central border of Kansas is located the congregation of Jewell, situated in the south-eastern part of Jewell County. It was organized from the Rubens and Holmwood congregation, in July, 1885. James M. Adams and S. Y. Hutcheson are correspondents.

HOLMWOOD. This is situated in the northern part of Jewell County, and not far from Mankato. It included Rubens, and was organized in September, 1881. J. B. Alexander, John A. McIntire and George M. Tippin, are elders.

STERLING. Near the center of the State, in Rice County, and upon the Arkansas river, is located the congregation of Sterling. It was organized in November, 1877, and the Rev. John M. Armour was in charge until May, 1885. The Rev. Preston H. Wylie became the pastor in April, 1887, and is now in charge. Among the principal families are those of W. J.

Connery, James Humphreys, R. H. Matthews, J. M. Davis, William Lemon, J. Selfridge, James Frem, William Davis and Nathaniel Patton.

ROCHESTER. Some forty miles south of Sterling is the young congregation of Rochester, in Kingman County. It was organized in December, 1886.

QUINTER. This newly organized congregation is situated in Gove County, and in the western part of the State. It was organized in July, 1887.

BURDETT. Some fifty miles west of Sterling, and not far from Larned, Pawnee County, lies the congregation of Burdett, organized in July, 1887. It is supplied by the Central Board of Missions.

NEBRASKA.

WAHOO. The town of Wahoo is the capital of Saunders County, and situated some forty miles directly west of the city of Omaha. The other society of the congregation is at Fremont, north-east of Wahoo, in Dodge County, and on the Platte river. They were long cultivated by the Central Board of Missions, and organized as the Wahoo and Fremont congregation, in December, 1871, with thirteen members. In October, 1877, the Rev. James A. Thompson became the pastor, and was released in May, 1880. The Rev. Dr. Hugh P. McClurkin, the present pastor, was installed in February, 1884. J. M. Lee, Joseph Manners and Frank L. McClelland are among the leading elders.

SUPERIOR. Situated around the growing town of Superior, in Nuckolls County, on the Republican river and near the Kansas line, is located this thriving congregation. It was organized in September, 1881, and the Rev. Robert C. Allen became the pastor in December, 1882, and was released in October, 1884. The congregation lost its organization in May, 1885, but was re-organized in August, 1885. The Rev. Patterson P. Boyd was installed pastor in March, 1888.

BEULAH. This congregation is situated in Webster County, on the Republican river, some fifteen miles west of Superior. It was organized in September, 1881. The Rev. William S. Fulton has been pastor for a part of his time since March, 1885.

ECKLEY. Some miles north of Beulah, in Webster County, lies the congregation of Eckley, organized in November, 1878, with seventeen members. The Rev. William S. Fulton has been the pastor for part of his time since March, 1885. David and D. D. Mearns, Adam Orr and William H. Middleton are among the leading members and officers.

COLORADO.

EVANS. A colony of Covenanters, chiefly from Southern Illinois and lead by the Rev. Andrew C. Todd, settled around the town of Evans, in Weld County, in the northern part of this State, in the spring of 1871. The situation is some forty-five miles north of the city of Denver, and about twenty-five miles east of the base of the Rocky Mountains, and in full view of Long's Peak which is covered with perpetual snow. The congregation received an organization in August, 1871, and Mr. Todd continued to minister to them. They erected a neat brick church in the town of Evans. Mr. Todd was formally installed pastor in August, 1874.

LA JUNTA. This society is situated in Bent County, in south-eastern Colorado. This is a new field. There live the families of J. C. Dodds and J. M. Hill.

DENVER. A few families of Covenanters are living in this city, but no organization has yet been effected.

WASHINGTON TERRITORY.

SUNNYDALE. This society of Covenanters is situated near the villages of Sunnydale and Kent, some fifteen miles from the city of Seattle, on Puget Sound. In 1885, two families from Lake Reno, Minnesota, settled in this locality and they were joined by elder Dr. Ewing from Round Prairie, Minnesota, two years later. In October, 1887, they were visited by the Rev. N. R. Johnston, of California, who preached to them several Sabbaths. · These families of Covenanters hold society meetings, conduct a prosperous Sabbath School, and form the nucleus of a congregation. The principal families are those of Dr. W. H. Ewing, D. S. Elsey and S. G. Clark.

CALIFORNIA.

OAKLAND. Covenanters have reached the Golden Gate. In 1875, the Rev. N. R. Johnston and family removed to this city and opened a mission among the Chinese. A few scattered families of Covenanters reside in different parts of the State. In August, 1879, a mission congregation was organized in Oakland, by a Commission of Synod consisting of Rev. N. R. Johnston, and elders S. M. McCloy and David Mitchell, of Santa Anna. Twenty-two members were received, ten of whom were Chinese converts, and John Rice and Ju Sing were ordained ruling elders. Mr. Johnston was placed in charge. By the removal of elder Rice the congregation was disorganized in May, 1885, and Mr. Johnston continues to preach in connection with the mission.

No doubt in many of the States and Territories of the great West there are numerous scattered families of Covenanters, but so far as is known to collaters of statistics, all the organized societies have been noticed.

COVENANTERISM IN THE SOUTH.

During the persecution and banishment of the Covenanters from Scotland over two hundred years ago, many of them settled on the Eastern Shore of Maryland, in parts of Virginia and South Carolina, but they formed no separate societies, and in time went into the different Presbyterian Churches as they were formed in America. During the rapid flow of emigration to this country previous to 1770, the Covenanters were not distinguished by historians from the Scotch-Irish Presbyterians, and the early history of these people, as a distinct class, is lost.

MARYLAND.

BALTIMORE.   As early as the year 1797, a few families
of Covenanters resided in the city of Baltimore.   At
the formation of the Reformed Presbytery, in the spring
of 1798, the Revs. William Gibson and James McKinney
were directed to visit the people in this city.   In June,
1799, the Revs. Samuel B. Wylie and Alexander Mc-
Leod, at that time licensed, were appointed to preach
here, which they did as often as convenient.   In 1802,
the Rev. Samuel B. Wylie accepted a call to the united
congregations of Philadelphia and Baltimore, and was
installed in charge in November, 1803.*   Baltimore had
no organization and was in a feeble condition.   Mr.
Wylie continued to preach here until 1806, when he
demitted this branch and confined his labors to Philadelphia.   The society continued to increase by emigration,
chiefly from Scotland, and they continued faithful in
the society meetings.   In 1812, they bought the old
Associate Reformed Church, at the corner of Aisquith
and Fayette streets, and enjoyed regular supplies.   The
students of the Philadelphia Seminary were frequent in
their visits, and gave the Baltimoreans an opportunity
to choose a pastor.   In the spring of 1818, they invited
the Rev. John Gibson, then a licentiate, and who had
preached for them a few days, to return to Baltimore,
urging that the prospects for a large congregation
were very flattering.   This he declined to do; partly
from motives of delicacy, and partly because ordered
elsewhere by the direction of Presbytery.   A unanimous

---

* From the Congregational records and other sources.

call was made out in his favor in April, 1818, and accepted. In July, 1818, Mr. Gibson came to Baltimore and began his labors, but unforeseen circumstances delayed his ordination five months. The Baltimore congregation was regularly organized by Revs. Alexander McLeod, Robert Lusk and William Gibson, December 15, 1818, with forty members, and Rev. John Gibson was ordained and installed pastor. James McCauseland, John McLean and John Anderson were ordained ruling elders, and John Mortimer was appointed to read out the lines, and sing the few tunes selected by the Board of Trustees. Probably the first Covenanters in Baltimore were James Fletcher, James McCauseland, Robert Carothers and John McLean from Scotland; Mrs. James Black, John Anderson and Samuel Moody, from Ireland. In 1819, emigration from Europe began to flow in rapidly, and among those who were added to the Church this year were Samuel Boyd, Archibald McGill, Alexander McCracken, John Neilson and James Wooden. The sacrament of the Lord's supper was, for the first time, administered on December 19, 1819, and the pastor was assisted by Revs. Alexander McLeod and Robert Lusk. In 1820, John Milroy, William and Samuel Cumming, and Samuel Russell, from Scotland; and Patrick May and Patrick Boyd, from Ireland, were among those added to the congregation. In 1821, forty persons were added to the Church, among whom were the families of David Graham, Dr. J. Harper, John McElroy, John Wood, Walter Russell, James Kirkpatrick, John McElwee, Hugh Connell, Samuel Henry, James Logan, Willoughby Lewis, Robert Bates, John Little,

Joshua David, John Murphy and Arthur Baxter. In 1822, eighteen were added, among whom were James Crawford, John Campbell, Hugh McConnell, John Davis, James Brown, Samuel Morrison and Alexander Scott. Willoughby Lewis and David Graham were added to the session, May 18, 1822. In 1823, thirty-five more members were added to the roll, chiefly from Scotland. Of these emigrants were John Waugh, James Mc-Collum, Samuel Boyd, Edward Spence, Patrick Dickey, George Smith, John Boyd, John Fisher, James Chartiers, Alexander Hamilton, John Hamel, Daniel Loughridge, William Stavely, William Waddell, Moses Roney, William Johnston, James Dykes, Edward Hamilton, William Pettigrew, John McQuown and John Arnold. For five or six years the congregation added many members to its communion, and, in 1830, was one of the largest and wealthiest congregations in the body. There were over three hundred members. John Mortimer, Patrick Dickey and James Smith were ordained ruling elders in April, 1828. The church now became too small to accommodate the worshippers who flocked to hear the eloquence of Mr. Gibson. In 1829, the church at Aisquith and Fayette streets was sold, and the congregation bought a large and commodious church at the corner of Holliday and Saratoga streets. Here large audiences waited upon the services, and many were added to the Church. A laxness in discipline followed this great success, and members were not always excluded from secret societies and the privileges of citizens. As a natural consequence, during the division of the Church in 1833,

Mr. Gibson and nearly the whole congregation, left the principles of the Church, and went into the Presbyterian and other bodies. The faithful remnant were left in charge of the church property, but it was too large for them to use and a debt was upon it. They then organized themselves into a society, sold the church and paid off the debt, and the same year bought a little mission church on Gallow's Hill, without seats and a brick floor, which is the original of the present church building on Harford Avenue and Chase street. They spent a considerable sum on repairs, and asked for supplies. At the re-organization, November 10, 1833, there were about forty members, and James Hunter, Samuel Reid and Hugh Crocket were added to the session. During this year Patrick Morrow, John Dickson, David Warwick, Robert Mc-Rosey, William Laughlin and John McCrory were among those added to the Church. Soon they were followed by James Duncan, Patrick Hall, Andrew Mabin and William Robinson. The Rev. William L. Roberts was installed pastor in January, 1835. During this year Matthew Cowan, James Dickson, John Henry, James Jackson, Samuel Russell, William J. Dickey, James Ganston, Gregory Barrett, James Stewart and John Russell were added to the membership. John Ford and William Wylie were elected elders, January 23, 1837. During this year, Mr. Roberts made a protracted war upon the milk dealers who delivered milk upon the Sabbath day. As many influential members were engaged in this business, the Church suffered greatly by their suspension, and the abandon-

ment by others. Mr. Roberts resigned the charge in
October, 1837, and James Hunter, Hugh Crocket, and
others, went with him to Sterling, New York. Among
those who supplied during the next few years, was
Francis Gailey, whom they called. Mr. W. J. Dickey
was the commissioner to the Presbytery meeting in
New York to urge the call, but upon the way with
Mr. Gailey he discovered his duplicity, and that he
did not intend to accept their invitation. The call
was declined. Mr. Gailey frequently returned to Baltimore and preached, and, when he made defection and
was suspended in October, 1838, he took the great
majority of the members with him, and they retained
the church property. The congregation was again disorganized, and the few faithful Covenanters were left
without a house of worship. They resorted to the
prayer meetings, which were held from house to house,
and generally at the home of Mr. William Cumming
in the eastern suburb of the city. Preaching was
occasionally enjoyed, and they were visited by Revs.
David Scott, Thomas Hanna and Charles B. McKee,
The case of the right of the property entered the
civil courts, and the trial was postponed from time to
time. In 1842, the congregation was re-organized and
the Rev. Charles B. McKee, to whom all honor is due
for the existence of the congregation, was made stated
supply in 1844. He preached and taught a classical
school, and in this way the cause was maintained.
The small congregation now worshipped in Union Hall,
on the corner of Baltimore and Holliday streets, and
subsequently in the church of the New Jerusalem

Society at the corner of Baltimore and Exeter streets. At the re-organization of the congregation, July 17, 1842, James Wright and James Dickson were chosen ruling elders. The Rev. Charles B. McKee was installed pastor in December, 1846, and the congregation began to grow. After the church property had been in the courts for ten years, and every effort had been made to obtain possession of the church, a present member of the congregation entered the church and remained there until it was opened by the authorities, and when he was found in the building, the court decided that the Covenanters held the property by right of possession. After paying a part of the costs, the congregation has worshipped in their own house unmolested for forty years. The Rev. Charles B. McKee left the communion of the Church in December, 1852, and the congregation suffered another loss. They numbered about sixty members, and were determined to make an effort to obtain another pastor. The Rev. John Crawford was ordained and installed pastor in November, 1853. Henry Smyth and Patrick Morrow were added to the session in May, 1854. Mr. Crawford died in September, 1856, much lamented by the congregation and Church. The Rev. William W. McMillan was ordained and installed in charge in December, 1859. D. James Cumming and William McLean were ordained elders in November, 1860. Mr. McMillan had a great deal to contend with, as times were financially hard and the war of the rebellion was in progress. The city was in arms and many of the members had enlisted. Mr. McMillan resigned the charge in May,

23

1863, and for various reasons the congregation was greatly reduced. In August, 1864, the Rev. W. Pollock Johnston was installed in charge. In 1868, the church was wholly remodeled and a small Sabbath School room was put under the church. Matthew H. Wright and D. Oliver Brown were ordained elders in October, 1871. Mr. Johnston resigned the charge in July, 1873. The Rev. John Lynd was ordained and ·installed in charge in December, 1873, and resigned in November, 1877. In October, 1878, the Rev. Alfred D. Crowe was ordained and installed in charge. Captain James M. Shackelford and Joseph M. Smith were chosen ruling elders in November, 1880, and in October, 1881, James S. Mullen and George A. Maben were added to the session. Mr. Crowe resigned in August, 1884, on account of impaired health, and died a few months thereafter in Rochester, New York. In November, 1885, W. Melancthon Glasgow, the present pastor, was ordained and installed in charge. Among the members not already mentioned are recorded the names of George Crocket, John Cummings, John Coulter, Alexander Kinnear, John McGowan, Robert Lamb, John Rodgers, William Ross, John McLean, Professors James R., Hugh, and Alexander M. Newell, Dr. John Dickson, Alexander Harbison, John McKinney, Fergus and James Johnston, William Knox, John B. Crocket, William W. Russell, H. W. Calderwood, Thomas Moore, William Irwin, John Wright, James Maben, W. C. Purvis, Thomas McGowan, James Mitchell, Adam Wallace, W. J. Hughes, Robert Hunter, Robert Hughes, Captain William Hunt, George W.

Marshall, George B. and George M. Cummings, John
H. McGowan, Joseph Bowes, J. Renwick Cummings,
J. T. Plummer, Walter Nicholson, John F. Bachen.

VIRGINIA.

SUFFOLK. A few families from Western Pennsylvania
removed to the country below the Chesapeake Bay, and
near the town of Suffolk, in the south-eastern corner
of Virginia, and were organized as a mission station in
November, 1876. They were sustained chiefly by the
Philadelphia Presbytery; and the ministers of that court,
and the Rev. James L. Pinkerton supplied them for
some time. The mission was disorganized in May, 1881,
by the removal of some of the colony, and others going
into the United Presbyterian Church. Among the
families of this colony were those of John Haslett,
John Galbraith, Thompson Gilleland and John Steele.

TENNESSEE.

HEPHZIBAH. This once flourishing congregation was
situated along the Elk river, near Fayetteville, in
Lincoln County. As early as the year 1807, the families
of Alexander Morton, John Paul, John Murdoch, and
others, from South Carolina, located in this vicinity, and
were visited by the Rev. Thomas Donnelly.* In 1809,
and in 1810, other families from South Carolina joined
them, and the Rev. John Kell preached to them. The
congregation was organized June 12, 1812, as the Elk

* *Reformed Presbyterian Advocate*, 1872, p. 160.

congregation, by Rev. John Reilly, of South Carolina, and elder William Edgar, of Duck river, with eighteen members. At this time Samuel Little and Alexander Morton were chosen ruling elders. The sacrament of the Lord's supper was administered in the open woods, God's first temple, beneath the shade of a wide spreading beech. In 1815, they were visited by Robert Lusk, licentiate, and, in 1818, they called the Rev. Samuel Wylie, but he declined on account of the prevalence of slavery. In the spring of 1822, Hugh McMillan, and in the fall of the same year, Gavin McMillan, came and preached with much acceptance to the people. Rev. Gavin McMillan declined a call tendered him. The Rev. Robert Lusk dispensed the next communion in a grove, in October, 1822, at which time James Blair, John Carithers and James Morton were added to the session, the former elders having removed to Illinois. In 1823, they erected a log church. In 1825, the Rev. Robert McKee, licentiate, preached six months and received a unanimous call. He declined on account of the prevalence of slavery. In 1826, the Rev. James Faris visited them, and the congregation had grown to one hundred members. In 1828, Revs. James Faris and Ebenezer Cooper dispensed the sacraments, and Thomas Morton, Thomas Blair, Andrew Carithers and William Wyatt were added to the session. Mr. Cooper was now called to the pastorate, accepted, returned to the Northern Presbytery, and was ordained in June, 1828. When he came back to the congregation for settlement, which now changed its name from Elk to Hephzibah, he declined being installed pastor, giving as reasons the prevalence of slavery and the great distance from his ministerial brethren. In 1832, Mr. Cooper, and the great majority of the congregation, emigrated to Fayette County, Indiana, on account of the evils of slavery. In 1833, the society became identified with the New School body, and is now about extinct.

DUCK RIVER. A few families from South Carolina settled along Duck river, in Hickman County, southwest of the city of Nashville, in 1810, but afterwards removed to Illinois and Indiana.

RODGERSVILLE. A small colony from South Carolina, and emigrants from Ireland, settled along the Holston river, Hawkins County, in East Tennessee, in the early part of the present century. Some of them afterwards emigrated to Cincinnati, Ohio, and other free States. Among these families were Patrick Murphy, Dr. Archibald and Samuel McKinney.

ALABAMA.

SELMA. The city of Selma was selected by the Central Board of Missions as the seat of the Southern Mission in 1874, and the Rev. Lewis Johnston was placed in charge. The Selma congregation was organized May 21, 1875, with twenty-five members, four of whom were certified from the Baptist Church, three from the Presbyterian, one from the Methodist, and twelve were received from the world. Lewis Johnston, Sr., and George M. Elliot, previously ordained for the field, and Daniel W. Boxley were chosen elders. This was the first Covenanter congregation of the

sable race ever organized in America, and the Rev.
Lewis Johnston was installed pastor. Mr. Johnston
was suspended in November, 1876. The Rev. George
M. Elliot, the present pastor, was installed in December, 1877. John Willdee and James H. Pickens were
elected elders. The Revs. Hugh W. Reed and J. W.
Dill preached at Pleasant Grove, six miles from Selma,
where there is conducted a flourishing Sabbath School.

GEORGIA.

There was a society of Covenanters near the present
town of LOUISVILLE, in eastern Georgia, as early as
1780, to which the Rev. William Martin frequently
preached. At the meeting of the Committee of the
Reformed Presbytery at Rocky Creek, South Carolina,
in February, 1801, a petition was received from this
society for ministerial assistance. The Committee
directed the Rev. Thomas Donnelly to visit the society,
and if he found it practicable to attach it to the
Rocky Creek congregation; and if not, to endeavor
to send them supplies. There is no record, however,
of any organization in Georgia, although groups of
families lived within the limits of this State.

NORTH CAROLINA.

CHARLOTTE. A large number of Covenanters lived
within the bounds of Mecklenberg County, and were
visited by Rev. William Martin previous to 1785.
They gradually migrated back to South Carolina, and

other States, after the war of the Revolution, and no organization beyond the society meeting was ever effected.

STATESVILLE. Still farther north in Iredell County, and near the present village of Statesville, was a society of Covenanters in 1780, also visited by the Rev. William Martin. Indeed all through the southern and eastern parts of North Carolina there were a few societies occasionally visited by the ministers in the South, but were never formally organized into congregations or had a settled ministry.

SOUTH CAROLINA.

CHESTER DISTRICT. In the latter part of the seventeenth century a few banished Covenanters settled at Port Royal and in the vicinity of Charleston, but on account of the unhealthy condition of the country they either migrated to Chester District or returned to Scotland. Soon Chester District became the stronghold of Covenanterism in the South. In 1750, soon after the removal of the Rev. Alexander Craighead to the South, a few members of the "Craighead Society" at Octorara, Pennsylvania, and other Covenanters from Virginia and North Carolina, settled in this region. Among these were Hugh and John Mc-Donald. They settled along the Rocky Creek and were the pioneers of Chester.* John McDonald and his wife were both killed by the Cherokee Indians in 1761, and their children were made prisoners. In

*Sketch by D. G. Stinson per R. B. Elder, Guthriesville, S. C.

1755, emigrants from Ireland began to settle up the country, and among these were many Covenanter families. They built a union church and the Rev. William Richardson, of Waxhaws, became the preacher. The church was called "Catholic," because Presbyterians generally worshipped there, and this general meeting house was situated on the Rocky Mount road, some fifteen miles south-east of the town of Chester. In 1770, the Covenanters separated from the others and held society meetings. They then wrote to Ireland for a preacher and made every effort to obtain a minister. In accordance with their wishes, the Rev. William Martin, of Ballymoney, Ireland, came with a colony of his people in 1772, and settled along the Rocky Creek. No imaginary picture has been drawn when a description of the manners and customs of these patriotic Covenanters is given by Mrs. E. F. Ellet in her "Domestic History of the American Revolution," and written by Mr. Daniel G. Stinson, whose father was a member of this colony. This chapter of interesting Covenanter history will here be inserted:

An interesting glimpse into the life and character of the Scotch-Irish patriots of South Carolina at the period of the Revolution is afforded in the history of Mrs. Green, daughter of Robert Stephenson (or Stinson,) a native of Scotland, who was born in the County Antrim, Ireland, in 1750. The family was reared in the strictest tenents of the Covenanter faith, in the vicinity of Ballymoney, under the pastoral care of the Rev. William Martin, who, in 1772, emigrated to America, and settled on the Rocky Creek, South Carolina. Many of the congregation quitted their country with him, and followed their pastor under impulse of the same desire of the "freedom to worship God." Among these emigrants were James, William and Elizabeth Stinson, and their brother-in-law, William Anderson, who married Nancy

Stinson before the sailing of the ship. Her wedded life thus commenced with a voluntary renunciation of home and the society of
early friends, to seek a new country and to encounter unforeseen
privations and difficulties. Bounty lands had been bestowed by the
government as inducements to emigration, and those who received such
warrants, upon their arrival took great care to fix their location as
near as possible to a central point, where a meeting house might be
built. Their spirit was that of the ancient patriarch, who first built
an altar. The spot selected for this purpose was the dividing ridge
between Great and Little Rocky Creeks. Here, in the summer of 1773,
these pious Covenanters might be seen from day to day, felling trees
and clearing a space of ground upon which they reared a large log
meeting house, many of them living in tents at home, till a place
was provided in which they could assemble for religious service. A
number of log cabins soon rose in the neighborhood, each with a
patch of ground in which Indian corn was planted. The Irish
emigrants were ignorant of the manner of cultivating this grain; but
the first settlers, or "country-borns" were ready to offer assistance
and took pains to instruct them in its culture. The wants of small
families were supplied with small crops, for corn was only then used
for making bread, the woods affording abundant supplies of grass
cane and wild pea vines to serve their horses and cattle for provender
the whole year round. The streams abounded in shad and various
other fish in their season, and the trusty rifle that hung upon the
rack over the door, was never brought back without having performed
its duty in slaying the deer, or whatever small game might be sought
in the forest. Often have the old men who lived in that day spoken
of the abundance that prevailed; a good hunter, when he chose,
could make five dollars a day in deer skins and hams, while, if
generous, he might give away the remainder of the venison to the
poor. The hams and skins were sent to Charleston and exchanged
for powder, lead, and other necessary articles. The wealth of these
primitive Covenanters consisted in stock, their labors in tilling the
earth, felling the woods and fencing their fields, while they were
disturbed by none of the wants or cares created by a more advanced
state of civilization. Such was the condition of the Covenanters, who
had left their native Ireland, for the religious liberty found in the
wilds of America. During seven years after their settlement in the
woods, they enjoyed a life in which nothing of earthly comfort was

wanting. Year after year the patch enlarged, the field becoming to
the respectable dimensions of ten acres, and then a good clearing for
a farm. Every Sabbath morning the parents, in their "Sunday
clothes," with their neatly dressed and well-behaved little ones, might
be seen at the log meeting-house ; their pocket Bibles containing the
old Psalms in their hands, and, turning over the leaves, they would
follow the preacher in all the passages of Scripture cited by him, as
he commented upon the verses. Their simple, trustful piety caused
the wilderness to rejoice. But this happiness could not be lasting.
The rumour of war which had gone over the land, was heard even in
this remote section, and these refugees who had found peace could
not but sympathize with their oppressed brethren. Some, it is true,
from the vicinity, had been out in what was called "the Snow Cam-
paign," an expedition undertaken towards the close of 1775 against
the fierce Cherokee Indians and certain loyalists in the upper regions ;
and some had been present at the attack on Sullivan's Island in 1776,
and brought a report to those remaining at home. The desolation
that raged in the North ere long took its way Southward, and the
families which were unmolested, and had enjoyed the pure ordinances
of the gospel, were now disturbed. This immunity was of short
duration. John McClure, of Fishing Creek, came home and brought
the intelligence of the surrender of Charleston, and his own defeat at
Monk's Corner. Still worse news came from across the river—of the
inhuman massacre of Buford's command by Tarleton's corps at Waxhaws. This event gave a more sanguinary character to the war.
Directly after this appalling announcement, spread the rumour that a
strong party of British was posted at Rocky Mount, that the people
of Wateree were flocking to take protection as loyal subjects, and that
the conquerers were sending forces in every direction to reduce the
Province to subjection. Such was the aspect of affairs up to a certain
Sabbath in June, 1780. On the morning of this memorable Sabbath,
the different paths leading up to the log meeting house were unusually crowded. The old country folk were dressed with their usual
neatness, especially the women, whose braw garments, brought from
Ireland, were carefully preserved, not merely from thrift, but as a
memorial of the green isle of their birth. Their dresses of silk, chintz,
or Irish calico—fitted each wearer with marvelous neatness, and the
collars or ruffles of linen, white as snow, and the high-heeled shoes.
They wore fur hats with narrow rims and large feathers ; their hair

neatly braided, hanging over the shoulders or fastened by the black ribbon band around their heads, comprised their holiday attire. It was always a mystery to the dames, who had spent their lives or many years in the country, how the gowns of the late comers could be made to fit so admirably; their own, in spite of every effort, showing a sad deficiency in this respect. The men, on their part, appeared not less adorned in their coats of fine broadcloth, with their breeches, large knee buckles of pure silver, and hose of various colors. They wore shoes fastened with a large strap secured with a buckle, or white topped boots, leaving exposed three or four inches of the hose from the knee downward. It must be acknowledged that these people, so strict in their religious principles, were somewhat remarkable in their fondness for dress. They considered it highly irreverent to appear at church not clad in their best clothes, and though when engaged in labor during the week, they conformed to the customs of their neighbors, wearing the coarse homespun of their own manufacture, and on the Sabbath it was astonishing to see how much of decent pride there was in the exhibition of the fine clothes brought from beyond the seas. As the years rolled on many of the dresses and coats began to show marks of decay; but careful repairing preserved the hoarded garments, linked with such endeared associations, and only a few, who had married with the "country-born," had made any alteration in them. The peculiarity of dress gave the congregation, assembled for worship in that rude sanctuary, a strange and motely appearance—European finery being contrasted with the homespun gowns, hunting shirts and moccasins of the country people. It was always insisted upon as a point of duty by Covenanters, that children should be brought to church with parents. The little ones sat between the elders, that they might be kept quiet during Divine service, and also to be ready at the appointed hour to say the Catechism. The strict deportment and piety of this people had already done much to change the customs formerly prevalent. Men and women who used to hunt or fish upon the Sabbath day, now went regularly to meeting, and some notorious ones whose misconduct had been a nuisance to the community, now left the neighborhood. The Stroudes, Kitchens and Morrisses, formerly regarded as the Philistines of the land, were regular in their attendance upon Divine service. Upon this particular Sabbath, the whole neighborhood seemed to have turned out, and every face wore an expression of anxiety. Groups of men might be seen gathered together under shade trees in every direction, talking in loud and earnest tones, some laying down plans for the assent of their friends; some pale with alarm and listened to others telling the news; and some, transported with indignation, stamped the ground and gesticulated vehemently as they spoke. Everywhere the women mingled with the different groups, and appeared to bear an active part in what was going on. At eleven o'clock, precisely, the venerable form of William Martin, the preacher, came in sight. He was about sixty years of age, and had a high reputation for learning and eloquence. He was a large and powerful man, with a voice that might have been heard at the distance of half a mile. As he walked from the place where he hitched his horse, towards the stand (it being customary when the congregation was too large to be accommodated in the meeting-house, to have the service in the open air), the loud and angry words of the speakers must have reached his ears. The voices ceased as he approached, and the congregation was soon seated in silence upon the logs surrounding the stand. When he arose to speak every eye was fixed upon him. Those who had been most noisy expected a reproof for their desecration of the Sabbath, for their faithful pastor was never known to fail of rebuking those whose deportment was unsuited to the solemnity of the day. But at this time he also seemed absorbed with the great subject that agitated every bosom. "My hearers," he said, in his broad, distinct Irish dialect, "talk and angry words will do no good. *We must fight!* As your pastor, in preparing a discourse suited to this time of trial, I have sought for all light; I have examined the Scriptures and other helps in ancient and modern history, and have especially considered the controversy between the United Colonies and the mother country. Sorely have our countrymen been dealt with, till forced to their declaration of independence. Our forefathers in Scotland made a similar one, and maintained that declaration with their lives. It is now our turn, brethren, to maintain this at all hazards." After the prayer, and singing of the Psalms, he calmly opened his discourse. He cited many passages of Scripture to show that a people may lawfully resist wicked rulers; pointed to historical examples of princes trampling upon the rights of the people; painted in vivid colors the rise and progress of the Reformation in Scotland; and finally applied the subject by fairly stating the merits of the revolutionary controversy. Giving a brief sketch of the events of the war, from the first shedding of blood at Lexington, and, warming with the subject as he proceeded, his address became eloquent with the fiery energy of a Demosthenes. In a voice like thunder, frequently striking with his clenched first the clapboard pulpit, he appealed to the excited concourse, exhorting them to fight valiantly in defence of their liberties. As he dwelt upon the recent horrid tragedy—the butchery of Buford's men, cut down by the British dragoons while crying for mercy—his indignation reached its height. Stretching out his hand toward Waxhaws—"Go see," he cried, "the tender mercies of Great Britain! In that church you may find men, though still alive, hacked out of the very semblance of humanity; some deprived of their arms, some with one arm or leg, some with both legs cut off, and others with mutilated trunks. Is not this cruelty a parallel to the history of our Scottish forefathers, driven from their conventicles, and hunted as beasts of the forest? Behold the godly youth, James Nesbit, chased for days by the British for the crime of being seen on his knees upon the Sabbath morning, etc!" To this stirring sermon the whole assembly responded. Hands were clenched and teeth set in the intensity of feeling; every uplifted face expressed the same determination, and even the women were filled with the spirit that threatened vengeance upon the invaders. During the interval of Divine worship, they went about professing their resolution to do their part in the approaching contest; to plough the fields, and gather the crops in the absence of the men, aye, to fight themselves rather than submit. In the afternoon the subject was resumed and discussed with renewed energy, while the appeals of the preacher were answered by even more energetic demonstrations of feeling. When the worship was concluded, and the congregation separated to return homeward, the manly form of Captain Ben Land was seen walking among the people, shaking hands with every neighbor, and whispering in his ear the summons to the next day's work. As the minister quitted the stand, William Stroud stepped up to him. This man, with his sons, was noted for strength and bravery. They were so tall in stature, that like Saul, they overlooked the rest of the congregation. "He doubted not," he said, "that Mr. Martin had heard of his 'whipping the pets.'" "I rather think," he continued, "some people will be a little on their guard how they go to Rocky Mount for 'tection papers! Yesterday I was down at old deaf Lot's still house, and who do you think was there? John and Dick Featherston. John said he had been to Rocky Mount to see the fine fellows, and they were so good to him as to give him 'tection. "Do, John, tell me what that is," I asked. He said "it was a paper, and whoever had one was safe; not a horse, cow or hog would the British take without paying two prices for it. So John, says I, I know now who told the British about James Stinson's large stock of cows which they drove off yesterday—knocking down Mrs. Stinson for putting up old brindle in the horse stable, so as to keep one cow to give milk for the children! Now, John, as you have British 'tection, I will give you Whig 'tection." "With that I knocked him down. Dick came running up, and I just give him a kick and doubled him up. John got up and ran, and Dick begged like a whipped boy. I told him he might carry the news that 'tection paper men should be whipped, and have their cows taken from them to pay James Stinson for his. I think this is what you call the law of Moses. And as for these Britishers, if I don't make old Nelly take in their ears, and be *dad* to them!" "Excuse me for swearing this time, if you please. Now, Mr. Martin, here is old Bill—that is two; then here is young Will, Tom, Jack, Hamp, Erby, Ransom and Hardy." The manner in which this characteristic speech was delivered may be imagined. Mr. Martin showed his acceptance of the proffered help by taking William's hand and introducing him to Captain Land. As they passed away from the stand, and on their way home from the meeting, one of the sturdy Covenanters, William Anderson, was unusually silent, as if some weighty matter engaged his thoughts. His wife spoke first, after reflecting. "I think, William, little Lizzie and I can finish the crop, and gather it in if need be, as well as take care of the stock." "I am glad of that, Nancy," was the reply. "I was silent, for I did na ken how to let you know it, but to-morrow morning I leave home. The way is now clear; the Word of God approves, and it shall ne'er be said that the Covenanters, the followers of the Reformers of Scotland, would na lend a helpin' hand to the renewal of the Covenant in the land of America! Now, Nancy, Captain Land will be out before day, giving notice that up at the cross roads hard by, he will drill the men who are willing to fight; this was agreed upon as I left meeting." They journeyed home and ate their dinner. As they arose from the table, Mrs. Anderson said, "William, were you out at the Kirk in Bally-money, upon that Sabbath when Mary Martin, our minister's first wife, lay a corpse in his house? No one thought he could attend to preaching in his sore distress; but precisely at the striking of the hour, he was seen walking down the long aisle to the pulpit. I never shall forget the sermon! There was not a dry eye in the whole

congregation; old men and women fairly cried out. I thought of
that to-day when, after the sermon, old Stroud went up to him
as if he had been one of the elders. Did you see the man of
God clap Stroud on the shoulder? Our minister is a wonderful
man; he can persuade people to almost anything." Mr. Anderson
looked up quietly and asked, "Did he persuade you to marry him,
Nancy, when he went to your father's a courting?" "Na, indeed,
William, I could na think of an old man when I had you
fairly in my net. But I did a good turn in letting him know that
Jenny Cheny was setting her cap for him, and sure enough he took
my advice and they married." The Sabbath evening wore away amid
the accustomed religious services, but the conversation frequently
turned upon the war. Early upon Monday morning, the plough was
left standing in the furrow, and the best horse was bridled and saddled
and left standing at the door. Mrs. Anderson had been up since a
little after midnight, making hoe cakes upon the hoe, and corn dodger
in the oven, and while the cooking of meats was going on, she was
busily plying the needle sewing up sacks and bags to hold provisions
for man and horse upon a long journey. As soon as he had taken
his breakfast, William bade his wife farewell, mounted and rode off.
The effect of Mr. Martin's eloquence was speedily apparent. At an
early hour upon Monday morning, many of the conscientious Covenanters were seen drilling on the muster-ground seven miles from
Rocky Mount, under the brave Captain Ben Land, while two miles
above this, at the shop of a negro blacksmith, half a dozen more were
getting their horses shod. Those at the muster-ground were charged
upon by a party of British dragoons, having no previous notice of
their approach, and were dispersed. The man who carried to the
enemy the tidings of Mr. Martin's sermon and the meeting of the Covenanters to drill, did not die in his bed. Their Captain being overtaken
and surrounded by the dragoons, who attacked him with their broad
swords, defended himself with his sword to the last, and wounded
severely several of his enemies before he fell. The party at the blacksmith shop was also surprised, and one man killed. The dragoons then
crossed Rocky Creek, and soon found their way to the rude stone hut
which was the dwelling of Mr. Martin. They found the old divine in
his study preparing a sermon, which was to be a second blast, and
made him their prisoner, and carried him like a felon to Rocky Mount.
There he and Thomas Walker were bound to the floor in one of the
log huts. The enemy knew well what reason they had to dread the
effect of Martin's stirring eloquence.

This colony expected to settle down close together, but the situation necessitated them to select lands at a distance from one another. Among those who came with Mr. Martin in this first colony were Andrew and James Stevenson (Stinson); William Anderson and his wife Nancy; Alexander Brady and his wife Elizabeth; the several families of the Linns and Kells, and others.* They took up bounty land which entitled them to one hundred acres for each head of the family, and fifty for each member thereof. Mr. Martin bought a plantation one mile square of six hundred and forty acres, upon which he built a stone house. The first log church erected by Covenanters was in the spring of 1774, and was situated on the same road as the "Catholic" church, and two miles east of it. It was burned by the Tories in 1780. The hands and hearts of the Covenanters were in the trying scenes of the Revolution. The men shouldered the musket and went to the defence of the country, while the women remained at home and attended to the farms. Mr. Martin was their leader, and did much for the cause of the country in arousing all the inhabitants of Chester to their duty as citizens. As a zealous Whig, and an eloquent preacher, Mr. Martin threw all his influence on the side of the Colonists, for which he was apprehended in June, 1780, and imprisoned at Rocky Mount and Camden by the British. Here he was confined for over six months. In December, 1780, and on the day of his trial before Lord Cornwallis at Winnsboro, he stood before

---

* Sketch by D. G. Stinson per R. B. Elder, Guthriesville, S. C.

him erect, with his grey locks uncovered, his eyes fixed upon his lordship, his countenance marked with frankness and benevolence. "You are charged," said Lord Cornwallis, "with preaching rebellion from the pulpit. You, an old man, and a minister of the gospel of peace, are charged with advocating rebellion against your lawful sovereign King George the III. What have you to say in your defence?" Nothing daunting, Mr. Martin replied, "I am happy to appear before you. For many months I have been held in chains for preaching what I believe to be the truth. As to King George I owe him nothing but good will. I am not unacquainted with his private character. I was raised in Scotland; educated in her literary and theological schools; settled in Ireland, where I spent the prime of my days, and came to this country some eight years ago. As a King, he was bound to protect his subjects in the enjoyment of their rights. Protection and allegiance go together, and when the one fails, the other cannot be exacted. The Declaration of Independence is but a reiteration of a principle which our Covenanted fathers have always maintained, and have lead this nation to adopt. I am thankful you have given me liberty to speak, and will abide your pleasure whatever it may be."* After his release by Lord Cornwallis, Mr. Martin went over to Mecklenberg, North Carolina, where he preached for some time. It was here he baptized Isaac Grier, the first Presbyterian minister born in Georgia and the grandfather of William Moffat Grier, President of

---

* Howe's History of the Presbyterian Church in South Carolina.

24

Erskine College, Due West, South Carolina. When the news came to him that the British had evacuated Charleston, Mr. Martin carried the word to the neighborhood, adding the comment, "the British have taken shipping, and may the d—l go with them." In the Fairfield District there lived one John Phillips, who was a man of wealth and talent. During the war, however, he became a rank Tory and was called "Tory Colonel Phillips." He betrayed the cause of the Covenanters, and those who had often saved his life when he cast himself upon the mercy of the Whigs. He accompanied Tarleton to Little Rocky Creek, where he took Archibald McClurkin from his bed, when he was lying at the point of death with small-pox, and hanged him to a tree by the roadside. This barbarous act so aroused the righteous indignation of the Covenanters, that their military aid in behalf of the Colonists was thereby greatly increased. Many cold blooded deeds were attributed to this traitor Phillips. After the war he returned to Ireland, but was not there safe from the vengeance he had provoked in South Carolina. He was shot on the street in Bally-money by one of McClurkin's brothers, but not fatally injured. He lived in constant fear of the avenger of blood and died a drunkard, himself in despair, and his family wholly destitute.* In 1781, Mr. Martin returned to Rocky Creek and resumed his labors among the Covenanters, preaching in the "Catholic" meeting-house. He was dismissed for intemperate habits, in 1785, but did not cease preaching. He frequently preached at the

* Mrs. Ellet's "Women of the Revolution."

house of Edward McDaniel, at Jackson's Creek, in Fairfield District, at the house of Richard Gladney, and
across the Catawba river, at the house of William
Hicklin. A small society built him a church, two miles
east of the site of the one burnt by the Tories, and
he continued to preach there for many years. In 1804,
his stone house was burnt, and the rest of his days he
lived in a log cabin. He continued his intemperate
habits and died in 1806. In the summer of 1789, the
Rev. James Reid, of Scotland, came on a missionary
tour to America, and visited the societies in South
Carolina. He set in order the affairs of the Church as
the representative of the Scottish Presbytery, and
dispensed the sacraments. At that time he also organized the Rocky Creek congregation, and the elders were
Samuel Loughridge, Adam Edgar, John Wyatt, Thomas
Morton and James McQuiston. Soon afterwards, John
Kell, David Stormont, John Rock, Robert Hemphill,
Hugh McMillan and Archibald Coulter were added to
the session. They represented the different societies in
Chester, York and Fairfield Districts.* In 1791, the
Rev. James McGarragh was sent out by the Reformed
Presbytery of Ireland, and some members came with
him. He settled in the Beaver Dam society, a branch
of the Rocky Creek congregation. In 1792, the Rev.
William King arrived, having been sent out by the
Scottish Presbytery. After an extended tour through
the North and East, he settled on the south side of the
Beaver Dam, near the Mount Prospect church. In 1793,
Revs. McGarragh and King constituted a Committee to

---

* Sketch by Rev. D. S. Faris, in *R. P. & C.*, 1876, p. 51.

judicially manage the affairs of the Church in America. They restored Mr. Martin and the affairs of the Church began to wear a regular appearance.* The membership was large and scattered, and required all the time of the three ministers. The majority of the Covenanters in America were settling in the South, as the lands were cheap and adapted to farming and grazing. Mr. McGarragh had fallen into intemperate habits, and was suspended by the Committee in 1795. Mr. King died in August, 1798, and Mr. Martin was again left alone in the exercise of the ministry. In the spring of 1798, the Reformed Presbytery was re-organized in America, at Philadelphia, and the Revs. James McKinney and S. B. Wylie were sent upon a commission to South Carolina to rectify disorders, and to banish slaveholders from the pale of the Covenanter Church. This commission was constituted at the Rocky Creek meeting house, (widow Edgar's) January 28, 1801, by Revs. James McKinney and S. B. Wylie, with Mr. Thomas Donnelly, licentiate, who had been preaching here for over a year, and elders John Kell and David Stormont. During the sittings of this court, Thomas Donnelly was ordained and installed pastor of the societies ; S. B. Wylie was called as his colleague ; William Martin was deposed for holding slaves and becoming habitually intemperate ; James McGarragh's suspension was continued, and James Harbison, Alexander Martin, Hugh McQuiston, John Cunningham, David Smith, John Mc-Ninch, John Cooper, William Edgar, James Montgomery and Robert Black were chosen ruling elders.† At this

---

* Historical part of Testimony.   † Minutes of Reformed Presbytery.

time the communion was dispensed, of which all the Covenanters partook. Mr. Wylie declined the call, and Mr. Donnelly entered upon the work of supplying all the societies as best he could. In 1802, the Rev. James McKinney was translated from Galway, New York, and took charge of the "Brick Church" society. He died in a few months after his settlement. Mr. Donnelly was again left alone to minister to the scattered societies. He bought a farm, on the north side of the Big Rocky Creek, from Stephen Harman, and for eleven years was the sole Covenanter minister exercising his functions in South Carolina. In 1813, Mr. Donnelly received assistance in the settlement of the Rev. John Reilly over the Little Rocky Creek and Beaver Dam congregations. Mr. Reilly died in 1820. For two years Mr. Donnelly was again left alone, and his congregation was divided. In June, 1822, the Rev. Campbell Madden was ordained and installed pastor of the Richmond society, and also preached at the tent of John Orr, and taught a school at Glendon's Grove. At the same time, the Rev. Hugh McMillan took charge of the Brick Church, in which he also conducted a classical school. Dr. Madden died in August, 1828, and Hugh McMillan emigrated to Ohio with many of his congregation. About this time emigration to the northern free States set in, and during the next ten years the cause in the South became very weak on account of the prevalence of human slavery. Mr. Donnelly remained and preached to the scattered societies until his death in November, 1847. He was the last Covenanter minister in the

South, and soon the cause became extinct. At one time there were over five hundred Covenanters in South Carolina, and they composed the congregations of Rocky Creek, Big Rocky Creek, Little Rocky Creek, Beaver Dam and Bethesda. Among the names, not heretofore mentioned as members of the Church in South Carolina, are the different families by the names of McMillan, Cooper, McKelvy, Hemphill, Woodbourne, Montford, Nesbit, and others, of the Brick Church; those of Ewin, McHenry, Erwin, Todd, Kell, Rock, Linn, Little, McFadden, McClurkin and Simpson, of the Beaver Dam congregation; those of Martin, Dunn, Wright, Hood, Sproull, Henry, Stormont, Cathcart, Robinson, McMillin and Richmond, of the Richmond or Big Rocky Creek Church; those of McNinch and Crawford dwelt at the McNinch meeting house; those of Smith, Faris, McDonald, Coulter, Wright, Willson, Orr, Wylie, Black, Henkle, Hunter, Boyd, Neil and McDill at the Little Rocky Creek congregation. In the old Brick Church graveyard lie the remains of the Revs. William King, James McKinney, John Reilly and Thomas Donnelly. Rev. Dr. Campbell Madden was buried at Winnsboro, James McGarragh in Paul's graveyard, and William Martin in a private burying ground near his humble abode. The inscriptions upon some of the tombstones which mark these sacred graves are here inserted, that the names of these worthy fathers may be kept in remembrance.

It is understood that the inscriptions on the stones of Revs. King, McKinney, Reilly and Madden were prepared by Mr. Donnelly.

Sacred to the
Memory of the Rev'd.
WILLIAM KING ; who departed
this life Aug'st 24th, A. D. 1798, aged
about 50 years.
Within this humble tomb pale Death has laid
A King who mortal sceptre never swayed,
But he himself did rule by Jesus' laws ;
In grace and Holy life a pattern was.
In love to God and man he shone conspicuously,
And walked with God in deep humility.
In faithfulness and zeal for Jesus' cause
Few of his fellows to him equal was,
But zeal in him so mixed with moderation,
Made even foes him view with admiration.
Tho' deeply skilled in human learning, he
Taught truths divine with great simplicity,
That perfect God might make his saints thereby,
And through his means Christ's body edify.
The Pastor's, Husband's, Parent's care he shew'd,
While he in earthly house did make abode.
His loss by all bewail'd, tho' felt by none
So much as by this people left alone.
His clay here lies, his soul to heaven is fled ;
His people he left on God for to be fed.

Sacred to the
Memory of
The Rev. JAS. McKINNEY,
Who departed this life Sept. 16th,
A. D. 1802, aged about 45 years.
Death's hand, tho' cold, strikes a most certain blow
In wafting Zion's sons from toil below,
To place them in the Father's house above,
To see him in the fullness of his love.
Ecclesia wails her noble champion laid,
In this low tomb to Death his tribute's paid.
A husband kind, a tender parent he,
To friend and foes a friend he wish'd to be.

Tho' few in letters, human or divine,
Or grace or nature's gifts did so much shine,
Yet, hated by unworthy world, he
By God was thought above its company;
Amidst its threats his clay in quiet lies,
While his immortal part has reach'd the skies.
Truth's foes rejoiced to see her Hero fall,
That to their idols they may join withal.
Spare boasts, truth's foes, tho' whirling winds to heaven
Elijah bore, Elisha soon was given,
By him who in the greatest love can raise
Another champion in McKinney's place.

Sacred to the Memory of
The Revd. JOHN RILEY,
Who departed this life
25th August, 1820,
Aged 50 years.

This tomb contains his dust; no more
His voice is heard where it was heard before.
His wife, his people, mourn his labors' end,
And friendly neighbors a departed friend.
His gain their loss, his life by death secure
In endless mansions, where joys are pure.
Ye mourners look to Zion's sovereign Lord,
Who can to you another guide afford.

Sacred to the Memory of
Rev. C. MADDEN,
Who departed this life August 12, 1828,
Aged 33 years.

Insatiate death! thou sparest none;
To thy vast kingdom all must come.
Didst thou regard the widow's tears,
The orphans' helpless state and years;
Didst thou respect a lettered mind,
Formed to benefit mankind;
Didst thou regard a temper meek.

By grace refined his God to seek ;
Didst thou regard Mount Sion's peace,
Her cries to God for gospel grace ;—
Our Madden had with us remained,
And peace and joy to us proclaimed.
What hast thou done ? thou wast his friend ;
Him to his Father's house didst send,
Where he will sing to endless days
The triumph and the Saviour's praise.
His family, his flock, his friend,
To heavenly grace he did commend.
In the Chief Shepherd's hand they're safe
As long as they do live by faith.

In Memory of
Rev. THOMAS DONNELLY,
Who departed this life
The 28th November, 1847,
In the 76th year of his age,
And the 46th of his ministry.
He was a native of Ireland,
And for many years
Pastor of the Reformed Presbyterian Church
In this vicinity.
"For him to live was Christ—
To die, gain."

The descendants of the South Carolina Covenanters are now generally found in Ohio, Indiana and Illinois, whither they migrated, and are in connection with both branches of the Church. The few who lived in the South after the death of the Rev. Thomas Donnelly, went into the Associate Reformed and Presbyterian Churches. To Covenanters, South Carolina is sacred ground; and within her borders are the sepulchres of many worthy fathers. Chester District and Rocky Creek, where many a patriotic Covenanter fought for the preservation of his home and country, and maintained a faithful testimony for the rights of King Jesus, are places fraught with both tender and sad associations. Those Covenanter fathers either voluntarily forsook comforts beyond the ocean or were compelled to "flee to the land of the free, and the home of the brave" for their civil and religious liberty, and attained it at any cost. They maintained the purity of the Church, and left the comforts of the South on account of the evil influence of slavery. Rather than give up their principles they gave up their homes; and while not a single Covenanter is found in that country to-day, "they being dead" yet speak from the scores of flourishing congregations of the North-West where their works have followed them, and where their children rise up and call them blessed.

SUMMARY OF CONGREGATIONS.

ADAMSVILLE : *Jamestown, Mercer County, Pennsylvania.* Organized by Pittsburgh Presbytery, November 14, 1873. Disorganized, October 13, 1874.

AINSWORTH : *Ainsworth, Washington County, Iowa.* Organized by Iowa Presbytery, December 17, 1867. Disorganized, October 7, 1873.

ALBANY : *Albany, New York.* Organized by Northern Presbytery, June 6, 1815. James Christie, June 12, 1822, to May 17, 1830. J. R. Willson, September 17, 1830, to May 19, 1833. David Scott, June 7, 1836, to May 8, 1842. Disorganized, May 24, 1849.

ALLEGHENY : *Allegheny City, Pennsylvania.* Organized as Pittsburgh and Allegheny by Pittsburgh Presbytery, September 9, 1833, afterwards Allegheny and Pittsburgh, and since October 17, 1865, is Allegheny. Thomas Sproull, May 12, 1834, to October 13, 1868. D. B. Willson, November 29, 1870, to October 13, 1875. J. R. W. Sloane, June 6, 1877, to May 31, 1884. J. R. J. Milligan since October 15, 1885.

BALLIBAY : *Camptown, Bradford County, Pennsylvania.* Organized by Southern Presbytery as Wyalusing, December 16, 1832. Disorganized, May 24, 1837. Re-organized by New York Presbytery as Ballibay, August 28, 1875. Disorganized, June 5, 1886.

BALTIMORE: *Baltimore, Maryland.* Society formed in 1797. S. B. Wylie, 1803, to 1806. . Organized by Middle Presbytery, December 15, 1818. John Gibson, December 15, 1818, to August 7, 1833. W. L. Roberts, January 15, 1835, to October 9, 1837. C. B. McKee, December 2, 1846, to December 4, 1852. John Crawford, November 15, 1853, to September 3, 1856. W. W. McMillan, December 26, 1859, to May 5, 1863. W. P. Johnston, August 4, 1864, to July 13, 1873. John Lynd, December 4, 1873, to November 6, 1877. A. D. Crowe, October 10, 1878, to August 12, 1884. W. M. Glasgow since November 26, 1885.

BARNESVILLE: *Barnesville, Kings County, New Brunswick.* Organized by the New Brunswick and Nova Scotia Presbytery in 1846. J. R. Lawson, 1846, to October 17, 1856. J. R. Lawson, October 24, 1857, to April 12, 1882. Thomas Patton since May 26, 1887.

BARNET: *West Barnet, Caledonia County. Vermont.* Organized by New York Presbytery, July 9, 1872. D. C. Faris since June 25, 1873.

BEAR RUN AND MAHONING: *Marchand, Indiana County, Pennsylvania.* Organized by Pittsburgh Presbytery, October 15, 1870. J. F. Crozier since November 18, 1874.

BEAVER DAM: *Chester, Chester County, South Carolina.* Organized by Scottish Committee in 1792. William King, 1793, to August 24, 1798. Thomas Donnelly, supply. John Reilly, October 8, 1813, to August 27, 1820. Campbell Madden, June 18, 1822, to August 12, 1828. Disorganized in 1833.

BEAVER FALLS : *Beaver Falls, Pennsylvania.* Organized by Pittsburgh Presbytery, November 10, 1874. R. J. George since June 15, 1875.

BEECH WOODS : *Morning Sun, Preble County, Ohio.* Organized by Middle Committee in 1805, and supplied. John Kell, April 3, 1816, to October 6, 1819. Gavin McMillan, May 7, 1823, to October 7, 1836. Josiah Dodds, October 6, 1847, to October 10, 1865, when attached to Garrison.

BELLE CENTRE : *Belle Centre, Logan County, Ohio.* Organized by Lakes Presbytery, April 10, 1877. John Lynd, January 5, 1879, to April 14, 1885. J. J. Huston since April 30, 1886.

BELLEFONTAINE : *Bellefontaine, Logan County, Ohio.* Organized by Lakes Presbytery, October 11, 1876. F. M. Foster, May 13, 1880, to August 23, 1887. J. J. Huston, supply.

BETHEL : *Sparta, Randolph County, Illinois.* Organized by Western Presbytery, June 19, 1821. Samuel Wylie, June 19, 1821, to August 7, 1833. Hugh Stevenson, August 16, 1840, to May 15, 1846. James Milligan, October 14, 1848, to May 24, 1855. D. S. Faris since October 7, 1857.

BETHESDA : *Chester, Chester County, South Carolina.* Organized by Southern Presbytery, October 10, 1817. Thomas Donnelly, October 10, 1817, to November 1, 1847. Disorganized, 1848.

BEULAH : *Beulah, Webster County, Nebraska.* Organized by Kansas Presbytery, September 8, 1881. W. S. Fulton since March 27, 1885.

BIG ROCKY CREEK: *Chester, Chester County, South Carolina.* Organized by Scottish Committee in 1792. William King, 1792, to August 24, 1798. Thomas Donnelly, March 3, 1801, to April 10, 1816. Disorganized in 1817.

BIG SPRING: *Newville, Cumberland County, Pennsylvania.* Society formed in 1753. John Cuthbertson, 1753, to 1774. Matthew Linn, March 10, 1774, to November 1, 1782, when disorganized.

BLOOMINGTON: *Bloomington, Monroe County, Indiana.* Organized by Western Presbytery, October 10, 1821. James Faris, November 22, 1827, to May 20, 1855. D. J. Shaw since May 22, 1856.

BOSTON, FIRST: *Boston, Massachusetts.* Organized by New York Presbytery, July 12, 1854. J. R. Lawson, November 20, 1856, to October 22, 1857. William Graham since July 12, 1860.

BOSTON, SECOND: *Boston, Massachusetts.* Organized by New York Presbytery, November 21, 1871. David McFall since July 11, 1873.

BOVINA: *Bovina Centre, Delaware County, New York.* Organized by Northern Presbytery in 1814. M. B. Williams, April 15, 1820, to October 17, 1823. James Douglas, April 15, 1825, to March 15, 1857. J. T. Pollock, July 11, 1861, to March 10, 1864. Joshua Kennedy, January 11, 1865, to May 20, 1885. O. B. Milligan since June 22, 1887.

BROAD ALBIN: *Broad Albin, Fulton County, New York.* Organized by Northern Presbytery, May 10, 1818. S. M. Willson, October 14, 1821, to May 16, 1827. J. N. McLeod, December 29, 1829, to June 19, 1832.

A. S. McMaster, April 4, 1833, to August 7, 1833. Disorganized, October 10, 1838.

BROOKLAND: *Ingleside, Westmoreland County, Pennsylvania.* Organized by Pittsburgh Presbytery, May 9, 1822. Jonathan Gill, October 23, 1823, to August 7, 1833. Hugh Walkinshaw, April 15, 1835, to April 19, 1843. Oliver Wylie, June 24, 1846, to October 14, 1851. Robert Reed, June 21, 1854, to April 11, 1882. Attached to Parnassus under J. C. McFeeters since November 16, 1886.

BROOKLYN: *Brooklyn, New York.* Organized by New York Presbytery, June 15, 1857. J. M. Dickson, November 18, 1857, to May 20, 1862. J. H. Boggs, December 14, 1864, to November 29, 1880. S. J. Crowe, December 7, 1881, to October 28, 1884. J. F. Carson since May 20, 1885.

BROWNSVILLE: *Jolly, Monroe County, Ohio.* Organized by Pittsburgh Presbytery, July 12, 1854. Oliver Wylie supply, July 12, 1854, to October 24, 1856. J. A. Thompson, August 31, 1859, to June 10, 1865. Armour McFarland, supply. S. R. McClurkin, September 13, 1876, to October 17, 1877.

BRUSH CREEK: *Locust Grove, Adams County, Ohio.* Organized by Middle Presbytery as Chillicothe, May 8, 1812. Robert Wallace, October 12, 1814, to October 6, 1820. C. B. McKee, August 7, 1821, to September 10, 1822. James Blackwood, April 12, 1827, to April 9, 1829. David Steele, June 6, 1831, to September 18, 1840. Robert Hutcheson, September 29, 1842, to May 21, 1856. Disorganized, May 21, 1856. Re-organized by

Lakes Presbytery, November 16, 1881. William Mc-Kinney, R. J. Sharpe, T. C. Sproull, and others, supplies.

BUFFALO: *Buffalo, New York.* Organized by Western Presbytery, November 17, 1838. Disorganized, May 26, 1854.

BURDETT: *Burdett, Pawnee County, Kansas.* Organized by Kansas Presbytery, July 13, 1887.

CARLETON PLACE: *Carleton Place, Ontario, Canada.* Organized by Northern Presbytery, September 9, 1830, as a part of Ramsey. Distinct congregation, August 29, 1837. Mission Station.

CARLISLE: *Carlisle, Cumberland County, Pennsylvania.* Organized in 1751, John Cuthbertson 1751, to 1774. Matthew Linn, March 10, 1774, to November 1, 1782, when disorganized.

CEDAR LAKE: *Ray, Steuben County, Indiana.* Organized by Lakes 'Presbytery, April 19, 1841. John French, September 23, 1850, to October 3, 1880. R. C. Wylie since October 31, 1884.

CEDARVILLE: *Cedarville, Green County, Ohio.* Organized by Middle Presbytery as Massie's Creek, June 19, 1810. John Kell, supply. Jonathan Gill, May 14, 1816, to April 6, 1823. Gavin McMillan, supply. Hugh McMillan, September 7, 1829, to August 7, 1833. Disorganized, August 18, 1841. Re-organized as Cedarville by Lakes Presbytery, June 1, 1850. H. H. George, June 23, 1858, to August 4, 1866. Samuel Sterrett, May 16, 1868, to October 20, 1878. P. P. Boyd, May 22, 1872, to July 20, 1871. T. C. Sproull since June 10, 1881.

CENTRAL ALLEGHENY: *Allegheny City, Pennsylvania.* Organized by Pittsburgh Presbytery, October 24, 1870. J. W. Sproull since April 24, 1871.

CENTREVILLE: *Centreville, Mercer County, Pennsylvania.* Organized by Pittsburgh Presbytery, September 18, 1879. S. J. Crowe, September 18, 1879, to April 12, 1881. J. R. Wylie, July 3, 1882, to November 8, 1887.

CHURCH HILL: *Coultersville, Randolph County, Illinois.* Organized by Illinois Presbytery, October 10, 1854. W. F. George, March 5, 1860, to May 17, 1871. J. M. Faris, June 19, 1873, to May 30, 1884. John Teaz since July 8, 1885.

CINCINNATI: *Cincinnati, Ohio.* Organized by Western Presbytery, October 16, 1816. Archibald Johnston, supply. Samuel Robinson, October 10, 1818, to August 20, 1821. C. B. McKee, November 18, 1822, to October 17, 1831. Disorganized, August 7, 1833. Re-organized by Lakes Presbytery, August 22, 1844. J. R. Willson, supply. Disorganized, October 6, 1852. Re-organized, February 24, 1853. H. H. George, June 23, 1858, to August 18, 1872. R. M. Sommerville, supply, one year. J. M. Foster, December 29, 1877, to April 14, 1886.

CLARINDA: *Clarinda, Page County, Iowa.* Organized by Illinois Presbytery, December 17, 1855. Joseph McCracken, July 6, 1857, to October 16, 1858. David McKee since September 20, 1862.

CLARKSBURGH: *Clarksburgh, Indiana County, Pennsylvania.* Organized by Pittsburgh Presbytery, October 8, 1867. J. A. Black, November 18, 1868, to April

11, 1882. J. J. McClurkin, stated supply, since May 16, 1884.

COLDENHAM : *Coldenham, Orange County, New York.* Society formed by John Cuthbertson in 1753. Organized by the Reformed Presbytery, as Wallkill, August 10, 1798. Alexander McLeod, July 6, 1801, to September 8, 1803. James Milligan, June 10, 1812, to April 17, 1817. J. R. Willson, August 10, 1817, to September 17, 1830. J. R. Willson, November 21, 1833, to June 26, 1840. J. W. Shaw, May 29, 1844, to October 26, 1881. R. H. McCready, March 6, 1884, to May 22, 1888.

CONOCOCHEAGUE : *Fayetteville, Franklin County, Pennsylvania.* Society formed in 1751, by John Cuthbertson. Matthew Linn, March 10, 1774, to November 1, 1782. Organized by Middle Committee, June 16, 1802. Robert Lusk, August 12, 1816, to October 15, 1823. S. W. Crawford, August 26, 1824, to May 10, 1831. Thomas Hanna, December 8, 1842, to October 29, 1844. Joshua Kennedy, November 5, 1845, to May 1, 1860.

CORNWALLIS : *Somerset, Kings County, Nova Scotia.* Organized by New Brunswick and Nova Scotia Presbytery, September 13, 1843. William Sommerville, 1835, to September 28, 1878. Thomas McFall since August 25, 1881.

CRAFTSBURY : *East Craftsbury, Orleans County, Vermont.* Organized by Northern Presbytery, September 14, 1816. James Milligan, September 26, 1817, to August 6, 1829. S. M. Willson, May 19, 1833, to May 10, 1845. R. Z. Willson, November 17, 1846, to December 18, 1855. J. M. Armour, September 23, 1857, to October 31, 1865. A. W. Johnston, August 5,

1868, to October 31, 1871. J. C. Taylor since December 17, 1873.

DAVENPORT: *Davenport, Iowa.* Organized by Iowa Presbytery, September 14, 1864. Disorganized, May 26, 1869.

DETROIT AND NOVI: *Detroit, Michigan.* Organized by Lakes Presbytery, April 16, 1854. Boyd McCullough, September 19, 1855, to May 14, 1871. Disorganized, May 14, 1871. Mission Station until May 27, 1880.

DUANESBURGH: *Duanesburgh, Schenectady County, New York.* Organized under Reformed Presbytery of Ireland in 1794. James McKinney, May, 1798, to April 4, 1802. Gilbert McMaster, August 8, 1808, to August 7, 1833. Disorganized, October, 1836.

EAST END, PITTSBURGH: *Pittsburgh, Pennsylvania.* Organized by Pittsburgh Presbytery, November 24, 1887.

ECKLEY: *Beulah, Webster County, Nebraska.* Organized by Kansas Presbytery, November 13, 1878. W. S. Fulton since March 10, 1885.

ELKHORN: *Oakdale, Washington County, Illinois.* Organized by Western Presbytery, July 30, 1834. Samuel McKinney, April 15, 1835, to May 24, 1840. William Sloane, September 13, 1840, to May 9, 1858. A. C. Todd, July 1, 1859, to May 17, 1871. D. G. Thompson since October 9, 1872.

ELLIOTA: *Canton, Fillmore County, Minnesota.* Organized by Iowa Presbytery, November 5, 1868. J. S. Buck, 1867, to October 13, 1870. J. W. Dill, April 26, 1878, to May 25, 1881. Robert Clyde since February 12, 1886.

ESKRIDGE: *Eskridge, Wabaunsee County, Kansas.* Organized by Kansas Presbytery, April 15, 1884. N. M. Johnston since August 4, 1886.

EVANS: *Evans, Weld County, Colorado.* Organized by Illinois Presbytery, August 10, 1871. A. C. Todd since August 21, 1874.

FAIRGROVE: *Fairgrove, Tuscola County, Michigan.* Organized by Lakes Presbytery, December 7, 1878. J. Ralston Wylie, November 1, 1879, to October 12, 1887.

GALWAY: *West Galway, Fulton County, New York.* Organized as a part of Duanesburgh, in 1794. James McKinney, May, 1798, to April 4, 1802. Gilbert Mc-Master, August 8, 1808, to May 10, 1818. Organized as Galway distinct, May 10, 1818. S. M. Willson, October 14, 1821, to May 16, 1827. J. N. McLeod, December 29, 1829, to June 19, 1832. A. S. McMaster, April 4, 1833, to August 7, 1833, when disorganized. Re-organized by Western Presbytery, November 9, 1835. Disorganized, April, 1842.

GARRISON: *Glenwood, Fayette County, Indiana.* Organized by Middle Committee in 1805. John Kell, April 3, 1816, to October 6, 1819. Gavin McMillan, May 7, 1823, to October 7, 1836. Josiah Dodds, October 6, 1847, to October 10, 1865. T. P. Robb, May 16, 1871, to April 12, 1874. J. J. McClurkin, August 14, 1880, to March 13, 1884. Disorganized, September 9, 1884.

GREENFIELD: *Greenfield, Harrison County, Ohio.* Organized by Pittsburgh Presbytery, October 16, 1822. William Sloane, November 16, 1829, to October 23,

1838. James Love, June 29, 1839, to May 11, 1847. Disorganized, May 24, 1849.

GREENSBURGH: *Greensburgh, Westmoreland County, Pennsylvania.* Organized by Middle Presbytery in 1813, John Cannon, September 16, 1816, to February 2, 1836. James Milligan, November 23, 1839, to October 16, 1841. S. O. Wylie, May 17, 1843, to November 18, 1844. R. B. Cannon, May 5, 1847, to April 4, 1854. A. M. Milligan, May 6, 1856, to April 10, 1866. Attached to New Alexandria, October 8, 1867.

GROVE HILL: *Grove Hill, Bremer County, Iowa.* Organized by Illinois Presbytery, October 2, 1861. Robert Hutcheson, April 17, 1863, to May 8, 1867. Disorganized, May 26, 1869.

HEBRON: *Idana, Clay County, Kansas.* Organized by Kansas Presbytery, November 9, 1871. J. S. T. Milligan, supply. S. M. Stevenson, October 30, 1874, to April 17, 1876. Matthew Wilkin, November 11, 1876, to July 12, 1880. J. R. Latimer since August 18, 1882.

HEPHZIBAH: *Fayetteville, Lincoln County, Tennessee.* Organized as Elk by Southern Presbytery, June 12, 1812. Supplied by John Kell, Thomas Donnelly, Robert McKee, and others. Ebenezer Cooper, 1828, to 1832. Disorganized, August 7, 1833.

HICKORY GROVE: *Avery, Monroe County, Iowa.* Organized by Iowa Presbytery, October 13, 1865, as Albia. James Love, April 16, 1866, to September 14, 1881. J. A. Thompson since September 17, 1882.

HOLMWOOD: *Mankato, Jewell County, Kansas.* Organized by Kansas Presbytery, September 1, 1881.

HOPKINTON: *Hopkinton, Delaware County, Iowa.* Organ-

ized by Illinois Presbytery, April 10, 1856, as Maquo-
keta. W. L. Roberts, May 9, 1860, to December 7,
1864. D. H. Coulter, April 18, 1867, to October 14,
1874. R. C. Wylie, June 15, 1875, to Ootober 3, 1882.
T. H. Acheson since September 23, 1886.

HORTON: *Grand Pre, Hants County, Nova Scotia.*
Organized by New Brunswick and Nova Scotia Presbytery, May, 1835. William Sommerville, May 16, 1835,
to September 28, 1878. Thomas McFall, August 25,
1881, to June 5, 1886, when disorganized.

HOULTON: *Houlton, Aroostook County, Maine.* Organ-
ized by New Brunswick and Nova Scotia Presbytery,
May 16, 1859. Supplied occasionally. J. A. F. Bovard,
April 12, 1880, to March 10, 1884.

INDIANAPOLIS: *Indianapolis, Indiana.* Organized by
Lakes Presbytery, May 10, 1867. John Crozier stated
supply. Disorganized, May 25, 1870.

JEWELL: *Rubens, Jewell County, Kansas.* Organized
by Kansas Presbytery, July 15, 1885.

JONATHAN'S CREEK: *White Cottage, Muskingum County,
Ohio.* Organized by Lakes Presbytery, August 23, 1853,
as Eden and Irville. Armour McFarland, August 23,
1853, to April 12, 1876. T. C. Sproull, supply. R. B.
Cannon since September 9, 1886.

JUNKIN TENT: *Kingston, Cumberland County, Pennsylvania.* Society formed in 1750. John Cuthbertson,
1751, to 1774. Matthew Linn, March 10, 1774, to
November 1, 1782. A part of Conococheague, 1802,
to 1860.

KORTRIGHT: *West Kortright, Delaware County, New
York.* Organized by Northern Presbytery in 1814. M.

B. Williams, April 15, 1820, to August 31, 1831. James Douglas, supply. S. M. Willson, October 22, 1845, to January 21, 1864. J. O. Bayles since January 10, 1866.

KOSSUTH : *Kossuth, Des Moines County, Iowa.* Organized by Iowa Presbytery, September 9, 1865. Robert Johnson, January 7, 1868, to July 27, 1875. Disorganized, April 30, 1879.

LAKE ELIZA : *Le Roy, Lake County, Indiana.* Organized by Lakes Presbytery, September 6, 1852. P. H. Wylie, May 14, 1855, to October 9, 1860. R. M. Thompson, September 9, 1865, to September 13, 1881. Robert Clyde, supply in 1884. Disorganized, June 1, 1887.

LAKE RENO : *Glenwood, Pope County, Minnesota.* Organized by Iowa Presbytery, October 29, 1869. E. G. Elsey since July 17, 1882.

LANSINGBURGH : *Lansingburgh, Rensselaer County, New York.* Organized by Northern Presbytery, June 17, 1828. Robert McKee, December 29, 1830, to May 26, 1835. Disorganized, October 16, 1848.

LIND GROVE : *Mediapolis, Des Moines County, Iowa.* Organized by Illinois Presbytery, September 10, 1856. C. D. Trumbull, January 29, 1864, to April 1, 1874. M. A. Gault, May 20, 1875, to October 4, 1877. J. W. Dill, July 6, 1881, to September 19, 1887.

LISBON : *Flackville, St. Lawrence County, New York.* Organized as a society in 1823. Disorganized, August 7, 1833. Re-organized by Rochester Presbytery, October 5, 1840. John Middleton, February 8, 1844, to April 11, 1854. James McLachlane, July 16, 1856, to

November 19, 1864. William McFarland since May 11, 1871.

LITTLE BEAVER : *New Galilee, Beaver County, Pennsylvania.* Organized by Middle Presbytery, May, 1814. Robert Gibson, September 6, 1819, to October 16, 1830. George Scott, April 19, 1831, to August 7, 1833. James Blackwood, May 24, 1834, to October 10, 1838. J. W. Morton, November 27, 1845, to June 3, 1847. Samuel Sterrett, June 21, 1848, to May 16, 1860. N. M. Johnston, April 14, 1864, to June 3, 1886. J. R. Wylie since May 18, 1888.

LITTLE ROCKY CREEK : *Chester, Chester County, South Carolina.* Settled in 1772, by William Martin and a colony from Ireland. William Martin, 1772, to 1789. James McGarragh, 1791, to 1795. William King, 1795, to August 24, 1798. James McKinney, May 10, 1802, to September 4, 1802. Thomas Donnelly, supply. John Reilly, February 23, 1813, to August 27, 1820. Campbell Madden, June 18, 1822, to August 12, 1828. Disorganized, 1832.

LOCHIEL : *Brodie, Ontario, Canada.* Society formed with Ramsey in 1816. Organized by Rochester Presbytery, July 14, 1861, as Glengary. Robert Shields, supply, 1865, to 1883. R. C. Allen since October 18, 1887.

LONDONDERRY : *Londonderry, Guernsey County, Ohio.* Organized by Pittsburgh Presbytery, October 16, 1822. Robert Wallace, supply. William Sloane, November 16, 1829, to October 23, 1838. James Love, June 27, 1839, to October 5, 1864. J. A. Thompson, October 3, 1866, to September 1, 1875. J. R. Latimer, May 19, 1880, to May 27, 1882.

LONG BRANCH: *Blanchard, Page County, Iowa.* Organized by Kansas Presbytery, April 16, 1877. M. A. Gault, supply. M. A. Gault, October 1, 1880, to October 25, 1882. B. M. Sharp since October 13, 1887.

LOWER CHANCEFORD: *Chanceford, York County, Pennsylvania.* Society formed in 1751. John Cuthbertson, 1751, to 1782, when disorganized.

MACEDON: *Macedon, Mercer County, Ohio.* Organized by Lakes Presbytery, July 5, 1852. W. F. George, Septembor 26, 1853, to April 20, 1858. P. H. Wylie, November 14, 1860, to March 1, 1887. Disorganized, June 2, 1888.

MANSFIELD: *Mansfield, Ohio.* Organized by Ohio Presbytery, October 11, 1878. S. A. George since November 20, 1878.

MCKEESPORT: *McKeesport, Pennsylvania.* Organized by Pittsburgh Presbytery, April 27, 1882. J. H. Wylie, June 30, 1885, to June 27, 1887.

MIAMI, FIRST: *Northwood, Logan County, Ohio.* Organized by Western Presbytery, October 16, 1831. J. B. Johnston, June 10, 1834, to November 10 1858. J. C. K. Milligan, July 1, 1853, to April 20, 1858. J. L. McCartney, November 12, 1861, to September 1, 1875. Consolidated into United Miami, April 14, 1877.

MIAMI, SECOND: *Northwood, Logan County, Ohio.* Organized by Synod under Lakes Presbytery, August 9, 1851. William Milroy, October 12, 1854, to November 15, 1876. Consolidated into United Miami, April 14, 1877.

MIDDLETOWN: *Hooker, Butler County, Pennsylvania.*

Organized by Pittsburgh Presbytery, November 16, 1886, and was known as the North Washington Branch of Brookland congregation, since 1825.

MIDDLE WHEELING: *Roney's Point, Ohio County, West Virginia.* Organized by Pittsburgh Presbytery, April 26, 1860, and formerly supplied by pastors of Miller's Run. Armour McFarland, April 4, 1866, to April 12, 1873. S. R. McClurkin since September 13, 1876.

MILLER'S RUN: *Venice, Washington County, Pennsylvania.* Organized by Middle Committee, October 19, 1806, as Canonsburgh. John Black, supply. William Gibson, October 23, 1817, to May 26, 1826. G. T. Ewing, October 23, 1827, to May 16, 1830. John Crozier, May 12, 1834, to October 9, 1842. William Slater, May 24, 1843, to April 14, 1887.

MILTON: *Milton, Northumberland County, Pennsylvania.* Organized by Philadelphia Presbytery, October 13, 1830. William Wilson, August 6, 1832, to August 7, 1833, when passed into New School body.

MONCTON: *Moncton, New Brunswick.* Organized by New Brunswick and Nova Scotia Presbytery, September 15, 1885.

MONONGAHELA: *Elizabeth, Allegheny County, Pennsylvania.* Society formed in 1794. John Black, supply. Organized by Middle Committee, October, 1806. William Gibson, October 23, 1817, to May 26, 1826. G. T. Ewing, October 23, 1827, to May 16, 1830. John Crozier, May 12, 1834, to April 12, 1865. J. W. Sproull, April 10, 1866, to April 11, 1871. T. C. Sproull, October 3, 1871, to May 26, 1876. W. J.

Coleman, June 13, 1879, to July 5, 1881. John M. Wylie, April 27, 1883, to April 9, 1884. Robert Reed, supply, 1885, to 1887.

MORNING SUN: *Morning Sun, Louisa County, Iowa.* Organized by Iowa Presbytery, July 9, 1873. C. D. Trumbull since April 14, 1874.

MUDDY RUN: *McCall's Ferry, York County, Pennsylvania.* Formed into a society in 1743. John Cuthbertson, 1751, to 1782.

MUSKINGUM AND TOMICA : *Dresden, Muskingum County, Ohio.* Organized by Pittsburgh Presbytery, October 9, 1831. John Wallace, April 14, 1833, to April 4, 1855. J. C. K. Faris, December 6, 1865, to April 13, 1871. W. S. Fulton, December 5, 1877, to April 11, 1883. John M. Wylie since January 21, 1885.

NEW ALEXANDRIA : *New Alexandria, Westmoreland County, Pennsylvania.* Organized by the Pittsburgh Presbytery, July, 1822. John Cannon, 1819, to February 2, 1836. James Milligan, November 23, 1839, to October 14, 1848. A. M. Milligan, November 24, 1848, to October 4, 1853. A. M. Milligan, May 6, 1856, to April 10, 1866. T. A. Sproull, June 17, 1868, to April 8, 1878. J. L. Pinkerton, May 17, 1881, to October 9, 1883. J. F. Carlisle, June 20, 1884, to January 26, 1888.

NEWARK : *Newark, New Jersey.* Organized by New York Presbytery, June 17, 1874. D. H. Coulter, December 10, 1874, to October 27, 1875. Disorganized, October 30, 1878.

NEWBURGH, FIRST : *Newburgh, New York.* Society formed, November 8, 1802. Organized by Northern Presbytery, February 16, 1824. J. R. Johnston, Sep-

tember 6, 1825, to October 17, 1829. Moses Roney,
June 8, 1830, to October 10, 1848. Samuel Carlisle,
November 15, 1849, to July 3, 1887.

NEWBURGH, SECOND: *Newburgh, New York*. Organized by New York Presbytery, December 13, 1854. J. R.
Thompson since December 19, 1855.

NEW CASTLE: *New Castle, Pennsylvania*. Organized
by Pittsburgh Presbytery, January 9, 1871. S. J.
Crowe, May 21, 1872, to April 12, 1881. J. Milligan
Wylie, June 22, 1883, to December 26, 1887. W. R. Laird
since May 10, 1888.

NEW CONCORD: *New Concord, Muskingum County,
Ohio*. Organized by Pittsburgh Presbytery, June 13,
1821, as Salt Creek. Robert Wallace, October 9, 1823,
to July 19, 1849. H. P. McClurkin, October 15, 1850,
to October 8, 1856. H. P. McClurkin, December 2,
1858, to October 4, 1882. J. M. Faris since July 3,
1884.

NEW HARTFORD: *New Hartford, Oneida County, New
York*. Organized by Southern Presbytery, October 10,
1837. Disorganized, May 15, 1843.

NEW YORK, FIRST: *New York City, New York*.
Organized by Rev. William Gibson, December 26,
1797. Alexander McLeod, July 6, 1801, to February
17, 1833. James Christie, November 16, 1836, to
October 15, 1856. J. C. K. Milligan since June 16,
1858.

NEW YORK, SECOND: *New York City, New York*.
Organized by Northern Presbytery, June 11, 1830.
Robert Gibson, May 31, 1831, to December 22, 1837.

Andrew Stevenson, November 14, 1839, to May 17, 1875. R. M. Sommerville since December 14, 1875.

NEW YORK, THIRD: *New York City, New York.* Organized by New York Presbytery, March 14, 1848. John Little, June 5, 1849, to April 20, 1852. J. R. W. Sloane, May 26, 1856, to October 27, 1868. David Gregg, February 23, 1870, to October 28, 1885. David Gregg, December 6, 1885, to January 25, 1887. F. M. Foster since September 7, 1887.

NEW YORK, FOURTH: *New York City, New York.* Organized by New York Presbytery, February 21, 1870. James Kennedy since November 13, 1870.

NORTH CEDAR: *North Cedar, Jackson County, Kansas.* Organized by Kansas Presbytery, October 23, 1871. J. S. T. Milligan since October 8, 1872.

NORTH SALEM: *Sugar Tree, Guernsey County, Ohio.* Organized by Ohio Presbytery, April 2, 1879. J. R. Latimer, October 10, 1880, to May 27, 1882.

NORTH UNION: *Valencia, Butler County, Pennsylvania.* Organized by Pittsburgh Presbytery, April 11, 1870, from Union and Pine Creek, and John Galbraith has since continued pastor.

OAKLAND: *Oakland, California.* Organized by Synod under Kansas Presbytery, August 28, 1879, as a mission congregation with N. R. Johnston in charge. Disorganized, May 21, 1885.

OCTORARA: *Octorara, Lancaster County, Pennsylvania.* Society formed in 1740. Alexander Craighead, 1743, to 1749. John Cuthbertson, August 11, 1751, to November 1, 1782, when disorganized.

OIL CITY: *South Oil City, Pennsylvania.* Organized

by Pittsburgh Presbytery, August 19, 1865. David McFall, May 8, 1871, to April 8, 1873. J. A. F. Bovard since June 11, 1884.

OIL CREEK: *Titusville, Crawford County, Pennsylvania.* Organized by Pittsburgh Presbytery, February 14, 1860. Daniel Reid, December 19, 1861, to March 31, 1875. J. A. F. Bovard since June 12, 1884.

OLATHE: *Olathe, Johnston County, Kansas.* Organized by Illinois Presbytery, April 16, 1865. W. W. McMillan, March 10, 1866, to October 14, 1885. J. H. Wylie since October 21, 1887.

OLD BETHEL: *Houston, Randolph County, Illinois.* Organized by Western Presbytery, October 15, 1836. James Wallace, August 16, 1840, to May 15, 1867. W. J. Gillespie, October 13, 1869, to August 6, 1870. P. P. Boyd, July 20, 1874, to December 12, 1887.

PARNASSUS AND MANCHESTER: *Parnassus, Pennsylvania.* Organized by Pittsburgh Presbytery, June 20, 1870. J. M. Johnston, June 15, 1871, to January 3, 1873. J. C. McFeeters since June 19, 1874.

PATERSON: *Paterson, New Jersey.* Organized by Northern Presbytery, October 10, 1818. W. L. Roberts, May 19, 1824, to December 18, 1825. William Gibson, 1826, to 1832. Disorganized, October 7, 1836.

PAXTANG: *Paxton, Dauphin County, Pennsylvania.* Society formed in 1740. John Cuthbertson, August 15, 1751, to March 10, 1774. Matthew Linn, March 10, 1774, to November 1, 1782, when disorganized.

PEQUEA: *Pequea, Lancaster County, Pennsylvania.* Society formed in 1750. John Cuthbertson, August 14, 1751, to November 1, 1782, when disorganized.

PERTH, FIRST: *Perth, Ontario, Canada.* Organized under Scottish Synod, April 29, 1836. James McLachlane, August 29, 1837, to October 8, 1855, when disorganized. Re-organized by Rochester Presbytery, July 14, 1861. Robert Shields, supply, July 13, 1865, to August 28, 1883.

PERTH, SECOND: *Perth, Ontario, Canada.* Organized by Rochester Presbytery, June 12, 1852. John Middleton, October 19, 1854, to October 8, 1856, when disorganized.

PHILADELPHIA, FIRST: *Philadelphia, Pennsylvania.* Organized by Rev. William Gibson, January 28, 1798. Samuel B. Wylie, November 20, 1803, to August 7, 1833. J. M. Willson, November 27, 1834, to October, 28, 1862. T. P. Stevenson since May 5, 1863.

PHILADELPHIA, SECOND: *Philadelphia, Pennsylvania.* Organized by Southern Presbytery, August 10, 1842. S. O. Wylie, December 5, 1844, to August 22, 1883. J. K. McClurkin, October 9, 1884, to August 25, 1887.

PHILADELPHIA, THIRD: *Philadelphia, Pennsylvania.* Organized by New York Presbytery, January 16, 1851. A. M. Milligan, December 8, 1853, to October 14, 1855. John Middleton, November 18, 1856, to May 17, 1862. R. J. Sharpe, April 6, 1866, to April 10, 1879. J. M. Crozier, May 6, 1880, to September 7, 1881. R. C. Montgomery since March 27, 1883.

PHILADELPHIA, FOURTH: *Philadelphia, Pennsylvania.* Organized by New York Presbytery, July 13, 1853. David McKee, July 5, 1854, to August 4, 1859, when disorganized.

PINE CREEK AND UNION: *Valencia, Butler County, Pennsylvania.* Society organized in 1806, as a part of Ohio congregation. Matthew Williams, 1807, to 1815. Organized by Pittsburgh Presbytery, October 8, 1815. Matthew Williams, October 8, 1815, to October 16, 1825. T. C. Guthrie, April 26, 1826, to August 7, 1833. Hugh Walkinshaw, April 15, 1835, to October 16, 1841. John Galbraith, June 29, 1843, to April 11, 1870. Alexander Kilpatrick since May 17, 1876.

PITTSBURGH: *Pittsburgh, Pennsylvania.* Organized by Middle Committee, December 18, 1800, as Ohio. John Black, December 18, 1800, to August 7, 1833, when disorganized. Re-organized by Pittsburgh Presbytery, October 17, 1865. A. M. Milligan, May 14, 1866, to May 7, 1885. David McAllister since October 20, 1887.

PLEASANT RIDGE: *Olathe, Johnston County, Kansas.* Organized by Illinois Presbytery, April 16, 1865. W. W. McMillan, March 10, 1866, to August 11, 1871. Matthew Wilkin, May 8, 1874, to July 12, 1880. R. M. Thompson since October 12, 1881.

POLAND AND NORTH JACKSON: *Canfield, Mahoning County, Ohio.* Organized by Middle Presbytery, May 17, 1814, as Austintown, and attached to Little Beaver until its separate existence, May 16, 1860. Samuel Sterrett, May 16, 1860, to October 7, 1867. R. J. George, May 19, 1870, to April 14, 1875. T. C. Sproull, July 8, 1876, to April 8, 1879. Changed to Youngstown, October 12, 1885.

PRINCETON: *Princeton, Gibson County, Indiana.* Organized by Middle Presbytery, October 14, 1813. John Kell, June 21, 1820, to August 7, 1833. Robert

Lusk, supply. J. J. McClurkin, June 2, 1843, to May 22, 1849. John Stott, October 13, 1851, to June 2, 1868, when disorganized. Re-organized by Illinois Presbytery, April 21, 1869. D. C. Martin, November 7, 1872, to April 12, 1888.

PRINCETOWN: *Princetown, Schenectady County, New York*. Organized by James McKinney, in 1794, as a part of Duanesburgh. James McKinney, May, 1798, to April 4, 1802. Gilbert McMaster, August 8, 1808, to August 7, 1833, when disorganized.

QUINTER: *Quinter, Gove County, Kansas.* Organized by Kansas Presbytery, July 7, 1887.

RAMSEY: *Almonte, Ontario, Canada.* Organized by James Milligan, September 9, 1830. Disorganized, August 7, 1833. Re-organized by James McLachlane, October 9, 1833. James McLachlane, October 9, 1833, to October 8, 1856, when disorganized. Re-organized by Rochester Presbytery, July 14, 1861. Robert Shields, July 13, 1865, to August 28, 1883. E. M. Coleman since May 9, 1888.

REHOBOTH: *Marchand, Indiana County, Pennsylvania.* Organized by Pittsburgh Presbytery, November 16, 1847, as Warsaw and Montgomery. R. J. Dodds, June 18, 1852, to May 24, 1856. T. M. Elder, May 11, 1859, to April 10, 1866. J. F. Crozier since November 18, 1874.

REHOBOTH: *Wyman, Louisa County, Iowa.* Organized by Illinois Presbytery, October 19, 1854. R. B. Cannon, December 14, 1854, to December 17, 1867. E. G. Elsey, August 14, 1874, to April 12, 1881. J. A. Black since February 9, 1886.

ROCHESTER : *Rochester, New York.* Organized by Southern Presbytery, July 21, 1831. John Fisher, July 21, 1831, to April 17, 1835. C. B. McKee, May 14, 1837, to August 29, 1842. David Scott, July 11, 1844, to July 19, 1862. R. D. Sproull, May 14, 1863, to October 6, 1880. John Graham since June 22, 1881.

ROCHESTER : *Rochester, Kingman County, Kansas.* Organized by Kansas Presbytery, December 4, 1886.

ROCK CREEK : *Gettysburgh, Adams County, Pennsylvania.* Society formed in 1742, as Marsh Creek. John Cuthbertson, 1751, to 1774. Alexander Dobbin, March 10, 1774, to November 1, 1782, when disorganized.

ROCKY CREEK : *Chester, Chester County, South Carolina.* The parent society in the South, formed about 1750. In 1770, called "Edgar's Meeting House." William Martin, 1772, to 1789. William King, 1792, to 1798. Thomas Donnelly, March 3, 1801, to April 10, 1816. Hugh McMillan, June 18, 1822, to April 6, 1829, when disorganized.

ROCKY SPRING : *Chambersburgh, Franklin County, Pennsylvania.* Original of Conococheague, formed in 1751. John Cuthbertson, August 31, 1751, to March 10, 1774. Matthew Linn, March 10, 1774, to November 1, 1782. Organized as Conococheague, June 16, 1802.

ROUND PRAIRIE : *Round Prairie, Todd County, Minnesota.* Organized by Iowa Presbytery, May 12, 1873. .

RUSHSYLVANIA : *Rushsylvania, Logan County, Ohio.* Organized by Lakes Presbytery, November 17, 1853. J. R. W. Sloane, January 13, 1855, to May 21, 1856. P. H. Wylie, November 13, 1860, to May 25, 1876. H. H. George, May 3, 1878, to May 18, 1880. John

Lynd, August 12, 1880, to April 14, 1885. J. J. Huston, July 30, 1886, to April 9, 1888.

RYEGATE : *Ryegate, Caledonia County, Vermont.* Organized by Reformed Presbytery, October, 1798. William Gibson, July 10, 1799, to April 13, 1815. James Milligan, September 26, 1817, to May 17, 1839. J. M. Beattie, June 20, 1844, to May 17, 1882. H. W. Reed, January 19, 1883, to September 21, 1886.

SAINT JOHN : *Saint John, New Brunswick.* Society formed, May, 1821. Organized by Alexander Clarke, March, 1828. Alexander Clarke, August, 1827, to April 25, 1832. A. M. Stavely, August 16, 1841, to July 26, 1879. A. J. McFarland since August 4, 1882.

SAINT JOHNSBURY : *Saint Johnsbury, Caledonia County, Vermont.* Organized by New York Presbytery, July 29, 1879. W. R. Laird, June 15, 1880, to May 1, 1888.

SAINT LOUIS : *Saint Louis, Missouri.* Organized by Illinois Presbytery, April 2, 1846. A. C. Todd, July 29, 1852, to April 12, 1857. Joseph McCracken, October 14, 1859, to September 2, 1874. J. R. Hill, September 28, 1877, to April 15, 1885. E. M. Smith since May 16, 1887.

SALEM : *Stanton, Jefferson County, Pennsylvania.* Organized by Pittsburgh Presbytery, October 31, 1860. A. J. McFarland, February 5, 1862, to April 11, 1882. H. W. Temple since July 14, 1887.

SANDUSKY : *Crestline, Crawford County, Ohio.* Organized by Lakes Presbytery, October 10, 1843. J. C. Boyd, May 13, 1847, to November 6, 1867. Disorganized, April 12, 1876.

SCHENECTADY : *Schenectady, New York.* Organized in 1794, with Duanesburgh. James McKinney, May, 1798, to April 4, 1802. Gilbert McMaster, August 8, 1808, to May 16, 1831, when received separate organization. John McMaster, January 25, 1832, to August 7, 1833, when disorganized.

SELMA : *Selma, Dallas County, Alabama.* Organized by Pittsburgh Presbytery, May 21, 1875, as a mission congregation. Lewis Johnston, May 21, 1875, to November 14, 1876. G. M. Elliot since December 14, 1877.

SHARON: *Linton, Des Moines County, Iowa.* Organized by Illinois Presbytery, September 26, 1846. J. M. McDonald, May 17, 1851, to June 19, 1872. T. P. Robb since July 6, 1874.

SHENANGO AND NESHANNOCK : *Neshannock Falls, Lawrence County, Pennsylvania.* Organized by Pittsburgh Presbytery, October 25, 1829. A. W. Black, January 18, 1832, to August 7, 1833, when disorganized.

SLIPPERY ROCK AND PORTERSVILLE : *Rose Point, Lawrence County, Pennsylvania.* Society formed in 1806, and a part of Little Beaver. Organized by Pittsburgh Presbytery, April 12, 1834. James Blackwood, May 24, 1834, to October 8, 1851. Thomas Hanna, November 17, 1852, to October 29, 1861. J. C. Smith since April 16, 1863.

SOUTHFIELD : *Birmingham, Oakland County, Michigan.* Organized by Ohio Presbytery, May 10, 1834. James Neill, May 18, 1843, to October 6, 1851. J. S. T. Milligan, November 11, 1853, to April 11, 1871. J. R. Hill, May 10, 1872, to May 25, 1876. Joseph McCracken since June 15, 1878.

SPRINGFIELD: *Balm, Mercer County, Pennsylvania.* Organized by Pittsburgh Presbytery, August 4, 1852. J. J. McClurkin, September 8, 1854, to October 14, 1873. J. Renwick Wylie, June 29, 1877, to April 10, 1888.

STAUNTON: *Staunton, Macoupin County, Illinois.* Organized by Illinois Presbytery, July 14, 1863. John Middleton, May 23, 1865, to August 9, 1870. W. F. George, May 13, 1872, to April 14, 1880. E. M. Smith since May 12, 1887.

STERLING: *Sterling Valley, Cayuga County, New York.* Organized by Northern Presbytery, November 17, 1823. W. L. Roberts, November 16, 1826, to October 6, 1830. W. L. Roberts, October 19, 1837, to May 26, 1855. Matthew Wilkin, October 23, 1856, to October 2, 1867. S. R. Galbraith, July 7, 1870, to October 1, 1871. T. J. Allen, November 11, 1875, to June 1, 1887. J. C. B. French since January 12, 1888.

STERLING: *Sterling, Rice County, Kansas.* Organized by Kansas Presbytery, November 5, 1877. J. M. Armour, April 1, 1877, to May 26, 1885. P. H. Wylie since April 15, 1887.

SUPERIOR: *Superior, Nuckolls County, Nebraska.* Organized by Kansas Presbytery, September 1, 1881. R. C. Allen, December 8, 1882, to October 15, 1884. Disorganized, May 22, 1885. Re-organized, August 27, 1885. P. P. Boyd since March 16, 1888.

SYLVANIA: *Sylvania, Dade County, Missouri.* Organized by Illinois Presbytery, August 10, 1871. Josiah Dodds since May 9, 1878.

SYRACUSE: *Syracuse, New York.* Organized by Rochester Presbytery, October 10, 1849. John Newell, May 7, 1851, to May 26, 1853. J. M. Johnston, May 13, 1859, to August 11, 1866. J. M. Armour, June 8, 1867, to September 9, 1873. S. R. Wallace since December 8, 1874.

TABOR: *Clay Centre, Clay County, Kansas.* Organized by Kansas Presbytery, October 12, 1873. S. M. Stevenson since October 30, 1874.

TOPSHAM: *Topsham, Orange County, Vermont.* Organized by Northern Presbytery, September 6, 1818. William Sloane, October 14, 1820, to April 17, 1829. N. R. Johnston, November 10, 1852, to May 16, 1865. J. M. Faris, September 1, 1869, to May 22, 1872. J. C. K. 'Faris since December 2, 1874.

TORONTO: *Toronto, Canada.* Organized by Rochester Presbytery, May 27, 1851. Robert Johnson, November 4, 1852, to November 7, 1859. Disorganized, May 27, 1868. Re-organized, January 23, 1872. Disorganized, May 26, 1875.

TROY: *Troy, New York.* Organized by Northern Presbytery, June 17, 1828. Robert McKee, December 29, 1830, to May 26, 1835. Disorganized, April 13, 1849.

UNITED MIAMI: *Northwood, Logan County, Ohio.* Organized by Lakes Presbytery, April 14, 1877, by consolidation of First and Second Miami. George Kennedy, May 23, 1878, to June 15, 1882. Ruther Hargrave since May 27, 1886.

UTICA: *Utica, Licking County, Ohio.* Organized by Middle Presbytery, October 12, 1814, as Licking.

Robert Wallace, October 12, 1814, to May 10, 1820.
Armour McFarland, October 5, 1837, to May 23, 1855.
J. C. Boyd, November 26, 1856, to October 4, 1882.
W. J. Coleman, 'April 15, 1886, to November 17,
1887.

UTICA: *Utica, New York.* Organized by Southern
Presbytery, October 10, 1837. Disorganized, October
13, 1840.

VERNON: *Waukesha, Waukesha County, Wisconsin.*
Organized by Rochester Presbytery, October 18, 1848,
as Waukesha. Disorganized, November 8, 1850. Re-
organized by Illinois Presbytery, September 16, 1856,
as Vernon. Robert Johnson, 'November 7, 1859,
to December 17, 1867. R. B. Cannon, September 13,
1872, to May 28, 1878. Isaiah Faris since November
22, 1878.

WAHOO AND FREMONT: *Wahoo, Saunders County,
Nebraska.* Organized by Kansas Presbytery, December
19, 1871. J. A. Thompson, October 18, 1877, to May
18, 1880. H. P. McClurkin since February 29, 1884.

WALNUT CITY: *Walnut City, Appanoose County, Iowa.*
Organized by Iowa Presbytery, March 18, 1868.
Isaiah Faris, September 21, 1870, to May 23, 1877.
Disorganized, April 9, 1884.

WALNUT RIDGE: *Salem, Washington County, Indiana.*
Organized by Western Presbytery, May 13, 1822.
Robert Lusk, October 7, 1824, to August 10, 1825.
Robert Lusk, May 9, 1835, to September 18, 1840.
J. J. McClurkin, June 2, 1843, to April 10, 1851.
Disorganized, May 28, 1862.

WALTON: *Walton, Delaware County, New York*. Organized by New York Presbytery, June 11, 1861. David McAllister, December 16, 1863, to September 6, 1871. David McAllister, June 23, 1875, to October 24, 1883. S. G. Shaw since July 8, 1884.

WASHINGTON: *Washington, Washington County, Iowa*. Organized by Iowa Presbytery, November 27, 1863. S. M. Stevenson, February 15, 1865, to October 4, 1871. W. P. Johnston, October 10, 1873, to August 4, 1881. T. A. H. Wylie since December 7, 1882.

WEST HEBRON: *West Hebron, Washington County, New York*. Society formed in 1764. Organized by Northern Presbytery, October, 1814, as Argyle. J. W. Stewart, October 13, 1825, to April 5, 1832. Disorganized, May 24, 1862. Re-organized by New York Presbytery, August 29, 1866, as West Hebron. J. A. Speer since July 28, 1875.

WHITE LAKE: *White Lake, Sullivan County, New York*. Organized by Northern Presbytery, April 15, 1820. M. B. Williams, April 15, 1820, to May 16, 1821. J. B. Williams since November 14, 1850.

WILKINSBURGH: *Wilkinsburgh, Allegheny County, Pennsylvania*. Organized by Pittsburgh Presbytery, July 14, 1848. Thomas Hanna, supply. Joseph Hunter, April 13, 1852, to September 9, 1882. W. W. Carithers since June 20, 1883.

WILMINGTON: *Wilmington, Delaware*. Organized by Philadelphia Presbytery, December 25, 1832. S. M. Gayley, December 25, 1832, to August 7, 1833. Disorganized, October, 1834.

WILMOT : *Wilmot, Annapolis County, Nova Scotia.*
Organized by New Brunswick and Nova Scotia Presbytery, November 13, 1849. Robert Stewart, November
13, 1849, to May 28, 1881.

WINCHESTER : *Winchester, Jefferson County, Kansas.*
Organized by Iowa Presbytery, September 7, 1868.
Josiah Dodds, November 7, 1868, to October 17, 1876.
D. H. Coulter since August 17, 1877.

XENIA : *Xenia, Ohio.* Organized by Middle Presbytery,
June 19, 1810. John Kell, supply. Jonathan Gill, May
14, 1816, to April 6, 1823. Gavin McMillan, supply.
Hugh McMillan, September 7, 1829, to August 7, 1833.
Disorganized, August 18, 1841.

YORK : *York, Livingstone County, New York.* Organ-
ized by Northern Presbytery, November 17, 1823. W.
L. Roberts, November 16, 1826, to October 6, 1830.
John Fisher, July 21, 1831, to July 22, 1845. Samuel
Bowden, December 31, 1846, to November 21, 1876.
W. C. Allen since September 26, 1882.

YOUNGSTOWN : *Youngstown, Ohio.* Organized by Pittsburgh Presbytery, October 12, 1885, as remnant of
Poland and North Jackson. H. W. Reed since May 4,
1888.

THE MINISTRY.

THOMAS HOUSTON ACHESON:

Son of John and Nancy (Caskey) Acheson, was born in New Galilee, Beaver County, Pennsylvania, August 10, 1861. He received his early education in the schools of his native town, and, in due time, entered Westminster College, where he remained until his junior year, and graduated from Geneva College in 1882. He studied theology in the Allegheny Seminary, and was licensed by the Pittsburgh Presbytery, April 15, 1885, and labored for six months in Kansas and Nebraska. He was ordained by the Iowa Presbytery, and installed pastor of the congregation of Hopkinton, Delaware County, Iowa, September 23, 1886, where he is in charge. He married Miss Minnie Hill, of Crystal Park, Colorado, August 24, 1886. In 1880, he became an editor of the *College Cabinet* for two years.

WILLIAM ANDREW ACHESON:

Son of William and Margaret (Graham) Acheson, was born in the city of New York, July 28, 1815. He was early furnished with the opportunity of acquiring a liberal education in the best schools, and graduated from the University of the City of New York

in 1836. He engaged in teaching, and other employments, for several years. He studied theology under
the direction of the Rev. James Christie, D. D., and
also in the Allegheny Seminary, and was licensed
by the New York Presbytery, December 3, 1847. He
travelled generally throughout the Church, but especially
supplied the vacancies in the South and West, where
his labors were very acceptable. While on his way to
Princeton, Indiana, he was attacked with cholera, and
died in three days thereafter, in Evansville, Indiana,
November 26, 1850. He never married. Few young
men possessed a more robust constitution, and the
abilities which are peculiarly adapted to missionary
work. He was endowed with a fine mind, and the
elements of a popular preacher. He was warm in his
attachments, easy in his manners, kind in his deportment, and unaffected in his devotion to the cause of
Christ.

JOHN STEVENSON ALLEN:
    Son of Cochran and Elizabeth (Willson) Allen,
was born in Balm, Mercer County, Pennsylvania,
October 20, 1857. He received his preparatory course
of literary training in Grove City College, and graduated from Westminster College in 1882. He studied
theology in the Union Seminary of New York City,
and was licensed by the New York Presbytery, May
20, 1885. He preached in but a few of the vacancies,
and connected with the Presbyterian Church, being
received by the Presbytery of the City of New York,
February 8, 1886. He was ordained by the West
Chester Presbytery of that body, and installed pastor

of Throgg's Neck congregation, West Chester, West
Chester County, New York, May 13, 1886, where he
is in charge.

NATHANIEL ALLEN, M. D.:

Son of Robert and Ann (Gillespie) Allen, was
born near Andes, Delaware County, New York, June
14, 1810.   In early life he was cast upon his own
resources, and, with great difficulty, obtained a liberal
education, and taught school in Orange County, New
York, with marked success for many years.   He pursued
his classical studies in the Academy of Coldenham, New
York, under the Rev. J. R. Willson, D. D., and graduated from the Oneida Institute, Whitesboro, New
York, in 1838.   He studied theology in the Coldenham
and Allegheny Seminaries, and was licensed by the
Pittsburgh Presbytery, June 29, 1843.   He preached
within the bounds of this Presbytery for two years,
and, when transferred to the Lakes Presbytery in
1845, he was refused appointments and complained to
Synod.   For the want of that aptness to teach which
is essential in the ministry, his license was withdrawn
by the authority of Synod, May 31, 1847.   In 1848,
he entered the Ohio Medical College, Cincinnati, completed the three years' course, and settled in Princeton,
Indiana, where he practiced medicine as a successful
physician for several years.   In 1855, he memorialized
the Synod to consider his case, but failed to receive
his license to preach, and returned to Princeton,
Indiana, where he died of hemorrhages of the lungs,
March 29, 1857.   He married Miss Eliza J. Reid, of
Rushville, Indiana, March 18, 1846.   He was a skilled

physician and sympathetic to every trouble. He was a good man, a true Covenanter, scrupulously conscientious in the discharge of all religious duties and persevering in his purpose, but failed to attain the grand object of his desires—the Christian ministry. He received the degree of Doctor of Medicine from the. Ohio Medical College in 1851. He published a sermon, "The Help of the Church," 1851, pp. 16.

ROBERT CAMERON ALLEN:

Son of Samuel and Mary (Gilmore) Allen, was born in Balm, Mercer County, Pennsylvania, May 4, 1848. He received his elementary literary training in what is now Grove City College, graduated from Westminster College in 1875, and engaged in teaching. He studied theology in the Allegheny Seminary, and was licensed by the Pittsburgh Presbytery, April 8, 1879, and labored in the far West, under the direction of the Central Board of Missions. He was ordained by the Kansas Presbytery, and installed pastor of the congregation of Superior, Nuckolls County, Nebraska, December 8, 1882, and was released October 15, 1884. He was installed pastor of the Lochiel congregation, Brodie, Ontario, Canada, October 18, 1887, where he is in charge. He married Miss Lizzie S. Little, of West Fairfield, Pennsylvania, June 28, 1878.

THOMAS JOHN ALLEN:

Son of Robert and Jane (Willson) Allen, was born in Findley, Mercer County, Pennsylvania, July 18, 1848. He received his early education in what is now Grove City College, and graduated from Westminster College in 1871. He studied theology in the Allegheny

Seminary, and was licensed by the Pittsburgh Presbytery, April 15, 1874. He was ordained by the Rochester Presbytery, and installed pastor of the congregation of Sterling, Cayuga County, New York, November 11, 1875, and resigned this charge, June 1, 1887, and removed to Balm, Pennsylvania. Recently he has engaged in evangelistic work with fruitful results. He married Miss Nannie Ramsey, of Oakdale, Illinois, August 28, 1877.

WILLIAM COCHRAN ALLEN:

Son of Cochran and Elizabeth (Willson) Allen, was born in Balm, Mercer County, Pennsylvania, November 7, 1854. He received his rudimentary literary education in what is now Grove City College, and graduated from Westminster College in 1877. He studied theology in the Allegheny Seminary, and was licensed by the Pittsburgh Presbytery, April 13, 1881, and labored for some time in Lake Reno and Round Prairie, Minnesota. He was ordained by the Rochester Presbytery, and installed pastor of the congregation of York, Livingston County, New York, September 28, 1882, where he is in charge. He married Miss Jeanie A. Black, of London, Pennsylvania, June 1, 1882.

JOHN McLAUGHLIN ARMOUR:

Son of Thomas G. and Mary A. (Cathcart) Armour, was born in Sparta, Randolph County, Illinois, October 9, 1825. He received his early education in the schools of his native village, and in the city of St. Louis, Missouri, and graduated from Geneva College in 1852. He studied theology in the Cincinnati Seminary, and at the same time with his literary course in the Northwood Seminary, and was licensed by the Lakes Presbytery,

April 16, 1852. He was ordained by the New York Presbytery, and installed pastor of the congregation of Craftsbury, Orleans County, Vermont, September 23, 1857, and resigned October 31, 1865, and took charge of the Freedmen's Mission in Washington, D. C. He was installed pastor of the congregation of Syracuse, New York, June 8, 1867, and resigned September 9, 1873. He removed to Northwood, Logan County, Ohio, and was a supply for three years. He took charge of the congregation of Sterling, Rice County, Kansas, April 1, 1877, and resigned May 26, 1885. He removed to the city of Philadelphia, Pennsylvania, where he is devoting himself to the work of an author and supplying vacant pulpits. He married Miss Mary E. Sudborough, of Hamilton, Canada, March 21, 1856. Among his publications are: "Atonement and Law," 1885, pp. 240, three editions. "The Divine Method of Life," 1887, pp. 250.

JOHN OWEN BAYLES:

Son of Stephen and Martha (McVey) Bayles, was born in Cherry Fork, Adams County, Ohio, February 4, 1835. He received his early education in that vicinity, and with the family removed to Northwood, Logan County, Ohio, where he graduated from Geneva College in 1857. He studied theology in the Allegheny Seminary and was licensed by the Pittsburgh Presbytery, April 25, 1860. He supplied vacant congregations and mission stations, and, in the spring of 1864, took charge of the Freedmen's Mission in Washington, D. C. He was ordained by the New York Presbytery, and installed pastor of the Kortright congregation, West Kortright,

Delaware County, New York, January 10, 1866, where he is in charge. He married Miss Martha B. Floyd, of Philadelphia, Pennsylvania, November 30, 1865.

JOSEPH BEATTIE, D. D.:

Son of John and Eliza (McKinney) Beattie, was born in Saint Andrews, Orange County, New York, October 17, 1830. His mother was a daughter of the Rev. James McKinney, and his father a pious Covenanter and an elder in the Coldenham congregation. He pursued his preparatory literary studies in the schools of his native county and graduated from Union College in 1852. He studied theology in Philadelphia, under the direction of the Rev. James M. Willson, D. D., and was licensed by the Philadelphia Presbytery, May 26, 1856. The next week he was chosen by Synod as a Missionary to Syria. Accepting this appointment, he was ordained *sine titulo* by the New York Presbytery, September 23, 1856, and, with Dr. R. J. Dodds and others, sailed for that foreign land, October 16, 1856. He first settled in Damascus, where he pursued his studies in the Arabic language, and became a proficient scholar in that tongue. After exploring many parts of the Holy Land, he finally settled in Latakia in 1859, where suitable buildings were subsequently erected, and where he spent the rest of his life in the proper work of a Missionary. He visited the United States three times—in 1863, 1876 and 1878, and in those visits he lectured through all parts of the Church and awakened an interest in the Foreign Mission. Upon his last visit he left his wife to educate his children in this country, but scarcely had he reached the sacred soil of Syria, when he received the distressing intelligence of her death, and he immediately returned to his motherless children. He soon afterwards returned to Syria, and, in 1880, opened a Theological School for the training of a native ministry. He died at his home in Latakia, Syria, of gastric fever, October 8, 1883. He was a man of fine personal appearance, of ripe experience and of sound judgment, to whom the missionaries, as well as the native scholars, looked for counsel and direction. He was a faithful minister, a most judicious teacher, and one universally beloved for his kindness to his fellow-teachers and sympathy for the distressed heathen. He was a man firm in his convictions and unyielding in his fidelity to truth and duty. He did yeoman service in establishing the Syrian Mission, and was instrumental in bringing many souls to a saving knowledge of Christ. He married Miss Martha E. Lord, of Camden, Delaware, September 16, 1856. He was honored with the degree of Doctor of Divinity by Union College in 1878. He was Moderator of the Synod of 1876.

JAMES MILLIGAN BEATTIE:

Son of John and Sarah (Haines) Beattie, was born in Saint Andrews, Orange County, New York, September 24, 1811. He was a half-brother to Rev. Joseph Beattie, D. D., and received an equally strict religious training in the home of his pious parents. He received his preparatory literary studies in the Coldenham Academy of his native County, and graduated from Union College in 1834. He studied theology in the Coldenham Seminary under the Rev. James R. Willson,

27

D. D., one year. In 1840, he went to Scotland and studied theology in the Paisley Seminary, and was licensed by the Paisley Presbytery, of the Covenanter Church, April 13, 1843. He returned to this country the same year, was ordained by the New York Presbytery, May 29, 1844, and installed pastor of the united congregations of Ryegate and Barnet, Caledonia County, Vermont, June 20, 1844. At the organization of the Barnet congregation, he resigned that branch, May 24, 1872, and on account of declining strength he was released from Ryegate, May 17, 1882. For two years he endured much severe suffering of the body, and died at his home in Ryegate, Caledonia County, Vermont, March 9, 1884. He married Miss Margaret S. Nelson, of Ryegate, Vermont, December 25, 1855. He was a sound theologian, an instructive preacher, and a faithful shepherd of the flock which Christ gave him. He was studious in his habits, reserved in his manners, and exemplary in his deportment. He was peculiarly gifted in prayer, conscientiously regular in the performance of Christian duties, and thoroughly devoted to the work of the Master.

ANDREW WATSON BLACK, D. D.:

Son of Rev. Dr. John and Elizabeth (Watson) Black, was born in the city of Pittsburgh, Pennsylvania, April 24, 1808. He received a strict religious training in the home of his distinguished father, pursued his preparatory literary course in the Pittsburgh Academy under Dr. Robert Bruce, and graduated from the Western University of Pennsylvania in 1826. He studied theology in the Philadelphia Seminary, and was licensed by the Pittsburgh Presbytery, February 10, 1828. He itinerated throughout the vacancies and travelled extensively through Tennessee and South Carolina. He was ordained by the Pittsburgh Presbytery, and installed pastor of the united congregations of Shenango, Mercer and Neshannock, Neshannock Falls, Lawrence County, Pennsylvania, January 18, 1832. In August, 1833, he, and the majority of the congregation, became identified with the New School branch of the Covenanter Church. He resigned his congregation August 10, 1838, and removed to the city of Pittsburgh. He was installed pastor of a colony of his father's congregation in the city of Allegheny, Pennsylvania, May 16, 1839, and also performed the duties of Chaplain in the Western Penitentiary. In 1855, he resigned these charges, and became agent for the American Bible Society. In May, 1858, he was chosen by his Church to the chair of theology in the Philadelphia Seminary, and, while preparing to enter upon the duties of this important office, he was taken with dysentery, and died very suddenly at his home in Sewickleyville, in Allegheny County, Pennsylvania, September 10, 1858. He was a fine scholar, a forcible writer, and a popular preacher. He took a prominent part in all Church work, and was interested in many literary institutions and benevolent societies of his native city. He married Miss Margaret Roseburgh, of Pittsburgh, Pennsylvania, January 1, 1835. He was honored with the degree of Doctor of Divinity by Rutgers College in 1852. He was Moderator of the General Synods of 1842 and 1853.

JOHN BLACK, D. D.:

Son of John and Margaret (McKibbin) Black, was born in Ahoghill, County Antrim, Ireland, October 2, 1768. He received the rudiments of a classical education in the schools of his native country, and graduated from the University of Glasgow, Scotland, in 1790. He returned to Ireland where he engaged in teaching, and also began the study of theology. He came to America in the fall of 1797, as an exile for liberty at the time of the Irish insurrection. He was employed for some time as a teacher of the classics near the city of Philadelphia, Pennsylvania, and subsequently in connection with the University of Pennsylvania. He resumed his theological studies, and was licensed by the Reformed Presbytery, at Coldenham, Orange County, New York, June 24, 1799. Being assigned by this court to labor in Western Pennsylvania, he soon afterwards gathered the Ohio congregation, centering in Pittsburgh, and including all the societies of Covenanters west of the Allegheny mountains. He was ordained by the Reformed Presbytery, and installed pastor of this extensive congregation, December 18, 1800. In 1806, the congregation was divided into three parts, and he remained pastor of the portion in and around the city of Pittsburgh, which soon became a large and influential charge. He also was engaged as a classical teacher, and, in 1820, was elected Professor of Latin and Greek in the Western University of Pennsylvania, and resigned in 1832, when he visited Europe. He was President of Duquesne College one year. At the division of the Church in August, 1833, he became identified with the New School branch of the Covenanter Church. He remained pastor of a majority of his former congregation until his death, at his residence in Pittsburgh, Pennsylvania, October 25, 1849. He was a remarkably proficient scholar, especially in the languages, and spent most of his life in teaching. He was identified with almost all the literary and charitable institutions of his adopted city, and was a zealous advocate of every reform. He was the first Covenanter minister settled west of the Allegheny mountains, and the pioneer missionary in the new West. During the suspension of the Theological Seminary after 1828, he taught a class in theology in connection with his other duties. He was a great man. His preaching talents were of a high order. He possessed a lively imagination and dwelt largely in allegory, sometimes enrapturing his audience with descriptions of Scripture figures and scenery. He was a ready and forcible extemporaneous speaker on all subjects, and never refused an invitation to preach. His life was too busy with collegiate and ministerial duties to effect much as an author, yet he published some valuable articles in the newspapers and magazines of the Church in his day. Among his publications are: "Church Fellowship," 1819, pp. 109. "The Bible against Slavery," 1839, pp. 36. "The Baptist Controversy," 1846, pp. 52. "The Duration of the Mediatorial Dominion," 1848, pp. 32. The "Directory of Worship" is from his pen, and he wrote the Latin Introduction to Rabbi Leeser's issue of the Hebrew

Bible. He married Miss Elizabeth Watson, of Pittsburgh, Pennsylvania, in 1802. He was honored with the degree of Doctor of Divinity by Washington College in 1824. He was Moderator of the Reformed Presbytery in 1801, and previous to 1833, the stated Clerk of Synod for many years. He was Moderator of the General Synod in 1837.

JOHN BLACK, JR.:

Son of Rev. Dr. John and Elizabeth (Watson) Black, was born in the city of Pittsburgh, Pennsylvania, April 9, 1806. He received his preparatory course of literary training in the Pittsburgh Academy under Dr. Robert Bruce, and graduated from the Western University of Pennsylvania in 1825. He studied theology in the Philadelphia Seminary, and also under the direction of his distinguished father, and was licensed by the Pittsburgh Presbytery, April 22, 1828. His trial discourses were the last he delivered, for at that time he was greatly reduced by consumption, from which disease he died at the house of his uncle, the Rev. Dr. S. B. Wylie, in Philadelphia, Pennsylvania, August 15, 1828. He was unmarried. He was a large and exceedingly muscular man, and possessed a commanding appearance. His scholarly attainments and natural endowments gave ample promise that, had he been spared, he would have become a powerful preacher and an able divine.

JAMES ALEXANDER BLACK:

Son of Samuel and Elizabeth (Bell) Black, was born near Dromore, County Down, Ireland, * * * He came with his parents to America in 1841, and settled in the city of Pittsburgh, Pennsylvania, where he received his early education in the public schools, and graduated from Allegheny City College in 1862. He studied theology in the Allegheny Seminary, and was licensed by the Pittsburgh Presbytery, May 23, 1867. He was ordained by the same Presbytery, and installed pastor of the congregation of Clarksburgh, Indiana County, Pennsylvania, November 18, 1868, and resigned this charge, April 11, 1882. In the fall of 1882, he accepted the Presidency of the Polytechnic Institute, Allegheny City, Pennsylvania, which position he occupied three years. He was installed pastor of the Rehoboth congregation, Wyman, Louisa County, Iowa, February 9, 1886, where he is in charge. He married Miss Tirzah M. Cannon, of New Alexandria, Pennsylvania, June 8, 1876.

JAMES BLACKWOOD:

Son of Thomas and Martha (Akin) Blackwood, was born in Ardstraw, County Tyrone, Ireland, August 14, 1793. He was early dedicated to the work of the gospel ministry, and received his preparatory course of study in the schools of his native County. In 1811, he entered the University of Glasgow, Scotland, where he remained three years, and then engaged in teaching. In 1818, he repaired to Belfast, Ireland, where he resumed his literary and theological studies, and was licensed by the Southern Presbytery, Ireland, May 10, 1822. He came to America in 1824, with other members of the family, and settled in Belmont County, Ohio, and missionated throughout Western Pennsylvania and Ohio for several years. To fully meet the exigencies of his work, he was ordained *sine titulo* by the Pittsburgh Presbytery, May 8, 1826. He was installed pastor of the Brush Creek congregation, Locust Grove, Adams County, Ohio, April 12, 1827, and was released April 9, 1829. He remained unsettled for nearly five years, during most of which time he was actively engaged in missionary work. He was installed pastor of the united congregations of Little Beaver, Austintown, Camp Run, Slippery Rock, Greenville and Sandy Lake, principally in Beaver and Lawrence Counties, Pennsylvania, May 24, 1834. In 1838, Little Beaver, Austintown and Greenville, and in 1850, Sandy Lake, became separate congregations, and he confined his labors to Slippery Rock and Camp Run until his death. In 1850, his health began to decline, and, at times, he was unable to fully attend to his ministerial duties. His sufferings were often intense, and his disease took the form of dropsy, from which he died at his home near Portersville, Pennsylvania, October 8, 1851. He was a clear and instructive preacher, a faithful pastor, and a rigid disciplinarian. He possessed an ardent temperament, and was strong in his attachments as well as decided in his antipathies.* With strangers he was somewhat formal and distant, but, when he discovered in them true manhood, honesty and piety, they were received into his friendship. He was exceedingly tender in his feelings, and peculiarly sympathetic to those in suffering or in sorrow from bereavement. He was social and lively in his disposition, and made the hour of relaxation teem with pleasantry. He was a good Presbyter, and was not absent from a meeting of Synod during his ministry, where his opinion upon

---

* Sprague's Annals, p. 78, by Rev. Dr. T. Sproull.

ecclesiastical questions was highly regarded. He married Miss Jemima Calderwood, of Philadelphia, Pennsylvania, August 18, 1833. He was Moderator of the Synod of 1838.

JOHN HASLETT BOGGS:

Son of John and Annabella (Haslett) Boggs, was born in the city of Allegheny, Pennsylvania, December 7, 1837. He received his preparatory course of study in the public schools of his native city, and graduated from Allegheny City College in 1860. He studied theology in the Allegheny Seminary, and was licensed by the Pittsburgh Presbytery, April 12, 1864. He was ordained by the New York Presbytery, and installed pastor of the congregation of Brooklyn, New York, December 14, 1864, and resigned this charge, November 19, 1880. He connected with the Presbyterian Church, and was received by the Philadelphia Presbytery of that body, April 6, 1881. He was installed pastor of the Hermon congregation, Frankford, near Philadelphia, Pennsylvania, April 26, 1881, and resigned June 4, 1887. He spent some time in California for his health, with the expectation of returning to the East. He married Miss M. A. Taylor, of Allegheny City, Pennsylvania, January 6, 1865. He was an editor of *Our Banner* from 1874, to 1880. He published " Why Covenanters do not Vote," 1872, pp. 15.

JOHN ALEXANDER FINLEY BOVARD:

Son of George and Jane (Finley) Bovard, was born in the city of Philadelphia, Pennsylvania, March 7, 1851. In early life his parents removed to Lake County, Indiana, where he received his early education in the schools of Hebron and Crown Point. He resumed

his classical studies in Geneva College, and graduated
from the State Normal School, Valparaiso, Indiana, in
1877. He studied theology in the Allegheny Seminary,
and was licensed by the Pittsburgh Presbytery, April 13,
1880. He was ordained *sine titulo* by the New Brunswick and Nova Scotia Presbytery, as a missionary to
Houlton, Maine, July 28, 1881, where he labored
three years. He was installed pastor of the united
congregations of Oil Creek and Oil City, Pennsylvania,
June 12, 1884, where he is in charge. He married
Miss Mary J. Jamison, of Allegheny City, Pennsylvania,
January 15, 1880.

SAMUEL BOWDEN:

Son of Andrew and Rose (Witherspoon) Bowden,
was born in the city of New York, New York,
August 26, 1822. He received his preparatory literary
training in the private schools of his native city, and
graduated from Columbia College in 1840. He studied
theology in the Allegheny Seminary, and was licensed
by the New York Presbytery, October 29, 1844. He
was ordained by the Rochester Presbytery, and installed
pastor of the congregation of York, Livingston County,
New York, December 31, 1846, and resigned this
charge, November 21, 1876. He withdrew from the
communion of the Covenanter Church, October 6, 1880,
and connected with the Presbyterian Church, being
received by the Rochester Presbytery of that body,
April 19, 1881. He took charge of the congregation
of Tonawanda, Wyoming County, New York, May 6,
1883, and resides in Le Roy, Genesee County, New
York. He was twice married. First to Miss Maria

O. Beattie, of St. Andrews, New York, October 24, 1848 ; and second to Miss Mary E. Donnan, of York, New York, April 20, 1864. He was Moderator of the Synod of 1864.

JOHN CALVIN BOYD :

Son of Robert and Mary (McMaster) Boyd, was born in the city of Steubenville, Ohio, June 27, 1814. His father was an accomplished scholar and teacher, and his mother was distinguished for her piety and traits of Christian character. His religious and literary training early fitted him for becoming a teacher of others, and in this occupation he began in Utica, Licking County, Ohio, where he became a successful teacher and prosecuted his classical studies. In 1840, he entered Miami University, where he remained two years. He studied theology under the Rev. Armour McFarland, and also in the Cincinnati Seminary, and was licensed by the Lakes Presbytery, May 7, 1846. He was ordained by the same Presbytery, and installed pastor of the Sandusky congregation, Cresline, Crawford County, Ohio, May 13, 1847, and also of the congregation of Utica, Licking County, Ohio, November 26, 1856. He resigned the Sandusky branch, November 6, 1867, and devoted his whole time to Utica. He resigned this charge on account of impaired health, October 4, 1882, and supplied throughout the Ohio Presbytery as his health would permit. He died at his home in Utica, Ohio, of nervous chills and typhoid fever, June 3, 1886. He married Miss Jane McCune, of Philadelphia, Pennsylvania, May 30, 1850. He was a well-read theologian of the old school, a most logical reasoner, and an instructive preacher. He was a fearless advocate of the cause of the slave, hazarded his interests and even his life for the overthrow of human slavery, and bore constant testimony against the evils of both Church and State. He was well grounded in the truth of the Word of God, most decided in his convictions, and punctual in the performance of all religious duties. He was recognized in Church courts for his clear discussion and sound judgment on questions pertaining to the good of Zion. He was highly esteemed in the community where he labored, and the quiet, yet exemplary, life which he lived, was a strong testimony to the power of the gospel which he so successfully preached. He published some sermons and articles of importance in the papers and magazines of the Church.

PATTERSON PROUDFIT BOYD:

Son of James and Jane (Speer) Boyd, was born near Londonderry, Guernsey County, Ohio, August 2, 1842. In 1852, his parents removed to Oskaloosa, Iowa, and were devoted members of the Associate Church, in which he was reared. Here he received his early education in Oskaloosa College, and in 1865, entered Muskingum College, where he graduated in 1868. He studied theology in the Allegheny Seminary, and was licensed by the Ohio Presbytery, April 12, 1871. He was ordained by the Lakes Presbytery, and installed pastor of the congregation of Cedarville, Greene County, Ohio, May 22, 1872, and resigned this charge, April 8, 1874. He was installed pastor of the Old Bethel congregation, Houston, Randolph County, Illinois, July 20, 1874, and resigned this charge, December 12, 1887. He was installed pastor of the congregation of Superior, Nuckolls County, Nebraska, March 16, 1888, where he is in charge. He married Miss Laura C. Foster, of Cedarville, Ohio, October 17, 1872.

JAMES BROWN:

Was born in Penpont, Dumfries Shire, Scotland, July 18, 1812. He received his early education in the best schools of his native village, and graduated from the University of Glasgow, Scotland, in 1835. He studied theology in the Seminary of Paisley, Scotland, under the direction of the Rev. Andrew Symington, and was licensed by the Paisley Presbytery, April 28, 1840. He preached with a good degree of success in that country for many years. He came to America in the fall of 1855, and preached for several years in the vacancies. He returned to Scotland, and was for some years a Chaplain to an institution in Edinburgh, and finally was lost sight of by the Church, and ceased preaching. In the latter part of his life he returned to his native Shire of Dumfries, where he died, September 8, 1883. He was a good man, a fair scholar, but, upon the whole, unappreciated as a preacher.

JAMES STEWART BUCK:

Son of John and Jane (Stewart) Buck, was born near De Kalb, Richland County, Ohio, June 24, 1835. His parents were members of the Associate Reformed Church, with which he also connected in his nineteenth year. He began his classical studies in Oberlin College, resumed them in Hayesville Academy, of his native County, and, in 1857, entered Jefferson College, but was not permitted to complete the full course on account of failing health. In 1858, he removed to New Galilee, Beaver County, Pennsylvania, where he opened an Academy. Not being satisfied with the Associate Reformed Church as to her position on civil government, he acceded to the Covenanter Church in the fall of 1860. He studied theology in the Allegheny Seminary, and was licensed by the Pittsburgh Presbytery, April 23, 1864. He missionated in Oil City, Pennsylvania, and other parts of the Church, until frequent and severe hemorrhages of the lungs compelled him to cease preaching. After a much needed rest, he was ordained *sine titulo* by the Pittsburgh Presbytery, May 21, 1867, and sent by the Central Board of Missions as a missionary to the North-West region. He soon afterwards settled in Elliota, Fillmore County, Minnesota, where he labored amid many discouragements and much weakness of body for nearly three years. While on his way to Synod in May, 1870, his strength failed, and he was but able to reach the home of his father-in-law, near Rose Point, Lawrence County, Pennsylvania, where he lingered a few months, and died from consumption, October 13, 1870. He married Miss M. J. Davis, of Rose Point, Pennsylvania, in 1859. He was an able, studious and conscientious preacher of the gospel; a humble, unassuming Christian, and from a rich experience declared the truth to dying men. He was most diligent and prayerful in his work, kind and attentive to all the members of his congregation, cheerful and hopeful in every trial. In appearance he was tall, slender, bent, and emaciated with disease. He often spoke with great difficulty, leaning upon the pulpit or sitting upon a chair, and his discourses were highly evangelical and deeply impressive. Among his publications are numerous letters to the Mission Board, and a posthumous tract, "Position of the Reformed Presbyterian Church," 1871, pp. 16.

JOHN CANNON:

Son of Hugh and Mary (Thompson) Cannon, was born in Dungiven, County Londonderry, Ireland, November 19, 1784. His parents were exemplary members of the Presbyterian Church, who emigrated to America in 1787, and settled in Westmoreland County, Pennsylvania. Becoming dissatisfied with the use of human psalmody in the worship of God, the family connected with Associate Reformed Church in 1788. He received his early literary instructions under private teachers, and graduated from Jefferson College in 1810. During his college course he espoused the principles of the Covenanter Church, and decided to study for the ministry. He studied theology in the Philadelphia Seminary, and was licensed by the Middle Presbytery, May 23, 1815. He was ordained by the same Presbytery, and installed pastor of the congregation of Greensburgh, Westmoreland County, Pennsylvania, September 16, 1816, where he continued to labor until his death. During the unpleasant controversy and division of the Church in 1833, he stood firm to the Covenanted cause, and was chosen Moderator of that notable Synod, showing the high esteem and confidence which his brethren placed in him. For a number of years before his death, he labored under a disease of the liver, which was aggravated by the fatigue and exposure which he was called upon to endure in reaching his places of preaching. His last public ministrations were during the communion season in August, 1835, when his disease exhibited the symptoms of dropsy, and he gradually declined until his death, at his home near Greensburgh, Pennsylvania, February 2, 1836. He married Miss Martha Brown of Greensburgh, Pennsylvania, May, 1818. In appearance he was of medium size, well proportioned, dark complexion, and possessed a grave and pleasing countenance. He was a very acceptable preacher, and his pastoral labors were signally blessed in the gathering of several societies which are now flourishing congregations. He was apt to teach, practical in applying truth, and prudent in managing difficult cases of discipline. He possessed a noble generosity of spirit, firmness of purpose, and amiability of manners. He was Moderator of the Synods of 1819 and 1833.

ROBERT BROWN CANNON, D. D.:

Son of Rev. John and Martha (Brown) Cannon, was born near Greensburgh, Westmoreland County, Pennsylvania, October 4, 1821. He received his early education under the direction of his father, studied the classics under the Rev. Hugh Walkinshaw, finished the classical course in the Greensburgh Academy, and graduated from the Western University of Pennsylvania in 1842. He was Principal of the Darlington Academy one year. He studied theology in the Allegheny and Cincinnati Seminaries, and was licensed by the Lakes Presbytery, May 7, 1846. He was ordained by the

Pittsburgh Presbytery, and installed pastor of the united congregations of Greensburgh, Westmoreland County, and Clarksburgh, Indiana County, Pennsylvania, May 5, 1847, and resigned this charge, April 4, 1854. He was installed pastor of the Rehoboth congregation, Wyman, Louisa County, Iowa, December 14, 1854, and resigned December 17, 1867. He was installed pastor of the congregation of Vernon, Waukesha County, Wisconsin, September 13, 1872, and resigned May 28, 1878. He removed to Cameron, Clinton County, Missouri, and labored under appointment of the Central Board of Missions, and also preached for two years gratuitously to the colored people of that place. He was installed pastor of the Jonathan's Creek congregation, White Cottage, Muskingum County, Ohio, September 9, 1886, where he is in charge. He was twice married. First to Miss Juliett H. Willson, of Cincinnati, Ohio, November 9, 1846; and second to Miss Elizabeth Biggam, of New York City, New York, June 10, 1856. He was honored with the degree of Doctor of Divinity by Iowa University in 1868.

WILLIAM WORK CARITHERS:

Son of Andrew T. and Mary (Reid) Carithers, was born near Linton, Des Moines County, Iowa, December 19, 1854. He received his early education in the Academy of Morning Sun, Iowa, and entered Geneva College, where he tutored, and graduated in 1878. He studied theology in the Allegheny Seminary, and was licensed by the Iowa Presbytery, April 13, 1882. He was ordained by the Pittsburgh Presbytery, and installed pastor of the congregation of Wilkinsburgh, Allegheny County, Pennsylvania, June 20, 1883, where he is in charge. He married Miss Ella M. George, of Venice, Pennsylvania, May 1, 1883.

JOHN FENTON CARLISLE:

Son of Rev. Samuel and Margaret M. (Fenton) Carlisle, was born in the city of Newburgh, New York, September 21, 1858. He received his early education in the public schools, and also in the Banks Classical School of his native city, and graduated from Columbia College in 1880. He studied theology in the Allegheny Seminary, and was licensed by the New York Presbytery, May 16, 1883. He was ordained by the Pittsburgh Presbytery, and installed pastor of the congregation of New Alexandria, Westmoreland County, Pennsylvania, June 16, 1884, and resigned this charge, January 26, 1888.

SAMUEL CARLISLE:

Son of Rev. Samuel and Letitia (Craig) Carlisle, was born in Ballibay, County Monaghan, Ireland, May 4, 1828. His father was an eminent minister of the Covenanter Church, and he was reared in the most careful manner by a pious parentage. He received his early education in the Coleraine Academy, and graduated from Belfast College in 1847. He studied theology in the Seminary of Paisley, Scotland, and was licensed by the Northern Presbytery, Ireland, May 4, 1848. In the following spring he came to America, was ordained by the New York Presbytery, and installed pastor of the First congregation of Newburgh, New York, November 15, 1849, where he spent the remainder of his life. On January 4, 1887, he was stricken with paralysis, which completely disabled his left side, and laid him prostrate upon his bed. For a time his life was in jeopardy, but in the spring he rallied, and was able to walk out, attended church and preached once. In order that he might be relieved from the excitement of the meeting of Synod in Newburgh, he was advised to leave the city. Accordingly, accompanied by his wife, he repaired to Ocean Grove, New Jersey, where he seemed to improve and where everything was done for his comfort. But, as he expressed it, "his work was done." A second stroke rendered him unconscious for four days, and he lay motionless until his death, at Ocean Grove, New Jersey, July 3, 1887. His body was taken back to Newburgh and buried in Cedar Hill Cemetery. He married Miss Margaret M. Fenton, of Newburgh, New York, May 10, 1853. He was an able preacher of the gospel. He was a careful Bible student, thoroughly conscientious in preparing for the pulpit, and consecrated his whole life to the service of his Master. IIis labors mct with general appreciation, and he exerted an influence for good in the community where he spent the whole of his ministerial life. He possessed a good physical constitution, a clear and sonorous voice, and preached with a seriousness and directness that never failed to impress his hearers. He was pre-eminently a man of prayer. He was fearless in attacking evil and prudent in presenting Reformation principles. He identified himself with every good work of the city and was held in the highest esteem by his fellow citizens. The work of preaching Christ he did conscientiously, faithfully and successfully. He was a public spirited man. He was a Director of the Newburgh Bible Society, a Manager of the Home of the Friendless, and prominent in the local National Reform and Temperance movements. Among his publications are a "Centennial Sermon," preached at Washington's Headquarters, Newburgh, 1876, pp. 20. "A History of the Reformed Presbyterian Church of Newburgh, and a Characteristic sketch of Dr. James R. Willson," 1885, pp. 10. He was Moderator of the Synod of 1886.

JOHN FLEMING CARSON:

Son of William and Margaret (Fleming) Carson, was born in the city of Philadelphia, Pennsylvania, January 28, 1860. He received his early education in the public schools and in the West Philadelphia Academy, and completed a special classical course in the University of Pennsylvania. He studied theology in the Allegheny Seminary, and was licensed by the Philadelphia Presbytery, April 28, 1884. He was ordained by the New York Presbytery, and installed pastor of the congregation of Brooklyn, New York, May 20, 1885, where he is in charge. He married Miss Rebecca McKnight, of Philadelphia, Pennsylvania, February 9, 1886.

JAMES CHRISTIE, D. D.:

Son of Major James and Mary (Weygand) Christie, was born in the city of New York, New York, February 20, 1786.* His father was a distinguished Revolutionary officer, and his mother a saintly woman abounding in deeds of chairty. They were exemplary members of the Associate Reformed Church, with which

* Sketch by Rev. John Forsythe, D. D., Newburgh, N. Y.

he also connected in early life under the pastoral care of the Rev. John M. Mason, D. D. He received a careful religious training in the home, a thorough literary education in the best schools of the city, and graduated from Columbia College in 1806. He became a prosperous merchant in New York City, and soon afterwards connected with the Dutch Reformed Church. In 1812, he abandoned commercial life and resolved to devote himself to the work of the gospel ministry. In the autumn of 1812, he began the study of theology in the Seminary of the Associate Reformed Church in New York, under Dr. John M. Mason, as a student of the Dutch Reformed Church, and was licensed by the Classis of New York, April 13, 1815. He was ordained by the Classis of Washington, and installed pastor of the congregation of Union Village (now Greenwich), Washington County, New York, November 18, 1816. In the spring of 1818, he connected with the Associate Reformed Church, and was installed pastor of the congregation of Newburgh, New York, September 6, 1818. While laboring in this charge he became intimately associated with the Rev. James R. Willson, D. D., whose influence and arguments produced a change in his former views, and he acceded to the communion of the Covenanter Church, being received by the Northern Presbytery, October 12, 1821. He was installed pastor of the congregation of Albany, New York, June 12, 1822. Here he founded the Albany Grammar School, which soon became a flourishing classical institution. He resigned the Albany congregation, May 17, 1830, and devoted himself to teaching, and preached frequently

in Troy and Lansingburgh, New York. In the controversy of 1833, he was in the hottest of the battle,
and stood firm and unyielding to the Covenanted cause
which he had espoused. He was installed pastor of the
First congregation of New York City, New York,
November 16, 1836, and resigned this important charge
October 15, 1856, and accepted the chair of Systematic
Theology in the Allegheny Seminary, where he continued with great acceptance for two years. He was
deposed from the ministerial office and privileges in the
Covenanter Church, on a charge of immorality, by the
New York Presbytery, November 3, 1858. He removed
to Brooklyn, New York, and was afterwards restored to
private membership in the Dutch Reformed Church, and
where he died, November 17, 1863. He married Miss
Margaret Nicholson, of New York City, in 1807.. He
was a profound theologian, a proficient linguist, a
thorough scientist, and an impressive evangelical preacher
of the gospel. He was acknowledged as a scholar and
theologian on both sides of the Atlantic. He was a
prominent minister of the Church, deeply interested in
all her schemes and missionary operations, and held
many responsible positions, which he discharged with
ability and satisfaction. He published " Strictures upon
Dr. Mason's Plea for Sacramental Communion on Catholic
Principles," 1821, pp. 212, which was afterwards repub-
lished in Europe with a commendatory preface by Dr.
McCrie, the biographer of John Knox. He was also
the author of many scientific and theological articles
published in the reviews and magazines of his day.
He was honored with the degree of Doctor of Divinity

by Jefferson College in 1855. He was Moderator of the Synods of 1828 and 1849.

ALEXANDER CLARKE, D. D.:

Son of William and Elizabeth (Craig) Clarke, was born near Kilrea, County Londonderry, Ireland, July 16, 1793.* His parents were pious Covenanters and he early embraced the principles of that Church, and defended them successfully in several debates. After passing through the accustomed rudimentary studies in the classical school of Mr. Ferris, he entered Belfast College, and graduated from Glasgow University, Scotland, in 1819. He was chosen by the Synod of Ireland to go as a missionary to the North American British Provinces, and for this purpose, after having studied theology privately and at Paisley, Scotland, was licensed and ordained, May 24, 1827. He arrived in St. John, New Brunswick, August 23, 1827, and, after some explorations, in the following November, selected Amherst, Nova Scotia, as the centre of missionary operations. He travelled extensively through all parts of the Maritime Provinces, and established some fifteen mission stations. In 1831, he was joined by the Rev. William Sommerville, and they were instrumental in bringing many souls to a saving knowledge of Christ and to accept the principles of the Covenanter Church. Desiring the liberty and privileges of citizenship in Nova Scotia, Mr. Clarke, and all the congregations he represented, became identified with the New School branch of the Covenanter Church, October 14, 1847, and were united to the General Synod of the

---

* Items furnished by the Rev. Nevin Woodside, Pittsburgh, Pa.

United States. He continued to labor in Amherst, Nova Scotia, and the vicinity, until shortly before his death, caused by general debility and old age, March 15, 1874. He married Miss Catharine McMillan, of Belfast, Ireland, May 22, 1821. He was a sound theologian, a true philanthropist, and an able soldier of the Cross. He was highly esteemed by men who did not agree with him in his religious beliefs, because of his fearless proclamation of the truth as he accepted it. He was a powerful controversialist. His masterly irony, clear and logical deductions and unanswerable Scriptural arguments, together with his wonderful memory, command of language and versatility of thought, gave him a power over his opponents seldom surpassed. He was a large well-built man, capable of undergoing many hardships, and the type of a man adapted in every way as a pioneer missionary. He was honored with the degree of Doctor of Divinity by the University of Pennsylvania in 1856. He was Moderator of the General Synod of 1856.

ROBERT CLYDE:

Son of Robert and Nancy (Harrison) Clyde, was born in Dervock, County Antrim, Ireland, May 6, 1851. His parents were members of the Presbyterian Church and connected with the Covenanter Church in 1853. He received his early education in the schools of his native County. He came to America in 1865, and settled in the city of Philadelphia, Pennsylvania, where, in 1870, he connected with the Reformed Presbytery, and in 1874, he returned to the Covenanter Church. He received his classical education under the direction of Dr. Steele, under whom also he studied theology one year, prosecuted his studies another year in the New School Seminary, and two years in the Allegheny Seminary, and was licensed by the Philadelphia Presbytery, May 27, 1879. He supplied generally throughout the Church for several years. He was ordained by the Iowa Presbytery, and installed pastor of the Elliota congregation, Canton, Fillmore County, Minnesota, February 12, 1886, where he is in charge. He married Miss Bella Dougherty, of Philadelphia, Pennsylvania, August 21, 1878.

EUSEBIUS McLEAN COLEMAN:

Son of John M. and Margaret (Brown) Coleman, was born near Dayton, Armstrong County, Pennsylvania, July 5, 1859. In early life his parents removed to the neighboring vicinity of Elder's Ridge, Indiana County, Pennsylvania, where he received his early education in the Elder's Ridge Academy. He engaged in teaching in South Buffalo, and, in the fall of 1880, entered Geneva College, where he graduated in 1883. He became Principal of the Normal Academy at McKeesport, Pennsylvania, and at the same time studied theology in the Allegheny Seminary, was licensed by the Pittsburgh Presbytery, April 12, 1887, and preached for some months in Canada. He was ordained by the Rochester Presbytery, and installed pastor of the Ramsey congregation, Almonte, Ontario, Canada, May 9, 1888, where he is in charge.

WILLIAM JOHN COLEMAN:

Son of John and Mary (Glass) Coleman, was born in Lisbon, St. Lawrence County, New York, May 12,

1851. He received his preparatory course of literary training in the Academy of Ogdensburgh, New York, and graduated from Geneva College in 1875. He studied theology in the Allegheny Seminary, and was licensed by the Rochester Presbytery, April 15, 1878. He was ordained by the Pittsburgh Presbytery, and installed pastor of the Monongahela congregation, Mc-Keesport, Pennsylvania, June 13, 1879, and resigned this charge April 12, 1881. He accepted an appointment as Secretary of the National Reform Association, July 1, 1881, and removed his residence to Beaver Falls, Pennsylvania. He resigned this position, April 1, 1886. He was installed pastor of the congregation of Utica, Licking County, Ohio, April 15, 1886, and resigned this charge, November 17, 1887. He accepted the chair of Political Science in Geneva College, November 29, 1887, where he is engaged in teaching. He married Miss Lizzie S. George, of Venice, Pennsylvania, May 29, 1879. The pages of the *Christian Statesman* and the *Christian Nation* bear testimony to his work as a lecturer, and he contributed an exposition of the Sabbath School lessons to the latter paper.

SAMUEL GEORGE CONNER:

Son of William and Nancy (George) Conner, was born near Midway, Washington County, Pennsylvania, December 11, 1855. He received his early education in the schools of Hickory, and graduated from Geneva College in 1885. He studied theology in the Allegheny Seminary, was licensed by the Pittsburgh Presbytery, April 11, 1888, and preached within the bounds of the Pittsburgh Presbytery.

EBENEZER COOPER:

Son of John and Mary (Martin) Cooper, was born in the Chester District, South Carolina, August 8, 1795. Giving evidence of early piety, and having the work of the ministry in view, he passed through the academical course of study in the classical school of Mr. John Orr, and graduated from South Carolina College, Columbia, in 1817. He studied theology in Philadelphïa, Pennsylvania, under the direction of Rev. S. B. Wylie, D. D., and was licensed by the Philadelphia Presbytery, May 4, 1822. He preached for several years in the vacancies with general acceptance, and devoted much time to the societies in Tennessee and South Carolina. He was ordained by the Northern Presbytery, June 18, 1828, and took charge of Hephzibah congregation, Fayetteville, Lincoln County, Tennessee. The congregati· ˙ .ì called him, but he refused to be installed pastor on account of the prevalence of slavery and the isolation from his ministerial brethren, and, in 1832, he and the majority of the congregation, removed to Fayette County, Indiana. During the division of the Church in 1833, he became identified with the New School branch of the Covenanter Church. He continued to preach in that body to vacant congregations as his health would permit for twenty years. In the spring of 1857, he removed to Cedarville, Green County, Ohio, where he died of dropsy on the chest, November 13, 1858. He married Miss Jane McMillan, of Chester, South Carolina, in 1820. He was a very mild and pleasing preacher. He possessed a most kind and peaceful disposition, and was held in high esteem for his integrity.

DAVID HACKSTON COULTER:

Son of James and Mahala (Skeggs) Coulter, was born in Coultersville, Randolph County, Illinois, March 15, 1833. He received his early education in the school of his native village, and also in Sparta Academy, and graduated from Geneva College in 1857. He taught in Geneva College before and after his graduation for some time. He studied theology in the Allegheny Seminary, and was licensed by the Illinois Presbytery, June 28, 1864. He was ordained by the Iowa Presbytery, and installed pastor of the congregation of Hopkinton, Delaware County, Iowa, April 18, 1867, and resigned this charge, October 14, 1874. He was installed pastor of the congregation of Newark,. New Jersey, December 10, 1874, and resigned October 30, 1875, and accepted the chair of Natural Science in Lenox College, Iowa. He was installed pastor of the congregation of Winchester, Jefferson County, Kansas, August 17, 1877, where he is in charge. He married Miss Martha A. Forsythe, of Northwood, Ohio, July 10, 1856.

ALEXANDER CRAIGHEAD:

Son of Rev. Thomas and Margaret Craighead, was born near Donegal, Ireland, March 18, 1707.* His father was a Presbyterian minister, came to America in 1715, and settled in Freetown, Massachusetts. In 1721, he, with his parents, removed to New Jersey, thence, in 1724, to White Clay Creek, Delaware, and finally, in 1733, to Octorara, Lancaster County, Pennsylvania. He received his classical education under the direction of

---

* Craighead Genealogy. Dr. Foote's Sketches of North Carolina.

his father, under whom, also, he studied theology, and was licensed by the Donegal Presbytery of the Presbyterian Church, October 16, 1734. He supplied "the first congregation over the river," at Meeting House Springs, two miles north of Carlisle, Pennsylvania, and was the first minister to preach west of the Susquehanna river. He was ordained by the Donegal Presbytery, and installed pastor of the Middle Octorara congregation, Lancaster County, Pennsylvania, November 20, 1735. He was an earnest fervid preacher, and a zealous promoter of revivals. He was a great admirer of Whitefield, and accompanied him upon some of his tours. His zeal, however, was not always tempered with prudence, and he contended that his ministerial brethren were too liberal in their views and lax in the application of discipline. He insisted upon new terms of communion, which required parents, when they presented their children for baptism, to adopt the Solemn League and Covenant, as the Church across the Atlantic had always done. He frequently absented himself from Church courts because of the failure of his brethren to adhere to the practices of the Church of his fathers, and for this cause a complaint was lodged against him in 1740, and the Presbytery met by appointment in his church to investigate the charges. When the members of the court came to the church, they found him, preaching from the text, "Let them alone, they be blind leaders of the blind." In the report to Synod, the Presbytery spoke of the sermon as a "continued invective against Pharisee preachers, and the Presbytery as given over to judicial blindness and hardness." At its close, the people and Presbytery were invited to repair to "the tent" to hear his defence read. The Presbytery declined to attend, and were proceeding to business in the church when such a tumult was raised that they were compelled to withdraw. At the meeting the next day he appeared and read his protest, in which he declined the jurisdiction of the Presbytery, whereupon he was suspended for contumacy, "directing, however, that if he should signify his sorrow for his conduct to any member, that member should notify the Moderator, who was to call the court together and take off the suspension." With an ardent love of personal liberty and freedom of opinion, he was far in advance of his brethren; also, in his views on civil government. These "advanced views" he gave to the public in pamphlet form, and attracted so much attention that Thomas Cookston, one of his majesty's justices in Lancaster County, had him arraigned for treason, and laid the pamphlet, in the name of the Governor, before the Synod of Philadelphia. Though the publication was anonymous, its authorship was very generally attributed to Mr. Craighead. The Synod unanimously agreed that the pamphlet was "full of treason and sedition," and made haste to declare their abhorrence of the paper, and with it all principles and practices that tend to destroy the civil and religious rights of mankind, or to foment and encourage sedition or dissatisfaction with the British government, or encourage anything that is disloyal." At the meeting of Synod in May, 1741, the Church was divided, and he went with the New Brunswick party, but did not remain long with them, because they refused to acknowledge the validity of the Solemn League and Covenant sworn by the Church in Scotland. In 1742, he published his reasons for withdrawing from the American Presbyterian Church; the chief of which was, that "neither the Synod nor the Presbyteries had adopted the Westminster Standards as a public act," and, in the fall of 1742, he joined the languishing cause of the Covenanters. They formed a General Meeting, over which he presided, and he was instrumental in building them a church in Octorara. In the fall of 1743, he gathered all the Covenanters of Eastern Pennsylvania together and they renewed the Covenants. He also opened up a correspondence with the Reformed Presbytery of Scotland, and solicited "helpers who might come and assist him to maintain the principles of the Scottish Reformation." He, however, lacked stability. Before any Covenanter minister could be induced to join him from Scotland, and having labored with great acceptance among the scattered societies for seven years, he returned to the Presbyterian Church, and, in 1749, removed to the Cowpasture river, in Augusta County, Virginia, where he enjoyed more freedom in proclaiming his views of independence from the British government. Here he remained among some families who had removed from Octorara, and he ministered to their spiritual wants for six years. In 1755, on account of the disturbed state of the country by Indians, he crossed the Blue Ridge mountains with a colony of his people, and settled on the Catawba river, in what is now Mecklenberg County, North Carolina. He was installed pastor of the congregation of Rocky River and Sugar Creek, Mecklenberg County, North Carolina, September 19, 1758. In this beautiful and peaceful valley, the solitary minister between the Yadkin and the Catawba, he passed the remainder of his days. Here he freely imbued the minds of his people with the idea of independence, whose hands and hearts were in the trying scenes of the Revolution. The members who formed the Convention at Charlotte, North Carolina, and framed the First Declaration of Independence (Mecklenberg, May, 1775), were all members of the Churches which he had founded and instructed, and incorporated the principles which he so uncompromisingly advocated. He died at his home within three miles of Charlotte, Mecklenberg County, North Carolina, March 12, 1766, and was buried in the old graveyard adjoining the church where he preached. Tradition says the two sassafras trees at the head and foot of the grave, sprung from the two sticks upon which the coffin was borne.

JOHN CRAWFORD:

Son of James and Jane (McAuley) Crawford, was born in Carncullough, County Antrim, Ireland, May 27, 1828. In early life he evinced decided evidence of a literary taste, and he was sent to the school in Dervock, where he received his preparatory training. In 1839, he began the study of the languages in Derry Keva, and continued them in Ballymoney. In 1845, he entered Belfast College, where he took several prizes for proficiency, and engaged in teaching. In 1849, he entered the College of Edinburgh, Scotland, where he attended some classes and waited on the lectures of Dr. Cunningham, of the Free Church Seminary, on Systematic Theology, and was for some time employed as a missionary among the Papists in Edinburgh. He studied theology in the Seminary of Paisley, Scotland, one year, when his health failed. Following the advice of physicians and friends, he emigrated to America, January 15, 1852, and settled in the city of Philadelphia, Pennsylvania, whither his parents had preceeded him. He resumed his theological studies under the direction of Drs. J. M. Willson and S. O. Wylie, and was licensed by the New York Presbytery, May 24, 1853. He was ordained by the Philadelphia Presbytery, and installed pastor of the congregation of Baltimore, Maryland, November 15, 1853. A few weeks preceeding his death, he contracted a cold resulting in a violent toothache, at the time occasioning no alarm; but the disease extended rapidly to the lungs, causing congestion, from which he died, at the residence of Mr. James Smith, in Baltimore, Maryland, September 3, 1856, and was buried in Philadelphia. He was unmarried. He possessed a weak body but a strong mind. His voice was soft and musical, his style dignified and chaste, and his illustrations beautiful and appropriate. The chief and most striking characteristic of his preaching was his intense earnestness and evident sincerity. He lived in view of death, and his preaching and prayers were singularly characterized by consolatory views of heaven. He was a most kind and faithful pastor, and especially interested in the young. He was a spiritually minded man, and piety was a living principle in him. He prayed as freely and involuntarily as he breathed. The

29

hearts of the pastor and people were closely knit together in Christian love, and in his untimely death the congregation lost an endeared pastor, and the Church a most devoted and able minister of the gospel. At the time of his death he was a member of the Board of Foreign Missions.

SAMUEL WYLIE CRAWFORD, D. D.:

Son of Nathan and Margaret (Wylie) Crawford, was born in the Chester District, South Carolina, October 14, 1792. His parents were from Scotland and died when he was quite young. In 1800, he was brought by his uncle, the Rev. S. B. Wylie, D. D., to the city of Philadelphia, Pennsylvania, where he received his education in the public schools and the University of Pennsylvania. In 1814, he began the study of medicine, but in a short time abandoned it for that of theology. He studied theology in the Philadelphia Seminary, and was licensed by the Middle Presbytery, April 10, 1818. He preached with general acceptance in the vacancies in the eastern part of the Church, and also to the inmates of the Walnut street Prison, Eastern Penitentiary and House of Refuge in the city of Philadelphia. He was ordained *sine titulo* by the Northern Presbytery, at Duanesburgh, New York, May 15, 1823, and was installed pastor of the Conococheague congregation, Chambersburgh, Franklin County, Pennsylvania, August 26, 1824. He soon afterwards became Principal of the Chambersburgh Academy, where he remained until April 10, 1831, when he resigned both congregation and school, and accepted the position of Principal of the Academical

Department of the University of Pennsylvania. At the division of the Church in August, 1833, he became identified with the New School branch of the Covenanter Church. In 1835, he was installed pastor of the Fairmount congregation of that body, in the suburbs of Philadelphia, and resigned this pastorate in 1846. He was installed pastor of the Fourth congregation of Philadelphia, August 17, 1848, and resigned October 11, 1856, on account of impaired health. For some time he was a teacher of theology in the Philadelphia Seminary, supplied vacant pulpits, and during the war of the rebellion was a chaplain in the army. In 1868, he retired to his country home near Chambersburgh, Pennsylvania, and where he died, June 12, 1876. He possessed a splendid physique, of a military bearing, and made an imposing appearance in the pulpit. He was a man of scholarly attainments and an earnest evangelical preacher of the gospel. He was distinguished as a philanthropist and abounded in deeds of charity. He was highly appreciated in all the educational and pastoral charges which he held, and was an influential member of Church courts. He married Miss Jane Agnew, of New York City, New York, August 28, 1821. Among his publications is a sermon on "Creeds and Confessions," 1826, pp. 44. He was honored with the degree of Doctor of Divinity by the University of Indiana in 1844. He was Moderator of the Synod of 1831, and the General Synod of 1863.

ALFRED DEAN CROWE:

Son of Samuel and Mary (Dean) Crowe, was born near Glade Mills, Butler County, Pennsylvania, December 1, 1848. He received a strict religious training in the home, and pursued his literary studies in the schools of his native County, and, in 1868, entered Geneva College, where he graduated in 1874. He studied theology in the Allegheny Seminary, and was licensed by the Pittsburgh Presbytery, April 11, 1877. He was ordained by the Philadelphia Presbytery, and installed pastor of the congregation of Baltimore, Maryland, October 10, 1878. He never possessed a very robust constitution, and in the winter of 1881, he contracted a severe cold which settled in his throat and frequently prevented him from preaching. From this time he began to decline and suffered from a hemorrhage of the lungs in January, 1884. On account of his failing health, he resigned the congregation, August 12, 1884, and resorted to the cooler climate of Western New York, where he improved to some extent. In the autumn, however, it was very evident that that fell disease, consumption, had fastened upon him, and he died at the home of his father-in-law, Mr. Abram Ernisse, in the city of Rochester, New York, December 20, 1884. He married Miss Susie A. Ernisse, of Rochester, New York, November 3, 1880. He was a good preacher. His pulpit exhibitions were carefully prepared, neatly arranged, and eloquently delivered. He was a student of Philosophy in Johns Hopkins University, and a constant reader of choice literature. He was a vigilant pastor, guarded carefully the walls of Zion, and the few years of his ministerial labor in Baltimore have left their impress upon the hearts of a devoted people.

SAMUEL JOHN CROWE:

Son of Samuel and Mary (Dean) Crowe, was born near Glade Mills, Butler County, Pennsylvania, September 1, 1843. He received his early education in the district schools, studied the languages under the direction of the Rev. John Galbraith, and graduated from Westminster College in 1866. He studied theology in the Allegheny Seminary one year, when he was appointed Principal of Geneva College, September 1, 1867, which position he held for four years, most of which time he continued his studies privately for the ministry. He was licensed by the Pittsburgh Presbytery, April 12, 1871, and attended the Allegheny Seminary one more year. He was ordained by the Pittsburgh Presbytery, and installed pastor of the congregation of New Castle, Pennsylvania, May 21, 1872. He was also installed pastor of the congregation of Centreville, Mercer County, Pennsylvania, September 18, 1879, and he resigned these charges, April 12, 1881. He was installed pastor of the congregation of Brooklyn, New York, December 7, 1881, and resigned October 28, 1884. In the spring of 1885, he removed to Warren, Ohio, where he was employed with the Equitable Life Assurance Company, and preached as his health would permit. He removed to New Brighton, Pennsylvania, in the fall of 1887, and accepted the position of Financial Agent for Geneva College, and supplied vacant pulpits. He married Miss Amanda R. Geddes, of New Bedford, Pennsylvania, October 31, 1866.

JOHN CROZIER:

Son of John and Jane (Cowser) Crozier, was born near Smithfield, Fayette County, Pennsylvania, in 1802.

His parents were originally Presbyterians, and, in the
latter part of the past century, joined the Associate
Reformed Church, in which he was reared. With
great difficulty, and much self-denial, he obtained his
early education amid the toil of farm life, and in due
time entered the Western University of Pennsylvania,
where he graduated in 1828. Largely through the
influence of family friends and his associations at college with professors and students, he espoused the
principles of the Covenanter Church, and resolved to
prepare for the ministry. He studied theology under
the direction of the Rev. John Black, D. D., of Pittsburgh, and was licensed by the Pittsburgh Presbytery,
April 7, 1831, and preached with acceptance in the
vacancies for two years. He was ordained *sine cura*
by the same Presbytery, as a Home Missionary, April
4, 1833. He was installed pastor of the united congregations of Monongahela, Allegheny County, and
Canonsburgh, Washington County, Pennsylvania, May
12, 1834. He was released from the Canonsburgh
branch, October 9, 1842, and from Monongahela,
April 12, 1865. He removed to the city of Indianapolis, Indiana, where he built up a congregation and
remained in charge until May 25, 1870. He returned
to Elizabeth, Allegheny County, Pennsylvania, where
he has since made his home and preached as his
health would permit. He was twice married. First to
Miss Anne Fletcher, of Baltimore, Maryland, January
19, 1836; and second to Miss Margaret H. Parkhill, of
Elizabeth, Pennsylvania, April 5, 1847. He has been
largely connected with the work of the Covenanter

Church for over half a century, and published some articles in the magazines of the Church. He was Moderator of the Synod of 1861.

JOHN FLETCHER CROZIER:

Son of Rev. John and Anne (Fletcher) Crozier, was born in Elizabeth, Allegheny County, Pennsylvania, * * * He received his early education in the schools of his native County, and graduated from Westminster College in 1870. He studied theology in the Allegheny Seminary, and was licensed by the Pittsburgh Presbytery, April 9, 1872. He was ordained by the same Presbytery, and installed pastor of the united congregations of Rehoboth, Bear Run and Mahoning, Marchand, Indiana County, Pennsylvania, November 18, 1874, where he is in charge.

JOHN McMILLAN CROZIER:

Son of Robert and Jane (Stott) Crozier, was born in the city of Allegheny, Pennsylvania, February 29, 1852. He passed through the accustomed studies in the public schools, and graduated from the Western University of Pennsylvania in 1871. He studied theology in the Allegheny Seminary, and was licensed by the Pittsburgh Presbytery, April 15, 1874. He itinerated with much acceptance among the vacancies in this country for several years, and visited the Churches in Ireland and Scotland. He was ordained by the Philadelphia Presbytery, and installed pastor of the Third congregation of the city of Philadelphia, Pennsylvania, May 6, 1880, where he died very suddenly of inflammation of the bowels, September 7, 1881. He was unmarried. He was a young man possessing a robust and strong constitution; a vigorous and well-cultivated mind; and was a fearless, practical and forcible preacher of the gospel. He was bold to denounce sin in every form, yet anxious to restore the repenting wanderer to his privileges in the Church. He manifested a true missionary spirit; encouraging the young to confess Christ, and the old to prepare for the change that awaits mankind. He was a kind pastor, peaceful and cheerful in his disposition, prayerful in his labor of love, and thoroughly devoted to the distinctive principles of the Church.

JOHN CUTHBERTSON:

Was born near Ayr, Ayrshire, Scotland, April 3, 1718.* He was reared in the strictest manner by a pious parentage, who were exemplary members of the persecuted Church of Scotland. He received his early training, preparatory to entering upon the work of the ministry, from private instructors. He studied theology under the Rev. John McMillan, who, with Rev. Thomas Nairn and ruling elders, constituted the Reformed Presbytery of Scotland, August 1, 1743, by which court he was licensed, May 16, 1745. He was ordained *sine titulo* by the same court, at Braehead, May 18, 1747, and labored among the scattered societies of Scotland. He was Moderator of the Reformed Presbytery in 1750, at which time, with Rev. Thomas Cameron, he was sent as a missionary to the scattered societies of Covenanters in Ireland. In the spring of 1751, he was sent as a missionary to the Covenanters in America, and landed at New Castle, Delaware,

---

* Principal items from his own diary.

August 5, 1751, having been forty-six days at sea from Derry Loch. He was the first Covenanter minister who came to America, and settled in Middle Octorara, Lancaster County, Pennsylvania, the scene of most of his labors, although he made extended missionary tours upon horseback through New York, Vermont, New Hampshire, Connecticut, New Jersey, Maryland, Virginia, and all parts of Pennsylvania as far west as the Ohio river. In the winter of 1773, he was joined by Revs. Matthew Linn and Alexander Dobbin, and they organized the Reformed Presbytery of America, at Paxtang, Dauphin County, Pennsylvania, March 10, 1774. He was then assigned to the Middle Octorara charge, although he exercised a superintending control over all the societies. With some others, July 2, 1777, he swore allegiance to the cause of the Colonies, and cast in his lot with those who were struggling to cast off the British yoke in America. In the following September, without consulting or informing the Reformed Presbytery in Scotland, he began the conferences with the Associate Church, which, after five years of agitation, culminated in the union of these two branches, forming the Associate Reformed Church. The articles were signed at Pequea, Lancaster County, Pennsylvania, June 13, 1782, and the Synod was constituted in Philadelphia, November 1, 1782. Many of the private members of the Covenanter Church went with the ministers, the faithful remnant resorting to the society meetings, and for eight years or more were left without a minister. Mr. Cuthbertson continued in charge of the Octorara congregation until his release, March 20, 1783,

when he took charge of the Associate Reformed congregation of Lower Chanceford, York County, Pennsylvania, where he labored until his death, March 10,
1791. The cause and circumstances of his death are
unknown. He was buried in the Lower Octorara graveyard connected with the church where Alexander
Craighead preached. His gravestone bears the following inscription: "Here lies the body of the Rev. John
Cuthbertson, who, after a labor of about forty years
in the ministry of the Gospel among the Dissenting
Covenanters of America, departed this life, 10th of
March, 1791, in the 75th year of his age. Psalm
112:6, The righteous shall be in everlasting remembrance." There are two mistakes in this inscription.
He was a Covenanter minister but thirty years; and
he says more than once in his diary that he was born
April 3, 1718, making him nearly seventy-three years
of age. He married Miss Sally Moore, near Philadelphia, Pennsylvania, February 25, 1756. He endured
many hardships as a pioneer missionary. According to
his diary, during the thirty-nine years he was engaged
in active service, he preached on two thousand four
hundred and fifty-two days; baptized one thousand eight
hundred and six children; married two hundred and
forty couples; rode on horseback seventy thousand miles,
or nearly equal to three times around the world. And
this travelling was done in those days when there
were no roads or bridges. Blazed trees marked the
pathway, and horse and rider swam the swollen streams.
He rode through the unbroken forests, past the lair of
the wild beast and the wigwam of the savage; under

the hot sun, through the pelting rain or drifting snow, and often without the necessities of life. For all this work, however, he was peculiarly adapted and providentially sustained. From the texts recorded in his diary, it is evident that he was a forcible evangelical preacher, and a man of deep convictions and fervent piety. As was too frequently the custom in those days, however, he indulged occasionally too freely in the glass, and at one time he was suspended for four weeks for intemperance, and received a rebuke from the Presbytery.

WILLIAM McCONNELL DAUERTY:

Son of William J. and Margaret (Cowan) Dauerty, was born near New Texas, Allegheny County, Pennsylvania, May 11, 1847. He received his preparatory education in the Wilkinsburgh Academy, Newell Institute, Western University of Pennsylvania, and graduated from the College of New Jersey, Princeton, in 1874. He studied theology in the Allegheny Seminary, and was licensed by the Pittsburgh Presbytery, April 9, 1878. He preached for three years in the vacancies, and engaged in clerical work in Pittsburgh, Pennsylvania. He was chosen to fill the chair of Latin and Greek in Curry Institute and Union Business College, Pittsburgh, November 10, 1883, which position he now occupies. He married Miss Rida A. Mullen, of Baltimore, Maryland, December 31, 1885. He is Superintendent of the Chinese School, and an officer in the Pittsburgh Covenanter congregation.

JAMES MILLIGAN DICKSON, D. D.:

Son of Robert and Janet (Lenny) Dickson, was born in Ryegate, Caledonia County, Vermont, February

6, 1831. After the usual rudimentary course in the common schools, he studied the classics under the direction of his pastor, the Rev. J. M. Beattie, and entered Peacham Academy. In the fall of 1849, he entered Geneva College, where he remained until his senior year, and graduated from Dartmouth College in 1853. He studied theology in the Northwood Seminary one year, three years in the Union Seminary of New York City, and a short term in the Allegheny Seminary, and was licensed by the New York Presbytery, May 20, 1857. He was ordained by the same Presbytery, and installed pastor of the congregation of Brooklyn, New York, November 18, 1857. He was released from this charge, May 20, 1862, when he connected with the Presbyterian Church, being received by the Third Presbytery of New York. He was installed pastor of the Sixth Presbyterian Church, of Newark, New Jersey, October 10, 1862, ·and resigned April 16, 1869. He was installed pastor of the Good-will Presbyterian Church, Montgomery, Orange County, New York, September 12, 1869, and resigned this charge, April 16, 1883. He connected with the Dutch Reformed Church, and was installed pastor of the Thirty-Fourth Street Dutch Reformed Church, New York City, New York, May 1, 1883, where he is in charge. He married Miss Annott M. Nelson, of Ryegate, Vermont, April 7, 1858 ; and as his second wife, Miss Helen A. West, of Brooklyn, New York, September 30, 1863. He was honored with the degree of Doctor of Divinity by Drury College in 1884. He published "The Goodwill Memorial," 1880, pp. 160.

JOHN WALKINSHAW DILL:

Son of Richard and Esther (White) Dill, was born near Kittanning, Armstrong County, Pennsylvania, September 19, 1846. He received his early education in the common schools, completed the course in the Dayton Union Academy in 1868, and graduated from Westminster College in 1871. He taught in the Academy of Lumber City, Pennsylvania, one year. He studied theology in the Allegheny Seminary, was licensed by the Pittsburgh Presbytery, April 14, 1875, and labored in Minnesota two years under appointment of the Central Board of Missions. He was ordained by the Iowa Presbytery, March 20, 1878, and installed pastor of the congregation of Elliota, Fillmore County, Minnesota, April 26, 1878, and resigned this charge, May 25, 1881. He was installed pastor of Lind Grove congregation, Mediapolis, Des Moines County, Iowa, July 6, 1881, and was released September 19, 1887. He accepted the Assistant Principalship of Knox Academy, Selma, Alabama, October 10, 1887, and became Principal, January 1, 1888, where he is engaged in teaching. He married Miss Maggie J. Getty, of Kossuth, Iowa, January 1, 1880.

ALEXANDER DOBBIN:

Son of John Dobbin, a pious sailor, was born in the city of Londonderry, Ireland, February 4, 1742.[*] His parentage was Scotch, and, imbued with the religious spirit of the ancestors, early directed his mind towards the Christian ministry. He studied the classics in his native city, and in due time entered the University of

---

[*] Sprague's Annals. Dr. J. A. Chancellor, Belfast, Ireland.

Glasgow, Scotland, where he graduated in 1771. He attended the theological lectures also in Glasgow, and resumed his studies privately under the direction of the ministers in Ireland, and was licensed by the Reformed Presbytery of Ireland, July 6, 1772. He was ordained *sine titulo* by the same court, at Conlig, near New-townards, County Down, Ireland, August 20, 1772, as a missionary to the Covenanters in America. In company with the Rev. Matthew Linn, he sailed from Londonderry and landed in New Castle, Delaware, December 13, 1773. He, with Revs. John Cuthbertson and Matthew Linn, constituted the Reformed Presbytery of America, at Paxtang, Dauphin County, Pennsylvania, March 10, 1774, at which time he was assigned to labor in the Rock Creek (Gettysburg) congregation, Adams County, Pennsylvania. He was among the first and most desirous of the ministers to countenance the union of the Associate and Covenanter bodies, and took a prominent part in the conferences which resulted in the formation of the Associate Reformed Church, November 1, 1782. He continued in charge of the Rock Creek congregation, or as many as went with him, and was also installed for half-time in the Marsh Creek congregation, September 9, 1785, and thus divided his time and continued his labor until his death. In October, 1808, while on his way to Gettysburg to preach, he ruptured a blood vessel by coughing, and was unable to fill his appointment. His disease settled into a quick consumption, from which he died, at his home in Gettysburg, Adams County, Pennsylvania, June 1, 1809, and was buried in the Marsh Creek graveyard. He was twice married. First to Miss Isabella Gamble, of County Down, Ireland, July, 1772; and second, to Mrs. Mary (Irvin) Agnew, of Adams County, Pennsylvania, in 1801. He was an interesting and instructive preacher of the extemporaneous style. He was a distinguished linguist, especially in Hebrew, and established in his own house the first classical school west of the Susquehanna river. More than sixty of his pupils became professional men, and not less than twenty-five entered the ministry. Before the establishment of the Theological Seminary of the Associate Reformed Church, he was the preceptor for many years, and his services were of great value. He was remarkably punctual at Church courts, where his opinion was regarded, and he was honored with the Moderatorship several times. He was a small man, with a bright black eye, a large pointed nose, and was by no means imposing in his appearance. He possessed a strong and sonorous voice, and his gestures in the pulpit were not always the most graceful. He dressed in knee pants and wore the wig. He was a very social man, cheerful in his disposition, and his countenance continually wore a smile. He adapted himself to all company, and his intercourse was much enjoyed for his wit and good humor.

JOSIAH DODDS:

Son of John and Elizabeth (McKee) Dodds, was born in Ballibay, County Monaghan, Ireland, March 3, 1819. His parents came to America the following year and settled near Lucesco, Westmoreland County, Pennsylvania, and, in 1829, removed to Butler County, in the vicinity of Bakerstown. Here he received his

early education, studied the classics under the Rev.
Hugh Walkinshaw, and graduated from the Western
University of Pennsylvania in 1842. He studied theology in the Allegheny and Cincinnati Seminaries, and
was licensed by the Pittsburgh Presbytery, April 13,
1846. He was ordained by the Lakes Presbytery,
and installed pastor of the united congregations of
Beech Woods, Preble County, Ohio, and Garrison,
Fayette County, Indiana, October 6, 1847, and resigned
this charge, October 10, 1865. He missionated in the
West for two years, principally in the station which
became the congregation of Winchester, Jefferson County,
Kansas, over which he was installed pastor, November
7, 1868, and was released, October 18, 1876. He
was installed pastor of the congregation of Sylvania,
Dade County, Missouri, May 9, 1878, where he is in
charge. He was thrice married. First to Miss Matilda
Cannon, of Greensburgh, Pennsylvania, June 28, 1847;
second, to Miss Mary Milligan, of Fayetteville, Indiana,
March 29, 1853; and third, to Miss Belle Torrence, of
Northwood, Ohio, August 12, 1857.

ROBERT JAMES DODDS, D. D.:

Son of Archibald and Margaret (Davison) Dodds,
was born near Freeport, Armstrong County, Pennsylvania, August 29, 1824. Possessed from his youth
with integrity of character and amiability of disposition he was dedicated to God for the work of the
ministry. At an early age he began his classical
studies under the direction of his pastor, the Rev.
Hugh Walkinshaw, and made such rapid progress and
proficiency in all the departments of literature taught

in a College, that he was recommended as sufficiently advanced to begin the study of theology in the spring of 1844. He studied theology in the Allegheny and Cincinnati Seminaries, and was licensed by the Pittsburgh Presbytery, June 21, 1848. At the meeting of Synod in 1847, the Mission of Hayti was organized, and he was chosen as a missionary for that foreign field, for which purpose, he was ordained *sine titulo* by the Pittsburgh Presbytery, November 24, 1848. The Mission, however, was soon afterwards abandoned, he was not sent out, and he preached in the vacancies for a few years. He was installed pastor of the Rehoboth congregation, Stanton, Jefferson County, Pennsylvania, June 18, 1852. He travelled extensively in this field, and was exposed to many inconveniences; yet by his missionary spirit and zeal for the cause, he built up a flourishing congregation of many branches. At the meeting of Synod in 1856, the Syrian Mission was established and he was unanimously chosen as one of the Missionaries. Accepting the appointment, he was released from the congregation, May 24, 1856. With the Rev. Joseph Beattie, their families and others, he sailed for Syria, October 16, 1856. He first settled in Damascus, where he learned the Arabic language, and in October, 1857, removed to Zahleh, a town at the foot of Mount Lebanon. In May, 1858, he was compelled to abandon the work in this place on account of the threats and persecution of the bigoted priesthood. Making a tour of exploration through Northern Syria, as far as Antioch, he passed through Latakia, and, being favorably impressed with its loca-

30

tion, began to perfect arrangements for its occupation. In the autumn of 1859, he removed thither, followed by Dr. Beattie and others, where suitable buildings were secured, and where he labored for eight years with good success. An unexpected opening occurred in Aleppo, and, the Mission deeming it advisable to enter in and possess it, Dr. Dodds was appointed to this field in May, 1867. Here he remained constantly busied with the proper work of the Mission until his death. During the summer of 1870, he visited the Mission in Latakia, and while there suffered an attack of fever. During a subsequent journey to Idlib, he contracted a severe cold which adhered to him. In the beginning of December following, he suffered from a slight hemorrhage of the lungs, intensified by typhoid fever, from which he died, at his home in Aleppo, Syria, December 11, 1870. He was twice married. First to Miss Amanda Cannon, of Greensburgh, Pennsylvania, January 2, 1849; and second to Miss Letitia M. Dodds, of Valencia, Pennsylvania, August 12, 1856. As a preacher, his sermons were rich in Scriptural truth and illustration. He was not a popular orator owing to a hesitancy in his speech, and he was more spiritual than ornate; more thoughtful than rhetorical; more anxious about conviction than elegance of style. He was admirably adapted with every qualification for a successful Missionary. He was a good classical scholar, and made such proficiency in the study of the Arabic tongue that he was able to preach a sermon in that language in eighteen months after beginning the study of it. He was a remarkably cheerful man, uniform in his feelings and sympathetic in his disposition. His intellectual character was marked with keen and vigorous reasoning powers, a retentive memory, and the ability to concentrate his ideas. Among his earlier publications is, "A Reply to Morton on Psalmody," 1851, pp. 140. His writings are principally letters to the Foreign Mission Board and are published in the Church magazines. He translated the Shorter Catechism into the Arabic language, and was engaged in writing and translating other works for the use of the Mission. He was honored with the degree of Doctor of Divinity by Monmouth College in 1870. He was Moderator of the Synod of 1866.

THOMAS DONNELLY:

Son of Thomas and Nancy (Moore) Donnelly, was born near Donegal, County Donegal, Ireland, January 13, 1772.* In early life he evinced a strong desire for an education, and after passing through the accustomed studies in the schools of his native County, he entered the University of Glasgow, Scotland, in the fall of 1788, where he remained two years. He came to America in the spring of 1791, and settled in the Chester District, South Carolina. The following year he entered Dickinson College, where he graduated in 1794, and returned to South Carolina, where he was engaged in teaching. He studied theology under the direction of the Rev. William King, and, in 1798, under the care of the Reformed Presbytery, and was licensed by that court, at Coldenham, Orange County, New York, June 24, 1799. He was assigned to labor in South Carolina,

---

* Sketch by Mr. Thomas Smith, Bloomington, Ind., in Sprague's Annals.

whither he returned, was ordained by a commission of the Reformed Presbytery, and installed pastor of the Rocky Creek congregation, Chester District, South Carolina, March 3, 1801. Over this extensive field he exercised pastoral functions, and frequently made tours to the scattered societies of Covenanters in Tennessee, North Carolina and Georgia. In 1816, he was released from a part of his first charge, and remained pastor of what was known as the Brick Church. He often found great difficulty in applying the principles of the Church in a slave country. His was often denominated " Mr. Donnelly's congregation," afterwards the Bethesda congregation, to which faithful one and adjacent societies, he continued to preach and exercise pastoral oversight, in accordance with the direction of Synod, the residue of his life. The strong opposition of the Covenanter Church to the institution of slavery caused many of the members to migrate to the free States of Ohio, Indiana and Illinois. He, however, felt the infirmities of age rapidly creeping upon him, and, realizing his inability to fully discharge the pastoral duties required in a new congregation, remained in the South, and continued to minister to the few scattered societies which were the last of the Covenanters in the Carolinas. In 1847, he suffered from a stroke of paralysis, which affected both his mind and his body, from which he never fully recovered. In the fall of the same year he was prostrated with a bilious affection, from which he died, at his home on Rocky Creek, Chester District, South Carolina, November 27, 1847. He married Miss Agnes Smith, of Chester, South Carolina, March 6, 1801.

He enjoyed the reputation of being a sound theologian and a fine classical scholar. In his preaching he had some of the old Scotch-Irish sing song, but he never gave sound for sense. He was a radical and decided enemy to the whole system of human slavery, and maintained the principles of the Church in their purity. He possessed a large amount of generosity and nobleness of heart, and was largely connected with the benevolent societies of his country. He was a strict disciplinarian, and he had few equals for strength of judgment in managing judicial affairs in troublous times. He was Moderator of the Synod of 1818.

JAMES DOUGLAS:

Son of John and Dorathy (Barwise) Douglas, was born in Castle Douglas, Lanarkshire, Scotland, April 10, 1779.* He was blessed with a pious parentage who instructed him in the principles of the Covenanter Church, with which he connected in 1793, under the pastoral care of the Rev. James Reid. With a view to the work of the ministry he passed through the accustomed rudimentary studies, and graduated from the University of Glasgow, Scotland, in 1807. He was appointed as teacher of Greek in the University after the death of the Professor of that language. He studied theology in the Stirling Seminary, under the direction of the Rev. John McMillan, and was licensed by the Glasgow Presbytery, May 18, 1813. He preached with much acceptance for several years, received calls, but declined, having determined to come to America. He came to America in September, 1818, and settled

---

* Principal items from his son, Mr. A. B. Douglas, Brooklyn, N. Y.

in the city of New York, New York, where he was
engaged as a teacher in a classical school, and preached
as occasion was afforded.   Some difficulties arising
between him and his ministerial brethren in that city,
which afterwards resulted in an exoneration from fault
of the subject of this sketch, he was suspended by
their influence by the Northern Presbytery, April 17,
1822, and pursued his vocation as a teacher.   In the
fall of 1824, he received an invitation from the Scotch
people of Bovina, Delaware County, New York, to
come and preach to them, which he accepted, and
began his labors among them, April 15, 1825.   The
difficulty now arose in dispensing the sacraments without the formal act of ordination.   The majority of the
people considered that as he had given trials for
ordination in Scotland, and they had been sustained,
and as he possessed every other requisite, the imposition of hands, in the present circumstance, might be
dispensed with.   To remove all difficulties, however, the
people agreed to petition the True Reformed Dutch
Church for ordination, which request was granted, and
he was formally set apart to the ministerial office by
that body, June 9, 1831.*   He continued to minister
to the people of Bovina until he was restored, and
his ordination recognized as valid, by the New York
Presbytery, October 14, 1846.   He was formally installed
pastor of the congregation of Bovina, Delaware County,
New York, November 3, 1847, where he continued to
labor until his death, March 15, 1857.   He was thrice
married.   First to Miss Alice Thompson, July 6, 1819;

* Bovina sessional records.

second to Miss Mary Qua, October 18, 1827; third to Miss Ann C. Duncan, November 16, 1842. He was a fine classical scholar and possessed the qualifications of a proficient and successful teacher. He was well versed in the old theology, an earnest and profound preacher, and his discourses were the fruit of mature study and fervent prayer. He was a strict disciplinarian, guarded carefully the walls of Zion, and rebuked wickedness of every form. He was sympathetic to every trouble and consolatary in the hour of bereavement. The American Bible Society, the Bovina Temperance Society, and other benevolent institutions and reform associations, found in him a firm and generous friend, and a fearless and able advocate. Among his publications are: "A Reply to an Anonymous Letter in the *Evangelical Witness*," 1824, pp. 68. "An Address on Temperance," delivered before the Bovina Temperance Society, 1834; and a few magazine articles and contributions to the local press.

HENRY EASSON:

Son of Henry and Jane (Bryce) Easson, was born in Dunblane, Perthshire, Scotland, April 20, 1841. The following year his parents came to America and settled in the vicinity of Walton, Delaware County, New York, where he received his early education. He pursued his preparatory studies in the Delaware Literary Institute, Franklin, New York, and nearly completed the course in Union College. He studied theology in the Allegheny Seminary, and, in the spring of 1872, being chosen as a Missionary to Syria, he was licensed and ordained *sine titulo* by the Pittsburgh

Presbytery, October 12, 1872. He sailed, with his family and others, for that foreign field, November 22, 1872, since which time he has been engaged in the work of a Missionary in Latakia, Syria. He married Miss Mary J. Beebe, of Schenectady, New York, January 20, 1870. He visited the United States in 1882, and lectured throughout the Church and returned to Syria. He translated the doctrinal part of the Reformed Presbyterian Testimony into the Arabic language for the use of the Mission Church in Syria.

THOMAS McCONNELL ELDER:

Son of Thomas and Mary (McConnell) Elder, was born near New Alexandria, Westmoreland County, Pennsylvania, March 24, 1826. He received a good common school education and began the study of the classics under the direction of his pastor, the Rev. James Milligan, D. D.; and, in 1847, became Principal of Loyal Hanna Institute of his native County. In 1851, he became a teacher in Geneva Female Institute, Northwood, Ohio, and graduated from Geneva College in 1854. He studied theology in the Northwood and Allegheny Seminaries, and was licensed by the Pittsburgh Presbytery, April 21, 1858. He was ordained by the same Presbytery, and installed pastor of the Rehoboth congregation, Dayton, Armstrong County, Pennsylvania, May 11, 1859. In 1862, he became Principal of Dayton Union Academy, which became a flourishing preparatory school. In 1863, he was appoined by Synod to take charge of the Mission among the Freedmen, at Fernandina, Florida, where he also served as Chaplain to the Eleventh Regiment of Maine Volunteers. In 1864, he was transferred to the Mission at Washington, D. C., where he remained in charge one year. He returned to his congregation and school in Dayton, which he resigned, April 10, 1866, and became Principal of the Dayton Soldiers Orphan School. In the fall of 1868, while witnessing a game of base ball among the students, he was accidently struck upon the head with one of the ball bats, and so seriously injured that he was compelled to cease preaching, and also resigned the school in 1871. He subsequently retired from all active service and became interested in secular pursuits. He withdrew from the communion of the Covenanter Church, May 16, 1883. He is editor of the *Dayton News*, a local journal. He married as his first wife, Miss Tirzah Mason, of New Alexandria, Pennsylvania, September 14, 1848; and as his second, Miss Mary P. Lindsay, of Philadelphia, Pennsylvania, October 10, 1854.

GEORGE MILTON ELLIOT: (COLORED.)

Son of Winslow and Mary A. (Bowser) Elliott, was born near Isle of Wight, Isle of Wight County, Virginia, June 4, 1849. In 1861, his parents removed to Pickereltown, Logan County, Ohio, where he received his early education, and graduated from Geneva College in 1873. He studied theology in the Allegheny Seminary, and was licensed by the Pittsburgh Presbytery, April 12, 1876. He was ordained by the same Presbytery, August 21, 1877, and installed pastor of the congregation of Selma, Alabama, December 14, 1877, where he is in charge. In 1876, he became Principal of Knox Academy, Selma, Alabama, and resigned this office, October 4, 1886, and devoted himself to missionary work. He was twice married. First to Miss Sarah R. Miller, of Pittsburgh, Pennsylvania, June 19, 1878; second to Miss Hattie L. Davis, of Selma, Alabama, April 21, 1885. In March, 1886, he became editor of the *Guiding Star*, a weekly and monthly paper, devoted to the moral and religious welfare of the colored race.

EDWARD GRAHAM ELSEY:

Son of John H. and Susan (French) Elsey, was born in Reynoldsburgh, Franklin County, Ohio, March 22, 1830. He received his early education in the schools of that vicinity, and in Northwood, Ohio. He subsequently removed to California, Branch County, Michigan, where he was engaged in farming and teaching for many years. Having an earnest desire to preach the gospel, he removed to Northwood, Ohio, and resumed his studies in Geneva College, graduating in 1870. He studied theology in the Allegheny Seminary, and was licensed by the Lakes Presbytery, April 14, 1873. He was ordained by the Iowa Presbytery, and installed pastor of the Rehoboth congregation, Wyman, Louisa County, Iowa, August 14, 1874, and resigned this charge, April 13, 1881. He was installed pastor of Lake Reno congregation, Glenwood, Pope County, Minnesota, July 17, 1882, where he is in charge. He married Miss Phebe T. Dobbin, of West Hebron, New York, October 19, 1861.

WILLIAM MORRISON ENGLES, D. D.:

Son of Silas and Anna (Patterson) Engles, was born in the city of Philadelphia, Pennsylvania, October

12, 1797.* He received a liberal education in the schools of his native city, and graduated from the University of Pennsylvania in 1815. He studied theology in the Philadelphia Seminary, and was licensed by the Middle Presbytery, October 21, 1818. He preached with much acceptance as a supply to the mission stations of Wyoming and Mauch Chunk, Pennsylvania, for several months. He connected with the Presbyterian Church, being received by the Presbytery of Philadelphia, November 10, 1819, and preached to the Old Scotch congregation, which became the Seventh Presbyterian Church of Philadelphia, Pennsylvania, over which he was ordained and installed pastor, July 6, 1820. A serious throat disease caused him to resign this charge, September 4, 1834, and he became editor of the *Presbyterian*, in which capacity he continued until his death. In 1838, he was appointed editor of the Presbyterian Board of Publication, a position which he discharged with great ability until his resignation in 1863. He finally became a subject of heart disease, from which he died, at his residence in the city of Philadelphia, Pennsylvania, November 27, 1867. He was a mild, instructive and thoroughly evangelical preacher. His usefulness as an editor was very great. His extensive reading of books of theology, and thorough discrimination of works of science were largely the means of the popularity and success of the Presbyterian Publishing House. He revised and abridged many old works which found a ready sale. He was the author of many tracts and books published anony-

* *Presbyterian Historical Almanac*, Vol. 10, p. 87.

mously. His "Sick Room Devotions" and "The Soldier's Pocket Book," were especially valuable, and found a large circulation at the time of the war of the rebellion. He married Miss Margaret Schott, of Philadelphia, Pennsylvania, in 1822. He was honored with the degree of Doctor of Divinity by Lafayette College in 1838. He was Moderator of the General Assembly in 1840, and Stated Clerk for many years.

GORDON THOMPSON EWING:

Son of John and Mary (Thompson) Ewing, was born near Maghera, County Londonderry, Ireland, July 17, 1798.* His parents were members of the Anti-Bounty Associate Church, and, being the only son, was the object of peculiar parental solicitude. Having completed his rudimentary education, he was placed under the tuition of his pastor, the Rev. John Bryce, and, in 1816, he made a profession of his faith in the Associate Church. In 1818, he entered the College of Belfast, Ireland, where he graduated with honor in 1821. He came to America in the spring of 1822, and landed in the city of Philadelphia, Pennsylvania, where he made the acquaintance of the Rev. Samuel Wylie, and accompanied him to his home near Kaskaskia, Illinois, and opened a classical school. While teaching in this place he espoused the principles of the Covenanter Church, and began the study of theology under the care of the Rev. Samuel Wylie. In the fall of 1824, he resumed his studies in the Philadelphia Seminary, and was licensed by the Pittsburgh Presbytery, May 9, 1825. He was ordained by the

---

* Principal items from a Sketch in *Banner of the Covenant*, 1848.

Pittsburgh Presbytery, and installed pastor of the congregation of Canonsburgh, Washington County, Pennsylvania, October 23, 1827, and resigned this charge, May 16, 1830, on account of impaired health. In the fall of 1830, he returned to Ireland, and, in the spring of 1831, was called to the congregation of Londonderry; but, as he thought of returning soon to America, he did not accept it, but engaged as stated supply for one year, which arrangement was repeated for eight years. He was installed pastor of the congregation of Grange, Ireland, July 20, 1840, and resigned, November 9, 1841, when he returned to America. The Church in America had passed through the division of August, 1833, and, after due consideration, he became identified with the New School branch of the Covenanter Church. He was installed pastor of the Second congregation of Pittsburgh (situated in the suburb of Bayardstown), Pennsylvania, September 9, 1842, where he continued until his death. Having fallen into the weakness of Irish character, and being a constant sufferer from malaria for many years, atrophy ensued with direful effects. In March, 1848, he embarked for New Orleans, Louisiana, thence intending a coasting voyage to New York, but his strength yielded to the pressure of his disease, and he died on board the steamer "General Pike," one hundred miles above New Orleans, Louisiana, March 21, 1848. He married Miss Margaret Black, of Pittsburgh, Pennsylvania, March 13, 1828. He possessed a solemn and imposing appearance, and was a genial and pleasant companion. As a preacher, he was interesting and instructive, and at times most eloquent. He was a fluent speaker, a proficient scholar, and his acquisitions were considerable in theology and science. He was Moderator of the General Synod in 1847.

DANIEL CARGILL FARIS:

Son of Rev. James and Nancy (Smith) Faris, was born in Bloomington, Monroe County, Indiana, June 21, 1843. He received his early education in the common schools, and under the direction of his father, and graduated from the University of Indiana in 1863. He was a teacher, for some time, in the Mission School at Natchez, Mississippi. He studied theology in the Allegheny Seminary, was licensed by the Illinois Presbytery, April 21, 1869, and labored for two years in Lake Reno and Round Prairie, Minnesota. He was ordained by the New York Presbytery, and installed pastor of the Barnet congregation, West Barnet, Caledonia County, Vermont, June 25, 1873, where he is in charge. He married Miss Mary A. Russell, of Round Prairie, Minnesota, November 15, 1870.

DAVID SMITH FARIS:

Son of Rev. James and Nancy (Smith) Faris, was born in Bloomington, Monroe County, Indiana, November 11, 1830. He received his early education in the common schools, and under the direction of his distinguished father, and graduated from the University of Indiana in 1851. He studied theology privately during the suspension of the Seminary, and was licensed by the Illinois Presbytery, October 10, 1855. At the reorganization of the Allegheny Seminary, in 1856, he attended one session. He was ordained by the Illinois

Presbytery, and installed pastor of the Bethel congregation, Sparta, Randolph County, Illinois, October 7, 1857, where he is in charge. He was twice married. First to Miss Jane McAfee, of Philadelphia, Pennsylvania, May 8, 1861; and second, to Mrs. Hester (Edgar) Finley, of Sparta, Illinois, March 30, 1871. He is the author of a pamphlet, "A Defense of the Old School Covenanters as Dissenters from the United States Constitution," 1864, pp. 33, and many historical articles in the magazines of the Church, bearing upon the history of the Covenanters in South Carolina. He was Moderator of the Synod of 1883.

ISAIAH FARIS:

Son of Rev. James and Nancy (Smith) Faris, was born in Bloomington, Monroe County, Indiana, April 25, 1846. He received his early literary training in the schools of his native city, and graduated from the University of Indiana in 1863, and was engaged in teaching in Natchez, Mississippi. He studied theology in the Allegheny Seminary, and was licensed by the Illinois Presbytery, April 21, 1869. He was ordained by the Iowa Presbytery, and installed pastor of the congregation of Walnut City, Appanoose County, Iowa, September 21, 1870, and resigned this charge, May 23, 1877. He was installed pastor of the congregation of Vernon, Waukesha County, Wisconsin, November 22, 1878, where he is in charge. He was twice married. First to Miss Anna M. Pauly, of Sparta, Illinois, March 29, 1871; and second, to Miss Julia McLaughlin, of Vernon, Wisconsin, October 26, 1880.

JAMES FARIS:

Son of James and Mary A. (Becket) Faris, was born near Chester, Chester District, South Carolina, May 15, 1791.* His father died when he was very young, and he was brought up by his aunt, Mrs. Agnes Smith. He received a liberal common school education, which prepared him for teaching, and by this means he prepared himself for college, and graduated from South Carolina College, Columbia, in 1816. He immediately afterwards assumed the position of Principal of the Academy of Pendleton, South Carolina, a flourishing classical school patronized by John C. Calhoun, and in which several congressmen and eminent legislators were educated. He resigned the school in June, 1822, and devoted himself to the study of theology, under the direction of the Rev. Thomas Donnelly, and was licensed by the Southern Presbytery, January 21, 1824. He attended one session in the Philadelphia Seminary, and made an extended preaching tour through the South and West. He was ordained by the Western Presbytery, and installed pastor of the congregation of Bloomington, Monroe County, Indiana, November 22, 1827, where he continued to labor until his death, from a stroke of paralysis, May 20, 1855. He married Miss Nancy Smith, of Chester, South Carolina, April 29, 1823. He was a plain, didactic preacher, a logical reasoner, and a sound theologian. He made no pretense at oratory, and was unaffected in his pulpit manners. He was an excellent scholar and especially proficient in mathematics. He was born a reformer, and knew the evils

---

* Principal items from his son, the Rev. D. S. Faris, Sparta, Illinois.

of slavery from observation. He endeavored to have the Legislature of South Carolina pass a law by which benevolent slaveholders might free their slaves; but in this he failed, and removed from the South that his family might be free from the contaminating influence of the accursed institution of human slavery. His house was the home of the anti-slavery lecturer, and for many years an important station upon the "Underground Railroad." He was advanced in his views upon all reforms, and took an early stand upon temperance. He was a devout and pious man, peculiarly fond of religious conversation, thoroughly devoted to the principles of the Church and the work of the ministry. In order that he might glean in his Father's vineyard, he sacrificed the fame and remuneration of the scholar and teacher, and also gave four sons to the same work of preaching the gospel of Christ.

JOHN CALVIN KNOX FARIS:

Son of James and Nancy (Smith) Faris, was born in Bloomington, Monroe County, Indiana, April 11, 1833. He received his early education in the common schools, and under the direction of his father, graduating from the University of Indiana in 1853, and engaged in teaching. He studied theology in the Allegheny Seminary, and was licensed by the Pittsburgh Presbytery, April 18, 1859. He attended the Ohio Medical College, Cincinnati, Ohio, one session, and preached generally throughout the Church. He was appointed a Missionary to Natchez, Mississippi, February 16, 1864, where he remained in charge of the Freedmen's Mission for over a year. He was

31

ordained by the Ohio Presbytery, and installed pastor
of the Muskingum and Tomica congregation, Dresden,
Muskingum County, Ohio, December 6, 1865, and
resigned on account of impaired health, April 13, 1871.
He spent two years, principally in Colorado, in regain-
ing his health, and occasionally preached.   He was installed
pastor of the congregation of Topsham, Orange County,
Vermont, December 2, 1874, where he is in charge.
He married Miss Elizabeth J. McKnight, of Pittsburgh,
Pennsylvania, April 25, 1865.

JAMES MELVILLE FARIS:

Son of David and Elizabeth (Smith) Faris, was
born in Bloomington, Monroe County, Indiana, April
14, 1840. He received his early education in the
public schools, graduated from the University of
Indiana in 1862, and engaged in teaching. He studied
theology in the Allegheny Seminary, and was licensed
by the Illinois Presbytery, May 26, 1868. He was
ordained by the New York Presbytery, and installed
pastor [of the congregation of Topsham, Orange County,
Vermont, September 1, 1869, and resigned this charge,
May 22, 1872. He was installed pastor of the Church
Hill congregation, Coultersville, Randolph County,
Illinois, June 19, 1873, and resigned May 30, 1884.
He was installed pastor of the congregation of New
Concord, Muskingum County, Ohio, July 3, 1884,
where he is in charge. He was twice married. First
to Miss Jennie Smith, of Bloomington, Indiana, October
15, 1868; and second to Miss Jennie Watson, of
Utica, Ohio, January 28, 1886.

JAMES MELVILLE FINLEY:

Son of William and Elvira (Gault) Finley, was born in Hill Prairie, Randolph County, Illinois, September 12, 1854. He received his early education in the Plumb Creek school and Coultersville Academy of his native County, and graduated from Geneva College in 1879. He studied theology in the Allegheny Seminary, was licensed by the Illinois Presbytery, April 12, 1882, and preached generally throughout the Church. He married Miss Mary E. Caskey, of Allegheny, Pennsylvania, March 28, 1882. He has resided in Coultersville, Illinois, and Allegheny, Pennsylvania, and is preaching for the Presbyterian Church of New Sharon, Iowa.

JOHN FISHER:

Son of Robert and Jane (Porter) Fisher, was born in Cremore, County Armagh, Ireland, October 10, 1797. His parents were pious members of the Covenanter Church, with which he also connected in early life, and he was given the opportunity of attending the best schools in that vicinity. He came to America in June, 1820, and settled in Coldenham, Orange County, New York, where he was soon engaged as a teacher, and pursued his classical course in the Montgomery Academy. He studied theology in the Philadelphia Seminary, and was licensed by the Philadelphia Presbytery, April 16, 1828. He preached in many of the vacancies and made an extended visit among the Covenanters of South Carolina, who were anxious for his settlement among them. He was ordained by the Northern Presbytery, and installed pastor of the united congregations of York, Livingston

County, and Rochester, New York, July 21, 1831. He resigned the Rochester branch, April 17, 1835, and devoted his whole time to York, where he labored with great diligence and success until his death. In 1843, that dangerous disease, bronchitis, began to develop itself, and by its progress he was, for a time, unable to perform his ministerial duties. In May, 1845, he suffered from a severe hemorrhage of the lungs, from which he died, at his home near York, New York, July 22, 1845. He married Miss Catherine Balfour, of York, New York, May 16, 1831. He was not what is now termed a finished scholar nor a polished speaker, but he was a powerful preacher of the gospel, and a zealous advocate of the principles of the Covenanter Church. He was frequently absent from the meetings of Synod, and for this cause was not so well known throughout the Church as he deserved to be. He was devoted to the spiritual welfare of his own flock, and was a most tender and faithful pastor. He was distinguished for his integrity and uprightness of character, and was highly regarded as a model man in the community. The anti-slavery reform and the temperance cause found in him an active worker and an efficient advocate. His position was fully tested during the controversy and division of the Church in August, 1833, when most of his friends abandoned the Testimony, but his love for the truth, and the attainments of the Reformation cause, prevailed over all personal attachments, and he held fast the profession of his faith without wavering.

FINLEY MILLIGAN FOSTER:

Son of Samuel M. and Joan (Kyle) Foster, was born in Cedarville, Green County, Ohio, December 1, 1853. He received his early education in the schools of his native village and in Geneva College, and graduated from the University of Indiana in 1876. He studied theology in the Allegheny Seminary, and was licensed by the Lakes Presbytery, April 11, 1879. He was ordained by the same Presbytery, and installed pastor of the congregation of Bellefontaine, Ohio, May 13, 1880, and was released from this charge, August 23, 1887. He was installed pastor of the Third congregation of the city of New York, New York, September 7, 1887, where he is in charge. He married Miss Sallie C. Neer, of Bellefontaine, Ohio, May 30, 1883. He is the author of many articles published in the Church magazines.

JAMES MITCHELL FOSTER:

Son of Samuel M. and Joan (Kyle) Foster, was born in Cedarville, Green County, Ohio, September 22, 1850. He received the accustomed rudimentary training in the schools of his native town, and graduated from the University of Indiana in 1871. He studied theology in the Allegheny Seminary, and was licensed by the Lakes Presbytery, April 12, 1876. He was ordained by the same Presbytery, and installed pastor of the congregation of Cincinnati, Ohio, December 27, 1877, and resigned this charge, April 13, 1886. He accepted the position of Secretary of the National Reform Association, July 1, 1886, which position he now occupies. He married Miss Laura L. Turner, of Bloomington,

Indiana, September 24, 1878. He is a voluminous writer upon various subjects, and contributes to the magazines and papers of the Church.

JOHN FRENCH:

Son of John and Jane (Graham) French, was born near Malone, Franklin County, New York, June 12, 1815. In 1816, his parents removed to Reynoldsburgh, Franklin County, Ohio, where he received his early education in the common schools. He was engaged in teaching for many years in different parts of Ohio, and attended Miami University a few sessions. He studied theology privately, and in the Cincinnati Seminary, and was licensed by the Lakes Presbytery, September 5, 1849. He was ordained by the same Presbytery, and installed pastor of the Cedar Lake congregation, California, Branch County, Michigan, September 23, 1850, where he labored diligently until his death. About two years before his decease his health began to decline, and he asked to be relieved from his pastoral charge on account of his inability to attend fully to all ministerial duties, but before this was done, he was released by sudden death, from ulceration of the bowels, October 3, 1880. He married Miss Lydia Carithers, of California, Michigan, December 5, 1850. He was a very large man, of a commanding appearance, and an energetic speaker. He was an earnest and instructive preacher, a genial conversationalist, and a faithful pastor. He was universally beloved as an exemplary Christian, and in his death the Church lost one of her worthy and esteemed ministers.

JOHN CALVIN BOYD FRENCH:

Son of Rev. John and Lydia (Carithers) French, was born in California, Branch County, Michigan, May 29, 1858. He received his early education in the schools of his native County, and entered Geneva College in 1873, where he remained two years. He engaged in teaching in his native County for some time, and finally resumed his studies in, and graduated from, Geneva College in 1883. He taught in the Normal Academy of McKeesport, Pennsylvania, two years, and at the same time studied theology in the Allegheny Seminary, was licensed by the Pittsburgh Presbytery, April 14, 1886, and preached for a few months in Blanchard, Iowa, and other parts of the Church. He was ordained by the Rochester Presbytery, and installed pastor of the congregation of Sterling, Cayuga County, New York, January 12, 1888, where he is in charge. He married Miss Agnes M. Steele, of McKeesport, Pennsylvania, August 13, 1885.

WILLIAM STEELE FULTON:

Son of James and Mary (Stewart) Fulton, was born near Northwood, Logan County, Ohio, March 17, 1849. He received his early education in the common schools, and graduated from Geneva College in 1873. He studied theology in the Allegheny Seminary, and was licensed by the Lakes Presbytery, April 12, 1876. He was ordained by the Ohio Presbytery, and installed pastor of the Muskingum and Tomica congregation, Dresden, Muskingum County, Ohio, December 5, 1877, and resigned this charge, April 11, 1883, and removed to Belle Centre, Ohio. He was installed pastor of the united congregations of Beulah and Eckley, Bostwick, Webster County, Nebraska, March 14, 1885, where he is in charge. He married Miss Jennie L. French, of California, Michigan, August 27, 1877.

FRANCIS GAILEY:

Was born in Killilastian, County Donegal, Ireland, March 14, 1802. His parents were poor but respectable members of the Covenanter Church. He came to America in 1816, and settled in Orange County, New York, where he was employed upon a farm. Naturally a bright and promising youth, he was induced to study for the ministry by the Rev. J. R. Willson, D. D., and pursued a literary course in the Academy of Coldenham, New York. He studied theology privately under the direction of Dr. J. R. Willson, and was licensed by the Northern Presbytery, May 14, 1830. He preached with great acceptance for a few years in the vacancies throughout the eastern part of the Church, and received several calls, none of which he would accept, and hence never was ordained, although he assumed ministerial functions. Feeling that he was unfairly treated by his brethren in several ecclesiastical transactions, he became embittered against the Church, and, for disorderly conduct and using abusive language, his license was cancelled, and he suspended by the authority of Synod, October 6, 1838. He continued to preach, however, and formed what was termed the "Safety League." He began the publication of the *American Reformed Covenanter* in 1839, a pamphlet issued every two months, through which he expressed his contempt for the Church and stigmatized her ministry as "malignants." He claimed that he was the true representative and only apostle of the Covenanters, and that the whole body had made defection from the attainments of the Reformation. He made some disciples in Baltimore, New York, and Southern Ohio, and re-baptized all his converts. He was soon shorn of his influence, however, and his followers repented and returned to the Church of their fathers. He was a resident of the city of New York, New York, for thirty-five years, where he died in Bellevue Hospital, friendless and alone, May 21, 1872. He married Miss Jane Wylie, of Baltimore, Maryland, July 9, 1847. He was a bright and intellectual man, a very acceptable preacher, a forcible speaker and a racy author. He was winning in his manners, but by no means imposing in his personal appearance. He gave evidence of holding a prominent position in the Church, had he been possessed of the true Christian spirit, with malice toward none and charity for all.

JOHN GALBRAITH:

Son of James and Margaret (McClure) Galbraith, was born in Edenmore, County Antrim, Ireland, April 6, 1818. His parents were worthy members of the Covenanter Church, and he received his early education in the schools of his native land. He came to America, April 6, 1832, and settled near Burgettstown, Washington County, Pennsylvania, where he continued his studies, and graduated from the Western University of Pennsylvania in 1838. He studied theology in the Allegheny Seminary, and was licensed by the Pittsburgh Presbytery, June 1, 1842. He was ordained by the same Presbytery, and installed pastor of the united congregation of Union, Pine Creek and Lovejoy, Valencia, Butler County, Pennsylvania, June 29, 1843. The congregation was divided, April 11, 1870, since which time he continues pastor of North Union, a part of his original charge. He married Miss Sarah Wylie, of Elizabeth, Pennsylvania, July 11, 1843. He was Moderator of the Synod of 1874.

SAMUEL RENWICK GALBRAITH:

Son of Rev. John and Sarah (Wylie) Galbraith, was born near Valencia, Butler County, Pennsylvania, August 25, 1844. He received his early literary training in the common schools, and under the direction of his father, graduating from Westminster College in 1866. He studied theology in the Allegheny Seminary, and was licensed by the Pittsburgh Presbytery, April 13, 1869. He was ordained by the Rochester Presbytery, and installed pastor of the congregation of Sterling, Cayuga County, New York, July 7, 1870. At the meeting of Synod in May, 1871, he was chosen to fill the vacancy in the Syrian Mission occasioned by the death of Rev. R. J. Dodds, D. D. He accepted the appointment, and resigned the pastoral charge of Sterling, October 4, 1871. He, with other Missionaries, embarked for Syria, November 4, 1871, and arrived in Latakia early in January, 1872. With enthusiastic devotion he began the study of the Arabic language, in which he made rapid progress. He soon began to suffer from severe headaches, which were followed by an attack of fever peculiar to that country. From this sickness he rallied, and repaired to Beyrout, to

seek the bracing air of Mt. Lebanon. While in Beyrout
a relapse of the fever set in, with symptoms of
softening of the brain, from which he died, 'June 21,
1872, and was buried in the Prussian Cemetery, under
the shadow of Mt. Lebanon, Syria. He married Miss
Anna Martin, of Lisbon Centre, New York, September 19, 1871. He was a pleasing and impressive
preacher. By his accurate scholarship, studious habits,
manly independence and earnest Christian character,
he was eminently fitted for the work which he had
undertaken. His discourses were carefully prepared,
methodically arranged, and chaste in style. He was
faithfully and conscientiously engaged in duty when
his Master called him.

MATTHEW AUGUSTINE GAULT:

Son of John and Martha (Adams) Gault, was born
in Coleraine, County Londonderry, Ireland, May 2,
1845. In 1847, his parents came to America,
settled near Brockport, Monroe County, New York,
and in 1852, they removed to Waukesha, Waukesha
County, Wisconsin. Here he connected with the Covenanter Church, and received his early education,
graduating from Monmouth College in 1870. He
studied theology in the Allegheny Seminary, and was
licensed by the Pittsburgh Presbytery, April 15, 1874.
He was ordained by the Iowa Presbytery, installed
pastor of Lind Grove congregation, Mediapolis, Des
Moines County, Iowa, May 20, 1875, and resigned this
charge, October 4, 1877. He became stated supply
to the Long Branch congregation, Blanchard, Page
County, Iowa, and was installed the pastor October 1,

1880. He resigned this charge, October 25, 1882, since which time he has been engaged as a Secretary of the National Reform Association, with his residence in Blanchard, Iowa. He married Miss Maggie P. Turner, of Waukesha, Wisconsin, September 17, 1871. His letters are printed in the Church magazines, and papers of the National Reform Association.

SAMUEL MAXWELL GAYLEY:

Son of Andrew and Margaret (Crawford) Gayley, was born in Creevy, County Tyrone, Ireland, June 4, 1802.* His parents were Scotch Presbyterians, from whom he received a strict religious education, and at ten years of age began a classical course of study with the ministry in view. In 1814, he lost his father by death, which event so frustrated his plans for the ministry that he abandoned that idea and commenced the study of medicine with Dr. Samuel Snodgrass of Castlederg. He remained in this study over a year ; in the meantime losing his devoted mother by death, his mind was again turned to the ministry, and he resumed his classical studies under the direction of the Rev. Andrew Maxwell, where he remained over two years. He came to America in May, 1823, and landed in the city of Philadelphia, Pennsylvania, an absolute stranger. He connected with the Covenanter Church, soon afterwards began the study of theology in the Philadelphia Seminary, and was licensed by the Philadelphia Presbytery, April 4, 1828. He labored for some time as stated supply at Conococheague, Pottsville and Mauch Chunk, in Eastern Pennsylvania. In 1831, he repaired to

* *Presbyterian Historical Almanac,* Vol. 6.

Wilmington, Delaware, where he gathered a congregation, over which he was ordained by the Philadelphia Presbytery and installed pastor, December 25, 1832. At the division of the Church in the following year, he became identified with the New School branch of the Covenanter Church, and took most of the congregation with him into that body. He connected with the Presbyterian Church, June 13, 1837, and was installed pastor of the congregation of Rockland, Delaware, where he remained sixteen years, most of which time he was Principal of a Classical School. In 1854, he removed to Media, Pennsylvania, and founded Media Classical Institute, which is still a flourishing school, and remained its Principal until his death, December 19, 1862. He was a clear, logical, and interesting preacher, with a great amount of missionary spirit. He was a thorough classical scholar, and in his Schools he educated a number of men who became eminent in Church and State. He wrote largely for the press and educational monthlies, and by correspondence with legislators was efficient in procuring the improved system of common school education.

HENRY GEORGE, D. D.:

Son of Henry and Maria (Dolman) George, was born in Cumberland, Muskingum County, Ohio, February 20, 1833. In 1839, his parents removed to Locust Grove, Adams County, Ohio, where he received his early education in the common schools, graduating from Geneva College in 1853. He became a Tutor of Greek in this institution, and, in 1856, Professor of Greek. He studied theology in the Northwood and

Allegheny Seminaries, and was licensed by the Lakes Presbytery, June 4, 1857. He was ordained by the same Presbytery, and installed pastor of the united congregations of Cedarville, Green County, and Cincinnati, Ohio, June 23, 1858. He resigned the Cedarville branch, August 4, 1866, the Cincinnati charge, August 18, 1872, and accepted the Presidency of Geneva College, which position he now occupies. In addition to his collegiate duties, he was installed pastor of the congregation of Rushsylvania, Logan County, Ohio, May 3, 1878, and resigned May 18, 1880. In the fall of 1880, Geneva College was removed from Northwood, Ohio, to Beaver Falls, Pennsylvania, whither he removed, and it is largely through his personal efforts that the institution enjoys its present prosperity. He married Miss Sarah Brown, of Cincinnati, Ohio, December 27, 1864. Among his numerous publications in the interests of Reformation, is an "Address on Secret Societies," 1872, pp. 40. He was honored with the degree of Doctor of Divinity by the Ohio Central College in 1874. He was Moderator of the Synod of 1871.

ROBERT JAMES GEORGE :

Son of John and Jane (Slater) George, was born near Venice, Washington County, Pennsylvania, July 15, 1844. He received his early education in the High School of Hickory, attended the Academy of Dayton, Pennsylvania, one year, and graduated from Westminster College in 1866. He studied theology in the Allegheny Seminary, and was licensed by the Pittsburgh Presbytery, April 13, 1869. He was ordained by the same Presbytery, and installed pastor of the Poland and

North Jackson congregation, Canfield, Mahoning County, Ohio, May 19, 1870, and resigned this charge, April 14, 1875. He was installed pastor of the congregation of Beaver Falls, Pennsylvania, June 15, 1875, where he is in charge. He married Miss Maggie R. Hamilton, of Putneyville, Pennsylvania, October 28, 1868. He was instrumental in locating and building up Geneva College in its present site, and is the Secretary of its Board and that of the Superintendents of the Theological Seminary. In the fall of 1886, he was appointed temporary Professor of Theology in the Allegheny Seminary as successor to the late Rev. J. R. W. Sloane, D. D., and, in the spring of 1887, was elected by Synod as Professor of Systematic Theology, but declined that honor to remain with his congregation.

SAMUEL ALEXANDER GEORGE:

Son of Michael and Hannah (Hutcheson) George, was born in Locust Grove, Adams County, Ohio, September 28, 1851. In early life his parents removed to Rushsylvania, Logan County, Ohio, where he received his early education in the public schools, graduating from Geneva College in 1873. He studied theology in the Allegheny Seminary, was licensed by the Lakes Presbytery, April 12, 1876, and labored as a Missionary in Mansfield, Ohio, and built up that congregation. He was ordained by the Ohio Presbytery, and installed pastor of the congregation of Mansfield, Ohio, November 20, 1878, where he is in charge. He married Miss Jemima Blackwood, of Rose Point, Pennsylvania, September 2, 1875.

WILLIAM FINNEY GEORGE:

Son of Alexander and Martha (Finney) George, was born near Venice, Washington County, Pennsylvania, November 19, 1821. He acquired the basis of a classical education in the schools of his native County, and graduated from Franklin College in 1845. In 1846, he became Professor of Languages in Muskingum College, where he remained two years. He studied theology in the Cincinnati and Northwood Seminaries one year each, and, in 1850, accepted the Presidency of Geneva College. He continued his theological studies in the Northwood Seminary, was licensed by the Lakes Presbytery, April 24, 1851, and, in the following winter, resigned his position in the College that he might devote himself to the work of the ministry. He was ordained by the Lakes Presbytery, at Utica, Ohio, May 12, 1853, and installed pastor of the congregation of Macedon, Mercer County, Ohio, September 26, 1853, resigning this charge on account of impaired health, April 20, 1858. He was installed pastor of the Church Hill congregation, Coultersville, Randolph County, Illinois, March 5, 1860, and resigned May 17, 1871. He was installed pastor of the congregation of Staunton, Macoupin County, Illinois, May 13, 1872, where he labored under many trials of body and mind, until he was taken away in death, by that wasting disease—consumption, April 14, 1880. He married Miss Martha Speer, of New Concord, Ohio, September 2, 1847. He was an earnest and interesting preacher, and a kind and attentive pastor. He was a scholar of considerable ability and possessed an aptness to teach. With a large family in a new

country, he had a good many difficulties to contend
with, and in addition to his ministerial work, taught
school with marked success, and practiced medicine with
much usefulness. He was a public-spirited man, took
an active part in Church courts, ably advocated the
reforms of his day, and was closely attached to the
principles of the Covenanter Church.

JOHN GIBSON:

Son of Rev. William and Rebecca (Mitchell) Gibson, was born in Ballymena, County Antrim, Ireland,
August 14, 1791. He came with his parents to America
in 1797, and settled in the city of Philadelphia, Pennsylvania; and, in 1799, removed to Ryegate, Caledonia
County, Vermont. He received a very careful religious
training from his distinguished parents, pursued his
classical studies under the direction of his father, and
attended the University of Vermont. He studied
theology in the Philadelphia Seminary, was licensed
by the Middle Presbytery, May 19, 1817, and preached
in Western Pennsylvania and Ohio for one year. He
was ordained by the Middle Presbytery, and installed
pastor of the congregation of Baltimore, Maryland,
December 15, 1818. He built up a flourishing congregation in this city, and also conducted a classical
school, in which the sons of the best families in the
city were educated. At the division of the Church
in August, 1833, he went out, but did not formally
connect, with the New School branch of the Covenanter Church. He joined the Presbyterian Church, being
received by the Presbytery of Baltimore, October 10,
1833, and took the great majority of the congregation

32

with him. He preached in Baltimore a short time without any charge. In 1834, he committed forgery to meet the monetary obligations contracted by an extravagant family, for which cause he was apprehended, but being a minister he was allowed his freedom provided he immediately left the State never to return.* He went to the West, and supplied vacant pulpits and taught school for many years. In 1858, he was stated supply at Belleville, Illinois ; in 1862, at Mt. Vernon ; and in 1866, he removed to Sparta, Illinois. In 1868, he went to Cincinnati, Ohio, and soon afterwards retired to the home of his brother, the Rev. W. J. Gibson, D. D., at Duncansville, Blair County, Pennsylvania, where he died, June 3, 1869. He married Miss Elizabeth Jamieson, of Baltimore, Maryland, in 1821. He was a forcible and interesting preacher, and in his earlier years very popular. He was a proficient classical scholar, and an apt and successful teacher. He possessed considerable ability, was a kind and social man, but rather liberal in his views. He was Moderator of the Synod of 1821.

ROBERT GIBSON :

Son of Rev. William and Rebecca (Mitchell) Gibson, was born in Ballymena, County Antrim, Ireland, October 1, 1793. His parents came to America in 1797, settled in the city of Philadelphia, Pennsylvania, and, in 1799, removed to Ryegate, Caledonia County, Vermont. Here he received his rudimentary training in the common schools, and, with the ministry in view, pursued the classics under the direction of his distin-

---

* Facts from some Baltimore parishioners.

guished father, and became an excellent scholar. He studied theology in the Philadelphia Seminary, was licensed by the Middle Presbytery, June 5, 1818, and his first pulpit efforts awakened more than ordinary attention. He was ordained by the Pittsburgh Presbytery, and installed pastor of the Little Beaver congregation, New Galilee, Beaver County, Pennsylvania, September 6, 1819. Large audiences gathered from all parts of the country to hear him whenever he was announced to conduct a preaching service, and, by his faithful and eloquent presentation of the gospel, the congregation flourished. In this new and extensive field he travelled much, and was subjected to great exposure in reaching the various places of preaching; and he contracted an insipient disease of the lungs, necessitating a change, and he resigned this charge, October 16, 1830. He was installed pastor of the Second congregation of the city of New York, New York, May 18, 1831. Here his ministrations were hailed with large and appreciative audiences three times a Sabbath, and the congregation grew in numbers and practical godliness. At the division of the Church in August, 1833, he was in the midst of the controversy, and although sorely tried, stood faithful to the Covenanted Testimony. In 1834, his health again began to decline, and, in 1836, he visited his old home among the evergreen hills of Vermont, but, on account of the frequency of his preaching among his admirers and old acquaintances, his health was not improved. In the spring of 1837, he made a visit to his native land and other parts of Europe, where the people received him gladly. He returned the same autumn not much benefitted, and gradually declined with that fatal disease, consumption, until his death, at his residence in the city of New York, New York, December 22, 1837. He was twice married. His first wife was Miss Mary A. Harvey, of Philadelphia, Pennsylvania, 1817; the second, Miss Mary A. Lindsay, of the same city, 1827. He is justly ranked among the most eloquent and popular preachers of the Covenanter Church. His appearance was prepossessing; above the medium in height, of dark complexion, and of an open and agreeable countenance. He had a splendid voice, soft in melody, flexible in tone, distinct in articulation, and a manner that attracted the masses of the people. While he may not be ranked among the profound theologians, yet his mode of thinking, his manner of address, and his forms of expression were all in sympathy with the popular mind. He was bold, faithful and magnanimous in declaring the truth of God, and in rebuking all error and vice. He was peculiarly zealous and successful in the maintenance of the Calvinistic system against the Arminian errors and Hopkinsian subtleties. Opposition but increased his ardor and added fresh vigor to his enlightened zeal, and his powers of persuasion were peculiarly effective. He took a prominent part in all Church work, and was among the number of sterling integrity who maintained the principles of the Church in their purity. In 1832, he became an associate editor of the *American Protestant Vindicator*, a weekly paper published in New York, and devoted to the cause of Protestantism against

Roman Catholicism. He also published three ably written pamphlets in vindication of the position of the Old School Covenanter Church during the controversy of 1833, which are unanswerable. He was Moderator of the Synod of 1834.

WILLIAM GIBSON:

Son of Robert and Susannah (McWhirr) Gibson, was born near Knockbracken, County Down, Ireland, July 1, 1753. His parents were members of the Presbyterian Church, but on account of the departure of that body from the attainments of the Reformation, he connected with the Covenanter Church in early life. He passed through the accustomed routine of studies in the national schools, and under private instructors, and graduated from the University of Glasgow, Scotland, in 1775. He studied theology in Edinburgh, and privately, and was licensed by the Reformed Presbytery of Ireland, May 19, 1781. He preached with great acceptance in the vacancies for a few years, and was ordained by the Reformed Presbytery, and installed pastor of the united congregations of Kellswater and Cullybackey, County Antrim, Ireland, April 17, 1787. His labors were signally blessed by the gathering of a large congregation, and in his fidelity to truth, and the doctrine of Christ's Headship over the Church, he rendered himself obnoxious to a tyrannical government. His ardent love for personal liberty led him to encourage those associations formed in Ireland to throw off the British yoke. The Insurrection of 1797 marked a trying period in the history of Ireland, and the Covenanters were often suspected by governmental agents as countenancing the association of "United Irishmen." During this rebellion, the oath of allegiance was required, but the Covenanters refused to take it. A magistrate living in the vicinity of Mr. Gibson's congregation, administered the oath to two men who waited upon his ministrations, and one of them remarked that Mr. Gibson would censure them for what they had done. This observation reached the ear of the magistrate, who declared with a profane oath, that Mr. Gibson should either take the oath of allegiance or his life should go for it. This was the reason he found an asylum, with hundreds of others, in America, and not because he was a member of the "United Irishmen." According to his own testimony he never was a member of that association.* He fled for safety to America, and landed in the city of Philadelphia, Pennsylvania, October 18, 1797, and resided, with his family, in this city nearly two years. He supplied the small societies of Covenanters in Philadelphia, Coldenham, New York, and in Vermont. He, with the Rev. James McKinney and ruling elders, constituted the Reformed Presbytery of America, at Philadelphia, Pennsylvania, May, 1798. He was installed pastor of the congregation centering in Ryegate, Caledonia County, Vermont, July 10, 1799. This field was very extensive and in a severely cold and uncultivated section of country, but his labors were accompanied with manifest tokens of the Divine blessing. The congregation became divided into several branches, and he resigned the charge, April 13, 1815. He was installed pastor of the congregation of Canonsburgh, Washington

* *American Reformed Covenanter.*

County, Pennsylvania, October 23, 1817, and resigned on account of the infirmities of age, May 27, 1826. He took charge of the congregation of Paterson, New Jersey, for several years. In May, 1834, he removed to the city of Philadelphia, Pennsylvania, where he resided two years. During the controversy and division of the Church in August, 1833, he remained among the faithful brethren who held the principles of the Covenanter Church as they have always been applied. In 1836, he removed to the city of New York, New York, and supplied the pulpit of his son, the Rev. Robert Gibson, who was in feeble health. In the summer of 1838, disease and the extreme infirmities of age rendered him unable to sustain himself under the fatigue of the usual pulpit labors, and he gradually declined until his death, at his home in the city of New York, New York, October 15, 1838. Although in his eighty-fifth year, he preached twice upon the Sabbath, and his reason and memory were unimpaired. He married Miss Rebecca Mitchell, of Londonderry County, Ireland, in 1788. He was a well-read theologian and a fine classical scholar. His discourses were distinguished for soundness of doctrine, Scriptural illustration, and practical application. He was not a brilliant speaker and yet a most instructive preacher. He was especially interesting upon sacramental occasions, when it was evident that he had drunk deeply at the fountain of Divine truth, and he dispensed the waters of life with a copiousness and richness of sanctified thought seldom surpassed. He was a large, fine-looking man, venerable and imposing in his appearance. He was the honest and upright

man in all his transactions; naturally benevolent in
disposition, warm and unchanging in his friendships,
and void of anything like dissimulation. He effected
little as an author. He published a pamphlet in the
form of a dialogue concerning the Calvinistic doctrine
of the Atonement against Hopkinsianism, 1802, pp. 80;
also a sermon, "When the Enemy shall come in like a
Flood," 1803, pp. 47. He was Moderator of the first
Synod of 1809, and also in 1816 and 1832.

JONATHAN GILL:

Son of John and Jane (Shaw) 'Gill, was born near
Huntingdon, Huntingdon County, Pennsylvania, August
9, 1777. His childhood and youth were characterized
by many of the deprivations of a new country, and
with difficulty he obtained the rudiments of an education, and engaged in teaching. After some time he
resumed his studies in the Canonsburgh Academy, and
graduated from Jefferson College in 1810. He studied
theology in the Philadelphia Seminary, and was licensed
by the Middle Presbytery, May 9, 1814. He was
ordained by the Western Presbytery, and installed
pastor of the united congregations of Xenia and
Massie's Creek, Green County, Ohio, May 14, 1816,
and resigned this charge, April 6, 1823. He was
installed pastor of the Brookland congregation,
including Puckety and Thompson's Run societies,
Lucesco, Westmoreland County, Pennsylvania, October
20, 1823. At the division of the Church in August,
1833, he became identified with the New School branch
of the Covenanter Church, and the pastoral relation
was dissolved. He was restored, October 16, 1834,

but soon returned to that body, and his name was stricken from the roll by the authority of Synod, October 7, 1836. In 1835, he became Professor of Languages in the Western University of Pennsylvania, and subsequently Principal of an Academy. He connected with the Associate Reformed Church, being received by the Monongahela Presbytery of that body, May 24, 1840. He died of pneumonia, at his home in the vicinity of the city of Pittsburgh, Pennsylvania, April 20, 1846. He married Miss Rachael M. Steen, of Philadelphia, Pennsylvania, in 1815. He was an acceptable preacher, a proficient scholar, and a successful teacher, to which latter profession he mostly devoted his energies. He distinguished himself as a linguist in the translation of the Hebrew Bible, which is considered an excellent work.

WILLIAM JOHN GILLESPIE:

Son of John and Sarah (Gillespie) Gillespie, was born in Ballynahinch, County Down, Ireland, October 3, 1841. His parents were members of the Seceder Church, and sent him to the classical school of Wishaw, Scotland, where he received his early education. He came to America, May 14, 1857, and settled in Newburgh, New York, where he resumed his studies, and connected with the Covenanter Church. In 1862, with a view to the ministry, he entered Westminster College, where he graduated in 1866. He studied theology in the Allegheny Seminary, was licensed by the Pittsburgh Presbytery, April 15, 1868, and labored in Minnesota for some time. He was ordained by the Illinois Presbytery, and installed pastor of the Old Bethel congregation, Sparta, Randolph County, Illinois, October 13, 1869. He connected with the United Presbyterian Church, being received by the Southern Illinois Presbytery, August 6, 1870. He was installed pastor of the congregation of Sparta, Illinois, September 11, 1870, and resigned August 14, 1877. He was installed pastor of the Charles Street congregation, New York City, New York, August 30, 1877, and resigned June 16, 1879. He was installed pastor of the congregation of Jordan's Grove, Randolph County, Illinois, December 16, 1879, and resigned October 24, 1882. He was installed pastor of the Union congregation, Sparta, Illinois, January 18, 1883, and resigned May 31, 1886. He took charge of a Mission enterprise in Leavenworth, Kansas, June 5, 1886, and is Chaplain of the National Home for Disabled Volunteer Soldiers. He married Miss Jennie Wier, of Sparta, Illinois, October 1, 1872.

WILLIAM MELANCTHON GLASGOW:

Son of Moses T. and Martha W. (Thompson) Glasgow, was born in Northwood, Logan County, Ohio, July 1, 1856. The following year his parents removed to Belle Centre, Ohio, where he received his early education in the public schools. In March, 1872, he was employed in connection with the *Cincinnati Daily Star*, and, in 1874, was agent and reporter for the same paper in Dayton, Ohio. He resumed his studies in Geneva College, where he graduated in 1880, and was employed in Boston, Massachusetts, for two years. He studied theology in the Allegheny Seminary, was licensed by the Pittsburgh Presbytery, April 9, 1884, and made a tour of the British Maritime Provinces. He was ordained by the Philadelphia Presbytery, and installed pastor of the congregation of Baltimore, Maryland, November 26, 1885, where he is in charge. He was an editor of the *College Cabinet* two years, beginning with its establishment in 1878. He published the "History of the Reformed Presbyterian Church in America," 1888.

DAVID GRAHAM:

Son of Thomas and Mary (De Witt) Graham, was born in Coleraine, County Londonderry, Ireland, September 8, 1779.* He received his preparatory literary course in the schools of his native County, and graduated from the University of Glasgow, Scotland, in 1799. He studied theology in the Seminary of Paisley, Scotland, and was licensed by the Reformed Presbytery of Ireland, March 9, 1804. He was ordained by the same court, and installed pastor of the congregation of Magherafelt, County Londonderry, Ireland, October 16, 1805. Becoming embarrassed in some worldly affairs he went to London, England, in 1807, and during his absence in that city he was deposed from the ministerial office, by the Reformed Presbytery of Ireland, for abandoning his charge and for mistreating his people.† He came to America, February 8, 1808, and settled in the city of New York, New York, where he was engaged as a teacher of the languages. He made application for admittance into the Covenanter Church and for the exercise of his ministerial functions. After a full con-

* Principal items from his son, Hon. John Graham, New York City.
† Minutes of Synod, 1809, p. 33.

fession of his conduct in Ireland, and renewing his pledges of fidelity to the Church, he was restored by the Northern Presbytery, at Milton, Northumberland County, Pennsylvania, August 12, 1809. He preached with great acceptance in the vacancies, and, in 1810, was called to the congregation of Canonsburgh, Pennsylvania, and accepted the call. Before his installation, however, he was arraigned by the Middle Presbytery for "withdrawing his profession of repentance, and employing his ministry to the injury of the Church." His trial was held in the Court House in the city of Pittsburgh, Pennsylvania, in August, 1811, and lasted eight days, attracting a large crowd of eager spectators from the country congregations, and many of the legal profession in the city. His fine address and persuasive eloquence drew to himself the sympathy of a numerous constituency, and the impression deepened that he was persecuted by the jealous spirit of his brethren whose known abilities as divines were far below his acquisitions. The charges, however, were all proven, whereupon he declined the authority of the court, and was deposed by the Middle Presbytery, August 20, 1811. With a number of followers he became identified with the Seceder Church, and preached for some time in Washington and Butler Counties, Pennsylvania. His preaching became too orthodox for them, when he advocated with unanswerable arguments and overwhelming eloquence that "Christ reigned as Mediator from the roofless heavens to the bottomless hell." Many of his followers returned to the Church of their fathers and the rest abandoned him. In 1818, he returned to New

York City, and began the study of law with Thomas Addis Emmett, one of the most distinguished members of the metropolitan bar, and he was admitted to the practice of law, November 9, 1820. He soon rose into prominence and became one of the leading lawyers in the city, as well as an influential member of the Lafayette Avenue Dutch Reformed Church. He was engaged as counsel, in 1833, in pleading for the property of the Covenanter Church. In the later years of his life he returned somewhat to intemperate habits, and died very suddenly of dysentery, at his home in the city of New York, New York, September 13, 1839. He married Miss Mary Hazleton, of Londonderry, Ireland, March 16, 1807. He was a fine classical scholar, a clear logician, and a most interesting and eloquent preacher. For many years he conducted a class in Hebrew, composed principally of clergymen, in New York. As a lawyer, he stood in the front rank, particularly as an advocate, and was remarkable for his powers of cross-examination. He was rather below the medium in height, corpulent, of a pleasing address and courteous manner. He published "A Treatise on the Law of New Trials," 1834, a standard work and still an authority.

JOHN GRAHAM:

Son of Hugh and Maria (Williams) Graham, was born in the city of New York, New York, May 14, 1857. In early life his parents removed to the city of Philadelphia, Pennsylvania, where he received his early education in the public schools, and attended the University of Pennsylvania two years. He studied theology in the Allegheny Seminary, and was licensed by the Philadelphia Presbytery, May 6, 1880. He also graduated from the National School of Elocution and Oratory, Philadelphia, June 8, 1881. He was ordained by the Rochester Presbytery, and installed pastor of the congregation of Rochester, New York, June 22, 1881, where he is in charge. He married Miss Emma Mehaffay, of Allegheny City, Pennsylvania, September 9, 1880.

WILLIAM GRAHAM:

Son of John and Dorathy (Martin) Graham, was born near Ballibay, County Monaghan, Ireland, July 7, 1826. He received his early education in the schools of his native County, came to America, December 1, 1847, and settled in the city of New York, New York, where he was engaged in business for many years. With the ministry in view, he resumed his classical studies, graduating from the University of the City of New York in 1859. He studied theology at the same time under the direction of the Rev. Andrew Stevenson, D. D., and was licensed by the New York Presbytery, November 1, 1859. He was ordained by the same Presbytery, installed pastor of the First congregation of Boston, Massachusetts, July 11, 1860, where he is in charge. He was married twice. First to Miss Elizabeth Bell, of New York City, March 26, 1856; and second to Miss Mary A. Dickson, of Ryegate, Vermont, December 3, 1862.

DAVID GREGG:

Son of David and Mary (Rafferty) Gregg, was born in the city of Allegheny, Pennsylvania, March 25, 1845. He received his early education in the public schools and in Westminster College of his native city, graduating from Jefferson College in 1865. He studied theology in the Allegheny Seminary, and was licensed by the Pittsburgh Presbytery, April 15, 1868. He was ordained by the New York Presbytery, and installed pastor of the Third congregation of the city of New York, New York, February 23, 1870, and resigned this charge, October 28, 1885. He was re-installed pastor, December 6, 1885, and released January 25, 1887. He connected with the Congregational Church, and was installed pastor of the Park street Church, Boston, Massachusetts, February 16, 1887, where he is in charge. He married Miss Katie Ethridge, of Rome, New York, October 12, 1870. He was an editor of *Our Banner* from 1874 until 1887; and contributed an exposition of the Sabbath School lessons to the *Christian Statesman* for several years. He was Moderator of the Synod of 1882.

THOMAS CATHCART GUTHRIE, D. D.:

   Son of Hugh and Margaret (Cathcart) Guthrie, was born near Broughshane, County Antrim, Ireland, August 7, 1796. He was trained in the strictest manner by a Covenanter parentage, and united with the Church in 1813, then under the pastoral charge of the Rev. W. J. Stavely, D. D., of Kellswater congregation. He came to America in 1817, for his health, and settled near the city of Pittsburgh, Pennsylvania, where he spent some time in recuperation. He resumed his studies in the Pittsburgh Academy, graduating from the Western University of Pennsylvania in 1823. He studied theology in the Philadelphia Seminary, and was licensed by the Pittsburgh Presbytery, April 14, 1825. He was ordained by the same Presbytery, and installed pastor of the united congregation of Pine Creek, Union and Camp Run, centering about Bakerstown, Allegheny County, Pennsylvania, April 26, 1826. At the division of the Church in August, 1833, he became identified with the New School branch of the Covenanter Church, and remained pastor of a portion of his former flock, until his resignation, May 23, 1855. During this year he went to Chicago, Illinois, and was about to remove his family to that city, when he was attacked with malarial fever, and returned to his former home. He was installed pastor of the congregation of Mount Pleasant, Westmoreland County, Pennsylvania, a part of his original charge, June 9, 1856. He, and the congregation, connected with the United Presbyterian Church, October 10, 1859. He resigned this charge, May 24, 1864, and spent the residue of his life in supplying pulpits as his health would permit. In 1874, he removed to Sparta, Randolph County, Illinois, where he died, March 22, 1876. He married Miss Elizabeth Caskey, of Pittsburgh, Pennsylvania, December 30, 1828, as his first wife; second, Mrs. Nancy (Gilleland) McLean, of Bakerstown, Pennsylvania, January 26, 1837; and third, Miss Mary Faun, of Allegheny City, Pennsylvania, June 1, 1849. He was an earnest and instructive preacher, and an attentive pastor. He was a proficient classical scholar and well-read in science and philosophy. His intellectual powers were considerable, and he possessed a most vivid imagination. He was honored with the degree of Doctor of Divinity by Franklin College in 1843. He was Moderator of the General Synod of 1844.

JOSEPH HAMILTON :

Son of Joseph and Susannah (Logan) Hamilton, was born in Belraugh, County Londonderry, Ireland, June 13, 1842. He received the rudiments of an education in the national schools, began the classics under the Rev. James Bryce, attended the Belfast Academy, and graduated from Queen's College in 1861. He studied theology in the Belfast Seminary, and was licensed by the Northern Presbytery, Ireland, January 30, 1866. He was ordained by the same court, and installed pastor of the congregation of Garvagh, County Londonderry, Ireland, November 7, 1867, and he resigned this charge, October 14, 1872. He came to America the following spring, and was received by the Rochester Presbytery, May 30, 1873. He supplied vacancies throughout the Church generally, but especially the Canadian societies of the Rochester Presbytery. While preaching in West Hebron, Washington County, New York, he was reckoned heretical in his teaching in the case of the man said to be possessed of an unclean spirit; in which discourse he denied the personality of the Devil. After a statement of his beliefs relative to the subject, which were deemed subversive to the teachings of the Scriptures and the Church, he was suspended by the Rochester Presbytery, October 5, 1875. He preached as opportunity afforded, without any ecclesiastical connection, and taught public and select schools in different parts of the country for

33

several years. He removed to the city of Allegheny, Pennsylvania, where for many years he was employed as an agent for several publishing houses, and engaged in selling religious and wholesome literature. In June, 1886, he became a teacher in the Naval Academy at Oxford, Maryland, where he remained some time.

THOMAS HANNA, D. D.:

Was born near Kilmarnock, Ayershire, Scotland, August 14, 1806. His parents were exemplary members of the Covenanter Church, from whom he received the best training. He received the elements of an excellent education, and graduated from the University of Glasgow, Scotland, in 1832. He studied theology in the Paisley Seminary, was licensed by the Glasgow Presbytery, March 4, 1835, and preached with much acceptance in the vacancies of Scotland for six years. He came to America in the summer of 1841, and was received as a licentiate, by Synod, October 6, 1841. He was ordained by the Southern Presbytery, and installed pastor of the Conococheague congregation, Fayetteville, Franklin County, Pennsylvania, December 8, 1842, and resigned this charge, October 29, 1844, and was stated supply at Wilkinsburgh, Pennsylvania, in 1850. He was installed pastor of the Slippery Rock and Camp Run congregation, Rose Point, Lawrence County, Pennsylvania, November 17, 1852, and resigned this charge, October 29, 1861. For many years he resided in Allegheny City, Pennsylvania, and occasionally preached. He connected with the United Presbyterian Church, being received by the Stamford Presbytery of that body, October 10,

1872, and he removed to Williamsford, Ontario, Canada, where he preached as opportunity afforded. Here he died of an acute form of inflammation of the lungs, June 7, 1881, and was buried in the Presbyterian graveyard at Chatsworth, Canada. He was thrice married. First to Mrs. Elizabeth (Mowry) McCracken, of Allegheny, Pennsylvania; second to Miss Margaret Sproull, of the same city; and third to Miss Kate McGilvray, of Wellsville, Ohio. He was a theologian and scholar of no ordinary attainments, an acceptable preacher and a devoted student of the Bible. In the later years of his life he became eccentric, and his mind weakened. During his residence in Canada he conducted religious services in his own house, and in such places as the people would gather to hear him.

RUTHER HARGRAVE:

Son of John and Mary (Cranston) Hargrave, was born in Madrid, St. Lawrence County, New York, September 3, 1855. He received his early education in the Academy of Potsdam, New York, and graduated from Union College in 1882. He studied theology in the Allegheny Seminary, was licensed by the Rochester Presbytery, March 26, 1885, and labored in Barnesville and Moncton, New Brunswick, for several months. He was ordained by the Lakes Presbytery, and installed pastor of the United Miami congregation, Northwood, Logan County, Ohio, May 27, 1886, where he is in charge. He married Miss Eliza A. Ballantine, of Lisbon Centre, New York, September 15, 1886.

HUGH HAWTHORNE:

Son of John and Mary (Graham) Hawthorne, was born in Kilkinamurry, County Down, Ireland, June 17,

1805.*. His parents were consistent members of the Covenanter Church, and early directed his mind towards the Christian ministry. After passing through the accustomed studies in the national schools, he pursued the classics under the direction of his pastor, the Rev. John Stewart, and graduated from Belfast Academical Institution in 1828. He studied theology in Belfast, and in the Seminary of Paisley, Scotland; came to America in May, 1830, finished the course under the Rev. S. B. Wylie, D. D., of Philadelphia, Pennsylvania, and was licensed by the Philadelphia Presbytery, May 17, 1831. He preached in the vacancies with general acceptance for three years. He connected with the Dutch Reformed Church, November 8, 1834, and preached that winter in the vacant pulpits of Albany, New York, and in the summer of 1835, supplied vacancies in the city of New York and vicinity. He was drowned while bathing in a river in New York, July 16, 1836, and a monument is erected to his memory. He was an acceptable preacher, a kind and social man, and was held in high esteem by those to whom he ministered.

JOHN HAWTHORNE:

Son of John and Mary (Graham) Hawthorne, was born in Kilkinamurry, County Down, Ireland, December 7, 1795. He was reared in the strictest manner by a Covenanter parentage distinguished for faithfulness to the cause of the Reformation. He received his early education in the national schools and under private instructors, and graduated from the Royal Academical Institution of Belfast, Ireland, in 1818. He studied

---

* Communications from Ireland.

theology in the Seminary of Paisley, Scotland, and was licensed by the Northern Presbytery, Ireland, March 10, 1821. He was ordained by the Western Presbytery, and installed pastor of the congregation of Bellenon, County Armagh, Ireland, June 6, 1822, and resigned July 17, 1846. In April, 1847, he sailed, with his family, for America, and died of a fever, in quarantine at Quebec, Canada, May 14, 1847. His intention was to first settle among relatives and friends in Muskingum County, Ohio, and to spend the residue of his life in preaching in America. The Pittsburgh Presbytery forwarded a letter of condolence to the widow and fatherless children. He married Miss Ann E. Boggs, of Ballylane, Ireland, in 1823. He was a laborious and successful minister of the gospel, and regarded as a sound theologian, an instructive preacher and a pious Christian. The Church in this country anticipated the accession of an able minister.

JOSEPH HENDERSON:

Was born in Penpont, Dumfries Shire, Scotland, November 16, 1802. IIis mind was early directed towards the ministry, and after passing through the preparatory course of study, was graduated from the University of Glasgow, Scotland, in 1824. He studied theology in the Paisley Seminary, and was licensed by the Paisley Presbytery, March 17, 1827. He was ordained by the Western Presbytery, and installed pastor of the congregation of Ayr, Scotland, September 8, 1830, and was released from this charge, April 16, 1844, on account of intemperate habits. He came to America in the spring of 1849, and, after a full statement of his case, confession of his wrong, and promise of reformation, he was restored by the New York Presbytery, October 3, 1849. He preached with acceptance for a few years in the vacancies, especially in the Canadian societies, and taught in Walden, New York. While preaching in Hamilton, Canada, he forsook the cause he had espoused, and connected with the Free Church of Canada, April 11, 1854. He preached in that city and other parts of the Dominion, and died in Hamilton, Canada, August 10, 1872. He married Miss Elizabeth Gould, of Edinburgh, Scotland, in 1828. He was a preacher of considerable ability, but vacillating. He was instrumental in gathering many scattered members into societies. He was Moderator of the Scottish Synod of 1841.

JAMES RENWICK HILL, M. D.:

Son of James and Mary (Kinnier) Hill, was born near Stanton, Jefferson County, Pennsylvania, March 26, 1842. He received his preparatory course of study in the Brookville Academy, finished the course in the Elder's Ridge Academy, and graduated from Westminster College in 1869. He studied theology in the Allegheny Seminary, and was licensed by the Pittsburgh Presbytery, April 12, 1871. He was ordained by the Lakes Presbytery, installed pastor of the congregation of Southfield, Oakland County, Michigan, May 10, 1872, and resigned this charge, May 22, 1876, and missionated in other parts of Michigan. He was installed pastor of the congregation of St. Louis, Missouri, September 28, 1877, resigned, April 15, 1885, and removed to Utica, Ohio, and for some time he was engaged in supplying vacancies. He connected with the Presbyterian Church, being received by the Zanesville Presbytery, and was installed pastor of the congregation of Pataskala, Licking County, Ohio, July 21, 1887, where he is in charge. He married Miss Maggie A. Kirkpatrick, of Utica, Ohio, May 23, 1870. He received the degree of Doctor of Medicine from the Homeopathic Medical College of Missouri in 1885. Among his publications are, "The Man of the Future," 1880, pp. 40. "True Temperance, and the Conditions of its Success," 1882, pp. 43.

JOHN HOLMES:

Son of John and Margaret (Galbraith) Holmes, was born in Ryegate, Caledonia County, Vermont, May 14, 1801. His parents came from Scotland and were among the first Covenanters in New England. He was carefully trained by a pious parentage, and, being lame and unable to work upon the farm, was the object of peculiar parental solicitude, and devoted himself to study with the gospel ministry in view. He received a liberal education in the common schools, studied the classics under the direction of his pastor, the Rev. James Milligan, D. D., and attended the University of Vermont. He studied theology in the Seminary of Andover, Massachusetts, where he graduated, September 11, 1833. He was licensed by the Northern Presbytery, May 19, 1834, and he preached generally throughout the Church for eight years. In 1842, he bought a farm near Jordan's Grove, Randolph County, Illinois, which his family cultivated, and he engaged most of his time in teaching school. Here he died, of pneumonia and erysipelas, January 19, 1854. He married Miss Jennie C. Elder, of Coultersville, Illinois, June 8, 1842. He was a scholar of considerable ability and a very successful teacher. He was unappreciated as a preacher on account of his eccentric mannerisms, peculiar voice, and inelegant style of delivery. When he became warmed up in his discourse, he was very energetic in gesticulation, and exceedingly high in the tone of the voice. His manners and peculiar style of preaching were not in harmony with the popular mind, and he frequently offended his hearers. He was a fearless advocate for the cause of the slave, and an efficient agent upon the "Underground Railroad," when it was exceedingly unpopular and often dangerous to hold such a position. He was honest and upright in all his dealings, and was held in high esteem as a citizen. In the later years of his life he manifested little or no attachment for the Church, although a believer in the Christian religion, and died in faith.

JOHN HOOD:

Son of Archibald and Mary (Kirkpatrick) Hood, was born near Oakdale, Washington County, Illinois, November 11, 1837. He received his early education in the schools of his native County, graduating from the University of Indiana in 1862. He entered the union army, where he endured many hardships upon the battle field and in cruel prison life. He studied theology in the Allegheny Seminary, and was licensed by the Illinois Presbytery, April 21, 1869. He connected with the Presbyterian Church, being received by the Alton Presbytery of that body, and by this court ordained and installed pastor of the congregation of Sparta, Randolph County, Illinois, June 17, 1869, and resigned this charge, April 11, 1878. He was installed pastor of the congregation of Cedar Rapids, Iowa, October 16, 1878, and resigned in 1885, and is State Agent for the American Bible Society, with his residence in that city. He married Miss Mary A. E. Gault, of Sparta, Illinois, April 25, 1871.

JOSEPH HUNTER:

Son of Alexander and Betsy (Anderson) Hunter, was born in Freeport, Armstrong County, Pennsylvania, August 25, 1816. His parents were among the early Covenanters of that section, and in his infancy removed into Westmoreland County, were he was reared under the pastoral care of the Rev. John Cannon. His preparatory course of study was pursued under the direction of the Rev. Jonathan Gill, subsequently under the Rev. Hugh Walkinshaw, and he graduated from Duquesne College in 1847. He studied theology in the Cincinnati Seminary, and was licensed by the Pittsburgh Presbytery, April 16, 1850. He was ordained by the same Presbytery, and installed pastor of the congregation of Wilkinsburgh and Deer Creek, Allegheny County, Pennsylvania, April 13, 1852. The Deer Creek branch was subsequently dropped, and he continued at Wilkinsburgh until impaired health caused him to resign this charge, September 23, 1882. His health declined under an affection of the heart, which caused a dilatation of that organ, aggravated by pneumonia, causing his death, at his residence in Wilkinsburgh, Pennsylvania, January 6, 1884. He married Miss Mary

A. Dennison, of Pittsburgh, Pennsylvania, June 21, 1852. He was in many respects a popular preacher, and well known throughout the Church. His style was earnest and impressive; his disposition genial, his manner social, and he was in these respects peculiarly fitted for the pastoral office which he discharged with faithfulness. He was a devout and pious man, but not demonstrative in regard to religious experience.

JOSIAH JAMES HUSTON:

Son of John and Susannah (Craig) Huston, was born near Glenwood, Fayette County, Indiana, May 15, 1858. In 1865, his parents removed to Roscoe, Des Moines County, Iowa, where he received his early education. He attended the High School of Morning Sun, finished the course in the Academy of Washington, Iowa, in 1879, and graduated from Monmouth College in 1881. He studied theology in the Allegheny Seminary, was licensed by the Iowa Presbytery, April 9, 1884, and preached in the West and other parts of the Church. He was ordained by the Lakes Presbytery, and installed pastor of the congregation of Belle Centre, Logan County, Ohio, April 30, 1886, and also of Rushsylvania, same County, July 30, 1886. He resigned the Rushsylvania branch, April 9, 1888, and, with Belle Centre, supplies Bellefontaine. He married Miss Bella W. Maginness, of Allegheny City, Pennsylvania, March 15, 1887.

ROBERT HUTCHESON:

Son of James and Sarah (Martin) Hutcheson, was born near Loughgilly, County Armagh, Ireland, April 24, 1810. His parents were members of the Secession Church, and he received his early education in the schools of his native country. He came to America in the spring of 1829, and settled near Cambridge, Guernsey County, Ohio, where he connected with the Covenanter Church, under the pastoral care of the Rev. William Sloane. He pursued his classical studies under the care of his pastor, and, in 1836, repaired to Westmoreland County, Pennsylvania, where he resumed them under the direction of the Rev. Hugh Walkinshaw. He studied theology in the Allegheny Seminary, and was licensed by the Pittsburgh Presbytery, May 8, 1839. He was ordained *sine titulo* by the same Presbytery, as a Home Missionary, September 10, 1841. He was installed pastor of the congregation of Brush Creek, Adams County, Ohio, September 29, 1842, where he labored faithfully, until the congregation was so reduced by emigration, that he resigned the charge, May 21, 1856. He soon afterwards removed to Bremer County, Iowa, and served the Church as a Home Missionary for several years. He was instrumental in building up the congregation of Grove Hill, Bremer County, Iowa, over which he was installed pastor, April 17, 1863, and was released, May 8, 1867, remaining stated supply for two years. In 1869, he repaired to the new stations of the North-West Mission, and was stated supply respectively at Elliota, Lake Reno, and Round Prairie, Minnesota, for several years. In 1878, his health began to fail, and he removed to Washington, Iowa, where he died of general debility, April 1, 1880. He was twice married. First to Miss Jane Walkinshaw, of Lucesco, Pennsylvania, in 1840; and second, to Mrs. Jane C. (Coulter) Andrews, of Princeton, Illinois, November 15,

1865. He was an interesting and instructive preacher, but not a pleasing speaker. He was an excellent classical scholar, a close thinker, a natural logician, active in Church courts, faithful in the discharge of pastoral duties, and a most earnest and sincere Christian. He was a strict disciplinarian, and bore constant testimony against the evils of the State and the innovations of the Church. He contributed able articles to *McClintock and Strong's Encyclopedia*, and essays, in the form of critical exegesis, to the magazines of the Church.

JACOUB JERRIDINIA:

Son of Salloom Feyad and Helana (Korani) Jerridinia, was born in Showifat, Lebanon, Syria, March 17, 1837. By trade he was a soapmaker, and labored in his native town. In October, 1870, he became converted to the Christian religion, and attended the American Mission Schools at Showifat and Obey. He became a teacher in connection with the School at Antioch and Suadea, and subsequently repaired to Latakia. Here he studied theology under the direction of the Rev. Joseph Beattie, D. D., and was licensed to preach the gospel by the Commission of the Syrian Mission, March 1, 1882. He married Miss Helana Corani, of Showifat, Syria, September 15, 1885. Since 1882, he has been engaged in teaching and preaching principally in connection with the Mission at Suadea.

ARCHIBALD JOHNSTON:

Son of Gavin and Elizabeth (Hunter) Johnston, was born in Truro, Nova Scotia, August 16, 1793.* His parents were sturdy Covenanters from Hamilton,

* Principal items from Rev. Dr. David Steele, Sr., Philadelphia, Pa.

Scotland. They removed from Nova Scotia in 1805, and settled in Lancaster, Lancaster County, Pennsylvania, where he received his early education and engaged in the printing business. In 1808, he abandoned secular pursuits and began studies preparatory to the Christian ministry, in the Canonsburgh Academy, graduating from Jefferson College in 1813. He studied theology in the Philadelphia Seminary, and was licensed by the Middle Presbytery, April 9, 1817. He visited Nova Scotia during the summer of 1817, and, after returning in the fall, supplied vacancies in the East for a few months. His health becoming impaired, he retired to the home of his parents, who were then living near Chillicothe, Ohio. In March, 1818, he became stated supply to the congregation of Cincinnati, Ohio, where he died of consumption, October 26, 1818, while yet a licentiate. Upon his death bed he married Miss Fannie Ferguson, of Cincinnati, Ohio, October, 1818, as she wanted to be his widow. He was a young man of great mental power. His discourses were characterized by a classical accuracy of expression, high poetical imagination, and replete with evangelical truth that at once bespoke a soul possessed of a deep and strong current of religious feeling. His graphic power was remarkable. His descriptions were those of a master, and appealed to the heart and conscience with such magnetic power that the attention of the auditor was completely enchained. Dr. Alexander McLeod said, "The time for the millennium has not come, and the world cannot stand before Archibald Johnston." Dr. John Black said,

"Archibald Johnston was the most accomplished orator ever licensed in the Covenanter Church." He published a poem entitled "The Mariner," in 1817, which was composed while on his tour to Nova Scotia. He was directed by the Synod of 1817, to write an article for the Testimony upon Messiah's Headship, which he entitled "Regnum Lapidis, or The Kingdom of the Stone." For some unaccountable reason it was not published. His father found a copy of the original article long after the death of the author, and printed it in the *Contending Witness*, Xenia, Ohio, in 1841.

ARCHIBALD WARRISTON JOHNSTON, M. D.:

Son of Samuel P. and Eleanor (Thomson) Johnston, was born near Hopedale, Harrison County, Ohio, November 26, 1844. His parents removed to Belle Centre, Logan County, Ohio, in 1851, where he received his preparatory education in Geneva College, graduating from the University of Indiana in 1864. He studied theology in the Allegheny Seminary, and was licensed by the Lakes Presbytery, April 19, 1867. He was ordained by the New York Presbytery, and installed pastor of the congregation of Craftsbury, Orleans County, Vermont, August 5, 1868, and resigned this charge, October 31, 1871. He removed to the city of Philadelphia, Pennsylvania, and entered upon the study of medicine in Jefferson Medical College, and took the first honor of his class. He is a practicing physician in that city and preaches occasionally. He married Miss Mary A. Willson, of Allegheny City, Pennsylvania, April 20, 1869. He received the degree of Doctor of Medicine from Jefferson Medical College in 1875.

JOHN BLACK JOHNSTON, D. D.:

Son of Nathan and Mary (Black) Johnston, was born near Clarksburgh, Indiana County, Pennsylvania, March 13, 1802. His parents were consistent members of the Seceder Church. They removed to Hopedale, Harrison County, Ohio, in 1805, where they connected with the Covenanter Church under the ministry of the Rev. Robert Wallace, and were prominent members in the Greenfield congregation, now extinct. He received his early training in the schools of this vicinity, and, in 1823, began his classical studies in Jefferson College, and graduated from Franklin College in 1829. He studied theology under the direction of the Rev. John Black, D. D., of Pittsburgh, Pennsylvania, and was licensed by the Pittsburgh Presbytery, October 3, 1832. He was ordained by the Ohio Presbytery, and installed pastor of the Miami congregation, Northwood, Logan County, Ohio, June 10, 1834. In 1841, he opened a classical school in his own house, which grew into Geneva College in 1848. In 1851, he also founded the Geneva Female Seminary, and erected the buildings for both these institutions. He was Principal of the College from 1848 to 1850, and Professor of Theology from 1852 until 1856. He resigned all his charges, and connected with the United Presbyterian Church, being received by the Sidney Presbytery, November 10, 1858. He was installed pastor of the congregation of St. Clairsville, Ohio, May 17, 1859, where he continued to labor until impaired health caused him to resign the charge, June 9, 1874. In 1870, he was appointed Postmaster at St. Clairsville, and resigned this office in 1881. His health gradually declined until his death, at his home in St. Clairsville, Ohio, October 24, 1882. He was twice married. His first wife was Miss Sarah Bruce, of New Athens, Ohio, April 29, 1828; and his second, Miss Elizabeth Boyd, of Cherokee, Ohio, November 2, 1841. He was a man of marked ability, of indomitable courage, and unceasing in his efforts to establish Christian education within the reach of all. He was a profound theologian, an apt teacher, and a proficient scholar. As a preacher of the gospel, a writer in the magazines, a lecturer on reforms, a public debater, and member of Church courts, he was deservedly in high repute, and discharged many important offices with acceptance. He was a fearless advocate of the cause of the slave, and was a distinguished conductor on the "Underground Railroad." He was not only a pioneer in the establishment of the literary institution of the Church, but in the work of the Foreign Mission as well. In 1846, he was sent to Hayti by Synod, to explore that Island as a probable field for missionary operations, and was prominently connected with work in this direction. He was piously attached to the principles of the Covenanter Church, and only left her communion on account of internal dissentions which frequently mar the fellowship of brethern. He never fully abandoned the Covenanted cause, and was held in high esteem by the Church in which he closed his earthly career. He was honored with the degree of Doctor of Divinity by Franklin College in 1869. Among his many able and valuable publications are "The Signs of the

Times," 1858, pp. 27. "Psalmody," 1868, pp. 172. "The Prayer Meeting," 1870, pp. 260. He was Moderator of the Synod of 1845.

JOSIAH MELANCTHON JOHNSTON:

Son of James H. and Mary (Hemphill) Johnston, was born near New Alexandria, Westmoreland County, Pennsylvania, September 12, 1830. His parents were exemplary members of the Covenanter Church, from whom he received the best of religious instruction. After receiving the rudiments of a liberal education, he entered Geneva College, where he graduated in 1854. He studied theology in the Associate Reformed Seminary, and also in the Covenanter Seminary of Allegheny, Pennsylvania, and was licensed by the Pittsburgh Presbytery, April 21, 1858. He was ·ordained by the Rochester Presbytery, and installed pastor of the congregation of Syracuse, New York, May 13, 1859. He was appointed by Synod, September 9, 1865, to take charge of the Freedmen's Mission in Natchez, Mississippi. He resigned the Syracuse congregation and the Natchez Mission, August 17, 1866, and became Principal of the Mission School in Washington, District of Columbia. Here he taught and preached among the colored people until his resignation, May 27, 1870. He was installed pastor of the congregation of Parnassus, Westmoreland County, Pennsylvania, June 15, 1871, and resigned January 3, 1873. He connected with the United Presbyterian Church, and was installed pastor of the Central congregation of Allegheny City, Pennsylvania, January 10, 1873, and resigned, June 16, 1874. He was installed pastor of the Fifth congregation of

34

Pittsburgh, Pennsylvania, November 19, 1874, and resigned, October 16, 1878. He was installed pastor of the congregation of Morning Sun, Preble County, Ohio, April 1, 1879, where he died of a fever, July 3, 1881. He married Miss Emily C. Jameson, of Belle Centre, Ohio, June 1, 1854. He was a very popular preacher, easy in his manner, and fluent in his speech. He possessed the power to enchain the attention of an audience, not so much by the matter of his discourse, as by his happy style and eloquent delivery.

JAMES RENWICK JOHNSTON:

Son of Nathan and Mary (Hunter) Johnston, was born in Truro, Nova Scotia, March 24, 1800, while his parents were on their way from Scotland to the United States.* In 1805, his parents removed to Pennsylvania, where he received his early education, and graduated from Jefferson College in 1822. He studied theology in the Philadelphia Seminary, and was licensed by the Philadelphia Presbytery, May 24, 1824. He was ordained by the Northern Presbytery, installed pastor of the congregation of Newburgh, New York, September 16, 1825, resigned this charge, October 17, 1829, and connected with the Presbyterian Church. In 1830, he went to Mobile, Alabama, where he was a pastor for four years. He was installed pastor of the congregation of Goshen, Orange County, New York, May 21, 1835, and resigned this charge in 1840, being without charge for four years. He was installed pastor of the congregation of Hamptonburgh, Washington County, New York, October 8, 1844, and resigned in 1849. In

* Principally from *Presbyterian Historical Almanac*, Vol. 8, p. 119.

1854, he removed to the city of Philadelphia, Pennsylvania, and preached as frequently as his health would permit. In 1862, he removed to Burlington, New Jersey, where he died of general debility, June 16, 1865. He married Miss Margaret A. McLeod, of New York, New York, June 8, 1827. He was a man of superior mind and cultivation, and few possessed more of the elements of the true ministerial character. He was devout and courteous, and adapted himself and his discourses to the circumstances of his people. He lived a life of usefulness, was patient under long and severe personal affliction, and died in peace with God and men when his work was done.

LEWIS JOHNSTON: (COLORED.)

Son of Lewis and Jane (Brunson) Johnston, was born in the city of Allegheny, Pennsylvania, December 11, 1847. His parents were members of the Covenanter Church then under the pastoral care of Rev. Thomas Sproull, and, in 1853, removed to Temperanceville, a suburb of Pittsburgh, Pennsylvania, and, in 1858, to Blairsville, Pennsylvania, where he was employed in the coal mines, and attended the common schools as opportunity was afforded. In 1864, he entered the Union army, where he remained until the close of the war. In the summer of 1865, he returned to Blairsville and resumed his work as a miner. Soon afterwards he began his classical studies under Dr. A. M. Milligan, of New Alexandria, with the ministry in view. In 1867, he entered Geneva College, where he graduated in 1870. He studied theology in the Allegheny Seminary, and was licensed by the Pittsburgh Presbytery, April 8,

1873. He was ordained *sine titulo* by the same Presbytery, October 14, 1874, as a Missionary among the Freedmen at Selma, Alabama. He built up the flourishing school which is now Knox Academy, and was installed pastor of the congregation of Selma, Alabama, May 21, 1875. He was suspended from the exercise of the ministerial office and privileges in the Church, November 14, 1876. He soon afterwards went to Little Rock, Arkansas, where he taught school for many years. In 1882, he turned his attention to the land agency, was clerk in the court, and employed in a newspaper office. He was restored to the exercise of his ministerial functions by the Pine Bluff Presbytery of the Presbyterian Church, May 24, 1883, engaged in mission work, and began the publication of the *Pine Bluff Reformer*. Since March 1, 1886, he is engaged in organizing Schools and Churches throughout the destitute portions of Arkansas. He married Miss Mercy A. Taborn, of Marysville, Ohio, March 2, 1870. He was the first colored Covenanter minister ever ordained.

NATHAN McMILLAN JOHNSTON:

Son of Samuel P. and Eleanor (Thomson) Johnston, was born near Hopedale, Harrison County, Ohio, March 23, 1832. He received his early education in the schools of his native County, and, in 1851, removed to Belle Centre, Logan County, Ohio. He resumed his studies in Geneva College, and, in the fall of 1858, entered the University of Michigan. He studied theology in the Allegheny Seminary, and was licensed by the Pittsburgh Presbytery, April 14, 1863. He was ordained by the same Presbytery, installed pastor of the Little Beaver congregation, New Galilee, Beaver County, Pennsylvania, April 14, 1864, and resigned this charge, June 3, 1886. He was installed pastor of the congregation of Eskridge, Wabaunsee County, Kansas, August 4, 1886, where he is in charge, and lectures in the interests of the National Reform Association. He married Miss Annie J. Hammond, of St. Clairsville, Ohio, August 4, 1857.

NATHAN ROBINSON JOHNSTON:

Son of Nathan and Mary (Black) Johnston, was born near Hopedale, Harrison County, Ohio, October 8, 1820. He received his early education in Richmond Academy, pursued the classical course in Miami University, and graduated from Franklin College in 1843. For two years he was Principal of the Academy of St. Clairsville, Ohio. In the fall of 1845, he began the study of theology in the Cincinnati Seminary, where he continued three sessions. In 1848, he was editor of the *Free Press*, an anti-slavery paper, published in New Concord, Ohio. In the fall of 1849, he resumed his theological studies in the Northwood Seminary, and was licensed by the Lakes Presbytery, April 29, 1850. He was ordained by the New York Presbytery, and installed pastor of the congregation of Topsham, Orange County, Vermont, November 10, 1852. In 1863, he was appointed by Synod as a Missionary to the contrabands of Port Royal, South Carolina. He resigned the Topsham congregation, May 16, 1865, and removed to Northwood, Ohio, where he resuscitated Geneva College, and was the Principal of that institution for two years. In the spring of 1867, he opened an

Academy in New Castle, Pennsylvania, and subse
quently in Blairsville and New Brighton. In 1871, he
was chosen a Professor in Geneva College, but resigned
May 28, 1872, and became a Home Missionary in
Elliota, and other parts of Minnesota. In 1875, he went
to California, and opened a Mission School among the
Chinese at Oakland, where he has built up a congregation, is a contributor to several papers, and is
actively engaged in the work of evangelizing the
Chinese of the Pacific coast. He married Miss Rosa-
mond Rodgers, of Albany, Vermont, March 1, 1861.

ROBERT JOHNSON:

Son of Robert and Margaret (Anderson) Johnson,
was born in Killygore, County Antrim, Ireland, November 17, 1810. He received the rudiments of a classical
education under the direction of his pastor, the Rev.
Clarke Houston, D. D., graduating from the Belfast
Academical Institution in 1836, with the honorary
degree of Master of Arts. He studied theology in the
Seminary of Paisley, Scotland, and was licensed by the
Northern Presbytery, Ireland, May 17, 1839. He was
ordained by a Commission of the Irish Synod, and
installed pastor of the mission congregation of Manchester, England, August 4, 1842, and resigned this
charge, April 9, 1849. The same spring he came to
America, and was received by Synod, May 23, 1849.
He was installed pastor of the congregation of Toronto,
Canada, November 4, 1852, and resigned, April 10,
1859. He was installed pastor of the congregation of
Vernon, Waukesha County, Wisconsin, November 7,
1859, and resigned this charge, December 17, 1867.

He was installed pastor of the congregation of Kossuth, Des Moines County, Iowa, January 7, 1868, and resigned on account of seriously impaired health, July 27, 1875. For several years he suffered from nephritic, and with intervals of partial cessation of extreme pain, his disease continued until it took an acute form, from which he died, at his home near Kossuth, Iowa, July 27, 1879. He never married. He was a man of excellent attainments both in literature and theology. He was able and eloquent as a preacher, warm-hearted and genial as a friend, pious and devout as a Christian. He was thoroughly indoctrinated in the gospel, took great delight in the sacred traditions of a martyred ancestry, and earnestly defended the principles and testimony of the Covenanter Church. He was a bold witness against the abounding evils of the day. While preaching in Toronto, Canada, he delivered a course of lectures to crowded houses against the Roman Catholic Church. Bishop Charbonnel denounced him in the Cathedral as a black heretic, worse than Satan, and warned the people against going to hear the "Villifier of the Holy Mother Church." The enraged priests at Rome sent him threatening letters, among others one with the picture of a coffin with a black seal, and under it the words, "*hic jacet.*" The Protestants of the city held him in high esteem as the champion for truth. His principal publications are, "The Absurdities of the Popish Dogma of the Immaculate Conception," 1855, pp. 73, and "Instrumental Music in Public Worship," 1871, pp. 80.

SAMUEL DELLMORE JOHNSTON:

Son of Rev. Nathan M. and Annie J. (Hammond) Johnston, was born near Belle Centre, Logan County, Ohio, April 17, 1862. His parents removed to New Galilee, Beaver County, Pennsylvania, in 1864, where he received his early education in the public schools. In the fall of 1877, he entered Geneva College, where he remained two years. He resumed his studies in, and graduated from, Geneva College in 1884. He studied theology in the Allegheny Seminary, was licensed by the Pittsburgh Presbytery, April 12, 1887, and preached for six months in Houlton, Maine. He was an editor of the *College Cabinet* two years beginning in 1882.

WILLIAM POLLOCK JOHNSTON:

Son of Samuel P. and Eleanor (Thomson) Johnston, was born near Hopedale, Harrison County, Ohio, January 26, 1839. He received his early education in this vicinity, and, in 1851, removed to Belle Centre, Logan County, Ohio. He entered Geneva College, where he remained until his senior year, graduating from Jefferson College in 1858. He studied theology in the Allegheny Seminary, and was licensed by the Lakes Presbytery, May 22, 1862. He was ordained by the Philadelphia Presbytery, installed pastor of the congregation of Baltimore, Maryland, August 4, 1864, and resigned this charge, July 13, 1873. He was installed pastor of the congregation of Washington, Iowa, October 10, 1873, and, in the fall of 1879, was chosen Principal of the Washington Academy. He resigned these charges, August 4, 1881, and accepted the chair of Latin and English Literature in Geneva College, Beaver Falls, Pennsylvania, and sub-sequently was appointed college pastor, which positions he now occupies. He married Miss Clara D. Anderson, of Washington, Iowa, June 17, 1874. He is a con-tributor to the *Geneva Cabinet.*

JOHN KELL:

Son of John and Jane (Morton) Kell, was born near Rocky Creek, Chester District, South Carolina, October 19, 1772.* Among the notable events of his childhood was the fact that his mother hid him and his little brother in the bushes, lest they would be burned with the house by the British soldiers. His youthful days were spent in labor upon his father's farm, and, in 1790, he began preparatory studies, with the ministry in view, in the classical school of Mr. John Orr. In 1801, he crossed the ocean and entered the University of Glasgow, Scotland, where he graduated in 1805. He studied theology in the Seminary of Stirling, Scotland, under the Rev. John McMillan, and, after visiting Ireland, returned to America in the fall of 1808. He was licensed by the Middle Presbytery, June 18, 1809, and was assigned to preach among the scattered societies in the West and South. He was ordained *sine titulo* by the Southern Presbytery, December 4, 1811, and missionated for four years in South Carolina, Tennessee, and in parts of Ohio, Indiana and Illinois. He was installed pastor of the Beech Woods congregation, Morning Sun, Preble County, Ohio, April 3, 1816, and resigned this charge, October 6, 1819. He was installed pastor of the con-

---

* Sprague's Annals.

gregation of Princeton, Gibson County, Indiana, June 21, 1820. At the division of the Church in August, 1833, he became identified with the New School branch of the Covenanter Church, and remained pastor of a portion of his former flock, until his resignation, September 24, 1838. He spent the residue of his life in preaching in vacancies as his health would permit, and died of an affection of the heart, at his home in Princeton, Indiana, November 6, 1842. He married Miss Jane Hartin, of Beech Woods, Ohio, November 10, 1811. In person he was large and portly, and in his youth was quite an athlete. He was a good scholar, and an instructive preacher. He was not an eloquent speaker, but there was an unction about his preaching that never failed to make an impression. His life was largely that of a Missionary, and to his untiring ministrations many congregations owe their existence. He constantly realized the responsibilities of the ministerial office, and discarded all books but the Bible, from the rich treasures of which he fed the people. He was a dauntless pioneer of the West, engaged in visiting lonely societies and families in the depths of the then wilderness, and brought to them the glad tidings of salvation. He was Moderator of the Synod of 1812.

GEORGE KENNEDY:

Son of Rev. James and Eliza (Conn) Kennedy, * * * He came to New York in 1870, and graduated from Columbia College in 1874. He studied theology in the Allegheny Seminary, and was licensed by the New York Presbytery, May 16, 1877. He was ordained by the Lakes Presbytery, installed pastor of the

United Miami congregation, Northwood, Logan County, Ohio, May 23, 1878, and resigned this charge, June 15, 1882. He accepted the chair of Greek in Geneva College, September 9, 1882, which position he now occupies. He is an occasional contributor to the *Genevan* and Church magazines, and is College librarian.

JAMES KENNEDY:

Son of George and Mary (Paul) Kennedy, was born near Bonn, County Londonderry, Ireland, August 15, 1818. He received his early training in the classical school of the Rev. James Bryce, and graduated from the Belfast Academical Institution in 1840. He studied theology in the Seminary of Paisley, Scotland, and was licensed by the Northern Presbytery, Ireland, May 10, 1842. He was ordained by the Western Presbytery, and installed pastor of the united congregations of Broadlane and Drimbolg, Newtonlimavady, County Londonderry, Ireland, May 18, 1843, and resigned this charge, August 2, 1870. He came to America the same summer, and was installed pastor of the Fourth congregation of New York City, New York, November 13, 1870, where he is in charge. He married Miss Eliza Conn, of Coleraine, Ireland, May 9, 1848. He published "Tekel," 1858, pp. 40. "Assurance of Grace and Salvation," 1877, pp. 48. He contributed a series of articles on "The Spiritual Senses" to *Our Banner*, 1878, and an exposition of the Sabbath School Lessons to the *Christian Nation*, 1885, and many other articles in the Church papers and magazines. He was Moderator of the Irish Synod in 1846, and of the American Synod in 1875.

JOSHUA KENNEDY, D. D.:

Son of James and Catharine (Cannon) Kennedy, was born in Newtonlimavady, County Londonderry, Ireland, August 22, 1815. He came with his parents to America in 1823, and settled near Shady Grove, Franklin County, Pennsylvania, where he received his early education in the Green Castle Academy, and graduated from Union College in 1841. He studied theology in the Allegheny Seminary, and was licensed by the Illinois Presbytery, May 12, 1844. He was ordained by the New York Presbytery, and installed pastor of the Conococheague congregation, Fayetteville, Franklin County, Pennsylvania, November 5, 1845. In 1852, he established the Fayetteville Academy, which was a flourishing school for many years. He resigned these charges, May 1, 1860, and during the war of the rebellion was a Missionary and Chaplain in Fernandina, Florida, and other parts of the South. He was installed pastor of the congregation of Bovina, Delaware County, New York, January 11, 1865, and resigned this charge on account of seriously impaired health, May 20, 1885. In the fall of 1885, he removed to Green Castle, Pennsylvania, where he is living in infirm health. He married Miss Mary J. Bell, of Carlisle, Pennsylvania, October 8, 1847.

ALEXANDER KILPATRICK:

Son of Daniel and Mary (McCaughan) Kilpatrick, was born in Bloomington, Monroe County, Indiana, January 20, 1847. His father was a member of the Presbyterian Church, and the family removed to Linton, Des Moines County, Iowa, in the fall of 1852, and connected with the Covenanter Church. He received his early education in the Morning Sun Academy, Iowa, also in Monmouth College, graduating from the University of Indiana in 1871, and taught school in Kansas one year. He studied theology in the Allegheny Seminary, and was licensed by the Pittsburgh Presbytery, April 14, 1875. He was ordained by the same Presbytery, and installed pastor of the united congregations of Pine Creek and Union, Valencia, Butler County, Pennsylvania, May 17, 1876, where he is in charge. He married Miss Ella Davidson, of Valencia, Pennsylvania, September 4, 1877.

WILLIAM KING:

Was born in Donegal, Donegal County, Ireland, January 6, 1747.* He received a liberal education in the schools of his native town, and graduated from the University of Glasgow, Scotland, in 1782. He studied theology in the Seminary of Stirling, Scotland, and privately, being licensed by the Reformed Presbytery of Scotland, March 16, 1784, and preached in Coleraine, County Londonderry, Ireland, for seven years. He was ordained *sine titulo* by the Reformed Presbytery of Scotland, at Wishaw, June 4, 1792, as a Missionary to America, sailing from Greenock for Charleston, South Carolina, in the brig "Samuel," July 10, 1792, and, in the fall of this year, settled in the Chester District, South Carolina. In 1793, he made a tour among the societies of Covenanters in the North and East, returned to South Carolina, and took charge of the Beaver Dam congregation in the spring of 1794. He labored, how-

---

* Communications from Ireland.

ever, among all the societies in the Carolinas, and, for the greater part of his time, was alone in the work. He faithfully discharged all the duties encumbent upon him by the Scottish Presbytery, and insisted upon the people freeing themselves from the sin of slavery. He was invited to meet a Committee from the North to organize the Reformed Presbytery in Alexandria, Virginia, in May, 1798, but on account of serious illness he was not permitted to meet his brethren, and died at his home in the Chester District, South Carolina, August 24, 1798. He married Miss Nancy Neil, of Chester, South Carolina, September, 1794. He was a most amiable and peaceful man ; a faithful and instructive preacher ; a scholar of considerable ability and well acquainted with the science of theology. He was a true Christian and a Covenanter of undaunting courage and sterling integrity.

WASHINGTON ROBERT LAIRD :

Son of Robert W. and Harriet M. (Angier) Laird, was born in Danville, Caledonia County, Vermont, April 22, 1855. He received his early education in the common schools, and in the Academy of McIndoes Falls, Vermont, graduating from Geneva College in 1876. He studied theology in the Allegheny Seminary, and was licensed by the New York Presbytery, May 27, 1879. He was ordained by the New York Presbytery, installed pastor of the congregation of St. Johnsbury, Vermont, June 15, 1880, and resigned May 1, 1888. He was installed pastor of the congregation of New Castle, Pennsylvania, May 8, 1888, where he is in charge. He married Miss Fannie E. Hadfield, of Allegheny City, Pennsylvania, August 23, 1877.

JAMES ROSS LATIMER:

Son of Samuel and Margaret (Smith) Latimer, was born in Bloomington, Monroe County, Indiana, July 14, 1851. He received his early education in the common schools of his native city, and graduated from the University of Indiana in 1873. He studied theology in the Allegheny Seminary two years, and taught Greek in Geneva College; resumed his studies in the Allegheny Seminary, and was licensed by the Lakes Presbytery, April 10, 1878. He was ordained by the Ohio Presbytery, and installed pastor of the congregation of Londonderry, Guernsey County, Ohio, May 19, 1880, and of the congregation of North Salem, same County, October 10, 1880. He resigned these charges, May 27, 1882. He was installed pastor of the Hebron congregation, Idana, Clay County, Kansas, August 18, 1882, where he is in charge. He married Miss Mary E. Copeland, of Clay Centre, Kansas, April 16, 1883.

JAMES REID LAWSON:

Son of James and Elizabeth (Reid) Lawson, was born in Rathfriland, County Down, Ireland, May 23, 1820. He received his early education in the schools of his native vicinity, and graduated from the Belfast Academical Institution in 1841. He studied theology in the Seminary of Paisley, Scotland, and was licensed by the Southern Presbytery, Ireland, March 4, 1845. He was ordained *sine cura* by the same Presbytery, September 18, 1845, as a Missionary to the British North American Provinces. He arrived in St. John, New Brunswick, the same fall, and, after visiting different parts of the Maritime Provinces, settled in South Stream, now Barnesville,.Kings County, New Brunswick, in the spring of 1846, when there were only two Covenanters in that vicinity. Here he labored faithfully for ten years, and gathered a congregation, which he resigned October 17, 1856. He was installed pastor of the congregation of Boston, Massachusetts, November 20, 1856, and resigned, October 22, 1857. He returned to Barnesville, New Brunswick, where he continued to labor until partial paralysis caused his resignation, April 12, 1882, and he is infirm health. He married Miss Margaret Hastings, of St. John, New Brunswick, July 1, 1851. In May, 1880, he began the publication of the *Advocate*, a monthly religious magazine. Among his published writings are : " The Character of Joseph, or The Young Man's Model," 1855, pp. 21. " The Millennium," 1864, pp. 24. " Correspondence on Psalmody with the Editor of the *St. John Telegraph*," 1880, pp. 42. " The British Elective Franchise," 1884, pp. 22, two editions.

MATTHEW LINN :

Son of Matthew Linn, was born at Corkermaine, near Cairn Castle, County Antrim, Ireland, August 10, 1731.* He was of Scotch parentage and a tiller of the soil. Brought up in the strictest manner by a Covenanter parentage, he received a careful religious training, and the elements of an education in the schools of that vicinity and under private instructors. In the spring of 1757, he was ordained a ruling elder, and the same fall entered the University of Glasgow, Scotland, where he graduated in 1760. He studied theology with the ministers of the Presbytery, and was licensed by the

---

* Sprague's Annals. Communications from Ireland.

Reformed Presbytery of Scotland, July 16, 1761. He was ordained at the organization of the Reformed Presbytery of Ireland, at Vow, and installed pastor of the societies of Bannside, Limavady and Aghadowey, County Londonderry, Ireland, August 21, 1763. After ten years of faithful labor in his native country, he was appointed to accompany Rev. Alexander Dobbin as a Missionary to America, and arrived in New Castle, Delaware, December 13, 1773. He, with Revs. John Cuthbertson and Alexander Dobbin, organized the Reformed Presbytery of America, at Paxtang, Dauphin County, Pennsylvania, March 10, 1774, at which time he was assigned to preach to the Churches of Paxtang, Dauphin County, and Stoney Ridge, Cumberland County, Pennsylvania. He abandoned the Covenanted cause and went into the Associate Reformed Church at its formation, November 1, 1782. In 1783, he removed to Franklin County, Pennsylvania, where he became pastor of the united congregations of Green Castle, Chambersburg, West Conococheague and the Great Cove. In 1797, he was thrown from his horse, and so seriously injured that he became unfit for ministerial duty, and resigned his charges, March 13, 1798. He died from a disease brought on by his injuries, at his home near Green Castle, Franklin County, Pennsylvania, April 21, 1800, and was buried in the old graveyard at Brown's Mills. He married a cousin of Robert Fulton, of steamboat fame, Miss Jennett Fulton, of County Antrim, Ireland, in 1769. He was large and corpulent in person, comely in his appearance, and winning in his manners. He was a laborious student all his life. He was an eloquent

35

speaker, and large audiences had their attention astonishingly rivited for hours, while with marked ability he unfolded the truths of the gospel. In private life he was an ornament to the Christian religion, and recommended the doctrines he so powerfully proclaimed by the silent energy of an eminently holy and exemplary life.

JOHN LITTLE:

Son of James and Esther (Allen) Little, was born in Ouley, County Down, Ireland, June 17, 1823. His parents were active and exemplary members of the Covenanter Church, by whom he was religiously instructed and dedicated to God for the gospel ministry. He received his preparatory literary studies in the schools of Rathfriland, graduating from the Belfast Academical Institution in 1843. He studied theology in the Seminary of Paisley, Scotland, and was licensed by the Southern Presbytery, Ireland, March 8, 1848. The same fall he came to America, was ordained by the New York Presbytery, and installed pastor of the Third congregation of New York City, New York, June 5, 1849. For causing defection and abandoning his charge, he was suspended by the New York Presbytery, April 20, 1852. He connected with the Presbyterian Church, and was received by the Presbytery of the City of New York, February 9, 1853. He preached but a short time, when, becoming despondent, he sickened and died in great distress, January 2, 1855. He never married. He was a diligent student, a clear and logical reasoner, an interesting and eloquent preacher. Being of a genial and open-hearted disposition, of an ambitious turn of mind, he was lead away from the faith of the Covenanter Church by a false knowledge of himself and the persuasion of a few admiring followers.

JAMES LOVE:

Son of David and Eleanor (Stevenson) Love, was born in Strasburgh, Franklin County, Pennsylvania, January 29, 1799. In the fall of 1800, his parents removed to Washington County, Pennsylvania, where he pursued his studies in the common schools and prepared himself for teaching, which vocation he followed for many years. He soon afterwards began the study of the classics with a view to the ministry under the direction of Rev. Samuel Ralston, D. D., a Presbyterian minister. In the fall of 1835, he began the study of theology under the direction of Rev. Thomas Sproull in Allegheny, Pennsylvania, and was licensed by the Pittsburgh Presbytery, April 10, 1838. He was ordained by the same Presbytery, and installed pastor of the united congregations of Greenfield and Londonderry, Guernsey County, Ohio, June 27, 1839. His field of labor here was very extensive, including the mission stations of McMahon's Creek, thirty-six miles distant, and Steubenville, forty-five miles from his home, and these wearisome journeys were made upon horseback through all kinds of weather. He resigned the Greenfield branch, May 11, 1847, and the Londonderry charge, October 6, 1864. In the spring of 1865, he removed to Monroe County, Iowa, and began a mission station with eight members, which soon grew into a congregation. He was installed pastor of this, the Albia congregation, now Hickory Grove, Avery, Monroe County, Iowa, May 16, 1866, and resigned on account of impaired health and old age, September 13, 1881. He removed to Morning Sun, Louisa County, Iowa, where he lived in retirement until his death of old age, November 12, 1886. He was twice married. First to Miss Jeanette Glenn, of Franklin County, Pennsylvania, in 1823 ; and second, to Miss Susan French, of California, Michigan, in 1868. He was a strong and valiant soldier of the Cross, endured many hardships and suffered many deprivations in proclaiming the gospel in new settlements. He possessed a large physique, a robust constitution, and retained his mental powers unimpaired until his death. He was a good classical scholar, a sound theologian and a forcible preacher.

ROBERT LUSK :

Son of William and Elizabeth (Holliday) Lusk, was born near the city of Londonderry, Ireland, March 8, 1781.* He came with his parents to America in 1792, and settled in Cumberland County, Pennsylvania. In early life he manifested a thirst for knowledge, which could not be gained very extensively in the primitive schools of his adopted neighborhood, and, in 1804, he repaired to the Academy of Greensburgh, Pennsylvania, where he received his preparatory course of study, and graduated from Jefferson College in 1810. He studied theology in the Philadelphia Seminary, and was licensed by the Middle Presbytery, May 9, 1814. He was ordained by the same Presbytery, and installed pastor of the Conococheague congregation, Chambersburgh, Franklin County, Pennsylvania, June 16,

---

* Items principally from the Rev. Dr. David Steele, Sr., Philadelphia, Pa.

1816, and resigned this charge, October 15, 1823. He was installed pastor of the congregation of Walnut Ridge, Washington County, Indiana, October 7, 1824. Upon the charge of having defrauded a neighbor, he was suspended by the authority of Synod, August 10, 1825. These weighty charges were thoroughly investigated by a Commission of Synod, and he was restored to his ministerial functions, October 15, 1834, and re-installed pastor of Walnut Ridge, May 9, 1835. He left the communion of the Church, June 24, 1840, and joined the Reformed Presbytery, and his name was stricken from the roll by the authority of Synod, September 18, 1840. He preached in the vicinity of his home as often as his health would permit, and died of erysipelas, December 14, 1845. He was twice married. First to Miss Margaret Thomson, of Conococheague, Pennsylvania, in 1816; and second, to Miss Mary Reid, of Walnut Ridge, Indiana, in 1824. He was not considered a pleasing speaker, yet he was a very instructive preacher and gifted in prayer. His literary acquisitions were both general and accurate, and he was a reputable scholar in science and medicine. In his pulpit exhibitions he had a style peculiarly his own, and aimed to "speak by punctuation and paragraphs." He was a diligent student of prophecy, and in this connection noted carefully the events of Providence. He published "Characteristics of the Witnessing Church," and "Characteristics of Surrounding Communities," in the *Contending Witness*, 1843. He was Moderator of the Synod of 1817.

JOHN LYND:

Son of Andrew and Rosa (Gilmore) Lynd, was born in Knockaduff, County Londonderry, Ireland, March 24, 1850. He received his preparatory course of literary training in the Aghadoey Classical School, and in the Coleraine Academy, graduating with honor from Magee College in 1871. He studied theology two sessions in Magee College, and one session in the Belfast Seminary. He came to America in April, 1873, and was licensed by the New York Presbytery, May 20, 1873. He was ordained by the Philadelphia Presbytery, installed pastor of the congregation of Baltimore, Maryland, December 4, 1873, resigned this charge, November 6, 1877, and accepted the chair of Greek and English Literature in Geneva College, Northwood, Ohio. He was also installed pastor of the congregation of Belle Centre, Logan County, Ohio, January 5, 1879. He resigned the professorate at the removal of the College, May 26, 1880, was installed pastor of the congregation of Rushsylvania, Logan County, Ohio, August 12, 1880, and resigned these united charges, April 14, 1885. He returned to Ireland in May, 1885, and was installed pastor of the Ballylaggan congregation, Ballymoney, County Antrim, Ireland, June 5, 1885, where he is in charge. He married Miss Belle Purvis, of Baltimore, Maryland, April 8, 1875. He was Moderator of the Irish Synod of 1886.

CAMPBELL MADDEN, M. D.:

Was born in Coleraine, County Londonderry, Ireland, September 8, 1795.* He received his early

---

* Communications from Ireland. Sprague's Annals.

education in the Coleraine Academy, graduating from the University of Glasgow, Scotland, in 1816. He studied theology privately, and was licensed by the Northern Presbytery, Ireland, June 1, 1819. He came to America in the fall of 1820, and settled in the Chester District, South Carolina. Having studied medicine in Glasgow, Scotland, for several sessions, he resumed his course in the College of Physicians and Surgeons, in Lexington, Kentucky, and finished the prescribed course with first honors. He returned to South Carolina, was ordained by the Southern Presbytery, and installed pastor of the Beaver Dam congregation, Chester District, June 18, 1822, where he preached and practiced medicine until his early decease. He possessed a fine physical constitution, but he was not cautious of the Southern climate, and, being constantly exposed to all kinds of weather in the performance of his professional duties, he was attacked with fever and ague, followed by repeated and severe hemorrhages of the lungs, from which he died, at his home in the Chester District, South Carolina, August 12, 1828. He married Miss Margaret Cathcart, of Chester, South Carolina, in 1821. He was a very useful man and an acceptable preacher of the gospel. He possessed a mind of considerable culture, and his reasoning was clear and logical. His voice was feeble, but he spoke with such distinctness and pathos that he never failed to interest and instruct his hearers. Modesty was a notable trait of his character, and he only failed to boldly denounce the evils of slavery more frequently than he did because he felt he was a stranger in this land. He received the degree of Doctor of Medicine from the College of Physicians and Surgeons, Lexington, Kentucky, in 1821.

DANIEL CARGILL MARTIN:

Son of John and Margaret (Dodds) Martin, was born near Eastbrook, Lawrence County, Pennsylvania, November 15, 1841. He received his preparatory course of study in what is now Grove City College, graduating from Westminster College in 1868. He studied theology in the Allegheny Seminary, was licensed by the Pittsburgh Presbytery, April 12, 1870, and, under appointment of the Central Board of Missions, he spent some time in exploring the Pacific coast from San Jose, California, to Vancouver's Island, gathering scattered Covenanters into societies. He was ordained by the Illinois Presbytery, installed pastor of the congregation of Princeton, Gibson County, Indiana, November 7, 1872, and resigned this charge, April 12, 1888. He is residing at Pine Creek Station, near the city of Allegheny, Pennsylvania. He married Miss Lucretia Mott McIntosh, of Allegheny City, Pennsylvania, September 22, 1869.

WILLIAM MARTIN:

Son of David Martin, was born at Ballyspollen, near Ballykelley, County Londonderry, Ireland, May 16, 1729.* In 1750, he entered the University of Glasgow, Scotland, where he graduated in 1753. He studied theology under the direction of the Rev. John McMillan, and was licensed by the Reformed Presbytery of Scotland, October 10, 1756. He was the first Covenanter minister ordained in Ireland, this act taking place at Vow,

---

* Communications from Ireland. Irish Testimony.

on the lower Bann, and he was installed pastor of the societies centering in Ballymoney, County Antrim, Ireland, July 13, 1757. In 1760, the societies were divided into two congregations, separated by the river, he chosing Kellswater congregation, and lived for many years in Bangor. He came to America with a colony of his people in 1772, and settled on Rocky Creek, Chester District, South Carolina, where he bought a tract of land one mile square, and his people took up bounty land. He was the first Covenanter minister settled in the South. In 1774, his people built a church two miles east of Catholic, where he preached, and was dismissed in 1777, on account of intemperate habits. His adherents built another church near by, which was burnt by the British in 1780. He suffered many annoyances from the British and Tories, and taught his people to fight for their liberty as *Americans*. In the spring of 1781, he went to Mecklenberg, North Carolina, on account of the disturbed state of the country in the Chester District, and, after the surrender of Lord Cornwallis at Yorktown, October 9, 1781, he returned to South Carolina, and resumed his charge around Catholic. In 1785, he was again dismissed for his conduct, and his services became unacceptable to the people. In 1793, he was restored to his privileges, and was made a member of the Committee of the Reformed Presbytery of Scotland, with Revs. King and McGarragh, to judicially manage the affairs of the Church in America. He continued to preach at the Jackson's Creek Church, Wolf Pen or Wolf Pit Meeting-House, Winnsboro, and at private houses in all the settlements between Statesville, North Carolina, and Louisville, Georgia. Co-incident with his good preaching he continued his bad habit until the meeting of the Reformed Presbytery of America, when seven charges were brought against him, among which were habitual drinking and the holding of slaves, and he was deposed from the ministerial office by that court, March 12, 1801.* He did not cease preaching, however, until shortly before his death. He sold all his land, and made over his effects to his relatives. He died of a fever, brought on by an injury received by falling from his horse, October 25, 1806, and he was buried in a small graveyard near his cabin. He was married three times, but the names of his wives are unknown. He was a large, fine-looking man, a proficient scholar, an eloquent preacher, and an able divine.

DAVID McALLISTER, D. D., LL. D.:

Son of David and Mary A. (Scott) McAllister, was born in the city of New York, New York, August 25, 1835. He received his early education in the public schools and learned the printing business. Resuming his studies under the direction of the Rev. J. B. Williams, of White Lake, New York, he graduated from Union College in 1860. He studied theology in the Allegheny Seminary, and one session in the Union Seminary, New York, being licensed by the New York Presbytery, May 20, 1863. He was ordained by the same Presbytery, and installed pastor of the congregation of Walton, Delaware County, New York, December 16, 1863, and resigned, September 6, 1871,

---

* Minutes of Reformed Presbytery.

and accepted the appointment of Secretary of the National Reform Association, in which capacity he was employed four years. He was re-installed pastor of Walton, June 23, 1875, and resigned, October 24, 1883, and accepted the chair of Political Science and History in Geneva College, Beaver Falls, Pennsylvania. He resigned this professorate, and was installed pastor of the congregation of Pittsburgh, Pennsylvania, October 21, 1887, where he is in charge. He married Miss Mary A. King, of New York City, New York, November 25, 1863. He was one of the founders and an editor of the *Christian Statesman* since 1867; Vice President of Geneva College four years; Treasurer of the National Reform Association; Member of the Board of Superintendents of the Theological Seminary, and also of the Foreign Mission. Among his numerous publications the most note-worthy are: "The National Reform Manual," 1871. "Christianity and Civil Government," 1888, pp. 400. He was honored with the degree of Doctor of Divinity by Muskingum College in 1884, and that of Doctor of Laws by Franklin College in 1884. He was Moderator of the Synod of 1880.

JOHN McAULEY:

Son of Daniel and Martha (Davis) McAuley, was born near Wytheville, Wythe County, Virginia, January 6, 1807.* His grandparents came from Scotland, in 1774, as members of the Mecklenberg Colony, and settled near Charlotte, North Carolina. His father was an elder in the Presbyterian Church, the family being brought up in that faith, and returned to North

---

* Rev. Robert Bruce in *Associate Presbyterian.*

Carolina in 1819. He received his early education in Charlotte, North Carolina, attended the High School of Christiansburgh, Virginia, and graduated from Greenville College, Tennessee, in 1833. While at College his outspoken condemnations of the institution of slavery would have prevented him from receiving a diploma, had not the President insisted that it would seriously injure the College to deny the degree to one whose scholarship was so high and satisfactorily attained. In the fall of 1833, he began the study of theology in the Presbyterian Seminary of South Hanover, Indiana, and finished the course in the spring of 1836. He did not see his way clear to remain in the Presbyterian Church, and was received into the Associate Reformed Church, and licensed by the Miami Presbytery of that body, November 16, 1836. He was ordained by the Allegheny Presbytery, and installed pastor of the united congregations of Jefferson, Upper Piney and Cherry Run, Sligo, Clarion County, Pennsylvania, July 14, 1838. He resigned Jefferson and Upper Piney in 1841, and devoted his whole time to Cherry Run, where he labored nearly thirty years. He, and his congregation, refused to go into the United Presbyterian Church in 1858, and he remained in the residuary Associate Reformed Church. Not being fully satisfied with this Church on the subject of civil government, he was suspended for insubordination, by the Clarion Presbytery, September 11, 1867. After a full statement of his beliefs, he connected with the Covenanter Church, being received by the Pittsburgh Presbytery, December 31, 1867. At the time of the taking of the Covenant in 1871, he became dissatisfied with the bond and some of the modes of procedure, and left the communion of the Covenanter Church, May 1, 1873. He next connected with the Reformed Presbytery, May 17, 1873, and was associated with the Rev. Dr. David Steele, Sr., until his death. His disease was a complicated paralysis, affecting both mind and body, causing a sore trial to his family and friends, from which he died, at his home in Sligo, Clarion County, Pennsylvania, August 16, 1883, and was buried in the old graveyard of Rimersburgh, near the scene of his labors. He married Miss Elizabeth Reed, of South Hanover, Indiana, February 8, 1838. He was a good man, a faithful pastor, and an instructive preacher.

GEORGE ROBB McBURNEY:

Son of J. R. and Elizabeth K. (Robb) McBurney, was born near Venice, Washington County, Pennsylvania, February 1, 1862. He received his early education in Ingleside Academy, and graduated from Geneva College in 1885. He studied theology in the Allegheny Seminary, was licensed by the Pittsburgh Presbytery, April 11, 1888, and preached within the bounds of the Pittsburgh Presbytery.

JOHN McCARTNEY:

Son of William and Isabella (McCreary) McCartney, was born near Cambridge, Guernsey County, Ohio, July 13, 1828. He received his early education in Muskingum College, graduating from Jefferson College in 1851. In the fall of 1851, he became Principal of the Academy of West Carlisle, Ohio. In 1852, he

was editor of the *Literary Cabinet*, published in Zanesville, Ohio, and in 1854, became Principal of the High
School of that city. In 1855, he was called to the
professorship of Mathematics in Muskingum College.
He studied theology one year in the Allegheny
Seminary, two years in Glasgow, Scotland, another
year in the Allegheny Seminary, and was licensed by
the Pittsburgh Presbytery, April 21, 1860. He was
ordained by the Lakes Presbytery, installed pastor of
the First Miami congregation, Northwood, Logan
County, Ohio, November 12, 1861, and resigned this
charge, September 1, 1875. In 1864, he was among
the philanthropists who revived Geneva College, and
threw her doors open for the education of the colored
race, and visited this and other lands in procuring
means to sustain the institution. In 1870, he was
chosen a professor in Geneva College, and, in 1872,
appointed to the chair of Natural Science. He spent
two years abroad, and resumed his position, which he
occupied in the same institution at Beaver Falls, Pennsylvania, until the fall of 1887, when he was assigned
to Natural History. He married Miss Catharine Robert-
son, of Glasgow, Scotland, August 11, 1868. Largely
through his personal exertions, Geneva College enjoys
its endowment fund and physical laboratory. In
December, 1887, he went to California, under appointment of the Central Board of Missions, and spent
some time in collecting together scattered Covenanters.
DANIEL McCLELLAND:

Was born in Boveragh, County Londonderry,
Ireland, in 1736.* He received his early education in

---

* Communications from Ireland. Cuthbertson's Diary.

this vicinity, and came to America. He returned to Ireland, where he began the study of theology, and was licensed by the Reformed Presbytery of Scotland, December 21, 1763. He was allowed to visit relations in Ireland, among whom he preached for some little time. He was ordained *sine titulo* by the Reformed Presbytery of Ireland, at Laymore, near Ballymena, July 13, 1765. He came to America as a Missionary in the spring of 1766, and settled among the scattered Covenanters in Connecticut. The Rev. John Cuthbertson says in his diary that Mr. McClelland assisted him at the dispensation of the Lord's Supper at Octorara, Pennsylvania, April 10, 1766. He also assisted at many other communions, and preached on different occasions. He assisted Mr. Cuthbertson again at Octorara, May 31, 1767, but his services were neither satisfactory to him nor acceptable to the people. He continued to preach to the scattered societies in Eastern Pennsylvania, until the spring of 1768, when he returned to New England. The remaining events of his life are unknown, but it is probable that he drifted away from the Church.

ALBERT WITSIUS McCLURKIN :

Son of Rev. Dr. Hugh P. and Jane (Orr) McClurkin, was born in New Concord, Muskingum County, Ohio, January 1, 1864. He received his early education in Muskingum College, and graduated from Geneva College in 1884. He taught school in Wahoo, Nebraska, one year. He studied theology in the Allegheny Seminary, was licensed by the Kansas Presbytery, April 3, 1888, and preached in Quinter, Kansas, for some months.

HUGH PARK McCLURKIN, D. D.:

Son of John and Elizabeth (Park) McClurkin, was born near Rocky Creek, Chester District, South Carolina, November 6, 1821. His parents were among the early Covenanters of the South, and removed from that country on account of slavery, in the fall of 1833, and settled near Sparta, Randolph County, Illinois. He received his early education in the schools of his native and adopted countries, and graduated from Duquesne College in 1845. He studied theology in the Cincinnati Seminary, and was licensed by the Lakes Presbytery, April 20, 1848. He was ordained by the Pittsburgh Presbytery, and installed pastor of the Salt Creek congregation (now New Concord), New Concord, Muskingum County, Ohio, October 15, 1850, and resigned this charge, October 8, 1856. He was re-installed pastor, December 2, 1858, and resigned, October 4, 1882. He was installed pastor of the congregation of Wahoo, Saunders County, Nebraska, February 29, 1884, where he is in charge. He married Miss Jane Orr, of Pittsburgh, Pennsylvania, January 17, 1843. He was for many years a Trustee of Muskingum College, and President *pro tem* of that institution for two years, beginning in 1859. He was honored with the degree of Doctor of Divinity by Muskingum College in 1879. He was Moderator of the Synod of 1868.'

JOHN JOHNSTON McCLURKIN:

Son of John and Elizabeth (Park) McClurkin, was born near Rocky Creek, Chester District, South Carolina, June 6, 1813. He received his early education in the schools of his native district, and entered South

Carolina College, Columbia, where he remained until his junior year. In the fall of 1833, he removed to Sparta, Randolph County, Illinois, and the following year resumed his studies, and graduated from the University of Indiana in 1836. He studied theology privately under the direction of Revs. Samuel McKinney and William Sloane, was licensed by the Illinois Presbytery, April 6, 1841, and attended the Allegheny Seminary one session. He was ordained by the Illinois Presbytery, and installed pastor of the united congregations of Princeton, Gibson County, and Walnut Ridge, Washington County, Indiana, June 2, 1843. He was released from Princeton, May 22, 1849, and from Walnut Ridge, April 10, 1851. He preached for two years in Southern Illinois as a Missionary, and also among the New School Covenanters and Associate Reformed brethern. He was installed pastor of the united congregations of Springfield, Greenville and Sandy Lake, Balm, Mercer County, Pennsylvania, September 8, 1854, and resigned this charge, October 14, 1873, and filled appointments for seven years. He was installed pastor of the Garrison congregation, Glenwood, Fayette County, Indiana, August 14, 1880, and resigned March 13, 1884. In 1885, he became stated supply to the congregation of Clarksburgh, Indiana County, Pennsylvania, where he is in charge. He was married four times. First to Miss S. A. Waddle, of Princeton, Indiana, July 29, 1839; second to Miss Maria Ferguson, of Walnut Ridge, Indiana, October 16, 1843; third to Mrs. Maria (Patton) Stevenson, of Sparta, Illinois, June 10, 1852 ; and fourth to Miss L. J. Ewing, of Bloomington, Indiana, April 5, 1881.

JOHN KNOX McCLURKIN, D. D.:

Son of Rev. J. J. and Maria S. (Patton) Stevenson McClurkin, was born in Sparta, Randolph County, Illinois, November 23, 1853. The next year his parents removed to Balm, Mercer County, Pennsylvania, where he received his early education, and graduated from Westminster College in 1873. He taught in that institution one year, and in the fall of 1874, accepted the chair of Greek in Geneva College, Northwood, Ohio. In the fall of 1875, he accepted the chair of Greek in Westminster College, and, in 1883, was elected President of Westminster College; and, although declining the honor, he was the acting President for one year. He studied theology in the Princeton and Allegheny Seminaries, and was licensed by the Pittsburgh Presbytery, April 12, 1881. He was ordained by the Philadelphia Presbytery, installed pastor of the Second congregation of the city of Philadelphia, Pennsylvania, October 9, 1884, and resigned this charge, August 25, 1887, accepting the chair of Systematic Theology in the Allegheny Seminary, where he is in charge. He was honored with the degree of Doctor of Divinity by Westminster College in 1887.

SAMUEL RUTHERFORD McCLURKIN:

Son of Thomas and Martha (Kirkpatrick) McClurkin, was born near Oakdale, Washington County, Illinois, September 12, 1848. He received his early education in the common schools, and attended respectively, Sparta Academy, Monmouth College, Iowa University, and graduated from Westminster College in 1872. He studied theology in the Allegheny Seminary, and was licensed by the Illinois Presbytery, May 26, 1875. He was ordained by the Ohio Presbytery, and installed pastor of the Middle Wheeling congregation, Roney's Point, Ohio County, West Virginia, September 14, 1876, where he is in charge. He married Miss Jennie M. Ferguson, of Brownsville, Ohio, October 24, 1878.

THADDEUS ZWINGLE McCLURKIN:

Son of Rev. Dr. H. P. and Jane (Orr) McClurkin, was born in Norwich, Muskingum County, Ohio, January 31, 1853. He received his early education in the public schools, and in Muskingum College, graduating from Westminster College in 1875. He studied theology in the Allegheny Seminary, and was licensed by the Ohio Presbytery, April 2, 1879. He preached generally throughout the States and the British Provinces. He connected with the Presbyterian Church, November 10, 1884, and preached respectively in Duncannon, Pennsylvania, Beaver Dam and Minneapolis, Minnesota, and Philadelphia, Pennsylvania. He married Mrs. Laura L. Coverleigh, of Duncannon, Pennsylvania, March 25, 1885.

THOMAS McCONNELL:

Son of Thomas and Jane (McConnell) McConnell, was born in Portglenone, County Antrim, Ireland, April 27, 1819. He enjoyed the advantages of an early religious training in the home, and under the pastoral care of the Rev. James Smyth. He came to America in 1837, and settled in the city of Allegheny, Pennsylvania. He resumed his classical studies under the care of the Rev. Hugh Walkinshaw, and graduated from Duquesne

College in 1847. Having studied theology privately, and in the Cincinnati Seminary, he was licensed by the Pittsburgh Presbytery, October 27, 1847. He preached with general acceptance in the vacancies for about one year, when seriously impaired health caused him to cease. In 1849, he removed to West Elizabeth, Allegheny County, Pennsylvania, but on account of an affection of the throat he was seldom able to preach. His disease gradually assumed a pulmonary type, causing hemorrhages of the lungs, from which he died at his home in West Elizabeth, Pennsylvania, May 3, 1850. He married Miss Mary J. Anderson, of Canonsburgh, Pennsylvania, February 10, 1848. He was possessed of an amiable disposition, a consistent and uniform character, and was strongly attached to the principles of the Covenanter Church. From the ability, piety and consecration which he manifested, high expectations of great usefulness in the ministry were entertained, and he was peculiarly fitted for occupying a prominent position in the Church.

JOSEPH McCRACKEN:

Son of William and Elizabeth (Hood) McCracken, was born in Rathfriland, County Down, Ireland, October 21, 1825. He came with his parents to America in 1832, and settled near York, Livingston County, New York, where he received his early education. He pursued his preparatory classical course in Temple Hill Academy, and graduated from Union College in 1848. He went abroad the following year, and studied theology in the Seminaries of Paisley and Edinburgh, Scotland, and was licensed by the Rochester Presbytery, May 13,

1853. He was ordained by the Illinois Presbytery at Linton, Iowa, October 29, 1856, and installed pastor of the congregation of Clarinda, Page County, Iowa, July 6, 1857, and resigned this charge, October 16, 1858. He was installed pastor of the congregation of St. Louis, Missouri, October 14, 1859, and resigned, September 2, 1874. He accepted the chair of Mathematics in Geneva College, Northwood, Ohio, and resigned, May 26, 1877. He was installed pastor of the Southfield congregation, Birmingham, Oakland County, Michigan, June 15, 1878, where he is in charge. He married Miss Harriet H. Rowan, of Argyle, New York, September 15, 1857. He was Moderator of the Synod of 1873.

ROBERT HOUSTON McCREADY:

Son of Robert and Margaret (Houston) McCready, was born in the city of Pittsburgh, Pennsylvania, July 12, 1853. He received his early education in the public schools, studied privately under Rev. Dr. J. R. W. Sloane, attended Geneva College until his senior year, graduating from the Western University of Pennsylvania in 1879. He studied theology in the Allegheny Seminary, with short terms at Yale Theological School and Union Seminary, New York, was licensed by the Pittsburgh Presbytery, April 11, 1882, and spent some time in the British Maritime Provinces and vacancies of the Church. He was ordained by the New York Presbytery, installed pastor of the congregation of Coldenham, Orange County, New York, March 6, 1884, and resigned May 22, 1888. He connected with the Presbyterian Church, being received by the Presbytery of the City of New York. He was installed pastor of the Prospect Hill Presbyterian Church, New York City, May 28, 1888, where he is in charge.

BOYD McCULLOUGH:

Son of William B. and Mary (Moffett) McCullough, was born in Rathfriland, County Down, Ireland, March 25, 1825. He came with his parents to America in 1832, and settled in Beech Woods, Jefferson County, Pennsylvania, where he received his early education in the common schools. He studied the classics under the direction of the Rev. James Milligan, D. D., graduating from Duquesne College in 1848. He studied theology in the Cincinnati and Northwood Seminaries, and was licensed by the Lakes Presbytery, April 16, 1852. He was ordained by the same Presbytery, installed pastor of the united congregations of Novi, Oakland County, and Detroit, Michigan, September 19, 1855, and resigned this charge, May 14, 1871. He made a lecturing and preaching tour throughout Great Britain and Ireland, and returned in the fall of 1872, preaching as a supply for three years. He connected with the United Presbyterian Church, August 13, 1875, and was stated supply at Caledonia, Minnesota, and Pepin, Wisconsin, for eight years. In the summer of 1886, he removed to Beech Tree, Pennsylvania, where he engaged in supplying vacant pulpits. He was twice married. First to Miss Julia A. Johnston, of Northwood, Ohio, November 19, 1850; and second to Mrs. Emily C. (Jameson) Johnston, of Belle Centre, Ohio, December 8, 1885. He contributed a series of articles to the *National Era*, in 1858, and on "Bible Characters" to the *Michigan Farmer*, in 1861. He is the author of a book of poems entitled "The Shamrock," 1882, pp. 192.

JAMES McGOWAN McDONALD, D. D.:

Son of John and Martha (Marshall) McDonald, was born near Winnsboro, Fairfield District, South Carolina, November 3, 1823. His parents removed from that country in 1837, on account of the prevalence of slavery, and settled near Sparta, Randolph County, Illinois. He was an only child and his father died shortly after arriving in Illinois. He took charge of the farm, and pursued his studies under the direction of his pastor, the Rev. James Wallace, and also under his uncles, Dr. Robert and Adam Marshall, and became a most proficient scholar, although he never attended an Academy or College. He studied theology in the Cincinnati and Northwood Seminaries, and was licensed by the Lakes Presbytery, April 29, 1850. He was ordained by the Illinois Presbytery, and installed pastor of Sharon congregation, Linton, Des Moines County, Iowa, May 17, 1851, and resigned this charge on account of failing health, June 19, 1872. For many years he was troubled with a spasmodic cough, which turned into a pulmonary affection, producing a disorganization of the lungs, from which disease he died at his home near Linton, Iowa, September 9, 1872. He married Miss Elizabeth Orr, April 16, 1849. He was an eloquent, fearless and earnest preacher, and his discourses were always well prepared. He was endowed with a most excellent memory, a quick and discriminating perception, and in an argument he was almost invincible.   He was a fine classical scholar, a sound theologian, and a logical reasoner. He took great delight in debate, and frequently lectured upon the distinctive principles of the Covenanter Church. Among his writings are: "The Dominion of Christ," 1848. "Capital Punishment," 1851. "Infant Baptism," 1852. "Review of Parker's Infant Baptism," 1853. "The Perfect Law of Liberty," 1860, and other articles published in the Church magazines. He was honored with the degree of Doctor of Divinity by Monmouth College in 1868.

ALEXANDER McDOWELL:

Was born in Coleraine, County Londonderry, Ireland, in 1727.* He came to America in early life, with his parents, who were strict Scotch Presbyterians, and settled in Eastern Connecticut. He received his early education in the schools of the new settlement and under private teachers, and graduated from Harvard College in 1748. He studied theology privately, and was licensed to preach in the spring of 1752. He was ordained and installed pastor of the Presbyterian congregation of Colerain, Franklin County, Massachusetts, September 28, 1753, and was dismissed in 1759, because he insisted on a strict adherence to the Solemn League and Covenant and other usages of the Church of Scotland. He then associated himself with the Covenanter societies in Massachusetts and Connecticut, and through his instrumentality they were gathered together and erected a log meeting house near Pelham. Little else is known of Mr. McDowell.

* Partially from Webster's History of Presbyterian Church. Cuthbertson's Diary.

The Rev. John Cuthbertson says in his diary that "on October 28, 1759, he preached in the meeting house at Pelham, Massachussetts, and that Alexander Mc-Dowell came thirty miles from his home east of the Connecticut river to meet him, took him to his home, treated him with true Christian hospitality, and that in all points they agreed in doctrine and had much Christian fellowship." Two years later Mr. McDowell made a preaching tour to the scattered Covenanters in New York and Eastern Pennsylvania, and frequently accompanied Mr. Cuthbertson on his preaching tours. He assisted at a communion at Rock Creek, (Gettysburgh) Adams County, Pennsylvania, October 4, 1761, and on October 12, 1761, this congregation made out a unanimous call for Mr. McDowell. He declined their invitation, however, and, in December, 1761, returned to Connecticut, and nothing more is known of him.

JAMES McDONALD McELHINNEY:

Son of Joseph and Nancy (McClure) McElhinney, was born near Linton, Des Moines County, Iowa, October 22, 1858. He received his early education in the schools of St. Louis, Missouri; and, in the fall of 1876, entered Geneva College, where he remained three years, graduating from Monmouth College in 1881. He was a teacher and Principal of the Academy of Morning Sun, Iowa, for two years. He studied theology in the Allegheny Seminary, was licensed by the Iowa Presbytery, April 7, 1886, and labored for six months in Superior, Nebraska, and Holmwood, Kansas. He accepted the appointment of a Missionary in the city of New York, May 1, 1887, where he is employed.

DAVID McFALL:

Son of James and Ann (Dunlap) McFall, was born near Dervock, County Antrim, Ireland, March 12, 1846. He received his early education in the schools of Coleraine, Ireland, came to America in 1867, and settled in the city of Allegheny, Pennsylvania. He soon afterwards resumed his studies, and graduated from Westminster College in 1869. He studied theology at the same time in the Allegheny Seminary, and was licensed by the Pittsburgh Presbytery, April 12, 1870. He was ordained by the same Presbytery, installed pastor of the congregation of Oil City, Pennsylvania, May 18, 1871, and resigned this charge, April 8, 1873. He was installed pastor of the Second congregation of Boston, Massachusetts, July 11, 1873, where he is in charge. He married Miss Clara B. Milligan, of Allegheny City, Pennsylvania, October 16, 1873. He has published numerous articles in the Church magazines, contributed an exposition of the Sabbath School Lessons to the *Christian Statesman*, lectured in the interests of the National Christian Association, and is Chaplain in the Cambridge Prison.

THOMAS McFALL:

Son of James and Ann (Dunlap) McFall, was born near Dervock, County Antrim, Ireland, August 23, 1848. He received his early education in the schools of his native country, came to America in 1867, and settled in the city of Allegheny, Pennsylvania. He received his preparatory studies in Westminster College, graduating from Geneva College in 1875. He was employed upon the *Christian Statesman* in Philadelphia,

Pennsylvania, one year. He studied theology in the Allegheny Seminary, and was licensed by the Pittsburgh Presbytery, April 8, 1879. He was ordained by the New Brunswick and Nova Scotia Presbytery, and installed pastor of the united congregations of Cornwallis and Horton, Somerset, Kings County, Nova Scotia, August 25, 1881. The Horton branch was dropped, June 3, 1886, and he continues in charge of Cornwallis. He married Miss Anna M. Lyons, of Philadelphia, Pennsylvania, September 16, 1879.

ARMOUR McFARLAND:

Son of Patrick and Eliza (Knox) McFarland, was born near Cookstown, County Tyrone, Ireland, March 8, 1808. He received his early education in the schools of his native country, and graduated with the honorary degree of Master of Arts from the University of Glasgow, Scotland, in 1828. He studied theology in the Seminary of Paisley, Scotland, and was licensed by the Western Presbytery, Ireland, October 21, 1830. He came to America in May, 1831, settled in West Bedford, Coshocton County, Ohio, and engaged in preaching. He was ordained by the Ohio Presbytery, installed pastor of the congregation of Utica, Licking County, Ohio, October 5, 1837, and also of Jonathan's Creek, Muskingum County, Ohio, October 6, 1847. He resigned the Utica branch, May 23, 1855, and devoted his whole time to Jonathan's Creek, to which was added the charge of Middle Wheeling, West Virginia, April 4, 1866. He resigned Middle Wheeling, April 12, 1873, and Jonathan's Creek, April 12, 1876, on account of impaired health, and retired to his country residence near Zanesville, Ohio, where he is living in the infirmities of age. He married Miss Sarah McCune, of Utica, Ohio, March 22, 1842.

ARMOUR JAMES McFARLAND:

Son of James and Martha (McNichol) McFarland, was born in West Bedford, Coshocton County, Ohio, September 18, 1836. He received his early education in the West Bedford Academy, entered Geneva College, where he remained until his senior year, and graduated from Miami University in 1858. He studied theology in the Allegheny Seminary, and was licensed by the Pittsburgh Presbytery, April 2, 1861. He was ordained by the same Presbytery, installed pastor of the Salem congregation, Stanton, Jefferson County, Pennsylvania, February 5, 1862, and resigned this charge, April 11, 1882. He was installed pastor of the congregation of St. John, New Brunswick, August 4, 1882, where he is in charge. He was twice married. First to Miss Matilda Gregg, of Allegheny City, Pennsylvania, April 29, 1862; and second, to Miss Mary C. Crozier, of Elizabeth, Pennsylvania, October 18, 1866.

JOSEPH McFARLAND:

Son of James and Martha (McNichol) McFarland, was born in West Bedford, Coshocton County, Ohio, June 18, 1839. He received his early education in the West Bedford Academy, entered Geneva College, where he remained until his junior year, and graduated from Miami University in 1859. He studied theology in the Allegheny Seminary two years, and engaged in farming three years. He resumed his studies in the Allegheny Seminary, and was licensed by the Pittsburgh Presbytery, May 23, 1867. After preaching a few months, he abandoned the work. In the fall of 1868, he removed to Dallas County, Iowa, where he engaged in farming. In the spring of 1876, he returned East, and settled upon a farm near Stanton, Jefferson County, Pennsylvania, where he is residing. He married Miss Mary J. Crawford, of Dresden, Ohio, September 3, 1868. He was elected an elder in the Salem congregation, April 9, 1878, and is actively engaged in Sabbath School work.

WILLIAM McFARLAND:

Son of James and Martha (McNichol) McFarland, was born in West Bedford, Coshocton County, Ohio, November 5, 1844. He received his early education in the West Bedford Academy, and graduated from Washington and Jefferson College in 1868. He studied theology in the Allegheny Seminary, and was licensed by the Pittsburgh Presbytery, April 12, 1870. He was ordained by the Rochester Presbytery, and installed pastor of the Lisbon congregation, Flackville, St. Lawrence County, New York, May 11, 1871, where he is in charge. He married Miss Martha E. McClure, of Oil City, Pennsylvania, October 4, 1871.

JAMES McFEETERS:

Son of Thomas and Mary (Fletcher) McFeeters, was born in Raphoe, County Donegal, Ireland, January 1, 1848. In 1850, his parents came to America and settled in Jamestown, Mercer County, Pennsylvania, where he received his early education in the Adamsville Academy, graduating from Westminster College in 1870. He studied theology in the Allegheny Seminary, and was licensed by the Pittsburgh Presbytery, April 8,

1873. He was ordained by the same Presbytery, and installed pastor of the united congregations of Manchester and Parnassus, Westmoreland County, Pennsylvania, June 19, 1874; the Brookland congregation being added, November 16, 1886, where he is in charge. He married Miss Nannie C. Dill, of Wyman, Iowa, February 25, 1875. He is editor of the Young Folk's department of the *Christian Statesman* since 1883; contributes an exposition of the Sabbath School Lessons to the same paper since 1885; is editor of "Old Arm Chair" in the *Christian Nation* since 1884; the Temperance department of the *St. Louis Midland* since 1884; and many articles in the magazines of the Church. He is President of the Board of Trustees of Geneva College.

JAMES McGARRAGH:

Was born in Donaghadee, County Down, Ireland, July, 1752.* He received the rudiments of an excellent education in the schools of his native County, and graduated from the University of Glasgow, Scotland, in 1781. He studied theology one year under the direction of the Rev. William Stavely, also in Scotland, and was licensed by the Reformed Presbytery of Scotland, at Bready, County Londonderry, Ireland, August 20, 1783. He preached with much acceptance to the scattered societies throughout Ulster for several years. In 1789, there arose a theological discussion between the Seceders and Covenanters in reference to the civil relations. The subject had long afforded a fruitful topic for debate, and the aid of the press had frequently been used in the discussion. The adherents

---

* Communications from Ireland.

of the two parties assembled in the vicinity of Ballibay to hear a *viva voce* discussion of its merits. On
the side of the Seceders appeared the Rev. John
Rodgers, who had challenged the first Covenanter
minister that came into the district; and the first
minister coming into the neighborhood was Mr. James
McGarragh, then a licentiate. On a platform erected
in the open air, not far from the meeting-house of
Cahans, and in the presence of an immense crowd of
auditors, these two disputants discussed this point of
polemic theology at great length. Immediately in front
of Mr. Rodgers stood a goodly pile of books, to
which he occasionally appealed in confirmation of his
statements; but Mr. McGarragh scorned the aid of
such auxiliaries and exhibited no volume but one—the
English Bible. The advocate of the Covenanters was
by no means deficient either in self-possession or
volubility of speech; and as the Seceders had recently
accepted *Regium Donum*, he did not neglect a topic
which afforded such scope for his powers of declama-
tion and argument. The discussion, however, produced
no practical change of opinion, as the two parties now
adhered more firmly than ever to the principles which
each had previously professed.* Receiving urgent
requests from the Covenanters in South Carolina to
come to that country, he decided to accept their call,
and was ordained at Bready, August 28, 1789. Late
in the fall of 1790, he sailed from Belfast for Charleston, South Carolina, and after a very tedious and
stormy passage arrived on the Southern shore of the

---

* Reid's History of the Presbyterian Church in Ireland.

United States of America. In the spring of 1791, he settled on the north side of the Beaver Dam, a branch of the Rocky Creek congregation, Chester District, South Carolina. His most excellent wife, Miss Elizabeth Clark, of County Down, Ireland, to whom he had been married some time before leaving his native land, died soon after his arrival in this country, and the second time he married an intemperate and worthless woman, who was his housekeeper, and who lead him to fall into intemperate habits, for which conduct he was suspended by the Committee, June 24, 1795.* He was deposed from the ministerial office by the Reformed Presbytery, February 5, 1801, but was afterwards restored to private membership. He taught school and cultivated a small farm for a livelihood, died in great despondency, September 6, 1816, and was buried in Paul's graveyard, near Mount Prospect, Chester District, South Carolina. He was a proficient scholar, an apt teacher, and a very acceptable preacher.

CHARLES BROWN McKEE:

Son of James and Agnes (Morrow) McKee, was born near Elder's Ridge, Indiana County, Pennsylvania, March 28, 1792. He received his early education in the neighboring Academy of Greensburgh, also in a classical school in Philadelphia, and attended the University of Pennsylvania. He studied theology in the Philadelphia Seminary, and under the direction of the Rev. S. B. Wylie, D. D., and was licensed by the Philadelphia Presbytery, December 28, 1819. He was ordained by the Pittsburgh Presbytery, installed pastor

---

* Rev. D. S. Faris in *R. P. &. C.*, 1876, p. 51.

of the Brush Creek congregation, Chillicothe, Ohio, August 7, 1821, and resigned, September 10, 1822. He accepted the chair of Languages in Cincinnati College, was installed pastor of the congregation of Cincinnati, Ohio, November 18, 1822, and resigned, October 17, 1831. He soon afterwards removed to the city of Rochester, New York, where he opened a classical school and preached as occasion was afforded. He was installed pastor of the congregation of Rochester, New York, May 14, 1837, and resigned, August 29, 1842. In 1844, he removed to the city of Baltimore, Maryland, where he opened a flourishing classical school, and was stated supply to the congregation for two years. He was installed pastor of the congregation of Baltimore, Maryland, December 2, 1846, and was released, December 4, 1852, when he connected with the Presbyterian Church. He built up the Twelfth Presbyterian Church of that city, and was the pastor for five years. In 1858, he took charge of the Presbyterian Church at Lewinsville, Virginia, where he labored until the rebels occupied that country in 1861. His sentiments and sympathies being wholly with the North, he found it necessary to resign the charge. He removed to the city of Washington, D. C., where he accepted an appointment in the War Department. This position he discharged with ability and acceptance, until stricken with paralysis at his desk, and, in three days thereafter died, at his home in Georgetown, D. C., June 5, 1866. He was twice married. First to Miss Julia H. Snyder, of Philadelphia, Pennsylvania, January 31, 1821 ; and second to Miss Hannah Adams, of

Rochester, New York, June 10, 1841. He was a most excellent and finished scholar, and was well known as a teacher of the classics. He was thoroughly versed in the ancient languages and biblical literature, and possessed rare capabilities for imparting instruction. As a preacher, he was most interesting and instructive, and at times quite eloquent. During his residence in Washington he preached much in the hospitals and camps of the soldiers, and also to the refugees who flocked around the city during the war of the rebellion. He made application for re-admission into the Covenanter Church, but died before his request could be acted upon by a constituted court. Among his publications are: "An Analysis and Defence of the Doctrines of the Westminster Confession of Faith," 1832; "The Hopkinsian Heresy," 1841; "Anti-Deacon," 1843. He was Moderator of the Synod of 1841.

DAVID McKEE:

Son of David and Jane (Smith) McKee, was born near Ballibay, County Monaghan, Ireland, April 10, 1821. He received his early education in his native country, came to America in 1836, and settled in Crawford County, Pennsylvania. He resumed his studies in the Mercer Academy, and graduated from Jefferson College in 1847. He studied theology in the Cincinnati Seminary, and privately, and was licensed by the Pittsburgh Presbytery, April 9, 1851. He was a Professor of Greek in Westminster College, two years. He was ordained by the Philadelphia Presbytery, installed pastor of the Fourth congregation of Philadelphia, Pennsylvania, July 5, 1854, and resigned this charge, August 4, 1859. He was installed pastor of the congregation of Clarinda, Page County, Iowa, September 20, 1862, where he is in charge. He married Miss Mary E. Gregg, of Allegheny City, Pennsylvania, September 3, 1856. He was Moderator of the Synod of 1885.

JOSEPH ANDERSON McKEE:

Son of John A. and Eleanor (Anderson) McKee, was born near Lucesco, Westmoreland County, Pennsylvania, February 6, 1838. In early life his parents removed to the city of Allegheny, Pennsylvania, where he received his early education in the public schools, and graduated from Westminster College in 1867. He connected with the United Presbyterian Church, studied theology in their Allegheny Seminary, and was licensed by the Allegheny Presbytery of that body, May 13, 1869. He preached for two years and returned to the Covenanter Church, being received as a licentiate by the Pittsburgh Presbytery, April 11, 1871. He died from a relapse of typhoid fever, at the home of his father, in Allegheny City, Pennsylvania, September 2, 1871. He was unmarried. Owing to the delicate state of his health he was not permitted to preach in many of the vacancies, but his efforts gave abundant evidence that, had he been spared, he would have become a useful and devoted minister.

ROBERT McKEE:

Was born in Ahoghill, County Antrim, Ireland, May 13, 1798. In early life he came to America, and settled in the city of New York, New York, where he received the best of an education in the public schools, and also in a private classical school. He engaged in teaching, with marked success, for many years. He studied theology in the Philadelphia Seminary, and was licensed by the Northern Presbytery, August 9, 1825. He was stated supply to the congregation of Fayetteville, Lincoln County, Tennessee, for some time. While in Nashville, Tennessee, he connected with the free mason lodge, for which cause he was suspended. After confessing his guilt, and abandoning the unfruitful works of darkness, he was restored by the Northern Presbytery, October 10, 1828. He was ordained by the same Presbytery, and installed pastor of the united congregations of Lansingburgh and Troy, New York, December 29, 1830, where he remained pastor for over four years. He connected with the Presbyterian Church, being received by the Presbytery of Albany, May 16, 1835. He preached for some time in the Eighth Presbyterian Church in Albany, New York, but devoted himself principally to teaching. He died in Albany, New York, July 13, 1840. He married Miss Hannah Thomson, of Conococheague, Pennsylvania, in 1820. He was a very acceptable preacher, but in the latter days of his life his mind became impaired, and he was often very eccentric and peculiar in his manners.

JAMES McKINNEY:

Son of Robert and Elizabeth (McIntyre) McKinney, was born in Cookstown, County Tyrone, Ireland, November 16, 1759.* After pursuing his preparatory studies in the schools of his native County, he entered the University of Glasgow, Scotland, where he graduated in 1778. He remained a few years longer in

---

* Sprague's Annals.

Glasgow, and took a full course in medicine and theology, and was licensed by the Reformed Presbytery of Ireland, May 19, 1783. He was ordained by the same court, and installed pastor of the congregation of Kirkhills or Dervock, County Antrim, Ireland, October 4, 1783. This charge was very extensive, and embraced the north-west portion of the County Antrim, and a large part of Derry. Here he labored faithfully for about ten years, and was known as a bold and fearless advocate of the rights of God and men. He deeply sympathized with the oppressed at the time of the Irish rebellion, and, although he did not belong to the society of "United Irishmen," yet he was charged with influencing and encouraging them to throw off the British yoke. The true cause of his leaving his native land was his sermon on the "Rights of God." This was denounced as treasonable by the secret spies of the British government. An indictment was found against him, and he, being feared by the government, and an object of jealousy, they determined to seize and imprison him. He was providentially away from home when the soldiers came to arrest him, and as bail on a charge of treason could not be accepted, he escaped to America in the summer of 1793. He travelled as a Missionary to all the scattered Covenanters from Vermont to the Carolinas, and organized many congregations. He received his family from Ireland in 1797, and resided in Philadelphia, Pennsylvania. He, with the Rev. William Gibson and ruling elders, constituted the Reformed Presbytery of America, at Philadelphia, May, 1798. At this time he took charge of the united congregations of Galway and Duanesburgh, New York, and also preached in other societies adjacent. In November, 1800, he, with the Rev. S. B. Wylie, constituted a Committee of the Reformed Presbytery to visit the Churches throughout the South to abolish slavery from the pale of the Covenanter Church. He resigned the charge at Duanesburgh, New York, April 4, 1802, and accepted the call to the congregation of Rocky Creek, Chester District, South Carolina, whither he removed, died in a few months thereafter, away from his family, September 16, 1802, and was buried in the old graveyard on Rocky Creek. He married Miss Mary Mitchell, of County Londonderry, Ireland, in 1784. For scholarship and eloquence combined he was not only the greatest man in the Covenanter Church in his day, but he was a great man among the men of that age. He lived in revolutionary times, and he was an ardent lover of civil and religious liberty. His sermons were a continuous stream of thought; and for grandeur of conception and impressiveness of delivery, such displays of eloquence were seldom heard. His diction was clear and copious, abounding in brilliant figures. He seemed to catch inspiration from the working of his mind upon divine truth, and then his keen perception and vivid imagination produced in energetic language an effect that was inexpressibly powerful upon his audience. He was a very kind and social man, and devoted to the spiritually of his people. He was courteous to his brethren and remarkably submissive to the authority of the Church court.

If at any time he was advised of a tresspass on decorum, he would say to the presiding officer, "You are right; I am a friend of good order, and bow to your authority." He had his trials and hardships in a new country. "In the place of his residence the help needed in the labors of the field could not always, even for wages, be obtained. In such cases he did not withhold his own hand. In his forest clearing, amidst the half burnt logs, in company with his hired man, he might be seen putting forth the strength of his muscular frame at the heaviest end of a log. But near by were the implements of the scholar and the man of reflection—the paper, the inkstand and the quill, and the table was the stump of the newly felled tree; and while the hired man was resting a moment from the common toils, Mr. McKinney was at his rude table making a record of his thoughts—those deep meditations on the rights of God, of Christ, of the Church, and of Humanity. Thus in the charcoaled field, with his frame blackened with its dust, the soul of this great man was roaming abroad among the works of Divinity, his mind winging its way to heaven, and the whole being was in constant communication with God." An eminent divine said, "I have met with many considerable, and some great, men, but not one equal to James McKinney." Another says, "He is like Leviathan—made without fear." Such are the testimonies of men on both sides of the Atlantic to the character of the "Great McKinney," who, when he came to die, and was amidst the pains of dissolution in a strange country, said as his last words:

"Now is the time to have the anchor cast within
the vail," and he fell asleep. The only specimen of
his writings extant is his "Rights of God," 1797, pp.
68, and the second edition emitted by the Rev. Robert
Gibson in 1833. The other portions of the contemplated work were the "Rights of Christ as
Mediator," "Rights of the Church," and the "Rights
of Men." Most of this manuscript was prepared for
the press, but was lost about the time of his death.

ROBERT McKINNEY:

Son of Robert and Eleanor (McGeorge) McKinney, was born near Ogle, Butler County, Pennsylvania,
December 10, 1846. He received the elements of an
education in the common and select schools of that
neighborhood, attended Westminster College one year,
and graduated from Geneva College in 1874. He
studied theology in the Allegheny Seminary, and
was licensed by the Pittsburgh Presbytery, April 11,
1877. During the summer of 1877, he contracted a
severe cold while on a preaching tour, which settled
upon his lungs and produced hemorrhages. Upon
resuming his studies in the Seminary in the fall, his
health gave way, and he repaired to Florida for
recuperation. The hemorrhages returning, his brother
went to bring him home, and succeeded in reaching the
home of his brother-in-law, Mr. Pierce, in Bellevue,
Allegheny County, Pennsylvania, where he died of
consumption, July 4, 1878, and was buried in the old
graveyard of Pine Creek, amidst the dust of his kindred.
He married Miss Hamie E. Gray, of Brownsdale,
Pennsylvania, September 6, 1877. He was a large and

PRESBYTERIAN CHURCH IN AMERICA. 605.

well-developed man, with intellectual talents and con-
versational powers which gave great promise of usefulness in the ministry.

SAMUEL McKINNEY:

Son of Samuel and Margaret (Findley) McKinney,.
and nephew of the Rev. James McKinney, was born
in Galway, County Galway, Ireland, March 10, 1807.*
He came with his parents to America in 1813, and
settled in Hawkins County, Tennessee, where his
youth was spent upon a farm. He attended the common schools and studied under private instructors,
graduating from the University of Pennsylvania in
1832. He studied theology under the care of the Rev.
S. B. Wylie, at Philadelphia, was licensed by the
Northern Presbytery, June 10, 1832, and preached with
great acceptance in the vacancies for a few years. He
was ordained by the Ohio Presbytery, installed pastor
of the Elkhorn congregation, Oakdale, Washington
County, Illinois, April 15, 1835, and resigned this
charge, May 24, 1840, and accepted a professorate in
Denmark College, Tennessee. In 1843, he was chosen
President of West Tennessee College, and the following
year connected with the Presbyterian Church. In 1850,
he was elected President of Austin College, Huntsville,
Texas, whither he removed, and continued to hold
this office until impaired health caused his resignation
in 1875. He then retired from active duty, and died
of dysentery, at his home in Huntsville, Texas, November 27, 1879. He married Miss Nancy W. Todd,
of Oakdale, Illinois, July 4, 1836. He was a most

* MS. from his son, Hon. A. T. McKinney, Huntsville, Texas.

acceptable preacher, and a man mighty in the Scriptures. He preached occasionally in the South, but was distinguished as a teacher, in which occupation he held a high rank both as to accurate scholarship and successful management.

WILLIAM McKINNEY:

Son of Robert and Margaret (Criswell) McKinney, was born near Ogle, Butler County, Pennsylvania, March 4, 1841. He received his early education in the common schools, and Westminster College, attending Yale College for some time. He studied theology in the Allegheny Seminary, and was licensed by the Pittsburgh Presbytery, April 12, 1876. He took charge of the newly organized Mission School in Camden, Alabama, January 1, 1877, but this field was abandoned in April, 1878. In 1879, he was stated supply at Lake Reno and Round Prairie, Minnesota, and, in 1881, at Saline Ridge, Kansas. Subsequently he supplied in other parts of the Church. He was twice married. First to Miss Myra McKee, of Allegheny, Pennsylvania, September 10, 1875; and second to Miss Lillie J. Gray, of Waukesha, Wisconsin, December 17, 1879. He preaches occasionally, and is engaged in farming near. Myoma, Pennsylvania.

JAMES McLACHLANE:

Was born in the city of Glasgow, Scotland, June 14, 1798. His parents were pious members of the Secession Church, with which body he also connected in early life. He received the best of an education in the schools of his native city, and graduated from the University of Glasgow in 1822. He studied theology in the Perth

Seminary, under the direction of the eminent Dr. Taylor, of the old Burgher section of the Secession Church, and was licensed by the Glasgow Presbytery of that body, April 19, 1826. He was ordained *sine cura* by the same court, November 16, 1826, and in the spring of 1827, went out to the Cape of Good Hope, to labor as a Missionary in the Caffraria region, under the auspices of the London Missionary Society. He returned to his native land the following year on account of the serious illness of his wife. In 1829, he received the appointment of Chaplain to the Seamen's Chapel, Glasgow, Scotland, which office he held for four years. He connected with the Covenanter Church, May 24, 1833. In the summer of the same year he came to Canada West, as a Missionary under the Synod of Scotland, and labored principally in Ramsey, Carleton Place and Perth. He took charge of the congregations of Ramsey and Perth, August 29, 1837, and continued in this pastoral relation for eighteen years. He was installed pastor of the congregation of Lisbon, St. Lawrence County, New York, July 16, 1856, where he continued to labor until his death, caused by an affection of the heart, November 19, 1864. He was twice married. First to Miss Jane Campbell, in 1825; and second, to Miss Christiana Hamilton, in 1833, both of Glasgow, Scotland. He was a devoted soldier of the Cross, and bore many hardships in presenting the gospel in new fields. He shrunk from no toil, however arduous, and most cheerfully performed every Christian duty. He was a very quiet, unassuming, and humble Christian, avoiding the very appearance of pomp or pride, and took his chiefest joy in silent meditation with his Saviour. While he was well-read in theology and the Puritan Divines, yet he had no taste for general reading and avoided public life. His discourses were carefully written and committed to memory before delivery. He was an acceptable speaker, but by no means eloquent.

ALEXANDER McLEOD, D. D.:

Son of Rev. Niel and Margaret (McLean) McLeod, was born at Ardcrisinish, in the Isle of Mull, Scotland, June 12, 1774.* His father was a distinguished minister of the Presbyterian Church of Scotland, whose parish embraced the famous Island of Iona, where Columba preached the pure gospel more than twelve centuries before him. The subject of this sketch, from his earliest years, evinced an earnest desire to be a preacher of the gospel. Being deprived of both his pious parents in early life, he was cast largely upon his own resources. He received the elements of an excellent classical education in his native Mull, and pursued them further in the parish school of Bracadila, in the Isle of Skye. At the age of eighteen he resolved to push his fortune in the New World, and came to America by the way of Liverpool, England, in the spring of 1792. Soon after his arrival in the city of New York, he ascended the Hudson to Albany, thence to Schenectady, New York, where, in the fall, he was employed as a teacher of Greek among a society of his own people. At the establishment of Union College, he became a student, and graduated with honor in 1798. Having connected with the Covenanter Church at Princetown, New York,

---

* Sprague's Annals. Memoir by Dr. S. B. Wylie.

under the eminent Rev. James McKinney, he studied theology under his direction, and was licensed by the Reformed Presbytery, at Coldenham, New York, June 24, 1799. In the fall of 1800, he was called to the pastorate of Coldenham and New York, but he declined to accept it on the plea that there were slave-holders among those who signed his call. The matter was taken before the Presbytery, which court enacted, without a dissenting voice, that "no slaveholder should be allowed the communion of the Church." After this deliverance he accepted the calls, and was ordained and installed pastor of the united congregations of Coldenham, Orange County, and New York City, New York, July 6, 1801. He was released from the Coldenham branch, September 8, 1803, and devoted his labors to the rapidly growing congregation in New York City. He soon became known for his remarkable powers as a writer and preacher, and took his place in the front rank of the scholars and preachers of his day. He was called by several denominations, and sought after by different institutions of learning, but he declined all these honors to remain among the devoted flock of his own gathering. In 1816, he went to Washington to aid in the organization of the American Colonization Society, and wrote its constitution. In 1824, he suffered from inflammation of the lungs, which was caused by exposure amid his manifold toils and excessive duties. In 1830, he visited Europe for his health, and returned much improved. During his absence he was elected Professor of Theology, and editor of a monthly magazine about to be established by the Covenanter Church. He accepted these appointments, heard classes in theology, and edited the *American Christian Expositor*, until his death. He died of heart disease, at his residence in New York City, New York, February 17, 1833. He married Miss Maria A. Agnew, of New York City, New York, September 16, 1805. He was possessed of superior mental endowments, the gifts of a learned man, and the graces of an eloquent preacher. He was a profound theologian, a distinguished metaphysician, and a clear logician. He was a lucid expositor of divine truth; close in his definitions, clear in his explanations, vigorous in his arguments, and practical in his applications. In labors he was abundant. Three discourses every Sabbath, an evening lecture every week, and the accustomed catechetical duties and pastoral visits occupied his time. He loved to preach, and he possessed the power to enchain the attention of an audience, and to bring conviction to the heart. He was the efficient patron, if not the originator, of various charitable institutions, and had no small honor in connection with the American Colonization Society, the New York Society for the Instruction of the Deaf and Dumb, and the American Society for Ameliorating the Condition of the Jews. He was a profuse writer, and as an author the following are among his publications extant: "Negro Slavery Unjustifiable," 1802. "Messiah, Governor of the Nations of the Earth," 1803. "Ecclesiastical Catechism," 1807, twelve editions. "Lectures upon the Prophecies of the Revelation," 1814, four editions. "View of the Late War," 1815, two editions. "The Life and Power of True Godliness," 1816, six editions. He also wrote

"Reformation Principles Exhibited," and most of the "Historical Part of the Reformed Presbyterian Testimony," and the "Book of Discipline." He edited the *American Christian Expositor*, a monthly, two volumes, 1830—1832. He contributed largely to the *Christian Magazine, Evangelical Witness, Evangelical Guardian and Review*, and other religious magazines and papers. He edited the "Larger Catechism with Proofs," the first book stereotyped in America. He was honored with the degree of Doctor of Divinity by Middleburg College in 1809. He was Moderator of the Synod of 1814.

JOHN NIEL McLEOD, D. D.:

Son of Rev. Dr. Alexander and Maria A. (Agnew) McLeod, was born in the city of New York, New York, October 11, 1806. He received a careful religious training in the home of his distinguished parents, a liberal education in the classical school of Mr. John Borland, and graduated from Columbia College in 1826. He studied theology in the Philadelphia Seminary, and was licensed by the Northern Presbytery, August 4, 1828. He was ordained by the same Presbytery, installed pastor of the united congregations of Galway, Saratoga County, and Broad Albin, Fulton County, New York, December 29, 1829, and resigned this charge, June 19, 1832. He was installed pastor, as his father's successor, of the First congregation of New York City, New York, January 14, 1833. At the division of the Church in August, 1833, he became identified with the New School branch of the Covenanter Church, and remained pastor of a portion of his former flock, until his death, of paralysis of the heart, at his residence in New York City, April 27, 1874. He married Miss Margaret Wylie, of Phila-delphia, Pennsylvania, June 13, 1830. He was a man of fine personal appearance, of commanding dignity, and earnest piety. He was an interesting preacher of the Scottish type, and well-read upon all subjects pertain-ing to the ministerial office. In 1851, he was chosen Professor of Theology in his Church, and held this office for many years. In 1862, he became Chaplain of the Eighty-fourth New York regiment during the war of the rebellion. He was known in New York as a philanthropist, and was a member of the American Bible Society, Chairman of the Revision Committee, Vice-President of the American Colonization Society, also of the Society for the Amelioration of the Con-dition of the Jews, and other charitable and benevolent associations. He was an editor of the *Banner of the Cross*, and wrote largely for the press and Church magazines. He was honored with the degree of Doc-tor of Divinity by Dickinson College in 1846. He was Moderator of the General Synods of 1836 and 1869, and was Stated Clerk for many years.

ALGERNON SYDNEY McMASTER, D. D.:

Son of Rev. Dr. Gilbert and Jane (Brown) Mc-Master, was born in Mercer, Mercer County, Penn-sylvania, November 17, 1807.* The following year his parents removed to Duanesburgh, New York, where he received a thorough literary education in the com-mon schools and under the direction of his father, and graduated from Union College in 1827. He studied

---

* Memorial Sermon by Dr. J. S. Grimes, Letonia, Ohio, 1882.

theology under the care of his father, and the Rev. S. B. Wylie, D. D., in Philadelphia, and was licensed by the Western Presbytery, January 3, 1833. He was ordained by the same Presbytery, and installed pastor of the united congregations of Galway and Schenectady, New York, April 4, 1833. At the division of the Church in August, 1833, he became identified with the New School branch of the Covenanter Church, and remained pastor of the majority of his former charge for five years. He connected with the Presbyterian Church, June 8, 1838, and was installed pastor of the Fourth congregation of Pittsburgh, Pennsylvania, where he remained four years. He was installed pastor of the congregation of Westfield, Lawrence County, Pennsylvania, April 12, 1843, and resigned November 9, 1854. He was installed pastor of the congregation of Poland, Mahoning County, Ohio, December 10, 1854, and resigned May 23, 1878, on account of impaired health, and where he died of general debility, September 30, 1882. He married Miss Elizabeth Chase, of Chatham, New York, June 6, 1833. He was an able and learned theologian. His ripe scholarship, and his clear logical mind, filled with a wealth of Scriptural knowledge, made him an able expositor of truth. His preaching was practical and edifying, his reading of Scripture peculiarly solemn and effecting, and his prayers were remarkable for their fervor and appropriateness. He took great delight in catechising the children, and was an attentive pastor to all his flock. As a presbyter, he was thoroughly versed in Church polity, and his influence was felt in the courts where he was heard with marked attention. He was honored with the degree of Doctor of Divinity by Washington College in 1857.

ERASMUS DARWIN McMASTER, D. D., LL. D.:

Son of Rev. Dr. Gilbert and Jane (Brown) McMaster, was born in Mercer, Mercer County, Pennsylvania, February 4, 1806.* In 1808, his parents removed to Duanesburgh, New York, where he was carefully trained in religious duties and literary studies by his father, graduating from Union College in 1827. He studied theology under the care of his father, was licensed by the Northern Presbytery, June 16, 1829, and preached in the vacancies a year. He connected with the Presbyterian Church, being received by the Albany Presbytery, October 18, 1830. He was ordained by the same Presbytery, installed pastor of the congregation of Ballston, New York, February 13, 1831, and resigned this charge, April 24, 1838. This was his only pastoral charge. He was inaugurated President of Hanover College, Indiana, November 7, 1838, where he continued in office for six years. He was inaugurated President of Miami University, Ohio, August 13, 1845, and resigned, August 9, 1849. The same fall he accepted the professorship of Systematic Theology in the Presbyterian Seminary of New Albany, Indiana, and was forced to abandon the office in 1858, because he was in favor of the abolition of human slavery, which system the Presbyterian Church heartily endorsed. It was in the General Assembly which met in Indianapolis, Indiana, May 30, 1859, that

---

* *Presbyterian Historical Almanac,* Vol. 9, p. 171.

he made his celebrated speech on the motion to postpone the election of Professors of Theology in the Chicago Seminary, because this question of slavery was agitating the minds of the public, and the Assembly had not the courage to come out in favor of abolition. For several years he lived * in comparative retirement at Monticello, Indiana. He removed to the home of his brother, the Rev. A. S. McMaster, D. D., in Poland, Ohio, where he resided three years. In the spring of 1866, he was unanimously elected professor of Systematic Theology in the North West Seminary, of Chicago, Illinois, where he was inaugurated with great demonstration, September 10, 1866. Soon afterwards he was prostrated with a severe attack of pneumonia, from which he died very suddenly, in Chicago, Illinois, December 10, 1866, and was buried, according to his wish, in the family burying ground near Xenia, Ohio. He never married. He was confessedly one of the great men of the Presbyterian Church in America. Endowed by nature with the noblest powers of intellect, blessed with the greatest advantage of receiving a thorough education, and early possessed with the grace of the Holy Spirit, he was enabled at an early period of his life to take a high position in the Church. As a scholar, theologian and preacher, he was of the first rank. He never forgot his early training in the Covenanter Church, and frequently made reference to the principles of that Church as the guide of his actions. He was a lifelong and consistent opponent of the whole system of human slavery, and, for the holding of this high position, frequently brought odium upon himself. His rare powers, profound humility, independence of thought, convictions of right, affectionate sympathy and Christian philanthrophy, marked him as one of the noblest servants of Christ. He was honored with the degree of Doctor of Divinity by Union College in 1841, and that of Doctor of Laws by Miami University in 1864.

GILBERT McMASTER, M. D., D. D. :

Son of James and Mary (Crawford) McMaster, was born in Saintfield, County Down, Ireland, February 13, 1778.* He received every opportunity of acquiring an education in his native land, came with his parents to America in 1791, and settled in Franklin County, Pennsylvania. He pursued a liberal course of study in the Franklin Academy, under the superintendence of the celebrated James Ross, LL. D. In 1798, he was engaged as a teacher in Shippensburgh, Pennsylvania, and soon afterwards entered Jefferson Academy at Canonsburgh, Pennsylvania, where he finished the course in 1802, just before the establishment of Jefferson College. He then began the study of medicine, finished the course in 1805, and settled as a physician in Mercer, Pennsylvania. In 1807, Drs. Alexander McLeod and S. B. Wylie sought an interview with him at Pittsburgh, and informed him that the Presbytery of which they were members had resolved to exercise their authority in persuading him to yield his scruples and enter upon the work of the ministry. In this case he recognized the voice of Providence, and he obeyed. Having studied theology a year or so under

---

* Sprague's Annals. *Presbyterian Historical Almanac,* Vol. **5,** p. 387.

the Rev. John McMillan, of Canonsburgh, and having read extensively the best theological writers, he was, after a close examination, licensed by the Reformed Presbytery, October 7, 1807. He was ordained by the Northern Committee of the same court, and installed pastor of the united congregations of Galway and Duanesburgh, New York, August 8, 1808. He was released from the Galway branch, May 10, 1818, and devoted his whole time to Duanesburgh, which became a flourishing congregation. At the division of the Church in August, 1833, he became identified with the New School branch of the Covenanter Church, and remained pastor of the majority of his former congregation, until his resignation April 17, 1840. He was installed pastor of the congregation of Princeton, Gibson County, Indiana, May 5, 1840, and resigned this charge on account of ill health, March 31, 1846. From this time until his death he lived with his son, the Rev. Dr. E. D. McMaster, at Oxford, Ohio, and in 1849, in New Albany, Indiana, where he died, March 17, 1854, and was buried in the old family graveyard near Xenia, Ohio. He married Miss Jane Brown, of Canonsburgh, Pennsylvania, June 13, 1803. As a preacher he was distinguished for the clearness of his method, the fullness of his expositions, the soundness of his doctrine, and the appropriateness of his application. He had a dignified and commanding appearance, but his speaking was not animated, and his style of delivery often faulty. He required the close and protracted attention of his audience, but he richly rewarded them for their patience. The cast of his intellectual character disposed him to delight in general and comprehensive principles, and the bearing of these upon the great interests of man and the kingdom of Christ, rather than in minute details. His ideas of the Church were broad and catholic. He was a man of great magnanimity, at once genial and generous, and he held a position of prominence in the Church to which he was attached. He was a learned and voluminous writer upon various subjects. Among his most valuable publications extant are the following: "Duty of Nations," 1810. "An Essay in Defence of some Fundamental Doctrines of Christianity," 1815, an octavo volume. "The Shorter Catechism Analyzed, with Proofs," 1815, three editions. "An Apology for the Book of Psalms, in Five Letters," 1818, four editions. "The Moral Character of Civil Government: Considered with Reference to the Political Institutions of the United States, in Four Letters," 1832. "A Brief Inquiry into the Civil Relations of Reformed Presbyterians according to their Judicative Acts," 1833. "Speech in Illustration of a Report on the Doctrine of Civil Government," 1835. "Thoughts on the Union of the Church," 1846. "The Upright Man in Life and Death," a sermon at the funeral of the Rev. Dr. S. B. Wylie, 1852. He published many other articles of minor importance in the magazines and papers of his day. He was honored with the degree of Doctor of Divinity by Union College in 1828. He was Moderator of the Synods of 1811 and 1827, and of the General Synod of 1851.

JOHN McMASTER, D. D.:

Son of Hugh and Eleanor (Barr) McMaster, was born in Donegon, County Antrim, Ireland, March 1, 1808.* He came with his parents to America in 1811, and settled in the city of Pittsburgh, Pennsylvania, where they connected with the Covenanter congregation under the care of the Rev. John Black. He received his preparatory studies in the public schools, and in the Pittsburgh Academy, graduating from the Western University of Pennsylvania in 1827. He studied theology under his pastor, the Rev. John Black, D. D., was licensed by the ' Pittsburgh Presbytery, April 8, 1830, and he visited the West and South during that year. He was ordained by the Western Presbytery, and installed pastor of the congregation of Schenectady, New York, January 26, 1832. At the division of the Church in August, 1833, he became identified with the New School branch of the Covenanter Church, and remained pastor of a portion of his former charge until his release, April 16, 1837. He was installed pastor of the congregation of Walnut Hill, Marion County, Illinois, November 4, 1837, and resigned, April 13, 1846. He was installed pastor of the congregation of Princeton, Gibson County, Indiana, June 4, 1846, and continued in this relation until he and the congregation went into the United Presbyterian Church, August 30, 1870. The congregation then became known as the Second Church; and, by the consolidation of the First and Second Churches, April 16, 1874, he was pastor of the First United

* Communications from his family.

Presbyterian congregation of Princeton, until his death, by apoplexy of the brain, July 11, 1874. He was thrice married. First to Miss Joanette McMaster, of Duanesburgh, New York, November 15, 1832; second to Miss Mary Milburn, of Walnut Hill, Illinois, March 22, 1841; and third to Miss Margaret Sterne, of Princeton, Indiana, June 5, 1862. He was a good scholar and in many respects a great preacher. He was a good conversationalist, exceedingly jovial and humorous. He was always interesting in his discourses, and whether in the pulpit or upon the platform, his influence was on the side of righteousness. He took a deep interest in public affairs, and was a zealous advocate of thorough Christian education. He was highly regarded as a preacher, pastor, and citizen, and earnestly desired the unity of the Church of Christ. He was honored with the degree of Doctor of Divinity by Jefferson College in 1864. He was Moderator of the General Synods of 1845 and 1866.

GAVIN McMILLAN:

Son of Hugh and Jane (Harvey) McMillan, was born in Dervock, County Antrim, Ireland, February 6, 1787.* He came with his parents to America in August of the same year, and settled in the Chester District, South Carolina, where his father was an honored elder in the Rocky Creek congregation. In 1810, he began his studies, with the ministry in view, under the direction of his pastor, the Rev. Thomas Donnelly, and also in the Classical School of Mr. John Orr, graduating with honor from South Carolina Col-

---

* *Reformed Presbyterian Advocate*, 1867, p. 108.

lege, Columbia, in 1817. He studied theology under the direction of the Rev. S. B. Wylie, D. D., in Philadelphia, was licensed by the Philadelphia Presbytery, October 13, 1821, and missionated in the South and West. He was ordained by the Pittsburgh Presbytery, and installed pastor of the Beech Woods congregation, Morning Sun, Preble County, Ohio, May 7, 1823. At the division of the Church in August, 1833, he hesitated about the step his brethren were taking, but finally became identified with the New School branch of the Covenanter Church. He remained pastor of a portion of his former charge until his death, caused by an inflammation of the kidneys, at his home in Morning Sun, Ohio, January 25, 1867. He married Miss Rosanna Reynolds, of Ryegate, Vermont, February 4, 1824. He was a didactic and practical preacher. He was neither a finished speaker, nor did his discourses display much rhetoric, but his utterances were warm and full of impassioned sentiment. The spiritually minded heard him gladly, for he came to them with his Bible and his heart full of truth and love for perishing souls. He was a man distinguished for prayer, and was warmly attached to Reformation principles. He deeply regretted the breach in the Church, and frequently sought to heal it. In all the relations which he sustained, he was affectionàte, laborious, and faithful. He was Moderator of the General Synods of 1839 and 1861.

HUGH McMILLAN, D. D.:

Son of Hugh and Jane (Harvey) McMillan, was born in the Chester District, South Carolina, February

8, 1794.* He received his early classical education in the school of Mr. John Orr, and graduated with first honor from the University of Pennsylvania in 1818. He was Professor of Languages in South Carolina College, Columbia, one year; but, having devoted himself to the work of the ministry, he returned to the study of theology under the direction of the Rev. S. B. Wylie, D. D., in Philadelphia, was licensed by the Philadelphia Presbytery, April 4, 1820, and for two years served the Church as a Missionary in the new settlements in the West and South. He was ordained by the Southern Presbytery, and installed pastor of the Rocky Creek congregation, Chester District, South Carolina, June 18, 1822. He soon afterwards opened an Academy in the old "Brick Church." Owing to his views on slavery and the position which the Covenanter Church had taken on the question, he proposed to his congregation to remove to one of the free States. With this end in view, he visited Southern Ohio, in the spring of 1828, and soon afterwards received a call from the united congregations of Xenia and Massie's Creek, Green County, Ohio, over which he was installed pastor, September 7, 1829. Many of his former flock joined him in Ohio, and, in 1830, he opened an Academy in Xenia. At the division of the Church in August, 1833, he became identified with the New School branch of the Covenanter Church, and the great majority of the congregation remained with him. In 1850, he resigned the Xenia branch, and continued pastor of Massie's Creek, until his death,

---

* *Xenia (Ohio) Torchlight*, October 17, 1860.

caused by lung fever, at Cedarville, Ohio, October 9, 1860. He married Miss Mary A. McClurg, of Brownstown, Pennsylvania, in 1821. He was a distinguished classical scholar and engaged in teaching most of his life. No less proficient was he in theology, being a preceptor in this department for many years. He was a preacher of recognized power and influence, and was largely connected with the literary and benevolent institutions of the Church. The success of the Bible cause in the County in which he lived may well be attributed to his indefatigable labors. He was highly regarded by all classes as a public-spirited man, and one thoroughly interested in any cause that would conduce to the welfare of humanity. He was honored with the degree of Doctor of Divinity by Miami University in 1857. He was Moderator of the General Synod of 1833.

WILLIAM WILLSON McMILLAN:

Son of John and Elizabeth (Morrow) McMillan, was born in Selma, Dallas County, Alabama, May 13, 1827. His parents were originally from South Carolina, and settled in Sharon, Noble County, Ohio, where he received his early education, and graduated from the University of Indiana in 1853. He studied theology in the Allegheny Seminary, and was licensed by the Pittsburgh Presbytery, April 18, 1859. He was ordained by the Philadelphia Presbytery, installed pastor of the congregation of Baltimore, Maryland, December 26, 1859, and resigned this charge, May 5, 1863. He labored three years in the far West as a Missionary. He was installed pastor of the united congregations of Olathe and

Pleasant Ridge, Johnston County, Kansas, March 10,
1866. He resigned the Pleasant Ridge branch, May 6,
1873, and Olathe, October 14, 1885. He is engaged in
gathering scattered Covenanters into societies, by appointment of the Central Board of Missions, with his residence in Olathe, Kansas. He married Miss Mary A.
McMunn, of Sharon, Ohio, November 22, 1859.

JOSEPH WYLIE McNAUGHER:

Son of Samuel and Jane (Steele) McNaugher, was
born in the city of Allegheny, Pennsylvania, January 14,
1861. He received his early education in the schools
of his native city, also in Newell Institute, Pittsburgh,
graduating from Geneva College in 1882, and engaged
in business with his father one year. He studied
theology in the Allegheny Seminary, and was licensed
by the Pittsburgh Presbytery, April 14, 1886. He soon
afterwards went abroad, and spent the summer in Europe.
In good health he sailed homeward, and took cold upon
the sea, causing inflammation of the bowels, from which
he died, on the vessel "City of Rome," within two days
of the New York harbor, September 8, 1886, his body
being brought home and interred in the Allegheny
Cemetery. He was an excellent scholar, of studious
habits, a sincere and pious Christian, and the upright
man in all his ways. He began the work of the
ministry with the right motive, and gave abundant
evidence of becoming an acceptable and faithful minister.
He was an editor of the *College Cabinet* two years,
beginning in 1880, and the efficient librarian of the
Theological Seminary.

DAVID METHENY, M. D.:

Son of Joseph and Jane (Sterrett) Metheny, was born near New Galilee, Beaver County, Pennsylvania, October 16, 1836. His parents died when he was in infancy, and he lived with his grandmother Metheny until he was fifteen years old. In 1851, he found a home with his uncle, Dr. S. A. Sterrett, of Pittsburgh, Pennsylvania, where he received a liberal education in the public schools and Allegheny City College. He studied medicine under the direction of Dr. S. A. Sterrett, and settled as a physician in the city of Allegheny, Pennsylvania. In the spring of 1864, he was chosen by Synod as a medical Missionary to Syria, and for this work he was ordained a ruling elder by the session of the Pittsburgh and Allegheny congregation, October 24, 1864. He, with others, sailed for Syria, November 2, 1864, where he labored at Latakia, and places adjacent, for nine years. In the spring of 1873, he visited America, was licensed and ordained by the Pittsburgh Presbytery, September 10, 1873, returned to Syria the same fall, and continued his work in the vicinity of Latakia for ten years. He established the Tarsus Mission, at Mersine, Asia Minor, December 28, 1883, where he is now laboring. He was twice married. First to Miss Emeline Gregg, of Allegheny City, Pennsylvania, April 29, 1862; and second, to Miss Mary E. Dodds, of Latakia, Syria, December 10, 1877. His writings are principally letters to the Board of Foreign Missions, and are published in the Church magazines. He was Moderator of the Synod of 1879.

JOHN MIDDLETON:

Son of William and Catharine (McArthur) Middleton,. was born in Johnstown, Fulton County, New York, January 31, 1811. His parents were members of the Presbyterian Church, with which body he also connected in early life. His childhood and youth were spent upon his father's farm, and his education was obtained as he had opportunity. He connected with the Covenanter Church in 1831. In 1835, he began classical studies with the ministry in view, and graduated from Jefferson College in 1839. He studied theology privately, also in the Allegheny Seminary, and was licensed by the Western Presbytery, May 15, 1842. He was ordained by the Rochester Presbytery, installed pastor of the congregation of Lisbon, St. Lawrence County, New York, February 8, 1844, and resigned this charge, April 11, 1854. He was installed pastor of the Second congregation of Perth, Canada, October 19, 1854, and resigned, April 11, 1856. He was installed pastor of the Third congregation of Philadelphia, Pennsylvania, November 18, 1856, and resigned this charge, May 17, 1862. He was installed pastor of the congregation of Staunton, Macoupin County, Illinois, May 23, 1865, and resigned this charge on account of failing health, August 9, 1870. From this time until his death he was almost constantly confined to the sick room, by a severe wasting disease, from which he died, at Staunton, Illinois, September 14, 1872. He married Miss Sibella Galbraith, of Burgettstown, Pennsylvania, September 29, 1839. He never possessed a robust constitution, and he suffered greatly from the rigor of the cold northern winters of New York and Canada. He was a plain, practical preacher, and made no attempt at oratory or eloquence. He was studious in his habits, took constant delight in searching the Scriptures, was a tender and affectionate pastor, and a pious and conscientious Christian.

ALEXANDER McLEOD MILLIGAN, D. D.:

Son of Rev. Dr. James and Mary (Trumbull) Milligan, was born in Ryegate, Caledonia County, Vermont, April 6, 1822.* Dedicated from his birth for the work of the gospel ministry, at a very early age he began classical studies under the direction of his father. He entered Craftsbury Academy to prepare for College, but on account of the removal of his parents, in 1839, to New Alexandria, Pennsylvania, his plans were frustrated, and he began teaching school near Blairsville, Pennsylvania. In 1841, he resumed his studies in the Western University of Pennsylvania, and graduated from Duquesne College in 1843. He studied theology in the Allegheny and Cincinnati Seminaries, and was licensed by the Pittsburgh Presbytery, April 14, 1847. He was ordained by the same Presbytery, and installed pastor of the united congregations of New Alexandria and Greensburgh, Westmoreland County, Pennsylvania, November 24, 1848, where he labored as his father's successor until his resignation, October 4, 1853. He was installed pastor of the Third congregation of Philadelphia, Pennsylvania, December 8, 1853, and resigned this charge, October 14, 1855. He was installed pastor of the united congregations of New Alexandria, Greensburgh and Clarksburgh, Pennsylvania, May 6, 1856,

* Memorial Volume.

and resigned these charges, April 10, 1866. He was
installed pastor of the congregation of Pittsburgh, Pennsylvania, May 14, 1866, where, by his rare powers as a
preacher, he built up one of the largest and most
influential congregations in the body, over which he
remained pastor until his death. His life was in jeopardy
in 1874, by reason of a dangerous tumor; and he was
restored from this critical condition in answer to prayer.
His health began to fail in the spring of 1884, having
spent a part of the previous winter teaching in the
Theological Seminary in addition to his pastoral duties.
In November, 1884, he repaired to the milder climate
of Southern California, to spend the winter. Disappointed
in the return of health, he turned his face homeward
to die among his kindred and friends, but departed this
life upon the overland train soon after it entered the
wilds of Wyoming Territory, May 7, 1885. His body
was enbalmed in Cheyenne, and brought home and
buried in the Bellevue Cemetery, Allegheny, in the
presence of a concourse of sorrowing people. His disease
was known as Addison's disease of the kidneys. He
was twice married. First to Miss Ellen Snodgrass,
June 24, 1847; and second, to Miss Belle A. Stewart,
August 24, 1871, both of New Alexandria, Pennsylvania.
He was a great and good man. In personal appearance
he was large and commanding, and his well cultivated
mind was filled with varied and useful knowledge,
gathered by close study and careful reading. He was
an eloquent and magnetic speaker. His voice was
musical, flexible, and powerful, and he often enchained
the attention of an audience for hours when he was

aroused upon such subjects as the cause of the slave or the rights of Christ as King of nations. He was a laborious, prudent, and affectionate pastor, devoted to the spiritual welfare of his flock. He was thoroughly in sympathy with the distinctive principles of the Covenanter Church, and fearlessly denounced the evils of society and the corruptions in high places. He did yeoman service as an abolitionist, received a good share of its reproachful honor, and wrote a consolatory letter to John Brown, in 1859, while he was incarcerated at Charlestown, Virginia. He was a leader in all reforms, especially the cause of National Reformation, in the interests of which he constantly preached and lectured. He was heard in Church courts with marked attention, and, as a public-spirited man, was prominent in the Church's work in all departments. He was a member of all the Mission Boards, as well as of the College and Seminary. The success of the establishment and endowment of Geneva College at Beaver Falls, Pennsylvania, was largely due to his personal exertions. He was a preacher rather than a writer, yet the pages of the Church magazines and the *Christian Statesman* contain many of his contributions. He was honored with the degree of Doctor of Divinity by Washington and Jefferson College in 1872. He was Moderator of the Synod of 1863.

ALEXANDER McLEOD MILLIGAN:

Son of Rev. Dr. A. M. and Ellen (Snodgrass) Milligan, was born in the city of Philadelphia, Pennsylvania, September 14, 1854. In 1856, his parents removed to New Alexandria, Pennsylvania, and, in 1866,

39

to Allegheny, Pennsylvania, where he received his early education in the public schools. He pursued his classical course in Geneva College, and also in Wheaton College, graduating from Geneva College in 1880. He studied theology in the Allegheny Seminary, was licensed by the Pittsburgh Presbytery, April 9, 1884, and has made preaching tours through the British Maritime Provinces, Canada, and the States.

EZRA McLEOD MILLIGAN:

Son of Rev. John C. K. and Rachael (Farrington) Milligan, was born in the city of New York, September 9, 1858. He received his early education in the schools of his native city, attended Geneva College, studied privately under his father, and engaged in business in New York for several years. He studied theology in the Allegheny Seminary, was licensed by the Pittsburgh Presbytery, April 11, 1888, and preached in La Junta, Colorado, for some months.

JAMES MILLIGAN, D. D.:

Son of John and Margaret (Milligan) Milliken, was born in Dalmellington, Ayershire, Scotland, August 7, 1785.* In early life he had very poor health and was supposed to be in consumption. His parents were members of the Established Church of Scotland, with which he also connected in 1799. His boyhood and youth were spent upon the moor in the duties of a shepherd boy, and he recited the classics to a private instructor twice a week. He came to America in 1801, and settled in Westmoreland County, Pennsylvania, where he engaged in selling general merchandise. He was

* *Presbyterian Historical Almanac*, Vol. 5, p. 398.

not satisfied with other Presbyterian Churches, and, after hearing the Rev. John Black preach and explain the principles of the Covenanter Church, he joined this body in 1805. He soon afterwards abandoned secular pursuits and began his classical studies in Jefferson College. In 1806, he opened an Academy in Greensburgh, Pennsylvania, which he taught but a short time, when he resumed his studies, and graduated with honor from Jefferson College in 1809. He became a teacher of the Languages in the University of Pennsylvania, also studied theology in the Philadelphia Seminary, and was licensed by the Northern Presbytery, April 4, 1811. He was ordained by the same Presbytery, installed pastor of the congregation of Coldenham, Orange County, New York, June 10, 1812, and resigned this charge, April 17, 1817. He was installed pastor of the congregation of Ryegate, Caledonia County, Vermont, September 26, 1817, and resigned the charge, May 17, 1839. He was installed pastor of the congregation of New Alexandria, Pennsylvania, November 23, 1839, which he resigned, April 16, 1848. He was installed pastor of the Bethel congregation, Sparta, Randolph County, Illinois, October 14, 1848, and resigned, May 24, 1855. He resided with his sons in Southfield, Michigan, and New Alexandria, Pennsylvania, for several years, and made missionary tours through different parts of the Church. He died at the home of his son, the Rev. J. S. T. Milligan, at Southfield, Michigan, of rheumatic paralysis, January 2, 1862. He married Miss Mary Trumbull, of Ryegate, Vermont, in 1820. He was an earnest and practical preacher, a distinguished linguist, a strict disciplinarian, and remarkably gifted in prayer. He was early in the field as a lecturer on slavery and temperance, and with fearlessness and success defeated the errors in doctrine taught throughout New England during his residence in that country. His labors in behalf of the slave were not confined to his Church, but he travelled all over the East awakening the sympathies of philanthropists, and exposing the complicity of the nation in this sin. He was the first to introduce the office of the deacon, and the practice of continuous singing in the Covenanter Church, which *improvements* brought him into many sharp controversies with his brethren. He suffered many hardships in dispensing gospel ordinances throughout the New England States and Canada, and made many extended preaching tours on horseback. Among his publications are: "A Defence of Infant Baptism," 1812. "A Narrative of the Secession Controversy in Vermont," 1823. "Grace and Free Agency," 1826. "Prospects of a True Christian in a Sinful World," 1827. He was honored with the degree of Doctor of Divinity by Muskingum College in 1850. He was Moderator of the Synod of 1825.

JOHN CALVIN KNOX MILLIGAN:

Son of Rev. Dr. James and Mary (Trumbull) Milligan, was born in Ryegate, Caledonia County, Vermont, February 1, 1829. In 1839, his parents removed to New Alexandria, Pennsylvania, where he received his early education in the common schools, and under the direction of his father. He studied the

classics in Allegheny, Pennsylvania, under the care of
Mr. William A. Acheson, graduating from the Western
University of Pennsylvania in 1848. He studied theology one year in the Cincinnati Seminary, and, in the
spring of 1849, became Principal of Geneva College,
and Professor of Mathematics. At the same time he
studied theology in the Northwood Seminary, and was
licensed by the Lakes Presbytery, April 16, 1852.
He was ordained by the same Presbytery at Utica,
Ohio, May 12, 1853, installed co-pastor of the First
Miami congregation, Northwood, Ohio, July 1, 1853,
and resigned the professorate and congregation, April
20, 1858. He was installed pastor of the First congregation of New York, New York, June 16, 1858,
where he is in charge. He married Miss Rachael W.
Farrington, of Newburgh, New York, October 3, 1854.
He is largely connected with the missionary and
educational interests of the Church, and has been
Chairman of the Board of Superintendents of the
Theological Seminary for several years. He established,
and is editor of, *Our Banner*, since 1874. He was
Moderator of the Synod of 1870.

JAMES RENWICK JOHNSTON MILLIGAN:
   Son of Rev. J. S. T. and Jane T. (Johnston)
Milligan, was born in Southfield, Oakland County,
Michigan, August 9, 1855. He received his early
education in the public schools of Birmingham, Michigan. In 1873, he entered Geneva College, where he
remained two years, and engaged in teaching. In
1876, he resumed his studies in, and graduated from,
Geneva College in 1880, and was employed in Boston,

Massachusetts, for two years. He studied theology in the Allegheny Seminary, was licensed by the Pittsburgh Presbytery, April 9, 1884, and preached in Kansas and Nebraska for some months. He was ordained by the Pittsburgh Presbytery, and installed pastor of the congregation of the city of Allegheny, Pennsylvania, October 15, 1885, where he is in charge. He was an editor of the *College Cabinet* in 1880.

JAMES SAURIN TURRETIN MILLIGAN:

Son of Rev. Dr. James and Mary (Trumbull) Milligan, was born in Ryegate, Caledonia County, Vermont, August 26, 1826. He received his early education in the schools of his native village, and, in 1839, his parents removed to New Alexandria, Pennsylvania, where he continued his classical studies under the direction of his father. In 1848, he began the study of theology in the Cincinnati Seminary, and, in 1849, took charge of the Grammar department of Geneva College, graduating from this institution in 1852. He at the same time pursued his theological studies in the Northwood Seminary, and was licensed by the Lakes Presbytery, April 16, 1852. He was ordained by the same Presbytery, installed pastor of the congregation of Southfield, Oakland County, Michigan, November 11, 1853, and resigned this charge, April 11, 1871. He was installed pastor of the congregation of North Cedar, Jackson County, Kansas, October 8, 1872, where he is in charge. He married Miss Jane T. Johnston, of Belle Centre, Ohio, June 16, 1853. In 1855, he was appointed to lecture upon "Bible Politics," and spent some time as the first

National Reform lecturer. In 1864, he organized the Mission among the contrabands at Washington, D. C. He has published many articles in the magazines and papers of the Church.

OSSAWATTOMIE BROWN MILLIGAN:

Son of Rev. Dr. A. M. and Ellen (Snodgrass) Milligan, was born in New Alexandria, Westmoreland County, Pennsylvania, November 4, 1861. In 1866, his parents removed to the city of Allegheny, Pennsylvania, where he received his early education in the public schools, also in Newell Institute, Pittsburgh, graduating from Geneva College in 1883. He studied theology in the Allegheny Seminary, and was licensed by the Pittsburgh Presbytery, April 14, 1886. He was ordained by the New York Presbytery, and installed pastor of the congregation of Bovina, Delaware County, New York, June 22, 1887, where he is in charge.

WILLIAM MILROY:

Son of James and Mary (McJerrow) Milroy, was born in York, Livingston County, New York, December 23, 1820. His parents were from Scotland, and early dedicated him for the work of the ministry. In early life he was sent to Scotland, where he laid the foundation of a thorough and accurate classical education in the Academy of Wigton, and returning to America, graduated from Union College in 1846. He studied theology in the Cincinnati Seminary, and under the care of the Rev. Samuel Bowden, being licensed by the Rochester Presbytery, June 10, 1851. He was ordained by the Lakes Presbytery, and installed pastor of the Second Miami congregation, Northwood, Logan

County, Ohio, October 12, 1854, where he spent the residue of his life. In 1870, he added to his pastorate the labors of Professor of Latin in Geneva College, which undoubtedly overtasked his strength, as he was not possessed of a robust constitution. In the fall of 1876, he was attacked with acute pleurisy, accompanied by extreme nausea, from which disease he died, at his home in Northwood, Ohio, November 15, 1876. He married Miss Isabella McCracken, of York, New York, October 6, 1854. He was a profound theologian and a most proficient classical scholar. He was not an attractive preacher, but he excelled in clear logic, complete exposition, and comprehensive treatment of the doctrines of grace and salvation. His blameless life, practical wisdom, and sagacious prudence gained to him the confidence and respect of all. He was a faithful pastor, an efficient teacher, and conscientiously regular in all his duties. He was heard with attention in Church courts, where his interpretations of Church polity conduced to the peaceful settlement of all questions. He was unambitious, and his retiring disposition prevented him from being as widely known as many others of less renown. He was Moderator of the Synod of 1872.

WILLIAM MILROY:

Son of James and Elizabeth (McGill) Milroy, was born in Freugh, Wigtonshire, Scotland, June 18, 1832. He received his preparatory classical education in the Academy of Newton-Stewart, Scotland, and, in 1853, came to America, settling in Ontario, Canada. He soon afterwards resumed his studies, and graduated from the

University of Toronto in 1858. He studied theology in the Allegheny Seminary, was licensed by the Pittsburgh Presbytery, April 3, 1861, and returned to Scotland the same fall. He was ordained by the Presbytery of Dumfries, and installed pastor of the congregation of Penpont, Scotland, August 7, 1862, where he remained in charge for fourteen years. In 1876, he, and most of the congregation, left the Covenanter Church and connected with the Free Church of Scotland, in which body he is an honored minister. Among his publications are: "Unity of the Church," 1864, pp. 28. "Conscience," 1866, pp. 24. "A Scottish Communion," 1882, pp. 212, and some magazine articles. He was Moderator of the Synod of the Free Church of Scotland in 1878.

WILLIAM McCRACKEN MILROY, B. D.:

Son of Rev. William and Isabella (McCracken) Milroy, was born in Northwood, Logan County, Ohio, August 25, 1855. He received his early education in the school of his native village, and graduated from Geneva College in 1877. In 1875, he was Tutor of Latin in Geneva College, and, in 1877, was made Professor of Latin as his father's successor. In 1879, he entered the Allegheny Seminary where he studied theology two years, and graduated from the Yale Divinity School in 1882. He studied another year in the Allegheny Seminary, and was licensed by the Lakes Presbytery, April 10, 1883. In the fall of 1883, he took up graduate work in the Union Seminary, New York City, and supplied the congregation of Brooklyn, New York, for several months. In 1884, he taught Greek in Westminster College, and, in 1885, entered the

Philological department of Johns Hopkins University, and is in charge of the Mission of the Central Presbyterian Church, Baltimore, Maryland. He received the degree of Bachelor of Divinity from Yale Seminary in 1882, and will receive that of Doctor of Philosophy from Johns Hopkins University in 1888.

ANDREW MONTGOMERY:

Son of James and Mary (Francie) Montgomery, was born in Conner, County Antrim, Ireland, July 2, 1824. He received his early education in his native land, came to America in March, 1846, and settled in New York City, New York. He resumed his studies in that city, and graduated from Geneva College in 1853. He studied theology at the same time in the Northwood Seminary, also under the Rev. Dr. James Christie, of New York, and was licensed by the New York Presbytery, November 9, 1854. He preached generally throughout the Church for eight years. He connected with the Presbyterian Church, being received by the Columbia Presbytery of that body, June 10, 1862. He preached throughout the State of New York, and as stated supply to the Congregational Church of Jefferson, Schoharie County, New York, for several years. In 1868, he was stated supply to the Presbyterian Church of Jewett, New York, and, in 1873, preached in Connecticut. In May, 1880, he went to Minnesota, and preached in many of the vacancies in that State, holding ecclesiastical communion in the Congregational Church. He suffered from a stroke of paralysis, and retired to the city of Minneapolis, Minnesota, where he is residing in enfeebled health.

He married Miss Mary C. Avery, of Jefferson, New York, in 1864.

ROBERT CAMERON MONTGOMERY:

Son of James and Margaret (Allen) Montgomery, was born in Pardoe, Mercer County, Pennsylvania, June 16, 1856. He received his early education in what is now Grove City College, and graduated from Westminster College in 1878. He studied theology in the Allegheny Seminary, and was licensed by the Pittsburgh Presbytery, April 13, 1881. He was ordained by the Philadelphia Presbytery, and installed pastor of the Third congregation of the city of Philadelphia, Pennsylvania, March 27, 1883, where he is in charge.

JOSEPH WASHINGTON MORTON:

Son of William and Hannah (Slemmons) Morton, was born near Rose Point, Lawrence County, Pennsylvania, January 3, 1821. His parents were members of the Presbyterian Church, with which body he connected in 1837. He received his early education in the schools of the neighborhood, studied the classics privately under the direction of Thomas Mehard and Ethan A. Stewart, and, in 1839, entered Beaver Academy, graduating from Brighton Institute in 1841. He studied theology in the Western Seminary at Allegheny, Pennsylvania, was licensed by the Beaver Presbytery, April 13, 1843, and was stated supply at Freedom and Concord, Pennsylvania, for two years. Chiefly on account of the refusal of the Presbyterian Church to testify against the sinful institution of human slavery, he left her communion, and connected with the Covenanter Church, being received as a licentiate by the

Pittsburgh Presbytery, May 29, 1845. He was ordained by the same Presbytery, installed pastor of the united congregations of Little Beaver, Jackson and West Greenville, centering near New Galilee, Beaver County, Pennsylvania, November 27, 1845, and resigned this charge, June 3, 1847. At the meeting of Synod in 1847, he was unanimously chosen as a Missionary to the newly organized Mission in the Island of Hayti, where he labored diligently for nearly two years. Coming in contact with the Missionary of the Seventh Day Baptist Church of Port au Prince, he changed his principles in reference to the Christian Sabbath, and became convinced that it was his duty to keep the seventh day of the week as the Christian Sabbath. He returned to the United States to lay his case before Synod, and was put upon trial for "denying the divine authority of the Christian Sabbath;" and, as the fact was not denied, he was suspended from the ministry and privileges in the Covenanter Church, by the authority of Synod, May 29, 1849. He soon afterwards connected with the Seventh Day Baptist Church, and began teaching in De Ruyter, Madison County, New York. He was pastor and teacher respectively in Plainfield, New Jersey, New York City, Vineland, New Jersey, and Ashaway, Rhode Island. He was pastor of the Seventh Day Baptist Church of Marlboro, New Jersey, for eight years; of Westerly and Pawtucket, Rhode Island, for two years; and for some length of time was engaged in secular pursuits in Vineland, New Jersey. In 1885, he became General Missionary of the Seventh Day Baptist Society, laboring in Illinois and Wisconsin, with his headquarters in Chicago, Illinois, and his residence in Milton, Wisconsin. He was twice married. First to Miss Mary J. Curry, of Beaver Falls, Pennsylvania, May 1, 1844; and second to Miss Jane C. Bond, of Milton, Wisconsin, September 17, 1885. Among his publications are: "The Psalter," 1847. "Le Catechism Abrege," 1848. "Vindication of the True Sabbath," 1850.

JAMES NEILL:

Son of Matthew and Jane (Black) Neill, was born in Aghadoey, County Londonderry, Ireland, March 16, 1811. He received his early education in that city under the direction of the Rev. J. P. Sweeney, graduating from the University of Glasgow, Scotland, in 1840, having studied theology one year in the Paisley Seminary. He came to America in May, 1840, resumed his studies in the Allegheny Seminary, and was licensed by the Pittsburgh Presbytery, April 7, 1842. He was ordained by the Lakes Presbytery, installed pastor of the congregation of Southfield, Oakland County, Michigan, May 18, 1843, and resigned this charge, October 6, 1851. He soon afterwards removed to Iowa, where he was employed for many years in the vacant congregations and mission stations. The exposure which he was required to endure in a new country and among scattered societies, caused inflammatory rheumatism, which completely wrecked his physical frame, and the last ten years of his life were spent in intense bodily suffering. While he was excluded from the active work of the ministry by this affliction, and to a great measure from social intercourse with his brethren, yet his mind lost none of its power, and he always manifested an interest in the work of the Church. He died from this painful disease, at his home in Hopkinton, Iowa, January 15, 1880. He married Miss Emeline McCartney, of Norwich, Ohio, May 30, 1843. He was a plain but earnest preacher of the gospel. He lost no opportunity to oppose looseness of discipline, and to controvert all forms of unbelief.

WILLIAM NEILL:

Was born in Garvagh, County Londonderry, Ireland, June 16, 1801. His parents were members of the Secession Church, and when he was quite young, came to America and settled in the vicinity of Farmington, Belmont County, Ohio, where they were under the pastoral care of the Rev. Alexander McCoy. He received his early education in this County, and attended Franklin College for several years. He studied theology under the direction of the Rev. Alexander McCoy, of West Virginia, and was licensed by the Reformed Dissenting Presbytery, May 13, 1829. He was ordained by the same court, April 19, 1831, and installed pastor of the societies of Three Ridges, Short Creek and Forks of Wheeling, in West Virginia, and Miller's Run in Washington County, Pennsylvania, October 18, 1831, where he preached for eight years. He was received into the Covenanter Church, by the Western Subordinate Synod, October 14, 1839, and labored for ten years in the vacancies of the Church. He joined the Associate Reformed Church, being received by the Chartiers Presbytery of that body, September 5, 1849. He afterwards lost his mind, was confined in an asylum in West Virginia for several years, and died, May 14, 1862. He was a man of considerable ability and theological education, but so eccentric that he was unappreciated as a preacher.

JAMES ROBERT NEWELL, PH. D.:

Son of Thomas and Elizabeth (Gregg) Newell, was born in the city of Belfast, Ireland, March 3, 1831. He received his early education in the public schools of his native city, and graduated from Queen's College in 1849. He came to America in the spring of 1850, and was employed as a teacher in a classical school in Baltimore, Maryland. In 1853, he was chosen to a professorship in Westminster College, Allegheny City, Pennsylvania, where he taught for eight years. In 1861, he became Professor of Languages in Allegheny City College, and subsequently founded Newell Institute, Pittsburgh, which became a flourishing preparatory and classical school. He studied theology in the Allegheny Seminary, and was licensed by the Pittsburgh Presbytery, May 23, 1867. He seldom preached beyond the vicinity of Pittsburgh, but devoted himself to teaching. He connected with the Presbyterian Church in 1871, and soon afterwards was chosen President of Mt. Auburn Female Seminary, Cincinnati, Ohio, where he died very suddenly of apoplexy, November 8, 1874. He married Miss Christiana W. Sproull, of Allegheny City, Pennsylvania, July 22, 1856. He was an acceptable preacher, but best known as a teacher. He was a fine classical scholar, well-read in educational matters, and possessed to a remarkable degree the gifts of imparting instruction.

He was honored with the degree of Doctor of Philosophy by Washington and Jefferson College in 1871.
JOHN NEWELL, D. D.:

Son of Thomas and Elizabeth (Gregg) Newell, was born in the city of Belfast, Ireland, August 18, 1824. He received his early education in the public schools of his native city, and graduated with honor from the Belfast Academical Institution in 1845. He studied theology in the Seminary of Paisley, Scotland, and was licensed by the Eastern Presbytery, Ireland, October 9, 1849. The following spring he came to America, was ordained by the Rochester Presbytery, installed pastor of the congregation of Syracuse, New York, May 7, 1851, and resigned this charge, May 26, 1853. In the fall of 1853, he accepted the Presidency of Westminster College, Allegheny City, Pennsylvania, where he remained in charge for seven years. In 1860, he resigned this position and returned, with his family, to Ireland. He was installed pastor of the congregation of Newtonards, County Down, Ireland, May 8, 1861, and resigned this congregation May 10, 1867. He was installed pastor of the congregation of Manchester, England, October 14, 1867, where he was pastor three years. He returned to the United States in May, 1871, taught in Newell Institute, Pittsburgh, and also preached in the vacancies adjacent. He died at his residence in Wilkinsburgh, Pennsylvania, of pericarditis, complicated with pneumonia, September 20, 1875. He married Miss Harriet Finlay, of Buffalo, New York, May 20, 1851. Gifted with mental endowments above the ordinary, and possessing a thorough classical education, he was a finished scholar and a successful teacher. He was a teacher rather than a preacher. He was, however, a well-read theologian, and his sermons were finished discourses and well prepared. His delivery was mild, but there was an unction and pathos in his voice that never failed to interest his hearers. Having travelled much, and stored his mind with useful knowledge, he was well posted in general information. He was honored with the degree of Doctor of Divinity by an institution in Baltimore, Maryland, in 1857. Among his publications are: "The Higher Law," 1851, pp. 39. "The Royal Priesthood of Messiah," 1858, pp. 20. He was Moderator of the Synod of Ireland in 1862.

ROBERT GAMBLE ORR:

Son of Robert and Elizabeth (Gamble) Orr, was born in Donascallion, County Londonderry, Ireland, July 8, 1787.* He attended the schools of his neighborhood, and entered the University of Glasgow, Scotland, where he graduated in 1810. He studied theology in the Seminary of Stirling, Scotland, and was licensed by the Western Presbytery, Ireland, March 16, 1813. He was ordained by the Northern Presbytery, installed pastor of the united congregations of Dumboc and Ballyrashane, Ireland, August 31, 1815, and was released from this charge, at the request of the congregation, July 26, 1820. He came to America in 1832, and, at the division of the Church in August, 1833, became identified with the New School branch of the Covenanter Church. He preached for some time at Ogdensburgh, New York. He died of mortification arising

---

* Communications from Ireland.

from an injury received in one of his feet, at Paterson, New Jersey, June 12, 1835. From the experiences through which he passed, it is evident that he was not highly regarded as a preacher.

JAMES PATTON:

Son of Joseph and Margaret (Kingston) Patton, was born in Sparta, Randolph County, Illinois, April 11, 1855. He received his early education in the High School of his native town, and graduated from Monmouth College in 1883. He studied theology in the Allegheny Seminary, was licensed by the Illinois Presbytery, April 14, 1886, preached for a few months in the British Provinces, and other parts of the Church.

THOMAS PATTON:

Son of Joseph and Margaret (Kingston) Patton, was born in Sparta, Randolph County, Illinois, December 19, 1852. He received his early education in the High School of his native town, and, in 1873, entered Geneva College, where he remained two years, and engaged in teaching near his home. In 1877, he resumed his studies in Westminster College, and graduated from Monmouth College in 1880. He studied theology in the Allegheny Seminary, was licensed by the Illinois Presbytery, April 11, 1883, and labored in Kansas, Nebraska, Minnesota, and the British Provinces. He was ordained by the New Brunswick and Nova Scotia Presbytery, and installed pastor of the congregation of Barnesville, Kings County, New Brunswick, May 26, 1887, where he is in charge. He married Miss Anna Carithers, of Linton, Iowa, June 10, 1885.

JAMES LOUGHRIDGE PINKERTON:

Son of Samuel and Mary (Warnock) Pinkerton, was born near West Hebron, Washington County, New York, March 28, 1849. In 1851, his parents removed to Waupaca, Wisconsin, where he connected with the Vernon congregation, and entered Monmouth College, where he graduated in 1873. He studied theology in the Allegheny Seminary, and was licensed by the Pittsburgh Presbytery, April 12, 1876. In 1877, while supplying the Mission at Suffolk, Virginia, he was prostrated by a severe attack of fever, affecting both body and mind. He retired to his home near Waupaca, Wisconsin, for some time, made an extended tour through Europe, and returned much improved after several years of rest. He was ordained by the Pittsburgh Presbytery, installed pastor of the congregation of New Alexandria, Westmoreland County, Pennsylvania, May 17, 1881, and resigned on account of enfeebled health, October 9, 1883, since which time he has retired from all active service, and is residing near Waupaca, Wisconsin.

WILLIAM ALEXANDER PINKERTON:

Son of Samuel and Margaret J. (Smith) Pinkerton, was born near Clarinda, Page County, Iowa, January 1, 1861. He received his preparatory education in the High School of Clarinda, graduating from Amity College in 1882, and engaged in teaching one year. He studied theology in the Allegheny Seminary, was licensed by the Kansas Presbytery, April 4, 1887, and preached a few months in Burdett, Kansas, and other localities. He married Miss Alice E. Whitehead, of Allegheny, Pennsylvania, December 22, 1887.

JAMES THOMSON POLLOCK:

Son of William and Fannie R. (Thomson) Pollock, was born near Leesville, Carroll County, Ohio, August 14, 1835. His parents were worthy members of the Covenanter Church, and removed to Belle Centre, Logan County, Ohio, in 1847. He received his early education in Geneva College, graduating in 1856. He studied theology two years in the Associate Seminary at Xenia, Ohio, two years in the Allegheny Seminary, and was licensed by the Lakes Presbytery, April 18, 1860. He was ordained by the New York Presbytery, and installed pastor of the congregation of Bovina, Delaware County, New York, July 11, 1861. He connected with the United Presbyterian Church, being received by the Wheeling Presbytery of that body, March 10, 1864. He was commissioned, July 14, 1864, to labor in the South among the soldiers, and was Chaplain of the Eighth Indiana regiment, during the war of the rebellion. In the summer of 1865, he returned North, supplied vacancies, and connected with the Presbyterian Church, September 17, 1866. He was installed pastor of the congregation of Osborn, Ohio, May 2, 1867, and has held charges respectively in Monroeville, Tiffin, Maumee City, Bucyrus, Utica, and is now pastor of the Presbyterian Church of Madisonville, Hamilton County, Ohio. He married Miss Elizabeth A. Andrews, of Dayton, Ohio, June 12, 1867.

HUGH WALKINSHAW REED:

Son of Rev. Robert and Mary (Walkinshaw) Reed, was born near Lucesco, Westmoreland County, Pennsylvania, July 26, 1855. He received his early education in the schools of his native County, graduating from Geneva College in 1878. He studied theology in the Allegheny Seminary, and was licensed by the Pittsburgh Presbytery, April 13, 1881. He was ordained by the New York Presbytery, installed pastor of the congregation of Ryegate, Caledonia County, Vermont, January 19, 1883, and resigned this charge, September 21, 1886. He was chosen Principal of Knox Academy, Selma, Alabama, October 4, 1886, where he taught and preached until January 1, 1888. He was installed pastor of the congregation of Youngstown, Ohio, May 4, 1888, where he is in charge. He was twice married. First to Miss I. Emma Robeson, of Dresden, Ohio, March 29, 1881; and second, to Miss Alice B. Miller, of Ryegate, Vermont, November 23, 1886.

ROBERT REED:

Son of Robert and Mary (Gibson) Reed, was born near Brandywine Manor, Chester County, Pennsylvania, June 13, 1821. His parents soon afterwards removed to the city of Pittsburgh, Pennsylvania, thence to Mifflin, near Pittsburgh, and finally to Londonderry, Guernsey County, Ohio. He received his early education in Madison College, graduating from Muskingum College in 1848. He studied theology in the Cincinnati and Northwood Seminaries, and was licensed by the Lakes Presbytery, April 16, 1852. He was ordained by the Pittsburgh Presbytery, installed pastor of the united congregations of Brookland and North Washington, Lucesco, Westmoreland County, Pennsylvania, June 21, 1854, and resigned, April 11, 1882. In May, 1884, he became stated supply to the

Monongahela congregation, Elizabeth, Pennsylvania, where he preached until shortly before his death. He was troubled with kidney disease for several years, resulting in sciatica and blood poisoning, which caused extreme suffering, and from which he died, at his home near Lucesco, Pennsylvania, October 31, 1886. He married Miss Mary Walkinshaw, of Lucesco, Pennsylvania, September 16, 1854. He was an earnest preacher of the gospel and strongly attached to the distinctive principles of the Covenanter Church. He was of a quiet and diffident disposition, never making himself prominent, but he was candid and decided in his opinions, and unswerving in his convictions of truth and uprightness. He was highly esteemed as a good Presbyter, a faithful pastor, and an exemplary Christian.

ROBERT CAMERON REED:

Son of Rev. Robert and Mary (Walkinshaw) Reed, was born near Lucesco, Westmoreland County, Pennsylvania, April 25, 1860. He received his early education in that vicinity, graduating from Geneva College in 1885. He studied theology in the Allegheny Seminary, was licensed by the Pittsburgh Presbytery, April 11, 1888, and preached within the bounds of that Presbytery.

DANIEL REID:

Son of Allan and Margaret (Millar) Reid, was born in Cedarville, Green County, Ohio, March 22, 1834. In early life his natural diffidence and timidity were so great, that his godly parents feared he would be prevented from prosecuting his studies for the ministry, to which they had dedicated him. In 1846, his parents removed to Harper, Logan County, Ohio, and he was the first student to enter Geneva College at its organization, from which institution he graduated in 1855. The next year he began the study of theology in the Associate Seminary at Xenia, Ohio, the following three years pursuing his course in the Allegheny Seminary, and was licensed by the Lakes Presbytery, April 18, 1860. He was ordained by the Pittsburgh Presbytery, and installed pastor of the Oil Creek congregation, Titusville, Crawford County, Pennsylvania, December 19, 1861, where he remained in charge until his death. This field of labor was very extensive, and he was constantly exposed to all kinds of weather. Here he labored diligently for his Master, until prostrated by pneumonia, followed by a malignant typhoid fever, from which he died, at his home near Titusville, Pennsylvania, March 31, 1875. He married Miss Agnes Wright, of Titusville, Pennsylvania, January 22, 1863. He was an earnest, instructive and evangelical preacher of the gospel. He was especially distinguished for his conscientiousness, humility, and piety. He was not an eloquent preacher, but he gave a sound and interesting presentation of divine truth, and was firm in his attachment to the principles of the Church. His reserved and timid disposition prevented him from holding a prominent position in the Church.

JAMES REID:

Was born in the parish of Shotts, Scotland, August 12, 1750.* He received the rudiments of an education

---

* *Reformed Presbyterian*, Vol. 3, p. 187.

in the schools of his native parish, and graduated from Edinburgh College in 1776. He studied theology in the Seminary of Stirling, Scotland, and was licensed by the Reformed Presbytery of Scotland, April 27, 1780. He was ordained by the same court, and installed pastor of the united congregations of Wigtown and Kirkcudbright, Scotland, July 10, 1783. It was during this period that the few faithful Covenanters in America were deprived of all their ministry by defection, and made urgent application to the Reformed Presbytery of Scotland for ministerial assistance. After much serious deliberation, Mr. Reid accepted the appointment to visit America, and left Scotland, August 4, 1789. He visited all the Covenanter societies from New York to the Carolinas, organized many congregations, and dispensed the sacraments. He returned to Scotland, July 16, 1790. He resumed his labors with renewed diligence among his flock, which was soon afterwards reduced by the Stranraer society being organized into a separate congregation, and he continued in charge of Newton-Stewart, Whithorn and Castle Douglas. In 1825, in consequence of a decision of the Synod to erase the particular mention of the Auchensaugh renovation of the Covenants from the terms of communion, he regarded it a departure from the Testimony, and withdrew, with a few followers, from the communion of the Reformed Presbyterian Church, and maintained a separate standing. In the spring of 1828, he removed to the city of Glasgow, Scotland, where he resided with his daughter, Mrs. Stewart, continued to preach to a few people until old age caused his strength to fail, and where he died of a severe illness, November 4, 1837. He married Miss Helen Bland, of Anworth, Scotland, December 26, 1786. He was a good man, full of the Holy Ghost and of faith. Notwithstanding the checkered career of his life, and the unfavorable circumstances for study, he was an acceptable and edifying preacher, and did not fail to raise his voice against personal and national evils. He was distinguished for his gravity of deportment, kindliness of manner, and regularity in the performance of religious duties. During his last days his eyesight failed him, yet he desired to have his books beside him, from which others read to him, imparting subjects for meditation and prayer. Among his publications extant are: " The Lives of the Westminster Divines," in two volumes. "The Divinity of Christ," 1792, pp. 60. "The Incarnation," 1794, pp. 68.

JOHN REILLY:

Was born in Ballibay, County Monaghan, Ireland, August 7, 1780.* He came to America in October, 1797, and settled in the city of Philadelphia, Pennsylvania, where he prosecuted his studies for becoming a teacher. In due time he entered upon his chosen vocation in Darby and Frankford, near Philadelphia. He was ordained a ruling elder in Dr. Wylie's congregation, August 5, 1801, and continued in this office until he entered upon the work of the ministry. Being deemed qualified, he entered upon the study of theology under the Rev. Dr. S. B. Wylie, and was licensed by the Middle Presbytery, May 24, 1809. He preached with great acceptance throughout the vacancies, and also in

* Sprague's Annals.

South Carolina, for three years. He was ordained *sine titulo* by the Middle Presbytery, February 23, 1813, and sent as a Missionary to South Carolina. He was installed pastor of the united congregations of Beaver Dam in Chester District, and Wateree in Fairfield District, South Carolina, October 8, 1813, where he labored the remainder of his life. He died of a bilious fever, at his home in Beaver Dam, South Carolina, August 27, 1820. He married Miss Jane Weir, of Philadelphia, Pennsylvania, in 1806. He was a plain, practical, and instructive preacher, and was popular among all classes of people. He was distinguished for his gentleness and kindness, being very attentive to the young. He was bold to speak against the evils of Church and State, and denounced with special severity the practice of holding slaves as chattels.

JOHN RICE:

Son of Samuel C. and Susan (Kessen) Rice, was born in Paisley, Scotland, February 23, 1824. He received his early education in the private school of Mr. J. K. Chalmers, and in the Grammar School of William Hunter, LL. D., graduating from the University of Glasgow, Scotland, in 1844. He studied theology in the Paisley Seminary, was licensed by the Paisley Presbytery, July 4, 1848, and preached for a few years in Scotland. He came to America in the spring of 1853, and preached one year, principally in the vacancies of the State of New York. He connected with the Presbyterian Church, being received by the Ohio Presbytery of that body, October 21, 1854. He was ordained by the Saltsburgh Presbytery, and installed pastor of the united congregations of Harmony, Mechanicsville and Union, Indiana County, Pennsylvania, in 1856, where he remained eight years. He was installed, in 1864, over the united congregations of Fairfield, Milledgeville and Sandy Lake, Mercer County, Pennsylvania, and remained nine years. In 1873, he took charge of the united congregations of Bethel, Onslow, Wayne and Scotch Grove, Jones County, Iowa, resigning in 1881, when he retired from active service, and is living upon his farm near Scotch Grove, Iowa. He was married twice. First to Miss Jessie H. Mowatt, of Syracuse, New York, in 1854; and second, to Miss Louisa M. Diven, of Penn Run, Pennsylvania, in 1857.

THOMAS PLANTS ROBB:

Son of George and Jane (George) Robb, was born near Venice, Washington County, Pennsylvania, April 5, 1843. He received a liberal education in the common schools of his native County, finished the course in the Dayton Union Academy in 1866, and graduated from Muskingum College in 1867. He studied theology in the Allegheny Seminary, and was licensed by the Pittsburgh Presbytery, April 12, 1870. He was ordained by the Lakes Presbytery, installed pastor of the Garrison congregation, Glenwood, Fayette County, Indiana, May 16, 1871, and resigned this charge, April 12, 1874. He was installed pastor of the Sharon congregation, Linton, Des Moines County, Iowa, July 6, 1874, where he is in charge. He married Miss Catharine Marshall, of Dayton, Pennsylvania, October 16, 1872.

WILLIAM LOUIS ROBERTS, D. D.:

Son of John and Mary (Smith) Roberts, was born near Franklin, Pendleton County, Virginia, (now in

West Virginia) June 27, 1798. His parents were members of the Associate Reformed Church, and removed
to Canonsburgh, Pennsylvania, in 1804, where he
received his early education. He pursued his preparatory course in the Academy of Bedford, Pennsylvania,
and graduated from Jefferson College in 1820. He
received the appointment as cadet in the United States
Military Academy at West Point, New York, but was '
finally persuaded to abandon military aspirations by
the Rev. Dr. J. R. Willson and connected with the
Covenanter Church. He studied theology under the
direction of the Rev. Dr. J. R. Willson at Coldenham,
New York, and was licensed by the Northern Presbytery, September 11, 1822. He was ordained by the
same Presbytery, installed pastor of the congregation of
Paterson, New Jersey, May 19, 1824, and resigned
this charge, December 18, 1825. He was installed
pastor of the united congregations of Clyde, Galen,
Caledonia and York, New York, November 16, 1826,
and resigned these societies, October 6, 1830. He
was installed pastor of the congregation of Baltimore,
Maryland, January 15, 1835, and was released, October
9, 1837. He was installed pastor of the united congregations of Clyde and Sterling, New York, October
19, 1837, and resigned this charge, May 26, 1855. He
removed to Hopkinton, Delaware County, Iowa, and
was stated supply to the newly organized congregation of that place for five years, being installed pastor,
May 9, 1860, where he remained until his very sudden death of heart disease, December 7, 1864. He
was twice married. First to Miss Margaret. Milliken,

of Walden, New York, in 1821; and second to Miss
Anna Acheson, of New York City, New York, in
1830. He was a learned, eloquent and earnest preacher
of the gospel. By many he was regarded as one of
the great preachers of the Covenanter Church, and
was known to a large circle of professional men as
a public-spirited minister. He was a keen controversialist and a great debater. He was held in high esteem
by those who differed from his sentiments, for his
candid opinions and unwavering tenacity to Bible
principles of government. He was a talented author,
a forcible writer, and did much with his voice and
pen to strengthen the members of the Church in her
distinctive principles. Among his writings extant are:
"Submission to the Powers that Be," 1828, pp. 140.
"The Higher Law," 1851, pp. 32. "The Reformed
Presbyterian Catechism," 1853, pp. 188. He was
honored with the degree of Doctor of Divinity by
Jefferson College in 1846. He was Moderator of the
Synod of 1853.

SAMUEL ROBINSON:

Son of John and Sarah (McElroy) Robinson, was
born near Dervock, County Antrim, Ireland, in 1780.*
He was brought up under the pastoral care of the
Rev. James McKinney. He came to America in 1791,
and settled in the Chester District, South Carolina,
where he received his early education, and entered the
Philadelphia Academy. He studied theology in the Philadelphia Seminary, was licensed by the Middle Presbytery, May 9, 1814, and preached with great acceptance

---

* Communications from relatives and acquaintances.

in the South and West for several years. He was
ordained by the Western Presbytery, installed pastor
of the congregation of Cincinnati, Ohio, October 10,
1818, and, for constant intemperate habits, was deposed
by the same court, August 20, 1821. He was afterwards restored in the Associate Reformed Church, and
preached as a supply to the Second Presbyterian Church
of Cincinnati, Ohio. He connected with the New
School Covenanter Church, preached in Cincinnati, and
frequently lectured in the Mechanic's Institute. He
died a reformed man, at the home of his brother,
near Oxford, Preble County, Ohio, August 15, 1845.
He was thrice married. First to Miss Margaret Miller,
of Philadelphia, Pennsylvania; second to an intemperate
woman who was the cause of his trouble; and third
to Mrs. Camp, of Cincinnati, Ohio, who was a great
worker in the Methodist Church. He was a man of
a commanding appearance, a popular preacher, and
an eloquent lecturer. He was a well-read historian,
proficient in Biblical literature, possessing a mind well
stored with useful knowledge, and was frequently
engaged as a lecturer as well as a preacher.

MOSES RONEY:

Son of James and Jane (McWhirter) Roney, was
born near Canonsburgh, Washington County, Pennsylvania, September 20, 1804.* His parents were descended
from a long line of Covenanter ancestry, and their
first settlement in America was in South Carolina,
where tradition says they prospered. Their princ... es
being so antagonistic to the institution of human

* MS. from his son, Hon. J. B. Roney, Philadelphia, Pa.

slavery, they left their home in the South and emigrated to Western Pennsylvania—then the "great wilderness West." Here they made a new home, building a house (still standing) from logs cut in the forest and hewn into shape by the immediate ancestors of Moses Roney. His parents were most exemplary members of the Covenanter Church, who gave him a strict religious training and instilled into his mind those principles of civil and religious liberty which bore fruit throughout the whole of his after life. In 1818, he entered Canonsburgh Academy, and graduated with first honors from Jefferson College in 1823. Soon afterwards he left his home with a parental blessing, and as his outfit with which to begin the battle of life—a horse, saddle, bridle and the saddle-bags of the day. Turning his face eastward he rode to Baltimore, Maryland, where he sold his travelling outfit, and taught in a classical school for two years, during which time he was a member of the Baltimore congregation. He then repaired to Coldenham, New York, where he studied theology under the direction of the Rev. Dr. J. R. Willson, and was licensed by the Pittsburgh Presbytery, June 8, 1829. He was ordained by the Northern Presbytery, and installed pastor of the congregation of Newburgh, New York, June 8, 1830. He was chosen by Synod as the editor of the *Reformed Presbyterian*, and continued as editor of that magazine from its first issue in March, 1837, until his death, with the exception of the year 1848, when he was in the South. In 1843, he contracted a severe cold while engaged in his untiring efforts in behalf of his congregation and the people by whom he was surrounded. The immediate cause of it was his pastoral visits, on one of which occasions he was going homeward in midwinter from an overheated room whither he had been summoned on an errand of charity, and was kept out in the cold winter air until morning in returning. This reception of cold was followed by an inflammation of the lungs and hemorrhages, but he continued actively engaged in his pastoral duties. During this period the bold spirit of his ancestors came to the front, and he became a recognized, though quiet, leader of the abolitionists of the neighborhood, entertaining at his house, when hotels were closed against them, the leaders in the movement. It is related of him that upon one occasion when an anti-slavery meeting was to be held in his church at which he was to be present, a number of his fellow-citizens called upon him and warned him of his danger. With the courage that always distinguished him, after thanking them, he went to the meeting, and it is said his personal presence prevented an outbreak which threatened to be serious, as he was held in high esteem by those who differed from his political as well as religious views. In 1847, his disease had made such rapid progress that he was advised by his physicians to spend the winter in a warmer climate. Unwilling to leave his post of duty, he went to Baltimore and consulted one of the most eminent physicians of that city, who had been his friend in earlier years. Acting upon his advice he immediately went to Aikin, South Carolina, to which place also he returned the following winter. Being thus compelled to abandon pastoral duties, he resigned the Newburgh congregation, October 10, 1848. In the summer of 1849, he accepted the Presidency of Westminster College, Allegheny City, Pennsylvania, and removed his family to that city, where he continued to labor, until his death by consumption, July 3, 1854, and was buried in the old graveyard of Coldenham, New York. He married Miss Elizabeth F. Beattie, of Coldenham, New York, in 1831, whose mother was descended from the famous Belknap family of that region. He was one of the most fascinating pulpit orators of his day. He was eloquent both in sentiment and expression, and possessed a full loud voice. His whole bearing was intellectual, and one calculated to carry influence and dignity into every department of Church work. As a teacher in Baltimore, pastor and editor in Newburgh, professor and editor in Allegheny, his voice and his pen were always used to their full extent in the furtherance of truth and righteousness. While many differed with him in sentiment, none ever doubted his sincerity. His was a master mind. Endowed as his birthright with the sense of true honor, and possessing an unyielding devotion and unwavering attachment to the distinctive principles of the Covenanter Church, he lived as he died, in the full belief that no less to the Covenanters of Scotland than to the Puritans of England, America owed her manifold blessings of civil and religious liberty. Religiously he was so strong in his deep-rooted conviction of the truth of the principles, that when the ordeal

41

came through which the Church passed in 1833, he was the leader who called together those who held intact the testimony of the Church. He was Moderator of the Synod of 1843.

THOMAS ALEXANDER RUSK:

Son of Thomas and Mary (Westby) Rusk, was born in the city of New York, New York, December 16, 1859. He received his early education in the public schools, and in the Columbia Grammar School, graduating from Columbia College in 1880. He studied theology two years in the Allegheny Seminary, and engaged in clerical work in New York. In the fall of 1883, he resumed his studies in the Union Seminary, New York, where he graduated in May, 1885. He was licensed by the New York Presbytery, May 20, 1885, and preached in New Brunswick, and other parts of the Church.

WILLIAM LLOYD CUMMINGS SAMSON:

Son of Henry F. and Isabella M. (McKenery) Samson, was born in Wyman, Louisa County, Iowa, December 31, 1863. His parents removed to Washington, Iowa, in 1881, where he received his early education in the Washington Academy, graduating from Geneva College in 1885. He studied theology in the Allegheny Seminary, was licensed by the Iowa Presbytery, April 4, 1888, and preached in Houlton, Maine, for some time.

DAVID SCOTT:

Son of William and Margaret (Gregg) Scott, was born in Pollockshaws, near Glasgow, Scotland, July 17, 1794. In very early life he entered upon a thorough classical course of study, graduating from the University of Glasgow, Scotland, in 1820, having spent two years in the study of medicine. He studied theology in the Paisley Seminary, was licensed by the Glasgow Presbytery, June 10, 1824, and preached and taught in his native land for five years. He came to America in the spring of 1829, and preached with much acceptance for three years. He was ordained *sine titulo* by the Southern Presbytery, as a Home Missionary, November 1, 1832, and visited many of the Mission Stations. He was installed pastor of the congregation of Albany, New York, June 7, 1836, and resigned this charge, May 8, 1842. He was installed pastor of the congregation of Rochester, New York, July 11, 1844, and was released, July 19, 1862. With the exception of the winter of 1866, when he taught in the Allegheny Theological Seminary, he labored within the bounds of the Rochester Presbytery the remainder of his life. He was long afflicted with asthma, but died of an affection of the heart, at his home in Rochester, New York, March 29, 1871. He married Miss Eliza Walker, of New York City, May 13, 1833. He was an unassuming preacher and made no display, but excelled in clear logic and lucid expositions. His discourses were characterized by a faultless arrangement, appropriate Scriptural illustrations, and were the fruit of careful study. He was a learned man and a most instructive preacher, never allowing any affair to interfere with his pulpit preparation. He was a man of sound judgment, wise legislation, and well acquainted with the history of the Church. During the controversy of 1833, he stood firmly to the principles of the Church, advocated fearlessly their truth and practicability, and succeeded in vindicating the Church against the attacks of her ablest opponents. He was very punctual in his attendance upon Church courts, was never absent from a meeting of Synod, and but once from Presbytery, during the forty years of his ministry. He was a proficient historian, and wrote many historical and controversial articles for the magazines of the Church. Among his publications are: "A Calm Examination of Dr. Gilbert McMaster's 'Civil Government,'" 1832, pp. 44. "An Exposure of Dr. Gilbert McMaster's 'Brief Inquiry,'" 1833, pp. 28. "Extract of the Minutes of the Division of 1833," 1833, pp. 38. "Distinctive Principles," 1841, pp. 324. "Argument on the Church," 1854, pp. 60. "Narrative of the Division of 1833," 1863, pp. 28, and a few minor pamphlets. He was Moderator of the Synods of 1840 and 1851.

GEORGE SCOTT, D. D.:

Son of William and Agnes (Henry) Scott, was born in Crevah, County Monaghan, Ireland, July 26, 1805.* In early life he began the study of the classics under the direction of the Rev. Samuel Carlisle, and subsequently under Rev. Thomas Cathcart. He came to America in 1822, and soon afterwards settled in the city of Philadelphia, where he opened a classical school, and recited in the advanced studies to the Rev. Dr. S. B. Wylie. He studied theology under the direction of the Rev. S. B. Wylie, D. D., was licensed by the

---

* Communications from the family.

Philadelphia Presbytery, April 14, 1830, and made an extensive tour through the South and West. He was ordained by the Pittsburgh Presbytery, and installed pastor of the Little Beaver congregation, New Galilee, Beaver County, Pennsylvania, April 19, 1831. At the division of the Church in August, 1833, he became identified with the New School branch of the Covenanter Church, and remained pastor of a portion of his former charge, which was known as the Darlington congregation, where he remained until his resignation, October 10, 1863. For five years he preached in the vacancies as his health would permit. He connected with the Presbyterian Church, October 7, 1868, and, in 1878, removed to New Brighton, Pennsylvania, where he was honorably retired from active service, and where he died, December 16, 1881. He was thrice married. First to Miss Mary Brown, of Greensburgh, Pennsylvania, June 18, 1832; second, to Miss Duisa A. Forbes, of Petersburgh, Ohio, November 28, 1843; and third, to Mrs. Maria C. Lindsley, of New York City, May 20, 1873. He was an interesting evangelical preacher of the gospel, and his pulpit exhibitions were profoundly solemn and frequently eloquent. He was a faithful and successful pastor, a pious and sincere Christian. He was long connected with Darlington Academy, and prominently connected with the literary and missionary operations of his denomination. He was honored with the degree of Doctor of Divinity by Monmouth College in 1864. He was Moderator of the General Synod in 1852.

WALTER MOFFAT SHANKS:

Son of Samuel and Agnes (Rea) Shanks, was born in Ouley, County Down, Ireland, October 12, 1842. In early life he came to America, and settled in the city of New York, where he was cast upon his own resources. By incessant toil and prudent management he obtained his rudimentaay education in night schools, attended the free night school at Cooper Union, and graduated from Lafayette College in 1873. He studied theology in the Allegheny Seminary, and was licensed by the New York Presbytery, May 17, 1876. For five years he preached as stated supply at Detroit and Fairgrove, Michigan, and other parts of the Church. In the fall of 1881, he went to Scotland, where he was stated supply at Douglas Water. He held the view that the Covenanted work of Reformation, and the National and Solemn League and Covenant, have authority and obligation above all the renovations that have been made, and that the present Covenanter Church has followed defection. For these and other reasons he was suspended by the Synod of Scotland, March 6, 1883. After a careful examination of his peculiar beliefs, and finding nothing subversive to the position or interests of the Church, he was restored, December 5, 1883, and has been laboring in the congregation of Lanark, Scotland. He married Miss Isabella G. McQueen, of West Hebron, New York, January 1, 1878. Among his publications are: "Infant Baptism," "The Divine Ordinance of Praise," "Catholic Union," and "This Blessed Union and Conjunction," all of which are in tract form.

BYRON MELANCTHON SHARP:

Son of James and Mary (Thompson) Sharp, was born near New Galilee, Beaver County, Pennsylvania, February 17, 1853. His parents were members of the

Associate Church, and he connected with the Covenanter Church in 1877. He received his early education in the schools of his native village, also in the Darlington Academy, and graduated from Westminster College in 1879. He taught in the Academy of Frankfort Springs, and was employed by a mercantile agency two years. He studied theology in the Allegheny Seminary, was licensed by the Pittsburgh Presbytery, April 9, 1884, and preached in the Maritime Provinces and in the Mission Stations of the West. He was ordained by the Kansas Presbytery, and installed pastor of the Long Branch congregation, Blanchard, Page County, Iowa, October 13, 1887, where he is in charge.

ROBERT JAMES SHARPE :

Son of John and Sarah (Simpson) Sharpe, was born in Ahoghill, County Antrim, Ireland, December 11, 1835. He came with his parents to America in early life, and settled near Mahoning, Indiana County, Pennsylvania, where he received his early education, and graduated from Allegheny City College in 1861. He studied theology in the Allegheny Seminary, and was licensed by the Pittsburgh Presbytery, April 12, 1865. He was ordained by the Philadelphia Presbytery, installed pastor of the Third congregation of the city of Philadelphia, Pennsylvania, April 6, 1866, and resigned this charge, April 10, 1879. He removed to Elizabeth, and subsequently to Allegheny, Pennsylvania, and supplied throughout different parts of the Church for six years. He was suspended by the Pittsburgh Presbytery, December 22, 1885. He was partially restored, April 12, 1887, allowed to preach by invitation, and is residing in Elizabeth, Pennsylvania. He married Miss Martha J. Withrow, of Elizabeth, Pennsylvania, May 5, 1859.

DAVID JAMISON SHAW:

Son of James and Susannah (Patterson) Shaw, was born in Knockbracken, County Down, Ireland, May 14, 1821. He received his early education in the city of Belfast, Ireland, came to America in 1832, and settled near New Alexandria, Pennsylvania. He soon afterwards resumed his studies in the neighboring Academy of Elder's Ridge, and graduated from Geneva College in 1853. He studied theology at the same time in the Northwood Seminary, and was licensed by the Lakes Presbytery, April 12, 1854. He was ordained by the Illinois Presbytery, and installed pastor of the congregation of Bloomington, Monroe County, Indiana, May 22, 1856, where he is in charge. He married Miss Martha J. Hartin, of Belle Centre, Ohio, November 13, 1854.

JAMES WILLIAM SHAW:

Son of William and Martha (Gormley) Shaw, was born near Ardstraw, County Tyrone, Ireland, November 6, 1812. He received his early education in that vicinity, came to America in 1824, and settled in West Hebron, Washington County, New York, where he continued his education in the common schools. In 1837, he entered the Coldenham Academy, and subsequently attended Lafayette College. He studied theology in the Coldenham and Allegheny Seminaries, and was licensed by the Southern Presbytery, April 11, 1843. He was ordained by the New

York Presbytery, and installed pastor of the congregation of Coldenham, Orange County, New York, May 29, 1844, and resigned this his only charge on account of impaired health, October 26, 1881. He preached occasionally as his health would permit, and died at his home near Coldenham, New York, of a complicated kidney disease, November 27, 1886. He was twice married. First to Miss Margaret J. Burnside, of Pittsburgh, Pennsylvania, February 28, 1843; and second to Miss Elizabeth M. Finley, of Little Britain, New York, July 1, 1845. He was a man of considerable natural ability, of an acute and logical mind, of a keen perception, and a fond student of nature. As a preacher he was sound and instructive; a man of unbending conviction in regard to divine truth, and ever preached the gospel in its purity whether the subject was popular or not. He was conscientiously devoted to the work of the Master, and piously attached to Reformation principles. He was retired in his disposition, and for this reason was not so well known in the Church as he deserved to be. His many contributions to the magazines were always spirited and interesting. He also published a few sermons, among which are: "Attachment to Zion." "Our Banner set up." "The Sufferings and Glory of Christ."

SAMUEL GORMLEY SHAW:

Son of Rev. J. W. and Elizabeth M. (Finley) Shaw, was born in Coldenham, Orange County, New York, November 20, 1854. He received his early education in the schools of that vicinity, also in the Newburgh Classical Institute, graduating from Columbia

College in 1880. He studied theology in the Allegheny Seminary, was licensed by the New York Presbytery, May 16, 1883, and was a supply at Barnesville, New Brunswick, for several months. He was ordained by the New York Presbytery, and installed pastor of the congregation of Walton, Delaware County, New York, July 8, 1884, where he is in charge. He married Miss Sadie J. Hilton, of Newburgh, New York, February 11, 1885.

ROBERT SHIELDS:

Son of Alexander and Agnes (Young) Shields, was born in Glover, Orleans County, Vermont, September 30, 1827. He attended the common schools in his native County and the Craftsbury Academy, graduating from Geneva College in 1855. He studied theology at the same time in the Northwood Seminary, and was licensed by the Lakes Presbytery, May 17, 1855. He travelled as a licentiate throughout different parts of the Church for several years, and, in 1858, became a teacher in Geneva College. In 1862, he was sent as a Home Missionary to Fernandina, Florida, to minister to the spiritual wants of the oppressed contrabands. In 1863, he labored among the soldiers' camps at Little Rock, Arkansas, and, in 1864, was employed in the Freedmen's Mission in Washington, D. C. He was ordained by the Rochester Presbytery, and installed pastor of the Ramsey congregation, Almonte, Ontario, Canada, July 13, 1865, where he labored until his death, by heart disease, August 28, 1883. He married Miss Elizabeth Waddell, of Almonte, Canada, March 26, 1866. He was afflicted from his youth with a severe catarrhal trouble, which affected his general health and hindered his powers as a preacher. He was an intellectual man with a strong mind and a weak body. His sermons were carefully prepared, always clear and concise, and delivered with earnestness and spiritual unction. He was a wise and faithful pastor, a modest and pious Christian. He was a reputable botonist, having turned his attention somewhat to geology, and was at home among the flowers and rocks. He was so conscious of his entire dependence upon the God of all mercies, that he gave every fifth dollar he possessed to the Lord. He published some historical articles in the magazines of the Church, and printed a few pamphlets, among which are : "The Watchman's Word," 1873. "Tribute to Cæsar," 1874.

WILLIAM SLATER :

Son of James and Martha (Thompson) Slater, was born near Noblestown, Allegheny County, Pennsylvania, August 25, 1813. He received his early education in the schools of that vicinity, and while working at the tailor's trade, continued his studies, graduating trom the Western University of Pennsylvania in 1840. He studied theology in the Allegheny Seminary, and was licensed by the Pittsburgh Presbytery, June 1, 1842. He was ordained by the same Presbytery, and installed pastor of the Miller's Run congregation, Venice, Washington County, Pennsylvania, May 24, 1843, resigned this charge, April 13, 1887, and is living near Venice, Pennsylvania. He married Miss Margaret McCoy, of Roney's Point, West Virginia, February 25, 1851.

JAMES RENWICK WILLSON SLOANE, D. D.:

Son of Rev. William and Mary (McNeice) Sloane, was born in Topsham, Orange County, Vermont, May 29, 1823. From his earliest childhood his habits were characterized by seriousness and a fondness for books. In 1829, his parents removed from New England and settled near Greenfield, Ohio, where he attended the district school, and began the study of the classics under the direction of his distinguished father, with whom, also, he taught an Academy in Cadiz, Ohio. In 1840, his parents again removed and settled in Oakdale, Washington County, Illinois, where, in 1841, he connected with the Covenanter Church. In due time he entered Jefferson College, where he distinguished himself as a scholar and speaker, and graduated with first honor in 1847. He soon afterwards went to Hopkinsville, Kentucky, as a teacher, but his sentiments on the question of human slavery, and the condition of affairs in the South, caused him to turn his face Northward. In March, 1848, he became President of Richmond College, in Eastern Ohio, where he remained three years, and, in March, 1852, was inaugurated President of Geneva College, Northwood, Ohio. By extensive reading, and thorough training under his father in the science of theology, he was received as a candidate for the ministry, and licensed by the Lakes Presbytery, October 20, 1852. He was ordained by the Lakes Presbytery, and installed pastor of the congregation of Rushsylvania, Logan County, Ohio, January 13, 1855. The accumulated duties of teacher and pastor were cheerfully borne and successfully performed. Having been early dedicated by his parents, and possessing an earnest desire to preach the gospel, and devote himself wholly to the work of the ministry, he resigned the Presidency of Geneva College, and the pastorate of the Rushsylvania congregation, May 21, 1856. He was installed pastor of the Third congregation of the city of New York, New York, May 26, 1856. Here he won a national reputation as an evangelical preacher and a fearless advocate for the cause of the slave. He resigned this charge in New York, October 27, 1868, and accepted a professorship in the Theological Seminary of Allegheny, Pennsylvania, where the residue of his life was spent in training a ministry for the Covenanter Church. In addition to his duties in the Seminary, he accepted the pastorate of the congregation of Allegheny, Pennsylvania, June 6, 1877, and resigned this charge, May 31, 1884, on account of impaired health. During the winters of his last years he was frequently laid aside by illness, and his physical system gradually declined. On the evening previous to his very sudden death, he retired in comparative good health, and was found dead in his bed at his residence in Allegheny, Pennsylvania, on the morning of March 6, 1886. His disease proved to be an affection of the heart. He was buried in the Bellevue Cemetery, near his former home, and beside his life-long companion, Dr. A. M. Milligan. He was thrice married. First to Miss Margaret A. W. Milligan, of Eden, Illinois, October 23, 1849; second to Miss Margaret C. McLaren, of Geneva, New York, May 4, 1858; and third to Miss Frances B. Swanwick, of Warriston, Illinois, January 17, 1865. Dr. Sloane was

a profound theologian and a great preacher. He possessed a fine physical constitution, a dignified and
commanding appearance, and a deep, voluminous, flexible
voice, which at once mastered his audience the moment
he began to speak. During the dark days and discussion
of slavery in New York, his very appearance on the
platform would quell a mob which the police could not
silence. His preaching was highly evangelical and
Calvinistic. His manner was clear and concise, usually
doctrinal and exhortatory, and always forcible and impressive. He was neither imaginative nor passionate,
for he was so well informed, and so sufficiently learned,
that he needed not to turn aside for flowery illustrations.
He was habitually conscious of the sacredness and
responsibility of the ministerial office, and considered it
no small honor to speak for God to men. He was a
thorough Covenanter, and piously devoted to the principles of the Reformation. The cause of National
Reform was very dear to his heart, and often at great
sacrifices, and expenditure of husbanded strength, he
would go and speak in behalf of this great movement.
In slavery times he was a champion for the cause of
the oppressed. Upon the platform with Phillips,
Garrison, Cheever, and Beecher, he was no less distinguished for his powerful eloquence and convincing
arguments. Upon the great Christian principles of the
Bible in relation to civil government he rose to a height
that was truly majestic, his invincible logic and burning eloquence enrapturing the audiences he addressed.
He was a fine classical scholar, and a most successful
teacher. He had an extensive acquaintance with books,

and was well versed in science and theology. While he was humble and tender, he was also courageous and firm. His heart was as broad as humanity. Out of the fulness of his heart, and his love for sinners, he preached the gospel of Jesus to dying men. His life was blameless and free from guile or unmanliness. He was a good conversationalist. His classical taste gave a form to his sentiments which made his conversation as graceful as it was edifying. He had natural humor, but the disposition to indulge in it was generally repressed. His conversation was upon subjects which invited discussion, and upon themes of momentous import. He was always willing to consider the new, while maintaining attachment to the old, and was free from unreasonable prejudice. He was much interested in the cause of education; and the claims of Geneva College and the Theological Seminary received much of his attention. In Church courts he was heard with marked attention, for his opinion was regarded of value. With dignity he possessed humility; with gravity, simplicity; with candor, integrity; with modesty, boldness. After all he was human, and a brother man. He represented the Church in several ecclesiastical courts and councils. He was largely connected with the public work of the Church, and was regarded as a representative man. He did not effect much as an author, but his greatest works have been written upon human hearts, and published in the lives of his people. His principal writings will be found in the " Life and Work of J. R. W. Sloane, D. D.," 1888, pp. 440. He was honored with the degree of Doctor of Divinity by Westminster College in 1869. He was Moderator of the Synod of 1867.

WILLIAM SLOANE :
Son of William and Jane (Robinson) Sloane, was
born near Larne, County Antrim, Ireland, May ·12,
1787.* He was peculiarly studious, apt to learn, and
pursued the reading and study of the "Scottish Divines"
with pleasure at ten years of age. He attended the
schools of his native parish and finished the course in
the Larne Academy in 1808. For nine years he was
engaged in teaching, and also acquired extensive
knowledge of literature and theology. He came to
America in 1817, studied theology under the direction
of the Rev. Dr. J. R. Willson, of Coldenham, New
York, and was licensed by the Northern Presbytery,
April 4, 1820. He was ordained by the same Presbytery, installed pastor of the congregation of Topsham, Orange County, Vermont, October 14, 1820, and
resigned this charge, April 17, 1829. He was installed
pastor of the united congregations of Greenfield and
Londonderry, Ohio, November 16, 1829, and resigned,
October 23, 1838. He was installed pastor of the
Elkhorn congregation, Oakdale, Illinois, September 13,
1840, and resigned this charge on account of seriously
impaired health, May 9, 1858. During the last five
years of his life he preached occasionally as his health
would permit. Although in comparatively good health
the previous day, he was found dead in his bed on the
morning of December 3, 1863. He married Miss Mary
McNeice, of Carmany, Ireland, in 1816. He was not
what is termed a popular preacher, for he was neither
a rhetorician nor an orator, but he was always heard

* *R. P. & C.*, 1865, p. 184.   Life and Work of Dr. J. R. W. Sloane.

with great pleasure by the spiritually minded. His style was concise, perspicuous and forcible; generally argumentative and illustrative. His great excellence in preaching consisted in a clear and honest presentation of the truth, followed by a happy application. His knowledge of the classics was extensive, and he was well read in theology, often giving instructions to young men preparing for the ministry. He was mighty in the Scriptures, and his prodigious memory assisted him greatly in his pulpit exercises. He was an ardent abolitionist, and a fearless advocate for the cause of the slave. He was frequently drawn into controversy upon the Arminian and Universalist heresies while preaching in New England, and did valiant service in exposing the unfruitful works of secret societies. He did not take a prominent part in Church courts, but was regarded as a faithful minister of Christ and piously devoted to the principles of the Covenanter Church.

ELLSWORTH MONTGOMERY SMITH:

Son of Robert J. and Mary (Carson) Smith, was born in the city of St. Louis, Missouri, April 18, 1862. In early life his parents removed to Staunton, Macoupin County, Illinois, where he received his early education, and graduated from Geneva College in 1883. He studied theology in the Allegheny Seminary, was licensed by the Pittsburgh Presbytery, April 14, 1886, and labored in Maine and New Brunswick. He was ordained by the Illinois Presbytery, and installed pastor of the united congregations of Staunton, Illinois, May 12, 1887, and St. Louis, Missouri, May 16, 1887, where he is in charge. He was an editor of the *College Cabinet*, two years, beginning in 1881. 42

JOHN CALVIN SMITH:

Son of Thomas and Jane (Curry) Smith, was born in Bloomington, Monroe County, Indiana, October 29, 1831. He received his early education in the schools of his native city, graduating from the University of Indiana in 1851. He taught in the Academy of Bedford, Indiana, one year, and in the Model School connected with the University of Indiana, two years. In 1855, he taught Mathematics and Natural Science in Geneva College, Northwood, Ohio, and filled this position three years. He studied theology in the Allegheny Seminary, and was licensed by the Lakes Presbytery, May 22, 1862. He was ordained by the Pittsburgh Presbytery, and installed pastor of the Slippery Rock congregation, Rose Point, Lawrence County, Pennsylvania, April 16, 1863, where he is in charge. He married Miss Sarah McCartney, of Bellefontaine, Ohio, August 9, 1855. He has published many articles in the magazines of the Church, and spoken upon the reforms of the day.

ROBERT McGOWAN SOMMERVILLE:

Son of Rev. William and Sarah B. (Dickie) Sommerville, was born in Grand Pre, Nova Scotia, October 14, 1837. He received his early education under the direction of his father, and graduated from Queen's University, Belfast, Ireland, in 1860. He studied theology at the same time in the Belfast Seminary, and was licensed by the Eastern Presbytery, Ireland, January 3, 1861. He returned to America the same spring, was ordained by the New Brunswick and Nova Scotia Presbytery, and installed co-pastor with his father of the united congregations of Horton and Corn-wallis, Nova Scotia, October 16, 1861. He was released from the Cornwallis branch in 1862, and soon after-wards built a church in Wolfville, where he preached for many years. In 1866, he was also chosen Inspector of Schools for Kings County, Nova Scotia, and resigned all these charges, November 13, 1873, and came to the States. He was stated supply at Cincinnati, Ohio, one year, and to the Second congregation of New York City for six months. He was installed pastor of the Second congregation of New York City, December 14, 1875, where he is in charge. He married Miss Elizabeth Chipman, of Cornwallis, Nova Scotia, September 13, 1865. He is Corresponding Secretary of the Board of Foreign Missions, Assistant Clerk of Synod, and, since January, 1887, editor of the *Herald of Mission News.*

WILLIAM SOMMERVILLE:

Son of William and Jane (Kirk) Sommerville, was born in Ballyroney, County Down, Ireland, July 1, 1800.* He began the study of the classics with Rev. John Stewart, and continued them under the direc-tion of Rev. David McKee, graduating with honor from the University of Glasgow, Scotland, in 1820. He soon afterwards began the study of theology in the Seminary of Paisley, Scotland, and was licensed by the Southern Presbytery, Ireland, December 5, 1826. He was ordained *sine titulo* by the Southern Presbytery, Ireland, May 31, 1831, as a Missionary to the British North American Provinces, and sailed for St. John,

---

* Memoir by Rev. A. M. Stavely, 1878.

New Brunswick, August 16, 1831. After visiting different parts of the Maritime Provinces, he finally settled in the beautiful and fertile Cornwallis Valley, in Nova Scotia. Here his labors were devoted to Presbyterians generally, until other laborers came into the field, and then the lines were drawn more closely and soon confined to the Covenanter societies. The Presbyterians of Grand Pre agreed to sing the Psalms of David and conform to other peculiar usages of the Covenanter Church, and he became pastor of this congregation, May 16, 1833. Two years later a society sprung up in West Cornwallis, and desired a part of his time, which was granted, and he was installed pastor of this branch, May 9, 1835, and from this date to that of his death, he was pastor of the united congregations of Horton and Cornwallis, Nova Scotia. After a labor of forty-seven years as a pioneer missionary in this region, he died at his home in Somerset, Kings County, Nova Scotia, September 28, 1878. He was twice married. First to Miss Sarah B. Dickie, of Amherst, Nova Scotia, in 1832; and second to Mrs. Jane E. (Caldwell) Woodworth, of Grand Pre, Nova Scotia, September, 1854. His bodily vigor, mental endowments, and manly intrepidity fitted him peculiarly for missionary work. His abilities were those of a powerful evangelical preacher, and a resolute defender of Scripture doctrine. His genial spirit and earnest benevolence attracted many to the acceptance of the Covenanter faith. He met and measured spiritual weapons with all opponents of different denominations. His controversies were principally with the Baptists and their mode of applying water in the sacrament of baptism; and with other denominations for the exclusive use of the Psalms of David as a matter of praise in divine worship. He was a gifted controversialist, and his pen was seldom at rest. During at least twenty years of his pastoral labors he was engaged in teaching school. He visited his native country in 1840 and in 1858. Among his publications are: "Dissertation on the Nature and Administration of the Ordinance of Baptism," in two parts, two editions, 1845 and 1866, pp. 319. "Exclusive Use of the Psalms of David in Worship," 1855, pp. 189. "Rule of Faith," 1859, pp. 28. "Southern Slavery not founded on Scripture Warrant," 1865, pp. 26. "Social Position of the Cameronians," 1868, pp. 40. "Baptismal Immersion not of God," 1876, pp. 77. He also delivered a course of lectures before the Protestant Alliance of Nova Scotia, at Halifax, in 1858.

JAMES ALEXANDER SPEER:

Son of Robert and Sarah (Jamison) Speer, was born in New Concord, Muskingum County, Ohio, February 27, 1842. He received his early education in the schools of his native town, and entered Muskingum College in 1861. When the war of the rebellion broke out, he served in the army two years. In the fall of 1866, he became Principal of the Academy of Ontario, Ohio, and the following year taught in Muskingum College, where he graduated in 1868. He studied theology in the Allegheny Seminary, was licensed by the Pittsburgh Presbytery, April 8, 1873, and labored for some time in the West. He was ordained by the

New York Presbytery, and installed pastor of the congregation of West Hebron, Washington County, New
York, July 28, 1875, where he is in charge. He married Miss Nettie J. Black, of Allegheny City, Pennsylvania, December 27, 1876.

JOHN WALLACE SPROULL:

Son of Rev. Dr. Thomas and Magdalene (Wallace)
Sproull, was born in the city of Allegheny, Pennsylvania, January 17, 1839. He received his early education in the public schools and in Westminster College
of his native city, graduating from Jefferson College in
1858. He taught for some time in the Academies of
Neilsburgh and Fayetteville, Pennsylvania. He studied
theology in the Allegheny Seminary, and was licensed
by the Pittsburgh Presbytery, April 14, 1863. He was
ordained by the same Presbytery, installed pastor of
the Monongahela congregation, Elizabeth, Allegheny
County, Pennsylvania, April 10, 1866, and resigned
this charge, April 11, 1871. He was installed pastor
of the Central congregation of Allegheny City, Pennsylvania, April 24, 1871, where he is in charge.
He married Miss Anna M. Stewart, of New Alexandria, Pennsylvania, June 26, 1879. He has been
an editor of the *Reformed Presbyterian and Covenanter*
since 1868; is a member of the Central Board of
Missions, and Stated Clerk of Synod.

ROBERT DUNLAP SPROULL:

Son of Rev. Dr. Thomas and Magdalene (Wallace)
Sproull, was born in the city of Allegheny, Pennsylvania. * * * He received his early education in the
public schools and Westminster College of his native

city, graduating from Jefferson College in 1857. He studied theology in the Allegheny Seminary, and was licensed by the Pittsburgh Presbytery, April 3, 1861. He was ordained by the Rochester Presbytery, installed pastor of the congregation of Rochester, New York, May 14, 1863, and resigned this charge, October 6, 1880. He connected with the Presbyterian Church, being received by the Rochester Presbytery of that body, October 25, 1880, and preached in Cincinnati, Ohio, for some time. He took charge of the First Presbyterian Church of Providence, Rhode Island, January 16, 1883, resigned, January 14, 1886, and removed to Philadelphia. He was installed pastor of the Noble Street Presbyterian Church, Brooklyn, New York, October 14, 1886, where he is in charge. He married Miss Margaret A. Mc-Gormley, of Rochester, New York, April 19, 1864.

THOMAS SPROULL, D. D., LL. D.:

Son of Robert and Mary (Dunlap) Sproull, was born near Lucesco, Westmoreland County, Pennsylvania, September 15, 1803. He received his early education in a private Academy, and graduated from the Western University of Pennsylvania in 1829. He studied theology under the direction of the Rev. Dr. John Black of Pittsburgh, and was licensed by the Pittsburgh Presbytery, April 4, 1832. He was ordained *sine cura* by the same Presbytery, as a Home Missionary, April 4, 1833. He was installed pastor of the congregation of Pittsburgh and Allegheny, Pennsylvania, May 12, 1834, which became the Allegheny congregation, October 17, 1865, and continued in this charge until October 13, 1868. In 1838, he was chosen Professor of Theology in the Allegheny Seminary, and resigned in 1845. He was re-elected to the professorship in 1856; made Professor Emeritus in 1874, and continues to hear a class in pastoral theology. He was editor of the *Christian Witness*, an anti-slavery paper, two years, and also of the *Reformed Presbyterian* from 1855 until its consolidation with the *Covenanter* in 1863, and an editor of the *Reformed Presbyterian and Covenanter* until 1874. He has been actively connected with the missionary and educational institutions of the Church for over half a century. Besides his editorial work he published: "Duty of Social Covenanting," 1841, pp. 34. "Endless Punishment," 1856, pp. 64. "Augur and his Pupils," 1861, pp. 19. "Christianity and the Commonwealth," 1862, pp. 17. "Our Testimony," 1865, pp. 19. "The Loyal Archite," 1875, pp. 30. "Conditions of a Successful Pastorate," 1880, pp. 12. "Prelections on Theology," two editions, 1882, pp. 455. He also published a series of articles on the early history of the Reformed Presbyterian Church in America. He married Miss Magdalene Wallace, of Pittsburgh, Pennsylvania, July 1, 1834. He was honored with the degree of Doctor of Divinity by Westminster College in 1857, and that of Doctor of Laws by the Western University of Pennsylvania in 1886. He was Moderator of the Synod of 1847.

THOMAS ALEXANDER SPROULL:

Son of Rev. Dr. Thomas and Magdalene (Wallace) Sproull, was born in the city of Allegheny, Pennsylvania, October 13, 1842. His preparatory literary studies were pursued in the public schools and in Westminster College of his native city, graduating from Jefferson College in 1863. He studied theology in the Allegheny Seminary, and was licensed by the Pittsburgh Presbytery, May 23, 1867. He was ordained by the same Presbytery, and installed pastor of the congregation of New Alexandria, Westmoreland County, Pennsylvania, June 17, 1868, where he continued to labor until his last illness. His general health, and especially his voice, gave way some three years before his death, and he spent a summer in Colorado with great benefit. He resumed his work, but his weakness returning, in November, 1877, he repaired to the milder climate of Florida. This change, however, brought no relief, but more suffering in the form of a malignant fever, from which he died, in Gainesville, Florida, April 8, 1878, and he was buried in the old graveyard of New Alexandria. He married Miss Emma Stewart, of New Alexandria, Pennsylvania, May 20, 1869. He was a plain, solemn, impressive preacher, and made no display or attempts at oratory. He knew the Scriptures from his youth, and he experienced the power of the gospel of Christ which he touchingly presented to others. He was an unselfish and conscientious Christian, a most exemplary pastor, kind to the afflicted, and attentive to the aged. His whole course in life was that of genuine integrity of character, a consecrated devotion to the work of the ministry, and a faithful maintenance of the principles of the Church.

THOMAS CARGILL SPROULL:

Son of Thomas and Margaret (Dodds) Sproull, was born near Brownsdale, Butler County, Pennsylvania, October 29, 1840. He received his early education in the schools of that vicinity, and engaged in teaching. He resumed his studies in Allegheny City College, taught several terms, and graduated from Westminster College in 1868. He studied theology in the Allegheny Seminary, and was licensed by the Pittsburgh Presbytery, April 12, 1870. He was ordained by the same Presbytery, installed pastor of the Monongahela congregation, Elizabeth, Allegheny County, Pennsylvania, October 3, 1871, and resigned May 26, 1876. He was installed pastor of the united congregations of Poland and North Jackson, Mahoning County, Ohio, July 18, 1876, and resigned April 8, 1879. He was installed pastor of the congregation of Cedarville, Green County, Ohio, June 10, 1881, where he is in charge, and lectures in the interests of the National Reform Association. He married Miss Agnes S. Lowry, of New Alexandria, Pennsylvania, November 8, 1871.

WILLIAM SPROULL:

Son of Thomas and Margaret (Dodds) Sproull, was born near Brownsdale, Butler County, Pennsylvania, February 4, 1848. He received his early education in that vicinity, and graduated from Geneva College in 1874. He engaged in teaching near his home, one year. He studied theology in the Allegheny Seminary, was licensed by the Pittsburgh Presbytery, April 9, 1878, and supplied the pulpit of Cornwallis, Nova Scotia, for several months. He was ordained *sine titulo* by the Pittsburgh Presbytery, October 14, 1879, as a Missionary to Syria. He sailed for that foreign field, November 6, 1879, and was engaged in preaching and teaching in connection with the Latakia

Mission for over six years. He returned to the United States in June, 1886, and spent one year lecturing in the interests of the Foreign Mission. He resigned his connection with the Mission, June 3, 1887, and is supplying vacancies throughout the Church, with his residence in Mars, Pennsylvania. He married Miss Ella Campbell, of Bakerstown, Pennsylvania, October 23, 1879.

ALEXANDER McLEOD STAVELY:

Son of Rev. Dr. W. J. and Jane (Adams) Stavely, was born in Corkey, County Antrim, Ireland, June 19, 1816. His father was a distinguished Covenanter minister, under whom he received a careful training in religion and general literature. He began his classical studies in the Belfast Academy, attended Belfast College two years, and graduated from the University of Edinburgh, Scotland, in 1835. He studied theology two sessions under Dr. Thomas Chalmers, the remaining course in the Seminary of Paisley, Scotland, and was licensed by the Northern Presbytery, Ireland, March 16, 1839. He was ordained *sine titulo* by the same court, May 12, 1841, as a Missionary to St. John, New Brunswick. He came to this field in August, 1841, took charge of the congregation in St. John, laboring here and among the adjacent societies for thirty-eight years. He resigned this charge, June 16, 1879, and returned to his native land, where he preached in the vacancies for five years. He was installed pastor of the congregation of Ballyclare and Larne, County Antrim, Ireland, December 10, 1884, where he is in charge. He married Miss Margaret Cameron, of St. John, New Brunswick, April 21, 1852. Among his writings are the following:

" The Perpetuity of the Gospel." " Redeeming the Time."
" The Historical Position of the Covenanter Church."
" Life and Times of John Knox." " The Supremacy of
the Bible." " Memoir of the Rev. William Sommer-
ville." He was Moderator of the Irish Synod in 1880.
DAVID STEELE, D. D.:

Son of David and Sarah (Gailey) Steele, was born
in Upper Creevaugh, County Donegal, Ireland, November 2, 1803.* He received his early education in the
private and night schools of the vicinity, and labored
upon the farm until his sixteenth year. In 1820, he
entered the Academy of Londonderry, where he pursued
the regular course of study for three years. He came
to America in 1824, settled in Huntingdon, Pennsylvania, where he was engaged as a clerk in his uncle's
store, and also prosecuted his classical studies. In the
spring of 1825, he was engaged as a teacher in the
Academy of Ebensburgh, Pennsylvania, and the next
year entered the Western University of Pennsylvania,
graduating in 1827. He studied theology under the
direction of the Rev. Dr. John Black at Pittsburgh,
and was licensed by the Pittsburgh Presbytery, April
8, 1830. He was ordained by the Ohio Presbytery,
installed pastor of the congregation of Brush Creek,
Adams County, Ohio, June 6, 1831, where he continued
as pastor for nine years. He withdrew, with a few
followers, from the Covenanter Church, and organized
the Reformed Presbytery, June 24, 1840. He remained
in Adams County, Ohio, and preached to a few
adherents until 1859, when he removed to Hill Prairie,.

---

* Autobiography and Reminiscences, 1883.

Illinois. In October, 1866, he removed to Philadelphia, Pennsylvania, where he was engaged in preaching to a small congregation of his people and established a theological school. In 1885, he removed to Galesburgh, Illinois, and in the fall of 1886, returned to Philadelphia, where he died of old age and from the effects of a slight stroke of paralysis, June 29, 1887. He married Miss Eliza Johnston, of Chillicothe, Ohio, May 4, 1831. He was a learned and powerful preacher of the gospel, an adept in ancient languages, and an independent thinker. He held that the members of the Covenanter Church had departed from the attainments of the Reformation, especially in the matter of "voluntary associations." He spent the most of his life visiting the isolated families adhering to him, and centured the Church of his fathers for defection. It is regretted that he spent, what might have been a most useful life, in an isolated Church connection. He was a great controversialist, and manifested inflexibility of character. He died in the belief that the principles which he held and propagated would one day triumph in the earth. He edited the *Contending Witness*, a bimonthly, published at Xenia, Ohio, for many years. He also edited the *Reformation Advocate*, which was subsequently known as the *Original Covenanter*, from March, 1874, until 1884. Among his other publications are: "Supplement to Act, Declaration and Testimony of the Reformed Presbyterian Church," 1858. "The Two Witnesses," 1859. "Notes on the Apocalypse," 1870. "Reminiscences: Historical and Biographical," 1883. Previous to 1840, he was largely connected with the literary and theological institutions of the Church, and was stated Clerk of Synod for several years. He was honored with the degree of Doctor of Divinity by the Western University of Pennsylvania in 1884.

SAMUEL STERRETT:

Son of Joseph and Ann (Morrison) Sterrett, was born near Norwich, Muskingum County, Ohio, March 11, 1817. In early life he commenced the elementary classics under the direction of his pastor, the Rev. Robert Wallace, and entered upon a regular course of study in Franklin College, where he graduated in 1840. He studied theology in the Allegheny and Cincinnati Seminaries, his course being interrupted by impaired health, and was licensed by the Pittsburgh Presbytery, April 14, 1847. He was ordained by the same Presbytery, and installed pastor of the united congregations of Little Beaver, Pennsylvania, and Poland and North Jackson, Ohio, June 21, 1848. In 1860, the charge was divided, and he remained pastor of Poland and North Jackson, Ohio, until his resignation, October 7, 1867. He was installed pastor of the congregation of Cedarville, Green County, Ohio, May 16, 1868, where he died very suddenly, from an affection of the stomach, October 20, 1871. He married twice. First to Miss Elizabeth Kernohan, of Londonderry, Ohio, October 14, 1845; and second, to Miss Elizabeth McGeorge, of New Galilee, Pennsylvania, May 21, 1860. He was not an attractive speaker, but a sound theologian, and one remarkably versed in the doctrines of the Bible. He excelled in pastoral work, where his kind and amiable disposition won many to an attendance upon divine services and to embrace the principles he so faithfully advocated. He was highly regarded as a minister, Presbyter, and Christian, by all his brethren. He was Moderator of the Synod of 1857.

ANDREW STEVENSON, D. D.:

Son of John and Isabella (Brown) Stevenson, was born in Ballibay, County Monaghan, Ireland, January 10, 1810. His early life was full of trials and hardships. By the death of his godly father in 1818, the family was left in straightened circumstances, and, having acquired sufficient knowledge, he began to teach a private school in the neighborhood. By constant teaching and hard study he educated himself, and frequently recited to the Rev. J. P. Sweeny. In 1831, he was chosen by the Irish Synod as a Catechist to accompany the Rev. William Sommerville to the British North American Provinces. He accepted this appointment, and missionated for two years, principally among the societies of New Brunswick. In 1833, he came to the city of Philadelphia, Pennsylvania, where he opened a classical school, and conducted it successfully for several years. He studied theology privately under Revs. Drs. J. R. Willson and James Christie, and was licensed by the Southern Presbytery, May 15, 1839. He was ordained by the same Presbytery, and installed pastor of the Second congregation of the city of New York, November 14, 1839, where he continued to labor with marked success until impaired health caused him to retire from active duty as emeritus pastor, May 17, 1875. The illness which terminated his life was of long duration and intense suffering. He was almost entirely prevented

from attending the public ordinances for the last two
years of his life. After various attacks of pneumonia,
his disease assumed a chronic form, combined with senile
bronchitis, from which he died, at his residence in the
city of New York, June 24, 1881. He married Miss
Anna M. Willson, of Coldenham, New York, February
10, 1840. He was a man of fine personal appearance,
possessing the power of attracting others to him, and
impressing his individuality upon them. He was not
regarded as an eloquent preacher, but a clear, cogent,
and conscientious imparter of divine truth, whose discourses were practical, and forcibly applied. He was an
organizer. This is where his great success lay. He
always found something for every one to do. He took
a great interest in emigrants coming from the sister
Churches beyond the ocean, frequently finding them
employment, and by his kindness and attention gathered
them into the Church. He was closely attached to
Covenanter principles, and freely and fearlessly proclaimed them from the pulpit. His influence and power
in the Church will long be remembered, notwithstanding
he was frequently drawn into earnest debate with his
brethren. He was long and actively connected with the
Board of Foreign Missions, and other benevolent associations. He was honored with the degree of Doctor
of Divinity by the University of the City of New York
in 1865. He was Moderator of the Synod of 1869.

HUGH STEVENSON:

Son of Thomas and Mary (Bigum) Stevenson, was
born near Port Norris, County Armagh, Ireland, October 10, 1808. His parents were members of the Pres-

byterian Church. They came to America in 1820, and, after a short settlement near Erie, Pennsylvania, removed to New Concord, Muskingum County, Ohio, where they connected with the Covenanter Church. In early life he gave evidence of possessing a good mind and evinced a desire for an education. He made considerable progress in the schools of his adopted community, and graduated from Franklin College in 1836. He studied theology privately under the direction of the Rev. William Sloane, and was licensed by the Pittsburgh Presbytery, May 8, 1839. He was ordained by the Western Presbytery at Northwood, Ohio, July 13, 1840, and installed pastor of the Bethel congregation, Sparta, Randolph County, Illinois, August 16, 1840, where he faithfully labored until his untimely death. His last illness was protracted from the preceeding year with inflammatory rheumatism, followed by a bilious fever, from which he died, at his home in Sparta, Illinois, May 15, 1846. He married Miss Maria Patton, of Cadiz, Ohio, June 10, 1837. He may not be regarded as a great preacher, but he possessed a clear mind, sound judgment, and an affable manner, which attracted attention and rendered his services both acceptable and valuable. He was of a cheerful disposition, conscientious in the performance of duty, and closely attached to the principles of the Church, which he made prominent in all his ministrations.

SAMUEL McCUTCHEN STEVENSON:

Son of Archibald and Isabella (McCutchen) Stevenson, was born near New Concord, Muskingum County, Ohio, February 3, 1829. He received his early education

43

in the public schools and graduated from Muskingum College in 1856. In the fall of 1856, he became Principal of the Schools at Adamsville, Ohio, where he was engaged in teaching for three years. He studied theology in the Allegheny Seminary, and was licensed by the Pittsburgh Presbytery, April 14, 1863. He was appointed by Synod as a Missionary to the North-West, and spent a year in Iowa, Wisconsin and Minnesota, gathering scattered Covenanters into societies. He was ordained by the Iowa Presbytery, October 5, 1864, installed pastor of the congregation of Washington, Iowa, February 15, 1865, and resigned this charge, October 4, 1871. He missionated and taught in Clay Centre, Clay County, Kansas, for three years. He was installed pastor of the Tabor congregation, Idana, Clay County, Kansas, October 30, 1874, where he is in charge and engaged in teaching. He married Miss Aurilla M. Elliot, of Adamsville, Ohio, March 23, 1858.

THOMAS PATTON STEVENSON, D. D.:

Son of Rev. Hugh and Maria (Patton) Stevenson, was born in Cadiz, Harrison County, Ohio, April 2, 1838. In 1840, his parents removed to Sparta, Illinois, where he received his early education, graduating from Muskingum College in 1856. He studied theology one year in the Allegheny Seminary, and was Professor of Languages in Muskingum College for two years. He resumed his studies in the Allegheny Seminary in 1859, and was licensed by the Pittsburgh Presbytery, April 9, 1862. He was ordained by the Philadelphia Presbytery, and installed pastor of the First congregation of Philadelphia, Pennsylvania, May 5, 1863, where he is in charge. He married Miss Mary E. McClurkin, of New Concord, Ohio, May 17, 1862. In 1867, he became one of the editors of the *Christian Statesman*; was an organizer of the National Reform Association, and the Corresponding Secretary since the organization. He has for many years been a member of the Board of Foreign Missions, of the Superintendents of the Theological Seminary, of the Corporators of Geneva College, and of numerous important Committees, and lectures upon the great questions of reform. He was honored with the degree of Doctor of Divinity by Muskingum College in 1872. He was Moderator of the Synod of 1881.

JAMES SPEER STEWART:

Son of Alexander and Elizabeth (Speer) Stewart, was born near New Castle, Pennsylvania, May 13, 1856. He received his early education in the schools of his native County, and engaged in teaching. He resumed his studies in, and graduated from, Geneva College in 1880. He was Instructor of Latin and Greek in Geneva College one year; Professor of Mathematics in the Academy of Washington, Iowa, in 1882, and had charge of the Academy of Northwood, Ohio, two years. He studied theology in the Allegheny Seminary, and was licensed by the Pittsburgh Presbytery, April 12, 1887. He was ordained by the Pittsburgh Presbytery, as a Missionary to Syria, May 31, 1888. He married Miss Mary Love, of Beaver Falls, Pennsylvania, September 3, 1883.

JAMES WYLIE STEWART:

Son of John and Mary (Wylie) Stewart, was born in Ballibay, County Monaghan, Ireland, August 24,

1794.* His parents were of an old family of Covenanters, and he was reared in the strictest manner in
the home, and under the pastoral care of the Rev.
Thomas Cathcart. He received his early education in
Ballibay, and graduated from the Belfast Academical
Institution in 1815. He studied theology at the same
time in the Belfast Hall, and one year in the Seminary
of Stirling, Scotland, being licensed by the Southern
Presbytery, Ireland, December 3, 1816. He came to
America in May, 1823, and preached as a licentiate
for two years. He was ordained by the Northern
Presbytery, installed pastor of the Argyle congregation, now West Hebron, Washington County, New
York, October 13, 1825, and was released April 5,
1832. At the division of the Church in August, 1833,
he became identified with the New School branch of
the Covenanter Church. He preached to a few followers
and taught two years in the Academy of Salem, New
York. He connected with the Dutch Reformed Church,
June 19, 1835, was installed pastor of the congregation of Battenville, Washington County, New York,
and was Principal of the Jackson Academy. In 1838,
he became Principal of the Academy of Warwick,
Orange County, New York, and preached as opportunity
was afforded. He next connected with the Presbyterian
Church, October 16, 1844, and the following year was
installed pastor of the Union Church, of Philadelphia,
Pennsylvania, where he died after a short and severe
illness, March 1, 1849. He was twice married. First
to Miss Ruth Gifford, of New York, in 1827; second,

* Communications from Ireland. Church and Synodical Records.

to Miss Elizabeth Willard, of Salem, New York, in 1835. He was generally acceptable as a preacher, but caused a great deal of trouble in the Church. He was a proficient scholar, a very successful teacher, and, upon the whole, was regarded as a man of considerable ability.

ROBERT STEWART:

Son of William and Elizabeth (Beggs) Stewart, was born in Ballynaloob, County Antrim, Ireland, April 5, 1824. He received his early education in the schools of his native parish, and under the direction of the Rev. William Toland, graduating from the Royal Academical Institution of Belfast in 1843. He studied the Irish language under the tuition of M. Branningan; attended the Presbyterian Seminary in 1845; and the Covenanter Seminary of Paisley, Scotland, being licensed by the Northern Presbytery, Ireland, February 3, 1847. He labored in the Mission of Connaught, studied the Gaelic language with Rector Gage, and took the London prize for proficiency in that tongue. He was ordained *sine titulo* by the Synod of Ireland, July 12, 1849, as a Missionary to the North American British Provinces. The same fall he came to America, settled in the mission station of Wilmot, Annapolis County, Nova Scotia, and also preached in Margaretville and Lawrence-town for over thirty years. He resigned this charge, May 26, 1881, and supplied vacancies throughout the United States. His residence is in Wilmot, Nova Scotia, where he counsels in law and medicine, and instructs in the classics. He married Miss Margaret Morrison, of Melvern Square, Nova Scotia, November 7, 1855.

JOHN STOTT:

Son of Thomas and Jane (Hamilton) Stott, was born near Cremore, County Armagh, Ireland, May 17, 1808. He received his early education in the schools of his native parish, graduated from the Belfast Academical Institution in 1830, and was also engaged in the study of medicine. He studied theology in the Seminary of Paisley, Scotland, and was licensed by the Northern Presbytery, Ireland, March 9, 1834. He was ordained by the Western Presbytery, installed pastor of the congregation of Convoy, County Antrim, Ireland, July 15, 1835, and resigned, October 16, 1850. The following spring he came to America, and was received by Synod, May 28, 1851. He was installed pastor of the congregation of Princeton, Gibson County, Indiana, October 13, 1851, and was suspended June 2, 1868. He took a few of his former flock into an independent organization, occasionally preaches to them without any ecclesiastical connection, practices medicine and follows other pursuits in Princeton, Indiana. He was Moderator of the Synod of 1865.

ALEXANDER CHARLES STUART:

Son of Charles and Matilda (Buchanan) Stuart, was born near Londonderry, Ireland, July 17, 1823. His parents were members of the Secession Church and he was brought up under the ministry of the Rev. Dr. Rentoul. He received his early education in the English Academy and Raphoe Classical School, graduating from Belfast College in 1843. He studied theology three sessions in Belfast, Ireland, and finished the course in the Theological Hall of the Original Seceder Church in Edinburgh, Scotland, under the celebrated Dr. Thomas McCrie. He came to America in the spring of 1847, and settled in the city of St. John, New Brunswick, where he connected with the Covenanter Church. He was recognized as a theological student, and licensed by the New Brunswick and Nova Scotia Presbytery, September 26, 1847. He preached with a good degree of success in St. John, Mill Stream, Campbell, and other parts of New Brunswick, for three years. In 1850, he came to the United States and preached in the Covenanter congregations in New York, Philadelphia, and other vacancies, for two years. In 1852, he went to Montreal, Canada, where he connected with the United Presbyterian Church of Canada. He was ordained by the Montreal Presbytery of that body, and installed pastor of a congregation in the vicinity of the city of Montreal, September 9, 1853, where he remained in charge two years. He was installed pastor of the united congregations of Garafraxa, Caledonia and Hemingford, Ontario, Canada, January 10, 1856, and remained about two years. In 1859, he was pastor at Perrytown, and preached and taught at Port Hope, Canada. In 1861, he went into the union which formed the Presbyterian Church of Canada, and soon afterwards came to the States, preaching respectively in Southern Illinois, New York, Western Pennsylvania, Ohio and West Virginia. In 1871, he was called to the charges of Locust Bottom, Zion and Salt Peter, on the James river, in Botetourt County, Virginia, where he labored about two years. He then returned to West Virginia, where he preached nearly eight

years. In August, 1883, he was invited to look after
the interests of Presbyterianism at the head waters of
the Big Sandy river, in Kentucky, and has his residence in Pikeville, Pike County, Kentucky, where he is
preaching, and teaching a classical school. He married
Miss Eleanor Middleton, of Manorcunningham, Ireland,
August 15, 1844. He published a few articles against
Popery, and some expositions of the Minor Prophets.

JOHN HENDERSON SYMMES:

Son of Campbell and Abigail (Doying) Symmes,
was born in Ryegate, Caledonia County, Vermont,
October 4, 1801. He received his preparatory literary
education in the schools of his native town, and finished
the course in the Academy of Coldenham, New York,
in 1824. He studied theology in the Philadelphia
Seminary, and was licensed by the Philadelphia Presbytery,
May 22, 1827. Feeling the need of a thorough College
education, he resumed his studies in, and graduated
from, Dartmouth College in 1830. He preached with
much acceptance in the vacancies in New England and
Canada, and also as stated supply at Pottsville and
Mauch Chunk, Pennsylvania. He was ordained *sine
titulo* by the Philadelphia Presbytery, as a Home
Missionary, June 16, 1831, and labored in that capacity
for a short time. He connected with the Presbyterian
Church, being received by the Doylestown Presbytery
of that body, May 27, 1832. He was installed pastor
of the Presbyterian congregation of Columbia, Pennsylvania, November 8, 1833, and remained pastor seven
years. He was installed pastor of the First Presbyterian
congregation of Lansingburgh, New York, October 29,

1840, where he remained four years. In December, 1844, he became supply, and, April 9, 1845, pastor, of the First Presbyterian congregation of Cumberland, Maryland, and resigned this charge, April 2, 1862. Most of the families of wealth and influence in this congregation sympathized with the South during the rebellion, rendering his situation extremely unpleasant, as his sentiments were strongly in favor of the North. Being urged to become Chaplain of the Second Regiment of the Maryland Volunteer Infantry, composed mostly of men from Cumberland and vicinity, he accepted, and served in this capacity until the close of the war. In the summer of 1865, he returned North, and preached in the vacancies for two years. He was installed pastor of the First Presbyterian congregation of Conshohocken, Montgomery County, Pennsylvania, November 16, 1867, where he died of an enlargement of the heart, November 28, 1874. He married Miss Catharine McAdam, of Philadelphia, Pennsylvania, March 7, 1833. He was a most capable man, an eloquent preacher, and possessed many noble qualities of Christian character. He was an accomplished scholar, and drew from the storehouse of useful knowledge for the instruction and edification of his people. He possessed a kind and genial disposition; and, while he was strong in his convictions, he was mild in the utterance of them. He filled the prominent positions to which he was chosen with great acceptance, and was highly regarded as preacher, pastor, and Christian, by all his brethren.

JOHN CAMPBELL TAYLOR:

Son of John B. and Elizabeth (Campbell) Taylor, was born in Meigs, Muskingum County, Ohio, November

11, 1843. He received his early education in the schools of that vicinity, and graduated from Muskingum College in 1870. He studied theology in the Allegheny Seminary, and was licensed by the Ohio Presbytery, April 3, 1872. He was ordained by the New York Presbytery, and installed pastor of the congregation of Craftsbury, Orleans County, Vermont, December 17, 1873, where he is in charge. He was twice married. First to Miss Mary J. Hamill, of Allegheny City, Pennsylvania, July 1, 1873; and second, to Miss Ella S. Clark, of Norwich, Ohio, July 23, 1883.

JOHN TEAZ:

Son of Ezekiel and Lavinia (Cromie) Teaz, was born near Londonderry, Ireland, July 1, 1849. He received his rudimentary education in the schools of his native land. He came to America in June, 1869, and settled in the city of Brooklyn, New York, where he resumed his studies, graduating from Brooklyn Lay College in 1877. He studied theology in the Allegheny Seminary, and was licensed by the Pittsburgh Presbytery, April 12, 1881. With a preference for missionary work, he spent four years laboring principally under the direction of the Central Board of Missions in the Maritime Provinces and the West. He was ordained by the Illinois Presbytery, installed pastor of the Church Hill congregation, Coultersville, Randolph County, Illinois, July 7, 1885, where he is in charge.

DAVID TELFAIR:

Was born in Monteith, Scotland, in 1722. He was educated in Edinburgh, and licensed by the Associate Church in the spring of 1745.* He was

_____

* Publications in Philadelphia, Pa. Drs. Scouller and Lathan.

ordained by the same court, in 1746, and when the Synod divided in 1747, he adhered to the Burgher Synod of the Secession Church. He was installed pastor of the congregation of Bridge-of-Teith, Scotland, in 1749, where he remained several years. By appointment of the Burgher Synod he was sent as a Missionary to America in the spring of 1766, being directed to preach in Philadelphia, Pennsylvania, and Cambridge, New York, one year. He preached most of the time, however, to the Burgher congregation in Shippen street, Philadelphia, and, when the year was up, concluded to remain in America. He connected with the Associate Church, being received by the Presbytery of Pennsylvania, (Anti-Burgher,) June 9, 1767. In the spring of 1768, he returned to Scotland, and resumed for three years his charge at Bridge-of-Teith. He came back to America in 1771, and remained as an independent Burgher minister, preaching as opportunity was afforded. He connected with the Covenanter Church, being received by the Reformed Presbytery, at Stony Ridge, Pennsylvania, August 12, 1780. He preached with general acceptance to the scattered societies for two years. He went with the other ministers into the Associate Reformed Church at its formation, November 1, 1782, and soon afterwards took charge of his old congregation in Philadelphia, which he resigned, in 1788, on account of impaired health. He died in Philadelphia, Pennsylvania, April 29, 1789, and was buried in the old burying ground on Shippen street near Fourth. He was said to be a very acceptable preacher, but rather vacillating in principle.

HENRY WILLSON TEMPLE:

Son of John B. and Martha (Jameson) Temple, was born in Belle Centre, Logan County, Ohio, March 31, 1864. He received his early education in the public schools of his native village, and at an early age entered Geneva College, where he graduated in 1883. He studied theology in the Allegheny Seminary, was licensed by the Lakes Presbytery, April 14, 1886, and labored for several months in the West. He was ordained by the Pittsburgh Presbytery, and installed pastor of the Salem congregation, Stanton, Jefferson County, Pennsylvania, July 14, 1887, where he is in charge.

DAVID GLENN THOMPSON:

Son of Gordon and Eliza (Walker) Thompson, was born near Londonderry, Guernsey County, Ohio, April 2, 1845. He received his early education in his native County, and served a short period in the war of the rebellion. In 1865, he resumed his studies and graduated from Muskingum College in 1868. He studied theology in the Allegheny Seminary, and was licensed by the Ohio Presbytery, April 12, 1871. He was ordained by the Illinois Presbytery, and installed pastor of the Elkhorn congregation, Oakdale, Washington County, Illinois, October 10, 1872, where he is in charge. He was twice married. First to Miss Mattie A. McKitrick, of Antrim, Ohio, January 22, 1873; and second, to Miss Adda Foster, of Cedarville, Ohio, April 3, 1877.

JAMES ALEXANDER THOMPSON:

Son of Robert and Martha (Mechem) Thompson, was born near Athens, Athens County, Ohio, December 17, 1827. He received his early education in Utica, Ohio, under the Rev. J. C. Boyd, and graduated from Muskingum College in 1852. He studied theology in the Northwood Seminary, and privately, and was licensed by the Pittsburgh Presbytery, July 22, 1857. He was ordained by the same Presbytery, installed pastor of the congregation of Brownsville, Monroe County, Ohio, August 31, 1859, and resigned this charge, June 10, 1865. He was installed pastor of the congregation of Londonderry, Guernsey County, Ohio, October 3, 1866, and was released September 1, 1875. He was installed pastor of the congregation of Wahoo, Saunders County, Nebraska, October 18, 1877, and resigned, May 18, 1880. He was installed pastor of the Hickory Grove congregation, Avery, Monroe County, Iowa, September 17, 1882, where he is in charge. He married Miss Sarah M. McBride, of Mt. Stirling, Ohio, October 16, 1855.

JAMES RENWICK THOMPSON:

Son of William and Jane (Lawther) Thompson, was born near the city of Newburgh, New York, September 25, 1824. He received his preparatory course of education in the schools of Newburgh, graduated from the University of the City of New York in 1847, and taught one year in Brooklyn, New York. He studied theology in the Cincinnati and Northwood Seminaries, and was licensed by the Lakes Presbytery, April 16, 1852. He preached in the vacancies one year, and visited Europe for his health, returning in the autumn of 1854. He was ordained by the New York Presbytery, and installed pastor of the Second congregation of Newburgh, New York, December 19, 1855, where he is in charge. He married Miss Mary F. Lawson, of Newburgh, New York,

June 1, 1858. He published a sermon "A National
Bereavement," 1865, pp. 24, after the death of President
Lincoln, and many articles in the city press and Church
magazines. He was Moderator of the Synod of 1877.

JOHN SLATER THOMPSON:

Son of William G. and Christiana G. (Robb)
Thompson, was born near Canonsburgh, Washington
County, Pennsylvania, May 27, 1858. He received his
early education in the Canonsburgh Academy, and
graduated from Geneva College in 1885. He studied
theology in the Allegheny Seminary, was licensed by
the Pittsburgh Presbytery, April 11, 1888, and preached
in Burdett, Kansas, for some time.

RICHARD McCLURE THOMPSON, D. D.:

Son of Anthony and Rebecca (McClure) Thompson,
was born in Wolf Creek, Mercer County, Pennsylvania,
August 20, 1828. His opportunities for acquiring an
education were very meagre, and he studied in the
Select School of Mr. George McConnell. In 1846, he
began classical studies under the Rev. James Blackwood, and subsequently under the Rev. John Galbraith,
finishing the course in Westminster College in
1856. He studied theology two years in the Allegheny
Seminary, and, in 1858, founded what is now Grove
City College, where he taught two years. He resumed
his studies in the Allegheny Seminary, and was licensed
by the Pittsburgh Presbytery, April 9, 1862. He was
ordained by the Lakes Presbytery, installed pastor of
the Lake Eliza congregation, Winfield, Lake County,
Indiana, September 7, 1865, and resigned this charge,
September 13, 1881. He was installed pastor of the

Pleasant Ridge congregation, Olathe, Johnston County, Kansas, October 11, 1881, where he is in charge. He married Miss Susanna Magee, of Valencia, Pennsylvania, July 15, 1862, and a sermon was preached on the occasion. He was honored with the degree of Doctor of Divinity by Grove City College in 1885.

ANDREW CALVIN TODD:

Son of Andrew and Margaret (McLean) Todd, was born in Newberry, Newberry County, South Carolina, January 23, 1826. His parents removed from the South in 1827, on account of the prevalence of slavery, settled near Bloomington, Indiana, and, in 1831, removed to Oakdale, Washington County, Illinois. Here he received his early education in the public schools, and under private instructors, graduating from Jefferson College in 1847. He studied theology in the Cincinnati and Northwood Seminaries, and was licensed by the Illinois Presbytery, May 17, 1851. He was ordained by the same Presbytery, installed pastor of the congregation of St. Louis, Missouri, July 29, 1852, and resigned this charge, April 12, 1857. He was installed pastor of the Elkhorn congregation, Oakdale, Washington County, Illinois, July 1, 1859, was released May 17, 1871, and organized a colony of Covenanters which settled in Evans, Weld County, Colorado. He was installed pastor of the Evans congregation, August 21, 1874, where he is in charge. He married twice. First to Miss Margaret L. Willson, of Greensburgh, Pennsylvania, October 2, 1849; and second to Miss Ella A. Brown, of Iowa City, Iowa, July 6, 1880. In August, 1861, he organized a company of soldiers, went

to the defence of the country as the Captain of the
Tenth Missouri Volunteers, and returned in November,
1862, in obedience to an act of Synod.

CHARLES DE WITT TRUMBULL:

Son of John K. and Laura A. (Dunbar) Trumbull,
was born in East Craftsbury, Orleans County, Vermont,
April 4, 1837. He received his early education in the
schools of his native village, and removed with his
parents to Northwood, Logan County, Ohio, in 1851.
He resumed his studies in Geneva College, where he
remained until his senior year, graduating from Jefferson
College in 1858. He was a teacher and Assistant
Principal of Geneva College, for two years. He studied
theology in the Allegheny Seminary, and was licensed
by the Lakes Presbytery, April 21, 1863. He was
ordained by the Iowa Presbytery, installed pastor of the
Linn Grove congregation, Mediapolis, Des Moines County,
Iowa, January 29, 1864, and resigned this charge,
April 1, 1874. He was installed pastor of the congregation of Morning Sun, Louisa County, Iowa, April 14,
1874, where he is in charge. He married Miss Mary
Sproull, of Allegheny City, Pennsylvania, June 8, 1864.
He has published a few sermons and historical articles
in the magazines of the Church, and performed efficient
service as Chairman of several Boards and Committees.
He was Moderator of the Synod of 1878.

HUGH WALKINSHAW:

Son of John and Mary (Henry) Walkinshaw, was
born near Broughshane, County Antrim, Ireland, June
15, 1803. His parents, who were members of the
Presbyterian Church, designed him for the ministry,

and, in 1811, he began the classics with that end in view. In 1819, he came to America, settled in Belmont County, Ohio, and soon afterwards resumed his studies, graduating from Franklin College in 1827. He studied theology under the Rev. Dr. John Black in Pittsburgh, and also under the Rev. Dr. S. B. Wylie in Philadelphia, and was licensed by the Philadelphia Presbytery, June 17, 1832. He was ordained by the Pittsburgh Presbytery, and installed pastor of the Brookland congregation, Lucesco, Westmoreland County, Pennsylvania, April 15, 1835. This field was then very extensive, and included the adjacent branches of North Washington, Union, Pine Creek and Puckety. In 1841, the congregation was divided into two separate organizations, and he remained pastor of Brookland and North Washington until his death. A year before his decease he suffered from a fracture of one of his limbs, causing an organic disease of the liver, which finally developed into a dropsical affection, causing his death, at his home near Lucesco, Pennsylvania, April 19, 1843. He married Miss Lydia J. Sproull, of Lucesco, Pennsylvania, in 1835. He was a learned man and a diligent, prayerful student of God's Word. His preaching was more intellectual than emotional, his arguments being addressed to the judgment rather than the feelings. He was a faithful and attentive pastor, naturally fond of society, and abounded in deeds of genuine charity. He was closely attached to the distinctive principles of the Covenanter Church, and opposed to all voluntary associations with men of questionable character. He was rigid in his discipline, alert to every

44

transgression of ecclesiastical law, and profoundly jealous of the interests of the Church.

JAMES WALLACE:

Son of Rev. Robert and Margaret (King) Wallace, was born in Lisadier, County Armagh, Ireland, March 10, 1810. The following spring he was brought by his parents to America, who settled first in the city of Philadelphia, Pennsylvania, and, in 1814, in Norwich, Muskingum County, Ohio, where he received his early education under the direction of his godly father, graduating from Franklin College in 1834. He studied theology privately two years, and two years in the Coldenham Seminary, being licensed by the Southern Presbytery, May 10, 1838. He was ordained by the Western Presbytery at Northwood, Ohio, July 13, 1840, installed pastor of the Old Bethel congregation, Sparta, Randolph County, Illinois, August 16, 1840, and labored with great success until his resignation, May 15, 1867. At this time he accepted an appointment as Secretary of the National Reform Association, and the next ten years of his life were spent in travelling throughout the country proclaiming the glorious principles of Bible civil government. The disease which terminated his life was an organic affection of the heart, and he fell dead in his home, in the city of St. Louis, Missouri, May 1, 1877. He was thrice married. First to Miss Sarah Wright, of Adamsville, Ohio, in 1840; second, to Mrs. Mary J. (Sloane) McClurkin, of Warriston, Illinois, April 17, 1855; and third, to Mrs. Mary B. (Murdock) Trumbull, of Rochester, New York, in 1861. He was not an eloquent preacher, often becoming exceedingly tedious and monotonous; but those who waited upon his instructive services were fully rewarded for their patience. He understood well the Bible and its truths. He was a well-read theologian, and possessed the happy faculty of analysis and method. He was tender in his feelings, warm in his friendship, a close observer of human nature, and fond of religious conversation. He excelled as a pastor. He was a zealous reformer, and thoroughly enlisted in the cause of anti-slavery, temperance, and the different questions of the National Reform Association. He was Moderator of the Synod of 1862.

JOHN WALLACE:

Son of Rev. Robert and Margaret (King) Wallace, was born in Lisadier, County Armagh, Ireland, December 25, 1800. He received his early education in the schools of his native land, and came with his parents to America in 1811, who settled in the city of Philadelphia, Pennsylvania, where he resumed his studies in the public schools. In 1814, he removed to Norwich, Muskingum County, Ohio, where he continued his studies under the direction of his father, graduating from the Western University of Pennsylvania in 1829. He studied theology under the care of the Rev. Dr. John Black, of Pittsburgh, and was licensed by the Pittsburgh Presbytery, April 4, 1832. He was ordained by the Ohio Presbytery, installed pastor of the united congregations of Muskingum and Tomica, Dresden, Muskingum County, Ohio, April 14, 1833, and resigned this charge, April 4, 1855. He connected with the Associate Reformed Church, being received by the Second Presbytery of Ohio, October 27, 1857. In 1858, he went into the

United Presbyterian Church, was installed pastor of the congregation of Adamsville, Crawford County, Pennsylvania, May 6, 1862, and resigned this charge, May 1, 1866. He returned to the Covenanter Church, being received by the Pittsburgh Presbytery, October 16, 1866, and supplied throughout the vacancies as his health would permit. During the last years of his life he became almost blind, and died from a stroke of paralysis, at his home in Adamsville, Pennsylvania, January 7, 1880. He was twice married. First to Miss Jane E. Wylie, of White Cottage, Ohio, June 1, 1837; and second, to Miss Eleanor George, of White Cottage, Ohio, April 4, 1849. He was a very stern disciplinarian, and unbending in his convictions. He was not a pleasing speaker, but a faithful and sound evangelical preacher, and a sturdy soldier of the Cross, spending his whole life in missionary work.

ROBERT WALLACE:

Son of David and Mary (Brown) Wallace, was born in Loughgilly, County Armagh, Ireland, December 14, 1772. His parents were exemplary members of the Anti-Burgher Secession Church, with which he also connected in 1791. He received a liberal education in the public schools, and was engaged in teaching. In 1794, he connected with the Covenanter congregation of Ballylane. He devoted himself to the work of the gospel ministry; and, after many years of patient waiting until he had an opportunity of receiving a classical education, entered a private school, graduating from the University of Glasgow, Scotland, in 1810. The following spring he came to America with his family, and settled in the city of Philadelphia, Pennsylvania. He began the study of theology in the Philadelphia Seminary, and was licensed by the Middle Presbytery, May 9, 1814. He was ordained by the same Presbytery at Pittsburgh, Pennsylvania, and installed pastor of the united congregations of Licking and Chillicothe, Ohio, October 12, 1814. This field was very extensive, and included the nucleii of all the congregations in Eastern Ohio. The population of the country at that time was very scattered, and his journeys were long and exceedingly laborious. He was the pioneer Missionary in Ohio. He resigned the Licking branch, May 10, 1820, and removed to the Chillicothe branch, where he confined his labors mostly in Southern Ohio. He was installed pastor of the Salt Creek (now New Concord) congregation, Norwich, Muskingum County, Ohio, October 9, 1823, where he spent the rest of his life. He died in the infirmities of age, and from the effects of a fall from his horse, July 19, 1849. He was twice married. First to Miss Margaret King, of County Armagh, Ireland, in 1796; and second, to Mrs. Isabella (McCreary) McCartney, of Cambridge, Ohio, October, 1839. His preaching was characterized by plainness, boldness, and spiritual fervency; and he was clear, concise, and impressive in his delivery. While he was by no means eloquent in his pulpit exhibitions, yet there was a solemnity and persuasiveness in his manner that never failed to interest and convince. He was a most generous Christian, fearless in denouncing the evils of society, and the defections from the Church. During the division of the Church in 1833, not a single member of his charges left the fold. In pastoral and catechetical work he was most successful, and was held in high esteem by all his brethren.

SAMUEL RUTHERFORD WALLACE:

Son of David and Flora (Jamison) Wallace, was born in Norwich, Muskingum County, Ohio, August 19, 1849. He received his early education in the schools of his native town, and graduated from Muskingum College in 1870. He studied theology in the Allegheny Seminary, and was licensed by the Ohio Presbytery, April 2, 1873. He was ordained by the Rochester Presbytery, and installed pastor of the congregation of Syracuse, New York, December 8, 1874, where he is in charge. He married Miss Josie M. Williamson, of Cedarville, Ohio, October 29, 1875.

MATTHEW WILKIN:

Son of Matthew and Elizabeth (Duguid) Wilkin, was born near New Alexandria, Westmoreland County, Pennsylvania, August 2, 1809. His parents were pious members of the Associate Reformed Church, and, in 1811, removed to Harrison County, Ohio, where they connected with the Covenanter Church, under the Rev. William Sloane. Here he received a liberal education, engaged in teaching, and conducted a newspaper. He was subsequently chosen to the eldership, and served the Church in this relation until he entered the ministry. Having an earnest desire to preach the gospel, he removed to Northwood, Logan County, Ohio, in 1851, and began classical studies in Geneva College, where he finished the course in 1855. He studied theology at the same time in the Northwood Seminary, and was licensed by the Lakes Presbytery, May 17, 1855. He was ordained by the Rochester Presbytery, installed pastor of the congregation of Sterling, Cayuga County, New York, October 23, 1856, and resigned this charge, October 2, 1867. He removed his family to Northwood, Ohio, and served the Church as a Home Missionary and National Reform lecturer for six years. He was installed pastor of the congregation of Pleasant Ridge, Johnston County, Kansas, May 8, 1874, and also of Hebron, Clay County, Kansas, November 11, 1876, and exercised a joint pastorate over these charges until his death, July 12, 1880. He married Miss Elizabeth Mansfield, of Steubenville, Ohio, May 29, 1833. He was a clear, forcible, and profound preacher of the gospel. He possessed an intellectual and logical mind, which he used with rare power in the proclamation of the truth. His work was done conscientiously, and his characteristics were those of truthfulness and honest exaction. He was a rigid disciplinarian, attentive upon Church courts, and to the spiritual interests of his people. He was an earnest and successful advocate of the cause of temperance, and the claims of Christ as ruler of the Nation.

JOHN BLACK WILLIAMS:

Son of Rev. Matthew and Elizabeth (Parkhill) Williams, was born near Bakerstown, Allegheny County, Pennsylvania, February 24, 1825. He received his early education in Darlington Academy, completed the course in the Western University of Pennsylvania, and graduated from Muskingum College in 1844. He studied theology in the Cincinnati Seminary, and was licensed by the Pittsburgh Presbytery, October 3, 1849. He was ordained by the New York Presbytery, and installed pastor of the congregation of White Lake, Sullivan County, New York, November 14, 1850, where he is in charge. He has published many articles in the magazines of the Church, and is editor of the *White Lake Mirror*. He has educated many young men now occupying prominent positions, and has been a successful advocate of temperance and all reforms.

MATTHEW WILLIAMS:

Was born in Ballymena, County Antrim, Ireland, July 17, 1768. His parents were zealous adherents to the Seceder Church, and were most exemplary in their Christian character. At an early age he was sent to Edinburgh, Scotland, where he received a liberal classical education. He came with his parents to America in 1794, and settled in the Ligonier Valley, Westmoreland County, Pennsylvania, uniting with the Associate Reformed Church. He resumed his studies, and graduated from Jefferson Academy in 1801, just before the organization of Jefferson College. The following year he met the Rev. Dr. John Black, and, after hearing him preach, became convinced of the truth of the principles of the Covenanter Church, and united with the Miller's Run congregation. He studied theology under the Rev. Dr. John Black, of Pittsburgh, and was licensed by the Reformed Presbytery, September 20, 1804. The following year he settled on the banks of the Conoconessing, near Zenienople, Butler County, Pennsylvania, and labored as a Home Missionary for two years. His field of labor at that time was a part of the charge usually visited by the Rev. John Black, and included all the societies north of Pittsburgh. The country was an unbroken forest, and the wild beasts were often his companions. He rode on horseback almost incessantly, and was often away from his family for many weeks at a time. He was ordained by the Middle Committee of the Reformed Presbytery, and installed pastor of the united societies of Pine Creek, Union and Deer Creek, principally in Butler County, Pennsylvania, May 18, 1807. He removed to Pine Creek in 1815, and this was his principal charge and home the residue of his life. Literally worn out with the fatigue of travel, which brought on an incurable malady, he died at his home at Pine Creek, Pennsylvania, September 11, 1828. In the old burying ground, at that historic spot, may be seen upon a broad moss-covered stone, the following brief tribute to his memory: " He was a humble Christian, and a faithful minister of the gospel of Jesus Christ. He lived and died in the faith of that gospel which he had long preached." He married Miss Elizabeth Parkhill, of Elizabeth, Pennsylvania, in 1807. He was a man of medium stature, and his bearing was solemn and dignified. He was well versed in theology, a fair speaker of simple and choice language, and told no anecdotes in the pulpit. He was a creditable musician, a social and generous host, and his home was one of hospitable entertainment. He left no monument of literature, but his record as a faithful embassador for Christ is on high.

MELANCTHON BROWN WILLIAMS:

Son of Rev. Gershom and Phebe (Squire) Williams, was born in Cambridge, Washington County, New

York, July 16, 1797. His father was a distinguished minister of the Presbyterian Church, from whom he received a careful religious training. He received his first schooling in his native town, and could read before he was five years of age. In 1803, his parents removed to New Jersey, and he resumed his studies in the schools of Springfield and Newark, graduating from the College of New Jersey, at Princeton, in 1814, while yet in his sixteenth year. He immediately entered upon the study of law in New York City, where he read general law and did clerical work for two years. In the fall of 1816, he espoused the principles of the Covenanter Church, and immediately abandoned secular pursuits and entered upon the study of theology in the Philadelphia Seminary, being licensed by the Northern Presbytery, May 27, 1818. He continued his studies another year under the direction of the Rev. Dr. J. R. Willson at Coldenham, New York. He was ordained by the Northern Presbytery, and installed pastor of the united congregations of Kortright and Bovina, Delaware County, and White Lake, Sullivan County, New York, April 15, 1820. He resigned the White Lake branch, May 16, 1821 ; the Bovina charge, October 17, 1823, and continued to labor in Kortright until August 31, 1831, when he connected with the Presbyterian Church. In the fall of 1831, he took charge of a Congregational Church in the eastern part of Long Island. In 1832, he became Principal of the Academy of Bergen, New Jersey. He connected with the Dutch Reformed Church, and was installed pastor of the congregation of Betts'

Corner, near Auburn, New York, October 17, 1833, where he remained in charge two years. In 1835, he returned to the Presbyterian Church, and was stated supply at Weedsport, New York, for some time. In 1838, he became pastor of the Presbyterian congregation of Asylum, Bradford County, Pennsylvania. Owing to his radical principles on temperance and anti-slavery, he caused a division in this Church, and organized out of it an independent congregation which accepted his views. In waging war against these evils upon a Scriptural basis, he felt the need of a more thorough knowledge of the Hebrew language. He left the charge, December 14, 1840, and entered the Andover Theological Seminary, Massachusetts, where he studied and missionated until the spring of 1842, when he returned to his pastoral charge at Asylum, and for four years wielded his spiritual weapons effectively in battling against intemperance, slavery, and secretism. In 1848, he went Westward, remaining in Cincinnati, Ohio, for some time, and for a number of years labored as an independent missionary throughout Illinois and Wisconsin. In 1861, he returned East and located in Williamsburgh, Long Island, and became an editor of the *Principia* with William Goodell, afterwards with Rev. Dr. George B. Cheever, in which capacity he continued five years. He connected with the United Presbyterian Church, May 23, 1862, and, in 1866, retired to his birth place at Cambridge, New York, where he is living at an advanced age. He married twice. First to Miss Catharine Doig, of Albany, New York, June 10, 1820; and second, to Miss Agnes Beninger, of Salem, New York, March 22, 1854.

DAVID BURT WILLSON, M. D.:

Son of Rev. Dr. James M. and Rebecca (Burt) Willson, was born in Philadelphia, Pennsylvania, September 27, 1842. He received his early education in the public schools, and the Classical Institute of Rev. Dr. J. W. Faires, of his native city, graduating from the University of Pennsylvania in 1860. He studied medicine in the Jefferson Medical College, graduating in 1863, and for two years was a surgeon in the army. He studied theology in the Allegheny Seminary, and was licensed by the Pittsburgh Presbytery, April 15, ₁1868. He was ordained by the Pittsburgh Presbytery, installed pastor of the congregation of Allegheny, Pennsylvania, November 29, 1870, and resigned this charge, October 13, 1875, accepting the chair of Biblical Literature in the Allegheny Theological Seminary, which he now occupies. He was twice married. First to Miss Martha J. Grier, of Allegheny, Pennsylvania, August 16, 1873; and second, to Miss Mary R. Galbraith, of Valencia, Pennsylvania, August 14, 1883. He received the degree of Doctor of Medicine from Jefferson Medical College in 1863. He has been an editor of the *Reformed Presbyterian and Covenanter* since 1874, a member of the Central Board of Missions, and Clerk of Synod for several years. He was Moderator of the Synod of 1887.

JAMES McLEOD WILLSON, D. D.:

Son of Rev. Dr. James R. and Jane (Roberts) Willson, was born at "the forks of the Yough," near Elizabeth, Allegheny County, Pennsylvania, November 17, 1809. From childhood he was apt in the acquisition of learning and most diligent in his studies, his godly parents, who were uncompromising in their attachments to the principles of the Covenanter Church, being disposed to educate him for the ministry. He received instructions in the classics under his reputed father, who was Principal of the Academy of Bedford, Pennsylvania, and also attended classical schools taught by his father iñ Philadelphia, Pennsylvania, and Newburgh, New York. In due time he entered the senior class and graduated from Union College in 1829. He taught for some time in the Academy of Belair, Maryland, also in Schodack, New York, and was Principal of the High School in Troy, New York. He studied theology under the direction of his father, and was licensed by the Southern Presbytery, June 5, 1834. He was ordained by the same Presbytery, and installed pastor of the First congregation of Philadelphia, Pennsylvania, November 27, 1834. He was elected Professor of Theology in the Allegheny Seminary, May 31, 1859, which office he filled with great acceptance for three successive sessions while retaining his pastoral charge in Philadelphia. These accumulated labors, requiring a separation from his congregation for six months in the year, were too onerous, and he resigned the congregation, October 28, 1862. He removed to the city of Allegheny, Pennsylvania, where he continued to devote himself to the proper work of the Seminary until his death. He had long been a subject to headache, and the nervous energy and locomotion of his left side were impaired. This affliction was followed by a syncopal attack, terminating in a serious hypertrophy,

from which he died, at his residence in Allegheny,
Pennsylvania, August 31, 1866, and he was buried in
the Monument Cemetery at Philadelphia. He married
Miss Rebecca Burt, of Schenectady, New York, April
30, 1833. He was a clear, logical, and eminently
instructive preacher, but not an attractive speaker.
His discourses were always profoundly thought out, and
generally doctrinal, argumentative, and practical. He
was a faithful and kind pastor, and his strict dis-
ciplinary reproofs were in plainness of speech, though
not calculated to offend. His great power was in
debate, and he was a moulder of opinions upon the
floor of Synod. He always took an important part in
the discussions agitating the Church, and was almost
invincible in an argument. He was the representative
of the deacon question, and strongly discussed such
questions as slavery, voluntary associations, temperance,
and the issues of the war of the rebellion. His complete knowledge of the history and principles of the
Covenanter Church, together with his proficient scholarship and ripe experience, eminently fitted him for the
position which he held in the Theological Seminary.
Co-incident with his indefatigable labors as pastor and
professor, he edited the *Covenanter* from 1845 until its
consolidation with the *Reformed Presbyterian* in 1863,
and was an editor of the joint publication until his death.
Through this medium he fearlessly battled for truth
and righteousness against all opposition. Besides his
able editorial work, he emitted the following publications: "The Deacon," 1841, pp. 76. "Bible Magistracy,"
1842, pp. 122. "A Treatise on Psalmody," 1848, pp.

42. "Civil Government," 1853, pp. 162. "Social Religious Covenanting," 1856, pp. 36. "Witnessing," 1861, pp. 31, and other pamphlets of minor import. Being a public spirited man he was connected with all the Mission Boards, and literary and benevolent institutions. He was honored with the degree of Doctor of Divinity by Westminster College in 1865. He was Moderator of the Synod of 1859.

JAMES RENWICK WILLSON, D. D.:

Son of Zaccheus and Mary (McConnell) Willson, was born at "the forks of the Yough," near Elizabeth, Allegheny County, Pennsylvania, April 9, 1780. His ancestors were sturdy Covenanters who came to America in 1713, and settled in the Cumberland Valley in Eastern Pennsylvania. In 1769, the family removed to "the forks of the Yough." His father was a farmer, in which occupation he also engaged until his twenty-first year. In 1795, he connected with the Associate Reformed Church, but transferred his membership to the Covenanter Church in 1798. In 1801, he entered Jefferson Academy, and graduated with first honors from Jefferson College in 1805. His theological studies were pursued during his last collegiate year at Canonsburgh, Pennsylvania, under the direction of the Rev. Dr. John McMillan, also two years under the care of the Rev. Dr. Alexander McLeod, of New York, and he was licensed by the Middle Committee of the Reformed Presbytery, June 9, 1807. In 1809, he became Principal of the Academy of Bedford, Pennsylvania. In 1815, he took charge of a classical school in Philadelphia, and also established a Mission in "the Neck," where his labors were very successful. He was ordained by the Northern Presbytery, and installed pastor of the united congregations of Coldenham and Newburgh, Orange County, New York, August 10, 1817. In 1823, the Newburgh branch was dropped, and he remained at Coldenham until his resignation in 1830. He was installed pastor of the congregation of Albany, New York, September 17, 1830, and remained in charge three years. He returned to Coldenham, where he was re-installed November 21, 1833, and resuscitated the Coldenham Academy. He was chosen Professor of Theology in 1836, and the Eastern Seminary, located at Coldenham, New York, was established, October 12, 1838, where he was the preceptor for two years. At the union of the Eastern and Western Seminaries, creating the Allegheny Seminary, he resigned his charge at Coldenham, June 26, 1840, and accepted a professorate in the new institution. The Seminary was removed from Allegheny, Pennsylvania, to Cincinnati, Ohio, in 1845, where he was the sole Professor, and stated supply to the congregation of that city for four years. In 1849, the Seminary was removed to Northwood, Ohio, where he was exonerated from duty in 1851, and retired at Emeritus Professor. During the remaining two years of his life he resided with his son, the Rev. Dr. James M. Willson, in Philadelphia, and spent the summers in Coldenham, New York, where he died at the house of Mr. John Beattie, of old age, and under the affliction of a fractured limb, September 29, 1853. He lies buried in the graveyard of Coldenham, in the very spot above which stood the pulpit of the old church

where he so long preached. He married Miss Jane
Roberts, of Canonsburgh, Pennsylvania, in 1807. Without exception he was the most powerful preacher the
Covenanter Church in America has ever produced, and,
in intellectual grasp, classical scholarship, and pulpit
eloquence, ranked among the first preachers of the
country. He possessed every physical attribute of the
orator. His height was over six feet, his shoulders
broad, his voice sonorous, his eye brilliant; and, his
wide range of information in every department of
literature, his ready command of language, and his
intense earnestness, rendered him at once an attractive
speaker upon any subject. His was the career of a
great man. His style was generally distinguished for
perspicuity of statement, simplicity of method, and
beauty of illustration. His imagination was at once
active and elevated, and when it took possession of him
he was overwhelming in the majesty of his descriptions,
and the awful character of his denunciations. At the
time of his settlement in Newburgh, New York, there
existed a hot-bed of infidelity. The followers of Tom
Paine held sway, profaning sacred rites in the most
public and shameless manner—even administering the
symbols of the Saviour's death to dogs. He at once
inaugurated the battle. His boldness in proclaiming
the truth, the power of his arguments, the overwhelming force of his eloquence, the fearful warnings, and
clear prophetic denunciations, attracted the whole community as they hung upon his burning words. Some
shocking death-bed scenes, which seemed to be in
fulfilment of his threatenings, alarmed many, and

45

gradually the whole place became reformed. During his residence in Albany, he was frequently called upon to open the Legislature with prayer. His fame soon became known as he denounced the ungodliness of that body, and the wickedness of the city. The Legislature feared his prayers. When he preached his famous sermon "Prince Messiah," the Legislature discussed it for a whole sitting, and denounced the author in the most violent terms. The prayers of such a man were, by a unanimous vote, banished from the legislative halls; the sermon was consumed in a public bonfire, and the author burned in effigy before the State House door. He was prominent in the controversy that resulted in the division of the Church in 1833, and a champion of the portion adhering to the principles of the Church. He was a well-read historian, and published many articles on the history of the Church. He had a large acquaintance with public and religious men. He was eminently a man of prayer, and was accustomed to carry all matters to the throne of grace. He had no disrelish for social pleasantry, but his mind was usually occupied with themes of momentous import. He was a very successful teacher, and had knowledge of twelve languages, of most of which he was master. He was an American patriot, at the same time a consistent and ardent covenanting protestant against the evils of the country, and the infidelity of the Constitution of the United States. He was a public man, and an address from him at an anniversary, college commencement, or scientific association, was the attractive feature of the occasion. An address delivered at Newburgh, New

York, upon the occasion of the burial of the bones of
some revolutionary heroes, has been pronounced as one
of the most eloquent and beautiful discourses in the
English language. He left his impress as a great man
upon every department of literary work. He was a
profuse writer upon various subjects. The following are
his most valued publications extant: " Historical Sketch
of Opinions on the Atonement," 1817, pp. 350. "Subjection of Kings and Nations to Messiah," 1819.
" Civil Government," 1821. " Dr. Watts an Anti-Trini-
tarian," 1821. " Honour to Whom Honour is Due,"
1822. " The Book of Life of the Lamb," 1824. " The
Glory and Security of the Church of God," 1824.
" Political Danger," 1825. " The American Jubilee," 1825.
" The Sabbath, and the Duty of the Nation to Keep
it," 1829. " Prince Messiah's Claims to Dominion over
all Governments," 1832. " Tokens of Divine Displeasure
in the Conflagration of New York," 1835. " The Written
Law," 1840. " Public Covenanting," 1848. He was
editor of the *Evangelical Witness,* a monthly, 1822-26;
also of the *Albany Quarterly,* 1832-34. He was honored
with the degree of Doctor of Divinity by the Western
University of Pennsylvania in 1828. He was Moderator
of the Synod of 1823.

RENWICK ZACCHEUS WILLSON:

Son of Rev. Dr. James R. and Jane (Roberts)
Willson, was born in Bedford, Bedford County, Pennsylvania, June 19, 1813. In 1815, his parents removed
to Philadelphia, and, in 1817, to Coldenham, New York,
where he received his early education in the Academy
conducted by his distinguished father. Before he had

completed the prescribed course of study, he was afflicted with a disease of the eyes, which greatly impeded his progress in obtaining an education. He studied theology in the Coldenham and Allegheny Seminaries, and was licensed by the Pittsburgh Presbytery, April 7, 1842. He was ordained by the New York Presbytery, installed pastor of the congregation of Craftsbury, Orleans County, Vermont, November 17, 1846, and resigned this charge, December 18, 1855. He removed to Southern Illinois, and served the Church as a Home Missionary for several years. In 1867, he took charge of the New York City Mission, and in this capacity he labored until his death, at his home in the city of New York, from a relapse of typhoid fever, June 4, 1872. He married Miss Margaret Biggam, of New York City, November 10, 1846. He was not a popular preacher, but his discourses were profoundly intellectual, logical, and argumentative. He spent the best days of his life in the New York Mission. The character of the work changed the style of his preaching, and he became sympathetic, illustrative, and exhortatory in his manner. He saw so much of the misery and ruin entailed by strong drink, that he became exceedingly earnest in the cause of temperance. He was a man of truthfulness and uprightness in every transaction, much given to prayer, and evinced a rich Christian experience. He was well posted in Church law and order, and, understanding perfectly the government and history of the Church, was a safe and wise counsellor.

SAMUEL McCONNELL WILLSON:

Son of Zaccheus and Mary (McConnell) Willson, was born at "the forks of the Yough," near Elizabeth, Allegheny County, Pennsylvania, July 17, 1796. With the ministry in view he pursued his classical studies in the Bedford Academy, under the direction of his brother, the Rev. Dr. James R. Willson, and finished the course in the Philadelphia Academy in 1817. He studied theology under the direction of the Rev. Dr. S. B. Wylie, of Philadelphia, Pennsylvania, and was licensed by the Philadelphia Presbytery, June 19, 1820. He was ordained by the Northern Presbytery, installed pastor of the congregation of Galway, Saratoga County, New York, October 14, 1821, and resigned this charge, May 16, 1827. For five years he was engaged in teaching in Coldenham and Albany, New York, and also preaching as opportunity was afforded. He was installed pastor of the congregation of Craftsbury, Orleans County, Vermont, May 19, 1833, and resigned this charge, May 10, 1845. He was installed pastor of the congregation of Kortright, Delaware County, New York, October 22, 1845, where he continued to labor until his death, by a very painful disease, January 21, 1864. He was twice married. First to Miss Ann Barclay, of Montgomery, New York, in 1821; and second, to Miss Ann McClaury, of Kortright, New York, in 1854. He was a remarkably clear, concise, aad systematic preacher, but not an eloquent speaker. He was well-read in theological works. His style of presenting truth was not imaginative, and his discourses were unadorned with illustrations, except a few drawn from actual life. He excelled in prayer, and his soul was filled with the importance and preciousness of the doctrines of grace. During the division of the Church in 1833, he adhered, without faltering, to her true position. He was a bold and enthusiastic advocate of the cause of the oppressed slave, and entered with earnestness into the reforms where the welfare of men and the glory of God were to be promoted. He was a judicious counsellor, a wise legislator, and regular in his attendance upon Church courts, where his opinion was of weight. He was a true Christian, conscientious in the performance of religious duties, faithful to the ecclesiastical and social ties which bound him to his God, his Church, and his family. He was an associate editor of the *Albany Quarterly*, 1832–1834. He was Moderator of the Synods of 1836 and 1856.

WILLIAM WILSON, D. D., LL. D.:

Son of John and Lilly A. Wilson, was born in Findrum, County Donegal, Ireland, December 25, 1803.* He received his early education in the schools of Donegal, came with his parents to America in 1823, and settled in the city of New York. Here he enjoyed the advantages of an excellent classical education, and graduated from Union College in 1828. He studied theology in the Philadelphia Seminary, and was licensed by the Philadelphia Presbytery, April 14, 1830. He was ordained *sine titulo* by the same Presbytery, as a Home Missionary, June 16, 1831, and served in this capacity two years. He was installed pastor of the congregation of Milton, Northumberland County, Penn-

* Communications per Rev. J. Y. Boice, Philadelphia, Pa.

sylvania, August 6, 1832. At the division of the Church in August, 1833, he became identified with the New School branch of the Covenanter Church, remained pastor of the congregation, and became Principal of the Milton Academy, until his resignation, April 13, 1837. He returned to the city of New York, and, in 1838, removed to the city of Cincinnati, Ohio, where he preached to the congregation of that city until his installation as pastor, July 13, 1839. He was suspended for some irregularity, October 14, 1847, and organized an independent Church, which he styled the "Church of the Covenanters." After an ineffectual application to return to the true Covenanter Church, he returned to the New School body, May 17, 1854, and continued in this relation until shortly before his death. He was well informed in politics, took a patriotic stand at the time of the war of the rebellion, and was a Chaplain. After the war he returned to Cincinnati, Ohio, where he preached as his health would permit, and was Chancellor of the Cincinnati College for several years. During the winter of 1872, he slipped and fell upon the icy pavement, and fractured a limb, which developed into a disease which terminated his life, at his home in Cincinnati, Ohio, September 9, 1873. He married Miss Anna Campbell, of Cincinnati, Ohio, in 1853. He was an excellent classical scholar, and an interesting preacher of the gospel. His habits were not always in harmony with his profession, and he frequently came in collision with Church discipline. He possessed a mind of unusual power, which was stored with accurate and useful knowledge. He had a prodigious memory, and retained a vast amount of Scripture at his command. He was editor of the *American Christian Instructor*, a monthly, from 1833 to 1837. He was a profuse writer on political and religious subjects, and among his publications are the following: "The Blessed Nation," "Ministerial Heroism," "The Church and the New Age," "The Man for the Hour," "The Cause of the United States," "The Curse of Meroz," "A Nation Non-Plussed," "The Day of Small Things," and "Democracy versus Doulocracy." He published some essays on Geology in the *Presbyterian Witness*. He was honored with the degree of Doctor of Divinity by Franklin College in 1848, and that of Doctor of Laws by Cincinnati College in 1868. He was Moderator of the General Synod of 1843.

ALEXANDER WRIGHT:

Son of William and Eliza (Laughlin) Wright, was born in Craigs, County Antrim, Ireland, December 25, 1831. He received his early education in his native land, came to America in 1843, and settled in Eastern Pennsylvania, where he was engaged in farming and teaching for many years. By diligent study and constant teaching he prepared himself for College, graduating from Lafayette College in 1862. He studied theology in the Allegheny Seminary, and was licensed by the Pittsburgh Presbytery, May 23, 1867. Having preached with much acceptance for a short time in the Eastern part of the Church, he repaired to Minnesota, with the expectation of recovering his health which was seriously impaired. Finding no great benefit, he went to visit his relatives in Vernon, Waukesha County, Wisconsin, where he died of consumption, November 21, 1869. He never married. He was an earnest and practical preacher, giving evidence of great usefulness in the ministry. He was remarkably energetic, did not easily succumb to adverse circumstances, and by devoted labor and constant economy, not only sustained himself during the years of study, but acquired some property, and bequeathed a few thousand dollars to the Church.

JOSEPH HARVEY WYLIE:

Son of Rev. Preston H. and Mary A. (George) Wylie, was born in Winfield, Lake County, Indiana, November 13, 1858. In 1860, his parents removed to Rushsylvania, Ohio, and, in 1864, to Northwood, Ohio, returning to Rushsylvania in 1866, where he received his early education in the public schools, and studied in Geneva College three years. He engaged in teaching in Rushsylvania and West Mansfield, Ohio, graduating from Geneva College in 1881. He studied theology in the Allegheny Seminary, was licensed by the Pittsburgh Presbytery, April 9, 1884, and preached several months in Canada. He was ordained by the Pittsburgh Presbytery, installed pastor of the congregation of McKeesport, Pennsylvania, June 30, 1885, and resigned this charge, June 27, 1887. He was installed pastor of the congregation of Olathe, Johnston County, Kansas, October 21, 1887, where he is in charge. He married Miss Lizzie M. Adams, of Allegheny, Pennsylvania, January 19, 1886. He was an editor of the *College Cabinet* in 1881.

JAMES MILLIGAN WYLIE:

Son of James and Martha (Patterson) Wylie, was born near Rushsylvania, Logan County, Ohio, March 1, 1856. He received his early education in the public schools, and the Wright Normal School of his native village, graduating from Geneva College in 1878. He was engaged as a teacher of Mathematics in Geneva College the following year. He studied theology in the Allegheny Seminary, and was licensed by the Lakes Presbytery, April 12, 1882. He was ordained by the Pittsburgh Presbytery, installed pastor of the congregation of New Castle, Pennsylvania, June 22, 1883, and resigned this charge, December 26, 1887, accepting the appointment as General Secretary of Home Missions, with his residence in Kansas City, Missouri. He married Miss Lizzie M. Porter, of New Galilee, Pennsylvania, May 9, 1883.

JOHN WYLIE:

Son of Samuel and Mary (Speer) Wylie, was born in New Concord, Muskingum County, Ohio, October 18, 1848. In early life his parents removed to Washington, Iowa, where he received his early education, and engaged in teaching. He thus prepared himself for College, and graduated from the University of Iowa in 1870. He established and was Principal of the Academy of Aledo, Illinois, for eight years. He studied theology in the Allegheny Seminary, was licensed by the Iowa Presbytery, April 6, 1880, and missionated in the West. He was ordained by the Pittsburgh Presbytery, installed pastor of the Monongahela congregation, Elizabeth, Pennsylvania, April 27, 1883, and resigned this charge,

April 9, 1884. He was installed pastor of the united congregation of Muskingum and Tomica, Frazeysburgh, Muskingum County, Ohio, January 21, 1885, where he is in charge. He married Miss M. A. Smith, of New Concord, Ohio, June 23, 1875. He is a contributor of an exposition of the Sabbath School lessons to the *Zanesville Courier*.

JAMES RALSTON WYLIE:

Son of Thomas and Ann (Ralston) Wylie, was born near New Concord, Muskingum County, Ohio, November 7, 1847. He received his early education in his native County, and graduated from Muskingum College in 1872. In the fall of 1872, he accepted the Professorship of Mathematics in Geneva College, and, in 1875, taught Greek in the same institution. He studied theology in the Allegheny Seminary, and was licensed by the Lakes Presbytery, April 10, 1877. He was ordained by the same Presbytery, installed pastor of the congregation of Fairgrove, Tuscola County, Michigan, November 1, 1879, and resigned this charge, October 12, 1887. He married Miss Sarah E. George, of Rushsylvania, Ohio, September 7, 1875.

JAMES RENWICK WYLIE:

Son of Rev. Preston H. and Mary A. (George) Wylie, was born in Northwood, Logan County, Ohio, November 22, 1850. In 1855, his parents removed to Winfield, Lake County, Indiana, and, in 1860, to Rushsylvania, Ohio, where he received his early education and engaged in teaching. He resumed his studies in 1867, and graduated from Geneva College in 1873. He studied theology in the Allegheny Seminary, and was licensed by the Lakes Presbytery, April 12, 1876. He was ordained by the Pittsburgh Presbytery, installed pastor of the Springfield congregation, Mercer, Pennsylvania, June 29, 1877, and also of Centreville, Pennsylvania, July 3, 1882. He resigned the Centreville congregation, November 8, 1887, and Springfield, April 10, 1888. He was installed pastor of Little Beaver congregation, New Galilee, Beaver County, Pennsylvania, May 18, 1888, where he is in charge. He married Miss Nettie E. Armstrong, of Leechburgh, Pennsylvania, November 6, 1879.

OLIVER WYLIE: '

Son of Moses and Eleanor (Young) Wylie, was born near New Concord, Muskingum County, Ohio, October 15, 1817. After passing through the accustomed elementary training in the public schools, he graduated from Muskingum College in 1840. He studied theology in the Allegheny Seminary, and was licensed by the Pittsburgh Presbytery, April 18, 1845. While laboring in Illinois he contracted fever and ague, which fastened upon his constitution and clung to him throughout life. He was ordained by the Pittsburgh Presbytery, and installed pastor of the Brookland congregation, Lucesco, Westmoreland County, Pennsylvania, June 24, 1846. This charge was quite extensive, requiring much travelling, and constant exposure to all kinds of weather. His health being impaired by malaria and chronic bilious diseases, he was compelled to resign the congregation, October 14, 1851. With the hope of recruiting his health, he ceased preaching regularly for a time, and turned his attention to teaching. He became stated supply to the congregation of Brownsville, Monroe County, Ohio, April 17, 1853, where he continued to labor until his death, by a complication of diseases, October 24, 1856. He married Miss Isabella J. South, of Allegheny, Pennsylvania, July 16, 1846. He was a faithful and devout preacher of the gospel, and a close Bible student. He was closely attached to the principles of the Church, and a determined foe to all manner of oppression. He was a successful teacher, and, had his health permitted, would have become a most popular preacher, and held a place of influence in the Church.

PRESTON HARVEY WYLIE:

Son of William and Martha (Harvey) Wylie, was born near Somerset, Perry County, Ohio, April 16, 1822. In early life his parents removed into Muskingum County, Ohio, where he received his early education in the public schools, and began the classics under the Rev. John Wallace, with a view to the ministry. His plans were frustrated, however, for the time, by a weakness of the eyes. In 1850, he removed to Northwood, Ohio, where he resumed his studies, and graduated from Geneva College in 1853. He studied theology at the same time in the Northwood Seminary, and was licensed by the Lakes Presbytery, April 12, 1854. He was ordained by the same Presbytery, installed pastor of the Lake Eliza congregation, Winfield, Lake County, Indiana, May 14, 1855, and resigned this charge, October 9, 1860. He was installed pastor of the congregation of Rushsylvania, Logan County, Ohio, November 13, 1860, and also of Macedon, Mercer County, Ohio, January 10, 1861. He resigned the Rushsylvania branch, May 25, 1876, and the Macedon charge, March 1, 1887. He was installed pastor of the congregation of Sterling, Rice County, Kansas, April 15, 1887, where he is in charge. He married twice. First to Miss Mary A. George, of White Cottage, Ohio, March 12, 1844; and second, to Miss Rebecca A. Hays, of Cedarville, Ohio, May 6, 1862. He was Moderator of the Synod of 1884.

RICHARD CAMERON WYLIE:

Son of John and Maria (Wisher) Wylie, was born near Dresden, Muskingum County, Ohio, August 27, 1846. He received his early education in the schools of his native County, and in Muskingum College. In 1865, he removed to Oakdale, Washington County, Illinois, where he was engaged in teaching. In 1867, he became teacher of Latin and Greek in Muskingum College, and graduated from this institution in 1870. He again taught in Oakdale, Illinois, and spent some time in Colorado for his health. He studied theology in the Allegheny Seminary, and was licensed by the Illinois Presbytery, May 5, 1874. He was ordained by the Iowa Presbytery, installed pastor of the congregation of Hopkinton, Delaware County, Iowa, June 15, 1875, and resigned, October 3, 1882. He accepted the appointment as Secretary of the National Reform Association, and lectured for two years. He was installed pastor of the Cedar Lake congregation, Ray, Steuben County, Indiana, November 1, 1884, where he is in charge, and lectures upon National Reform. He married Miss Nannie Buchanan, of Lancaster, Ohio, June 6, 1876. His numerous letters and articles are published in the papers and magazines of the Church.

SAMUEL WYLIE, D. D.:

Son of Andrew and Elizabeth (Wylie) Wylie, was born in Moylarg, County Antrim, Ireland, February 19, 1790.* He was brought up under the pastoral care of the Rev. Simon Cameron, and received his early education in the best schools of his native land. He came to America in 1807, and settled in Philadelphia, Pennsylvania, where he resumed his studies in the University of Pennsylvania, graduating in 1811. He studied theology in the Philadelphia Seminary, and was licensed by the Middle Presbytery, May 23, 1815. He visited many of the vacancies the following year, and spent some time in the medical department of the University of Pennsylvania. In 1817, he went to the then "wilderness West," and explored new fields for missionary operations in the West and South. He was ordained *sine titulo* at the meeting of Synod, in Pittsburgh, Pennsylvania, May 26, 1818, and was sent as a Missionary to Southern Illinois. He began labor in Randolph, and parts of St. Clair and Washington Counties, and organized several societies, which soon became flourishing congregations. He was installed pastor of the Bethel congregation, Eden, Randolph County, Illinois, June 19, 1821, where he spent the rest of his life in the self-sacrificing duties of a pastor and missionary. At the division of the Church in August, 1833, he became identified with the New School branch of the Covenanter Church, and many of his former flock remained with him, over whom he exercised pastoral charge until his resignation, on account of the infirmities of age, February 20, 1870. He died

* Items principally from the family. Church Records.

at his home in Sparta, Illinois, March 20, 1872. He
married twice. First to Miss Margaret Millikin, of
Philadelphia, Pennsylvania; second, to Mrs. Margaret
(Black) Ewing, of Pittsburgh, Pennsylvania. He was a
faithful soldier of the Cross, and did much service for
his Master in establishing His kingdom upon earth.
He was a very acceptable preacher, and, in early times,
large audiences of people waited upon his ministrations.
He was not a bitter partisan, but always recognized the
step which the body had taken with which he was connected. He was a fearless advocate for the cause of
the slave, and enlisted the powers of his voice and pen
in their emancipation. He served his Church in many
important relations, and was recognized as a man of
influence, and an able divine. He published a "History
of the Reformed Presbyterian Churches in Southern
Illinois," in the *Presbyterian Historical Almanac*, 1859.
He was honored with the degree of Doctor of Divinity
by Washington and Jefferson College in 1868. He was
Moderator of the Synod of 1830, and the General Synod
of 1850.

SAMUEL BROWN WYLIE, D. D.:

Son of Adam and Margaret (Brown) Wylie, was
born in Moylarg, County Antrim, Ireland, May 21,
1773.* He received the rudiments of a thorough classical education in the vicinity of his home, and entered
the University of Glasgow, Scotland, where he distinguished himself as a scholar, and graduated with the
honorary degree of Master of Arts in 1797. He began
teaching a school in Ballymena, Ireland, but was com-

---

* Principally from Sprague's Annals.

pelled to flee from his native land in consequence of his connection with the efforts made in favor of Irish independence. He came to America, in October, 1797, settling in Philadelphia, Pennsylvania, where he was engaged as a teacher in Cheltenham. In 1798, he was appointed a Tutor in the University of Pennsylvania. He studied theology privately, and under the direction of the Rev. William Gibson, being licensed by the Reformed Presbytery, at Coldenham, New York, June 24, 1799. He was ordained *sine titulo* by the Reformed Presbytery, at Ryegate, Vermont, June 25, 1800, and was the first Covenanter minister ordained in America. He accompanied the Rev. James McKinney throughout the South to abolish slavery from the pale of the Covenanter Church. He preached for some time to the newly organized societies of Philadelphia, Pennsylvania, and Baltimore, Maryland. He was installed pastor of the congregation of Philadelphia, Pennsylvania, November 20, 1803, and frequently preached in Baltimore. At the organization of the Theological Seminary in Philadelphia, he was chosen the Professor, and entered upon the duties of the office, in 1810, resigning in 1817. He was re-elected in 1823, and resigned in 1828. In 1828, he was elected Professor of Latin and Greek in the University of Pennsylvania, and held this position for seventeen years, when he was retired as Emeritus Professor. At the division of the Church in August, 1833, he became identified with the New School branch of the Covenanter Church. A part of his congregation adhered to him, and he remained the pastor until shortly before his death, which event occurred appa-

46

rently without any disease, at his residence in Philadelphia, Pennsylvania, October 13, 1852. He married
Miss Margaret Watson, of Pittsburgh, Pennsylvania,
April 5, 1802. He was a life-long student, and one of
the best scholars the Covenanter Church has ever produced. He collected a valuable and rare library of
several thousand volumes, rich in theology, literature,
and science. He was not an eloquent preacher. His
voice was strong, but wanting in that flexibility and
modulation which is essential in effective speaking, and
his manner was modified by the necessity of having
to preach extemporaneously. He was a distinguished
teacher, to which occupation he devoted most of his
life and energies. His acquisitions as a linguist embraced
an understanding of fourteen languages, and he was
consulted in reference to this department of study by
scholars from all parts of the country. He was a generous and hospitable man, and gave of his abundance
for charitable and benevolent purposes. He was not
a profuse writer. His most noted publication is "The
Two Sons of Oil; or the Faithful Witness for Magistracy and Ministry upon a Scriptural Basis," 1803, pp.
81, two editions. This is the best presentation of the
position of the Covenanter Church that has been written, from which the author departed in 1833. His
sermon on the "Obligation of Covenants," 1804, pp.
117, was re-published in Europe. He is the author of
a Greek Grammar, 1838, and a "Memoir of Dr. Alexander McLeod," posthumously published, 1855, pp. 535.
He was honored with the degree of Doctor of Divinity
by Dickinson College in 1815. He was Moderator of the

Reformed Presbytery in 1800 and 1801, and largely connected with the legislative work of the early Covenanter Church in America. ·

SAMUEL OLIVER WYLIE, D. D. :

Son of Samuel and Mary (Patterson) Wylie, was born near Elizabeth, Allegheny County, Pennsylvania, July 14, 1819.* His parents were of a Covenanter ancestry, long in this country, and honorably connected with the history of the Church. Evincing a capacity for learning and a desire to enter upon the work of the ministry, he pursued his classical studies with this end in view, and graduated from the Western University of Pennsylvania in 1839. He studied theology in the Allegheny Seminary, and was licensed by the Pittsburgh Presbytery, June 1, 1842. He was ordained by the same Presbytery, installed pastor of the congregation of Greensburgh, Pennsylvania, May 17, 1843, and resigned November 18, 1844. He was installed pastor of the Second congregation of Philadelphia, Pennsylvania, December 5, 1844, and continued in this relation the residue of his life. For two years previous to his death, he was afflicted with dilatation of the heart, from which disease he died, at his home in Philadelphia, Pennsylvania, August 22, 1883. He married Miss Jean Wallace, of Pittsburgh, Pennsylvania, in 1844. He was an able, instructive, and practical preacher. His scholarship was of a high order. He was a close thinker, a logical reasoner, and thoroughly versed in theology and history. He was eminently successful as a pastor, and the spirited and

* Memorial Volume.

prosperous congregation which he left is the greatest monument to his indefatigable labors. He was an earnest advocate of the distinctive principles of the Covenanter Church, a courteous and dignified Presbyter, and a most humble and pious Christian. At the organization of the Foreign Mission in 1856, he was chosen Chairman of the Board, and to his mature judgment, wise management, and industrious correspondence, largely depended the success of the enterprize. In 1867, he was chosen Professor of Theology in the Allegheny Seminary, and taught one winter, but declined the office to remain among his devoted people. He was a member of the Executive Committee of the National Reform Association from its organization, and of the Board of Superintendents of the Theological Seminary for more than twenty years. He was Chairman of the Committee which drafted the Covenant of 1871, and, with a few changes, was adopted as it came from his pen. Among his publications are: "Truth's Pillar," 1856, pp. 40. "Messiah's Royal Beauty," 1860, pp. 40. He was honored with the degree of Doctor of Divinity by the Western University of Pennsylvania in 1871. He was Moderator of the Synod of 1855.

THOMAS ALEXANDER HENDERSON WYLIE:

Son of Rev. Preston H. and Mary A. (George) Wylie, was born near Zanesville, Muskingum County, Ohio, November 5, 1854. The following year his parents removed to Winfield, Lake County, Indiana, and, in 1860, to Rushsylvania, Logan County, Ohio, where he received his early education, and graduated from Geneva College in 1875. He was Principal of the Academy of Morning Sun, Ohio, one year. He studied theology in the Allegheny Seminary, was licensed by the Lakes Presbytery, April 1, 1879, and was stated supply respectively at St. John, New Brunswick, Brooklyn, New York, and Burlington, Iowa. He was ordained by the Iowa Presbytery, and installed pastor of the congregation of Washington, Washington County, Iowa, December 7, 1882, where he is in charge. He married Miss Mattie Murray, of Morning Sun, Ohio, February 21, 1882.

SUMMARY.

NATIVITY: Ireland, 90; Pennsylvania, 74; Ohio, 42; New York, 21; Scotland, 14; Indiana, 10; Vermont, 10; South Carolina, 9; Illinois, 8; Iowa, 4; Nova Scotia, 3; Virginia, 3; Michigan, 2; Alabama, 1; Missouri, 1; Syria, 1.

EDUCATION: Geneva College, 52; Privately Educated, 25;. Glasgow University, 25; Jefferson College, 24; Westminster College, 21; Belfast College, 17; Western University, 16; Muskingum College, 15; Indiana University, 14; Union College, 13; Franklin College, 8; University of Pennsylvania, 8; Columbia College, 7; Monmouth College, 6; Duquesne College, 5; Allegheny City College, 4; Coldenham Academy, 4; Edinburgh College, 4; Miami University, 3; University of the City of New York, 3; Dartmouth College, 2; Lafayette College, 2; Princeton College, 2; one each from Amity College, Dickinson College, Greenville College, Harvard College, Iowa University, Magee College, Oneida Institute, Toronto University, and Valparaiso Normal School.

Upon Leaving the Covenanter Church, the Following Ministers have either Died or are now in Connection with the Respective Denominations:—

Presbyterian Church: J. S. Allen, J. H. Boggs, Samuel Bowden, Alexander Craighead, W. M. Engles, S. M. Gayley, John Gibson, J. R. Hill, John Hood, J. R. Johnston, Lewis Johnston, John Little, Daniel McClelland, T. Z. McClurkin, R. H. McCready, Alexander McDowell, C. B. McKee, Robert McKee, Samuel McKinney, A. S. McMaster, E. D. McMaster, J. R. Newell, J. T. Pollock, John Rice, Samuel Robinson, George Scott, R. D. Sproull, J. W. Stewart, A. C. Stuart, J. H. Symmes.

New School Body: A. W. Black, John Black, Ebenezer Cooper, S. W. Crawford, G. T. Ewing, John Kell, J. N. McLeod, Gilbert McMaster, Gavin McMillan, Hugh McMillan, R. G. Orr, William Wilson, Samuel Wylie, S. B. Wylie.

United Presbyterian Church: W. J. Gillespie, T. C. Guthrie, Thomas Hanna, J. B. Johnston, J. M. Johnston, Boyd McCullough, John McMaster, M. B. Williams.

Associate Reformed Church: John Cuthbertson, Alexander Dobbin, Jonathan Gill, Matthew Linn, William Neill, David Telfair.

Without Ecclesiastical Connection: T. M. Elder, Francis Gailey, Joseph Hamilton, William Martin, James Reid, John Stott.

Dutch Reformed Church: James Christie, J. M. Dickson, David Graham, Hugh Hawthorne.

REFORMED PRESBYTERY: Robert Lusk, John Mc-Auley, David Steele.

CONGREGATIONAL CHURCH: David Gregg, Andrew Montgomery.

FREE CHURCH: Joseph Henderson, William Milroy.

SEVENTH DAY BAPTIST CHURCH: J. W. Morton.

STUDENTS OF THEOLOGY NOT COMPLETING THE PRESCRIBED COURSE IN REFORMED PRESBYTERIAN SEMINARY.

ROBERT H. ABRAHAM, of Toronto, Canada; Toronto University, 1876; Allegheny Seminary under Pittsburgh Presbytery, one session, ending in 1877; Free Church, and is settled in Hamilton, Canada.

JOSEPH J. ACHESON, of New York City, New York; University of the City of New York, 1833; privately under Southern Presbytery, three sessions, ending in 1836; studied medicine, and was a physician in Brooklyn, New York; died, November 4, 1873.

WILLIAM H. BARBER, of Brownsville, Ohio; Allegheny City College, 1861; received by Pittsburgh Presbytery in 1860; Presbyterian Church; died in 1862, while studying for the ministry in that body.

FRANCIS S. BEATTIE, of Philadelphia, Pennsylvania; Phiadelphia Academy, 1815; Philadelphia Seminary under Middle Presbytery, two sessions, ending in 1817; studied medicine, was a physician in Philadelphia, where he died in 1859.

JOHN K. BLACK, of Allegheny City, Pennsylvania; Allegheny City College, 1866; received as a student under Pittsburgh Presbytery in 1867; Presbyterian Church; settled minister in Cadiz, Ohio.

DANIEL W. BOXLEY, (Colored) of Rolla, Missouri; Geneva College, 1873; Allegheny Seminary under Illinois Presbytery, one session, ending in 1874; taught in Knox Academy, Selma, Alabama; studied medicine in Philadelphia; mail carrier in St. Louis, Missouri.

JOSEPH CONGER, of Newark, New Jersey; Union College, 1844; studied privately under New York Presbytery, two sessions, ending in 1846; Presbyterian Church; was a teacher in Schenectady, New York.

WILLIAM CUMMING, of Baltimore, Maryland; Johrs Hopkins University; Allegheny Seminary under Philadelphia Presbytery, one session, ending in 1881; Presbyterian Church; settled minister in Waverly, Baltimore, Maryland.

JOHN H. ECHOLS, (Colored) of Selma, Alabama; Geneva College, 1882; studied privately two sessions, ending in 1885; a teacher in Sparta, Georgia.

JAMES M. ELDER, of Clarksburgh, Pennsylvania; Geneva College; studied privately under Pittsburgh Presbytery, one session, ending in 1856; died in Clarksburgh, Pennsylvania, January 10, 1857.

ABOOD G. ESKER, of Latakia, Syria; Beirut College, in 1883; Allegheny Seminary, one session, ending in 1888; returned to Syria.

MOSES R. FRAZIER, of Newburgh, New York; Conell University, 1873; Allegheny Seminary under New York Presbytery, three sessions, ending in 1877; died in Newark, New Jersey, December 13, 1877.

ROBERT A. GEORGE, of New Concord, Ohio; Geneva College, 1879; Allegheny Seminary under Ohio Presbytery, two sessions, ending in 1881; engaged in clerical work in Kenton, Ohio.

ROBERT C. GIBSON, of Allegheny City, Pennsylvania; educated in an Academy; was received as a student under Pittsburgh Presbytery in 1847; went to Iowa, and engaged in teaching; died in 1856.

WILLIAM J. GIBSON, of Canonsburgh, Pennsylvania; Jefferson College, 1826; studied privately under his father, three sessions, ending in 1829; Presbyterian Church; settled minister in Philadelphia, Hollidaysburgh, Williamsburgh, Jacksonville and Duncansville, Pennsylvania; died October 18, 1883.

JAMES GRAY, of Clarksburgh, Pennsylvania; Westminster College, 1861; Allegheny Seminary under Pittsburgh Presbytery, two sessions, ending in 1863; died in Clarksburgh, Pennsylvania, February 22, 1864.

JOHN HAMILTON, of Columbiana, Ohio; Jefferson College, 1847; Cincinnati and Northwood Seminaries under Pittsburgh Presbytery, three sessions, ending in 1851; studied medicine, and is a physician in Allegheny, Pennsylvania.

WILLIAM R. HAMILTON, of Columbiana, Ohio; Jefferson College, 1849; Northwood Seminary under Pittsburgh Presbytery, one session, ending in 1851; studied medicine, and is a physician in Pittsburgh, Pennsylvania.

THOMAS S. HUGGART, of Pardoe, Pennsylvania; Westminster College, 1874; Allegheny Seminary under Pittsburgh Presbytery a part of the session ending in 1875; Presbyterian Church; settled at Lancaster, Ohio.

MARTIN HUTCHESON, of Londonderry, Ohio; educated in Geneva College; Allegheny Seminary under Ohio Presbytery, two sessions, ending in 1865; died in Cambridge, Ohio, October 25, 1867.

JAMES H. JOHNSTON, of Barnet, Vermont; Geneva College, 1854; Northwood Seminary under Lakes Presbytery, two sessions, ending in 1854; engaged in business in Huntsville, Ohio; removed to Iowa, where he was engaged in teaching.

JAMES B. MCCLELLAND, of Balm, Pennsylvania; Westminster College, 1878; Allegheny Seminary under Pittsburgh Presbytery, one session, ending in 1885; United Presbyterian Church, and is a Professor in Grove City College.

JAMES A. MCKELVY, of Coultersville, Illinois; Geneva College, 1883; Allegheny Seminary under Pittsburgh Presbytery, two sessions, ending in 1885; Presbyterian Church, and is an evangelist.

THOMAS MCKINLEY, of Philadelphia, Pennsylvania; University of Pennsylvania, 1826; Philadelphia Seminary under Philadelphia Presbytery, two sessions, ending in 1828; Tutor in University of Pennsylvania; died in Philadelphia, June 9, 1833.

ARCHIBALD MCKINNEY, of Rodgersville, Tennessee; University of Glasgow, Scotland; Philadelphia Seminary under Middle Presbytery, two sessions, ending in 1812; studied medicine and practiced in Cincinnati, Ohio, where he died about 1835.

ALEXANDER MOGEE, of Belfast, Ireland; Royal College, 1875; Allegheny Seminary under Philadelphia Presbytery, a part of the session ending in 1877; returned to Ireland; Presbyterian Church; settled minister in Ireland.

STEPHEN D. MONTGOMERY, of Morning Sun, Iowa; Monmouth College, 1885; Allegheny Seminary under Iowa Presbytery, one session, ending in 1886; United Presbyterian Church, and studied in their Allegheny Seminary; died of typhoid fever, at Allegheny General Hospital, November 30, 1887.

JOHN G. MURPHY, of Philadelphia, Pennsylvania; University of Pennsylvania, 1842; privately under Western Presbytery, two sessions, ending in 1844; studied medicine, and settled as a physician in Philadelphia, Pennsylvania, where he died, August 9, 1879.

LORENZO NEELEY, of Montgomery, New York; Union College, 1838; Coldenham Seminary under Southern Presbytery, one session, ending in 1840; Presbyterian Church; settled minister in Lansing, Michigan, where he died, April 4, 1853.

JAMES C. NIGHTINGALE, of New York City, New York; University of the City of New York, 1861; Allegheny Seminary under New York Presbytery, three sessions, ending in 1864; Presbyterian Church; an evangelist in Stamford, Connecticut.

LEVI B. PURVIS, of Bakerstown, Pennsylvania; Duquesne College, 1845; Cincinnati Seminary under Pittsburgh Presbytery, four sessions, ending in 1849; died in Bakerstown, Pennsylvania, November 21, 1849.

JOHN F. QUARLES, (Colored) of Atlanta, Georgia; educated in Geneva College; Westminster College, 1869; Allegheny Seminary under Pittsburgh Presbytery, two sessions, ending in 1871; studied law and practiced in New York; consul to Port Mahon; minister to Spain; politician; died in Flushing, New York, January 18, 1885.

JOHN ROBINSON, of Philadelphia, Pennsylvania; University of Pennsylvania; Coldenham Seminary under Southern Presbytery, two sessions, ending in 1840; studied law and practiced in Philadelphia.

THOMAS S. SLOANE, of Pittsburgh, Pennsylvania; Allegheny City College, 1860; Allegheny Seminary under Pittsburgh Presbytery, one session, ending in 1861; agent in Pittsburgh, Pennsylvania.

SAMUEL F. SMITH, of Tuscarora, Pennsylvania; Western University of Pennsylvania, 1823; Philadelphia Seminary under Philadelphia Presbytery, two sessions, ending in 1825; Associate Reformed Church; settled as a minister in Cochrantown, Pennsylvania, where he died, March 19, 1846.

THEOPHILUS SPROULL, of Allegheny City, Pennsylvania; Rochester University, 1872; Allegheny Seminary under Pittsburgh Presbytery, one session, ending in 1873; is a publisher in Pittsburgh, Pennsylvania.

WILLIAM O. SPROULL, of Allegheny City, Pennsylvania; Washington and Jefferson College, 1869; Allegheny Seminary under Pittsburgh Presbytery, two sessions, ending in 1871; Leipsic University, Germany; Presbyterian Church; Professor in Cincinnati University, Ohio.

GEORGE E. STEWART, of California, Michigan; Hillsdale College; Allegheny Seminary under Lakes Presbytery, one session, ending in 1870; taught in Texas many years; living in infirm health at Ray, Indiana.

SAMUEL B. TAGGART, of Canonsburgh, Pennsylvania; Jefferson College, 1856; Allegheny Seminary under Pittsburgh Presbytery, three sessions, ending in 1859; Presbyterian Church, and is stated supply at Uhrichsville, Ohio.

WILLIAM THOMPSON, of New York City, New York; Belfast College, 1848; studied privately under New York Presbytery, four sessions; engaged in teaching; died in New York City, January 23, 1853.

ROBERT TRUMBULL, of Craftsbury, Vermont; University of Vermont, 1834; taught in Albany, New York; studied theology privately under Northern and Southern Presbyteries, three sessions; Principal of Geneva Female Seminary, Northwood, Ohio, where he died, February 24, 1854.

CHARLES L. WILLIAMS, (Colored) of Coldenham, New York; Coldenham Academy; studied privately under Northern and Pittsburgh Presbyteries, two sessions; engaged in teaching in 1847; died in Xenia, Ohio, October 15, 1859.

ZACCHEUS G. WILLSON, of Elizabeth, Pennsylvania; Muskingum College; Northwood Seminary one session, and privately under Illinois Presbytery, two sessions, ending in 1854; Principal of Public Schools in St. Louis, Missouri, for many years; now living in Glenwood, Minnesota.

THE THEOLOGICAL SEMINARY.

At the meeting of the Reformed Presbytery, October 8, 1807, it was agreed upon to establish a Theological Seminary, and the Rev. Samuel B. Wylie was chosen Professor. The Seminary was organized, May 25, 1810, at Philadelphia. Mr. James Milligan was the first graduate in 1811. The Superintendents were Revs. John Black, Gilbert McMaster and Alexander McLeod. Mr. John Thomson, of Conococheague, was Treasurer.* Mr. Wylie resigned in 1817, and the students studied under the ministers of the Church. In 1823, the Seminary was resuscitated, Dr. Wylie re-elected Pro-

* For Constitution of Seminary see *R. P. & C.*, 1876, p. 106.

fessor, and the institution continued in Philadelphia. In 1827, it was again suspended by the resignation of Dr. Wylie. The students were again left to study privately under some minister. In 1836, the Seminary was re-organized and located at New Alexandria, Pennsylvania, with Rev. Dr. J. R. Willson as Professor. In 1838, this action was rescinded. Two Seminaries were now established—the Eastern at Coldenham, New York, with Rev. Dr. J. R. Willson, Professor; and the Western at Allegheny, Pennsylvania, with Rev. Thomas Sproull, Professor. In 1840, the Seminaries were united, and located in Allegheny, under the joint professorships of Drs. Willson and Sproull. In 1845, the Seminary was removed to Cincinnati, Ohio, and Dr. Sproull resigning, it continued under the sole charge of Dr. Willson. In 1849, it was again removed to Northwood, Ohio, where, in 1851, it was suspended, and Dr. Willson was retired as Emeritus Professor. The students prosecuted their studies under the Professors of Geneva Hall, and also under the care of their respective Presbyteries. In 1856, the Seminary was re-organized at Allegheny, Pennsylvania, where it has since remained. Revs. Drs. James Christie and Thomas Sproull were chosen Professors. Dr. Christie resigned in 1858, and Revs. John Newell and Joseph Hunter heard classes the following year. In 1859, Rev. James M. Willson was chosen Professor, and died in 1866. Rev. David Scott heard classes the following session. In 1867, Rev. S. O. Wylie was elected Professor, taught that year, but declined the appointment. In 1868, Rev. J. R. W. Sloane was chosen to the

GENEVA COLLEGE.

vacancy, and continued at his post until removed by death in 1886. In 1875, Rev. D. B. Willson was elected as Professor of Biblical Literature, and continues to fill that position. At that time Dr. Sproull was retired as Emeritus Professor, and continues to hear a class in Pastoral Theology. In 1873, the present Memorial Building was purchased. In 1884, Rev. Dr. A. M. Milligan heard some classes during the illness of Dr. Sloane. In 1886, Rev. James Kennedy was elected Professor, but declined. Rev. R. J. George acted as temporary Professor one session. In 1887, Rev. R. J. George was twice chosen to the professorate, but declined. The Rev. J. K. McClurkin was then chosen, and is in charge. The students are: *Fourth Year*—S. G. Conner, G. R. McBurney, A. W. McClurkin, T. A. McElwain, E. M. Milligan, R. C. Reed, W. L. C. Samson, J. S. Thompson. *Third Year*—R. J. Dodds, R. J. Gault, J. K. Reed, T. H. Walker. *Second Year*—J. M. Coleman, Solomon Kingston.

GENEVA COLLEGE.

Soon after his settlement in Northwood, Logan County, Ohio, in 1834, the Rev. J. B. Johnston began to teach a class of young men in his study. The diligence which they manifested, and the number attending his class, far exceeded his expectations, and he conceived the idea of founding a Grammar School. The matter was laid before the Presbytery several times, but not before the people until October, 1847. The project was very favorably received, and Geneva Hall was founded at Northwood, Ohio, April, 1848, when the Rev. J. B. Johnston was placed in charge. He erected, at his own risk, a substantial two-storied brick structure, containing five rooms. Attractive circulars were issued, and everything done to induce students to repair to the first Covenanter College established in America. In 1849, the Rev. J. C. K. Milligan was Professor of Mathematics and Languages, and the Rev. J. S. T. Milligan was Principal of the Preparatory department. The first Board of Inspection were: Revs. Armour McFarland, Robert Hutcheson, James Neill, J. C. Boyd, Josiah Dodds, J. B. Johnston, and elders, Henry George, M. T. Glasgow, John McDaniel, Samuel Jameson, Cornelius Jameson, William Pollock and J. S. Johnston. In 1849, the Rev. James M. Willson was chosen Principal, and Mr. Robert Trumbull a Professor. Mr. Willson declined. In 1850, the institution was wholly controlled by a Fiscal Board, and the Rev. W. F. George was chosen President of the College. Mr. David Paul, in addition to the other Professors, taught the Languages. In 1851, Rev. J. B. Johnston also founded Geneva Female Institute at Northwood, Ohio. Both these schools were well patronized by the Church. A large brick building was erected for the Ladies' Seminary. In March, 1852, the Rev. J. R. W. Sloane was inaugurated President of the College. In 1853, the College building was enlarged. A plan of endowment was devised in 1854, and a new charter was granted the institution the following year. By the resignation of Dr. Sloane in 1856, the Rev. J. C. K. Milligan was the Principal for two years. Messrs. J. C. Smith, H. H. George, S. B. Taggart and D. H.

Coulter taught in the College, and Misses Annie J. Hammond and Isabella Willson had charge of the Seminary. In 1858, the College became disorganized, and was conducted as an Academy for several years without a charter. Messrs. J. C. Smith, D. H. Coulter, Robert Shields and C. D. Trumbull were teachers. The school was suspended during the war. At the earnest solicitation of a few friends of the old institution, the Rev. N. R. Johnston revived the school in 1865, and the Rev. J. L. McCartney was instrumental in opening the new institution for the education of the colored race. Money was raised, and efficient Boards and Professors were chosen, and a large number of students were gathered. In 1867, Mr. S. J. Crowe was elected Principal, and associated with him in teaching were Revs. William Milroy, J. L. McCartney, P. H. Wylie, and Messrs. Wait Wright, T. C. Sproull, S. R. Galbraith, and others. In 1870, the Rev. William Milroy was chosen President, and Messrs. T. J. Allen and E. C. Simpson taught for a short time. In 1871, Rev. N. R. Johnston again took the charge for one year. In 1872, the Rev. H. H. George was chosen President, and has since continued in office. The institution received a new charter, and has since been known as Geneva College. The Professors were Rev. William Milroy, Rev. J. L. McCartney, J. R. Wylie, V. T. Herold and Miss Lotta Stewart. In 1873, J. S. Gamble and Miss Ida D. Gray were teachers. In 1874, the building was remodeled, and several boarding houses were erected. Rev. Joseph McCracken and Mr. J. K. McClurkin were chosen Professors. In 1875, Prof. McClurkin resigned, and Prof. McCartney

47

went abroad. In 1876, Mr. J. R. Latimer became a teacher, and W. M. Milroy filled the vacancy caused by the death of his father, the Rev. William Milroy. In 1877, the Rev. John Lynd was added to the corps, and Rev. David McAllister gave a course of lectures on Political Science. Tutors filled the vacancies in several departments. In 1878, Prof. McCracken resigned, and Mr. J. M. Wylie taught for one year. The *College Cabinet* was founded as an exponent of the College, and has since continued to be published. By an act of Synod, the College was removed from Northwood, Ohio, to Beaver Falls, Pennsylvania, in 1880, where a new building was erected at a cost of about $40,000, the plot of ten acres of ground being donated by the Economite Society. The first Professors in Beaver Falls were Revs. Profs. George, McCartney, McAllister, Thompson, Ritchie and Stewart. Dr. Sloane gave a course of lectures in Political Science. In 1881, Rev. W. P. Johnston was added to the corps of Professors, and Rev. George Kennedy, in 1882. Miss Mary E. Milligan was Principal of the Ladies' department, and Miss Eva McClurkin taught Music. In 1885, Miss Mary R. Bunn succeeded Miss Milligan. In 1887, Prof. S. B. Wylie succeeded Prof. McCartney, and Rev. W. J. Coleman was chosen to fill the vacancy caused by the resignation of Prof. McAllister in Political Science. The institution is well equipped with an able corps of Professors, and a sufficient endowment fund. A large number of the ministers of the Church have been students of and teachers in Geneva College. Her graduates are found in all the learned professions.

ALLEGHANY THEOLOGICAL SEMINARY
MEMORIAL BUILDING.

GENEVA FEMALE SEMINARY
1851.

SECOND BUILDING
OF GENEVA COLLEGE
1853.

FIRST BUILDINGS GENEVA COLLEGE 1848.

CROSS CUT EARLIEST ELECUTS

LATAKIA MISSION BUILDINGS.

KNOX ACADEMY
SELMA, ALABAMA

WESTMINSTER COLLEGE.

This institution was founded by the Pittsburgh Presbytery, in November, 1848, at Wilkinsburgh, Pennsylvania. A Female Seminary was established in connection with it. Rev. Moses Roney was chosen President. In 1850, the location was changed to Allegheny, Pennsylvania, where a suitable building was erected. Messrs. David McKee, John Hamilton, D. S. Faris, and others, were teachers. In 1853, Rev. John Newell succeeded Mr. Roney in the Presidency, and Mr. James R. Newell became a teacher. The College was disorganized in 1858, and the property donated by the Presbytery to the Theological Seminary.

ALLEGHENY CITY COLLEGE.

This institution succeeded Westminster College in 1858, and the Rev. John Newell was President, assisted in teaching by Profs. J. R. Newell, John Davis, F. L. Apel, Miss Aull, and others. In 1860, Prof. J. R. Newell took charge of the school, and, in 1863, changed it into Newell Institute, Pittsburgh, where it continued as a flourishing classical and preparatory school for many years.

KNOX ACADEMY.

This institution was founded at Selma, Alabama, in 1874, under the auspices of the Church, as a Mission School. (See Selma Mission.)

FOREIGN MISSIONS.

HAYTI.

PORT AU PRINCE. At the meeting of Synod in 1818, a Committee was appointed to inquire into the expediency of establishing a Foreign Mission. Nothing was done, however, until 1841, when a memorial from the brethren of the Philadelphia congregation lead to the approval of the plan, and, at the meeting in 1843, a Committee was appointed to select a field for operations. In 1845, the Island of St. Thomas was chosen, but the following year abandoned, and Hayti was selected. In the fall of 1846, the Rev. J. B. Johnston was sent out by the Board to inspect the field, and Port au Prince was designated as the centre of operations. In May, 1847, the Rev. J. W. Morton and A. M. Milligan, licentiate, were chosen Missionaries. Mr. Milligan declined, and Mr. R. J. Dodds, student of theology, was chosen. In the fall of 1847, Mr. Morton, with his family, repaired to the scene of his labors at Port au Prince. After preparing himself, and some books in the French language, he opened a successful school. While laboring here, Mr. Morton changed his views with reference to the Christian Sabbath, denying that the first day of the week was such. He returned to lay his case before Synod, and was suspended in May, 1849. The Mission was then abandoned, and Mr. Dodds was not sent out.

SYRIA.

LATAKIA. At the meeting of Synod in 1856, the cause of Missions was revived, and Syria was chosen as the field of operations. Revs. R. J. Dodds and John Crawford were chosen Missionaries. The latter declined, and Rev. N. R. Johnston was chosen. He declined, also, and Mr. Joseph Beattie, licentiate, was elected. He accepted. Revs. R. J. Dodds and Joseph Beattie, with their families, sailed for this foreign land in October, 1856. After spending some time in Damascus learning the Arabic language, they settled in Zahleh, a large town at the foot of Mt. Lebanon, in October, 1857. Mr. Dodds took charge of this field, Mr. Beattie continuing his studies at Damascus. In May, '1858, Mr. Dodds was compelled to abandon Zahleh on account of the threats of the Catholic priests, and, joined by Mr. Beattie, spent the following year in Bhamdun and Beirut. After several explorations, Latakia, a city on the Mediterranean, was selected in October, 1859, and where the Mission was permanently established. Three native teachers were employed, and the school opened with a bright outlook. The first convert was Hammud, a Fallahin, baptized by Mr. Dodds in December, 1861. In May, 1863, Mr. David B. Willson, physician, was chosen as a medical Missionary, but declined. Mr. Beattie and family visited America that year, and returned in 1864, with Dr. David Metheny, who had been chosen as a medical Missionary. Four mountain schools were now established, with native teachers. Mr. Dodds and family visited America in 1865, and returned the following year with Miss Rebecca Crawford, who

was placed in charge of the newly established Girls'
School. The new and present Mission buildings at
Latakia were erected in 1868, under the supervision
of Dr. Metheny. In May, 1867, Dr. Dodds took charge
of the new school at Aleppo, where he died in 1870.
In 1871, Revs. R. J. George and S. R. Galbraith were
chosen Missionaries. Mr. George declined, and Mr.
Galbraith, his wife, and Miss Mary E. Dodds, sailed
for Syria in the fall of this year. Mr. Galbraith died
in June, 1872, and his widow returned to America.
In 1872, Mr. Henry Easson was chosen and ordained
for this field. He arrived, with his family, in January,
1873. Dr. Metheny visited America in 1873, and was
ordained a minister, returning the same fall. The Mission was not without its troubles, as some of the converts were cruelly treated and imprisoned by the Turkish
Government. In 1875, Miss Mattie R. Wylie went as
a lady teacher, and the following year Dr. Beattie visited
this country. The building was now enlarged, and Mrs.
Metheny erected a beautiful memorial chapel. She died
in December, 1876. In June, 1878, Mrs. Beattie died
in Philadelphia, and Dr. Beattie now resigned his connection with the Mission and remained in America.
Two vacancies were created by the marriages of Misses
Mary E. Dodds and Rebecca Crawford, and Dr. Metheny
visited America for his health. He returned in October,
1879, with Rev. W. J. Sproull, his wife, and Miss
Mary Carson. By the sudden illness of Miss Carson,
Miss Wylie returned to America with her in August,
1880. Dr. Beattie returned in December, 1880, and
opened a theological school. Miss Wylie also returned

in May, 1881. In May, 1881, Dr. A. J. Dodds, his wife, and Miss Evadna Sterrett, were chosen Missionaries, and soon repaired to Latakia. Rev. Easson visited America in 1882, and returned the following year. Dr. Beattie died in October, 1883, and Dr. Metheny established the school at Tarsus. Mrs. A. J. Dodds died in April, 1885, necessitating the return to America of Dr. A. J. Dodds with his child. On his return to Syria, Dr. Dodds was drowned by the wreck of the "Sidon," off the coast of Spain, October 26, 1885. Rev. W. J. Sproull resigned in May, 1886, and returned with his family to America. In November, 1886, Miss Maggie B. Edgar arrived at Latakia as a lady teacher. In September, 1887, Dr. J. M. Balph and wife, and, in 1888, Rev. James S. Stewart and wife, accepted appointments to this field. At Latakia there are 177 communicants, 659 scholars, 21 schools, and 41 native teachers and employees.*

ALEPPO. This Mission was abandoned by the United Presbyterian Church of Scotland in May, 1867, at which time Dr. R. J. Dodds took charge of it. It consisted of two teachers and one hundred pupils. Dr. Dodds died here in December, 1870, and the field was abandoned.

SUADEA. The property of this Mission was donated by Mrs. William Holt Yates, in April, 1875, and called the "Dr. and Mrs. William Holt Yates Mission." A commodious new building was erected in 1876, by Mrs. Yates, and while under the supervision of Rev. Henry Easson, it has been taught by Jacoub Jerridinia and some native teachers.

---

* Report of Latakia Mission, 1888.

TARSUS. Dr. Metheny opened this Mission in Cilicia in December, 1882, and is now in charge of it. In February, 1883, Miss Evadna Sterrett, and in May, 1887, Miss Lillian B. Joseph accepted appointments, and are teaching in connection with this Mission.

CYPRUS. A Mission at Larnica, in the Island of Cyprus, has recently been established under the auspices of the Latakia Mission, and is in charge of two native teachers. There are now (1888) about thirty Syrians, Jews, and Cypriates, in attendance.

SKETCHES OF MISSIONARIES.*

JAMES McKINNISS BALPH, M. D.:

Son of Joseph and Sarah J. (McKinniss) Balph, was born near Butler, Pennsylvania, January 12, 1851. He received his early education in the Normal School of Edinboro, and continued his studies in Witherspoon Institute, Butler, Pennsylvania. He studied medicine under Dr. W. M. Clark, of Whitestown, and settled as a physician in Unionville, Pennsylvania. After practicing for three years, he resumed his studies in, and graduated from, the Cincinnati Medical College in 1877, and settled in Rose Point, Lawrence County, Pennsylvania, where he practiced medicine and discharged the duties of ruling elder in the Slippery Rock congregation. He married Miss Elzina J. Dodds, of Bakerstown, Pennsylvania, February 18, 1875. In the

* For Sketches of Revs. Joseph Beattie, R. J. Dodds, Henry Easson, S. R. Galbraith, Jacoub Jerridinia, David Metheny, William Sproull and J. S. Stewart see "The Ministry."

spring of 1887, he was chosen a medical Missionary to Syria, and sailed for that foreign field, September 7, 1887, where he is engaged in proper missionary work.

ELZINA J. (DODDS) BALPH:

Daughter of John A. and Margaret (Fife) Dodds, was born near Brownsdale, Butler County, Pennsylvania, May 7, 1854. She received her early education in the schools of that vicinity, and engaged in domestic duties until her marriage to Dr. J. M. Balph, February 18, 1875. She accompanied her husband to Syria.

MARTHA E. (LORD) BEATTIE:

Daughter of James and Martha (Lockwood) Lord, was born in Camden, Delaware, April 17, 1834. She received her education in a Select School taught by Friends, and resided in Camden until her marriage to Dr. Joseph Beattie, September 16, 1856. She sailed with her husband for the Syrian field, October 16, 1856, where she remained engaged in the proper work of domestic and missionary life, until impaired health caused her to come to America in 1876. She remained in this country to educate her children, her husband returning to Syria. She died of pneumonia, in Philadelphia, Pennsylvania, June 1, 1878. High testimonials are given of her Christian graces and consecration to the Master's service.

ARCHIBALD JOHNSTON DODDS, M. D.:

Son of Rev. Dr. R. J. and Letitia M. (Dodds) Dodds, was born in Damascus, Syria, May 26, 1857. He came to America in 1871, after his father's death, and settled in Lucesco, Westmoreland County, Pennsylvania. In 1872, he repaired to Allegheny, Pennsylvania, where he lived with Rev. Dr. J. R. W. Sloane, under whom he studied, and attended the public schools for three years. In 1875, he made his home with Dr. S. A. Sterrett, of Pittsburgh, and attended the Western University of Pennsylvania, where he graduated with first honor in 1879. He studied medicine in the Jefferson Medical College, Philadelphia, and graduated in 1881, taking the Chapman gold medal, the first prize in physiology. In May, 1881, he offered himself, and was appointed, medical Missionary to Syria. The same fall he sailed for that foreign field, where for four years he did valuable service as a physician, treasurer, and financial agent of the Mission. He married Miss E. Mizpah Metheny, of Kessab, Syria, September 26, 1882. By the death of his wife in the spring of 1885, he came to America to place his little son under the care of his mother, and returned to his work in Syria. While sailing on the steamship "Sidon," the vessel was wrecked off the coast of Spain, and he perished beneath the waters of the Atlantic, October 27, 1885. He was a proficient scholar, well-read in general literature, and thoroughly conversant with the different departments of the medical profession. He was devoted to the Mission, conscientious in the discharge of every duty, and remarkably successful in his labor for the Master.

E. MIZPAH (METHENY) DODDS:

Daughter of Rev. Dr. David and Emeline (Gregg) Metheny, was born in Allegheny, Pennsylvania, March 19, 1864. The same fall her parents went as Missionaries to Syria, and she spent the most of her life in Latakia. She married Dr. A. J. Dodds, September 26, 1882. Being in impaired health she contemplated a trip to America, but departed this life, in Latakia, Syria, April 14, 1885. She was a kind and devoted wife, and closely attached to the work in which her whole life was spent.

LETITIA M. (DODDS) DODDS:

Daughter of Robert and Letitia (Rowan) Dodds, was born near Valencia, Butler County, Pennsylvania, November 28, 1833. She received her early training in the schools of that vicinity, and was reared in the Union congregation. She married Rev. Dr. R. J. Dodds, August 12, 1856, and the same fall accompanied him to the Syrian Mission, where she was actively engaged in her proper duties at Latakia and Aleppo for fifteen years. After the death of her husband, she returned with her family to America, in 1871, and settled near Lucesco, Pennsylvania, removing to Beaver Falls, Pennsylvania, in the winter of 1887.

WILLIA A. S. DODDS:

Daughter of John A. and Margaret (Fife) Dodds, was born near Brownsdale, Butler County, Pennsylvania, March 3, 1859. She received her early education in the schools of her native County, and also in New Galilee, Beaver County, whither her parents removed, and she attended Geneva College some time. She went to Syria in April, 1887, and taught in the school at Mersine, in connection with the Tarsus Mission. She was appointed missionary teacher to Latakia, Syria, November 29, 1887.

MARY J. (BEEBE) EASSON:

Daughter of George and Laura (Williamson) Beebe, was born in Glenville, Schenectady County, New York,

March 19, 1848. She received her early education in her native village, and in the schools of Schenectady, New York. She was married to Rev. Henry Easson, January 20, 1870, and went to Syria, November 22, 1872, where she has since been engaged in connection with the Mission at Latakia and Suadea.

MARGARET B. EDGAR:

Daughter of William and Sarah (Moore) Edgar,. was born in Belfast, Ireland, June 25, 1861. In 1869,. she came with her parents to America and settled in Cincinnati, Ohio, where she attended the public schools. In 1881, the family removed to Cedarville, Green County, Ohio, and, in 1883, to Bellefontaine, Ohio,. where she resided until her departure for Syria, November 4, 1886. She is engaged in teaching in the Latakia Mission.

ANNA (MARTIN) GALBRAITH:

Daughter of Alexander and Mary J. (Coleman) Martin, was born in Lisbon, St. Lawrence County, New York, * * * She received her early education in the neighboring town of Ogdensburgh, and resided in Lisbon until her marriage to the Rev. S. R. Galbraith, September 19, 1871. She sailed for the Latakia Mission, in company with her husband, November 4, 1871.. After the death of her husband in June, 1872, she returned to this country, and has since resided in, Rochester, New York.

HELANA (CORANI) JERRIDINIA:

Daughter of Habib and Noor (Sheya) Corani, was born in Showifat, Lebanon, Syria, April 15. 1859. She attended the American Mission School at Beirut, and graduated from Showifat and Cripoli. She taught for some time in Cripoli and Showifat, and until her marriage to Jacoub Jerridinia, September 15, 1885, when she engaged with him in missionary work in Suadea and Latakia.

LILLIAN B. JOSEPH:

Daughter of Patterson O. and Helen A. (Dunbar) Joseph, was born in Hopkinton, Delaware County, Iowa, October 13, 1860. She received her early education in the public schools, and graduated from Lenox College in 1885. Accepting an appointment to labor in the Syrian Mission, she sailed from New York, April 27, 1887, and is engaged in teaching at Mersine, in connection with the Tarsus Mission.

REBECCA (CRAWFORD) MARTIN:

Daughter of William and Mary (Sterrett) Crawford, was born in Philadelphia, Pennsylvania, * * * She received her education in the public schools, where she graduated and taught, and was a member of the First congregation of Philadelphia. She accepted an appointment to the Syrian Mission, sailed for that foreign land, October, 1866, was connected with the Latakia Mission until her marriage to the Rev. Dr. James Martin, January 31, 1879, and, with her husband, is connected with the Mission at Antioch, Syria.

EMELINE (GREGG) METHENY:

Daughter of David and Mary (Rafferty) Gregg, was born in Allegheny, Pennsylvania, July 16, 1841. She received her education in the public schools of her native city, and was married to Dr. David Metheny, April 29, 1862. She accompanied her husband to the Syrian Mission, November 2, 1864. A weakness of the lungs became serious in the spring of 1876, and consumption continued its work until her death, at Latakia, Syria, December 17, 1876. She was always in delicate health, but her life was a living epistle. She was kind and attentive to all, and so much interested in the work of bringing the heathen to a saving knowledge of Christ, that she gave liberally to the maintenance of the Mission. She is buried beside the chapel and school rooms in Latakia, which were built at her expense.

MARY E. (DODDS) METHENY:

Daughter of Rev. Dr. R. J. and Amanda (Cannon) Dodds, was born near New Alexandria, Westmoreland County, Pennsylvania, December 27, 1849. Upon the death of her mother in 1853, she went to live with her grandmother Cannon, where she remained two years. In 1855, she went to live with her grandfather Dodds, near Freeport, Pennsylvania, where she attended the public schools, also the New Castle Academy, graduating from the Dayton Union Academy in 1871. Being appointed to assist in the Ladies' department of the Syrian Mission, she sailed for that foreign field, November 4, 1871, and taught in the Latakia Mission for six years. She was married to Rev. Dr. David Metheny, December 10, 1877, and is connected with the Tarsus Mission.

ELLA (CAMPBELL) SPROULL:

Daughter of Robert and Mary (Crawford) Campbell, was born near Bakerstown, Allegheny County, Pennsylvania, April 5, 1861. She received her education in that vicinity, and was married to Rev. William Sproull,

October 23, 1879. The following month she sailed with her husband for the Syrian Mission, where she resided for over six years. She returned to America with her husband in the spring of 1886, and resides in Mars, Pennsylvania.

EVADNA M. STERRETT:

Daughter of Dr. William and Sarah A. (Fife) Sterrett, was born in Tallycavey, Allegheny County, Pennsylvania, January 28, 1856. Her parents died when she was quite young, and she lived with her grandmother Fife, attending the common schools. She entered Curry Institute, Pittsburgh, where she graduated in 1878. In the spring of 1881, she was appointed to the Syrian Mission, and sailed for that field, August 20, 1881. She was a teacher in the Latakia School for over a year. In February, 1883, she was transferred to the Tarsus Mission, and, in 1884, opened a school in Mersine, where she has charge of a boarding school.

MARTHA R. WYLIE:

Daughter of Rev. Preston H. and Mary A. (George) Wylie, was born near White Cottage, Muskingum County, Ohio, December 14, 1846. In 1850, her parents removed to Northwood, Ohio; in 1855, to Winfield, Indiana, and, in 1860, to Rushsylvania, Ohio, where she received her early education, graduating from Geneva College in 1875. Accepting an appointment to the Syrian Mission, she sailed for that field in December, 1875, and, with the exception of a visit to America in 1880, has been actively engaged in the proper work of the Mission at Latakia, Syria.

DOMESTIC MISSIONS.

PORT ROYAL. In March, 1862, the Rev. N. R. Johnston, under appointment of the Domestic Board of Missions, repaired to Beaufort, South Carolina, but was prevented from establishing a Mission among the contrabands there by the soldiers. He then went to Port Royal, founded a Mission, and remained until fall. In October, 1862, Rev. Joshua Kennedy entered the Mission, but it was soon abandoned on account of the disturbed state of the country.

FERNANDINA. Revs. Joshua Kennedy and Robert Shields opened a Mission in Fernandina, Florida, in November, 1862. Mr. Shields was compelled to come North in February, 1863, but returned with Rev. T. M. Elder soon afterwards. On account of sickness, Revs. Shields and Elder came North in July, 1863, and Mr. Kennedy abandoned the Mission in April, 1864, when the authorities closed the Mission and Church on account of the ravages of small pox.

ST. AUGUSTINE. Rev. Joshua Kennedy visited St. Augustine, Florida, in December, 1862, and founded a Mission where he taught and preached for some time. It was abandoned in 1863.

LITTLE ROCK. Under appointment of the Board, the Rev. James Wallace visited the city of Little Rock, Arkansas, in November, 1863, for the purpose of founding a Mission. He was followed by the Rev. Robert Shields, who opened a Mission in the Penitentiary, which he taught for some months. The contrabands being removed to the farms, the Mission was abandoned in April, 1864.

Duvall's Bluff. Rev. Robert Shields came to this part of Arkansas, in April, 1864, erected a log school house, and conducted a mission among the colored population and the troops for a short time, when he returned North.

Natchez. By appointment of the Domestic Mission Board, the Rev. James Wallace established a Mission among the colored people of Natchez, Mississippi, in January, 1864. The City Hall was secured for school purposes, and a church for preaching services. Mr. J. C. K. Faris, and Misses Mary Sterrett and Lizzie Morrison were then appointed teachers. Soon afterwards, Mr. R. A. McGee and Misses Rebecca B. and Sarah J. Speer were added to the corps. Miss Jennie Holliday arrived in May, 1864. The teachers were then distributed over the city, and adjacent plantations on both sides of the Mississippi. A large number of pupils were gathered into these schools. In September, 1864, J. C. K. Faris became Superintendent, and the same fall, Messrs. Daniel C. and Isaiah Faris, and Misses Elizabeth Mc-Knight and M. J. Jamison became teachers. The male teachers all resigned, and, in September, 1865, Rev. J. M. Johnston was chosen Superintendent. A new building was now erected at a cost of $800. In October, 1866, the Mission was discontinued, and the property returned to those who had donated the most money for its construction.

Washington. In September, 1863, the Rev. James Wallace was directed by the Board of Domestic Missions to visit the city of Washington, D. C., as a prospective field for mission work. Revs. A. M. and

J. S. T. Milligan also thoroughly inspected the whole
field in February, 1864, and recommended the establishment of a Mission among the contrabands of this city.
A suitable lot was obtained one mile south of the
Capitol, and the Rev. J. S. T. Milligan superintended
the erection of buildings for school and tenement
purposes. The Mission was opened in April, 1864,
with Rev. J. O. Bayles in charge, and during this
year Mr. D. O. Brown, Mrs. James Gray and Miss
McKitrick were teachers. A large number of pupils
gathered into the school, and it promised to be a
successful project. In September, 1864, Rev. T. M.
Elder was appointed Superintendent, and the teachers
were Rev. J. O. Bayles, Misses M. B. Floyd and C.
S. Clough. The attendance was about four hundred.
Most of the teachers resigned in May, 1865. During
the summer a large and substantial building was
erected. Rev. J. M. Armour was chosen Principal,
and the teachers selected were Misses M. J. Divoll, S.
E. Morse and Helen M. Johnston. In October, 1866,
the Rev. J. M. Johnston was ' chosen Principal, and
the teachers were Rev. J. M. Armour, Misses S. E.
Morse, Helen M. Johnston, M. J. Jamison, Jennie E.
Smith, S. C. Clough, Eunice A. Jameson and Kate
Trumbull. The school was graded and divided into
departments as the city schools. At the communion
in October, 1867, four colored persons connected with
the Church. This service was held under the direction
of the Baltimore session, as no congregation was
organized in Washington. In 1869, John F. Quarles,
a colored man educated at Geneva College, became a

teacher. The Mission was disorganized May, 1870, on account of the failure of the Church to support it, and the property was sold to the best advantage.

SELMA. By the direction of the Board, Mr. Lewis Johnston, a colored licentiate, selected the city of Selma, Alabama, as the site of the new Southern Mission, in March, 1874, after an inspecting tour through the South. Mr. Johnston was chosen Principal, and Mr. George M. Elliott, Assistant. They opened the school in May, 1874, with fourteen scholars. In September, 1874, Mr. D. W. Boxley was made a teacher. In December, 1874, the present property was purchased. In May, 1875, a congregation was organized, with Rev. Lewis Johnston, pastor, and Lewis Johnston, Sr., and George M. Elliott, elders. D. W. Boxley was soon added to the session. In October, 1875, Mr. Welby Williams was chosen a teacher. In September, 1876, Misses Della Boyd and Anna E. Echols were chosen teachers. Mr. Johnston's connection with the Mission ceased in November, 1876. In October, 1877, Mr. G. M. Elliott became Principal, and John Willdee a teacher. A frame church building was erected in August, 1878. In 1879, P. A. W. Williams and wife became teachers. In 1880, the present commodious school building was erected by Mr. Robert Glasgow, of Pittsburgh, and the institution became known as Knox Academy. Mr. J. H. Pickens, and Misses Georgia Mallory and Maria Kingston now became teachers. Mrs. Elliott died in September, 1881, and Miss L. J. Cardoza taught that year. In 1882, Misses Ruth Hutcheson, Sadie R. and E. J. Guy

were added to the staff of teachers, and Rev. and Mrs.
J. M. Faris taught during the winter. In 1883, J. H.
Echols became a teacher, and during the winter, Mr.
J. M. Sloane and wife taught. Miss Anna E. Grinage
was added in 1884. Mr. Elliott resigned the Superin-
tendency in May, 1885, the congregation demanding
his whole time, and J. H. Echols filled the vacancy.
In October, 1886, Rev. H. W. Reed was chosen Principal, who was succeeded by Rev. J. W. Dill in
January, 1888. There are now ten teachers, and five
hundred pupils. At Pleasant Grove, six miles distant
from Selma, the Mission owns twenty-five acres of
ground, and is conducting a successful school under
Mr. S. H. Pickens.

CAMDEN. By the recommendation of Mr. Morrill, a
resident of Camden, Alabama, this city was selected as
a field for a Mission, November, 1876, and Mr. William
McKinney, licentiate, was appointed Missionary. He
repaired to this field, with his wife, in January, 1877,
and the first year gathered a school of about eighty
scholars. Mrs. McKinney died in October, 1877, and
Miss Mary E. Carson taught for some time. The Mission
being refused a share in the school fund by the newly
elected Democratic authorities in Camden, the school
was abandoned in April, 1878.

NEW YORK CITY. This Mission was first organized
by the New York Presbytery in October, 1867, and Rev.
R. Z. Willson was placed in charge. It was located in
East Fifty-Fourth street, near Third Avenue, and by
door to door visitation the Missionary gathered a large
school. In May, 1870, it was transferred from the Pres-

bytery to an Association called the "New York City Mission." Mr. Willson died in June, 1872, and the enterprise was abandoned. It was re-organized by the New York Presbytery in October, 1886, and since May, 1887, Mr. J. M. McElhinney, licentiate, has been in charge, and has done a good work. No permanent school has been established, but the work is done in connection with the several congregations of the city.

CHINESE. In August, 1875, the Rev. N. R. Johnston and family removed to Oakland, California, and opened a school among the Chinese. In May, 1877, it was recognized as a Mission of the Church. During the past decade twenty-nine Chinamen have been converted and baptized, and the school consists of over one hundred and fifty pupils. Besides Mr. Johnston, his daughter, Miss Monroe, Cheung Sing, and Ju Guy, have been teachers. In the congregations of Cincinnati, Pittsburgh, Allegheny, and New York, there are schools for the Chinese.

INDIAN. By direction of the Central Board, Mr. John R. Lee, of Wahoo, Nebraska, explored the Indian Territory as a field for the establishment of the new Indian Mission, in the fall of 1887, and selected Anadarko, near Fort Sill, among the Kiowa nation. Rev. J. Milligan Wylie, General Secretary of Home Missions, has the work under consideration. The Central Board of Missions assists many of the weak and rising congregations of the British Provinces and throughout the West, but all the permanent Missions have been noticed.

SYNODS AND PRESBYTERIES.

From the earliest settlement of Covenanters in America, those families residing in the same community organized themselves into a society or correspondence. All these societies or correspondences met by representation, annually or semi-annually, for the transaction of business or religious worship, as a Synod or Presbytery, and this was called "The General Meeting." Until the accession of a minister, these meetings were presided over by some prominent elder chosen by the people. From 1743 until 1749, they were presided over by the Rev. Alexander Craighead; and from 1751 until 1774, by the Rev. John Cuthbertson, and were usually held at Little Octorara, Lancaster County, Pennsylvania. The Reformed Presbytery was first organized in America by Revs. John Cuthbertson, Matthew Linn and Alexander Dobbin, with ruling elders, at Paxtang, Dauphin County, Pennsylvania, March 10, 1774.

MEETINGS OF THE REFORMED PRESBYTERY.

Date.	Place.	Moderator.	No. Min.	No. Elds.
March 10, 1774	Paxtang, Pa................	John Cuthbertson......	3	4
May 23, 1774.........	Rock Creek, Pa...........		2	3
November 23, 1774.	Pequea, Pa.............. ...		3	3
November 26, 1774.	Philadelphia, Pa...........	Matthew Linn...........	3	4
May 1, 1775..........	Octorara, Pa...........		3	5
May 22, 1775.........	Junkin Tent, Pa..........		3	6
May 20, 1776.........	Paxtang, Pa................		2	4
August 26, 1776......	Rock Creek, Pa...........	Alex. Dobbin...........	3	2
February 24, 1777..	Octorara, Pa................	John Cuthbertson......	3	5
August 18, 1777......	Lower Chanceford, Pa....			
September 30, 1777.	Donegal, Pa..........		2	4
March 31, 1778......	Pequea, Pa.................			
October 29, 1778....	Octorara, Pa................	John Cuthbertson......	3	4
June 9, 1779..........	Pequea, Pa.................		3	3
August 12, 1780......	Junkin Tent, Pa...........	John Cuthbertson......	4	7
March 21, 1781......	Pequea, Pa............		3	4
August 15, 1781......	Octorara, Pa................	Matthew Linn...........	4	6
November 28, 1781.	Paxtang, Pa.......		4	3
December 1, 1781...	Donegal, Pa..............		4	2
June 13, 1782.........	Pequea, Pa................	John Cuthbertson.....	4	6

The court was disorganized by the ministers going into the union which formed the Associate Reformed Church, November 1, 1782.

The Reformed Presbytery was re-organized by the Revs. William Gibson and James McKinney, with elders, at Philadelphia, Pennsylvania, May 18, 1798, and continued until the organization of the Synod, May 24, 1809.

MEETINGS OF THE REFORMED PRESBYTERY.

Date.	Place.	Moderator.	No. Min.	No. Elds.
May 18, 1798.........	Philadelphia, Pa...........	James McKinney.......	2	2
August 10, 1798......	New York, N. Y...........	William Gibson........	2	4
February 19, 1799..	New York, N. Y...........	James McKinney.......	2	
March 26, 1799.....	Philadelphia, Pa...........	William Gibson........	2	
June 21, 1799........	Coldenham, N. Y...........	James McKinney.......	2	6
June 24, 1800.......	Ryegate, Vt.................	William Gibson........	2	
June 27, 1800........	Duanesburgh, N.Y........	S. B. Wylie............	3	5
November 7, 1800..	Little Britain, N. Y......	S. B. Wylie............	2	2
December 4, 1800..	Elizabeth, Pa...............	James McKinney.......	2	1
December 18, 1800.	Pittsburgh, Pa.............	S. B. Wylie............	2	1
January 28, 1801....	Rocky Creek,. S. C........	S. B. Wylie............	2	2
April 7, 18c1.........	Greensburgh, Pa...........	S. B. Wylie............	3	1
July 3, 1801..........	Coldenham, N. Y...........	John Black.............	3	3
June 16, 1802........	New York, N. Y...........	William Gibson........	5	5
October 4, 1803.....	Conococheague, Pa........	Alexander McLeod....	4	5
September 18, 1804.	Conococheague, Pa........	Thomas Donnelly......	5	6
May 6, 1806.........	New York, N. Y...........	William Gibson........	5	4
October 6, 1807....	Conococheague, Pa........	Matthew Williams.....	6	5
May 16, 1809........	Philadelphia, Pa...........	Gilbert McMaster......	8	5

The Synod of the Reformed Presbyterian Church in America was constituted in the city of Philadelphia, Pennsylvania, May 24, 1809, by the oldest minister present, the Rev. William Gibson. The General Synod, composed of representatives from the several Presbyteries, was constituted in the city of New York, New York, August 2, 1825. The Presbyteries were divided into two Sub-Synods, August 12, 1831. Those East of the Allegheny Mountains composed the Eastern Subordinate Synod; and those West of the Allegheny Mountains, the Western Subordinate Synod, and the General Synod met bi-ennially. This division was abolished, June 26, 1840, and the Synod, composed of all the ministers in the Church, and a lay delegate from each session, was restored October 6, 1841, which is the Supreme Jndicatory of the Church, and has met annually since 1861.

SYNODS OF THE REFORMED PRESBYTERIAN CHURCH.

Session	Date.	Place.	Moderator.	No.Min.	No.Elds
1	May 24, 1809.........	Philadelphia, Pa.........	William Gibson..........	8	5
2	May 15, 1811........	New York, N. Y.........	Gilbert McMaster.......	7	5
3	August 11, 1812.....	Pittsburgh, Pa.	John Kell.................	10	10
4	May 4, 1814..........	Philadelphia, Pa.........	Alexander McLeod.....	11	7
5	May 16, 1816........	Philadelphia, Pa.........	William Gibson..........	9	4
6	September 3, 1817.	Coldenham, N. Y.......	Robert Lusk.............	7	6
7	May 26, 1818........	Pittsburgh, Pa...........	Thomas Donnelly......	13	6
8	August 10, 1819.....	Conococheague, Pa....	John Cannon............	13	5
9	October 7, 1821.....	Philadelphia, Pa.........	John Gibson..............	12	5
10	August 5, 1823.......	Pittsburgh, Pa...........	J. R. Willson.............	17	9
11	August 2, 1825.......	New York, N. Y.........	James Milligan..........	18	8
12	May 16, 1827........	Philadelphia, Pa.........	Gilbert McMaster.......	16	9
13	August 6, 1828.......	Philadelphia, Pa.........	James Christie..........	16	9
14	August 4, 1830.......	Pittsburgh, Pa...........	Samuel Wylie...........	21	10
15	August 3, 1831.......	Philadelphia, Pa.........	S. W. Crawford..........	19	14
16	August 16, 1833.....	Philadelphia, Pa.........	John Cannon.............	18	18
17	October 8, 1834.....	Pittsburgh, Pa...........	Robert Gibson...........	14	9
18	October 5, 1836.....	Allegheny, Pa............	S. M. Willson..........	17	10
19	October 2, 1838.....	New York, N. Y.........	James Blackwood.......	16	11
20	June 16, 1840........	Allegheny, Pa............	David Scott..............	16	14
21	October 6, 1841.....	Utica, Ohio	C. B. McKee............	23	19
22	August 15, 1843.....	Rochester, N. Y	Moses Roney............	26	19
23	May 19, 1845.........	Allegheny, Pa...........	J. B. Johnston..........	31	27
24	May 25, 1847.........	Allegheny, Pa........	Thomas Sproull	33	21
25	May 22, 1849........	Philadelphia, Pa.........	James Christie........	37	28
26	May 27, 1851.........	Allegheny Pa...........	David Scott.............	46	32
27	May 24, 1853.........	New York, N. Y.........	W. L. Roberts...........	46	34
28	May 22, 1855.........	Allegheny, Pa...........	S. O. Wylie.............	50	39
29	May 27, 1856........ .	Philadelphia, Pa.........	S. M. Willson............	47	38
30	May 27, 1857.........	Northwood, Ohio.......	Samuel Sterrett.........	53	47
31	May 24, 1859........	Allegheny Pa...........	J. M. Willson..........	51	42
32	May 28, 1861.........	New York, N. Y......	John Crozier.............	49	32
33	May 27, 1862.........	Allegheny Pa...........	James Wallace..........	58	40
34	May 28, 1863.........	Linton, Iowa.............	A. M. Milligan..........	51	28
35	May 24, 1864.........	Philadelphia, Pa.........	Samuel Bowden.........	60	34
36	May 24, 1865.........	Utica, Ohio................	John Stott................	64	47
37	May 23, 1866.........	Rochester, N. Y.........	R. J. Dodds............	60	34
38	May 22, 1867.........	Allegheny, Pa...........	J. R. W. Sloane.......	71	51
39	May 27, 1868.........	Northwood, Ohio......	H. P. McClurkin.......	70	60
40	May 26, 1869.........	Newburgh, N. Y.........	Andrew Stevenson.....	64	46
41	May 25, 1870.........	New York, N. Y.........	J. C. K. Milligan........	72	54

Session	Date.	Place.	Moderator.	No. Min.	No. Elds
42	May 24, 1871	Pittsburgh, Pa	H. H. George	79	72
43	May 29, 1872	York, N. Y	William Milroy	67	51
44	May 27, 1873	Northwood, Ohio	Joseph McCracken	74	58
45	May 27, 1874	Philadelphia, Pa	John Galbraith	80	60
46	May 26, 1875	Coulterville, Ill	James Kennedy	80	61
47	May 23, 1876	Allegheny, Pa	Joseph Beattie	84	66
48	May 22, 1877	Allegheny, Pa	J. R. Thompson	82	57
49	May 29, 1878	Linton, Iowa	C. D. Trumbull	71	62
50	May 28, 1879	New York, N. Y	David Metheny	86	55
51	May 26, 1880	Philadelphia, Pa	David McAllister	89	61
52	May 24, 1881	Pittsburgh, Pa	T. P. Stevenson	87	58
53	May 24, 1882	New Concord, Ohio	David Gregg	81	59
54	May 22, 1883	Allegheny, Pa	D. S. Faris	94	68
55	May 28, 1884	Northwood, Ohio	P. H. Wylie	88	61
56	May 27, 1885	Morning Sun, Iowa	David McKee	87	67
57	June 2, 1886	Rochester, N. Y	Samuel Carlisle	90	63
58	June 1, 1887	Newburgh, N. Y	D. B. Willson	91	62

THE PRESBYTERIES.

ILLINOIS PRESBYTERY: Organized September 14, 1840; including all the congregations West of Western Indiana; after June 3, 1863, all West and South to the Mississippi River.

IOWA PRESBYTERY: Organized June 3, 1863; including all the congregations West of the Mississippi River; after August 29, 1871, all in Eastern Iowa, Wisconsin and Minnesota.

KANSAS PRESBYTERY: Organized August 29, 1871; including all congregations in Western Iowa, Kansas, Missouri, Nebraska, Colorado, and West to the Pacific Ocean.

LAKES PRESBYTERY: Organized September 14, 1840; including all congregations West of the Scioto River in Ohio, to the Western Counties of Indiana, and North including the State of Michigan.

MIDDLE COMMITTEE AND PRESBYTERY: The Committee was organized June 22, 1802; including all congregations South of the Southern boundary of New York State and City, to the Northern boundary of North Carolina and Tennessee; changed to the Middle Presbytery May 24, 1809, and disorganized August 16, 1819.

NEW BRUNSWICK AND NOVA SCOTIA PRESBYTERY: Organized by the Irish Synod April 25, 1832; transferred to the American Synod, June 2, 1879; including all congregations in Maine, New Brunswick and Nova Scotia.

NEW YORK PRESBYTERY: Changed from Southern, August 22, 1843; including all congregations East of the Allegheny Mountains and Delaware County, New York, and South to Virginia; after October 11, 1853, all North of the Northern boundary of Pennsylvania and New Jersey; and after September 11, 1883, the Eastern limit was the Eastern boundary of New York State, including Massachusetts.

NORTHERN COMMITTEE AND PRESBYTERY: The Committee was organized June 22, 1802; including all congregations North and East of the Southern boundary of New York State; it was changed to the Northern Presbytery, May 24, 1809; after August 16, 1819, all North of the Southern boundary of New York State and East of New Jersey; after August 12, 1831, it was known as the Green Mountain Presbytery, including all East of the Green Mountains in Vermont; after August 7, 1833, all East of the Hudson River and North of the City of New York; and was disorganized and attached to the Southern Presbytery, May 17, 1839.

OHIO PRESBYTERY: Organized August 11, 1830; including all congregations in Ohio, West of the Muskingum River and the Canal North to Cleveland; after

October 5, 1838, all West of the Eastern Counties of Ohio to the Scioto River North to the Lake ; disorganized and attached to the Pittsburgh Presbytery, October 12, 1841. Re-organized, October 15, 1862, including all the congregations in Ohio, West of the Eastern Counties to the Scioto River and North to Lake Erie.

PHILADELPHIA PRESBYTERY : Organized August 16, 1819 ; including all the congregations East of the Allegheny Mountains and South of the Northern boundaries of Pennsylvania and New Jersey to North Carolina ; after August 12, 1831, all East of the Mountains to New York City and South ; disorganized, August 7, 1833. Re-organized, October 11, 1853, including all congregations in Eastern Pennsylvania, Maryland and Virginia.

PITTSBURGH PRESBYTERY : Organized August 16, 1819 ; including all the congregations West of the Allegheny Mountains to the Western boundary of Ohio ; after August 12, 1831, all West of the Allegheny Mountains to the Muskingum River in Ohio and Canal North to Cleveland ; after October 5, 1838, all West of the Mountains to the Eastern Counties of Ohio ; after October 12, 1841, all West of the Mountains to the Muskingum River and Canal North to Cleveland, in Ohio ; after October 15, 1862, all West of the Mountains to the Eastern Counties of Ohio.

ROCHESTER PRESBYTERY : Changed from Western Presbytery of the Eastern Subordinate Synod, August 22, 1843 ; including all the congregations in New York State, West of Delaware County and North embracing those in Canada West.

SOUTHERN COMMITTEE AND PRESBYTERY : The Committee was organized, June 22, 1802; including all the
congregations South of Virginia and Tennessee to the
Gulf of Mexico, and was changed to the Southern
Presbytery, May, 24, 1809. After May 20, 1816, all
South of the Northern boundary of North Carolina
and Tennessee ; and after August 12, 1831, was the
Southern Presbytery of the Western Subordinate Synod;
disorganized and attached to the Western Presbytery
of that Synod, October 5, 1838. The Southern Pres-
bytery of the Eastern Subordinate Synod was specified
August 12, 1831, sometimes called Albany, including
all the congregations North of the City of New York,
East of the Mohawk River, embracing Albany, to Vermont ; after August 7, 1833, all between the Hudson
River on the East, embracing New York City, West to
Lake Ontario and the Allegheny Mountains, to North
Carolina on the South ; after May 14, 1837, all in
New York State between the Hudson River and Dela-
ware County, and South to North Carolina, and was
changed to New York Presbytery, August 22, 1843.

VERMONT PRESBYTERY : Organized September 11,
1883; including all the congregations in the State of
Vermont.

WESTERN PRESBYTERY : Organized May 20, 1816;
including all the congregations in Ohio, West of the
Muskingum River; after August 16, 1819, all West of
the State of Ohio to the Pacific Ocean. The Western
Presbytery of the Western Subordinate Synod was specified August 12, 1831, including all the congregations
West of Ohio to the Pacific Ocean, and South to the

Cumberland Mountains; after October 5, 1838, all West of the Scioto River in Ohio to the Pacific Ocean, and was disorganized, September 14, 1840. The Western Presbytery of the Eastern Subordinate Synod was specified, August 12, 1831, sometimes called Mohawk, including all the congregations in New York State, West of the Hudson River, and was disorganized August 7, 1833. Reorganized, May 14, 1837; including all the congregations in New York State, West of Delaware County, and changed to Rochester, August 22, 1843.

THE PUBLICATIONS.

The Evangelical Witness, published in Newburgh, New York, under the patronage of the American Evangelical Tract Society; a monthly magazine; edited by Rev. James R. Willson, D. D.; first issued, August, 1822; price, $1.50 per annum. Discontinued, July, 1826.

The American Christian Expositor, published in New York, New York, as the organ of the Reformed Presbyterian Church; designed to promote the influence of sound principles and social order; a monthly magazine; edited by Rev. Alexander McLeod, D. D.; first issued, May, 1831; price, $2.00 per annum. Discontinued, April, 1833.

The Albany Quarterly, published in Albany, New York, under the patronage of the Albany Historical Society; a quarterly magazine; edited by Revs. James R. Willson, D. D., and Samuel M. Willson; first issued, January, 1832; price, $1.50 per annum. Discontinued, December, 1833.

The Reformed Presbyterian, published in Newburgh, New York, and authorized as the organ of the Reformed Presbyterian Church; a monthly magazine; edited by Rev. Moses Roney, A. M.; first issued, March, 1837; price, $1.50 per annum. The year 1848, the Rev. David Scott was editor. The Rev. Moses Roney died July 3, 1854. Rev. Thomas Sproull, D. D., became editor, March, 1855, and it was published in Pittsburgh, Pennsylvania. Consolidated with the *Covenanter*, January, 1863.

The Covenanter, published in Philadelphia, Pennsylvania, as a magazine of the Reformed Presbyterian Church; a monthly magazine; edited by Rev. James M. Willson, D. D.; first issued, August, 1845; price, $1.50 per annum. Consolidated with the *Reformed Presbyterian*, January, 1863.

The Reformed Presbyterian and Covenanter, published in Pittsburgh, Pennsylvania, as the organ of the Reformed Presbyterian Church; a monthly magazine; edited by Revs. Thomas Sproull, D. D., and James M. Willson, D. D.; first issued, January, 1863; price $1.00 per annum. Dr. J. M. Willson died August 31, 1866, and Dr. Sproull was the sole editor until January, 1868, when Rev. J. W. Sproull was the Associate. Dr. Thomas Sproull retired January, 1874, and Rev. D. B. Willson became an editor, with Rev. J. W. Sproull, under whose management it is published.

The Christian Statesman, published in Philadelphia, Pennsylvania, as the organ of the National Reform Association; a weekly paper; edited by Revs. T. P. Stevenson, D. D., and David McAllister, D. D., LL. D.;

first issued, August, 1867; price, $2.00 per annum. Mr. J. W. Pritchard was Business Manager for the year 1883, and Rev. J. H. Leiper since 1887.

Our Banner, published in New York, New York, and devoted to the principles of the Reformed Presbyterian Church; a monthly magazine; edited by Revs. J. C. K. Milligan, J. H. Boggs and David Gregg; first issued, January 15, 1874; price, $1.00 per annum. Rev. J. H. Boggs retired December, 1880, Rev. David Gregg, December, 1886, and Rev. J. C. K. Milligan is editor.

The College Cabinet, published at Northwood, Ohio, as the exponent of Geneva College; a monthly magazine; edited by D. G. Wylie and W. M. Glasgow; first issued, September, 1878; price, $1.00 per annum. The following have been the editors: 1878, D. G. Wylie and W. M. Glasgow; 1879, W. M. Glasgow and J. R. J. Milligan; 1880, (published at Beaver Falls, Pennsylvania,) J. H. Wylie, T. H. Acheson, J. W. McNaugher and D. G. Williamson; 1881, T. H. Acheson, J. W. McNaugher, D. G. Williamson and E. M. Smith; 1882, D. G. Williamson, E. M. Smith, S. D. Johnston and M. A. Parkinson; 1883, a Joint Stock Company organized, with ten editors and assistants, since which time the editorial staff has been annually elected. The name of the magazine was changed to the *Genevan*, September, 1886, and to the *Geneva Cabinet*, September, 1887.

The Monthly Advocate, published in St. John, New Brunswick, and devoted to the interests of Christian truth and morality; a monthly magazine; edited by

Rev. J. R. Lawson ; first issued May, 1880 ; price, 50 cents per annum. Discontinued, April, 1882.

The Christian Nation, published in New York, and endorsed by the National Reform Association; a journal of enlightened statesmanship, sound public morals, choice literature, and general information; a weekly paper; edited by John W. Pritchard; first issued, September, 1884; price, $2.00 per annum.

The Guiding Star, published in Selma, Alabama, and devoted to the moral and spiritual progress of the colored race; a weekly and monthly paper; edited by Rev. G. M. Elliot; first issued, March, 1886; price, 60 cents per annum. Discontinued, March, 1888.

Herald of Mission News, published in New York, with the approval of the Board of Foreign Missions of the Reformed Presbyterian Church; a monthly magazine; edited by Rev. R. M. Sommerville; first issued, January, 1887; price, 50 cents per annum.

FINIS.

JOSEPH BEATTIE, D. D.

JOHN BLACK, D.D.

SAMUEL BOWDEN

SAMUEL CARLISLE

JAMES CHRISTIE, D.D.

SAMUEL W. CRAWFORD, D.D.

JOHN CROZIER

ROBERT J. DODDS, D.D.

THOMAS DONNELLY

DAVID S. FARIS

JOHN GALBRAITH

HENRY H. GEORGE, D.D.

JOHN GIBSON

ROBERT GIBSON

DAVID GREGG

JOHN B. JOHNSTON, D.D.

JAMES KENNEDY

DAVID McALLISTER, D.D., L.L.D.

HUGH P. McCLURKIN, D.D.

JOSEPH McCRACKEN

CHARLES B. McKEE

DAVID McKEE

ALEXANDER McLEOD, D.D.

GILBERT McMASTER, D.D.

DAVID METHENY, M.D.

A. McLEOD MILLIGAN, D.D.

JAMES MILLIGAN, D.D.

JOHN C. K. MILLIGAN

WILLIAM MILROY

WILLIAM L. ROBERTS, D.D.

MOSES RONEY

DAVID SCOTT

JAMES R. W. SLOANE, D.D.

THOMAS SPROULL, D.D., L.L.D.

SAMUEL STERRETT

ANDREW STEVENSON, D.D.

THOMAS P. STEVENSON, D.D.

J. RENWICK THOMPSON

CHARLES D. TRUMBULL

JAMES WALLACE

DAVID B. WILLSON

JAMES M. WILLSON, D.D.

JAMES R. WILLSON, D.D.

SAMUEL M. WILLSON

PRESTON H. WYLIE

SAMUEL WYLIE, D.D.

SAMUEL B. WYLIE, D.D.

SAMUEL O. WYLIE, D.D.

www.ingramcontent.com/pod-product-compliance
Lightning Source LLC
Chambersburg PA
CBHW070643150426
42811CB00050B/515